T0183000

Lecture Notes in Computer Science 9697

Commenced Publication in 1973
Founding and Former Series Editors:
Gerhard Goos, Juris Hartmanis, and Jan van Leeuwen

More information about this series at http://www.springer.com/series/7407

Julian M. Kunkel · Pavan Balaji
Jack Dongarra (Eds.)

High Performance Computing

31st International Conference, ISC High Performance 2016
Frankfurt, Germany, June 19–23, 2016
Proceedings

 Springer

Editors
Julian M. Kunkel
Deutsches Klimarechenzentrum
Hamburg
Germany

Jack Dongarra
University of Tennessee
Knoxville, TN
USA

Pavan Balaji
Argonne National Laboratory
Lemont, IL
USA

ISSN 0302-9743   ISSN 1611-3349   (electronic)
Lecture Notes in Computer Science
ISBN 978-3-319-41320-4   ISBN 978-3-319-41321-1   (eBook)
DOI 10.1007/978-3-319-41321-1

Library of Congress Control Number: 2016942512

LNCS Sublibrary: SL1 – Theoretical Computer Science and General Issues

This Springer imprint is published by Springer Nature
The registered company is Springer International Publishing AG Switzerland

Preface

ISC High Performance, formerly known as the International Supercomputing Conference, was founded in 1986 as the Supercomputer Seminar. Originally organized by Hans Meuer, Professor of Computer Science at the University of Mannheim and former director of the computer center, the seminar brought together a group of 81 scientists and industrial partners who all shared an interest in high-performance computing. Since then the annual conference has become a major international event within the HPC community, and accompanying its growth in size over the years, the conference has moved from Mannheim via Heidelberg, Dresden, Hamburg, and Leipzig to Frankfurt. With 2,846 attendees and 153 exhibitors from over 56 countries in 2015, we were happy to see that this steady growth of interest also turned ISC High Performance 2016 into a powerful and memorable event.

In 2007, we decided to strengthen the scientific part of the conference by presenting selected talks on relevant research results within the HPC field. These research paper sessions began as a separate day preceding the conference, where slides and accompanying papers were made available via the conference website. The research paper sessions have since evolved into an integral part of the conference, and this year the scientific presentations took place over a period of three days.

For the past several years, the ISC High Performance conference has presented an ISC-sponsored award to encourage outstanding research in high-performance computing and to honor the overall best research paper submitted to the conference. Last year, this annual award was renamed as the Hans Meuer Award in memory of the late Dr. Hans Meuer, general chair of the ISC conference from 1986 through 2014, and co-founder of the TOP500 project. From all research papers submitted, the Research Papers Program Committee nominated the three papers with the highest review scores for the award and, in a face-to-face meeting, elected the best paper.

For ISC High Performance 2016, the call for participation was issued in Fall 2015, inviting researchers and developers to submit the latest results of their work to the Program Committee. In all, 60 papers were submitted from authors all over the world. This year, again a significant effort was made to improve the overall process. The Research Papers Program Committee consisted of 54 members selected from several countries throughout the world. Furthermore, 17 external expert reviewers were invited from the community to help with paper reviews of specific topics. After initial reviews were in place, a rebuttal process was made in which authors were given an opportunity to respond to reviewers' questions and help clarify issues the reviewers might have. To come to a final consensus on the papers to be accepted, we introduced a face-to-face meeting where each paper was discussed. Finally, the committee selected 25 papers for publication and for presentation in the research paper sessions.

We are pleased to announce that many fascinating topics in HPC are covered by the proceedings. The papers address the following issues in regards to the development of an environment for exascale supercomputers:

- Cost-efficient data centers
- Scalable applications
- Advancements in algorithms
- Scientific libraries
- Programming models
- Architectures
- Performance models and analysis
- Automatic performance optimization
- Parallel I/O
- Energy efficiency

We believe that this selection is highly appealing across a number of specializations.

Three award committees selected papers considered to be of exceptional quality and worthy of special recognition:

- The Hans Meuer Award honors the overall best research paper submitted to the conference. The award went to:
  "Mitigating MPI Message Matching Misery" by Mario Flajslik, James Dinan, and Keith D. Underwood.
- PRACE, the Partnership for Advanced Computing in Europe, awards a prize to the best scientific paper by a European student or scientist. This year's award was granted to:
  "Dynamic Sparse-Matrix Allocation on GPUs" by James King, Thomas Gilray, Robert M. Kirby and Matthew Might.
- The Gauss Centre for Supercomputing sponsors the Gauss Award. This award is assigned to the most outstanding paper in the field of scalable supercomputing and went to:
  "Predictive Modeling for Job Power Consumption in HPC Systems" by Andrea Borghesi, Andrea Bartolini, Michele Lombardi, Michela Milano and Luca Benin.

We would like to express our gratitude to all our colleagues for submitting papers to the ISC scientific sessions, as well as to the members of the Program Committee for organizing this year's attractive program.

June 2016

Julian M. Kunkel
Pavan Balaji
Jack Dongarra

Organization

Research Papers Program Committee

David Abramson	Monash University, Australia
Ilkay Altintas	San Diego Supercomputer Center, USA
Pavan Balaji	Argonne National Laboratory, USA (Co-chair)
Thomas Bönisch	High Performance Computing Center Stuttgart, Germany
Mahdi Bohlouli	University of Siegen, Germany
Ron Brightwell	Sandia National Laboratories, USA
Eva Burrows	University of Bergen, Norway
Xing Cai	Simula Research Laboratory, Norway
Ewa Deelman	USC Information Sciences Institute, USA
Jack Dongarra	University of Tennessee and Oak Ridge National Laboratory, USA (Chair)
Tomas Flouri	Heidelberg Institute for Theoretical Studies, Germany
Holger Fröning	University of Heidelberg, Germany
Lutz Gross	University of Queensland, Australia
Daniel Hackenberg	Technische Universität Dresden, Germany
Bilel Hadri	KAUST Supercomputing Lab, Saudi Arabia
Mary Hall	University of Utah, USA
David Ham	Imperial College London, UK
Frank Hannig	Friedrich-Alexander-Universität Erlangen-Nürnberg, Germany
Magne Haveraaen	University of Bergen, Norway
Stephan Herhut	Google, Denmark
Weicheng Huang	National Center for High-Performance Computing, Taiwan
Zhiyi Huang	University of Otago, New Zealand
Volodymyr Kindratenko	University of Illinois at Urbana-Champaign, USA
Julian M. Kunkel	Deutsches Klimarechenzentrum, Germany (Proceedings Chair)
Dong Li	University of California, Merced, USA
Fang-Pang Lin	National Center for High-Performance Computing, Taiwan
Qing Liu	Oak Ridge National Laboratory, USA
Hatem Ltaief	KAUST, Saudi Arabia
Thomas Ludwig	Deutsches Klimarechenzentrum, Germany
Arthur Maccabe	Oak Ridge National Laboratory, USA
M. Manjunathaiah	University of Reading, UK
Simon Mcintosh-Smith	University of Bristol, UK
Richard Membarth	DFKI and Saarland University, Germany
Marek Michalewicz	A*Star Computational Resource Center, Singapore

Bernd Mohr	Jülich Supercomputing Center, Germany
Alexander Moskovsky	RSC SKIF, Russia
Matthias Müller	RWTH Aachen University, Germany
Kengo Nakajima	University of Tokyo, Japan
Julio Ortega	Universidad de Granada, Spain
Dhabaleswar Panda	Ohio State University, USA
Huynh Phung	A*STAR, Singapore
Thomas Poulet	CSIRO, Australia
Ying Qian	East China Normal University, China
Francisco Rodrigo	Universidad Carlos III de Madrid, Spain
Sven-Bodo Scholz	Heriot-Watt University, UK
Federico Silla	Technical University of Valencia, Spain
Yogesh Simmhan	Indian Institute of Science, India
Alexandros Stamatakis	Technische Universität München, Germany
Osamu Tatebe	University of Tsukuba, Japan
Michela Taufer	University of Delaware, USA
Jeyan Thiyagalingam	University of Liverpool, UK
Yuichi Tsujita	RIKEN AICS, Japan
Jeff Vetter	Oak Ridge National Laboratory, USA
Xavier Vigouroux	Bull, France
Vladimir Voevodin	Lomonosov Moscow State University, Russia
Thomas Wild	Technische Universität München, Germany
Peter Ziegenhein	Institute of Cancer Research, UK

PHD Forum Program Committee

Lorena Barba	George Washington University, USA (Chair)
Anshu Dubey	Argonne National Laboratory, USA
Anne Elster	Norwegian University of Science and Technology, Norway
Fernanda Foerter	Oak Ridge National Laboratory, USA
Georg Hager	Friedrich-Alexander-Universität Erlangen-Nürnberg, Germany
Paul Kelly	Imperial College London, UK
Kengo Nakajima	University of Tokyo, Japan
Amanda Randles	Duke University, USA
Michelle Mills Strout	University of Arizona, USA
Ana Lucia Varbanescu	University of Amsterdam, The Netherlands
Michela Taufer	University of Delaware, USA
Richard Vuduc	Georgia Institute of Technology, USA
Gerhard Wellein	Friedrich-Alexander-Universität Erlangen-Nürnberg, Germany (Co-chair)
Felix Wolf	Technische Universität Darmstadt, Germany
Rio Yokota	Tokyo Institute of Technology, Japan

Research Poster Session Program Committee

Alvaro Aguilera	ZIH/TU Dresden, Germany
Mahdi Bohlouli	University of Siegen, Germany
Thomas Bönisch	HLRS, Germany
Xing Cai	Simula Research Laboratory, Norway
Javier Garcia Blas	Universidad Carlos III de Madrid, Spain
David Ham	Imperial College London, UK
Khalid Hasanov	IBM Research, Ireland
Weicheng Huang	National Center for High-Performance Computing, Taiwan
Julian Kunkel	Deutsches Klimarechenzentrum, Germany
Ravindranath Reddy Manumachu	UCD School of Computer Science, Ireland
Simon McIntosh-Smith	University of Bristol, UK
Richard Membarth	Intel Visual Computing Institute, Saarland University, Germany
Kengo Nakajima	University of Tokyo, Japan
Gabriel Noaje	A*STAR Computational Resource Centre, Singapore
Julio Ortega	University of Granada, Spain
Andrej Sozykin	Ural Federal University, Russia
Osamu Tatebe	University of Tsukuba, Japan
Jeyarajan Thiyagalingam	Oxford University, UK
Vladimir Voevodin	Moscow State University, Russia (Chair)
Peter Ziegenhein	The Institute of Cancer Research, UK

HPC in Asia Program Committee

Taisuke Boku	University of Tsukuba, Japan (Chair)
Ralph Bording	Pawsey, Australia
Horst Gietl	ISC Group, Germany
R. Govindarjan	IISC, India
Weicheng Huang	NCHC, Taiwan
Zhong Jin	CAS, China
Jysoo Lee	KISTI, Korea
Yutong Lu	NUDT, China
Martin Meuer	ISC Group, Germany
Marek T. Michalewicz	A*STAR, Singapore
Hiroshi Nakashima	Kyoto University, Japan
Nages Sieslack	ISC Group, Germany

Tutorials Committee

Pavan Balaji	Argonne National Laboratory, USA
Rosa M. Badia	BSC, Spain

Franck Cappello	INRIA and UIUC, France
James Dinan	Intel, USA
Ganesh Gopalakrishnan	University of Utah, USA
Bill Gropp	University of Illinois at Urbana-Champaign, USA (Chair)
Torsten Hoefler	ETH Zurich, Switzerland
Elizabeth Jessup	University of Colorado, USA
Fred Johnson	SAIC, USA
Alice Koniges	LBNL, USA
Michael Resch	HLRS, Germany
Rajeev Thakur	Argonne National Laboratory, USA

BoFs Committee

David Bader	Georgia Institute of Technology, USA
Natalie Bates	Energy Efficient HPC Working Group, USA
Costas Bekas	IBM Research Zurich, Switzerland
Alfred Geiger	T-Systems Solutions for Research, Germany
Horst Gietl	ISC Group, Germany (Chair)
Georg Hager	Friedrich-Alexander-Universität Erlangen-Nürnberg, Germany
Peter Kogge	University of Notre Dame, USA
Julian Kunkel	Deutsches Klimarechenzentrum, Germany
Jysoo Lee	KISTI, Korea
Pekka Lehtovuori	CSC – IT Center for Science, Finland
Cynthia R. McIntyre	Washington Technology Partners, USA
Marek Michalewicz	A*STAR Computational Resource Center, Singapore
Bernd Mohr	Jülich Supercomputing Center, Germany
Jean-Philippe Nominé	CEA, France
Marie-Christine Sawley	Intel, France
Martin Schulz	Lawrence Livermore National Laboratory, USA
Rainer Spurzem	Chinese Academy of Sciences and University of Heidelberg, Germany
Vladimir Voevodin	Moscow State University, Russia
Heike Walther	ISC Group, Germany
Michele Weiland	EPCC - The University of Edinburgh, UK
Gerhard Wellein	Friedrich-Alexander-Universität Erlangen-Nürnberg, Germany
Jan Wender	science+computing, Germany
Andreas Wierse	SICOS BW, Germany

Workshop Committee

Rosa M. Badia	BSC, Spain
Francois Bodin	Irisa, France
Bronis R. de Supinski	LLNL, USA
Craig Lucas	NAG, UK

Gerald F. Lofstead II   SNL, USA
Naoya Maruyama   RIKEN AICS, Japan
Bernd Mohr   JSC, Germany (Co-chair)
Marie-Christine Sawley   Intel, France
Seetharami R. Seelam   IBM Research, USA
John Shalf   NERC, USA
Michela Taufer   University of Delaware, USA (Co-chair)
Antonino Tumeo   PNNL, USA

Additional Reviewers for the Research Papers

Cihan Altinay   The University of Queensland, Australia
Lucas Czech   Heidelberg Institute for Theoretical Studies, Germany
Minh Dinh   University of Queensland, Australia
Tingxing Dong   AMD, USA
Joel Fenwick   University of Queensland, Australia
Yuhua Guo   Virginia Commonwealth University, USA
Dan Huang   University of Central Florida, USA
Siddhartha Jana   University of Houston, USA
Chao Jin   University of Queensland, Australia
Hideyuki Kawashima   University of Tsukuba, Japan
Jialin Liu   Lawrence Berkeley National Lab, USA
Sarah Lutteropp   Karlsruhe Institute of Technology, Germany
Radhika Nath   Reading University, UK
Hoang Nguyen   University of Queensland, Australia
Milos Puzovic   STFC, Hartree, UK
Joseph Schuchart   TU Dresden, Germany
Huadong Xia   MicroStrategy, USA

Contents

Autotuning and Thread Mapping

An Analytical Model-Based Auto-tuning Framework for Locality-Aware Loop Scheduling

Rengan Xu[1]([⊠]), Sunita Chandrasekaran[2], Xiaonan Tian[1],
and Barbara Chapman[1]

[1] Department of Computer Science, University of Houston, Houston, TX, USA
{rxu6,xtian2,bchapman}@uh.edu
[2] Department of Computer and Information Sciences,
University of Delaware, Newark, DE, USA
schandra@udel.edu

Abstract. HPC developers aim to deliver the very best performance. To do so they constantly think about memory bandwidth, memory hierarchy, locality, floating point performance, power/energy constraints and so on. On the other hand, application scientists aim to write performance portable code while exploiting the rich feature set of the hardware. By providing adequate hints to the compilers in the form of directives appropriate executable code is generated. There are tremendous benefits from using directive-based programming. However, applications are also becoming more and more complex and we need sophisticated tools such as auto-tuning to better explore the optimization space. In applications, loops typically form a major and time-consuming portion of the code. Scheduling these loops involves mapping from the loop iteration space to the underlying platform - for example GPU threads. The user tries different scheduling techniques until the best one is identified. However, this process can be quite tedious and time consuming especially when it is a relatively large application, as the user needs to record the performance of every schedule's run. This paper aims to offer a better solution by proposing an auto-tuning framework that adopts an analytical model guiding the compiler and the runtime to choose an appropriate schedule for the loops, automatically and determining the launch configuration for each of the loop schedules. Our experiments show that the predicted loop schedule by our framework achieves the speedup of 1.29x on an average against the default loop schedule chosen by the compiler.

1 Introduction

Heterogeneous architectures that comprise of CPU processors and computational accelerators such as GPUs have been increasingly adopted for scientific computing. The low-level programming models CUDA and OpenCL for GPUs offer users programming interfaces with execution models closely matching that of GPU architectures. Effectively using these interfaces for creating highly optimized applications require programmers to thoroughly understand the underlying architecture, as well as significantly change the program structures and algorithms.

© Springer International Publishing Switzerland 2016
J.M. Kunkel et al. (Eds.): ISC High Performance 2016, LNCS 9697, pp. 3–20, 2016.
DOI: 10.1007/978-3-319-41321-1_1

This affects both productivity and performance. Standardized directive-based models such as OpenACC [3] and OpenMP for accelerators [5] require developers to insert directives and runtime calls into the existing source code offloading portions of Fortran or C/C++ codes to be executed on accelerators.

Directives are high-level language constructs that programmers can use to provide useful hints to compilers to perform certain transformations and optimizations on the annotated code region. The use of directives can significantly improve programming productivity. Users can still achieve high performance of their program comparable to code written in CUDA or OpenCL, subjected to the requirements that a 'careful' choice of directives and compiler optimization strategies be made. One such scenario encountered quite commonly in a program is loop scheduling.

Loop scheduling defines the mapping of loop nest(s) to the underlying architecture. Consider the architecture is a GPU that consists of a number of GPU threads with complex topology settings; it is a daunting task to determine mapping strategies of the loop nest to those threads in order to achieve better performance. Different loop schedules reflect different memory access orders. Loop transformations change memory access orders that results in exploiting better locality - temporal and spatial. The reuse distance model [4] is a classic model predominantly used for CPUs to capture both types of locality in CPU architectures. However we cannot apply this model directly on GPUs due to the significant architectural differences between the CPUs and the GPUs. This paper aims to extend the reuse model to suit its applicability for GPUs.

The main contributions of this paper include:

– To the best of our knowledge, we are the first to propose a locality-aware auto-tuning framework to address the GPU loop scheduling issue.
– In the proposed framework, we extend the classic reuse distance model to GPU architecture in order to estimate GPU cache hit rate accurately.
– Our results demonstrate that our proposed framework chooses the loop schedule producing better performance compared to the default loop schedule chosen by default by the compiler.

The organization of this paper is as follows: Sect. 2 gives an overview of GPU architecture and OpenACC model. Section 3 provides a motivating example illustrating the performance impact of different loop schedules. In Sect. 4, we explain in detail the proposed auto-tuning framework on how to choose a loop schedule with better locality. Performance results are discussed in Sect. 5. Section 6 highlights the related work in this area. We conclude our work in Sect. 7.

2   GPU Architecture and OpenACC Directives

GPU architectures differ significantly from that of traditional processors. Employing a Single Instruction Multiple Threads (SIMT) architecture, NVIDIA GPUs have hundreds of cores that can process thousands of software threads simultaneously. GPUs organize both hardware cores and software threads into two-level of parallelism. Hardware cores are organized into an array of Streaming Multiprocessors (SMs), each SM consisting of a number of cores named as Scalar Processors (SPs). Each SM has its own L1 cache which is not cache coherent, and all SMs share an unified L2 cache.

The compute-intensive part of an application, called kernel, is offloaded to GPUs for parallel execution. The GPU launches massive threads to execute that kernel. The thread unit in GPU scheduling is called a warp (a warp size has 32 threads for NVIDIA GPUs). Multiple warps form a thread block and multiple thread blocks form a grid. Both the thread block and grid can be 1D, 2D, or 3D. For programmers, the challenge to efficiently utilize the massive parallel capabilities of GPUs is to map the kernels to the thread hierarchy, and efficient data layout in the GPU memory hierarchy to maximize coalesced memory access for the threads.

Directive-based high-level programming models for accelerators, e.g. OpenACC and OpenMP extensions for accelerators, have been designed to address the programmability challenge of GPUs. Using these programming models, programmers insert compiler directives into a program to annotate portions of code to be offloaded onto accelerators for executions. This approach relies heavily on the compiler to generate efficient code for thread mapping and data layout. It could be potentially challenging to extract the optimal performance using such an approach rather than using other explicit programming models. However, the directive-based models simplify programming on heterogeneous systems thus saving development time, while also preserving the original code structure assisting in code portability.

OpenACC allows users to specify three levels of parallelism in a data parallel region: gang, worker and vector parallelism to map the loop nests to the multiple-level thread hierarchy of GPUs. Programmer provides hints to map these three-level parallelism to GPU threads but the effectiveness of the mapping relies on the compiler and runtime implementation strategies. We use a high quality, open-source, validated OpenACC compiler called OpenUH [18]. Adhering to OpenACC standards, this compiler maps "gang" to thread block, "worker" to Y-dimension of thread block and "vector" to X-dimension of thread block [3].

3   A Motivating Example

Matrix multiplication has been widely used in scientific computing. We use this application to illustrate the importance of loop scheduling in GPU. The square-matrix multiplication we used is $C = AB$ where the size of matrix A, B, and C is $n \times n$. The elements in matrix C are $C_{i,j} = \sum_{k=1}^{n} a_{i,k} b_{k,j}$ where both the indices i and j loops from 1 through n. A double nested loop was constructed to solve this matrix multiplication. Multiple ways could be adopted to map this loop nest to the underlying GPU threads using directive-based programming model. Table 1 shows how this loop nest could be mapped in so many different ways to GPU threads. The table also indicates different launch configurations. The launch configuration specifies the thread block and grid shape and size that are used to

Table 1. The performance difference for matrix multiplication with different loop schedules and launch configurations

Loop schedule number	Loop schedule detail	Performance (ms)
0	bx(1)/tx(128)	3.24
1	by(1)/bx(1) tx(128)	3.36
2	by(1) ty(128)/bx(1) tx(1)	11.04
3	by(1) ty(64)/bx(1) tx(2)	5.87
4	by(1) ty(32)/bx(1) tx(4)	4.28
5	by(1) ty(16)/bx(1) tx(8)	3.47
6	by(1) ty(8)/bx(1) tx(16)	3.09
7	by(1) ty(4)/bx(1) tx(32)	3.16
8	by(1) ty(2)/bx(1) tx(64)	3.19
9	by(1) ty(1)/bx(1) tx(128)	3.28

run a loop. All of the 10 loop schedules in the table use only one thread block with 128 threads. However, since the loop nest is mapped to threads differently, there are differences in their performance. The loop schedule 0 is the default loop schedule chosen by the compiler. However, we notice that there are other loop schedules demonstrating better performance than the default schedule that the compiler chose. What are the strategies to choose an optimal or sub-optimal loop schedule and its corresponding launch configuration? Our proposed auto-tuning framework discussed in the rest of the paper provides suitable proven answers to this question.

We would like to keep the notations used for our framework as general as possible and not tie it to any specific programming model/language:

- bx, by and bz: denote X, Y and Z dimension of the grid, respectively
- tx, ty and tz: denote X, Y and Z dimension of the thread block, respectively
- num_bx, num_by and num_bz: denote the size of X, Y and Z dimension of the grid, respectively
- num_tx, num_ty and num_tz: denote the size of X, Y and Z dimension of the thread block, respectively

4   Auto-tuning for GPU Loop Scheduling

4.1   The Auto-tuning Framework

In this section, we describe our auto-tuning framework and the analytical model proposed that enables the identification of the appropriate loop schedule, and the launch configuration used for each of the loop schedules. Figure 1 gives an overview of the auto-tuning framework. The compiler generates multiple kernel files with different loop schedules. The loop schedule is chosen from a set of

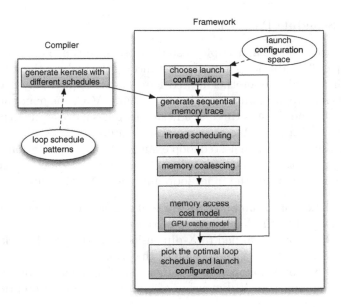

Fig. 1. The framework of auto-tuning for loop scheduling

loop schedule patterns which covers both double and triple nested loops. The framework chooses a launch configuration from the launch configuration search space which depends on the iteration space of each loop. The search of launch configuration is guided by the rule of maximizing the GPU occupancy. Before applying the framework, an application needs to run once on CPU to generate a sequential memory trace. Based on the loop schedule and the launch configuration, all memory accesses in the memory trace are assigned to GPU threads. This step defines the access of memory references for GPU threads. Next, the thread scheduling defines the execution order of the memory accesses in the trace.

In the execution of memory accesses, the memory coalescing is very critical. In GPU, a warp (the smallest execution unit) defines a set of consecutive threads. If consecutive threads access consecutive memory addresses, then the memory accesses are coalesced meaning they are merged into fewer memory transactions. We simulate the memory coalescing behavior in GPU architecture in our model. For instance, if the memory addresses referenced by all threads in a warp are in one cache line, then these memory access requests will be merged into only one memory request.

After memory requests are coalesced, the memory trace is fed into the memory access cost model where a memory access cost is computed, with the cache model. This process is repeated until the framework iterates over all loop schedules and the launch configuration space. Finally, the framework picks the optimal loop schedule and the corresponding launch configuration that has the minimal memory access cost. The compiler then recompiles the same program using the selected loop schedule. The major components in this framework will be discussed in the following sub-sections:

4.2   Loop Schedule Patterns

We only consider double and triple nested loops. Note that here the loop nest level means parallelizable loop nest. For instance, in the body of the parallelizable loop nest, there could be another nested loop that is sequentially executed. In the current GPU programming models such as OpenACC, the maximum level of the parallelizable loop nest is three. If a nested loop has more levels to parallelize, it can be collapsed into double or triple nested loop.

Listing 1.1 shows a double nested loop example. Using the notations described in the previous Sect. 3, we now introduce three loop schedules for the double nested loop (use x-loop for the inner loop and y-loop for the outer loop):

- schedule 2_1: x-loop is mapped to the X-dimension of a thread block, and y-loop is mapped to the X-dimension of the grid.
- schedule 2_2: x-loop is mapped to X-dimension of both thread block and grid, and y-loop is mapped to Y-dimension of the grid.
- schedule 2_3: x-loop is mapped to X-dimension of both thread block and grid, and y-loop is mapped to Y-dimension of both thread block and grid.

These loop schedule directives are implicitly added by the compiler. The graphical explanation for these loop schedules are shown in Figs. 2, 3 and 4. The detailed mapping function from the loop iterations to GPU threads for double nested loop are shown in Listings 1.3, 1.4 and 1.5. The purpose of schedule 2_2 is to overcome the GPU hardware threads limit within a block. In both schedule 2_1 and 2_2, the threads computing the outer loop are in different thread blocks, which are likely to be scheduled to different GPU SMs (Streaming Multiprocessor). This may not exploit the data locality efficiently. So how do we improve data locality? We consider the loop schedule 2_3 that allows some threads computing the outer loop iterations to remain in the same block thus improving data locality. For triple nested loop, a code example is shown in Listing 1.2 and other similar loop schedules are designed. Because of the space limit, we only illustrate the graphical representation for one loop schedule in Fig. 5, in which x-loop, y-loop and z-loop refer to the inner most loop, the middle loop and the outer most loop, respectively. The loop schedule in Fig. 5 means x-loop is mapped to X-dimension of thread block, y-loop is mapped to Y-dimension of thread block and z-loop is mapped to X-dimension of the grid.

```
#pragma acc loop
for(j = j_{start}; j < j_{end}; j++){
    #pragma acc loop
    for(i = i_{start}; i < i_{end}; i++){
        ......
    }
}
```

Listing 1.1. Double nested loop example

```
#pragma acc loop
for(k = k_{start}; k < k_{end}; k++){
    #pragma acc loop
    for(j = j_{start}; j < j_{end}; j++){
        #pragma acc loop
        for(i = i_{start}; i < i_{end}; i++){
            ......
        }
    }
}
```

Listing 1.2. Triple nested loop example

```
#pragma acc loop bx(num_bx)
for(j = j_start; j < j_end; j++){
    #pragma acc loop tx(num_tx)
    for(i = i_start; i < i_end; i++){
        ......
    }
}
mapping function to CUDA:
```

$j = j_{start} + blockIdx.x + t * gridDim.x, \quad (t = 0, 1, ..., \frac{j_{end}-j_{start}}{gridDim.x} - 1)$

$i = i_{start} + threadIdx.x + t * blockDim.x, \quad (t = 0, 1, ..., \frac{i_{end}-i_{start}}{blockDim.x} - 1)$

Listing 1.3. Loop schedule 2_1

```
#pragma acc loop by(num_by)
for(j - j_start; j < j_end; j++){
    #pragma acc loop bx(num_bx) tx(num_tx)
    for(i = i_start; i < i_end; i++){
        ......
    }
}
mapping function to CUDA:
```

$j = j_{start} + blockIdx.y + t * gridDim.y$

$(t = 0, 1, ..., \frac{j_{end}-j_{start}}{gridDim.y} - 1)$

$i = i_{start} + threadIdx.x + blockIdx.x * blockDim.x + t * blockDim.x * gridDim.x$

$(t = 0, 1, ..., \frac{i_{end}-i_{start}}{blockDim.x*gridDim.x} - 1)$

Listing 1.4. Loop schedule 2_2

```
#pragma acc loop by(num_by) ty(num_ty)
for(j = j_start; j < j_end; j++){
    #pragma acc loop bx(num_bx) tx(num_tx)
    for(i = i_start; i < i_end; i++){
        ......
    }
}
mapping function to CUDA:
```

$j = j_{start} + threadIdx.y + blockIdx.y * blockDim.y + t * blockDim.y * gridDim.y$

$(t = 0, 1, ..., \frac{j_{end}-j_{start}}{blockDim.y*gridDim.y} - 1)$

$i = i_{start} + threadIdx.x + blockIdx.x * blockDim.x + t * blockDim.x * gridDim.x$

$(t = 0, 1, ..., \frac{i_{end}-i_{start}}{blockDim.x*gridDim.x} - 1)$

Listing 1.5. Loop schedule 2_3

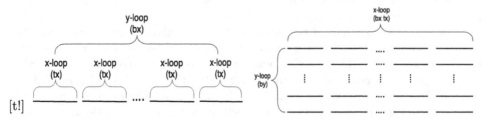

Fig. 2. Loop schedule 2_1   **Fig. 3.** Loop schedule 2_2

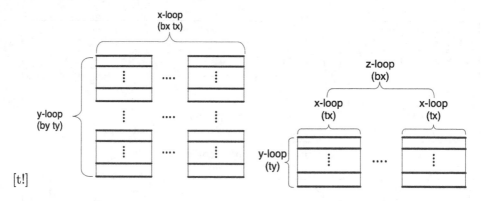

Fig. 4. Loop schedule 2_3   **Fig. 5.** Loop schedule 3_1

4.3   Thread Scheduling

The memory trace is defined for how the memory is accessed by threads, which is further defined for how the thread blocks are scheduled into different SMs and how the threads are scheduled within each SM. When the GPU launches a grid of threads for a kernel, that grid is divided into 'waves' of thread blocks. For example let us assume there are 15 SMs. Each SM has 2 thread blocks hence 30 thread blocks in total. Thread block 0 and thread block 15 will be assigned to SM0. Thread block 1 and thread block 16 will be assigned to SM1. If there was a scenario with 60 thread blocks and each SM allows at most 2 blocks (30 blocks for 15 SMs), we will need to assign these blocks into two waves; 30 thread blocks to the first wave and the other 30 thread blocks to the second wave. We use round-robin scheduling mechanism to schedule the thread blocks to all SMs in all waves. The number of threads scheduled is independent of the grid size. For instance, if the grid size is 2048 and only 128 threads are scheduled, then each thread will process 2048/128=16 elements.

Figure 6 shows thread scheduling mechanism. It highlights two waves scheduled to one SM. Each wave has two thread blocks; each thread block has two warps; each warp has two threads; each thread has five memory accesses. We access the memory references in a round-robin manner. This memory access pattern gives us the memory trace.

The equation to calculate the number of waves is given in Eq. 1. The number of waves is obtained by dividing the total number of thread blocks by the active thread blocks per SM times the number of SMs. The active blocks per SM is given in Eq. 2. For instance, in Kepler GPU, the $max\_threads\_per\_SM$ is 2048 and $max\_thread\_blocks\_per\_SM$ is 16 and upon knowing the number of thread blocks in the kernel, which is specified by the launch configuration, we can determine the number of waves.

$$waves = \frac{thread\_blocks}{active\_blocks\_per\_SM \times \#SMs} \tag{1}$$

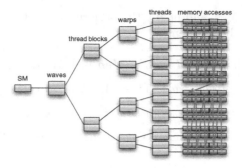

Fig. 6. Thread scheduling used in the auto-tuning framework

$$active\_blocks\_per\_SM =$$
$$min(max\_threads\_per\_SM/block\_size, max\_thread\_blocks\_per\_SM) \quad (2)$$

4.4   Memory Access Cost Model

After memory coalescing, the memory trace is fed into the memory access cost model which computes the memory access cost for a specific loop schedule and launch configuration. The metric used in this model is presented as

$$Cost_{mem} = \sum_{i}^{\#levels} (N_i \times L_i) \quad (3)$$

where N_i means the number of transactions happened in level i of the memory hierarchy, and L_i means the latency of memory level i.

The rationale behind this metric is the memory hierarchy in GPU architecture which is shown in Fig. 7. When the kernel needs to access a global memory address, it needs to load that address from L1 cache. If the data is already in L1 cache, then the access is a hit. If the data is not in L1 cache, then the access is a miss and it needs to load the data from L2 cache. If the data is not in L2 cache, then it needs to further load the data from DRAM. So the formula after expanding the Eq. 3 is shown in Eq. 4, which is the sum of memory access cost from L1, L2 and DRAM. The formula for calculating each individual cost is given in Eqs. 5, 6 and 7. The '4' in Eqs. 6 and 7 explains the number of global memory load transaction that is increased by 1 every 128 bytes in L1 cache, but every 32 bytes in L2 cache and DRAM. Since the memory access latency order from high to low - DRAM, L2 cache and L1 cache, we would like to access higher order memory as less as possible. In other words, we would like to have few global loads and low L1 and L2 cache miss rates as possible. When there is intra-thread data reuse or inter-thread data reuse, different loop schedules have different cache miss rates, and finally the performance of the kernels using those loop schedules would be different.

$$Cost_{mem} = Mem_{L1} + Mem_{L2} + Mem_{DRAM} \tag{4}$$

$$Mem_{L1} = global\_loads * (1 - L1\_miss\_rate) * L1\_latency \tag{5}$$

$$Mem_{L2} = global\_loads * L1\_miss\_rate * 4 * L2\_latency \tag{6}$$

$$Mem_{DRAM} = global\_loads * L1\_miss\_rate * L2\_miss\_rate * 4 * DRAM\_latency \tag{7}$$

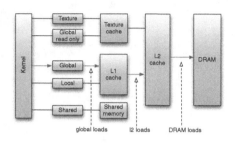

Fig. 7. GPU memory hierarchy   **Fig. 8.** L1 cache modeling

The key factors of the model are to estimate the global memory loads, L1 and L2 cache miss rates. To estimate L1 and L2 cache miss rate, we use reuse distance model [4]. It is a classic model to model the cache misses in CPU applications. The primary reasons for cache misses are cold/compulsory, conflict, capacity misses, famously termed as the 3 C model. The **cold miss** occurs when there is no data in the cache, no matter how big the cache is. The **conflict miss** usually occurs in direct-mapped caches and set-associative caches. Two cache lines may map to the same cache slot even though there may be empty slots. The **capacity miss** happens when there are no more available slots in the cache. The reuse distance model assumes that a LRU replacement fully associative cache is used. So it can only predict cold miss and capacity miss.

To the best of our knowledge, there is no existing work that discusses GPU L2 cache modeling. We found a couple of other related research work discussing GPU L1 cache modeling. Tang et al. [17] applied the reuse distance theory to model the GPU L1 cache. However, there were a few weaknesses and limitations in their approach: (1) they assumed only one thread block is active in one SM which is not true in the real hardware; (2) they modeled the cold miss and conflict miss but did not model capacity miss, however some research have shown that only a minority of the misses are conflict misses in both CPU [6] and GPU [14]; (3) they validated their model against a GPU simulator which is not a real hardware per se. Nugteren et al. [14] also used the reuse distance to model GPU L1 cache. However, in their implementation, all thread blocks were scheduled into only one SM which is not the case in a real hardware. Our thread scheduling mechanism overcomes the drawbacks of the above two papers discussed.

The reuse distance theory can measure both spatial locality and temporal locality if the distance is measured with cache line granularity. The spatial locality defines that the nearby memory addresses are likely to be referenced again in the near future. The temporal locality defines that the same data is likely to be referenced again in the near future.

The spatial locality is reflected by the memory coalescing level in the GPU kernel. If a GPU kernel has coalesced memory accesses, then it has better spatial locality than the kernel that has uncoalesced memory accesses. This is because the coalesced memory accesses allow the nearby data elements to be accessed at the same time the current data is accessed.

The temporal locality is reflected by the loop schedule. Different loop schedules pose different temporal locality since the execution order of the threads are different. The reuse distance theory can capture both the spatial locality and temporal locality effectively. Table 2 shows a reuse distance example. In this example, assume the cache line is of 16 bytes. If the data is accessed first or when a cold miss happens, the reuse distance is recorded as ∞. The reuse distance is a metric that defines the *distinct* memory accesses between the current memory access and the last access. If the reuse distance is larger or equal to the total number of cache lines, then a data reference is missed in the cache. The cache hit rate can be obtained by diving the hits by the total number of hits and misses.

Table 2. Reuse distance example. Assume cache line has 16 bytes and the cache size is 32 bytes. The reuse distance is based on cache line granularity

Address	0	8	16	96	8	16	17	104
Cache line	0	0	1	6	0	1	1	6
Reuse distance	∞	0	∞	∞	2	2	0	2
Cache hit/miss	Miss	Hit	Miss	Miss	Miss	Miss	Hit	Miss

Although the classic reuse distance model can predict the cache miss rate in CPU, it cannot be simply applied as-is on the GPU since the architectures are significantly different. The most important difference is that in GPU, the threads in a warp execute in lock-step manner and therefore memory coalescing is important in the memory accesses of a warp. If the memory addresses referenced by all the threads in a warp are in a cache line, then the memory accesses are merged into one memory access. Another difference is the parallel processing feature including parallel memory processing in GPU. Therefore in our implementation, the L1 modeling includes parallel memory processing. But we also compare it with the base implementation. The difference of "Base" and "Modeled" are shown in Fig. 8. In Base version, the memory coalescing is applied to the memory trace. Then the memory requests from different warps are processed in order. If the memory requests in a warp are not coalesced, then they are also processed in order within a warp. In Modeled version, we also apply memory coalescing, but we further add a timestamp. The timestamp is added to the following warps but it is also added to the threads in the same warp if their memory requests are not coalesced.

In the reuse distance model implementation, a key factor is the input, which is a memory trace. In our analytical model, the memory traces are different for different loop schedules. This is because different loop schedules assign the loop iterations into GPU threads differently, therefore the memory traces are different, and eventually the cache misses are different.

For L2 cache modeling, we must first apply L1 cache modeling for all SMs and record the cache misses in their individual list. Then the memory trace is processed in round-robin manner which is similar to the description in Fig. 6.

5   Performance Evaluation

The experimental platform is Intel Xeon processor E5520 with frequency 2.27 GHz and 32 GB main memory and an Nvidia Quadro K6000 GPU card which uses K40 architecture. L1 and L2 cache sizes are 16 KB and 1.5 MB, respectively. The cache line size for both L1 and L2 is 128 bytes. The proposed framework is implemented within the OpenUH compiler. The actual L1 and L2 cache hit rates are obtained from l1_cache_global_hit_rate and l2_l1_read_hit_rate metrics in CUDA profiler nvprof and the actual global memory loads are obtained from gld_transactions metric.

To evaluate our auto-tuning framework, we consider several benchmarks: two synthetic benchmarks (x-reuse and y-reuse), four from kernelGen OpenACC Performance Test Suite [2] (Matrix Multiplication, Jacobi, Laplacian and Divergence), one from CUDA SDK (Matrix Transpose) and one from EPCC OpenACC benchmarks [1] (Himeno). We test different data reuse patterns using the two synthetic benchmarks. Figure 9 shows these two benchmarks along with another pattern i.e. xy-reuse, a classic Matrix Multiplication case. The "x" here refers to the inner loop and "y" refers to the outer loop in a double nested loop. In the x-reuse benchmark, the inner loop reuses the common data; while in the y-reuse benchmark, the outer loop reuses the common data. The third case is the xy-reuse where both the inner and the outer loop reuse some common data.

x-reuse

y-reuse

Fig. 9. Data reuse patterns

Figure 10 shows results for L1 cache hit modeling for some of the benchmarks discussed above. Figure 10(a) and (b) are results for the two synthetic benchmarks and Fig. 10(c) and (d) are results for a couple of benchmarks from kernelGen suite. (Results for other benchmarks were quite similar, so due to space constraints we have not included them in the paper). The results indicate that modeled result is more accurate than "Base" version since it considers the parallel memory processing. Figure 10(a) shows that cache hit rates are high for all loop schedules. This is because for all iterations in x loop, the data they share are in one row and in the same contiguous memory section. Figure 10(b) shows that the shared data are in the same column and therefore they are not contiguous in memory. This leads to relatively lower cache hit. Figure 10(c), results for Matrix Multiplication, show that there is data reuse in both x and y loops and therefore the shape of cache hit results seem like a combination of x-reuse and y-reuse. Figure 10(d), results for Jacobi show that, the overall hit rate is slightly lesser than x-reuse. This is because the data, the threads share are stencil-like. For instance considering a 4-point stencil, for different points, the data that the threads access are not in contiguous memory locations, however for a specific point the data, the threads share, are still in contiguous memory location. As a result the cache hit rates are still relatively high. If the cache hit is high, the indication is that the threads will take lesser time to fetch data from high-latency memory.

The GPU L2 cache modeling result is shown in Fig. 11. We show the results for partial benchmarks including Laplacian, Divergence and Himeno. The results indicate that some loop schedules have low L2 cache hit while other loop schedules have high L2 cache hit. This illustates the importance of choosing the right loop schedules. The error percentage between the actual and the modeled L2 hit is only 4.37 %, 13.72 % and 2.76 % for Laplacian, Divergence and Himeno, respectively. The low error percentages indicate that our model can capture the L2 locality for different loop schedules accurately.

Figure 12 shows the global memory loads of kernels for the four benchmarks discussed in Fig. 10. The plots show that the modeled loads (before kernel launch) are exactly the same as the actual loads (profiled results) thus indicating that our proposed model is accurately predicting the memory loads. Figure 12(b) indicates that for y-reuse synthetic benchmark, no matter what the loop schedule is, the memory access appears to be fully coalesced leading to the same number of global memory loads all the time. In the other three plots, the tallest bars indicate the loop schedules for which the memory accesses are fully uncoalesced, while the shortest bars indicate the loop schedules for which memory accesses are fully coalesced, and the bars between the tallest and the shortest bars indicate partial memory coalescing. (Results for other benchmarks in kernelGen suite and EPCC were quite similar, so due to space constraints we have not included them in the paper). Higher the global memory loads, higher the time taken by the threads to process the memory requests.

Figure 13 shows several plots that demonstrate close correlation of kernel performance and the memory access cost modeling. We use the coefficient of

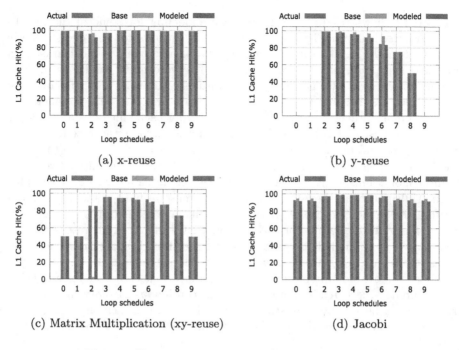

Fig. 10. GPU L1 cache modeling (Color figure online)

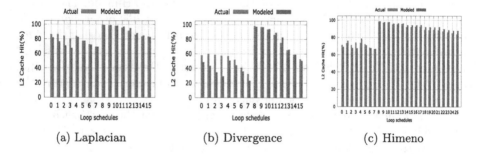

Fig. 11. GPU L2 cache modeling (Color figure online)

determination R^2 to measure the strength of the relationship between the kernel performance and the memory access cost in the model. R^2 is a popular indicator on how well a variable can be used to predict the value of another variable. The values of R^2 range from 0 (poor indicator) to 1 (excellent predictor). The R^2 value for all benchmarks are listed in Table 3 and the average value is 0.93 indicating the strong correlation between the kernel performance and the memory access cost modeling. Based on the memory access cost modeling, an optimal or a sub-optimal loop schedule is chosen by the framework. For all benchmarks tested, the speedup of the loop schedule chosen by the model against the default loop

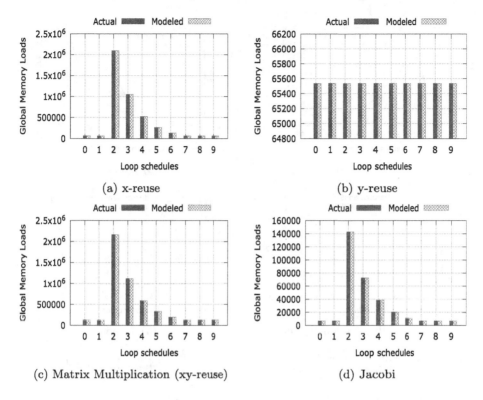

Fig. 12. Global memory loads (Color figure online)

schedule chosen by the compiler are listed in Table 3 and the average speedup is 1.29x. This proves the effectiveness of the proposed framework.

6   Related Work

To the best of our knowledge, there were only a few similar research on how to solve the loop scheduling issues on a GPU. Siddiqui et al. [16] presented how to choose the optimal loop schedule with machine learning approach. They used exhaustive search to find the optimal and sub-optimal loop schedules for the training data sets and stored those information into a database. For the new test benchmark, they found the closest training benchmark and applied its loop schedules to that test benchmark. Their approach, however, could only be used for different problem sizes in same application because it was difficult to define how close two applications are. Instead of exhaustive search, Montgomery et al. [13] used more efficient search approach such as direct search to find the optimal loop schedule. Their approach required to execute the kernels with different loop schedules. Our approach, however, only needs to run the kernel once on CPU because the model predicts the optimal loop schedule before the kernel's execution on GPU. This is one of the major highlights of our proposed framework.

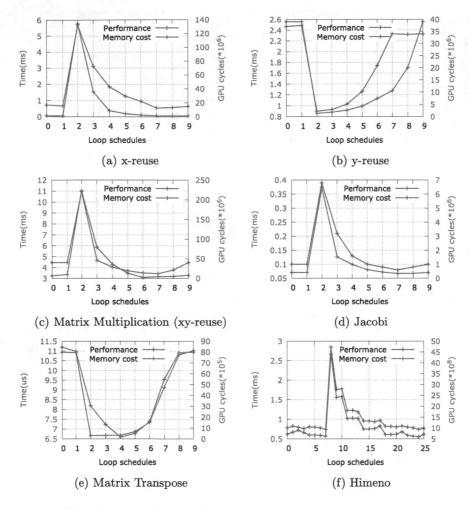

Fig. 13. Plots demonstrating correlation of performance vs memory access cost modeling (Color figure online)

Table 3. Evaluation results

Benchmark	Source	Nested loop type	R^2	Speedup
x-reuse	Synthetic	Double	0.927	1.0
y-reuse	Synthetic	Double	0.683	2.74
Matrix multiplication	Performance test suite	Double	0.913	1.03
Jacobi	Performance test suite	Double	0.998	1.1
Laplacian	Performance test suite	Triple	0.999	1.05
Divergence	Performance test suite	Triple	0.999	0.96
Matrix transpose	CUDA SDK	Double	0.943	1.37
Himeno	EPCC	Triple	0.994	1.09

Lee et al. [11] presented a framework to automatically and efficiently map a nested loop to GPU using Domain Specific Language (DSL). The parameters that form the search space included the dimension of the nested loop, the block size and degree of parallelism, which is essentially the grid size. They applied some hard constraints and soft constraints to restrict the search space. For all loop schedules we consider, many of them have the same software constraints such as the level of memory coalescing. The cache locality, which is a key factor, was not considered in their model.

We looked into some of the other related work on auto-tuning, [8,9,12]; these papers obtained the performance of auto-tuning the kernels by running those kernels. Our goal is different from them since we use an analytical model to predict the loop schedule without running the kernel. Hu et al. [10] and Baghsorkhi et al. [5] used analytical models to predict the performance of a kernel. Our work, however, do not need to predict the execution time of a kernel accurately because the computation part is the basically the same for all loop schedules and the difference of the performance part is the memory cost. Other research include the effect of cache on GPU applications. Picchi and Zhang [15] applied L2 cache locking mechanism to improve GPU application performance. Choi and Kim [7] analyzed the L1 and L2 cache behavior for some benchmarks with a GPU simulator.

7   Conclusion and Future Work

This paper discusses the importance of auto-tuning loop scheduling for GPU computing. We propose an analytical model-based auto-tuning framework to find the optimal or sub-optimal loop schedule that is better than the default loop schedule chosen by the compiler. The model used in the framework is locality-aware as it can predict the cache locality for each loop schedule. The model also predicts the total number of global memory loads and based on these information it obtains a memory access cost for each loop schedule. The framework iterates over all loop schedule patterns and launch configuration space and picks the loop schedule with the least memory access cost. We analyze the proposed framework with multiple benchmarks. The results indicate that the memory access cost modeling has strong correlation with the kernel performance and the loop schedule picked by the framework can achieve 1.29x speedup over the default loop schedule chosen by the compiler. For the future work, we will integrate more factors into the model to improve the prediction of the loop schedule that is as close as the optimal loop schedule.

References

1. EPCC OpenACC Benchmarks (2015). https://www.epcc.ed.ac.uk/research/ computing/performance-characterisation-and-benchmarking/epcc-openacc-bench mark-suite
2. KernelGen Performance Test Suite, December 2015. https://hpcforge.org/plugins/ mediawiki/wiki/kernelgen/index.php/Performance_Test_Suite

3. OpenACC (2016). http://www.openacc.org
4. Almási, G., Caşcaval, C., Padua, D.A.: Calculating stack distances efficiently. In: ACM SIGPLAN Notices, vol. 38, pp. 37–43. ACM (2002)
5. Baghsorkhi, S.S., Delahaye, M., Gropp, W.D., Wen-mei, W.H..: Analytical performance prediction for evaluation and tuning of GPGPU applications. In: Workshop on EPHAM2009, in Conjunction with CGO, Citeseer (2009)
6. Beyls, K., Hollander, E.D.: Reuse distance as a metric for cache behavior. In: Proceedings of the IASTED Conference on Parallel and Distributed Computing and Systems, vol. 14, pp. 350–360 (2001)
7. Choi, K.H., Kim, S.W.: Study of cache performance on GPGPU. IEIE Trans. Smart Process. Comput. **4**(2), 78–82 (2015)
8. Cui, X., Chen, Y., Zhang, C., Mei, H.: Auto-tuning dense matrix multiplication for GPGPU with cache. In: IEEE 16th International Conference on Parallel and Distributed Systems (ICPADS), pp. 237–242. IEEE (2010)
9. Grauer-Gray, S., Xu, L., Searles, R., Ayalasomayajula, S., Cavazos, J.: Auto-tuning a high-level language targeted to GPU codes. In: Innovative Parallel Computing (InPar), pp. 1–10. IEEE (2012)
10. Hu, Y., Koppelman, D.M., Brandt, S.R., Löffler, F.: Model-driven auto-tuning of stencil computations on GPUs. In: Proceedings of the 2nd International Workshop on High-Performance Stencil Computations, pp. 1–8 (2015)
11. Lee, H., Brown, K.J., Sujeeth, A.K., Rompf, T., Olukotun, K.: Locality-aware mapping of nested parallel patterns on GPUs. In: 47th Annual IEEE/ACM International Symposium on Microarchitecture (MICRO), pp. 63–74. IEEE (2014)
12. Mametjanov, A., Lowell, D., Ma, C.-C., Norris, B.: Autotuning stencil-based computations on GPUs. In: IEEE International Conference on Cluster Computing (CLUSTER), pp. 266–274. IEEE (2012)
13. Montgomery, C., Overbey, J.L., Li, X.: Autotuning openACC work distribution via direct search. In: Proceedings of the 2015 XSEDE Conference: Scientific Advancements Enabled by Enhanced Cyberinfrastructure, p. 38. ACM (2015)
14. Nugteren, C., van den Braak, G.-J., Corporaal, H., Bal, H.: A detailed GPU cache model based on reuse distance theory. In: High Performance Computer Architecture (HPCA), pp. 37–48. IEEE (2014)
15. Picchi, J., Zhang, W.: Impact of L2 cache locking on GPU performance. In: SoutheastCon, pp. 1–4. IEEE (2015)
16. Siddiqui, S., AlZayer, F., Feki, S.: Historic learning approach for auto-tuning openACC accelerated scientific applications. VECPAR-2014. LNCS, vol. 8969, pp. 224–235. Springer, Heidelberg (2014)
17. Tang, T., Yang, X., Lin, Y.: Cache miss analysis for GPU programs based on stack distance profile. In: 31st International Conference on Distributed Computing Systems (ICDCS), pp. 623–634. IEEE (2011)
18. Tian, X., Xu, R., Yan, Y., Yun, Z., Chandrasekaran, S., Chapman, B.: Compiling a high-level directive-based programming model for GPGPUs. LCPC 2013. LNCS, vol. 8664, pp. 105–120. Springer International Publishing, New York (2014)

Performance, Design, and Autotuning of Batched GEMM for GPUs

Ahmad Abdelfattah[1]([✉]), Azzam Haidar[1], Stanimire Tomov[1], and Jack Dongarra[1,2,3]

[1] Department of Electrical Engineering and Computer Science, University of Tennessee, Knoxville, USA
{aahmad2,haidar,tomov,dongarra}@eecs.utk.edu
[2] Oak Ridge National Laboratory, Oak Ridge, USA
[3] University of Manchester, Manchester, UK

Abstract. The general matrix-matrix multiplication (GEMM) is the most important numerical kernel in dense linear algebra, and is the key component for obtaining high performance in most LAPACK routines. As batched computations on relatively small problems continue to gain interest in many scientific applications, a need arises for a high performance GEMM kernel for batches of small matrices. Such a kernel should be well designed and tuned to handle small sizes, and to maintain high performance for realistic test cases found in the higher level LAPACK routines, and scientific computing applications in general.

This paper presents a high performance batched GEMM kernel on Graphics Processing Units (GPUs). We address batched problems with both fixed and variable sizes, and show that specialized GEMM designs and a comprehensive autotuning process are needed to handle problems of small sizes. For most performance tests reported in this paper, the proposed kernels outperform state-of-the-art approaches using a K40c GPU.

Keywords: GEMM · Batched GEMM · HPC · GPU computing · Autotuning

1 Introduction

Scientific computing applications extract their high-performance (HP) and efficiency through fast linear algebra libraries, and most notably the GEMM routine. Indeed, in the area of dense linear algebra (DLA), algorithms are designed as much as possible to use GEMM, e.g., as in the LAPACK library. For example, direct solvers for large dense linear system and least squares problems require $O(n^3)$ floating point operations (flops), of which $O(n^3)$ are in GEMM. Consequently, they run as fast/efficiently as running GEMM. Application areas that rely on DLA, and therefore GEMM, are computational electromagnetics, material science, fluid dynamics, applications using boundary integral equations, computational statistics, econometrics, control theory, signal processing, curve fitting, and many more. Therefore, even a slight improvement in GEMM, is extremely valuable and has great impact.

© Springer International Publishing Switzerland 2016
J.M. Kunkel et al. (Eds.): ISC High Performance 2016, LNCS 9697, pp. 21–38, 2016.
DOI: 10.1007/978-3-319-41321-1_2

Aside from scientific computing that requires large DLA, numerous other applications, that will normally require sparse linear algebra computations, use domain decomposition type frameworks where the overall computation is cast in terms of many, but small enough, problems/tasks to fit into certain levels of the machines' memory hierarchy. Many times it is advantageous to represent these small tasks as DLA problems on small matrices, as in applications such as astrophysics [16], metabolic networks [11], CFD and the resulting PDEs through direct and multifrontal solvers [22], high-order FEM schemes for hydrodynamics [5], direct-iterative preconditioned solvers [9], and some image [17] and signal processing [3]. Moreover, even in the area of DLA itself, large dense matrices can be broken into tiles and the algorithms expressed in terms of small tasks over them [2]. Also note that, implementation-wise, large GEMMs are parallelized on current computing architectures, including GPUs, as many small GEMMs. Under these circumstances, the only way to achieve good performance is to find a way to group these small inputs together and run them in large "batches." The most needed and performance-critical kernel here is a batched GEMM [4,7,8]. Finally, tensor contractions, used to model multilinear relations in areas of recent interest like big-data analytics and machine learning, as well as large scale high-order FEM simulations, can also be reduced to batched GEMMs [1].

To address the needs for batched linear algebra on new architectures, as outlined above, we designed high-performance batched GEMM algorithms for GPUs. We consider batched problems with both fixed and variable sizes. While we leverage optimization techniques from the classic GEMM kernel for one multiplication at a time, we also developed a different design scheme for the tuning process that can flexibly select the best performing set of tuning parameters. For variable size problems, we propose new interfaces, as well as techniques, to address the irregularity of the computation. We show that aside from the performance critical algorithmic designs and innovations, a comprehensive auto-tuning process is needed in order to handle the enormous complexity of tuning all GEMM variants resulting from our designs. The complexity is further exacerbated by targeting problems for entire ranges of small sizes (*vs.* for a few discrete sizes). Using a K40c GPU, the proposed kernels outperform state-of-the-art approaches (e.g., cuBLAS and MKL libraries) in most of the performance tests reported in this work.

2   Related Work

To enable GPUs for a large-scale adoption in the HP scientific computing arena, a fast GEMM had to be developed. This became feasible with the introduction of shared memory in the GPUs. While general purpose GPU computing was possible before that, performance was memory bound, as data - once read - could not be reused in many computations. The availability of shared memory made data reuse possible, and the first compute-bound GEMM for GPUs was developed in 2008 [21]. As the GPUs continued improving, new GEMM algorithms had to be developed to better use to the evolving architecture, especially its memory hierarchy. In particular, [18] presented a GEMM algorithm and implementation (in MAGMA, later incorporated in cuBLAS) that applied hierarchical communications/blocking on all memory levels available at the time, including a new register blocking. Blocking sizes, along with other performance-critical choices were parametrized and used in autotuning frameworks [12,14], but improvements were limited to certain very specific matrix sizes. Coding these multilevel blocking types of algorithms in native machine language was used to overcome some limitations of the CUDA compiler or warp scheduler (or both) to achieve better performance [19]. Similarly, assembly implementations [6,13] are used today in cuBLAS for Kepler and Maxwell GPUs to obtain higher performance than corresponding CUDA codes.

Besides the batched GEMM in cuBLAS, there have been a number of research papers on batched GEMM, developed as needed for particular applications. For example, a batched GEMM for very small sizes (up to 16) was developed for a high-order finite element method (FEM) [10]. Tensor contraction computations for large scale high-order FEM simulations were reduced to batched GEMM [1], obtaining close to peak performance for very small matrices (90+% of a theoretically derived peak) using some of the techniques that we developed and describe in detail here. Matrix exponentiation from the phylogenetics domain was reduced to batched GEMMs on small square matrices [15], obtaining very good performance for fixed sizes (4, 20, and 60) in single precision.

3   Batched GEMM Design and Implementation Details

This section discusses the main design and tuning approaches for batched GEMM kernels that support both fixed and variable sizes. From now on, variable size batched GEMM is abbreviated as *vbatched* GEMM. Our goal is to minimize coding effort and to design one kernel that could be easily adapted for use in both fixed and variable size batched GEMM. We begin by considering only fixed size batched problems. We then discuss the modifications we incorporated to handle a variable size problem at the end of the section.

Routine Interface. Each GEMM in a batch routine has the form of the standard BLAS GEMM:

$$C = \alpha \cdot op(A) \times op(B) + \beta \cdot C,$$

where A, B, and C are matrices, α and β are input scalars, and $op()$ specifies whether an input matrix is transposed. The interface of a batched/vbatched kernel must manage independent multiplications of matrices that are not necessarily stored contiguously in memory. As a result, the batched kernel requires the address of every individual matrix. It also requires the size and the leading dimension of every matrix. While such information can be passed using single integers in the fixed sizes case, arrays of integers are needed for the vbatched problems. Our kernels support multiplications with different values for α and β. We also add an extra input argument batchCount that indicates the number of matrices in the batch. Table 1 summarizes an example of the interface written in the C language for the batched/vbatched DGEMM routine.

Table 1. Interface of batched and vbatched matrix multiplication kernel against standard BLAS interface (GEMM: $C = \alpha \cdot op(A) \times op(B) + \beta \cdot C$).

Argument	Description	BLAS	Batched	Vbatched
TRANSA	$op(A)$	char	char	char
TRANSB	$op(B)$	char	char	char
M	Rows of $op(A)/C$	int	int	int*
N	Columns of $op(B)/C$	int	int	int*
K	Columns of $op(A)$/rows of $op(B)$	int	int	int*
α	Alpha	double	double*	double*
A	Input matrix	double*	double**	double**
LDA	Leading dimension of A	int	int	int*
B	Input matrix	double*	double**	double**
LDB	Leading dimension of B	int	int	int*
β	Beta	double	double*	double*
C	Input/output matrix	double*	double**	double**
LDC	Leading dimension of C	int	int	int*
batchCount	Number of matrices	N/A	int	int

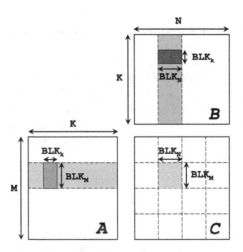

Fig. 1. Example of blocking in the GEMM kernel.

Kernel Design. To design a GEMM kernel in CUDA and take advantage of the available threads, thread blocks and multiprocessors of a GPU, the computation must be partitioned into blocks of threads (also called thread blocks, or simply TBs) that execute independently from each other on the GPU multiprocessors. To do that, as shown in Fig. 1, the matrix C can be subdivided into rectangular blocks of size $\text{BLK}_M \times \text{BLK}_N$, and each of these blocks computed by one TB.

Specifics on how to do this efficiently, e.g., using hierarchical blocking of both communications and computations, as noted in Sect. 2, are given in a design by Nath et al. [18], which is also available in the MAGMA library [20]. We use these ideas to build an extended CUDA kernel that is efficient for batched computations (note that the batched GEMM in cuBLAS also uses this early MAGMA GEMM kernel). However, some rules change here in the case of small matrices. For example, the standard GEMM kernel design tries to maximize the use of shared memory while for batched small GEMM, we should minimize the use of shared memory to allow more than one TB to be executed on the same multiprocessor. The results obtained by our autotuning framework, described below, prove this choice.

The TBs computing a single matrix C can be specified as a 2D grid of size $(\lceil \frac{M}{\mathtt{BLK}\_M} \rceil, \lceil \frac{N}{\mathtt{BLK}\_N} \rceil)$. A TB processes an entire slice of A and an entire slice of B to perform the necessary multiplication. The reading from global memory is blocked, so that the kernel loads a $\mathtt{BLK}_M \times \mathtt{BLK}_K$ block of A and a $\mathtt{BLK}_K \times \mathtt{BLK}_N$ block of B into shared memory, where the multiplication can benefit from the fast shared memory bandwidth. Moreover, a double buffering technique is used to enforce data prefetching into registers, where the computation is additionally blocked. For multiple/batched GEMMs, each C can be computed independently by its 2D grid of TBs, similarly to the standard case. Thus, we design a batched GEMM for a 3D grid of TBs, where one dimension specifies a particular GEMM, and the 2D subgrid specifies the TBs for computing that particular GEMM.

The kernel has many tuning parameters such as the BLK_M, BLK_N, and BLK_K illustrated in Fig. 1, and DIM_X and DIM_Y used to configure the number of threads in a TB, among others to specify algorithmic variations. For example, a key distinction with the case of single GEMM is that matrices can be very small, e.g., sub-warp in size. Therefore, instead of having multiple TBs working on a single C matrix, we have parametrized the basic kernel to allow configurations where a TB computes several GEMMs. This design is critical for obtaining close to peak performances for very small sizes [1].

Search Space Generation and Pruning. The MAGMA batched GEMM kernel has a total of 10 tuning parameters, which can produce millions of combinations if we use a brute-force generator. In can be computationally infeasible to search in an enormous design space like this. Therefore, to reduce it, we use generator rules that accept two sets of constraints in order to prune the parameter space. The first set corresponds to the hardware constraints, as defined by the GPU generation and model. Two examples of such constraints are the maximum number of threads in a TB (e.g., $1,024$ for a Kepler GPU), and the amount of shared memory required per TB (48 KB). Violation of hardware constraints usually leads to compilation errors or kernel launch failures.

The second set represents soft constraints that rule out kernel instances that are unlikely to achieve good performance for batched workloads. Violation of such constraints can still produce runnable kernels, but they are predictably not good candidates from a performance perspective. Specifying the rules is important in order to avoid mispredicting and consequently ruling out good candidates. For example, our experience shows that configurations that use a small number of threads per TB and small amounts of shared memory can be very efficient for batched computations. The explanation for this observation is that multiple TBs can run concurrently on the same Streaming Multiprocessor (SM), thus maximizing throughput. Therefore, we consider kernels that use a number of threads as small as 32, and rule out kernels that tend to maximize the occupancy per TB, e.g., the ones using more than 512 threads per TB. We point out that this is the opposite of a previous work that targeted classic GEMM operations [12], where the soft constraints were set to rule out kernels using less than 512 threads. Our search space generator ended up with 6, 400 eligible GEMM kernels. Since the autotuning experiment is performed once per a GPU model, we found that a brute-force approach is feasible to test all the eligible kernels within a reasonable amount of time.

Test Cases. A classical test case for a GEMM kernel is to tune for square matrices which is a good choice if only large matrices are targeted. However, this scenario rarely appears in higher-level LAPACK routines, such as the LU and QR factorizations, where the multiplication usually involves rectangular matrices (tall-skinny and short-wide matrices), with relatively small values of K compared to M and N. For small matrices computation, K gets even smaller. For example, the batched LU factorization [7] uses a panel of width up to 128, but it performs the panel factorization recursively as two panels of width 64, each factorized as two panels of width 32. Eventually, each panel of width 32 is factorized as four panels of size 8. Figure 2 shows this recursive nested blocking in the batched LU factorization for small matrices. As a result, in addition to the square sizes, we define our test cases as having discrete small values of K (8, 16, 32, etc.), while varying M and N.

For simplicity, all performance tests are conducted for fixed size batched computations, so that we can specify a winning kernel instance for every tested size. The vbatched GEMM kernel is assumed to have the same tuning decision as the fixed size batched GEMM.

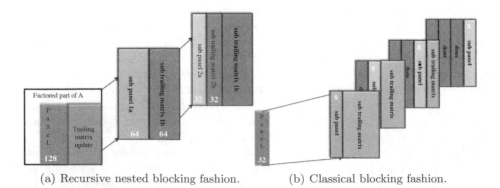

(a) Recursive nested blocking fashion.   (b) Classical blocking fashion.

Fig. 2. Recursive nested panel factorization in batched LU.

Autotuning Output Analysis. For every test case – specified by precision, a transposition mode that we call *shape*, and (M, N, K) sizes – we run all eligible GEMM kernels. We developed an automated selection process that sorts all kernels according to their performances at each data point, and stores the ID of the kernel instance with the best performance. After repeating the same step for all data points, the automated process selects the five (this number can be chosen by the user) most frequent kernel instances that scored the best performance across all data points. We also plot the maximal and the minimal performance obtained by all the kernels at every data point. For a fixed size GEMM: for every shape (e.g., NN, NT, etc.), every test case (e.g., square, tall-skinny $K = 8$ tall-skinny $K = 32$, wide, etc.), one or multiple winning versions can be selected in such a way as to provide the best performance for the entire range of sizes. For variable size GEMM: for every shape, we select one winning version that scores a performance within 5–10% of the best achievable performance and that fits all the sizes for a specific test case. The details for these choices are described below.

Performance Sensitivity and Software Framework. Figure 3 shows example performance graphs for some test cases, where the five best performing kernel instances are nominated by our selection process. We observe that not only different test cases have different winning versions, but also a single test case may have two or three winning versions according to the ranges of M and N. Unlike tuning for big matrices [12], which ended up with four kernels across all test cases, we observe that the performance is very sensitive for small matrices, and an efficient software framework that can call the correct winning version for each test case is required. Such a framework should be able to handle a large number of versions while preserving reasonable programming and coding effort. It should also provide an easy-to-modify code structure for future tuning experiments.

Template-Based Design. The original tuning of the classic GEMM kernels [18] resulted in finding a few versions, best for different cases. Each version is instantiated in a separate file where the corresponding tuning parameters are listed using compile-time macros (**#define**). This structure is impractical if many kernel versions are considered. Another drawback of such a design is that a kernel version must have all shapes covered. This is an unnecessary restriction, since we might need more kernels for the NN shape than for the NT shape, for example. It is more flexible to decouple GEMM shapes from each other.

Therefore, we use CUDA C++ templates to enable a unified code base for the batched/vbatched GEMM kernels. Templates enable an easy instantiation of a kernel with specific precision and tuning parameters. Figure 4 shows an example for the DGEMM routine using templates. Each set of tuning parameters is described as an array of integers. In addition, switching among versions becomes as simple as changing a single number, namely the kernel ID passed to the **instance** macro. We point out that the condition list in Fig. 4 is relatively short in practice, since our experiments show that we need less than a handful of versions per precision. The only cost, which is paid once, is the need to generate all possible combinations of tuning parameters using the space generator. Once this step is finished, any future changes to the code in Fig. 4 become very

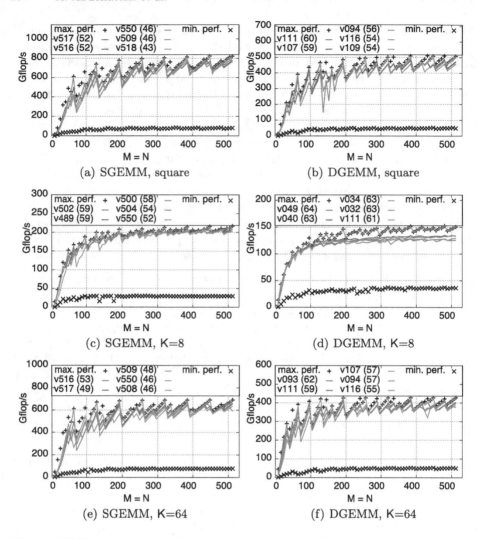

Fig. 3. GEMM performance of the five most frequent, best performing kernels in selected test cases. Each instance is associated with an ID and the number of occurrences. batchCount = 500. (Color figure online)

simple. In addition, there is no need to keep the same number of kernels across all shapes, or keep different DGEMM versions in separate files.

Now we describe how we move from the fixed size batched GEMM to the **vbatched GEMM**. There are two main approaches to address a vbatched problem on GPUs. The first assumes that a vbatched kernel is launched directly from the CPU side. Since the launch involves configuration of TBs, the kernel must be configured to accommodate the largest matrix dimensions in the batch. As a result, subgrids assigned to smaller matrices will have some threads (or even full TBs) with no work. We developed *Early Termination Mechanisms (ETMs)* to solve this problem. An ETM is a lightweight software layer that, at the beginning

```
1  #define NN_V_0    2, 32, 16, 8, 1
2  #define NN_V_1    4,  8, 32, 4, 1
3
4  #define NT_V_0    4, 16, 32, 4, 0
5  #define NT_V_1    8, 24, 16, 2, 1
6  /* other version definitions */
7
8  #define instance(shape,v) shape ## _V_ ## v
9  #include "gemm_kernel_template.h"
10
11 void dgemm(/* input arguments */){
12     /* some code */
13     switch(shape)
14     {
15         case "nn":
16         if(/* condition nn-1 */)
17             gemm_template<double, instance(NN,0)>(/* arg */);
18         else if (/* condition nn-2 */)
19             gemm_template<double, instance(NN,1)>(/* arg */);
20         /* other conditions */
21         break;
22         case "nt":
23         if(/* condition nt-1 */)
24             gemm_template<double, instance(NT,0)>(/* arg */);
25         else if (/* condition nt 2 */)
26             gemm_template<double, instance(NT,1)>(/* arg */);
27         /* other conditions */
28         break;
29         /* Repeat for all shapes */
30     }
31     /* some code */
32 }
```

Fig. 4. DGEMM routines using templates with flexible switching.

of a kernel launch, identifies threads with no work and immediately terminates them to avoid over-occupancy and memory access violations. ETMs are implemented at the level of a thread, so that each thread can independently determine whether it should proceed with the execution or not. Note that such an approach requires these maximal dimensions to be known on the CPU side prior to the kernel launch.

The second approach is based on the relatively new CUDA GPUs technology called *dynamic parallelism*. It enables a GPU kernel to launch another GPU kernel. In this case, a vbatched kernel is launched from the GPU side. The CPU role is to launch a *parent kernel* with a total number of CUDA threads equal to the number of matrices in the batch. Each CUDA thread then launches a GPU GEMM kernel for one matrix based on its dimensions. As opposed to the first approach, dynamic parallelism waives the need to know the largest dimensions across all matrices. However, it assumes that the underlying CUDA runtime will schedule execution of the *child kernels* efficiently on the GPU, which is not always the case, as described in Sect. 4. Dynamic parallelism is a technology that is available only on GPUs with compute capability 3.5 (Kepler) or higher.

The vbatched GEMM kernel uses the same code base as the fixed size batched routine, with the use of either ETMs or dynamic parallelism. Examples for both approaches are highlighted in Fig. 5. Shown are the output matrices of three independent GEMMs. The first approach (ETMs) requires knowledge about the maximum values of M, N, and K across all matrices. Note that such values do not necessarily belong to one matrix. Based on these values, it determines the GEMM kernel version to be called. As shown in Fig. 5(a), all matrices are processed using a single kernel that is called from the CPU. Each subgrid is responsible for one matrix. All matrices are subdivided using the same blocking size. The ETM layer is responsible for terminating TBs marked by ×, which do not have any work. The second approach, which is based on dynamic parallelism, lets the CPU launch a parent kernel with a number of *master threads*. Each master thread launches a GEMM kernel for its assigned matrix, and it chooses the best working GEMM instance for it. Consequently, this approach allows matrices to be subdivided using different blocking sizes.

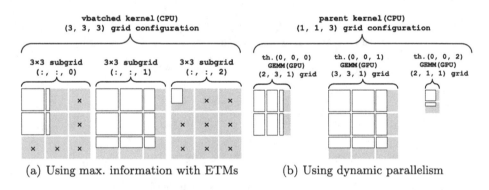

(a) Using max. information with ETMs   (b) Using dynamic parallelism

Fig. 5. Approaches for vbatched GEMM.

4   Performance Results and Analysis

System Setup. Performance tests are conducted on a machine equipped with two 8-core Intel Sandy Bridge CPUs (Intel Xeon E5–2670, running at 2.6 GHz), and a Kepler generation GPU (Tesla K40c, running at 745 MHz, with ECC on). CPU performance tests use Intel MKL Library 11.3.0. GPU performance tests use CUDA Toolkit 7.0. Due to space limitations, we show results for double precision only. We point out that the proposed tuned kernels support all other precisions, with roughly similar performance behavior. The performance of the MAGMA GEMM kernel is compared against the cuBLAS batched GEMM kernel, the cuBLAS classic GEMM kernel offloaded to concurrent streams, and the MKL GEMM kernel running on 16 CPU cores. The MKL library is configured to assign

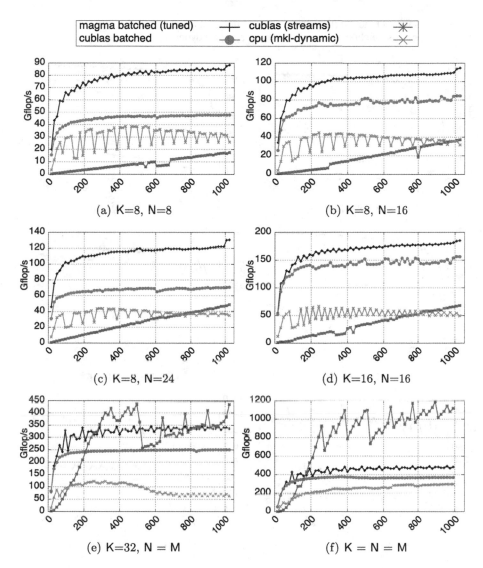

Fig. 6. Fixed size batched DGEMM performance for shape NN. (Color figure online)

one core per matrix at a time, and is used within an OpenMP parallel loop that is dynamically unrolled to balance the workload among cores.

Fixed Size. Figure 6 shows the performance for the NN shape, with different problem sizes that are typically used in higher-level factorization and solve algorithms. The tuned MAGMA kernel achieves the best performance when K is small, regardless of M, and N. In Figs. 6(a) through 6(d), it scores speedups of up to 87 %, 38 %, 86 %, and 26 % against the best competitor (cuBLAS batched), respectively. Starting K = 32, the MAGMA DGEMM kernel loses its advantage to the streamed GEMM, except for the small range of M and N, which is of particular

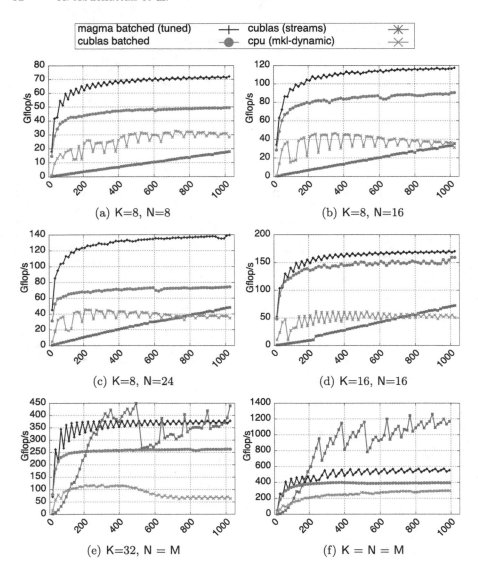

Fig. 7. Fixed size batched DGEMM performance for shape NT. (Color figure online)

importance for batched computation. In Fig. 6(e) and (f), MAGMA is generally faster than the batched cuBLAS kernel, achieving up to 43 % and 35 % speedups, respectively. However, the streamed GEMM, apart from some drops in Fig. 6(e), becomes the best performing kernel when M and N are around 200. A similar behavior is observed in Fig. 7 for the NT shape. MAGMA scores speedups up to 48 %, 39 %, 96 %, and 16 % against the batched cuBLAS kernel, for Figs. 7(a) through 7(d), respectively. When K gets larger as in Fig. 7(e) and (f), MAGMA has the advantage for relatively small values of M and N, with a 45 % speedup against batched cuBLAS for K = 32, and a slightly better better performance

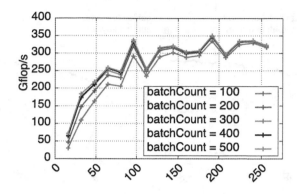

Fig. 8. Impact of batchCount on performance (DGEMM, shape NN, K=32, N=M). (Color figure online)

for the square case. Otherwise, the streamed cuBLAS kernel mostly achieves the best performance, except for the midrange in Fig. 7(e), where MAGMA takes over.

Figure 8 shows an example of the effect of batchCount on performance. As expected, a larger batchCount can affect the performance significantly for small matrix sizes, with at least 40 % performance difference for sizes less than 50. This is because the GPU is not saturated with enough work for small batchCount of such size range. Such performance difference decreases consistently as the sizes get larger. We observe that, in most of our tests, there is negligible impact of batchCount on performance after size 256.

Variable Size. Now considering the matrix test suites for the vbatched GEMM, each point M on the x-axis in Figs. 9 and 10 represents a distribution of sizes. Given a maximum value of M, the interval [1:M] is sampled randomly according to a certain distribution in order to generate the sizes. In this paper, we show results for uniform and Gaussian distributions.

Figure 9 shows the performance for the vbatched DGEMM kernel against a uniform distribution for the NN shape, while Fig. 10 considers the NT shape. In both shapes, the MAGMA DGEMM based on ETMs has a clear advantage in Figs. 9(a) through 9(d), and 10(a) through 10(d). The MAGMA DGEMM kernel based on dynamic parallelism is either equal to or better than the former approach for relatively large sizes in the cases of K = 32 and square matrices. The asymptotic speedups scored by the ETM-based kernel against streamed GEMM/MKL are $6.73\times/5.47\times$, $5.45\times/2.18\times$, $3.75\times/10.20\times$, and $4.34\times/11.06\times$ in Figs. 9(a) through 9(d), and $8.34\times/10.52\times$, $4.82\times/7.86\times$, $4.20\times/9.38\times$, and $3.80\times/9.86\times$ in Figs. 10(a) through 10(d), respectively. In Figs. 9(e) and 10(e), there is no winning kernel for all sizes. The two MAGMA kernels outperform other competitors for Maximum M up to 300. The streamed GEMM dominates the midrange, and then gets nearly matched or slightly outperformed by the

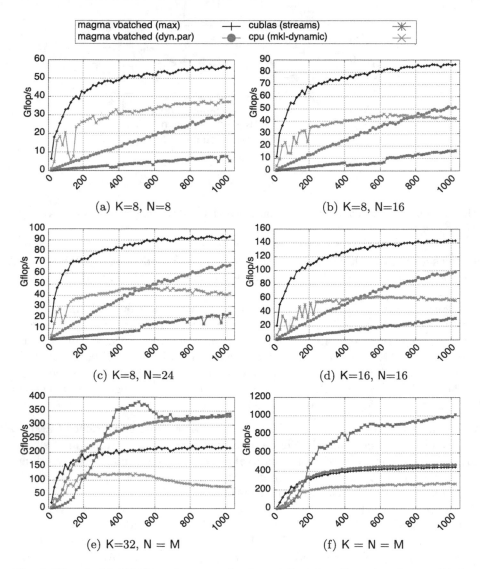

Fig. 9. Vbatched DGEMM performance for shape NN with uniform distribution. (Color figure online)

MAGMA kernel based on dynamic parallelism. For the case of square matrices (Figs. 9(f) and 10(f)), the streamed GEMM achieves the best performance unless matrices are too small, where the ETM-based MAGMA kernel is the best choice. We observe a similar behavior when we repeat all the above test cases based on the Gaussian distribution. For space limitations, we highlight only two test cases for the NN shape in Fig. 11.

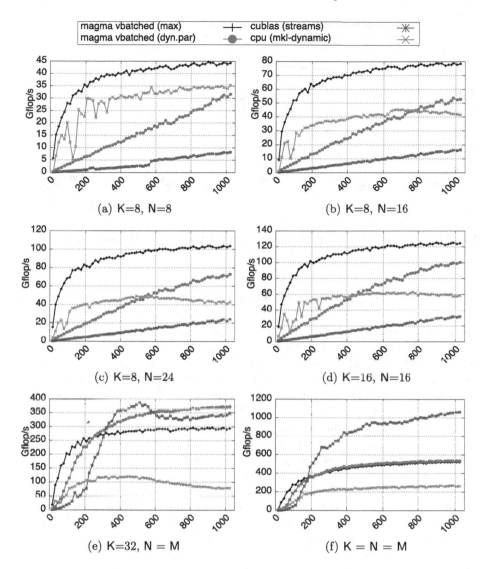

Fig. 10. Vbatched DGEMM performance for shape NT with uniform distribution (Color figure online)

Sub-warp Sizes. Finally, we want to point out that the framework presented was also used to find batched GEMM kernels for very small (sub-warp in size) matrices. Performance there is memory bound and can be modeled. Results show that we obtain close to peak performance [1] (90+% of the theoretically derived peak) to significantly outperform cuBLAS on GPUs and MKL on CPUs.

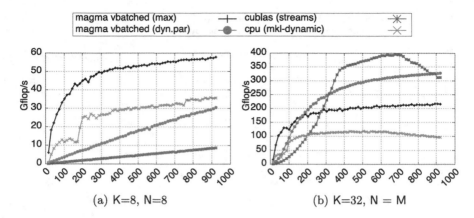

Fig. 11. Vbatched DGEMM performance for shape NN with Gaussian distribution (Color figure online)

5   Conclusion and Future Work

This paper presented a design and autotuning framework for fixed and variable size batched matrix-matrix multiplication using GPUs. Similarly to the GEMM routine, batched GEMMs on small matrices are needed in many applications from big-data analytics to data mining, and more. The work focused on the algorithmic design and performance autotuning for small fixed and variable sizes on test cases found in batched LAPACK factorization and solve algorithms. With a comprehensive autotuning process and a flexible software framework, we are able to find and call the best kernel configuration (within our design space) according to many deciding factors. The flexible software scheme ensures minimal coding effort if future changes are required, and can be used efficiently for other computational kernels that have a large number of tuning parameters.

Future directions include adding support for multiplications with different shapes within the same GPU kernel, thorough testing of the vbatched routine against different size distributions, and performance analysis and profiling of the dynamic-parallelism based kernels in order to analyze and understand their behavior and overhead. Work on applying and tuning the batched GEMMs in specific applications, e.g., using application-specific knowledge, especially in computing applications requiring variable sizes like direct multifrontal solvers for sparse matrices, is of high interest and subject to future work.

Acknowledgment. This work is based upon work supported by the National Science Foundation under Grants No. ACI-1339822 and CSR 1514286, NVIDIA, the Department of Energy (LLNL subcontract under DOE contract DE-AC52-07NA27344), and in part by the Russian Scientific Foundation, Agreement N14-11-00190.

References

1. Abdelfattah, A., Baboulin, M., Dobrev, V., Dongarra, J., Earl, C., Falcou, J., Haidar, A., Karlin, I., Kolev, T., Masliah, I., Tomov, S.: High-performance tensor contractions for GPUs. In: International Conference on Computational Science (ICCS 2016). Elsevier, Procedia Computer Science, San Diego, CA, USA, June 2016
2. Agullo, E., Demmel, J., Dongarra, J., Hadri, B., Kurzak, J., Langou, J., Ltaief, H., Luszczek, P., Tomov, S.: Numerical linear algebra on emerging architectures: the PLASMA and MAGMA projects. J. Phys.: Conf. Ser. **180**(1), 012037 (2009)
3. Anderson, M., Sheffield, D., Keutzer, K.: A predictive model for solving small linear algebra problems in GPU registers. In: IEEE 26th International Parallel Distributed Processing Symposium (IPDPS) (2012)
4. Dong, T., Haidar, A., Luszczek, P., Harris, A., Tomov, S., Dongarra, J.: LU Factorization of small matrices: accelerating batched DGETRF on the GPU. In: Proceedings of 16th IEEE International Conference on High Performance and Communications (HPCC 2014) August 2014
5. Dong, T., Dobrev, V., Kolev, T., Rieben, R., Tomov, S., Dongarra, J.: A step towards energy efficient computing: redesigning a hydrodynamic application on CPU-GPU. In: IEEE 28th International Parallel Distributed Processing Symposium (IPDPS) (2014)
6. Gray, S.: A full walk through of the SGEMM implementation (2015). https://github.com/NervanaSystems/maxas/wiki/SGEMM
7. Haidar, A., Dong, T., Luszczek, P., Tomov, S., Dongarra, J.: Batched matrix computations on hardware accelerators based on GPUs. Int. J. High Perform. Comput. Appl. (2015). http://hpc.sagepub.com/content/early/2015/02/06/1094342014567546.abstract
8. Haidar, A., Dong, T.T., Tomov, S., Luszczek, P., Dongarra, J.: A framework for batched and GPU-resident factorization algorithms applied to block householder transformations. In: Kunkel, J.M., Ludwig, T. (eds.) ISC High Performance 2015. LNCS, vol. 9137, pp. 31–47. Springer, Heidelberg (2015)
9. Im, E.J., Yelick, K., Vuduc, R.: Sparsity: optimization framework for sparse matrix kernels. Int. J High Perform Comput. Appl. **18**(1), 135–158 (2004). http://dx.doi.org/10.1177/1094342004041296
10. Jhurani, C., Mullowney, P.: A GEMM interface and implementation on NVIDIA GPUs for multiple small matrices. CoRR abs/1304.7053 (2013). http://arxiv.org/abs/1304.7053
11. Khodayari, A., Zomorrodi, A.R., Liao, J.C., Maranas, C.: A kinetic model of escherichia coli core metabolism satisfying multiple sets of mutant flux data. Metab. Eng. **25C**, 50–62 (2014)
12. Kurzak, J., Tomov, S., Dongarra, J.: Autotuning GEMM kernels for the Fermi GPU. IEEE Trans. Parallel Distrib. Syst. **23**(11), 2045–2057 (2012)
13. Lai, J., Seznec, A.: Performance upper bound analysis and optimization of SGEMM on Fermi and Kepler GPUs. In: Proceedings of the 2013 IEEE/ACM International Symposium on Code Generation and Optimization (CGO), CGO 2013, pp. 1–10. IEEE Computer Society, Washington, DC, USA (2013). http://dx.doi.org/10.1109/CGO.2013.6494986
14. Li, Y., Dongarra, J., Tomov, S.: A note on auto-tuning GEMM for GPUs. In: Allen, G., Nabrzyski, J., Seidel, E., van Albada, G.D., Dongarra, J., Sloot, P.M.A. (eds.) ICCS 2009, Part I. LNCS, vol. 5544, pp. 884–892. Springer, Heidelberg (2009)

15. Lopez, M., Horton, M.: Batch matrix exponentiation. In: Kindratenko, V. (ed.) Numerical Computations with GPUs, pp. 45–67. Springer International Publishing (2014), http://dx.doi.org/10.1007/978-3-319-06548-9_3
16. Messer, O.E.B., Harris, J.A., Parete-Koon, S., Chertkow, M.A.: Multicore and accelerator development for a leadership-class stellar astrophysics code. In: Manninen, P., Öster, P. (eds.) PARA 2012. LNCS, vol. 7782, pp. 92–106. Springer, Heidelberg (2013)
17. Molero, J., Garzón, E., García, I., Quintana-Ortí, E., Plaza, A.: Poster: a batched Cholesky solver for local RX anomaly detection on GPUs, PUMPS (2013)
18. Nath, R., Tomov, S., Dongarra, J.: An improved magma GEMM for fermi graphics processing units. Int. J. High Perform. Comput. Appl. **24**(4), 511–515 (2010). http://dx.doi.org/10.1177/1094342010385729
19. Tan, G., Li, L., Triechle, S., Phillips, E., Bao, Y., Sun, N.: Fast implementation of DGEMM on Fermi GPU. In: Proceedings of 2011 International Conference for High Performance Computing, Networking, Storage and Analysis, SC 2011, pp. 35:1–35:11. ACM, New York (2011). http://doi.acm.org/10.1145/2063384.2063431
20. Tomov, S., Dongarra, J., Baboulin, M.: Towards dense linear algebra for hybrid GPU accelerated manycore systems. Parellel Comput. Syst. Appl. **36**(5–6), 232–240 (2010)
21. Volkov, V., Demmel, J.: Benchmarking GPUs to tune dense linear algebra. In: SC 2008: Proceedings of the 2008 ACM/IEEE conference on Supercomputing, pp. 1–11. IEEE Press, Piscataway (2008)
22. Yeralan, S.N., Davis, T.A., Ranka, S.: Sparse mulitfrontal QR on the GPU. Technical report, University of Florida Technical Report (2013). http://faculty.cse.tamu.edu/davis/publications_files/qrgpu_paper.pdf

TCU: A Multi-Objective Hardware Thread Mapping Unit for HPC Clusters

Ravi Kumar Pujari$^{(\boxtimes)}$, Thomas Wild, and Andreas Herkersdorf

Institute for Integrated Systems, Technische Universität München,
Munich, Germany
{ravi.kumar,thomas.wild,herkersdorf}@tum.de

Abstract. Meeting multiple, partially orthogonal optimization targets during thread scheduling on HPC and manycore platforms simultaneously, like maximizing CPU performance, meeting deadlines of time critical tasks, minimizing power and securing thermal resilience, is a major challenge because of associated scalability and thread management overhead. We tackle these challenges by introducing the Thread Control Unit (TCU), a configurable, low-latency, low-overhead hardware thread mapper in compute nodes of an HPC cluster. The TCU takes various sensor information into account and can map threads to 4–16 CPUs of a compute node within a small and bounded number of clock cycles in round-robin, single- or multi-objective manner. The TCU design can consider not just load balancing or performance criteria but also physical constraints like temperature limits, power budgets and reliability aspects. Evaluations of different mapping policies show that multi-objective thread mapping provides about 10 to 40 % less mapping latency for periodic workloads compared to single-objective or round-robin policies. For bursty workloads under high load conditions, a 20 % reduction is achieved.

The TCU macro has a mere 9 % hardware area overhead and achieves more than 150 k thread mappings per second on an FPGA prototype of a RISC quad-core compute node operating at moderate 50 MHz. A 45 nm technology ASIC realization of TCU can operate well above 1 GHz and support up to 3.15 million thread mappings per second.

Keywords: Hardware scheduler · Thread mapper · Multi-objective · MPSoC · HPC · Manycore systems

1 Introduction

Supercomputers were traditionally built by connecting many single CPU motherboards over Ethernet. Advancements in fabrication technology resulted in increased integration density in terms of number of transistors per die area. System-on-chip (SoC) architectures with manycore processor [8,9,15] connected over bus or network on chip evolved. High Performance Computing (HPC) clusters are now realized by interconnecting many such multi-socket multiprocessor SoC nodes over Ethernet backplane or InfiniBand switches [1].

© Springer International Publishing Switzerland 2016
J.M. Kunkel et al. (Eds.): ISC High Performance 2016, LNCS 9697, pp. 39–58, 2016.
DOI: 10.1007/978-3-319-41321-1_3

Along with the advent of many flavors of multiprocessor systems, algorithms with parallel programming constructs like tasks, processes and threads were developed. Threads represent a unit of code which can be run in parallel on a processor. Most of the modern day application programs are modeled as single or multiple threads and are designed to exploit the thread level parallelism. Compute resources are shared among multiple threads either by (a) temporal multiplexing on a uniprocessor system using a timer tick and/or (b) spatial multiplexing as done in symmetric multi-processor systems (SMP). OpenMP (for SMP) and/or MPI (for NUMA) library constructs are used to program multi-threaded applications for HPC. These applications are written with performance as an optimization goal. Efficiency in terms of meeting deadlines, higher throughput or higher MIPS are the main objectives while mapping threads.

Thermal, power and reliability [2, 6, 11] concerns on these many-processor compute platforms favor spatial multiplexing of threads. On one hand we have the dynamics of chip status like power consumption, heat dissipation, temperature gradients leading to hotspots or reliability issues, and on the other hand the changing application workloads results in differential utilization of processor cores and variations in cache hit/miss rates and memory or IO bandwidth requirements. Not just sheer performance but power or thermal resilience also have to be considered while mapping threads on such manycore HPC systems. We deal here with optimization problems with orthogonal requirements: applications want faster or guaranteed performance while from the hardware's health perspective it is desirable to run slower and cooler. Meeting multiple objectives while operating so many processors in an HPC cluster is a burden for the conventional software-based middleware or operating systems.

Figure 1 shows an HPC cluster architecture wherein compute nodes are connected over a backplane board or infiniBand switches. Each of these compute nodes are multi-socket, multicore processing systems with reconfigurable fabric. This paper mainly deals with the architectural support needed for better coupling between these compute nodes and presents the Thread Control Unit (TCU), a hardware multi-objective thread mapper realized using the reconfigurable logic blocks on each compute node. A Fast, tunable, multi-objective in-hardware thread mapping strategy which considers multiple sensors while assigning threads to processors is the central idea of the TCU. For pragmatic reasons and to limit the feasibility proof for the TCU in this work, an integrated multi-core FPGA prototype design comprising of two compute nodes connected over a NoC link is developed.

In the following section we first present the prior art of different software- and hardware-based approaches employed in thread mapping and their objectives or optimization goals. Next we introduce our multi-objective thread mapping strategy which makes use of multiple sensors followed by concrete realization of the TCU on an FPGA prototype design. In a later section the performance evaluation of the TCU using different synthetic workloads is shown, and we conclude with the merits and outlook for this work.

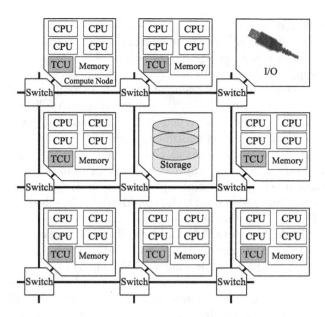

Fig. 1. TCU placed within HPC compute nodes

2   Related Work

Resource management on multi-processor systems is conventionally performed in the software layers like programming language libraries, middleware software or operating system (OS). In particular, the mapping of threads on to cores is done by a resource manager. A time sharing, pre-emptive or cooperative OS scheduler performs this by means of system calls. Searching and allocating processor cores to map threads, the context switches due to system calls add up as additional time overhead to each thread.

This delay overhead would become a severe bottleneck [12]; about 30 % for fine grained parallel application threads which are of just a few 1000 s of CPU clock cycles. In order to avoid frequent context switches, the resource management is done in a layer higher in the software stack, namely in user space. Cilk [7], a C/C++ library extension, for example uses spawning of many lightweight user level threads being managed by one worker thread per core. Similarly, OpenMP [5], Intel thread building blocks [13] and MPI are language/library extensions implementing run time support for spawning and unrolling of *loop parallel* programs. Erlang [14] runtime system similarly provides implementation of lightweight threads/processes which are run on top of a single OS scheduled process per core. Each OS scheduled process has its own ready queue (FIFO). The runtime systems of these languages/libraries make use of spawn-sync mechanisms to create threads and manage inter-thread communication. A central aspect of all these programming extensions is the ready queue management by worker threads. Many other OS processes can coexist along with these application-specific worker threads. Thus only a share of the time slice of the processor as allocated and allowed by the underlying pre-emptive/cooperative operating system is used by the worker thread. Load balancing among the worker threads is achieved by means of a work stealing approach or active migration of jobs.

As an OS support provided in the programming stack, Tessellation [3], a thin, hypervisor-like resource management solution, employs two-stage scheduling namely (a) resource allocation, (b) resource usage. Applications are built in resource containers (cells) and scheduling of threads is done within a cell boundary by a software user level runtime system. Cells can be non-multiplexed (exclusive access to hardware resources), time-triggered, event-triggered and best effort. This two-stage scheduling approach to manage hundreds of cores is welcome, but the non-functional physical aspects of the underlying chip like temperature, power or reliability also need to be considered while scheduling. Similarly, in Cilk, OpenMP and MPI libraries load balancing criteria do not consider these non-functional physical aspects. The objective is to be as fast as possible and purely performance-centric. Accounting for the physical effects is mainly left to the underlying hardware abstraction layer (HAL) of the OS.

Static temperature-aware task scheduling based on Integer Linear Programming (ILP) problem formulation running on a eight-core UltraSPARC T1 processor is presented in [4]. Dynamic techniques for load balancing as an extension to Solaris scheduler is also presented wherein the threads are moved among ready queues per cores. This thread migration is done at the interval of 20 s. Obtaining an ILP solution for every new thread spawned is not a feasible approach if the problem domain is expanded to hundreds of cores with large volumes of fast fluctuating sensor data. ILP helps if there is a-priori knowledge of threads incarnation and execution pattern. If not just temperature, but also power, reliability sensors, performance counters, etc. are also to be considered for ILP, then the search space of resource management would grow exponentially.

Carbon [10] tries to address the user space ready queue management for user level threads by having dedicated on-chip hardware extensions in the form of Local and Global Thread Units (LTU, GTU). The essence of load balancing is in pulling threads from GTU into LTU if the LTU FIFOs are free. The GTU and LTU are modeled as hardware blocks and evaluated using an in-house ISA simulator. The software layers are agnostic to the underlying load balancing.

Hardware extensions like Carbon follow an inherent optimization policy of "faster the better", when mapping threads. Physical constraints like thermal limitations, power budget (dark silicon) aren't considered. Software optimizations which address these have very large time constants of load balancing. Hence there is a need for a fast, scalable and multi-objective thread mapping strategy in 100+ core architectures which doesn't add additional overhead. A pure software-only approach is not sufficient, instead adequate hardware support is needed to mitigate the overhead of optimization while mapping threads. We address these deficiencies in this paper by employing an in-hardware thread mapping strategy and introduce our TCU. The TCU takes the physical runtime characteristic of chip into account while mapping threads and can be augmented to existing parallel programming constructs like OpenMP, Cilk or MPI.

3 Hardware Accelerated Thread Assignment

In this paper, we address the problem of thread management with compute nodes of HPC clusters as shown in Fig. 1. We assume applications are broken down into multiple independent threads and these threads can be run to completion on any of the CPUs. An application in need of computational resources requests the operating system or resource manager to identify and allocate compute nodes. The resource manager can identify the currently free compute nodes as done in current conventional HPC clusters. To mitigate the mapping overhead and enable a mapping that takes current load, temperature and dependability monitoring infrastructure into account, we propose that actual mapping and ready queue management of the threads be offloaded to dedicated hardware.

We introduce hardware extension in the compute nodes in the form of thread control units (TCU) (Fig. 1). Applications send jobs or threads to the compute nodes allocated to them. Incoming threads are assigned to cores by the dedicated TCU present in each node. The threads are sent to the TCU directly from an application running on a CPU on a remote node. The next section elaborates the mapping principle of the TCU.

3.1 Multi-objective Thread Assignment

To achieve synergy between performance and physical operating limitations, applications need to express their demands and hardware should try to give differential quality of service at the expense of associated cost. Figure 2 illustrates this problem concretely in the context of mapping the incoming threads on to ready queues of processors. We address this thread mapping problem in the following section.

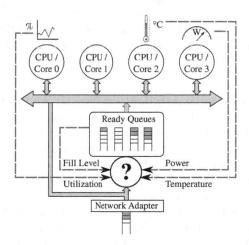

Fig. 2. Thread mapping problem

Sensors and Monitors in a Multi-processor System: Different approaches are used to measure the performance of an application. We considered both performance counter-based monitors and sensors for physical effects like power consumption, temperature, etc. Table 1 lists some of the available sensors/monitors per processor core.

Table 1. Sensors per core in a compute node

Sensors	V_{min}	V_{max}	Bits	Unit
Ready queue fill level	0	64	7	(-)
CPU utilization (measure of pipeline stalls)	0	100	16	(%)
CPU temperature	22	85	8	(°C)
CPU power	10	46	16	MW
Arrival rate (of threads)	0	1000	16	Threads/ms
Service rate (per core)	0	1000	16	Threads/ms

An application may have objective functions like high performance operation (implying higher CPU utilization and higher service rate) which can be orthogonal to lower power mode of operation (lower temperature and power values). At any given point in time, these monitors can have arbitrary values based on the current/past run-time behavior of applications. As a consequence, (a) it is really difficult for an application programmer to express the exact values for these sensors that are suitable for the application to run and (b) also for the OS, the search space would be prohibitively large to find a processor matching all the hardware monitoring conditions as desired by an application. Finding a processor meeting the right balance of the required sensor values is an NP hard problem. Studies on NoC-based MPSoCs [12] show that even a single hop radius search within the same chip can cost considerable runtime overhead. This overhead can be even larger for multi-socket off-chip many-processor compute platforms. Thus to tackle this scalability problem hardware assistance is used.

Coupling Sensor Data with Application Needs: Applications can't express the exact sensor values they need in order to run properly. Instead applications can easily express the relative importance of the different sensors. To express the application needs with respect to the desired sensor values, we classify the applications into finite set of different classes.

Table 2 depicts the application classification based on the relative importance of each of these monitors under different classes. Each class is defined by a set of sensor weights, which are pre-set or tuned by the runtime software. Class 0 implements a simple round-robin scheme, whereas classes 1, 2 and 3 are single-objective giving preference to only one of the sensors. Classes 4 and 5 represent multi-objective assignment policies which consider multiple sensors simultaneously. The number of classes can be extended based on other sensors like cache

Table 2. Application class configuration matrix with weights for different sensors

Class	ID	Sensors				
		Fill level	CPU Util.	CPU Temp.	Arrival rate	Service rate
Round-robin	0	0	0	0	0	0
Low-latency	1	1	0	0	0	0
Compute-intensive	2	0	1	0	0	0
Low-temperature	3	0	0	1	0	0
Multi-objective	4	0.3	0.3	0.3	0	0
Multi-objective	5	1	0	0	0.3	0.3

miss counters etc. Applications express their hardware needs by specifying their class_id as part of the thread descriptor. We assume a thread descriptor having a 3-tuple data structure *(void * thread, void * argv, char class_id)* with the memory footprint of just 9 bytes. As a concrete example, the *#pragma* in OpenMP could be extended with an additional class_id field as shown in the below code snippet. A similar adaptation can be done for Cilk or MPI programming constructs to provide the class_id of the threads being spawned.

```
omp_set_num_threads(READY_QUEUE_SIZE * NUM_CPU);
#pragma omp parallel for class_id(compute_intensive)
{
    unsigned int i,j,k;
    for (i = 0; i < N; i++)
        for (j = 0; j < M; j++)
            for (k = 0; k < P; k++)
                c[i][j] = a[i][k] * b[k][j];
}
```

Figure 3 depicts that different normalized sensors are weighted to identify the core to map new threads spawned by an application. This multi-objective thread mapping strategy addresses the problem in Fig. 2. Based on the weights applied and the current sensor value of each core, the thread mapper assigns incoming threads to the core with the minimum cost. The cost of running the thread on each core is computed on every new thread arrival using the up-to-date sensor values. If multiple cores have the same minimum cost, then a round-robin selection policy is employed among all the cores that have the same minimum cost. To keep the thread mapper design simple, fast and HW realizable we restricted to using only linear cost function. A higher order cost computation depending on history of sensor data can be employed which would result in higher implementation overhead. In the next section we present the design details of the TCU which performs the multi-objective thread mapping.

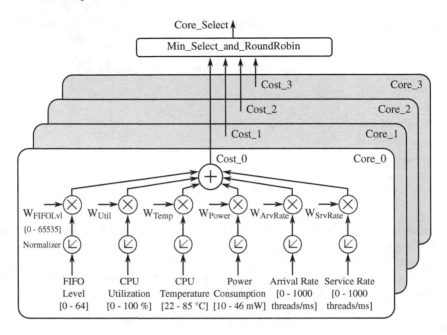

Fig. 3. Thread mapper: multi-objective sensor data-based thread assignment

3.2   Thread Control Unit

The Thread Control Unit (TCU) performs multi-objective thread assignment on an HPC compute processor node using multiple sensors. These sensors have to be either extracted or emulated per core (Table 1). For evaluation purpose, we prototyped two compute tiles, similar to compute nodes on an HPC rack, connected over an NoC [8] link on an FPGA. Each node consists of four Leon3 RISC processor cores. We enhanced each tile by adding a TCU block. Figure 4 shows the TCU comprising of the monitor aggregator (to collect the sensor values), queue selector (realizing the thread mapper (Fig. 3)), ready queues (Fig. 2) and the application class configuration matrix (Table 2). The design decision and the implementation details of each block are as follows:

Ready Queues: 64-bit-wide hardware FIFOs per core are used as ready queues. Selecting the appropriate FIFO depth is critical as smaller size means frequent overflows while larger queues are costly in terms of hardware. The optimum size of the FIFO can be determined using the network calculus if the application's injection rates and service/execution time are fixed. As the thread spawning is non-deterministic, for the FPGA prototype we set the FIFO depth to 64. Thus 64 threads per core can be stored in the ready queue and a maximum of 256 threads (64×4 cores) can be sent on a parallel loop unrolling. The underflow signal is used to power down cores and save power when no more threads are lying in the FIFOs.

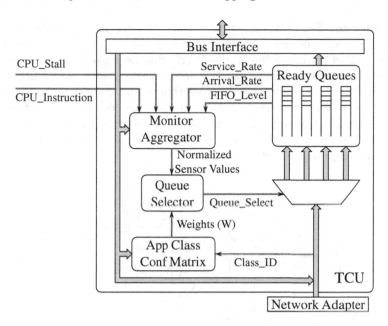

Fig. 4. TCU block diagram

Monitor Aggregator: This block provides all the different sensors per core to perform queue selection logic. A direct numerical comparison of the different monitor values from Table 1 is not possible as the meaning, their bit widths and units are different. A linear normalizer equation to convert each of these M sensor values (V_{ij}) of N cores to a uniform 16-bit-wide value as shown below is applied within this block.

$$V_{ij\_norm} = \left[\frac{(V_{ij} - V_{jmin})}{(V_{jmax} - V_{jmin})}\right] \cdot [2^{16} - 1] \,\bigg|\, \forall i \in N, \forall j \in M$$

As many sensors/monitors are needed they had to be built into the prototype design. Some of the sensors are already available such as the fill level of the ready queues. The derivative of fluctuations in the fill level of the ready queue is used to obtain the arrival and service rates. The number of clock cycles a CPU is stalled in each millisecond is used to calculate the CPU utilization. The power and temperature sensors are emulated based on the switching activity within the core.

Application Class Configuration Matrix: For the prototype, design the number of classes that are available in the configuration matrix is set to 8. Thus the total class configuration matrix is a memory mapped 8×32-bit RAM. Table 2 shows the normalized values in decimal format, but the actual weights to be applied to each sensor is quantized to 16 levels (0 to 15) and hence 4 bits per weight.

Queue Selector: Figure 3 suggests that the cost computation be done in parallel for each core and the normalization and weighting for each sensor also be done in parallel. An implementation trade-off criterion here would be the area overhead (number of multipliers, critical path) vs. performance (number of clocks, parallel/pipelined computation). Due to resource constraints on the FPGA, the costs are computed using a single MAC (multiply and accumulate) in a pipelined fashion as shown in Fig. 5. Each of the M sensors' normalized values (V_{ij}_norm) is read out from the monitor aggregator sequentially and the costs for all the N cores is also computed one after the other.

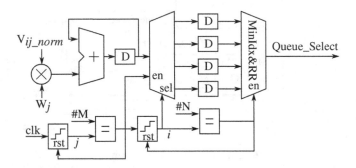

Fig. 5. Queue selector: pipelined cost computation

Governing access to critical sections, namely the ready queues, is a major concern in any SMP system. In conventional OS, the ready queues are realized as data structures located in memory. Any update (addition/deletion) of threads in the data structures is generally done using locks under a critical section of code. These accesses to critical sections are costly and performance hindering. In a compute tile, threads can be enqueued from the network adapter and the local cores simultaneously. The enqueue logic has to be atomic, i.e. store thread descriptors from each enqueuer simultaneously. Hence separate memory-mapped temporary buffers for thread descriptors from each enqueuer are incorporated to avoid any blocking calls in software. This provides atomicity and lock-free synchronization of multi-word enqueues.

3.3   TCU Prototype

Figure 6 shows the block diagram of two tiled MPSoC prototyped on a Virtex6 FPGA platform. For simplicity reasons, memory controller and IO peripherals are not shown, but are part of the prototype.

Resource Utilization: On the FPGA prototype design, ready queue FIFOs are mapped on the BlockRAM resources and the rest of the TCU components are synthesized using FPGA slices. Table 3a shows the resource utilization in

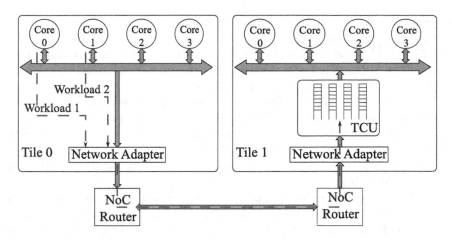

Fig. 6. Evaluation set-up for the TCU; Cores on tile 0 send two workloads to tile 1

comparison to a compute tile consisting of four Leon3 cores. The major share of FPGA slices were used to realize the registers to store the sensor data, weights and the temporary storages for incoming threads from the network adapter and local cores. Queue selection logic (Fig. 5) consumed only 285 slices. The TCU's share within the compute tile is about 9 % of slices. The TCU is completely realized in the TSMC 45 nm technology with worst case operating conditions. We synthesized using Synopsys design compiler to get the area, frequency and power estimates as shown in Table 3b. We let the tool synthesize FIFO RAM blocks using gates and as expected almost 80 % of the area is used to realize the FIFOs. The area of the TCU scales linearly with the number of cores. As evident from the synthesis results, the major area is consumed by the ready queue FIFOs (non-combinatorial) and increases with an increasing number of cores. Hence the TCU's share remained constant at about 9–10% even for designs with 8 and 12 cores per compute tile. Designs beyond 12 cores where not feasible to realize due to limited FPGA resources. We verified this scalability on the CHIPit multi-FPGA prototyping platform where we implemented a 2 × 2 tile design consisting of five cores each.

Table 3. Resource utilization on FPGA and ASIC synthesis

(a) Virtex6 xc6vlx240t FPGA

Component	Slices
4 Leon3 cores	16245
TCU	2659
Network Adapter	3502
Router	5980
Compute tile	29773
Two-tile MPSoC	55248

(b) TCU synthesis using TSMC 45 nm library

Cell Count	76160
Combinatorial Area	43334.776485 μm^2
Non-combinatorial Area	141782.915146 μm^2
Total Area	185117.691631 μm^2
Operating Voltage	1.1 V
Power	87.8611 mW
Maximum Frequency	1050 MHz

Performance Metrics: The FPGA prototype of two compute tiles with four core each operates at a moderate clock frequency of 50 MHz. The TCU takes 72–112 clock cycles to evaluate the cost of assigning each incoming thread onto a core. Hence the maximum latency for each incoming thread is $112 \times 20\,\text{ns} = 2.24\,\text{ms}$ for operating at 50 MHz.

The end-to-end latency is measured by continuously sending threads from cores in tile 0 to tile 1 over the NoC. The number of threads spawned on the target tile (among all the cores) was about 9000854 in 60 s i.e. 150k thread mappings per second. This corresponds to 6.668 ms per thread for a single hop over NoC including the delay in driver code. On ASIC, this corresponds to 317 ns at 1050 MHz (Table 3b).

The gist of this high transfer rate discussion is to show that an on-chip TCU can map about 3.15 million (150k × 1050 MHz/50 MHz) arbitrarily small threads each running for just a few 300–400 ns. Also, a standalone TCU realized off-chip on an FPGA fabric can operate at well above a 50 MHz clock rate and thus can cater to embarrassingly parallel programming needs on HPC clusters. For example, RDMA (remote DMA) feature of InfiniBand interconnect switches can be used to transfer threads spawned from one compute node on *loop unrolling* to another, and the TCU can be used to map the incoming threads at the receiving node without any OS or software intervention.

4   Experimental Validation

TCU evaluation has been performed on the two-tile FPGA prototype shown in Fig. 6 and introduced in the previous section. Cores in tile 0 send threads to tile 1 over a 128-bit-wide NoC interconnect. Threads are sent as a single NoC packet of 68 bits payload consisting of 32 bit thread pointer, 32 bit data pointer and 4 bit class_id. The class weights are set as in Table 2.

Workload Generator: Two workloads 1 (short runner) and 2 (long runner) are generated from core 0 and core 1 of tile 0 and sent to tile 1. The injection and execution periods of the threads are varied to mimic the periodic and bursty nature of applications with varying workloads. Table 4 shows the parameters set for workload generation. Workload 1 generates periodic threads while workload 2 can send a burst of threads that are spawned on the target tile. This mimics spawning of threads by real applications on say *loop unrolling*.

Table 4. Workload generator parameters

Workload		Type	Burst Size	Injection Period (ms)	Execution Period (ms) (±10%)
1	Short Runner	Periodic	1	10	10–40
2	Long Runner	Periodic / Bursty	1–11	250	250–1000

The two workloads can represent two different parallel phases of a single generic application requiring different execution times, or can be multiple competing applications running simultaneously on a compute node. The execution time here includes the binary or data transfer time as required for send/receive constructs in MPI or load/store time in OpenMP in NUMA architectures. For observability, we keep the injection period fixed, and vary the execution period of threads to generate different load situations on target tiles. For example, the execution time of threads from workload 1 can be varied from 10–40 ms or workload 2 from 250–1000 ms to generate 25–100 % of average load.

Single Periodic Workload: Figs. 7, 8 and 9 show the measured responses of the TCU for a single periodic workload generating 50 % average CPU load when single-objective mapping policies (classes 1,2 and 3) were applied. Also depicted are zoom out sections of the steady state responses between 60–64th second.

Class 1 (see Table 2) gives minimum latency, i.e. minimum fill level of ready queue (Fig. 7) and uses only two out of four cores. If an application is cache-sensitive and prefers to keep all its threads on the same cores, then class 1 is best suited. But this leads to a large difference in CPU utilization and temperature gradient among the four cores.

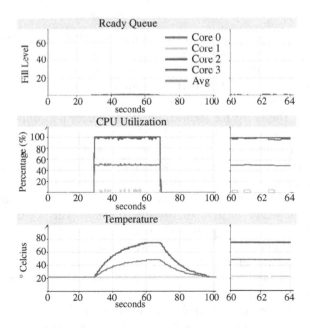

Fig. 7. Class 1: Minimize ready queue fill level

Class 2 (Fig. 8) utilizes all the cores equally by frequently changing its mapping decision for the incoming threads. The mean temperature was about

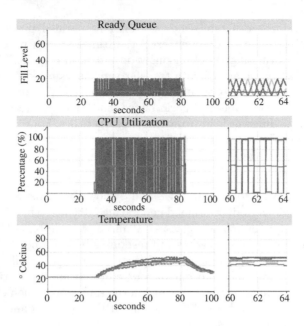

Fig. 8. Class 2: Optimize load distribution

48–50°C but the temperature gradient was about 10°C. Also, the number of threads having to wait in queue is increased by an average of five (maximum up to 20) threads, adversely affecting the performance.

Next, in class 3 (Fig. 9), the TCU attempts to operate all the cores at the same temperature and reduces the temperature gradient ($\leq 1°C$) by switching off some or all of the cores for some time. This causes non-uniform utilization of cores and thus the number of threads in ready queue is increased drastically to an average of 10 with a peak of 40 threads in waiting. Though class 3 gives minimum temperature gradient, its performance in comparison to classes 1 and 2 is worsened and isn't suitable for compute intensive tasks.

Classes 1, 2, and 3 perform very well in meeting only a single objective at the expense of other objectives. Figure 10 shows the TCU's response to threads belonging to multi-objective class 4. The steady state response (zoom out section) in the figure shows that TCU tries to keep the average FIFO level as low as possible by using all the CPUs, thus distributing the load and minimizing the temperature gradient. It offers the optimum operating point considering all the three sensors simultaneously.

Even when the average workload was increased to 75 %, the mean temperature increased to 65°C, but the steady state characteristics of the classes nevertheless showed similar behaviour. The class 1 was good on the latency aspect as no threads were pending in the FIFOs, while class 2 showed better utilization and class 3 had minimal temperature gradient. Multi-objective class 4 offered minimum temperature gradient with better utilization and minimum FIFO levels.

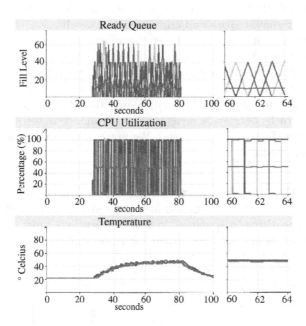

Fig. 9. Class 3: Minimize temperature gradient

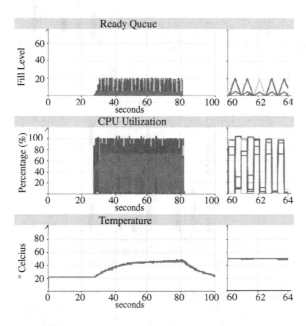

Fig. 10. Class 4: Multi-objective with FIFO level, CPU utilization and temperature

Note any other multi-objective mapping policy can be deployed using TCU, making use of different sensors and corresponding weights.

A single periodic workload is á very simplistic model for representing a real application. Class 3 (Fig. 9, temperature-aware) and class 4 (Fig. 10, multi-objective) minimized the temperature gradient at the expense of thread latency when compared to class 1 (Fig. 7, compute-intensive). Hence to compare the benefit of using multi-objective (class 4 or 5) over round-robin (class 0) or single-objective (class 1 or 3) policies, a measure of performance in terms of minimizing thread latency was further investigated. We present this evaluation next, using two different workloads.

Two Periodic Workloads: Short and long runners are generated from tile 0 and sent to tile 1. The two workloads are assigned to different classes and the latency for all the threads spawned in a 60-s duration under steady state is logged. The experiments are performed for three different scenarios. First, a

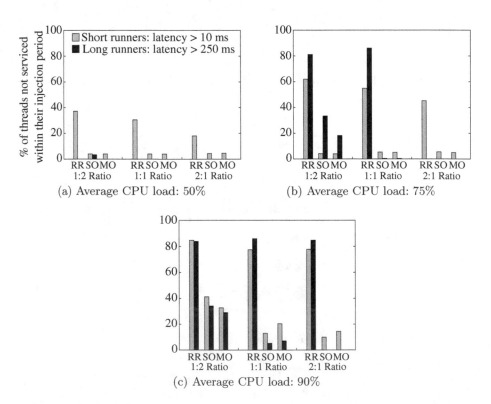

Fig. 11. Workload mix of short and long runners under different load conditions on four cores is varied in proportion of 1:2, 1:1 and 2:1 ratio. Latency observed by the two periodic workloads on employing different policies. RR: Round-robin; SO: Single-objective considering only FIFO level; MO: Multi-objective with FIFO level, CPU utilization and temperature

round-robin (RR) policy is used for both workloads by assigning them to class 0. The second scenario is single-objective (SO) wherein short runners are assigned to class 1 (fill level-sensitive) and long runners to class 3 (temperature). In the third multi-objective (MO) scenario, in order to benefit from multiple sensors, long runners are assigned to class 4. The total load produced by both workloads is varied from 50 %, 75 % to 90 % and the individual contribution of load due to short and long runners is mixed in the ratio of 1:2, 1:1 and 2:1 respectively. Since the total load in below 100 % (work-conserving), an ideal mapper could always assign incoming threads to one of the free cores without any latency.

Figure 11 shows the percentage of threads that experience delay beyond their injection period due to the TCU's mapping decisions. For moderate loads of about 50 %, at least 20 to 38 % of the threads had to wait in one of the ready queues before being serviced using RR. When the load was increased to about 75 %, almost 50–60 % of short runners and 80 % of long runners weren't serviced on arrival using RR. The situation was even worse for peak loads, with almost 80 % of threads for both short and long runners having to wait. In comparison to RR, only 4 % of short runners and worst case 4 % long runners had to wait with single or multi-objective for 50 % load situation. For high load situations of 75 % and 90 %, long runners are better served with MO than SO when they are in the majority. When long runners are in the minority, they experience just about 1 % performance degradation with MO compared to SO. Hence for an application generating long running threads, MO would be the preferred choice rather than the RR or SO policy.

Periodic and Burst Workloads: We further investigated the effect of the bursty or sporadic nature of applications. For this, first a baseline steady state load of 25 % is generated by sending periodic short runner threads. Second, a burst of long runners (with execution time 250 ms) of burst size 4, 8 or 11 is sent every second. Short runners experience no delay only if a bursty workload is not sent. We logged for about 60 s all the threads that experienced latency on arrival.

Figure 12 shows that about 45–95 % of short runners experience delay. This is because RR policy is being fair to all the arriving threads, hence caters to incoming long runner threads as well. Short runners are better isolated from bursty long runners when single- or multi-objective MO1 (class 4), MO2 (class 5) policies are used. For low bursts (Fig. 12a), less than 2 % of short runners are delayed using MO2 against SO (5 %) or MO1 (4 %). For medium bursts (size 8), MO1 outperforms the other policies. For high burst (Fig. 12c), the benefit of MO1 or MO2 over SO is not significant.

RR being fair, it very well serves all the bursty long runner threads upon arrival (Fig. 12a and b) without delay. But for high bursts (Fig. 12c), only 18 % of long runners are delayed with multi-objective (MO1) as against 24 % with RR. Thus for highly bursty workloads, MO1 outperforms RR. Overall, MO1 is better in serving bursty long runners while isolating the periodic short runners simultaneously.

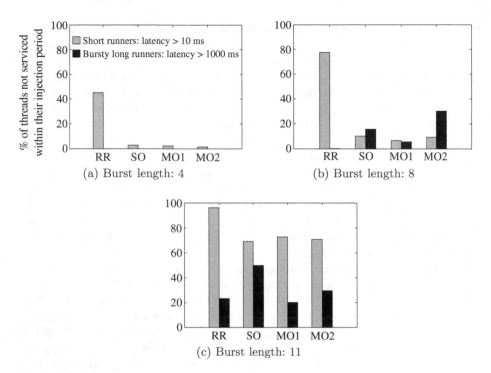

Fig. 12. Effect of bursty long runners of varying burst length on periodic short runner threads. RR: Round-robin; SO: Single-objective considering only FIFO level; MO1: Multi-objective with FIFO level, CPU utilization and temperature; MO2: Multi-objective with FIFO level, thread arrival and service rates

5   Conclusion

A multi-objective hardware-based thread control unit (TCU) for mapping threads on many-processor compute nodes of HPC clusters is presented. Fast and up-to-date sensors-based cost evaluation is the central idea of the TCU. The benefits of mapping threads in a compute node using multiple sensors simultaneously as against using a single sensor are illustrated. Round-robin, single- or multi-objective mapping policies are evaluated using concurrent multiple application workloads. Applications spawning threads in a periodic manner experience minimum mapping latency with multi-objective policies in comparison to round-robin or single-objective policies. They are better isolated from other bursty applications. Even for bursty and long-running applications, a high service rate is achieved using a multi-objective policy.

About 150 K thread mappings per second are achieved by the TCU on an FPGA prototype operating at a moderate frequency of 50 MHz. Very short running threads of just a few instructions can be spawned from one compute node, and can be mapped on the fly almost at the link rate onto processor cores on another compute node by the TCU. The design of the TCU is generic and extendible to HPC platforms that provide fast and direct access to its sensor data. For example cache or TLB hit/miss rates can be directly fed to TCU as additional sensors, and it can map successive train of threads to cores having higher hit rates thereby benefiting from data locality. The TCU's thread mapping policy can be tailored to meet any other application-specific needs or objectives by using different sensors/performance counters available on the compute platform. TCU acts as a dedicated hardware accelerator for offloading OS thread scheduling and mapping services. A small area footprint (9 % overhead per four-CPU compute node) and high performance justify implementing the TCU as an on-chip ASIC solution. Our current work in progress is evaluation of the TCU using NAS benchmarks on a 2×2 compute node design prototyped on a multi-FPGA platform.

Acknowledgement. This work was supported by the German Research Foundation (DFG) as part of the Transregional Collaborative Research Center "Invasive Computing" (SFB/TR 89).

References

1. Association, I.T.: InfiniBand Architecture Specification, Release 1.0 (2000). http://www.infinibandta.org/specs
2. Borkar, S.: Designing reliable systems from unreliable components: the challenges of transistor variability and degradation. IEEE Micro **25**(6), 10–16 (2005). http://dx.doi.org/10.1109/MM.2005.110
3. Colmenares, J., Eads, G., Hofmeyr, S., Bird, S., Moreto, M., Chou, D., Gluzman, B., Roman, E., Bartolini, D., Mor, N., Asanovic, K., Kubiatowicz, J.: Tessellation: refactoring the OS around explicit resource containers with continuous adaptation. In: 2013 50th ACM/EDAC/IEEE Design Automation Conference (DAC), pp. 1–10, May 2013
4. Coskun, A., Rosing, T., Whisnant, K., Gross, K.: Static and dynamic temperature-aware scheduling for multiprocessor SoCs. IEEE Trans. Very Large Scale Integr. VLSI Syst. **16**(9), 1127–1140 (2008)
5. Dagum, L., Menon, R.: OpenMP: an industry standard API for shared-memory programming. IEEE Comput. Sci. Eng. **5**(1), 46–55 (1998). http://dx.doi.org/10.1109/99.660313
6. Esmaeilzadeh, H., Blem, E., St. Amant, R., Sankaralingam, K., Burger, D.: Dark silicon and the end of multicore scaling. In: Proceedings of the 38th Annual International Symposium on Computer Architecture, pp. 365–376, ISCA 2011. ACM, New York, NY, USA (2011). http://doi.acm.org/10.1145/2000064.2000108
7. Frigo, M., Leiserson, C.E., Randall, K.H.: The implementation of the Cilk-5 multithreaded language. SIGPLAN Not. **33**(5), 212–223 (1998). http://doi.acm.org/10.1145/277652.277725
8. Henkel, J., Herkersdorf, A., Bauer, L., Wild, T., Hubner, M., Pujari, R., Grudnitsky, A., Heisswolf, J., Zaib, A., Vogel, B., Lari, V., Kobbe, S.: Invasive manycore architectures. In: 2012 17th Asia and South Pacific Design Automation Conference (ASP-DAC), pp. 193–200, January 2012

9. Howard, J., Dighe, S., Hoskote, Y., Vangal, S., Finan, D., Ruhl, G., Jenkins, D., Wilson, H., Borkar, N., Schrom, G., Pailet, F., Jain, S., Jacob, T., Yada, S., Marella, S., Salihundam, P., Erraguntla, V., Konow, M., Riepen, M., Droege, G., Lindemann, J., Gries, M., Apel, T., Henriss, K., Lund-Larsen, T., Steibl, S., Borkar, S., De, V., Van Der Wijngaart, R., Mattson, T.: A 48-core IA-32 message-passing processor with DVFS in 45 nm CMOS. In: 2010 IEEE International Solid-State Circuits Conference Digest of Technical Papers (ISSCC), pp. 108–109, February 2010

10. Kumar, S., Hughes, C.J., Nguyen, A.: Carbon: architectural support for fine-grained parallelism on chip multiprocessors. SIGARCH Comput. Archit. News **35**(2), 162–173 (2007). http://doi.acm.org/10.1145/1273440.1250683

11. Li, Y., Skadron, K., Brooks, D., Hu, Z.: Performance, energy, and thermal considerations for SMT and CMP architectures. In: 11th International Symposium on High-Performance Computer Architecture, HPCA-11 2005, pp. 71–82, February 2005

12. Pujari, R.K., Wild, T., Herkersdorf, A., Vogel, B., Henkel, J.: Hardware assisted thread assignment for RISC based MPSoCs in invasive computing. In: 2011 13th International Symposium on Integrated Circuits (ISIC), pp. 106–109, December 2011. http://doi.acm.org/10.1109/ISICir.2011.6131920

13. Reinders, J.: Intel Threading Building Blocks, 1st edn. O'Reilly & Associates Inc., Sebastopol (2007)

14. Virding, R., Wikström, C., Williams, M.: Concurrent Programming in ERLANG, 2nd edn. Prentice Hall International (UK) Ltd., Hertfordshire (1996)

15. Wentzlaff, D., Griffin, P., Hoffmann, H., Bao, L., Edwards, B., Ramey, C., Mattina, M., Miao, C.C., Brown III, J.F., Agarwal, A.: On-chip interconnection architecture of the tile processor. IEEE Micro **27**(5), 15–31 (2007). http://dx.doi.org/10.1109/MM.2007.89

Data Locality and Decomposition

Dynamic Sparse-Matrix Allocation on GPUs

James King$^{(\boxtimes)}$, Thomas Gilray, Robert M. Kirby, and Matthew Might

University of Utah, Salt Lake City, USA
{jsking2,tgilray,kirby,might}@cs.utah.edu

Abstract. Sparse matrices are a core component in many numerical simulations, and their efficiency is essential to achieving high performance. Dynamic sparse-matrix allocation (insertion) can benefit a number of problems such as sparse-matrix factorization, sparse-matrix-matrix addition, static analysis (e.g., points-to analysis), computing transitive closure, and other graph algorithms. Existing sparse-matrix formats are poorly designed to handle dynamic updates. The compressed sparse-row (CSR) format is fully compact and must be rebuilt after each new entry. Ellpack (ELL) stores a constant number of entries per row, which allows for efficient insertion and sparse matrix-vector multiplication (SpMV) but is memory inefficient and strictly limits row size. The coordinate (COO) format stores a list of entries and is efficient for both memory use and insertion time; however, it is much less efficient at SpMV. Hybrid ellpack (HYB) compromises by using a combination of ELL and COO but degrades in performance as the COO portion fills up. Rows that use the COO portion require it to be completely traversed during every SpMV operation.

In this paper we introduce a new sparse matrix format, dynamic compressed sparse row (DCSR), that permits efficient dynamic updates. These updates are significantly faster than those made to a HYB matrix while maintaining SpMV times comparable to CSR. We demonstrate the efficacy of our dynamic allocation scheme, evaluating updates and SpMV operations on adjacency matrices of sparse-graph benchmarks on the GPU.

1 Introduction

Sparse matrix-vector multiply (SpMV) is the workhorse operation of many numerical simulations and has seen use in a wide variety of areas such as data mining [1] and graph analytics [2]. In these algorithms, a majority of the total processing is often spent on SpMV operations. Iterative computations such as the power method and conjugate gradient are commonly used in numerical simulations and require successive SpMV operations [3]. The use of GPUs has become increasingly common in computing these operations as they are, in principle, highly parallelizable. GPUs have both a high computational throughput and a high memory bandwidth. Operations on sparse matrices are generally memory bound; this makes the GPU a good target platform due to its higher memory bandwidth compared to that of the CPU, but it is still difficult to attain high performance with sparse matrices because of thread divergence and noncoalesced memory accesses.

© Springer International Publishing Switzerland 2016
J.M. Kunkel et al. (Eds.): ISC High Performance 2016, LNCS 9697, pp. 61–80, 2016.
DOI: 10.1007/978-3-319-41321-1_4

Some applications require dynamic updates to the matrix; generally construed, updates may include inserting or deleting entries. Fully compressed formats such as compressed sparse row (CSR) cannot handle these operations without rebuilding the entire matrix. Rebuilding the matrix is orders of magnitude more costly than performing an SpMV operation. The ellpack (ELL) format allocates a fixed amount of space for each row, allowing fast insertion of new entries and fast SpMV, but limits each row to a predetermined number of entries and can be highly memory inefficient. The coordinate (COO) format stores a list of entries and permits both efficient memory use and fast dynamic updates but is unordered and slow to perform SpMV operations. The hybrid-ellpack (HYB) format attempts a compromise between these by combining an ELL matrix with a COO matrix for overflow. This compromise requires examination of the overflow matrix for SpMV operations and efficiency suffers.

Matrix representations of sparse graphs sometimes exhibit a power-law distribution (when the number of nodes with a given number of edges scales as a power of the number of edges). This distribution results in a long tail in which a few rows have a relatively high number of entries whereas the rest have a relatively low number. Important real-world phenomena exhibit the power-law distribution. Their corresponding matrices can represent adjacency graphs, web communication, and finite-state simulations. Such a matrix is also the pathological case for memory efficiency in the ELL format and requires significant use of the COO portion of a HYB matrix, making neither particularly well suited for dynamic sparse-graph applications.

One motivating application for our work is control-flow analysis (CFA): a general approach to static program analysis of higher-order languages [4,5]. These algorithms use an approximate interpretation of their target code to yield an upper bound on the propagation of data and control through a program across all possible actual executions. A CFA involves a series of increasing operations on a graph (extending it with nodes and edges), terminating when a fixed point is reached (a steady state in which the analysis is self-consistent).

Recent work has shown how to implement this kind of static analysis as linear-algebraic operations on the sparse-matrix representation of a function [6,7]. Other recent work shows how to implement an inclusion-based points-to analysis of C on the GPU by applying a set of semantic rules to the adjacency matrix of a sparse-graph [8]. These algorithms may be likened to finding the transitive closure of a graph encoded as an adjacency matrix. The matrix is repeatedly extended with new entries derived from SpMV until a fixed point is reached (no more edges need to be accumulated). Each of these approaches to static analysis on the GPU is very different; however, both require high performance sparse-matrix operations and dynamic insertion of new entries.

1.1   Contributions

Existing matrix formats are ill-suited for such dynamic allocation, with many being fully compressed or otherwise unable to be efficiently extended with new entries. Our contribution in this paper is to present a fast, dynamic method for sparse-matrix allocation:

1. **We present a new sparse matrix format, *dynamic compressed sparse row* (DCSR), that allows for efficient dynamic updates, exhibits easy conversion with standard CSR, and has fast SpMV.**
2. **We implement an open-source library for DCSR and demonstrate its efficacy, benchmarking SpMV and insertions using the adjacency matrices for a suite of sparse-graph benchmarks.**

2 Background

In this paper we are concerned with dynamic updates to sparse matrices. As SpMV is arguably the most important sparse-matrix operation, we want to maintain efficient times for the problem $Ax = y$. A major goal of sparse-matrix formats is to reduce irregularity in the memory accesses. We provide a brief overview of some of the most commonly used sparse-matrix formats.

The *coordinate* (COO) format is the simplest sparse-matrix format. It represents a matrix with three vectors holding the row indices, column indices, and values for all nonzero entries in the matrix. The entries within a COO format must be sorted by row in order to efficiently perform an SpMV operation. SpMV operations are conducted in parallel through segmented reductions over the length of the arrays. Tracking which thread has processed the final entry in a row requires explicit inter-thread communication.

The *compressed sparse row/column* (CSR/CSC) formats are similar to COO in that they have arrays that fully store two of the three sets, either the column indices or the row indices in addition to the values. Either the rows or columns (in CSR or CSC, respectively) are compressed to store only offsets corresponding to the row/column locations in the other two arrays. For CSR, entry i and $i+1$ in the row offsets array will store the starting and ending offsets for row i. CSR has been shown to be one of the best formats in terms of memory usage and SpMV efficiency due to its fully compressed nature, and thus it has become widely used [9]. CSR has a greater memory efficiency than COO, which is a significant factor in speeding up SpMV operations due to decreased memory bandwidth usage.

The *ellpack* (ELL) format uses two arrays, each of size $m \times k$ (where m is the number of rows and k is a fixed width), to store the column indices and the values of the matrix [10,11]. These arrays are stored in column-major order to allow for efficient parallel access across rows. This format is best suited for matrices that have a fixed number of entries per row.

Allocating enough memory in each row to store the entire matrix is prohibitively expensive for ELL when a matrix contains even one long row. The *hybrid-ellpack* (HYB) format offers a compromise by using a combination of ELL and COO. It stores as much as possible in an ELL portion, and the overflow from rows with a number of entries greater than the fixed ELL width is stored in a COO portion. ELL and HYB have become popular on SIMD architectures due to the ability of thread warps to look through consecutive rows in an efficient parallel manner [12].

The diagonal format (DIA) is best suited for banded matrices. It is formed by two arrays that store the nonzero data and the offsets from the main diagonal. The nonzero values are stored in an $m \times k$ array where m is the number of rows in the matrix and k is the maximum number of nonzeros of any row in the matrix. The offsets are stored with respect to the main diagonal, with positive offsets to the right and negative offsets to the left. The SpMV parallelization of this format is similar to that of ELL with one thread/vector assigned to each row in the matrix. The values array is statically sized, similar to ELL, which restricts its ability to handle dynamic insertions.

A number of other specialized sparse-matrix formats have been developed, including diagonal (DIA), jagged diagonal storage (JDS), block diagonal (BDIA), skyline storage (SKS), tiled COO (TCOO), block ELL (BELL), and sliced-ELL (SELL) [13], which offer improved performance for specific matrix types. Blocked variants of these and other formats work by storing localized entries in blocks for better data locality and a reduction in index storage. "Cocktail" frameworks that mix and match matrix formats to fit specific subsets of the matrix have been developed, but they require significant preprocessing and are not easily modified dynamically [14]. Garland et al. have provided detailed reviews of the most common sparse-matrix formats [10,11,15], as well as an analysis of their performance on throughput-oriented many-core processors [16].

Block formats, such as BRC [17] and BCCOO [18] that use blocking, have limited ability to add in additional entries. BRC can add new entries only if those entries correspond to zeros within blocks that have been stored. BCCOO can handle the addition of new entries, but it suffers from many of the same problems as COO. Also, new insertions will not always follow a blocked structure, so additional blocks may be sparse, which lowers memory efficiency.

Many sparse-matrix formats are fully compressed and do not allow additional entries to be added to the matrix dynamically. Adding additional entries to a CSR matrix requires rebuilding the entire matrix, since there is no free space between entries. Of existing formats, COO is the most amenable to dynamic updates because new entries can be placed at the end of the data structure. However, updating a COO matrix in parallel requires atomic operations to keep track of currently available memory locations. The ELL/HYB formats allow for some additional entries to be added in a limited fashion. ELL cannot add in more entries per row than the given width of the matrix, and while the HYB format has a COO matrix to handle overflow from the ELL portion, it cannot be efficiently updated in parallel since atomic operations are required and the COO portion must maintain the sorted property.

A great deal of research has been devoted to improving the efficiency of SpMV, which has been studied on both multi-core and many-core architectures. Williams et al. demonstrated the efficacy of using architecture-specific data structures to optimize performance [19,20]. As SpMV is a bandwidth-limited operation, research has also produced other methods, such as automatic tuning, blocking, and tiling, to increase cache hit rates and decrease bandwidth usage [21–23].

Graph applications often use sparse binary adjacency matrices to represent graphs and translate graph operations to linear algebraic operations [24]. A common graph algorithm is finding a transitive closure by repeated multiplication of its adjacency matrix. The transitive closure of an adjacency matrix R calculates $R^+ = \bigcup_{i \in \{1,2,3,\dots\}} R^i$, where R^i is the ith power of the matrix. This operation results in R^i having a nonzero between any pair of nodes that are connected by a path of length i. The union (addition/binary-or) of all $R, \dots R^n$ will have a nonzero entry for every pair of nodes that are connected by a path of length $\leq n$. This process of unioning successive powers of R can be continued until a fixed point is reached and all nodes that are connected by a path of any length will be marked in the matrix.

3   Dynamic Compressed Sparse Row (DCSR)

We present a dynamic sparse-matrix allocation method that allows for efficient dynamic updates while maintaining fast SpMV times. Our dynamic allocation uses a *row offset array*, representing a dense array of ordered rows, and for each a fixed number of *segment offsets*. The column indices and values are stored in arrays that are logically divided into these data segments in the same way that CSR row offsets partition the column indices and values. Each such segment is a contiguous portion of memory that stores entries within a row. Segments may contain more space than entries to allow for future insertions. The contiguous arrangement of entries within the set of segments for a given row is equivalent to the CSR format. In the following subsection we illustrate how dynamic allocation is performed, after which we provide details of how DCSR operations are implemented.

Initializing the matrix can be accomplished in one of two ways. Either a matrix can be loaded from another format (e.g., COO or CSR), or the matrix can be initialized as blank. In the latter case, each row is assigned an initial number of entries (an initial segment size) in the column indices and values arrays. The row offset array is initialized with space for k segment offset pairs, with either no allocated segments or a single allocated segment of size μ per row. In the latter case this allocation consumes the same amount of memory as an ELL matrix with a row width of μ, except in row-major order instead of column-major order. A memory buffer with excess space maintained, using a simple bump-pointer allocation method to add new segments, to allow for dynamic allocation. This allocation pointer is set to the end of the currently used space ($rows \times \mu$ in the case of a new matrix). A maximum size of memory buffer for the columns and values arrays is specified by the user. Figure 1 provides an illustrative comparison of CSR, HYB, and DCSR formats.

In total, the format consists of four arrays for column indices, values, row offsets, and row sizes, in addition to a memory allocation pointer. The row offsets

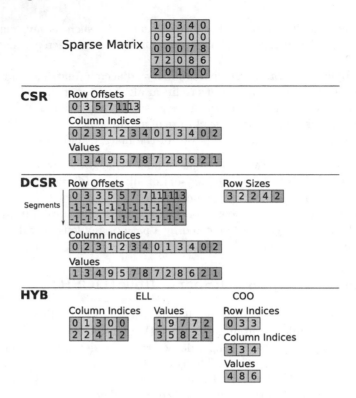

Fig. 1. Comparison of CSR, DCSR, and HYB formats. (Color figure online)

array functions in a manner similar to that of its CSR counterpart, except that both a beginning and ending offset are stored and space exists for up to k such pairs per row. This table is encoded as a strided array where the starting and ending offsets of segment k in row i are indexed by $(i*2+k*pitch)$ and $(i*2+k*pitch+1)$, respectively. The *pitch* may be defined as a value convenient for cache performance such that $pitch \geq 2*rows$. This pitch value is chosen to ensure memory aligned accesses. The number of memory segment offset pairs (the max k) is an adjustable parameter specified at matrix construction. The column indices and values correspond 1:1, just as in CSR. Unlike CSR, however, there may be more than one memory segment assigned to a given row and these segments need not be contiguous. As the last segment for a row may not be full, the actual row sizes are maintained so the used portion of each segment is known.

Explicitly storing row sizes allows for optimization techniques such as *adaptive CSR* (ACSR) [25] (of which we take advantage). This optimization implements customized kernels to process bins of specified row-lengths. During this binning process, we create a permuted set of row indices that are sorted according to these bin groupings. We launch each bin-specific kernel with these permuted indices on its own stream, which allows each kernel to easily access the rows that it needs to process without scanning over the matrix.

When inserting new elements within a row, the last allocated segment for that row is located, and if space is available the new elements are inserted in a contiguous fashion after the current entries. If that segment does not have enough room, a new segment will be allocated with the appropriate size plus an additional amount α. The α value represents additional "slack space" and allows for a greater number of entries to be inserted without the creation of a new segment. Although we experimented with setting α to be a factor of the previous segment size, for our tests we settled on a value of μ (average row size of matrix). When a new segment is allocated, the memory allocation pointer is atomically increased by the size of the new segment. A hard limit on these additions, before defragmentation is required, is fixed by the number of segments k. The defragmentation operation always reduces the number of segments in each row to one, which allows the format to scale to an arbitrary number of allocations. Pseudo-code for new segment allocation is provided by Algorithm 1.

When inserting new elements into the matrix, it is possible that duplicate nonzero entries (i.e., two or more entries with the same row and column index) will be added. Duplicate entries are handled in one of two ways. The first method is to simply let the accumulation occur, as it does not pose a problem for many operations. SpMV operations are tolerant of duplicate entries since the reduction relies on associative operations. This result will be correct to within floating point tolerance. For binary matrices, the row-vector inner products will produce the same result irrespective of duplicate nonzeros. A second solution is to perform a segmented reduction on the entries after sorting by row and column. This operation combines all duplicate entries into a single entry but is generally not needed when performing only SpMV and addition operations. In our tests, we let the values accumulate for all formats as they do not hinder the SpMV operations that are performed. Pseudo-code for an insertion operation is given by Algorithm 2.

An SpMV operation works as follows. Initially the first pair of segment offsets is fetched. The entries within the corresponding segment are multiplied by the appropriate values in x according to the algorithm being used (CSR-scalar, CSR-vector, etc.). If the row size is greater than the capacity of the current memory segment, the next pair of offsets is fetched. If the size of the current segment plus the running sum of the previous segment sizes is greater than or equal to the row size, the final segment of that row has been found. If the final segment is not full, the location of the last entry can be determined by the difference of the row size and the running sum. This process continues until the entire row has been read. This is illustrated in Algorithm 3.

As the matrix accumulates more segments, SpMV performance decreases slightly. A fixed number of segments also means this process cannot continue forever. Our solution to both problems is to implement a defragmentation operation that compacts all entries within the column indices and values arrays, eliminating empty space. This operation compacts all segments in a row into a single segment. The defragmentation may be invoked periodically, or more conservatively when a row has reached its maximum capacity of segments. In practice we do the latter and set a flag when any row reaches its maximum segment count. At this point we consider defragmentation to be required.

Algorithm 1. Allocate Segments

Input: sizes, offsets, Aj, Ax, B_offsets, B_cols, B_vals
Output: sizes, offsets, Aj, Ax

1 $row \leftarrow vid$; // vector ID
2 **while** $row < n\_rows$ **do**
3 $\quad$ $sid \leftarrow 0$; // segment index
4 $\quad$ $rl \leftarrow$ sizes$[row]$; // row length
5 $\quad$ $idx \leftarrow 0$; // thread row index
6 $\quad$ $start \leftarrow$ offsets$[row * 2]$; // starting segment offset
7 $\quad$ $end \leftarrow$ offsets$[row * 2 + 1]$; // ending segment offset
8 $\quad$ $free\_mem \leftarrow 0$;
9 $\quad$ $B\_start \leftarrow$ B_offsets$[row * 2]$;
10 $\quad$ $B\_end \leftarrow$ B_offsets$[row * 2 + 1]$;
11 $\quad$ $rlB \leftarrow B\_row\_end - B\_row\_start$;
12 $\quad$ **if** $rlA \geq 0$ **then**
13 $\quad\quad$ **while** $A\_idx < rlA$ **do**
14 $\quad\quad\quad$ $idx \leftarrow idx + (A\_end - A\_start)$;
15 $\quad\quad\quad$ **if** $idx < rlA$ **then**
16 $\quad\quad\quad\quad$ $sid \leftarrow sid + 1$;
17 $\quad\quad\quad\quad$ $A\_start \leftarrow$ offsets$[sid*$pitch$+row * 2]$;
18 $\quad\quad\quad\quad$ $A\_end \leftarrow$ offsets$[sid*$pitch$+row * 2 + 1]$;

19 $\quad\quad$ $idx \leftarrow A\_end + rlA - idx$;

20 $\quad$ **else**
21 $\quad\quad$ $idx \leftarrow A\_start$;

22 $\quad$ $free\_mem \leftarrow A\_end - A\_start$;
23 $\quad$ **if** $lane = 0$ **AND** $free\_mem < rlB$ **AND** $rlB > 0$ **then**
$\quad\quad$ // allocate new space
24 $\quad\quad$ $size \leftarrow rlB - free\_mem + \alpha$;
25 $\quad\quad$ $addr \leftarrow$ atomicAdd(sizes[n_rows], $size$);
$\quad\quad$ // allocate new row segment
26 $\quad\quad$ offsets$[(sid + 1)*$pitch $+ row * 2] \leftarrow addr$;
27 $\quad\quad$ offsets$[(sid + 1)*$pitch $+ row * 2 + 1] \leftarrow addr + size$;

$\quad$ // Allocate new entries (Algorithm 2)
28 $\quad$ Insert_Elements();
29 $\quad$ $row \leftarrow row +$ num_vectors;

Defragmentation performs the equivalent to a sort-by-row operation on the entries of the matrix; however, we formulated a method that does not require an actual sort and is significantly faster than doing so. We perform a prefix-sum operation on the row sizes to calculate the new row offsets in a compacted CSR form. After this, the entries are shuffled from their current indices to their new indices in newly allocated column indices and values buffers, after which we set a pointer in our data structure to these new arrays and free the old buffers (shallow copy). By using the knowledge of the row sizes to compute resulting offsets and indices, we eliminate the need to do any comparisons in this operation, which greatly improves performance. The defragmentation process is described by Algorithm 4.

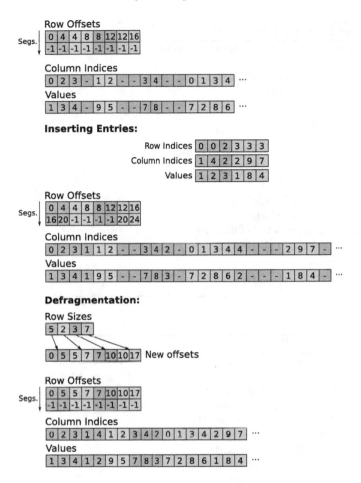

Fig. 2. Illustration of insertion and defragmentation operations with DCSR. (Color figure online)

Figure 2 illustrates an example of inserting new elements into a DCSR matrix. Initially the matrix has four populated rows with the memory allocation pointer being 16. Row 0 can insert one additional entry in its current segment before a new segment needs to be allocated. Rows 1 and 2 have enough room for two additional entries, and row 3 is full. Figure 2 shows a set of new entries that are inserted into rows 0, 2, and 3. In this case a new segment of size 4 is allocated for row 0 and row 3. The additional segments need not be consecutive nor in order of row since the exact offsets are stored for each segment. Finally, the defragmentation operation computes new segment offsets from the row sizes. The entries are shuffled to their new indices, which results in a single compacted segment for each row.

Algorithm 2. Insert Elements

Input: sizes, offsets, Aj, Ax, B_cols, B_vals
Output: sizes, Aj, Ax

1 $B\_idx \leftarrow B\_start +$ lane ; // add thread lane
2 **while** $B\_idx < B\_end$ **do**
3   **if** $idx \geq A\_end$ **then**
4          $pos \leftarrow idx - A\_end$;
5          $sid \leftarrow sid + 1$;
6          $A\_start \leftarrow$ offsets$[sid*$pitch$+row*2]$;
7          $A\_end \leftarrow$ offsets$[sid*$pitch$+row*2+1]$;
8          $idx \leftarrow A\_start + pos$;
9   Aj$[idx] \leftarrow$ B_cols$[B\_idx]$;
10   Ax$[idx] \leftarrow$ B_vals$[B\_idx]$;
11     $B\_idx \leftarrow B\_idx +$ VECTOR_SIZE;
12     $idx \leftarrow idx +$ VECTOR_SIZE;
13 **if** $lane = 0$ **then**
14   sizes$[row] \leftarrow$ sizes$[row] + rlB$;

Algorithm 3. DCSR SpMV

Input: sizes, offsets, Aj, Ax, x, y
Output: y

1 $tid \leftarrow$ thread index ; // thread ID
2 $lane \leftarrow tid \% Vec\_Size$; // lane ID
3 $vid \leftarrow tid / Vec\_Size$; // vector ID
4 **for** $row \leftarrow vid$ **to** num_rows, $row\ +=\ num\_vecs$ **do**
5      $idx \leftarrow 0$; // thread row index
6      $rl \leftarrow$ sizes$[row]$; // row length
7      $sid \leftarrow 0$; // segment index
8   **while** $idx < rl$ **do**
9          $start \leftarrow$ offsets$[sid*$pitch$ + row*2]$;
10         $end \leftarrow$ offsets$[sid*$pitch$ + row*2+1]$;
        /* accumulate local sums   */
11   **for** $j \leftarrow start$ **to** end, $j\ +=\ Vec\_Size$ **do**
12   sum $+=$ Ax$[j]$ * x$[$Aj$[j]]$;
13         $idx\ +=\ (end - start)$;
14   y$[row] =$ sum;

As CSR is the most commonly used sparse matrix format, we designed DCSR to be compatible with CSR algorithms and to allow for easy conversion between the formats. Minimal overhead is required to convert from CSR to DCSR and vice versa. When converting from CSR to DCSR, the column indices and values arrays are copied directly. For the row offsets array, the ith element is copied to indices $i*2-1$ and $i*2$ for all elements except the first and last one.

Algorithm 4. Defragment DCSR

    Input: sizes, offsets, Aj, Ax
    Output: offsets, Aj, Ax
    `/* prefix sum on row sizes`   `*/`
1   exclusive_scan(sizes, temp_offsets);
2   new T_cols(size(Aj)), new T_vals(size(Ax));
3   CompactIndices(T_cols, T_vals, temp_offsets, Aj, Ax, offsets, sizes);
    `/* shallow copy, old arrays deleted`   `*/`
4   Aj = &T_cols, Ax = &T_vals;
5   SetRowOffsets(offsets, sizes, temp_offsets);

A simple subtraction must be performed to calculate the row sizes from the row offsets. Converting back to CSR is equally simple, assuming the matrix is first defragmented; the column indices and values arrays are copied back, and the starting segment offset from each row is copied to the row offsets array.

4 Experimental Results

In our tests we used an Intel Xeon E5-2640 processor running at 2.50 GHz, 128 GB of memory, and 3 NVIDIA Tesla K20c GPUs. For additional scaling tests, we used an Intel Xeon E5630 processor running at 2.53 GHz, 128 GB of memory, and 8 NVIDIA Tesla M2090 GPUs. We compiled using $g++$ 4.7.2, CUDA 5.5, and Thrust 1.8, comparing our method against modern implementations in Nvidia CUSP [26]. Table 1(a) provides a list of the matrices that we used in our tests as well as their sizes, number of nonzeros, and row entry distributions. All the matrices can be found in the University of Florida sparse-matrix database [27].

Memory consumption is a major concern for sparse matrix formats, as one of the primary reasons for eliminating the storage of zeros is to reduce the memory footprint. The ELL component of HYB is best suited to store rows with an equal number of entries. If there is a large variance in row size, much of the ELL portion may end up storing many zeros, which is inefficient. We provide a comparison of memory consumption for HYB, DCSR (using 2, 3, and 4 segments), and CSR formats in Table 1(b). We compute the storage size of the HYB format using an ELL width equal to the average number of nonzeros per row (μ) for the given matrix. CSR has the smallest memory footprint since its row indices have been compressed to the number of rows in the matrix. We see that DCSR has a significantly smaller memory footprint in almost all test cases. Test cases such as AMA and DBL have lower memory consumption for HYB than for DCSR (with 3 and 4 segments), because these matrices have a low variance in row size. This low variance in row size makes them well suited for DCSR with 4 segments uses 20 % less memory on average than HYB.

The conversion time between formats is often a key factor when determining the efficacy of a particular format. High conversion times can significantly hinder

Table 1. (a): Matrices used in tests. NNZ: total number of nonzeros, μ: average row size, σ: standard deviation of row sizes, max: maximum row size. (b): Comparison of memory consumption among HYB, CSR, and DCSR formats. Size of HYB is listed in bytes (using ELL width of μ), and sizes for DCSR and CSR are listed as a percent of the HYB size.

Matrix	Abbr.	NNZ	Rows \ Cols	μ \ σ \ Max
amazon-2008	AMA	5M	735K	7 \ 4 \ 10
cnr-2000	CNR	3M	325K	9 \ 21 \ 2716
dblp-2010	DBL	807K	326K	2 \ 4 \ 154
enron	ENR	276K	69K	3 \ 28 \ 1392
eu-2005	EU2	19M	862K	22 \ 29 \ 6985
flickr	FLI	9M	820K	11 \ 87 \ 10K
hollywood-2009	HOL	57M	1139K	50 \ 160 \ 6689
in-2004	IN2	16M	1382K	12 \ 37 \ 7753
indochina-2004	IND	194M	7414K	26 \ 216 \ 6985
internet	INT	207K	124K	1 \ 4 \ 138
kron-18	KRO	10M	262K	40 \ 261 \ 29K
ljournal-2008	LJO	79M	5363K	14 \ 37 \ 2469
rail4284	RAL	11M	4K \ 1M	2633 \ 4K \ 56K
soc-LiveJournal1	SOC	68M	4847K	14 \ 35 \ 20K
webbase-1M	WEB	3M	1000K	3 \ 25 \ 4700
wikipedia-2005	WIK	19M	1634K	12 \ 31 \ 4970

(a) Matrices

Matrix	HYB size	DCSR 2 segs.	DCSR 3 segs.	DCSR 4 segs.	CSR
AMA	54M	0.924	1.026	1.128	0.77
CNR	47M	0.626	0.679	0.732	0.547
DBL	12M	0.86	1.052	1.245	0.572
ENR	4M	0.653	0.762	0.871	0.489
EU2	236M	0.675	0.703	0.731	0.633
FLI	160M	0.546	0.585	0.624	0.487
HOL	859M	0.531	0.541	0.551	0.516
IN2	229M	0.654	0.7	0.746	0.585
IND	2791M	0.571	0.591	0.612	0.541
INT	4M	0.761	0.969	1.177	0.449
KRO	171M	0.493	0.505	0.516	0.475
LJO	1152M	0.594	0.63	0.665	0.541
RAL	149M	0.577	0.577	0.577	0.576
SOC	1009M	0.595	0.631	0.668	0.54
WEB	40M	0.966	1.155	1.344	0.682
WIK	276M	0.635	0.68	0.725	0.567

(b) Memory Occupancy

performance. Architecture-specific formats may provide better performance, but unless the rest of the code base uses that format, the conversion time must be accounted for. We provide the overhead required to convert to and from CSR and COO matrices in Table 2(a). The conversion times have been normalized against the time required to copy CSR → CSR. The conversion times to DCSR are only slightly higher compared to that of CSR. HYB requires significant overhead as the entries must first be distributed throughout the ELL portion and the remaining overflow entries distributed to the COO portion.

4.1   Matrix Updates

To measure the speed of dynamic updates, we ran two series of tests that involved streaming updates and iterative updates. In the streaming updates test, we incrementally build up the matrix by continuously inserting new entries. The elements are first buffered into three arrays for the rows, columns, and values. We initialize the matrix sizes according to the average number of nonzeros for the given input. Afterward, the entries are added in a streaming parallel fashion to the matrices.

Updating a HYB matrix first requires checking the ELL portion, and if the row in question is full, inserting the new entry into the COO portion. Any updates to the COO portion require atomic operations to ensure synchronous writes between multiple threads. These atomic updates are prohibitive to fast parallel updates as all threads are contending to insert entries onto the end of the COO matrix.

Table 2. (a): Comparison of relative conversion times. Conversions are normalized against time to copy CSR→CSR. (b): Overhead of DCSR defragmentation and HYB sorting is measured as the ratio of one operation against a single CSR SpMV. Update time is measured as the ratio of 1000 updates to a single CSR SpMV. (∞ means this test was unable to complete within machine resource limits)

From To	COO CSR	COO DCSR	COO HYB	CSR DCSR	CSR HYB	DCSR CSR
AMA	2.93	3.03	9.22	1.06	9.25	0.9
CNR	2.24	2.62	14.84	1.04	13.62	0.87
DBL	4.34	5.74	18.07	1.17	16.83	1.1
ENR	5.56	5.95	27.15	1.29	26.95	1.14
EU2	2.1	2.29	16.08	1.06	15.67	0.99
FLI	2.13	2.5	23.29	1.06	19.74	0.96
HOL	1.82	1.9	20.37	1.01	20.3	0.99
IN2	2.15	2.42	18.12	1.06	18.15	0.98
IND	1.93	1.98	∞	1.03	∞	1.01
INT	12.07	13.74	21.38	1.3	15.12	1.0
KRO	1.78	2.09	24.01	1.0	20.14	0.91
LJO	2.09	2.19	19.96	1.02	19.97	0.98
RAL	1.73	2.03	20.67	1.0	17.97	0.91
SOC	2.22	2.35	20.47	1.06	20.41	1.01
WEB	2.89	3.19	11.45	1.16	11.56	0.86
WIK	2.18	2.42	20.13	1.07	20.11	0.98

(a) Conversion Times

Matrix	DCSR defrag	HYB sort	DCSR update	HYB update
AMA	3.9	2.12	2.02	4.89
CNR	5.13	6.75	3.77	15.26
DBL	5.69	4.66	3.6	10.23
ENR	5.49	8.0	2.21	18.2
EU2	2.32	4.28	2.65	12.05
FLI	1.58	4.22	1.94	10.01
HOL	1.54	5.57	2.55	12.45
IN2	2.58	5.85	3.14	13.34
IND	2.15	∞	3.36	∞
INT	6.74	6.19	1.76	8.78
KRO	1.02	3.43	1.82	11.3
LJO	1.45	3.02	1.34	6.1
RAL	0.72	2.04	1.82	13.61
SOC	1.05	3.74	1.02	5.74
WEB	2.65	1.93	2.54	7.39
WIK	1.39	2.54	1.32	5.49

(b) Sorting Overhead

Updating a DCSR matrix requires finding the last occupied (current) segment within a row. If that segment is not full, the new entry is added into it and the row size is increased. When the current segment for a row fills up, a new segment is allocated dynamically. Since atomic operations are required only for the allocation of new segments, and not for each individual element, synchronization overhead is kept low. By allowing for dynamically sized slack space within a row, we dramatically reduce the number of atomic operations that are required to allocate new entries. In this way, DCSR was designed to be updated in an efficient parallel manner.

The number of segments, initial row width, and α value can be tuned for the problem to give a reasonable limit on updates. In our tests we used four segments and α value of μ (average row size of the matrix). When a row nears its limit, a defragmentation is required in order to reduce that row to a single segment.

Figure 3 provides the results of our iterative and streaming matrix update tests. We do not compare to CSR in the latter case, since it is not possible to dynamically add entries without rebuilding the matrix. The goal of this operation is to load the matrix; insertion checks are not performed. DCSR saw an average speedup of 4.8× over HYB with streaming updates. In the case of IND, only DCSR was able to perform the operation within memory capacity.

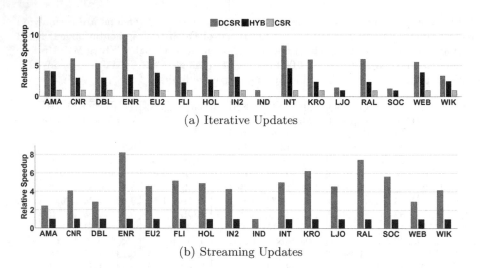

(a) Iterative Updates

(b) Streaming Updates

Fig. 3. Top: relative speedup of DCSR compared to HYB for iterative updates with SpMV operations. The speedup is compared to a normalized CSR baseline. Bottom: relative speedup of DCSR compared to HYB for matrix updates. (Color figure online)

We also executed an iterative update test to compare the abilities of the formats to perform a combination of dynamic updates and SpMV operations. This test is analogous to what would be performed in a graph application (such as CFA) where the graph is updated at periodic intervals. In the iterative updates test we perform a series of iterations consisting of a matrix addition operation ($A = A + B$) followed by several SpMV operations $Ax = y$. Part (a) of Fig. 3 provides the results for our iterative updates. Within each iteration, the matrix is updated with an additional 0.2 % random nonzeros followed by 5 SpMV operations, which is repeated 50 times, yielding a total increase of 10 % to the number of nonzeros. We compare the DCSR and HYB results to a normalized CSR baseline. In the CSR case a new matrix must be created to update the original matrix, which causes a significant amount of overhead (in terms of computation and memory). In the cases of LJO and SOC, CSR was not able to complete within memory capacity, so we normalized against HYB.

DCSR shows significant improvement over HYB on streaming updates in all test cases (in some by as much as 8×). DCSR also outperforms HYB in all test cases on iterative updates, and in some cases by as much as 2.5×. The Amazon-2008 matrix has a low standard deviation, and the majority of its entries fit nicely into the ELL portion, which greatly speeds up SpMV operations. However, even in this case DCSR slightly outperforms HYB on iterative updates due to having lower overhead for defragmentation. In all other cases DCSR exhibits noticeable performance improvements over HYB and CSR.

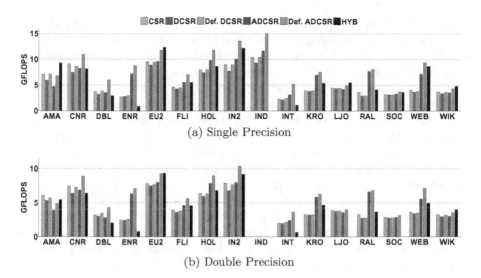

(a) Single Precision

(b) Double Precision

Fig. 4. FLOP ratings of SpMV operations for CSR, DCSR, and HYB. (Color figure online)

4.2 SpMV Results

In the SpMV tests we take the same set of matrices and perform SpMV operations with randomly generated dense vectors. We performed each SpMV operation 100× times and averaged the results. Figure 4 provides the results for these SpMV tests using both single and double precision floating-point arithmetic. We implemented an adaptive binning optimization [25] (labeled ACSR), which requires relatively little overhead and provides noticeable speed improvements by using specialized kernels on bins of rows with similar row sizes. In these tests we compare across several variants of our format, including DCSR, defragmented DCSR, ADCSR, and defragmented ADCSR, in addition to standard implementations of HYB and CSR.

The fragmented DCSR times are 8 % slower than the defragmented DCSR times on average. When the DCSR format is defragmented, it sees SpMV times competitive with those of CSR (1 % slower on average). With the adaptive binning optimization applied, we see that ADCSR outperforms HYB in many cases. On average, ADCSR performed 9 % better than HYB across our benchmarks.

4.3 Post-processing Overhead

Post-processing overhead is a concern when dealing with dynamic matrix updates. Dynamic segmentation allows for DCSR to be updated with new entries without requiring the entries to be defragmented. SpMV operations can be performed on the DCSR format regardless of the order of the segments, unlike HYB matrices, where a sort is required anytime an entry is added to the COO portion. The SpMV operation for HYB matrices assumes the COO entries are sorted

by row (without this property the COO SpMV would be dramatically slower).
Table 2 provides post-processing times for HYB and DCSR formats relative to a
single SpMV operation. In the case of IND, HYB was unable to sort and update
due to insufficient memory overhead (represented as ∞).

The defragmentation operation can internally order rows by row size at no
additional cost. This ordering is similar to the row sorting technique illustrated
in [28], although we use a global sorting scope as opposed to a localized one.
In addition, the internal order of segments may be changed arbitrarily, and
this permutation remains invisible from the outside because starting and ending segment indices are managed explicitly. To accomplish this optimization we
permute row sizes according to the permuted row indices (which have already
been binned and sorted by row size). The permuted row sizes can then be used
to create new offsets for the monolithic segments produced by defragmentation.
This operation has the effect of internally reordering column and value data by
row size at no additional cost. We observed this internal reordering provides a
noticeable SpMV performance improvement of 12 %. This improvement is from
an increased cache-hit rate via better correlation between bin-specific kernels
and the memory they access.

The DCSR defragmentation incurs a lower overhead than HYB sort because
entries can be shuffled to their new index without a sort operation. DCSR defragmentation is $2\times$ faster on average than HYB sorting, and this step is infrequently
required (while HYB sorting must be performed at every insertion). These factors allow DCSR to have significantly lower post-processing overhead.

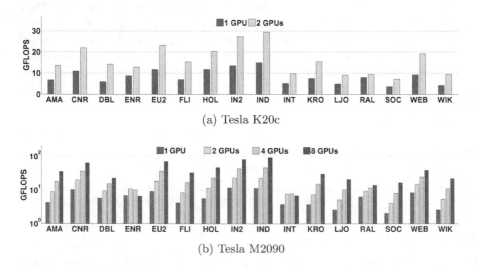

(a) Tesla K20c

(b) Tesla M2090

Fig. 5. Scaling results for SpMV with 1 and 2 K20 GPUs (upper) and 1, 2, 4, and 8
M2090 GPUs (lower). (Color figure online)

4.4   Multi-GPU Implementation

DCSR can be effectively mapped to multiple GPUs. The matrix can be partitioned across n devices by dividing rows between them (modulo n) after sorting by row size. This mapping provides a roughly even distribution of nonzeros between the devices. Figure 5 provides scaling results for DCSR across two Tesla K20c GPUs and up to eight Tesla M2090 GPUs. We see an average speedup of 1.93× for the single precision and 1.97× for double precision across the set of test matrices. The RAL matrix sees a smaller performance gain due to our distribution strategy of dividing up the rows. The added parallelism is split across rows but, in this case, the matrix has few rows and many columns. We see nearly linear scaling for most test cases.

For the matrices INT and ENR we see reduced scaling due to small matrix sizes. In these cases the kernel launch times account for a significant portion of the total time due to a relatively small workload. The total compute time can be roughly represented as $c + \frac{x}{n}$, where c is the kernel launch overhead, and the workload x is divided among n devices (assuming x can be fully parallelized). As the number of devices increases, the work per device decreases whereas the kernel launch time remains constant. In our tests we perform 100× iterations of each kernel, which leads to poor scaling performance on small matrices. We performed additional tests in which we moved the iterations into the kernel itself and called the kernel once, eliminating the additional kernel launch times. In this case we see scaling for the INT matrix of 1.94×, 3.55×, and 6.03×, and for the ENR matrix we see scaling of 1.80×, 2.70×, and 3.76× for 2, 4, and 8 GPUs, respectively. These results indicate that the poor performance of those cases was primarily due to the low amount of work done relative to the kernel launch overhead.

5   Conclusion

We have described a fast, flexible, and memory-efficient strategy for dynamic sparse-matrix allocation. The design of current formats limits the extension of an existing matrix with new entries. As many applications require or would benefit from efficient dynamic updates, we have proposed a strategy of explicitly managed dynamic segmentation that makes this operation inexpensive. Our approach is presented and evaluated using a new format (DCSR) that provides a robust method for allocating streaming updates while maintaining fast SpMV times on par with that of CSR. The format gracefully degrades in performance upon dynamic extension, but does not require a sort to be performed after inserting new entries (as opposed to COO-based formats such as HYB).

Without defragmentation, SpMV times are only marginally slower than that of a fully constructed CSR matrix, and after defragmentation they are roughly equal. With adaptive binning applied, DCSR gives faster overall SpMV times as compared to the HYB format. DCSR is significantly more efficient in terms of memory use as well. ELL must allocate enough room in every row for the longest row in a matrix. HYB is a vast improvement, allowing long rows to overflow into its COO portion; however, DCSR exhibited lower memory consumption on every benchmark when set to allow 2 segments per row, and still used 20 % less memory on average when allowing 4 segments per row.

A key advantage of DCSR design is compatibility with CSR-scalar, CSR-vector, and other CSR algorithms. Only minor modifications are required to account for a difference in the format of the row offsets array. We have demonstrated how CSR-specific optimizations, such as adaptive binning, can be easily applied to DCSR. Other optimizations such as tiling and blocking could also be used. This compatibility also means that minimal overhead is required to convert to and from CSR. Numerous sparse-matrix formats have been developed that are specifically tailored to GPU architectures. These formats offer improved performance, but require converting from whatever previous format was being used. As CSR is the most commonly used sparse-matrix format, and large amounts of software already incorporate it into their code bases, it is often not worth the conversion cost to introduce another format. DCSR reduces this barrier to use with a low cost of conversion.

To the best of our knowledge, no other work has created a dynamic format such as DCSR for iterative updates to sparse matrices. Some dynamic graph algorithms, such as approximate betweenness centrality [29], require dynamic updates but do not specify how the graph should be represented and modified— a matrix encoding would require a dynamic format to be efficient. Dynamic insertion algorithms, like that described in [30], use a modified insertion sort that disperses gaps throughout the data in order to reduce insertion time from $O(n)$ to $O(log\ n)$ with high probability. This method probabilistically reduces the overall cost of the insertion sort from $O(n^2)$ to $O(n\ log\ n)$. The defragmentation operation we implement can be done in $O(n)$ and insertions require $O(1)$, which is better than insertion sort. Also, leaving many intermittent gaps between the data would slow SpMV times. We mitigate this problem by grouping entries contiguously within segments.

We believe our strategy lends itself well to certain operations and problems, such as graph algorithms that require periodically updating the graph with new entries. These applications have not previously been well addressed by sparse-matrix formats. Our work also opens up a number of interesting research questions as to whether existing algorithms that rebuild matrices between iterations could be improved by a matrix format that permits dynamic updates directly.

References

1. Im, E., Yelick, K.: Optimization of sparse matrix kernels for data mining. In: First SIAM Conference on Data Mining (2000)
2. Gilbert, J., Reinhardt, S., Shah, V.: High-performance graph algorithms from parallel sparse matrices. In: Kågström, B., Elmroth, E., Dongarra, J., Waśniewski, J. (eds.) Applied Parallel Computing. State of the Art in Scientific Computing. LNCS, vol. 4699, pp. 260–269. Springer, Heidelberg (2007)
3. Saad, Y.: Iterative Methods for Sparse Linear Systems, 2nd edn. Society for Industrial and Applied Mathematics, Philadelphia (2003). Saad:2003:IMS

 4. Shivers, O.: Control-Flow Analysis of Higher-Order Languages. Carnegie-Mellon University, Pittsburgh (1991)
 5. Midtgaard, J.: Control-flow analysis of functional programs. ACM Comput. Surv. **44**(3), 10:1–10:33 (2012)
 6. Gilray, T., King, J., Might, M.: Partitioning 0-CFA for the GPU. In: Workshop on Functional and Constraint Logic Programming, September 2014
 7. Prabhu, T., Ramalingam, S., Might, M., Hall, M.: EigenCFA: accelerating flow analysis with GPUs. In: Proceedings of the Symposium on the Principals of Programming Languages, pp. 511–522 (2010)
 8. Mendez-Lojo, M., Burtscher, M., Pingali, K.: A GPU implementation of inclusion-based points-to analysis. ACM SIGPLAN Not. **47**(8), 107–116 (2012)
 9. Greathouse, J.L., Daga, M.: Efficient sparse matrix-vector multiplication on GPUs using the CSR storage format. In: Proceedings of the International Conference for High Performance Computing, Networking, Storage and Analysis, SC 2014, pp. 769–780. IEEE Press, Piscataway (2014)
10. Garland, M.: Sparse matrix computations on manycore GPU's. In: Proceedings of the 45th Annual Design Automation Conference, DAC 2008, pp. 2–6. ACM, New York (2008)
11. Garland, M., Kirk, D.B.: Understanding throughput-oriented architectures. Commun. ACM **53**(11), 58–66 (2010)
12. Bell, N., Garland, M.: Efficient Sparse Matrix-Vector Multiplication on CUDA. NVIDIA Corporation (2008). NVR-2008-004
13. Monakov, A., Lokhmotov, A., Avetisyan, A.: Automatically tuning sparse matrix-vector multiplication for GPU architectures. In: Patt, Y.N., Foglia, P., Duester-wald, E., Faraboschi, P., Martorell, X. (eds.) HiPEAC 2010. LNCS, vol. 5952, pp. 111–125. Springer, Heidelberg (2010)
14. Su, B.Y., Koutzer, K.: clSpMV: a cross-platform OpenCL SpMV framework on GPUs. In: Proceedings of the 26th ACM International Conference on Supercomputing, ICS 2012, pp. 353–364. ACM, New York (2012)
15. Vuduc, R.W.: Automatic Performance Tuning of Sparse Matrix Kernels. University of California, Berkeley (2003). AAI3121741
16. Bell, N., Garland, M.: Implementing sparse matrix-vector multiplication onthroughput-oriented processors. In: SC 2009, Proceedings of the Conference on High Performance Computing Networking, Storage and Analysis, pp. 1–11. ACM, New York (2009)
17. Ashari, A., Sedaghati, N., Eisenlohr, J., Sadayappan, P.: An efficient two-dimensional blocking strategy for sparsematrix-vector multiplication on GPUs. In: Proceedings of the 28th ACM International Conference on Supercomputing, ICS 2014, pp. 273–282. ACM, New York (2014)
18. Yan, S., Li, C., Zhang, Y., Zhou, H.: yaSpMV: yet another SpMV framework on GPUs. In: Proceedings of the 19th ACM SIGPLAN Symposium on Principles and Practice of Parallel Programming, PPopp 2014, pp. 107–118. ACM, New York (2014)
19. Williams, S., Oliker, L., Vuduc, R., Shalf, J., Yelick, K., Demmel, J.: Optimization of sparse matrix-vector multiplication on emerging multicore platforms. In: Proceedings of the ACM/IEEE Conference on Supercomputing, SC 2007, pp. 38:1–38:12. ACM, New York (2007)
20. Liu, X., Smelyanskiy, M., Chow, E., Dubey, P.: Efficient sparse matrix-vector multiplication on x86-based many-coreprocessors. In: Proceedings of the 27th International ACM Conference on International Conference on Supercomputing, ICS 2013, pp. 273–282. ACM, New York (2013)

21. Yang, X., Parthasarathy, S., Sadayappan, P.: Fast sparse matrix-vector multiplication on GPUs: implications for graph mining. Proc. VLDB Endow. **4**(4), 231–242 (2011)
22. Choi, J.W., Singh, A., Vuduc, R.W.: Model-driven autotuning of sparse matrix-vector multiply on GPUs. SIGPLAN Not. **45**(5), 115–126 (2010)
23. Reguly, I., Giles, M.: Efficient sparse matrix-vector multiplication on cache-based GPUs. In: Innovative Parallel Computing (InPar), pp. 1–12 (2012)
24. Kepner, J., Gilbert, J.: Graph Algorithms in the Language of Linear Algebra. Society for Industrial and Applied Mathematics, Philadelphia (2011)
25. Ashari, A., Sedaghati, N., Eisenlohr, J., Parthasarathy, S., Sadayappan, P.: Fast sparse matrix-vector multiplication on GPUs for graph applications. In: Proceedings of the International Conference for High Performance Computing, Networking, Storage and Analysis, SC 2014, pp. 781–792. IEEE Press, Piscataway (2014)
26. Bell, N., Garland, M.: CUSP: generic parallel algorithms for sparse matrix and graph computations (2012). Version 0.3.0
27. Davis, T.A., Hu, Y.: The University of Florida sparse matrix collection. ACM Trans. Math. Softw. **38**(1), 1–25 (2011)
28. Kreutzer, M., Hager, G., Wellein, G., Fehske, H., Bishop, A.R.: A unified sparse matrix data format for modern processors with wide SIMD units. CoRR. abs/1307.6209 (2013)
29. McLaughlin, A., Bader, D.A.: Revisiting edge and node parallelism for dynamic GPU graph analytics. In: IEEE International on Parallel Distributed Processing Symposium Workshops (IPDPSW), pp. 1396–1406 (2014)
30. Bender, M.A., Farach-Colton, M., Mosteiro, M.A.: Insertion sort is O(n log n). Theor. Comput. Syst. **39**(3), 391–397 (2006)

An Efficient Parallel Load-Balancing Framework for Orthogonal Decomposition of Geometrical Data

Bruno R.C. Magalhães[1]([✉]), Farhan Tauheed[2], Thomas Heinis[2],
Anastasia Ailamaki[2], and Felix Schürmann[1]

[1] Blue Brain Project, École Polytechnique Fédérale de Lausanne (EPFL),
Biotech Campus, 1202 Geneva, Switzerland
bruno.magalhaes@epfl.ch
[2] Data-Intensive Applications and Systems Laboratory,
École Polytechnique Fédérale de Lausanne (EPFL),
1015 Lausanne, Switzerland

Abstract. The accurate subdivision of spatially organized datasets is a complex problem in computer science but specifically important for load balancing in parallel environments. The problem is to (a) find a partitioning where each partition has the same number of elements and (b) the communication between partitions (duplicate members) is minimized. We present a novel parallel load-balancing framework — *Sort Balance Split* (SBS) — the first to our knowledge to perform accurate parallel partitioning of multidimensional data, while requiring a fixed number of communication steps independent of network size or input data distribution. When compared to the state of the art sampling and parallel partitioning methods adopted by HPC problems, it delivers better load balancing on a shorter time to solution. We analyse four partitioning schemes that SBS can be applied to, and evaluated our method on 4096 nodes of an IBM BlueGene/Q supercomputer partitioning up to 1 trillion elements, and exhibiting almost-linear scaling properties.

Keywords: Geometric partitioning · Spatial partitioning · Recursive bisection · Jagged partitioning · Load balancing

1 Introduction

Geometrical domain decomposition has been widely applied in several scientific fields. An accurate decomposition is important, as the best performance on a network of computing nodes is achieved with good data distribution across all processing entities and by the reduction of intra-network communication. In the case where we have a parallel and homogeneous architecture, if the processing time for each element is equal, the best load balancing has an even distribution across all processing entities. Most domain partitioning methods of static geometrical data rely either on connection or geometry-based decompositions.

© Springer International Publishing Switzerland 2016
J.M. Kunkel et al. (Eds.): ISC High Performance 2016, LNCS 9697, pp. 81–97, 2016.
DOI: 10.1007/978-3-319-41321-1_5

Connectivity-based partitioning is based on the analysis of the connectivity of the elements and aims to equalize the weight of edges or nodes via graph or hypergraph partitioning [17]. A hypergraph is a generalization of a graph where edges can connect more than two vertices and are called hyperedges. Some hypergraph partitioning applications are numerical linear algebra [5], integrated circuit design [14] and web document categorization [3]. Scotch [18], METIS and ParMETIS [13] are the most commonly used large-scale graph partitioners. For hypergraph partitioning, Zoltan [4] is the most commonly used toolkit.

Geometry-based partitioning relies on the principle that spatially placed elements require neighbouring elements' information for the processing of data. Such methods tend to divide the universe in several regions and allocate one region per compute node. Most common are straight decomposition, surfaces and space filling curves [1]. For geometrically-based partitions, the simplest and fastest method to compute is the orthogonal slicing creating rectangular partitions, as it can be easily expressed, has a low memory overhead, and allows for efficient implementation of common operations such as spatial queries, indexing, intersection and inclusion of other shapes. Another common feature of these types of problems is that elements may require information about their neighbourhood which may be partially stored on other processors' main memory. This can be solved typically by copying those neighbouring elements to the local processor — a method typically termed *ghosting* and which requires more memory on these nodes holding duplicated (*ghost*) elements. Once a processor is allocated a region, its computation is performed independently; this parallel processing falls in the category of *pleasantly parallel tasks*. An alternative method of handling data dependency across several nodes is by actively communicating neighbourhood information to other nodes as required.

This document presents the **Sort Balance Split** (SBS), a novel parallel framework for geometric data division based on orthogonal cut planes, built from three core operations: distributed sorting, load balancing, and network split — hence the name. The SBS allows for the efficient parallel implementation of any slicing algorithm based on orthogonal slices. The SBS delivers accurate slicing cut points, good weak and strong scaling properties, and high speed-up and performance increase over the state of the art, particularly for large networks and datasets. Contrary to most spatial decomposition algorithms, the SBS allows for decoupling of the complexity/structure of the dataset from the scalability, and therefore the methods and execution times presented in this document are valid and applicable to any spatial decomposition problem. Moreover, this collection of features makes the SBS particularly adequate for highly dense and heterogeneous datasets requiring high precision partitioning for good work load balancing, such as the neuronal networks containing billions of elements handled internally in our project. We analyse the complexity of four slicing configurations that can be built with SBS: single axis, Non-Uniform Grid (NUG, General Block Distribution, or Rectilinear partitions), Sort Tile Recursive (STR, or Jagged Partitions), and Orthogonal Recursive Bisection (ORB) or Recursive Coordinate Bisection (RCB). The remainder of the document is organized as follows: Sect. 2 formalizes and analyses the complexity behind different slicing techniques and Sect. 3 presents the details of the parallel implementation. The testing results are detailed in Sect. 4. Section 5 presents our final conclusions.

1.1 Related Work and Applications

Previous applications of parallel and large scale domain decomposition of geometrical data targeting distributed computation include particle interaction in astrophysics (particularly N-body simulations on the Gordon Bell Prize (GBP) winners of 2009 [8], 2010 [9] and 2012 [12]), cardiac model simulations ([20] and the GBP 2015 finalist [19]), fluid dynamics (cloud cavitation on the GBP 2013 winner [22]), materials engineering (materials crystallization on the GBP 2011 winner [24]), weather forecasting [21] and direct volume rendering [16].

The most common serial partitioning methods – including several GBP winners mentioned above – perform domain decomposition based on a sample of data and repeat the procedure until a minimum quality threshold is reached [2]. Common methods rely on histograms of element distribution in all dimensions and calculate the partitioning cut planes based on the histogram bins [15]. Due to its low resolution, this approach is mostly suitable for quasi-uniformly distributed datasets. Alternative methods are based on approximated slicing positions given by a grid of workload per sub-section of the volume [23], which is unsuitable for data in a high dimensional space as the number of volumes required for a high resolution presents a bottleneck in memory required to store all data.

Parallel partitioning in very large networks has also been presented by [25], as a four step algorithm – local sorting, splitter finding, data redistribution and p-way merging – that provides *exact splitting*, yet requires several collective (AllReduce) operations and one broadcast per compute node. The most common parallel algorithm is the Recursive Coordinate Bisection, available in the Zoltan toolkit [4], computing the slicing cut point coordinates with a binary-search approach to find the median. The initial cut plane is taken as the average between the minimum and maximum on the cut direction. Afterwards, a parallel reduction operation computes the weights of all elements on both sides of the cut plane, and the cut is subsequently moved depending on the total weights. This process is repeated until both sides respect a given imbalance threshold. The space is then split into subgroups used for recursion. The communication cost is dependent on the depth of recursion i.e. network size. Data migration happens at every bisection, thus high data movement may be required during partitioning, depending on the initial data distribution. The parallel Multi-Jagged algorithm [6] (MJ, implemented in the Zoltan2 toolkit), to our knowledge the only parallel implementation of a multidimensional-jagged geometric partitioner, is a generalization of the RCB algorithm to multiple dimensions. The amount of communication and number of iterative steps is not predictable on either the RCB or MJ, as both depend on the initial data distribution.

In order to tackle the main issues of the aforementioned serial and parallel methods – high load imbalance, unpredictable (possibly high) number of communication steps, and/or high execution time – the SBS method we introduce guarantees low and fixed communication cost (6 collective calls) per dimension, precise slicing cut planes, and fixed complexity in terms of local computation (one sorting operation per dimension). This methodology is particularly efficient on low latency networks, and particularly those tuned for collective communication such as the BlueGene/Q architecture. The performance properties are independent of the network size and the data layout. This is a unique feature of the SBS, allowing decoupling of the complexity/structure of the dataset from the scalability, contrary to most common algorithms such as histogram-based (highly dependent on density and bin size) and sampling-based algorithms (dependent on the sampling set and size), or the parallel RCB as implemented in Zoltan toolkit (high variability in number of iterations based on the imbalance of each step therefore dependent on data distribution).

2   Model and Algorithms

For convenience, we will describe an orthogonal data division algorithm as a **slicing** method, each region termed a **slice**, and the coordinates that delimit the orthogonal lines separating the slices termed **slicing cut points**. The set of all elements in the multidimensional space is referred to as our **universe**.

2.1   Slicing Problem Definition

Let E be the ordered set of n elements $\{e_i\}_{i=1}^n$ to be processed. Each element $e \in E$ has a position $\underline{x}(e) \in \mathbb{R}^m$ with coordinates $x^d(e)$, for $d = 1...m$ and an extent $V(e) \subseteq \mathbb{R}^m$ such that $\underline{x}(e) \in V(e)$. When $V(e) = \{\underline{x}(e)\}$ then we have a *point dataset* E. The orthogonal slicing problem on a m-dimensional space aims at partitioning the elements in E across s slices or sub-sets $\{R_i\}_{i=1}^s$, satisfying the following properties:

1. Cover: $\bigcup R_i = E$;
2. Distinct: $R_j \bigcap R_i = \emptyset, \forall i \neq j$;
3. Let $B_j = [b_j^{1\triangledown}, b_j^{1\triangle}] \times [b_j^{2\triangledown}, b_j^{2\triangle}] \times ... \times [b_j^{m\triangledown}, b_j^{m\triangle}] \subseteq \mathbb{R}^m$ be the *axis-aligned* bounding volume of R_j such that $b_j^{d\triangledown} = \min\limits_{e \in R_j} x^d(e)$ and $b_j^{d\triangle} = \max\limits_{e \in R_j} x^d(e)$;
   then, bounding boxes have zero-volume intersection i.e.
   $vol(B_i \bigcap B_j) = \phi, \forall i \neq j$.
4. $|\#R_j - \#R_i| \leq 1$, where $\#$ is the cardinality, i.e. slices have equal size when s divides n, or difference 1 in size otherwise.

In brief, equally sized sub-sets cover the initial set of elements without overlapping in space. In the cases where E is not a point dataset but where the elements have spatial extent, it may not be possible to slice completely the volume in non-overlapping rectangles, therefore the second rule does not hold, i.e. $\exists R_i, R_j \subseteq E$ such that $R_i \bigcap R_j = Q$ and $Q \neq \emptyset$, where Q is the set of *ghost* elements that are duplicated among processors.

2.2   Elements Sorting on a Given Dimension

Sorting of a dataset E on a dimension $d = 1...m$ is the operation that returns a permutation of E so that $x^d(e_i) \leq x^d(e_j)$, $\forall i \leq j$.

2.3   Slices Coordinates Calculation

Let E be a sequence of n elements **sorted** on a particular dimension d, and in s slices. The subset E'_k (where $k = 1...s$) that contains all the elements of the kth slice of E in d can be determined as:

$$E'_k = E\left[\left\lfloor \frac{n}{s} \right\rfloor (k-1) + 1, \left\lfloor \frac{n}{s} \right\rfloor k \right] \tag{1}$$

where $E[first, last]$ denotes the ordered sub-set of E containing all elements from index $first$ to $last$ inclusive, and $\lfloor\ \rfloor$ denotes the *floor* operation.

2.4   Computational Complexity

From Sect. 2.3, it follows that the slicing cut point can be calculated in constant time if the set is represented as a vector of elements sorted beforehand. This can be explained by the access operation requiring a single memory access to the cut point position which can be performed in constant time. For the sorting operation, we will assume an average complexity of $O(n \cdot \log_2 n)$ typically found on a *mergesort* or average-case *quicksort* algorithm. Table 1 details and summarizes the complexity and limitations of each slicing configuration. This will be extended to a parallel implementation in the following section.

3   Sort Balance Split

The Sort Balance Split framework relies on a sequential three-step algorithm applied recursively to each dimension:

1. distributed parallel sorting (Sect. 3.1), a prerequisite for the calculation of cut points in constant time;
2. distributed load balancing (Sect. 3.2), to solve the data imbalance of the previous sort;
3. network split (Sect. 3.3), the basis of SBS recursivity;

The algorithm terminates when every processor is allocated a region of data (slice). The final datasets are guaranteed to be unique, disjoint and of equal sizes, as a result of the three steps. Figure 1 illustrates an example of an application of the SBS algorithm based on the Sort Tile Recursive method on a 2D space.

Table 1. Computational steps of the four slicing configurations applied to a total of s slices, covering a universe of dimensionality d and n elements. We assume a user-defined sorting operation with average-case time complexity of $O(n \cdot \log_2 n)$, and negligible time for the calculation of slice cut points.

	Scheme	Computation steps	Properties / Limitations
	Single Axis	$= n \cdot \log_2 n$	One sorting of all elements on a single direction, independently of the number of dimensions.
	Non-Uniform Grid	$= d \cdot n \cdot \log_2 n$	One sorting of all elements applied to each dimension, iteratively; slicing configuration for the d dimensions must decompose final number of slices s i.e. $\prod_{k=1}^{d} S_k = s$.
	Sort Tile Recursive	$= n \cdot \log_2 n$ $+ n \cdot \log_2 \frac{n}{S_1}$ $+ n \cdot \log_2 \frac{n}{S_1 S_2}$ $+ \dots$ $+ n \cdot \log_2 \frac{n}{S_1 S_2 \dots S_{d-1}}$ $= \sum_{i=1}^{d} n \cdot \log_2 \frac{n}{\prod_{k=0}^{i-1} S_k}$	One sorting for each subslice's data on each dimension, applied iteratively; sub-slices computations are independent; slicing configuration for the d dimensions must decompose final number of slices s i.e. $\prod_{k=1}^{d} S_k = s$; Faster than NUG as each new dimension requires sorting across smaller datasets; we assume $S_0 = 1$ i.e. the initial universe is a single slice including all elements.
	Orthogonal Recursive Bisection	$= n \cdot \log_2 n$ $+ n \cdot \log_2 \frac{n}{2}$ $+ n \cdot \log_2 \frac{n}{4}$ $+ n \cdot \log_2 \frac{n}{8}$ $+ \dots$ $+ n \cdot \log_2 \frac{n}{\log_2 s}$ $= \sum_{i=1}^{\log_2 s} n \cdot \log_2 \frac{n}{2^{i-1}}$	Total number of slices s must be a power of 2; requires one sorting of half of the elements of a slice per iteration for a total of $\log_2 s$ steps, therefore a slow method on large networks; sub-slices computations are independent.

3.1 Distributed Sorting

Let $A \oplus B$ represent the function that concatenates 2 sequences of elements A and B, and let $\bigoplus_{i=1}^{s} E_i = E_1 \oplus E_2 \oplus \dots \oplus E_s$ represent the concatenation of several sequences. The sequences $E_1', E_2', \dots, E_s'$ are the result of a distributed sorting of $E_1, E_2, \dots E_s$ iff:

1. $\bigoplus_{i=1}^{s} E_i'$ is a permutation of $\bigoplus_{i=1}^{s} E_i$;
2. $\bigoplus_{i=1}^{s} E_i'$ is sorted;

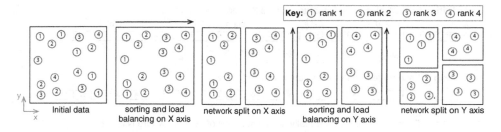

Fig. 1. A sample workflow (left to right) detailing the Sort Balance Split implementation of the Sort Tile Recursive applied to 16 points on a 2D space slices divided across 4 nodes on a 2 × 2 slicing configuration.

In practice, the distributed sorting algorithm re-distributes the elements spread across several compute nodes in such a way that all elements are sorted locally on each node's memory, and globally with respect to each node's rank on the network. In our application we implemented the parallel sample sort ([7], detailed in Fig. 2) due to its linear run time execution and scaling properties: the number of communications is fixed and independent of the network size. This method is *unstable* in the sense that it does not guarantee the same number of elements per node on the pre and post sorting phases. This is overcome by proceeding with a load balancing step after the sorting operation.

3.2 Distributed Load Balancing

A load balancing algorithm aims to balance the number of elements per node across a network while respecting the initial ordering of the elements.

The sequences $E'_1, E'_2, ...E'_s$ of sizes $n'_1, n'_2, ...n'_s$ are said to be the results of a load balancing of $E_1, E_2, ...E_s$ of sizes $n_1, n_2, ...n_s$ iff:

1. $\bigcup_{i=1}^{s} E_i = \bigcup_{i=1}^{s} E'_i$, the initial and final elements are the same;
2. $\bigoplus_{i=1}^{s} E'_i$ is not a permutation of $\bigoplus_{i=1}^{s} E_i$, i.e. order is preserved;
3. $|\#E'_j - \#E'_i| \leq 1$, where $\#$ is the size, i.e. sequences have equal size when s divides n, or difference 1 in size otherwise;
4. order of data across all nodes is preserved;

Figure 3 illustrates our implementation of the distributed load balancing algorithm.

3.3 Network Split

A network split operation divides a network of several compute nodes into several sub-networks of nodes, where each node belongs to one sub-network only. In our model, we enforce nodes with sequential ranks to be placed together in the new sub-network and in the same order as before the split. This guarantees that the global order of data across the network is respected. Given a compute node with

Initial data: 21 elements distributed across 3 nodes ranked 0 to 2

Step 1: Each node sorts its own data locally

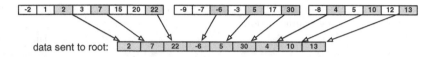

Step 2: Each node collects N equally distant samples of its data (where N is the total number of node), and sends them to a root node

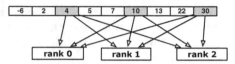

Step 3: root node sorts the received samples, takes N samples from them and broadcasts them to all nodes. The samples represent each processor's interval of data.

In practice: All ranks received the samples [4,10,13]. Therefore:
- rank 0 will receive all data from minimum to 4;
- rank 1 will receive all data between 4 and 10;
- rank 2 will receive all data from 10 to 30;

Step 4: Each node sends the portion of its segments to the corresponding destination, based on their intervals. Each receiver places the received data in the same order as sender rank - therefore final data will be already sorted.

Fig. 2. A top-to-bottom workflow and a practical example of a parallel implementation of the Sample Sort algorithm applied to 21 elements distributed among 3 computing nodes. Note that every node finishes the execution with a different (and unpredictable) number of elements compared to the initial state. On an MPI implementation, the method requires 3 collective operations: MPI_Gatherv, MPI_Bcast and MPI_Alltoallv.

a rank $node_{id}$, part of a network with an id $comm_{id}$ and holding $comm_{size}$ nodes, we calculate the new node rank and network id for the slicing of dimension d into S_d slices as:

$$node'_{id} \leftarrow \left\lfloor node_{id} \bmod \frac{comm_{size}}{S_d} \right\rfloor \tag{2}$$

and

$$comm'_{id} \leftarrow \left\lfloor node_{id} \, / \, \frac{comm_{size}}{S_d} \right\rfloor . \tag{3}$$

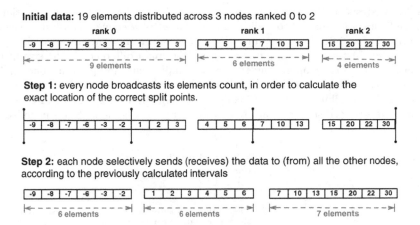

Initial data: 19 elements distributed across 3 nodes ranked 0 to 2

Step 1: every node broadcasts its elements count, in order to calculate the exact location of the correct split points.

Step 2: each node selectively sends (receives) the data to (from) all the other nodes, according to the previously calculated intervals

Fig. 3. A top-to-bottom workflow and a practical example of a parallel implementation of our load balancing algorithm, dividing 19 elements among 3 compute nodes. On an MPI implementation, the method requires 2 collective operations: `MPI_Alltoall` and `MPI_Alltoallv`.

For reference, Fig. 4 provides the implementation details for our network split algorithm.

3.4 Computational Complexity

From the previous sections, it follows that an MPI-based Sort Balance Split implementation based on a sample parallel sort followed by load balancing requires a total of 1 sorting operation of the data in local memory and 6 collective communication steps per dimension. Table 2 provides a comparison of the number of computational complexity between a serial implementation (from Table 1) and a parallel implementation of the four slicing schemes, with an extra

Initial data: data distributed across 8 nodes ranked 0 to 7 grouped in 1 comm. group

Step 1: each node calculates its new rank and sub-group id

Step 2: based on previous, split network in K independent networks, e.g:

Fig. 4. A sample implementation of a network split: 8 initial compute nodes are grouped in 4 sub-groups. On an MPI implementation, the method requires one collective call (`MPI_Comm_split`).

Table 2. Analysis of the serial and parallel implementation of the four mentioned slicing configurations applied to s slices and a dataset of n elements on d dimensions. The overhead of a collective communication operation involving p processors is represented as $\varphi(p)$. In terms of computation steps, the main difference is the size of the input data on the sorting operation: the parallel implementation performs one sorting of size n/s per node (first step of distributed sorting). The overhead of the remaining steps of the distributed sorting (3 collective calls), the load balancing (2 collective calls) and the network split (1 collective call) operations of the SBS are included on the communication steps.

Scheme	Serial implementation (from Table 1)	SBS-based parallel implementation	
		computation steps	communication steps
Single axis	$n \log_2 n$	$\frac{n}{s} \log_2 \frac{n}{s}$	$6 \cdot \varphi(s)$
		One sorting of a subset of n elements shared across s slices, and 6 global communications.	
Non-Uniform Grid	$d \cdot n \log_2 n$	$d \cdot \frac{n}{s} \log_2 \frac{n}{s}$	$6 \cdot d \cdot \varphi(s)$
		Same as single axis slicing applied to all the d dimensions.	
Sort Tile Recursive	$\sum_{i=1}^{d} n \cdot \log_2 \frac{n}{\prod_{k=0}^{i-1} S_k}$	$\sum_{i=1}^{d} \frac{n}{s} \log_2 \frac{n}{s}$	$6 \cdot \sum_{i=1}^{d} \varphi\left(\frac{s}{\prod_{k=0}^{i-1} S_k}\right)$
		Same steps and sorting size as NUG; the network size for a given dimension i is given by $\frac{s}{\prod_{k=0}^{i-1} S_k}$ instead (where $S_0 = 1$).	
Orthogonal Recursive Bisection	$\sum_{i=1}^{\log_2 s} n \log_2 \frac{n}{2^{i-1}}$	$\sum_{i=1}^{\log_2 s} \frac{n}{s} \log_2 \frac{n}{s}$	$6 \cdot \sum_{i=1}^{\log_2 s} \varphi\left(\frac{s}{2^{i-1}}\right)$
		Same rationale as STR applied to 2 sub-slices per dimension and for $log_2 s$ slicing steps; network size for a dimension i given by $\frac{s}{2^{i-1}}$.	

reference for the communication overhead. An initial analysis shows that the SBS speed-up over the serial case is more prominent as we increase the input data size and/or the network size. In practice this efficiency increment is due to the communication overhead being compensated by a faster (distributed) sorting, therefore it is required to have a *substantial* amount of data per node in order for this speed-up to be noticeable. These claims will be confirmed in our benchmarking results in the following section.

4   Results

The Sort Balance Split was tested in terms of load imbalance across the network, time to solution and scaling properties. The reference benchmarks are the most common histogram- and sampling-based on a serial architecture, and the Zoltan toolkit's RCB on a parallel environment. Section 4.3 details an initial analysis of the ghosting phenomena related to each of the four slicing schemas mentioned above, when applied to our dataset. The quality of our algorithm is measured in Sect. 4.4 where a small scale analysis of the load imbalance on 512 nodes compares the load imbalance of the best performant slicing schema with the histogram- and sampling-based approximation algorithms. Finally, Sect. 4.5 follows with a benchmark of the SBS against the most common serial and parallel algorithms (used on the Gordon Bell Prize winners mentioned initially) on a network of 16384 MPI ranks, where the SBS is shown to provide better load balancing on a lower time to solution. Finally, Sect. 4.6 shows very good (almost linear) weak and strong scaling properties of the SBS framework.

4.1 Testing Environment

The specifications of the BlueGene/Q environment used for testing are: 4096 nodes of A2 compute chip [10] for a total of 0.8 Petaflops theoretical peak, 16 GB DRAM/node for a total of 64 TB DRAM memory, standard IBM BlueGene/Q Compute Node Kernel. Testing results for networks of 8192 and 16384 MPI ranks were performed with a set-up of 2 and 4 MPI ranks per compute node, respectively. We believe such set-up of virtual MPI ranks does not degrade the quality of results as there were no differences in performance when applied to our network on 4096 or less compute nodes.

4.2 Data Representation

Our input data is a biologically inspired representation of a network of neurons with 3D morphologies (refer to [11] for details). The diversity of neurons is based on 1500 unique neuron morphologies which are cloned, rotated and tightly placed in space. A neuron (cell) is simplified as a central nucleus (soma) and a set of branches spreading out from several extremities of the soma. A branch is a sequence of connected compartments. A compartment's contour (its lipid bilayer forming a neuron membrane) is represented as a cylinder on a 3D space, and mentioned on this document as a **segment**. On a branch, a segment's end point serves as the following segment's start point. Other non-spatially defined characteristics of a compartment - e.g. ion channels, electrochemical gradients, ion pumps, transporters - are not relevant for the context of this document, thus we focus solely on the geometrical representation of such model. The geometrical distribution is highly heterogeneous: the center of a circuit is densely populated – having between 40–80 % of volume occupied by segments – and the endings of the branches may extend to sparse areas of the volumetric space. When partitioning a collection of neurons, the method aims at equalizing the number of segment points across all compute nodes. For the purpose of ghosting, the radius and length between two consecutive points provide the extent of the shape.

4.3 Slicing Schemes Load Imbalance

For the analysis of the load imbalance we applied the four mentioned slicing configurations to a circuit of 31 K neurons spread across 16384 domains, and we

Table 3. Analysis of the load imbalance of the four slicing configurations applied to a 31 K neurons circuit - approximately 449.5 Million segments - after partitioning on 16384 domains.

Segments Count	Base case	Single axis	Non uniform grid	Sort tile recursive	Orthogonal rec. bisec.
	Pre-ghosting	Post-ghosting	Post-ghosting	Post-ghosting	Post-ghosting
Max.	–	572307	89994	31423	31508
Min.	–	27509	5241	26687	27505
Max - Min	–	544798	84753	4736	4003
Avg.	27435	504678	31220	29853	30020
StdDev	–	117036	6529	905	774
Total count	449.5M	8268.8M	511.5M	489.1M	491.8M
Duplication	–	1739.3 %	13.7 %	8.8 %	9.4 %

present the results in Table 3. Our motivation is to understand how the overhead of the ghosting step applied to highly heterogeneous datasets is affected by different partitioning schemes. The results show the Sort Tile Recursive as the best performant slicing configuration: it allows for an accurate load balancing and a very low overhead added by ghost elements. It also runs very efficiently, only second to the single axis (which is impractical due to the high amount of ghosting). Finally, the STR adds the benefit of minimizing the communication overheard of the subsequent execution as it allows for a 3D slicing configuration that matches the physical nodes placement on the BlueGene/Q 5D torus network. Due to the high imbalance and the maximum number of elements across all domains, the Non-Uniform Grid is infeasible.

4.4   Load Imbalance of Approximation Methods

We perform an analysis of the load imbalance of the histogram-, sampling-, and SBS-based (no sampling) methods applied to four circuits of 10 K neurons on a network of 512 compute nodes. We measure how the imbalance provided by an approximation method affects the final data distribution, and consequently the total execution time defined by the compute node with the largest dataset. The workload distribution results are displayed in Fig. 5. Sampling elements are picked uniformly from equidistantly positioned indices of the input dataset. The histogram based partitioning implements the Non Uniform Grid configuration with 3000 equidistant bins per dimension, while the sampling- and the SBS-based partitioning were computed based on the Sort Tile Recursive configuration, shown previously to be the best performant for our input data. Our results exhibit poor histogram-based partitioning, driven by two main factors: the underlying NUG partitioning does not allow for an accurate balancing (also shown in Table 3), and the equidistant bins of the histogram lead to a low precision of slicing cut points, critical for the central areas of high density. The analysis of the other methods are straightforward: for any of the input sets tested, an increase of the sampling size taken from the input data leads to an decrease of the load imbalance. The study of load imbalance of these approximation methods on larger inputs and compute networks was limited by the high imbalance (thus high memory requirements) of the histogram-based method.

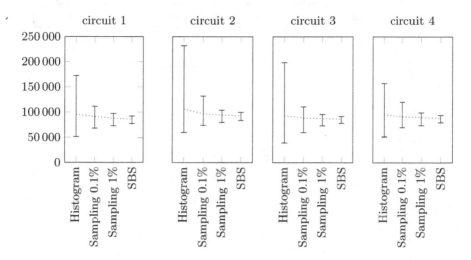

Fig. 5. Comparison of the workload distribution for histogram-, sampling-, and SBS-based slicing methods, applied to 512 compute nodes and 4 different circuits of 10 K neurons, after communication of ghost elements. Results provided as average (dotted) and min-max (vertical bar) number of segment points across all compute nodes.

4.5   Large Scale Runtime Analysis

Our large scale analysis focus on the most common approaches for orthogonal partitioning: the serial multi-jagged (STR) approach with sampling, the Zoltan-based parallel RCB, and the SBS-based multi-jagged/STR. Tests were run on a network ranging from 1024 to 16384 MPI ranks, as presented in Fig. 6. Due to the limitations of our synthetically-inspired data generation tools, the input data utilized is a set of randomly generated coordinates with an uniform distribution. This is in fact irrelevant, as the the execution time of the SBS method (contrarily to Zoltan) is independent of the data layout, therefore the application of SBS to any spatial decomposition problem yields similar execution time. Testing results show that the use of sampling in order to reduce the execution time provides a reduction of runtime proportional to the sampling rate. When compared to the serial implementation, the SBS-based STR allows a speed-up proportional to the increase of compute nodes. The SBS is shown to perform faster than the serial case with 0.1 % sampling for any network larger than 1024 ranks. On our largest tested network, the SBS outperformed the serial non-sampled implementation by 5 orders of magnitude, and achieved a speed-up of about 200× compared to the serial sampling from 0.1 % of the input data. The Zoltan-based implementation presents an inferior performance when compared to the SBS, particularly visible for smaller datasets on large networks. For large datasets, Zoltan yields a higher

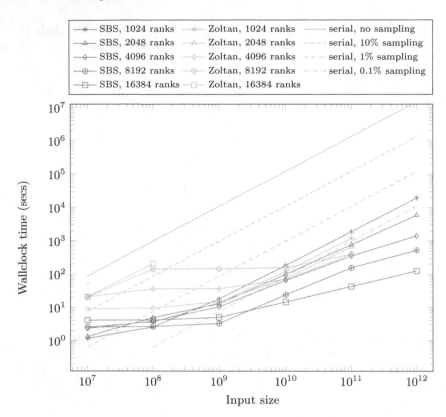

Fig. 6. Execution times for the serial sampling, Zoltan-based RCB and SBS-based Sort Tile Recursive slicing configurations. Sampling runtimes exclude the redistribution of the data based on the slicing cut points computed at the root node. Zoltan configured to allow an unbalancing threshold of 10 % (default value).

runtime, again most prominent for large networks. For the results with Zoltan we used the default configuration settings (e.g. imbalance threshold of 10 %) and it is conceivable that the results can improve if different settings were used. Due to an internal error it was not possible to perform a Zoltan partitioning on 1 trillion elements.

4.6 Weak and Strong Scaling

Weak scaling of the SBS has been tested for networks of 1024 to 16384 MPI ranks and different input sizes as displayed in Fig. 7. Weak scaling results (Fig. 7) show our method scaling across any number of compute nodes and problem sizes, and presenting nearly perfect weak scaling properties. Strong scaling results are presented in Fig. 8 where the SBS allows for almost ideal (linear) strong scaling. This feature is mostly prominent for large datasets as the communication overhead is almost negligible compared to the computation.

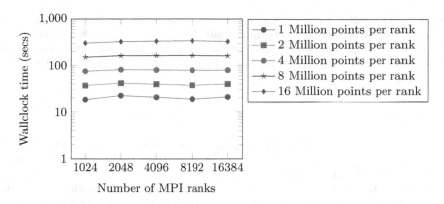

Fig. 7. Weak scaling of the Sort Balance Split framework applied to a 3D slicing based on the Sort Tile Recursive algorithm.

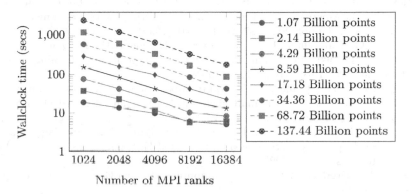

Fig. 8. Strong scaling of the Sort Balance Split framework applied to a 3D slicing based on the Sort Tile Recursive algorithm.

5   Summary and Conclusions

This paper presents and details the Sort Balance Split — a parallel framework for orthogonal domain decomposition based on a distributed load balancing, distributed sorting and network split algorithm — that serves as an efficient implementation of four slicing configurations: single axis, non uniform grid, sort tile recursive and orthogonal recursive bisection. We ran our methods on biologically inspired neural networks, and compared the SBS efficiency with the most common methods used in the large state of the art HPC problems and Gordon Bell Prize finalists, based on histogram, sampling, and parallel multi-jagged methods, where it provides a more accurate result on a shorter time to solution. At large scale, our method was shown to exhibit good weak and strong scale properties, and to scale linearly with input and network size, while running on a fixed number of communication steps independently of the network size or input data distribution.

Acknowledgements. The work was supported by funding from the ETH Domain for the Blue Brain Project (BBP). The BlueBrain IV BlueGene/Q system is financed by ETH Board Funding to the Blue Brain Project and hosted at the Swiss National Supercomputing Center (CSCS). We thank James King, Stuart Yates and Fabien Delalondre for technical discussions.

References

1. Aluru, S., Sevilgen, F.E.: Parallel domain decomposition and load balancing using space-filling curves. In: Proceedings of Fourth International Conference on High-Performance Computing, pp. 230–235. IEEE (1997)
2. Blackston, D., Suel, T.: Highly portable and efficient implementations of parallel adaptive n-body methods. In: Proceedings of the 1997 ACM/IEEE Conference on Supercomputing, SC 1997, pp. 1–20. ACM, New York (1997). http://doi.acm.org/10.1145/509593.509597
3. Boley, D., Gini, M., Gross, R., Han, E.H.S., Hastings, K., Karypis, G., Kumar, V., Mobasher, B., Moore, J.: Partitioning-based clustering for web document categorization. Decis. Support Syst. **27**(3), 329–341 (1999)
4. Boman, E.G., Catalyurek, U.V., Chevalier, C., Devine, K.D.: The Zoltan and Isorropia parallel toolkits for combinatorial scientific computing: partitioning, ordering, and coloring. Sci. Prog. **20**(2), 129–150 (2012)
5. Catalyurek, U.V., Aykanat, C.: Hypergraph-partitioning-based decomposition for parallel sparse-matrix vector multiplication. IEEE Trans. Parallel Distrib. Syst. **10**(7), 673–693 (1999)
6. Deveci, M., Rajamanickam, S., Devine, K., Catalyurek, U.: Multi-jagged: a scalable parallel spatial partitioning algorithm. IEEE Transactions on Parallel and Distributed Systems, PP(99), 1–1 (2015)
7. Grama, A.: Introduction to Parallel Computing. Pearson Education, Upper Saddle River (2003)
8. Hamada, T., Narumi, T., Yokota, R., Yasuoka, K., Nitadori, K., Taiji, M.: 42 tflops hierarchical n-body simulations on gpus with applications in both astrophysics and turbulence. In: Proceedings of the Conference on High Performance Computing Networking, Storage and Analysis, SC 2009, pp. 62:1–62:12. ACM, New York (2009). http://doi.acm.org/10.1145/1654059.1654123
9. Hamada, T., Nitadori, K.: 190 tflops astrophysical n-body simulation on a cluster of gpus. In: Proceedings of the 2010 ACM/IEEE International Conference for High Performance Computing, Networking, Storage and Analysis, SC 2010, pp. 1–9. IEEE Computer Society, Washington (2010). http://dx.doi.org/10.1109/SC.2010.1
10. Haring, R., Ohmacht, M., Fox, T., Gschwind, M., Satterfield, D., Sugavanam, K., Coteus, P., Heidelberger, P., Blumrich, M., Wisniewski, R., Gara, A., Chiu, G., Boyle, P., Chist, N., Kim, C.: The IBM blue Gene/Q compute chip. IEEE Micro **32**(2), 48–60 (2012)
11. Hill, S.L., Wang, Y., Riachi, I., Schürmann, F., Markram, H.: Statistical connectivity provides a sufficient foundation for specific functional connectivity in neocortical neural microcircuits. Proc. National Acad. Sci. **109**(42), E2885–E2894 (2012). http://www.pnas.org/content/109/42/E2885.abstract
12. Ishiyama, T., Nitadori, K., Makino, J.: 4.45 pflops astrophysical n-body simulation on k computer: The gravitational trillion-body problem. In: Proceedings of the International Conference on High Performance Computing, Networking, Storage and Analysis, SC 2012, pp. 5:1–5:10. IEEE Computer Society Press, Los Alamitos (2012). http://dl.acm.org/citation.cfm?id=2388996.2389003

13. Karypis, G.: METIS and ParMETIS. In: Padua, D. (ed.) Encyclopedia of Parallel Computing, pp. 1117–1124. Springer, Heidelberg (2011)
14. Karypis, G., Aggarwal, R., Kumar, V., Shekhar, S.: Multilevel hypergraph partitioning: applications in vlsi domain. IEEE Trans. Very Large Scale Integr. VLSI Syst. **7**(1), 69–79 (1999)
15. Kozloski, J., Sfyrakis, K., Hill, S., Schurmann, F., Peck, C., Markram, H.: Identifying, tabulating, and analyzing contacts between branched neuron morphologies. IBM J. Res. Dev. **52**(12), 43–55 (2008)
16. Kutluca, H., Aykanat, C., et al.: Image-space decomposition algorithms for sort-first parallel volume rendering of unstructured grids. J. Supercomput. **15**(1), 51–93 (2000)
17. Papa, D.A., Markov, I.L.: Hypergraph partitioning and clustering. In: Approximation Algorithms and Metaheuristics, pp. 61–1 (2007)
18. Pellegrini, F., Roman, J.: Scotch: a software package for static mapping by dual recursive bipartitioning of process and architecture graphs. In: Liddell, H., Colbrook, A., Hertzberger, B., Sloot, P.M.A. (eds.) HPCN-Europe 1996. LNCS, vol. 1067, pp. 493–498. Springer, Heidelberg (1996). http://dl.acm.org/citation.cfm?id=645560.658570
19. Randles, A., Draeger, E.W., Oppelstrup, T., Krauss, L., Gunnels, J.A.: Massively parallel models of the human circulatory system. In: Proceedings of the International Conference for High Performance Computing, Networking, Storage and Analysis, p. 1. ACM (2015)
20. Reumann, M., Fitch, B.G., Rayshubskiy, A., Keller, D.U., Seemann, G., Dossel, O., Pitman, M.C., Rice, J.J.: Orthogonal recursive bisection data decomposition for high performance computing in cardiac model simulations: dependence on anatomical geometry. In: Annual International Conference of the IEEE Engineering in Medicine and Biology Society, EMBC 2009, pp. 2799–2802. IEEE (2009)
21. Rodrigues, E.R., Navaux, P.O.A., Panetta, J., Fazenda, A., Mendes, C.L., Kale, L.V.: A comparative analysis of load balancing algorithms applied to a weather forecast model. In: 2010 22nd International Symposium on Computer Architecture and High Performance Computing (SBAC-PAD), pp. 71–78. IEEE (2010)
22. Rossinelli, D., Hejazialhosseini, B., Hadjidoukas, P., Bekas, C., Curioni, A., Bertsch, A., Futral, S., Schmidt, S.J., Adams, N.A., Koumoutsakos, P.: 11 PFLOP/s simulations of cloud cavitation collapse. In: Proceedings of the International Conference on High Performance Computing, Networking, Storage and Analysis, SC 2013, pp. 3:1–3:13. ACM, New York (2013). http://doi.acm.org/10.1145/2503210.2504565
23. Saule, E., Bas, E.Ö., Çatalyürek, Ü.V.: Load-balancing spatially located computations using rectangular partitions. CoRR abs/1104.2566 (2011). http://arxiv.org/abs/1104.2566
24. Shimokawabe, T., Aoki, T., Takaki, T., Endo, T., Yamanaka, A., Maruyama, N., Nukada, A., Matsuoka, S.: Peta-scale phase-field simulation for dendritic solidification on the tsubame 2.0 supercomputer. In: Proceedings of 2011 International Conference for High Performance Computing, Networking, Storage and Analysis. SC 2011, pp. 3:1–3:11. ACM, New York (2011). http://doi.acm.org/10.1145/2063384.2063388
25. Siebert, C., Wolf, F.: A scalable parallel sorting algorithm using exact splitting. Technical report, German Research School for Simulation Sciences GmbH (2010)

Parallel Community Detection Algorithm Using a Data Partitioning Strategy with Pairwise Subdomain Duplication

Diana Palsetia[1]([⊠]), William Hendrix[2], Sunwoo Lee[1], Ankit Agrawal[1], Wei-keng Liao[1], and Alok Choudhary[1]

[1] Northwestern University, Evanston, IL, USA
{drp925,slz839,ankitag,wkliao,choudhar}@eecs.northwestern.edu
[2] University of South Florida, Tampa, FL, USA
whendrix@usf.edu

Abstract. Community detection is an important data clustering technique for studying graph structures. Many serial algorithms have been developed and well studied in the literature. As the problem size grows, the research attention has recently been turning to parallelizing the technique. However, the conventional parallelization strategies that divide the problem domain into non-overlapping subdomains do not scale with problem size and the number of processes. The main obstacle lies in the fact that the graph algorithms often exhibit a high degree of data dependency, which makes developing scalable parallel algorithms a great challenge.

We present PMEP, a distributed-memory based parallel community detection algorithm that adopts an unconventional data partitioning strategy. PMEP divides a graph into subgraphs and assigns each pair of subgraphs to one process. This method duplicates a portion of computational workload among processes in exchange for a significantly reduced communication cost required in the later stages. After data partitioning, each process runs MEP on the assigned subgraph pair. MEP is a community detection algorithm based on the idea of maximizing equilibrium and purity. Our data partitioning method effectively simplifies the communication required for combining the local results into a global one and hence allows us to achieve better scalability over existing parallel algorithms without sacrificing the result quality. Our experimental results show a speedup of 126.95 on 190 MPI processes for using synthetic data sets and a speedup of 204.22 on 1225 processes for using a real-world data set.

1 Introduction

Data clustering is a branch of data mining algorithms that organizes a collection of data points into groups based on their similarity [10]. Clustering graph data, also known as community detection, usually refers to the identification of vertex subsets (clusters) that have significantly more internal edges than external ones [7]. Since the past few years, the volume of data has surpassed the

© Springer International Publishing Switzerland 2016
J.M. Kunkel et al. (Eds.): ISC High Performance 2016, LNCS 9697, pp. 98–115, 2016.
DOI: 10.1007/978-3-319-41321-1_6

capabilities of traditional sequential algorithms. For instance, CNM (Clauset, Newman, Moore), a popular community detection algorithm based on maximum modularity takes approximately 18 hours to process a social network data set containing 2,238,731 users and 14,608,137 connections [5,22]. Demands on high-performance solutions have encouraged researchers to develop heuristic and parallel algorithms for tackling large data problems.

Graph problems are data-driven, i.e., the memory access pattern in graph algorithms is often irregular and highly dependent on the network structure. Unlike spatial-based data clustering algorithms where the similarity of two data points can be determined by their distance, most graph algorithms must traverse the edges to calculate the affinity of a vertex to another. Thus, scalable performance can be difficult to achieve for a parallel algorithm because the graph structure is not known a priori [16]. In addition, graph clustering algorithms are iterative in nature with a high degree of data dependency. While there have been a few parallel graph clustering algorithms proposed recently, they suffer from frequent process synchronization and their result quality is affected by the processing order of vertex assignment to communities [1].

We propose a distributed-memory based parallel algorithm called PMEP which parallelizes MEP, a community detection algorithm based on the idea of maximizing equilibrium and purity of communities [23]. MEP has been demonstrated to produce high quality of results for medium to large graphs. To parallelize MEP, we use a data partitioning strategy that duplicates a portion of computational workload in exchange for a lower communication cost required in the later stage when combing local results into a global one. This strategy is motivated by the fact that graph problems are highly data dependent and it is unlikely for a data partitioner to produce subgraphs that can be processed independently on multiple processes without incurring a high cost of synchronization and communication. We employ the Parallel METIS (ParMETIS) graph partitioner [12,13] to break a graph into K subgraphs and assign each subgraph pair of all possible pairwise combinations to one of P processes, where $P = \binom{K}{2}$. This pairwise subgraph partitioning approach assigns each subgraph to $(K-1)$ processes, resulting in $(K-2)$ duplicated computation for processing the subgraph. Once received the assigned subgraph pairs, each process performs MEP on local data independently from other processes. The partial clustering results are then combined by resolving the conflicts on the community memberships found across all processes, which requires only one synchronization.

We used both synthetic and real-world data to evaluate PMEP. Using a synthetic data with 2 million vertices and 35.3 million edges, we achieved a speedup of 126.95 when running PMEP on 190 MPI processes. We evaluated the real-world data collected from Youtube using up to 1225 MPI processes and achieved a speedup of 204.22. We also compare the scalability of PMEP against the MPI implementation of parallel Louvain and observe that PMEP delivers a better performance.

2   Related Work

Fortunato gives a thorough overview of representative community detection algorithms, of which modularity-based methods are the most popular [7]. Since maximizing the graph modularity was proven to be an NP-complete problem [4], there have been several greedy approaches proposed [2,5,19]. Other than modularity-based methods, Zardi et al. introduced MEP, an algorithm that aims to maximize the equilibrium of communities [23]. This technique does not suffer from "resolution limit" problem that small communities are absorbed into large communities, an issue commonly seen in most of the modularity-based methods.

Riedy et al. use maximal matching to solve the parallel modularity maximization problem [17], based on CNM algorithm proposed by Clauset, Newman, and Moore [5]. This parallel approach was implemented using OpenMP and achieved a maximal speedup of $13\times$ on a Cray-XMT shared-memory machine using 80 compute cores and uk-2002 graph data set [3]. Louvain is another popular algorithm that addresses CNM drawbacks by using a hierarchical extraction process [2]. The majority of parallel implementations for Louvain are using OpenMP for shared-memory machines. Bhowmick and Srinivasan proposed a heuristic to eliminate some computations that can be implicitly obtained by computing the modularity [1]. Their OpenMP implementation creates a need for critical sections, which eventually limits the scalability. Staudt and Meyerhenke [18] parallelized the Louvain algorithm using an ensemble learning technique that combines multiple base classifiers or weak classifiers to form a strong classifier, as a preprocessing step. Lu et al. [15] use heuristics of coloring and vertex following to parallelize the Louvain algorithm. All of the above approaches achieved the maximal speedups of $8\times$ on 32 threads.

Wickramaarachchi et al. [21] implemented a distributed memory parallel Louvain algorithm using MPI and achieved the best speedup of $5\times$ on 128 processes. Similar to our approach, they also used a graph partitioning method. However, they only parallelized the first stage of Louvain.

3   MEP Algorithm

The Maximizing Equilibrium and Purity algorithm (MEP) is a community detection algorithm that identifies a community based on its internal and external connectivity [23]. Let $G = (V, E)$ be an undirected graph, where V and E are the sets of vertices and edges, respectively. MEP partitions G into k communities $C = \{C_1, \ldots, C_k\}$, where $\forall\, i, C_i \subseteq V$ and $\forall\, i \neq j, C_i \cap C_j = \emptyset$. In other words, $C_1, \ldots, C_k$ are non-overlapping communities. The computation of MEP consists of two phases: **region growing** and **community merging**. The region growing phase starts with each vertex as a community containing only itself and grows the communities based on the connectivity of vertices. The communities identified in this phase are the locally optimal solutions, which will later be examined and possibly combined in the merging phase.

In the rest of this paper, we refer $N(v)$ as the set of vertices that have edges directly connecting to vertex v. We denote $d(v)$ as the cardinality (or degree)

Algorithm 1. Region Growing Phase
Input: graph $G = (V, E)$
Output: Communities $C = \{C_1, C_2, \ldots, C_k\}$

1: **for each** $v_i \in V$ **do**
2:     $C_i \leftarrow \{v_i\}$ ▷ vertex starts out as a singleton
3: Create F, a free list, and add all vertices into F
4: Sort the vertices in F based on their degrees
5: **while** $F \neq \emptyset$ **do**
6:     Select v from F with the highest degree
7:     Delete v from F
8:     $\text{NFDN}(v) \leftarrow 0$
9:     $\text{comp}(v, 1 \cdots N(v)) \leftarrow 0$
10:     **for each** $u \in N(v)$ **do**
11:         **if** u is free **then**
12:             $\text{NFDN}(v) \leftarrow \text{NFDN}(v) + 1$
13:         **else**
14:             $\text{comp}(v, C_u) \leftarrow \text{comp}(v, C_u) + 1$
15:     Find C_x whose $\text{comp}(v, C_x)$ is the maximal
16:     **if** $\text{NFDN}(v) \leq \text{comp}(v, C_x)$ **then**
17:         Add v to C_x
18:     **else**
19:         RecuriveGrowth($N(v)$, C_v, F)   ▷ grows C_v

of v and $d(v) = |N(v)|$. A vertex v is referred as a *free* vertex, if it does not belong to any community but itself. The number of free, direct neighbors of vertex v is denoted as $\text{NFDN}(v) = |\{u | u \in N(v) \land u \text{ is free}\}|$. A vertex is said to be *compatible* to a community C_i if most of its direct neighbors are in C_i. Equation 1 defines the compatibility of vertex v to community C_i. The maximum compatibility of vertex v is the maximum among its compatibilities to all communities and its NFDN, as shown in Eq. 2. A vertex is defined as *pure* to a community C_i if and only if its compatibility to C_i is equal to its maximum compatibility.

$$comp(v, C_i) = |\{(v, u) | u \in N(v) \land u \in C_i\}| \tag{1}$$

$$comp_{max}(v) = \max\{\max_{C_i \in C} comp(v, C_i), \text{NFDN}(v)\} \tag{2}$$

$$v \text{ is pure to } C_i \text{ iff } comp(v, C_i) = comp_{max}(v) \tag{3}$$

3.1   Region Growing Phase

Algorithm 1 presents the region growing phase. Initially, all vertices start out as singleton communities and are marked as free in list F. The vertices in F are then sorted by their degrees in an increasing order. The algorithm grows communities starting from the vertex with the highest degree, v. If v's maximal compatibility is larger than $\text{NFDN}(v)$, then v is added to the community that has the maximal compatibility. Otherwise, the algorithm will grow C_v by adding direct neighbors of v if they are pure to C_v. For each newly added members, the algorithm recursively adds pure neighbors of those members (indirect connected neighbors of v) to grow C_v. The vertices are removed from the free list F once they were added to a community. This process iterates until the direct neighbors of v are exhausted, at which point the algorithm moves on to the vertex with next highest degree in F. At the end, the region growing phase produces an initial set of communities $C = \{C_1, C_2, \ldots, C_k\}$.

The community initialization in line 2 of Algorithm 1 takes $O(|V|)$ time. In line 4, we sort the vertices by their degree using a counting sort in $O(|V|)$ time. Starting from the vertex with the highest degree in F, we compute its compatibilities to the communities to which its (non-free) direct neighbors belong in lines 10–14. This takes $O(d)$ time. In the worst case, the time becomes $O(\Delta)$, where Δ as the maximum degree of a graph from the most connected vertex in the graph. The next step is to check the purity by comparing the maximal compatibility currently found against the number of free direct neighbors. If the number of free direct neighbors is larger, then we need to recursively check the purity for all the neighbors in line 19. The number of iterations to call procedure RecursiveGrowth is $O(d)$ and in the worst case $O(\Delta)$. Finding the maximal compatibility for each neighbor in line 3 takes $O(|V|)$ time. Thus, each call to RecursiveGrowth takes $O(\Delta|V|)$ time, which makes the complexity of entire recursive call $O(\Delta^2|V|)$. Assuming the while loop in line 5 repeats ℓ_1 times and $1 \leq \ell_1 \leq |V|/2$. The overall complexity of the region grow phase is $O(\ell_1\Delta^2|V|)$. The worst case, $\ell_1 = |V|/2$, happens when each vertex in the graph is connected to only one other vertex, making the complexity become $O(\Delta^2|V|^2)$. The best case, $\ell_1 = 1$, happens when every vertex is connected to every other vertex i.e. the graph being a clique, which makes the complexity become $O(\Delta^2|V|)$. Therefore, the complexity of region grow depends on how close the neighbors of a vertex v form a clique. This quantity can be measured and is commonly referred to the *local clustering coefficient*, denoted as *lcc*. A high average local clustering coefficient *alcc* of a graph is an indicator of the presence of dense subgraphs [20]. The *alcc* values range from 0 to 1. Value of ℓ_1 decreases as *alcc* value approaches to 1 and increases as *alcc* approaches to 0.

The region-growing phase exhibits a high degree of data dependency, because the processing of vertex v depends on the results of processing all the vertices with higher degrees than v. However, this priori information is not known. Such a high degree of data dependency exhibited in graph problems in general makes the parallelization of any graph clustering algorithm an extremely challenging task.

3.2   Community Merge Phase

This phase first checks whether the initial communities found in the region growing phase are in *equilibrium* or not. The concept of equilibrium is simply the definition of strong communities. A community is strong if it has more internal connections (also defined as *compactness*) than the average external connections (also defined as *separation*). Equation 4 defines *compactness* of a community as the number of edges within the community and Eq. 5 defines *separation* of two

Algorithm 2. Recursive Growth
Input: a set of vertices N, Community C, and free list F
Output: updated C and F

Procedure RecursiveGrowth(N, C, F)
  1: $newN \leftarrow \emptyset$
  2: **for each** $u \in N$ **do**
  3:    Find $comp_{max}(u)$
  4:    **if** $comp(u, C) = comp_{max}(u)$ **then**   ▷ if u is pure
  5:       Add u to C and delete u from F
  6:       Add u to $newN$
  7: **if** $newN \neq \emptyset$ **then**
  8:    RecursiveGrowth($newN, C, F$)

communities as the number of edges between them. Equation 6 defines the average separability of a community. Equation 7 describes the equilibrium condition for a community, i.e. its average separation over all other communities is less than its compactness. Communities that are not in equilibrium will be merged to the community with which it has the highest separation. After the merge, the overall purity of a community may decrease. In this case, the impure vertices are moved to communities in which they are pure. Algorithm 3 describes the community merge phase.

$$compact(C_i) = |\{(v, u)|(v, u) \in E, v \in C_i \wedge u \in C_i\}| \tag{4}$$

$$sep(C_i, C_j) = |\{(v, u)|(v, u) \in E, v \in C_i \wedge u \in C_j\}| \tag{5}$$

$$sep_{avg}(C_i) = \frac{1}{|C|} \sum_{j=1 \wedge j \neq i}^{|C|} sep(C_i, C_j) \tag{6}$$

$$sep_{avg}(C_i) < compact(C_i) \tag{7}$$

We denote $|C'|$ to be the number of communites after the region growing phase. Algorithm 3 initially populates a $|C'| \times |C'|$ matrix with the pairwise separability and calculates the compactness for each community in C'. It iterates through all the edges of the graph, which takes $O(|E|)$ time. Finding the maximum and average separability for each community, as well as updating the matrix for any merged community (lines 8–12), take $O(|C'|)$ time, for a total of $O(|C'|^2)$ time per iteration of the while loop in line 5. The algorithm iterates through all the vertices after each merge round for reassigning the membership (lines 15–18), at a cost of $O(|E|)$. While this while loop could potentially iterate $O(|C'|)$ times, we find empirically that the number of iterations is a small constant. If the number of iterations is ℓ_2, then the overall complexity for the merge phase becomes $O(\ell_2(|C'|^2 + |E|))$. This phase of the MEP algorithm has a high data dependency on the order of communities being processed, because when a community pair is merged, all connections with those two communities need to be updated.

Algorithm 3. Community Merge Phase

Input: graph $G = (V, E)$

Input: initial communities $C = \{C_1, C_2, \ldots, C_k\}$

Output: modified communities $C = \{C_1, C_2, \ldots, C_{k'}\}$

1: **for each** $C_i \in C$ **do**
2:      Calculate $compact(C_i)$
3:      **for each** $C_j \in C \wedge j \neq i$ **do**
4:          Calculate $sep(C_i, C_j)$
5: **while** true **do**
6:      merge_count $\leftarrow 0$
7:      **for each** $C_i \in C$ **do**
8:          **if** $sep_{avg}(C_i) > compact(C_i)$ **then**
9:              Find C_j in C where $sep(C_i, C_j)$ is maximal
10:             Merge C_i and C_j into a new $C_{k'}$
11:             Delete C_i and C_j from C
12:             Update $compact(C_{k'})$ and $sep(C_{k'})$
13:             Add $C_{k'}$ to C
14:             merge_count $\leftarrow$ merge_count $+ 1$
15:             **for each** v in $C_{k'}$ **do**
16:                 **if** $comp(v, C_{k'}) \neq comp_{max}(v)$ **then**
17:                     Find C_t in C that has $comp_{max}(v)$
18:                     Add v to C_t and delete v from $C_{k'}$
19:         **if** merge_count $= 0$ **then**
20:             break the while loop

4   Design and Implementation

Conventional parallelization strategies often consist of three steps: breaking the problem domain into a set of subproblems, solving subproblems independently and concurrently, and combining the subproblem solutions into a global solution for the original problem instance. Following the same principle, our parallelization divides a graph into subgraphs, detects communities within each subgraph independently using MEP, and merges the local communities to get the global solution. Contrary to the conventional approach that often seeks to generate non-overlapped subproblems, we adopt a data partitioning method that duplicates workload among processes. Our idea is motivated by the fact that graph problems are highly data dependent and it is unlikely for a data partitioner to produce subgraphs that can be processed independently without a high cost of process synchronization and communication at a later stage. For instance, if a non-overlapping partitioning is used, then the local results computed in each process must be sent to all other processes for merging, because any subgraph may have external edges connecting to all other subgraphs. Such a complete all-to-all personalized communication may be required multiple times when the algorithm traverses edges across multiple subgraphs to grow a community. Thus, a high communication cost is inevitable for such an approach. Owing to this, we design a strategy that duplicates a portion of computational workload among processes in exchange for a lower communication cost and hence heavier local computational workload. Our parallel algorithm consists of the following phases:

4.1 Parallel Read

The input graph data is stored in a file of compressed storage format (CSR), a widely used text format for storing graphs. In a CSR file, each line corresponds to a vertex and its adjacency list (vertex IDs of direct neighbors). This format is understood by ParMETIS [11], the data partitioner employed by our parallel algorithm (discussed in the next section). To enable parallel I/O, we convert the input file into a binary form but in the same data layout. During this off-line conversion, we also calculate the file starting offsets of adjacent lists and store the offsets in a separate file. In our parallel read phase, we partition vertices evenly into disjoint blocks among all processes. At first, all processes read the total number of vertices and edges to calculate the ranges of vertices to be assigned to individual processes. Through the offset file, each process can perform a file seek operation to jump to the file location containing the vertex subset to be read. We use an MPI collective read to read the graph data in parallel. A low cost is expected for this phase, as the I/O pattern from the above partitioning method is known to be highly scalable on state-of-the-art parallel file systems.

4.2 Graph Partitioning

There are several graph partitioning techniques proposed in the literature [8]. A high-quality partitioner can produce subgraphs that are well connected within each subgraph and fewer edges between them. Our parallel algorithm employs the Parallel METIS (ParMETIS) graph partitioner. METIS is a multilevel partitioning algorithm that produces high quality partitions by minimizing the resulting inter-subdomain connectivity and enforcing contiguous partitions [12,13]. Implemented using MPI, ParMETIS partitions a graph into K disjoint subgraphs in parallel, given K as a user input parameter.

Given P compute processes, one naive parallelization strategy is to partition a graph into P subgraphs and assign each subgraph to a process. However, when using this approach, the external edges between two subgraphs cannot be used to grow communities during the local computation, as processes possess no vertex data on the remote subgraphs connected through those external edges. To continue growing or merging the local communities, the intermediate results must be distributed among processes, which could involve multiple levels of data synchronization. Because a subgraph may have external edges connecting to all other subgraphs, a high communication cost is anticipated if this naive approach is used. To avoid such problem, we choose to duplicate a portion of computational workload in exchange for a lower communication complexity.

Our data partitioning method assigns every possible combination of subgraph pairs to a unique process. In this approach, the external edges between every two subgraphs can be used by a process to grow the communities. Given a graph and P processes, we call the ParMETIS library subroutine `ParMETIS_V3_PartKway` to partition the graph into K subgraphs such that $P = \binom{K}{2}$. A process is assigned all edges in subgraphs k_i, and k_j, along with the edges between them. This strategy requires the number of processes P to be $\binom{K}{2}$. For instance, when $K = 2$ we have one process, which is the serial case. When $K = 10$, our parallel program must run on $\binom{10}{2} = 45$ processes. This subgraph partitioning approach assigns each subgraph to exactly $(K - 1)$ processes, resulting in duplicated computation for detecting communities within the subgraph. This is the cost we intend to trade for achieving a lower communication cost later on.

The subroutine `ParMETIS_V3_PartKway` consists of three phases: graph coarsening, initial partitioning, and refinement. According to [11], coarsening and refinement take $O(|E|)$ time with $O(\log(|V|))$ stages. The partitioning phase takes $O(|E'|)$ time, where E' is the number of edges in the coarsened graph, and scales relative to $\sqrt{P}$. This partitioning function and hence our data partitioning phase takes $O(|E| \log(|V|) + |E'|/\sqrt{P})$ time.

4.3   Subgraph ID Distribution

The output of `ParMETIS_V3_PartKway` is an array in each process containing the subgraph IDs for the local vertices. Thus only the subgraph IDs of the local vertices assigned in the read phase are known. To achieve the pairwise subgraph duplication, we must also obtain the subgraph IDs for the vertices in the local vertices' adjacency lists. The subgraph IDs will be used to calculate the ranks of processes to which a vertex and its edges are to be duplicated. Because vertices are divided among processes in a block fashion in the read phase, the rank of a process that possesses the subgraph ID of a given vertex can be calculated by simply dividing the vertex ID by the block size.

In order to minimize the communication, we sort each list based on the vertex IDs and remove repeated vertices. The inter-process communication is carried out in three steps. First, an `MPI_Alltoall` is called to exchange the number of vertices to be sent and received among all processes. Next, send and receive buffers, one for each remote process, are allocated and a hash table lookup is performed to fill the send buffer with the requested subgraph IDs. The last step uses asynchronous communication calls (*isend* and *irecv*) to complete the communication. On average, each process is assigned $|E|/P$ edges and out of which $|V|/P$ vertices' subgraph IDs are already known. Thus, the complexity of this phase in terms of communication is $O(|E|/P)$.

4.4   Pairwise Subgraph Duplication

Given K subgraphs, there are $\binom{K}{2}$ combinations of subgraph pairs. We assign each process a pair of subgraphs along with the internal and external edges connecting the pair. If the two vertice of an edge belong to the same subgraph, the edge is internal. Otherwise the edge is external. An internal edge is identified when the subgraph IDs of its two vertices agree. To assign an external edge to a process, we use Eq. 8 to calculate the process rank p, where k_i and k_j

are subgraph IDs of the edge's two vertices, respectively. Using our duplication scheme, an external edge will be assigned to one and only one process and an internal edge is assigned in duplication to $(K-1)$ processes.

$$p = k_j * (k_j + 1)/2 - k_i - 1, \quad \text{for} \quad j > i \tag{8}$$

To start the duplication, each process first scans and packs all the edges from its local adjacency lists to send buffers if they are for remote processes. Adopting the similar communication method used in the previous phase, we call MPI asynchronous *isend/irecv* functions to distribute the workload. Edge scanning and packing takes $O(|E|/P)$ time. Assuming ParMETIS evenly divides the edges into K subgraphs, there are at most $O(|E|/K)$ external edges between each subgraph pair. Therefore, the complexity of this phase is $O(|E|/\sqrt{P})$ as $K = \sqrt{P}$.

4.5   Local Graph Construction

We use adjacency lists to represent the vertices and edges of the subgraph pair assigned to each process. To achieve a constant time for a vertex lookup in the later local MEP phase, we use a hash table to store the adjacency lists. The timing of creating a hash table depends on the efficiency of hashing function and the frequency of hash collision. In our implementation we use Jenkins' hash[1]. Assuming that it takes $O(h)$ time for adding an edge to the hash table, the time complexity of this phase is $O(h|E|/P)$, as each process is assigned $O(|E|/P)$ edges on average.

4.6   Local Region Growing

We implement the region growing phase of MEP algorithm using a union-find data structure to keep track of a vertex's community membership [6]. We also store the maximum compatibility (Eq. 3) of each vertex denoted as its *purity* and use it later in the global resolution phase to finalize the vertex's membership. The sequential complexity of this phase is $O(\ell_1 \Delta^2 |V|)$. Because of our duplication strategy, each subgraph is duplicated in $\sqrt{P}$ processes and thus the complexity of this phase is $O(\ell_1 \Delta^2 |V|/\sqrt{P})$.

4.7   Local Community Merge

We implement the community merge phase of MEP algorithm using a sparse community matrix M to represent the number of edges within and between the communities. As mentioned in Sect. 3.2, a vertex may change membership upon merging. When this happens, we update the vertex's *purity* value, which will be used in the next phase for resolving membership conflicts. As each process has $O(|E|/\sqrt{P})$ edges and $|C'|/P$ communities, where $|C'|$ denotes the number of communities found after the region growing phase, the time complexity of this phase is $O(\ell_2(|C'|^2/P + |E|/\sqrt{P}))$.

---

[1] http://burtleburtle.net/bob/.

4.8 Global Resolution

The locally detected communities are to be merged globally. Because each vertex is assigned to $(K - 1)$ processes, the memberships calculated by different processes may disagree. When such conflicts occur, we resolve them based on the vertex's purity. We divide this global resolution task among all processes based on the vertex IDs, in a block partitioning fashion. In other words, process rank i is responsible for vertices of IDs from $(|V|/P) \cdot i$ to $(|V|/P) \cdot (i + 1)$. All processes only redistribute the vertices' purities and their root IDs, using MPI asynchronous communication (*isend* and *irecv*). The overall communication message size exchanged among processes is $2|V|$ integers.

Each process receives $(K - 1)$ purities and root IDs for each of $|V|/P$ vertices it is responsible. To resolve a conflict, we let the community with higher purity win the conflict. Essentially, we treat the purity as the support of a vertex to a community. When root IDs differ but the purities are equal, we assign the vertex to the community with a larger root ID. Since the operation of finding the maximum is both associative and commutative, this strategy ensures the convergence, no matter in what order the resolution is performed on the partial results. Once all conflicts are resolved, we use an MPI collective write function to write the community IDs to a shared file in parallel. The computation time complexity of this phase is $O(K|V|/P) = O(|V|/\sqrt{P})$ and communication complexity is $O(|V|/P)$.

4.9 Complexity Analysis

The overall complexity of PMEP becomes $O(|E|log(|V|) + \ell_1\Delta^2|V|/\sqrt{P} + \ell_2(|C'|^2/P + |E|/\sqrt{P}))$, which corresponds to the graph partitioning and local MEP phases. Our complexity analysis implies that the computation time of PMEP is to be dominated by these two phases.

5 Experiments and Performance Evaluation

We implement PMEP in C using Message Passing Interface (MPI) for communication and I/O. Our experiments were carried out on Hopper, a Cray XE6 supercomputer at the National Energy Research Scientific Computing (NERSC) Center. Each compute node on Hopper contains two twelve-core AMD Magny-Cours 2.1-GHz processors and 32 GB of memory. We use both real-world and synthetic graph data sets. Table 1 provides some graph properties of the data sets used in our experiments, which include number of vertices ($|V|$), number of edges ($|E|$), maximum degree (Δ), number of ground truth communities ($|C|$), and average local clustering coefficient (*alcc*). Note that higher the *alcc* value, denser the graph [20].

5.1 Synthetic Graphs

For a better control on the quality of community results with various graph properties, we synthesize four large graphs, $g1$, $g2$, $g3$, and $g4$, with ground truth

Table 1. Graph properties of data set used in our experiments.

Graph	$|V|$	$|E|$	Δ	$|C|$	alcc
g1	2.00 M	35.37 M	88	39,685	0.111
g2	2.00 M	35.06 M	88	35,318	0.299
g3	6.00 M	88.88 M	75	122,750	0.299
g4	6.00 M	88.85 M	75	122,471	0.587
Youtube	1.13 M	2.99 M	28,754	8,385	0.081

M: million

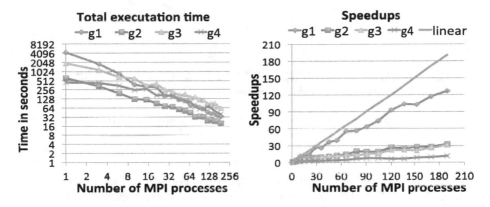

Fig. 1. Execution time and speedups for synthetic graphs (Color figure online).

using LFR benchmark [14]. The graphs become denser from $g1$ to $g4$ as the $alcc$ values increase. The LFR benchmark allows us to set $alcc$ values by changing the fraction of edges a vertex shares with others in different communities, while keeping other parameters constant, such as $|V|$, $|E|$, and Δ. Figure 1 presents the execution time and speedup of PMEP. Given two graphs of the same size, we observe that lower the $alcc$ value higher the execution time. For example, $g1$'s $alcc = 0.111$ is lower than $g2$'s 0.299 and $g1$ has a higher execution time than $g2$. Similarly, $g3$ has a smaller $alcc$ value than $g4$ and thus takes more time to complete. This performance trend matched our complexity analysis in Sect. 3 that the lower $alcc$ value corresponds to higher values in Δ, ℓ_1, ℓ_2, and $|C'|$. Given a fixed $alcc$ value, the execution time increases as the number of vertices and edges. In our experiment, graphs $g2$ and $g3$ have the same $alcc$ value, 0.299, and because $g3$ has more vertices and edges, its execution time is higher than $g2$.

Among the four graphs, we observe that $g1$ scales much better than the rest and $g4$'s speedups are the worst. To help understand the differences, we collected the timing breakdown for individual phases of PMEP. In Fig. 2, the upper four charts show the percentages of timing for all phases and the bottom four charts show the speedups for the top three phases that dominate the overall execution time. From the percentage charts, we can see that the top three phases are the

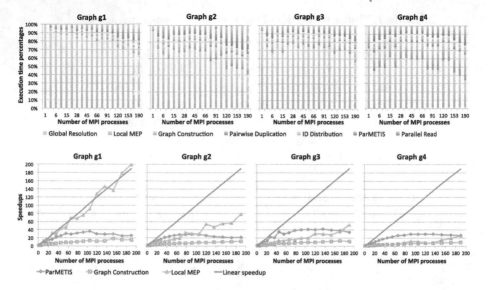

Fig. 2. Timing breakdown and speedup for individual phases of PMEP. (Color figure online)

local MEP, ParMETIS, and graph construction. For $g1$, the local MEP takes about 64 % to 93 % of the total time and because its speedup curve is quite close to the linear line, the overall speedups follow the similar trend. The best speedup for $g1$ is 126.95 when running 190 MPI processes.

For graphs $g2$, $g3$, and $g4$, the non-MEP phases start to take larger portions of the total time. However, since the local MEP still shows the dominant percentages in most of the cases, its scalability remains a strong influence to the overall speedup. The top three speedup charts show that the local MEP achieves lower speedups than the ones in $g1$'s chart and similar trends for the other two phases. The lower speedups altogether from the top three phases explain the lower overall speedups for $g2$, $g3$, and $g4$.

The high timing percentage of local MEP phase in $g1$ can be explained by its lower $alcc$ value. As discussed in Sect. 3, a smaller $alcc$ corresponds to a larger ℓ_1, meaning more iterations required on checking the compatibility and purity of a vertex's neighbors. In addition, the sparser graph $g1$ produces more fragmented intermediate communities $|C'|$ and hence a larger ℓ_2. Therefore, small $alcc$ in $g1$ makes both the region growing and community merging of the local MEP phase the most expensive phase. This behavior is consistent with the local MEP's complexity analysis.

As the number of processes increases, the timing percentages of graph partitioning phase (ParMETIS) increases proportionally, taking a significant percentage of the overall execution time. From its speedup charts, the scalability of ParMETIS flattens quickly as the number of processes reaches to 40. Recall that ParMETIS consists of three phases, among which only the initial partitioning phase scales with respect to $\sqrt{P}$, and the other two remain constant regardless of P. As the number of processes increases, the two non-scalable phases start to dominate and hence explain the speedup curve. This behavior implies the PMEP's overall performance could be limited by the scalability of ParMETIS.

The local graph construction phase noticeably takes a larger portion of the overall time for dense graphs. In addition, the percentages increase significantly as the number of processes. As we build the vertex adjacency lists into a hash table, the timing depends on the efficiency of the hash function and the frequency of hash collision. For dense graphs, a high number of hash collisions is expected because more vertices sharing the same neighbors. When using vertex IDs as hash keys, there is a high chance for a densely connected graph that the same keys (vertices) are used when inserting new edges to the hash table. The effect of increasing cost on hash collisions can be seen when comparing the percentages of $g2$ to $g1$ and $g4$ to $g3$.

The subgraph ID distribution phase occupies only a small fraction of the overall execution time and the main cost of this phase is the communication. Its complexity in term of communication amount is $O(|E|/P)$ per process. When there are sufficiently large workloads, this phase appears negligible compared to other phases. Both the pairwise subgraph duplication and global resolution phases are mainly communication tasks. The complexity of pairwise duplication phase $O(|E|/\sqrt{P})$ is the worst case scenario and in the real timing results show much smaller, as seen from the timing percentage breakdown charts for all the synthetic graphs. The global reduction phase also occupies very a small percentage of the execution time. The small communication amount complexity $O(|V|/P)$ explains the observed results. The I/O cost takes less than 1 % of the overall time. As we use MPI collective I/O to read/write files stored in the Lustre parallel file system on Hopper, the low I/O cost is expected.

5.2   Real World Data Set

The real-world dataset, *youtube*, used in our experiments was obtained from the collection of the Stanford Large Network Dataset Collection[2]. Although there are other real-world graphs that come with the ground truth communities, but most of them do not contain disjoint communities. This graph is considered sparse, it has very low *alcc* value 0.081. Figure 3 shows the overall execution time, speedups, percentage breakdown, and speedups of the top-three phases. The youtube graph has a small *alcc* value similar to the synthetic graph $g1$ and both numbers of vertices and edges are less than $g1$. However, the maximum degree ($\Delta = 28,754$) of youtube graph is much higher than all the synthetic graphs. According to the overall complexity derived in Sect. 4.9, such a high Δ value makes the local MEP workload much higher than the rest of phases. This effect can be seen from the breakdown percentage chart where the local MEP phase dominates the overall execution time. As the local MEP speedups show good scalability, the overall speedups follow the similar trend. The highest speedup

---

[2] http://snap.stanford.edu/data/index.html.

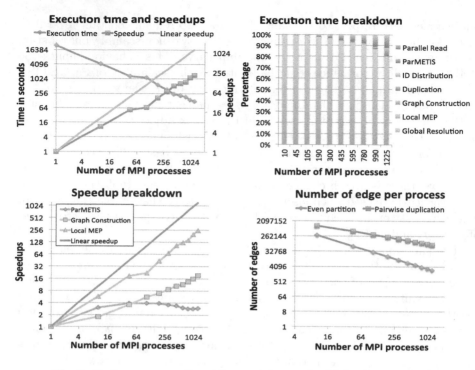

Fig. 3. Performance results of the youtube graph. (Color figure online)

achieved is 204.22 when running PMEP on 1225 MPI processes. Although this number is far from the linear speedup, we consider it a very good result for a parallel graph algorithm, given the fact that a high degree of data dependency in graph problems.

In Fig. 3, we also show the number of edges assigned to each process for our pairwise subgraph duplication strategy and the even data partitioning method. The number of edges per process for our approach is $O(|E|/\sqrt{P})$, while the even partitioning method is $O(|E|/P)$. As the number of processes increases, the chart shows the average number of edges of our approach deviates increasingly from the even partitioning method. This indicates that achieving a linear speedup is unlikely for PMEP if the computation workload of the graph problem is determined by the number of edges. However, our pairwise duplication approach produces a very small cost of inter-process communication, which is unlikely achievable by the even partitioning method.

5.3   Result Quality Analysis

In order to evaluate the quality of the community structures output from our algorithm against the known ground truth generated by the benchmark, we adopt a metric called adjusted rand index (ARI) [9]. Given two communities X and Y, the overlap between the two communities can be summarized by a contingency table where each entry t_{xy} denotes the number of vertices in

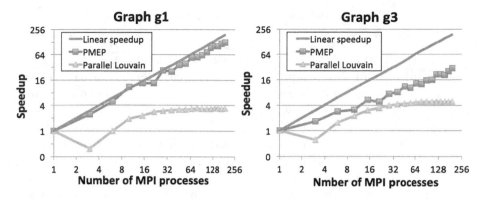

Fig. 4. Comparison between PMEP and parallel Louvain (Color figure online).

common between X and Y. ARI outputs a score ranging from -1 to 1, where 1 indicates that the two communities match perfectly and -1 indicates that two communities are in complete disagreement.

In terms of quality, we find PMEP results within 95 % accuracy to ground truth for both synthetic and real-world dataset. The quality results for graphs $g1$ to $g4$ for selected numbers of MPI process counts are shown in Table 2. These results demonstrate PMEP produces a high quality clustering solution when we increase the number of processes. Duplicating the internal edges implies that communities within the subgraphs are not split up, while still allowing to grow communities across multiple subgraphs. Thus, the heuristic used in our global resolution phase is shown to work well in producing high quality results.

5.4   Comparison with Parallel Louvain

We compare PMEP with the MPI implementation of parallel Louvain[3] [21]. Louvain is designed to minimize the value of modularity (Q), a popular metric in the graph community for measuring the strength of division of a graph into communities. Modularity is defined in Eq. 9, where e_i and a_i denote the fractions of internal and external edges in community C_i, respectively.

$$Q = \sum\nolimits_{i=1}^{|C|} (e_i - a_i^2) \tag{9}$$

Although the design goal of PMEP is different (PMEP is to maximize equilibrium and purity), we are interested to see the scalability of the parallel Louvain and its comparison to PMEP. Note that a direct comparison in execution time is not fair because MEP and Louvain are two completely different algorithms. In our experiments, we set the stop condition ϵ to 0.1, meaning when the change of modularity value from the previous iteration increases to more than ϵ. In Fig. 4, we present the speedup chart for $g1$ and $g3$. PMEP scalability is significantly

---

[3] https://github.com/usc-cloud/parallel-louvain-modularity.

Table 2. ARI and modularity for synthetic graphs.

P	g1			g2			g3			g4		
	ARI	Q	Q(PL)	ARI	Q	Q(PL)	ARI	Q	Q(PL)	ARI	Q	Q(PL)
1	0.997	0.504	0.504	1.000	0.700	0.703	1.000	0.700	0.701	1.000	0.899	0.900
3	0.999	0.504	0.502	0.999	0.699	0.695	1.000	0.700	0.699	1.000	0.899	0.900
10	0.986	0.501	0.504	0.998	0.699	0.698	0.980	0.700	0.699	0.998	0.899	0.900
28	0.957	0.504	0.503	0.974	0.699	0.700	0.964	0.700	0.700	0.991	0.899	0.900
55	0.946	0.504	0.504	0.969	0.700	0.699	0.950	0.700	0.698	0.988	0.899	0.900
91	0.962	0.502	0.504	0.980	0.700	0.699	0.955	0.700	0.700	0.985	0.899	0.900
136	0.950	0.502	0.504	0.994	0.700	0.700	0.972	0.700	0.700	0.985	0.899	0.900
190	0.971	0.504	0.500	0.998	0.700	0.700	0.982	0.700	0.700	1.000	0.899	0.900

better for both graphs and in the meanwhile the parallel Louvain's speedup curve starts to flatten when P reaches 32. We note that parallel Louvain currently only parallelizes its first phase that computes the initial communities based on modularity maximization. To show that PMEP can also deliver high quality results in term of modularity, the measured values are provided in Table 2. We observe PMEP's modularity measures are consistent with parallel Louvain (PL).

6 Conclusion

Community detection for large graphs is extremely challenging due to a lack of *a priori* information of the graph structure and a high degree of data dependency. The scalability and quality of a parallel algorithm is significantly impacted by the data partitioning scheme it employs. Our proposed PMEP addresses this challenge by adopting a pairwise subdomain duplication partitioning approach that aims to trade some additional computation workload for significant reduction in communication cost. The experimental results show that PMEP successfully achieves this goal and in the meanwhile maintains a high quality of clustering results. Our future work include the investigation of the ParMETIS and graph construction phases, as they have shown poor scalability in the timing breakdown charts.

Acknowledgment. This work is supported in part by the following grants: NSF awards CCF-1029166, IIS-1343639, CCF-1409601; DOE awards DE-SC0007456, DE-SC0014330; AFOSR award FA9550-12-1-0458; NIST award 70NANB14H012; DARPA award N66001-15-C-4036.

References

1. Bansal, S., Bhowmick, S., Paymal, P.: Fast community detection for dynamic complex networks. In: Mangioni, G. (ed.) CompleNet 2010. CCIS, vol. 116, pp. 196–207. Springer, Heidelberg (2011)

2. Blondel, V.D., Guillaume, J.L., Lambiotte, R., Lefebvre, E.: Fast unfolding of communities in large networks. J. Stat. Mech: Theory Exp. **2008**(10), P10008 (2008)
3. Boldi, P., Codenotti, B., Santini, M., Vigna, S.: Ubicrawler: a scalable fully distributed web crawler. Softw.: Pract. Experience **34**(8), 711–726 (2004)
4. Brandes, U., Delling, D., Gaertler, M., Görke, R., Hoefer, M., Nikoloski, Z., Wagner, D.: On finding graph clusterings with maximum modularity. In: Brandstädt, A., Kratsch, D., Müller, H. (eds.) WG 2007. LNCS, vol. 4769, pp. 121–132. Springer, Heidelberg (2007)
5. Clauset, A., Newman, M.E.J., Moore, C.: Finding community structure in very large networks. Phys. Rev. E **70**(6), 066111 (2004)
6. Cormen, T.H., Leiserson, C.E., Rivest, R.L., Stein, C.: Introduction to Algorithms, 3rd edn. The MIT Press, Cambridge (2009)
7. Fortunato, S.: Community detection in graphs. Phys. Rep. **486**(3–5), 75–174 (2010)
8. Hendrickson, B., Kolda, T.G.: Graph partitioning models for parallel computing. Parallel Comput. **26**(12), 1519–1534 (2000)
9. Hubert, L., Arabie, P.: Comparing partitions. J. Classif. **2**(1), 193–218 (1985)
10. Jain, A.K., Murty, M.N., Flynn, P.J.: Data clustering: a review (1999)
11. Karypis, G., Kumar, V.: Parallel multilevel k-way partitioning scheme for irregular graphs. In: Proceedings of the 1996 ACM/IEEE Conference on Supercomputing (1996)
12. Karypis, G., Kumar, V.: A fast and high quality multilevel scheme for partitioning irregular graphs. SIAM J. Sci. Comput. **20**(1), 359–392 (1998)
13. Karypis, G., Kumar, V.: Multilevel k-way partitioning scheme for irregular graphs. Parallel Distrib. Comput. **48**(1), 96–129 (1998)
14. Lancichinetti, A., Fortunato, S., Radicchi, F.: Benchmark graphs for testing community detection algorithms. Phys. Rev. E Stat. Nonlin. Soft Matter Phys. **78**(4 Pt 2), 046110 (2008)
15. Lu, H., Halappanavar, M., Kalyanaraman, A., Choudhury, S.: Parallel heuristics for scalable community detection. In: Proceedings of the International Workshop on Multithreaded Architectures and Applications (MTAAP), IPDPS Workshops (2014)
16. Meyerhenke, H., Gehweiler, J.: On dynamic graph partitioning and graph clustering using diffusion. In: Algorithm Engineering. Dagstuhl Seminar Proceedings, vol. 10261 (2010)
17. Riedy, E.J., Meyerhenke, H., Ediger, D., Bader, D.A.: Parallel community detection for massive graphs. In: Graph Partitioning and Graph Clustering, pp. 207–222 (2012)
18. Staudt, C., Meyerhenke, H.: Engineering high-performance community detection heuristics for massive graphs. In: ICPP, pp. 180–189 (2013)
19. Wakita, K., Tsurumi, T.: Finding community structure in mega-scale social networks:[extended abstract]. In: Proceedings of the 16th International Conference on World Wide Web, pp. 1275–1276. ACM (2007)
20. Watts, D.J., Strogatz, S.H.: Collective dynamics of'small-world'networks. Nature **393**(6684), 409–10 (1998)
21. Wickramaarachchi, C., Frincu, M., Small, P., Prasanna, V.: Fast parallel algorithm for unfolding of communities in large graphs. In: 2014 IEEE High Performance Extreme Computing Conference (HPEC), pp. 1–6, September 2014
22. Zafarani, R., Liu, H.: Social computing data repository at arizona state university. School Comput. Inf. Decis. Syst. Eng. (2009)
23. Zardi, H., Romdhane, L.B.: An $o(n^2)$ algorithm for detecting communities of unbalanced sizes in large scale social networks. Know.-Based Syst. **37**, 19–36 (2013)

TiDA: High-Level Programming Abstractions for Data Locality Management

Didem Unat[1]([⊠]), Tan Nguyen[2], Weiqun Zhang[2], Muhammed Nufail Farooqi[1], Burak Bastem[1], George Michelogiannakis[2], Ann Almgren[2], and John Shalf[2]

[1] Koç University, Istanbul, Turkey
dunat@ku.edu.tr
[2] Lawrence Berkeley National Laboratory, Berkeley, CA, USA

Abstract. The high energy costs for data movement compared to computation gives paramount importance to data locality management in programs. Managing data locality manually is not a trivial task and also complicates programming. Tiling is a well-known approach that provides both data locality and parallelism in an application. However, there is no standard programming construct to express tiling at the application level. We have developed a multicore programming model, *TiDA*, based on tiling and implemented the model as C++ and Fortran libraries. The proposed programming model has three high level abstractions, *tiles*, *regions* and *tile iterator*. These abstractions in the library hide the details of data decomposition, cache locality optimizations, and memory affinity management in the application. In this paper we unveil the internals of the library and demonstrate the performance and programability advantages of the model on five applications on multiple NUMA nodes. The library achieves up to 2.10x speedup over OpenMP in a single compute node for simple kernels, and up to 22x improvement over a single thread for a more complex combustion proxy application (SMC) on 24 cores. The *MPI+TiDA* implementation of geometric multigrid demonstrates a 30.9 % performance improvement over *MPI+OpenMP* when scaling to 3072 cores (excluding MPI communication overheads, 8.5 % otherwise).

1 Introduction

The energy cost for computation is improving at a faster rate than the energy cost of moving data on-chip [28]. However, current multicore programming models offer very little facility to express information about data locality or data movement in the memory hierarchy, while almost all parallel systems contain multiple nonuniform memory access (NUMA) nodes and multiple levels of caches. Current programming models fundamentally assume an abstract machine model, where processing elements within a compute node are equidistant. A data-centric model, on the other hand, can provide programming abstractions that describe how the data is laid out on the system and apply the computation to the data where it resides. Furthermore, as processor chips move towards hundred and even thousand-way parallelism, designs that cluster cores into NUMA regions,

© Springer International Publishing Switzerland 2016
J.M. Kunkel et al. (Eds.): ISC High Performance 2016, LNCS 9697, pp. 116–135, 2016.
DOI: 10.1007/978-3-319-41321-1_7

where cores within a region are cache-coherent but cores across regions are not, are expected to emerge [24]. Taking these architectural trends into the account, locality management will be the key to achieve scalability on the next generation computing systems. In response to these architecture changes, we have developed a tiling based programming model, which preserves data-locality in an application.

Tiling and domain decomposition are both well known methods that enhances both data locality and parallelism. Traditionally tiling, also known as cache blocking, is manually applied to loop iterations in a program. There is a plethora of prior work to automate tiling transformations that focus on iteration space tiling using traditional compiler analysis [17,19,25] and polyhedral compiler analysis for perfectly [1,20,22] and imperfectly nested loops [7,16]. However, there is only limited support for tiling in commercial compilers due to the complexity of generating optimized code without domain-specific knowledge or programmer intervention. Another issue with exclusively compiler-based approaches is that they are agnostic about how the parallel execution of tiles is mapped to the underlying architecture. Loop transformations are carried out independently per nested loop, without respecting data locality in the whole program. Application developers need to have a more direct approach in the programming model to manage memory affinity in a way that can be exploited by both the compiler and the runtime system. We argue that this crucial data locality optimization should be formalized and elevated to a fundamental feature of the programming model given its broad impact on application performance and programmer productivity.

We have developed a tiling based programming model, called TiDA, that provides a multi-language library interface to express parallelism and data locality using a handful of simple programming abstractions. In [26], we introduced the initial design principles of TiDA. In this paper, we describe the underlying abstractions for a generalized tiling-based programming model, present a more mature version TiDA library, unveil its implementation details and present extensive performance analysis on five applications. The over-arching tiling-based programming model enables a natural expression of data decomposition and data layout with *logical tiles* and *regional tiles*, so that an abstract *tile iterator* hides the thread management and mapping of tiles onto the underlying core topology. The implementation of the TiDA API achieves performance portability by isolating architecture specific information to a handful of program parameters, *tile size* and *region size*, and enables metadata to propagate to all loops and functions in the application. We show the effectiveness of the library with five structured grid applications including an advanced combustion proxy application and geometric multi-grid solver. Lastly, both the Fortran and C++ library implementations of TiDA are available online for download at https://bitbucket.org/tidaproject/public-source.

2   Programming Model

2.1   Data Locality Model

The energy cost of data movement is rapidly becoming a dominant factor, because the energy cost for computation is improving at a faster rate than the energy cost of moving data [28]. In fact, it is projected that with 11 nm technology the energy cost for transporting two floating-point operands for an addition just 5 mm on-chip will be comparable to a simple addition operation itself [24]. The design of on-chip networks poses not only energy but performance constraints as well because contention, latency, and throughput effects can have a significant impact on application execution time [10]. Therefore, given stringent power budgets and the increased cost of data movement, it will no longer be practical to continue to maintain the illusion of a flat and infinitely fast on-chip interconnect. Despite the changes in the abstract machine model of modern multicore architectures, the programming models still have the assumption of uniform distance between the compute units. For example, OpenMP assumes processing units are equidistant to each other and binding threads to the cores are left to the programmer or to the OS. In reality, compute units are not equidistant to each other and there is non-uniform interconnect topology as in Intel's Knights Landing, which has a 2D mesh-based network connecting 72 cores [2]. And yet our current on-chip threading and process models do not offer a natural abstraction for handling this non-uniformity.

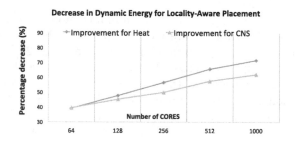

Fig. 1. Decrease in dynamic energy consumption for ghost cell exchange for the locality-aware placement compared to random placement of data on the chip.

As a motivating example, we quantify the gains in dynamic energy in on-chip data movement as a result of locality-management. We model the dynamic energy consumption of the ghost zone exchange using an analytical power model [3] for two applications: Heat and CNS, which are explained in Sect. 5. We model efficient direct communication between cores for the ghost zone exchange steps without accessing memory. This direct ghost zone exchange can be created by hardware-managed cache coherence or with explicit data movement for software managed coherence (such as GPUs or local-store architectures). Cores are assigned a 16^3 tile of double-precision floating point variables each. Locality-aware placement of data reduces the dynamic energy dissipated to complete the ghost zone exchange by 40–70 % compared to the random placement for the Heat and CNS applications as shown in Fig. 1. The energy gain for the locality-aware placement stems from reducing the average number of hops (communication distance). Reducing the number of hops reduces the number of channels and routers packets traverse which reduces the dynamic energy dissipated. The results on energy dissipation show the importance of correct data placement and the need for locality management support by a programming model. But for conventional threading/process models, both of these features must be handled manually by the programmer – a very unfriendly and non-portable interface.

2.2   Programming Abstractions

The primary design goal of TiDA is to provide simple programming abstractions for writing loop oriented code that offers options to describe different data decompositions and abstract away the details of how the data layout changes are implemented in each loop. We present two partitioning abstractions to handle locality as shown in Fig. 2 and an iterator to manipulate them:

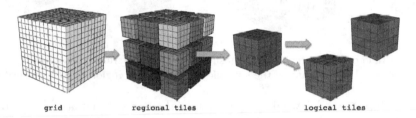

grid   regional tiles   logical tiles

Fig. 2. A grid is physically partitioned into regional tiles (regions). Each region is logically partitioned into logical tiles. 27 regions with 8 logical tiles in each are shown.

Region: is a physical partitioning of data into *regional tiles* where data within a region is contiguous, but each region is discontiguous with other regions. Such decomposition may introduce *halos* as shown in Fig. 3a, which consist of neighboring cells outside of the local domain at the boundaries that must be updated across computation phases, which will be discussed later. This abstraction is intended to address locality across NUMA nodes or regional coherence domains expected to emerge in exascale node architectures.

Tile: is a logical partitioning of data that is expressed in blocking of the iteration space. The *iteration space* is the order in which elements of a data array are visited by the iterations of a nested loop. Whereas repartitioning regional tiles to change working set sizes would require data reorganization to change the tile sizes, logical tiles can shrink the size of working sets to fit within available on-chip memory by changing the blocking factor of the iteration space without requiring data reorganization.

Tile Iterator: provides an interface to decouple the loop traversal from the loop body. It can hide complicated traversal orders, parallelization and execution strategies of tiles.

Figure 2 illustrates the partitioning of data and abstractions used for the partitioning. A grid is subdivided into regional tiles and region is locally partitioned into logical tiles.

2.3 Parameterization

Determining the optimal number of regions and size of a tile depend on the underlying machine's memory subsystem, the application itself, and other loop optimizations performed by the compiler. Therefore, it is important to support parameterization of the key elements of our tiling abstraction to facilitate performance portability in the programming model, and runtime retuning to support dynamically adaptive codes such as Adaptive Mesh Refinement (AMR).

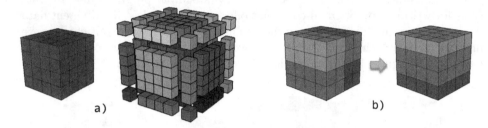

a)   b)

Fig. 3. (a) Halo cells of a regional tile is shown, (b) two different geometries of logical tiles in a regional tile. Dynamic tile size allows traversing a region in different orders.

An analytical model would argue that *local* tile sizes that are set at loop-by-loop basis would yield to optimal performance instead of program global tile sizes [27]. The advantage of local tile sizes is that the optimal tile size depends on array usage and loop content because different loops have different working set sizes. On the other hand, changing tile size may bring overhead because metadata needs to be reconstructed when tiling information is changed. Furthermore, different tile sizes can cause some of the threads to access non-local NUMA nodes because thread or memory pinning does not change loop-by-loop basis. Migrating threads to cores that are closer to the source NUMA node is an expensive process and can offset the benefits gained from using different tile sizes. Our programming model allows local tile sizes for logical tiles because logical tiles changes how the data space is viewed and traversed in the computation, can be also used to disable tiling for loops that do not exhibit any cache reuse. For example, in Fig. 3b, a regional tile is divided into logical tiles in two different ways. On the contrary, changing regional tile sizes requires reallocation of the data structures.

3 Implementation

3.1 Overview

We have developed TiDA as standalone C++ and Fortran libraries to make it easier to integrate into existing code frameworks. The library API provides an alternative to domain-specific languages or auto-tuning compilers that generate code variants. It also provides an alternative to C++ layout abstractions based on template metaprogramming, which do not interoperate well with other languages. Thus, converting existing applications over to use the TiDA abstractions is not as disruptive as completely rewriting the original application. In fact, the existing naively written loop nests in legacy codes largely remain intact with single line TiDA API calls used to annotate data array allocations as shown in Listing 1.1 and at the entry point to each loop nest or kernel invocation as shown in Listing 1.2. The programming abstractions are not tied to a particular language and can be incorporated into other languages such as Python or Julia.

Currently, the library supports programs operating on block-structured grid applications such as combustion, seismic, weather simulations and image processing. Such applications are generally limited by memory bandwidth on current systems [11,29], and expected to become even more memory bandwidth-constrained on future HPC as memory bandwidth improves more slowly than computational throughput [23]. These applications benefit greatly from tiling to improve cache reuse and from domain decomposition to increase parallelism. Indeed, the novelty of our approach is the generalization of best practices so that a single implementation can be applied for a broad array of codes. Although we are using structured stencils to motivate our demonstration, our generalized interfaces for domain decomposition and tiling are applied pervasively to support parallelization to other classes of algorithms such as dense and sparse linear algebra, particle-in-cell methods, and many others.

3.2 TiDA Types

The library provides new data types to embed the programming abstractions into a program. These are:

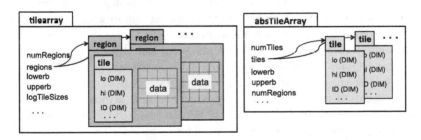

Fig. 4. Data structure of `tilearray` and `absTileArray` in TiDA

- `tilearray`: contains data and metadata. A `tilearray` is intended to replace the pure multidimensional array types in the original application that defines the values in a physical domain. The library extends an array with metadata that abstracts away details about data partitioning. The metadata follows the array through the code so that changes in partitioning strategy or mapping do not require any of the computation to be updated. `tilearray` has a pointer to an array of `regions`.

- **region**: represents a region in a `tilearray` and holds the actual data and its iteration space that the data is defined. Typically a TiDA programmer does not directly interact with regional tiles.
- **tile**: merely holds the low and high ends for a rectangular portion of the multidimensional array for logical or regional tiles and does not hold any data. Each `tile` is assigned an ID that uniquely identifies it.
- **absTileArray**: is used to build an abstract structure for `tilearrays` and to create a loop iterator. It defines a multidimensional iteration space through an array of `tiles`. Figure 4 illustrates the interaction of these four data types.
- **tileItr**: is created to iterate over set of tiles in an `absTileArray` or `tilearray`. If a logical tile size is passed to the build method of `tileItr`, then the iterator logically tiles the regions based on the provided tile size. `tileItr` is declared as private to a thread so that each `tileItr` object points to a distinct set of tiles in an `absTileArray`. At the build method, TiDA statically distributes tiles to threads based on thread IDs.

3.3   Supporting Parameterization

Selecting the tile size has a great impact on performance and its optimal value depends on the cache size and other loop optimizations such as loop fusion. Thus, being able to configure the tile size brings both performance and productivity benefits. In TiDA, the programmer has the option to specify logical tile size when the data structure is created or through environment variable, called (`TIDA_TILESIZE=tx,ty,tz`), which makes it trivial to tune tile size for an application. A programmer does not need to change any of the solvers as the metadata information propagates to all loops in the code following that array and transparently changes the loop iteration behavior. The geometry of the regions can be set in an environment variable (`TIDA_REGIONS=rx,ry,rz`) as well. The region size is then calculated in the library based on the problem size. For example, on a compute node with four NUMA nodes, choosing region geometry of 1,2,2 or 1,1,4 is expected to yield the best performance.

By default, logical tile size is global and does not change during execution. It is possible to change the global tile size per loop-basis by passing a tile size argument to the tile iterator. TiDA does not allow region size changes during execution except to re-allocate the array with the new layout, making the performance cost transparent to the programmer. In practice the search complexity to find optimal tile size per loop is too large for large-code basis and not desired by the application developers. We generally suggest using this feature only to disable tiling for loops where there is no data reuse because tiling can disrupt hardware prefetchers. The element-wise operations can illustrate the benefit of this feature because operations are performed on independent elements and the loops are highly compute bound. TiDA can be combined with an analytical model [27] to help select the optimal tile size for an application on a given architecture, which is out of scope of this paper.

3.4   Tile Boundaries

TiDA provides an interface, `fill_tileboundary()`, to update halos that is needed for structured grid problems. The depth of the halos can be specified in the `build` method when constructing a TiDA array. TiDA updates the halos of the region boundaries in regional tiling. This abstraction is important because it enables codes to migrate to machines with dramatically different memory consistency semantics, such as on software managed memory hierarchies and future systems with regional coherence models. TiDA relies on the programmer to place a call for `fill_tileboundary()` and to handle the inter-node communication (with e.g. MPI). This may introduce an extra copy overhead if the supplementary library is unaware of TiDA. However, this overhead can be eliminated by composing messages directly from a `tileArray`.

3.5   Thread and Memory Affinity

Data placement and thread binding play an important role in performance. Without NUMA-aware mapping and execution, the codes scale poorly due to the large memory access latency effects. A programmer using OpenMP can partly control affinity by setting KMP_affinity or GOMP_CPU_AFFINITY. This approach is prone to mistakes and is not portable across platforms. TiDA utilizes the HWLOC tool [15] to query available compute units and their physical numbering to automate thread binding. TiDA binds consecutive thread IDs to consecutive cores in a compact and balanced way. If there are fewer threads than cores, it will distribute them over the cores to increase memory bandwidth but place threads close to each to reduce the halo exchange latency.

In OpenMP programs, it is left to the operating system to bind pages to NUMA domains using the first touch policy. TiDA's region abstraction does not leave the binding to luck and the implementation assigns each region to a NUMA domain. In case a programmer creates only one region, then TiDA performs a parallel initialization to initialize data on NUMA systems, which also implements a first touch page mapping policy. Both thread binding and NUMA-aware mapping are currently static. Future work will look into user-controlled and dynamic affinity management where either thread or data is migrated to adapt the application execution.

4   Code Example

The code snippet in Listing 1.1 shows an example to illustrate how a `tilearray` is built in TiDA using the syntax of our Fortran library. Lines 1 and 2 declare variables with type `absTileArray` and `tilearray`. In the next line, `lo` and `hi` are declared as integer vectors defining the low and high ends of the index space of the grid. `tilesizes` and `numregions` are integer vectors for the tile sizes and number of regional tiles, respectively. They are optional arguments to the `_build` method of `absTileArray`. Their values can be read from the environment variables as well. Line 7 builds the metadata for array `A` and `B` with the index space and chops the space defined by `lo` and `hi` into tiles, and creates an array of `tiles`. Line 8 builds a `tilearray`, allocates its space based on the `absTileArray` and sets the depth of ghost zone. Line 9 builds another `tilearray` with the same structure. Finally, `destroy` in Lines 11–13 free the data structures.

```
1  type(tilearray)   :: A, B
2  type(absTileArray) :: abstractAB
3
4  integer :: lo(2), hi(2)
5  integer :: tilesizes(2), numregions(2)
6  ...
7  abstractAB= absTileArray_build(lo, hi, numregions, tilesizes)
8  A = tilearray_build(abstractAB, nGhosts)
9  B = tilearray_build(abstractAB, nGhosts)
10 ...
11 call destroy(abstractAB)
12 call destroy(A)
13 call destroy(B)
```

Listing 1.1. Building TiDA arrays in two dimensions

```
1  type(tileItr) : : ti
2  integer        : : tlo(2), thi(2), reglo(2), reghi(2)
3  integer        : : i, j
4  double precision, pointer : : ptrA(:,:)
5
6  !$OMP PARALLEL PRIVATE(ti, tlo, thi, reglo, reghi, i, j, ptrA)
7
8     ti = tileItr_build(abstractAB)
9     !ti = tileItr_build(abstractAB, logtilesize)
10
11    do while(next_tile(ti))                    !<--- Looping over logical tiles
12
13       ptrA =>dataptr(A, ti)          !
14       tlo  = get_lwb(ti)             ! metadata
15       thi  = get_upb(ti)             !
16
17       !Option 1: process a tile within a loop
18       do j = tlo(2), thi(2)          !
19          do i = tlo(1), thi(1)       !
20             ptrA(i,j) = compute(i,j)  ! Element
21             ...                       ! loops
22          end do                      !
23       end do                         !
24
25       !Option 2: process a tile within a function
26       reglo = get_lwb(get_region(A, ti))  !
27       reghi = get_upb(get_region(A, ti))  !
28
29       call compute_a_tile(ptrA, tlo, thi, reglo, reghi)
30
31    end do
32 !$OMP END PARALLEL
```

Listing 1.2. Operations on TiDA arrays

Listing 1.2 shows an example usage of TiDA. Line 1 declares a tile iterator, `ti`. At line 6, an OpenMP parallel region, spawning multiple threads, is started. In Line 8, `tileItr_build` returns a tile iterator that points to a set of tiles, private to the calling thread, in the tiled array `A`. Line 9 shows a variation of the `tileItr_build` function that creates a tile iterator with a different logical tile size than the one used for constructing `abstractAB`. This feature can be used for implementing function- or loop-specific tile size rather than program global tile size as illustrated in Fig. 3a.

In the do-while statement `next_tile` checks and increments the tile iterator if there are more logical tiles to process. In Line 13 through 15, the code
retrieves the `tilearray` metadata. Line 13, `dataptr` returns the pointer to the
floating point data for the current tile of the tile iterator `ti` in the tiled array
`A`. Depending on the `numregions`, this pointer points to a different location in
the grid but all this is hidden behind the TiDA interface. Line 14 and 15 get the
lower and upper bounds of the current logical tile in `ti`. Here we demonstrate
two different ways to process a `tile`. One way to process a `tile` is using the
element loops as shown in line 18 through 23. Element loops iterate over the
data points within a `tile`. TiDA does not modify the original loop bodies but
introduces tiling loops and new bounds for the element loops. Another way is to
process a `tile` within a function containing multiple nested loops as in line 29.
In this case, we pass the region sizes to a Fortran subroutine with an explicit-
shape array argument for performance reason instead of passing a pointer with
no explicit size information. `reglo` and `reghi` on Lines 26 and 27, contain the
low and high ends of the region, in which `ptrA` is defined.

Not all loops operate on the interior grid. Some loops may expand to sweep
a domain including the ghost zone, such as an initialization loop. For such loops,
TiDA provides the `expand_lwb(ti, expansion)` interface to expand lower (and
upper) bounds of a tile, where expansion is an integer vector. This function
returns expanded bounds of a tile depending on whether the tile resides at the
grid boundaries or not.

5   Experimental Evaluation

5.1   Evaluated Platforms

We use the "Hopper" supercomputer at the National Energy Research Scientific Computing Center (NERSC) for our experiments. A Hopper compute node
contains two sockets of 2.1 GHz 12-core Magny-Cours processors. Each socket
is comprised of two 6-core chips, totaling four NUMA nodes. The stream bandwidth is 51 GB/s for a Hopper node. All computations use double precision
arithmetic.

5.2   Performance Evaluation of Single-Mesh Applications

First, we evaluate TiDA performance on single-mesh applications, namely *Heat*,
Wave, *CNS*, and *SMC*, and compare performance against baseline implementations. The baseline versions perform no tiling and use OpenMP for outermost
loop parallelization. For the baseline versions, we set the thread affinities and
perform parallel initialization on the NUMA systems. TiDA programs use the
programming abstractions described in this paper and use no other manual code
optimizations. TiDA implementations use program global tile sizes. We have
tuned the logical tile sizes for each application and set the number of regions to
number of NUMA nodes for all applications. The characteristics of the applications are listed in Table 1. Figure 5 compares the TiDA library against OpenMP
(OMP) with no tiling for a problem size of 256^3 in double precision on Hopper.

Table 1. Characteristics of evaluated applications. #Loops indicate only 3D spatial loops in solvers. Byte/Flop ratios are for unlimited cache.

	Heat	Wave	CNS	SMC	miniMG
Stencil	7-point	13-point	27-point	27-point	7-point
#Halos	1	6	4	4	1
#Loops	1	4	14	28	5/grid level
#3D arrays	2	6	46	157	5/grid level
Flops/point	7	79	1625	15K	20
Byte/flop	3.43	1.14	1.32	0.82	2

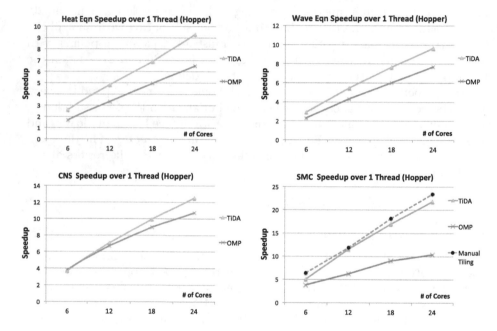

Fig. 5. Hopper speedups for *Heat, Wave, CNS and SMC* for problem size of 256^3.

1. **Heat** solves the heat transfer equation, given a constant heat conduction coefficient and no heat source. The solver iteratively updates a data point using 6 nearest neighbors, requiring three planes to be loaded into the cache for an update. Thus, its working set size is about 1.5 MB ($3 * 8 * 256^2$), far exceeding the size of the L2 cache on Hopper. Tiling greatly reduces memory traffic: for example, $256 * 16 * 16$ tiles that yield the best performance for Heat also reduces the working size to 90 KB, which falls within the limits of the L2. Smaller tiles come with a trade-off because the halos of each tile must be brought in the cache, leading to an increase in data movement to the point where tiling incurs more traffic than the untiled code.

2. **Wave** studies the constant speed wave equation solved with a third-order Runge-Kutta scheme for time stepping. *Wave* implements a star-shape, 13-

point stencil in a communication avoiding fashion where it expands its halos from 2 to 6 cells so it can compute 3 time steps in a row without exchanging halos. Since a region allocates its domain including its halos separately from other regions, it needs to exchange the deep ghost zone with other regions. Even though for this kernel, filling ghost zone accounts for 10 % of the execution time, TiDA still outperforms the OpenMP implementation.

3. **CNS**, developed by the Exascale Combustion Codesign Center, integrates the compressible Navier-Stokes equations and assumes constant transport properties. This application employs a 27-point stencil kernel. The TiDA improvement over OpenMP is about 17 % on 24 cores. CNS reaches out to four cells in all dimensions when it updates stencil grids in a Runge-Kutta step. However, the updates are performed one derivate at a time and there is reuse only in one of the dimensions in a loop. Because of this property, CNS would benefit from using different logical tile sizes for different loop nests. Moreover, in CNS some loops (4 out of 14) have no reuse and merely stream a number of arrays and perform point-wise operations. In such cases, tiling does not help and performance is ultimately bounded by memory bandwidth.

4. **SMC** [13] is an advanced proxy for the direct numerical combustion codes such as S3D [8]. SMC integrates the multicomponent reacting compressible Navier-Stokes equations with models for chemical species diffusion and kinetics. The dynamical core of SMC uses 8th-order stencil operations to approximate spatial derivatives, converting the system into a large set of ordinary differential equations that are integrated using a third-order, low-storage, TVD Runge-Kutta scheme. The computational cost of the algorithm depends on the number of chemical species and the number of reactions between the species. Our experiments use 9 chemical species.

TiDA is a clear winner for the SMC application, realizing 21.8x the performance on 24 cores as shown in Table 2 and Fig. 5. SMC is particularly challenging for OpenMP and good case study for TiDA because of the high number of data arrays used in the computation. The working set size is very large (about 256 MB for $N = 256$) even for 9 species. The exascale target for SMC is 50 or more chemical species, which will further increase the working set size. As chemical species are added to the simulation, the memory traffic required per Runge-Kutta step increases linearly. Thus, tiling in all dimensions is indispensable for SMC both in current and future machines. We also manually tiled SMC and compared our results on Hopper. The performance of the manual tiling is only 5 % better than TiDA. This indicates that the library introduces a small overhead on the application.

5.3   Region and Tile Size Parameters

The results in Fig. 5 in the previous section are obtained by using program global tile sizes and program global number of regions. Even though setting global values for these parameters is easy and provides reasonably good performance, TiDA provides APIs to use local tile sizes or array-specific region sizes. We study

Table 2. Hopper running time of TiDA and OpenMP for SMC.

	Time (sec) TiDA	Time (sec) OpenMP	Speedup TiDA	Speedup OpenMP
Baseline	553.1	553.1	1.0	1.0
6 threads	110.2	144.9	5.0	3.8
12 threads	48.0	89.1	11.5	6.2
18 threads	32.6	61.4	17.0	9.0
24 threads	25.4	53.3	21.8	10.4

impact of using local parameters on the CNS application because it has 14 loops and accesses 46 three dimensional arrays.

We first study the impact of using local tile sizes on performance. A programmer can set a different logical tile size for a loop nest or for a function when a tile iterator is created. The CNS application is implemented using four main functions, namely *Diffterm, Hypterm, CtoPrim* and *Update*. We created a different tile iterator with a different tile size for each function and measure the execution time. Figure 6 (Left) shows the performance improvement over the program global tile sizes for each function and overall speedup of the application. Two of the functions did not benefit from tile size changes because there is little or no reuse in these functions. *Diffterm* and *Hypterm* have a different optimal tile size than the program global tile size and enjoy 10 % and 6 % speedup, respectively. The overall performance improvement for function-specific tile sizes is 7 %.

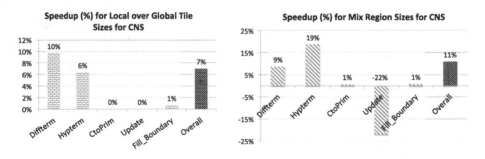

Fig. 6. Left: speedup for function-specific tile sizes over program global tile sizes. Right: speedup for array-specific region sizes over program global region sizes.

In TiDA, it is possible to use a different region size per array as long as an iterator uses the same logical tile size to iterate all the relevant arrays. This feature is particularly useful for arrays without halos because one can create smaller regional tiles than there are NUMA domains without paying the extra memory space cost for halos. In an extreme case a regional tile size can be equal to logical tile size. In CNS, 18 of the three dimensional arrays does not have halo cells. For those we choose a region size that is equal to the logical tile size. Figure 6 (Right) shows the performance improvement for the array-specific region size over program global region size. *Diffterm* and *Hypterm* benefit from array-specific region sizes and give 9 % and 19 % speedup, respectively. Using mix region size lowers the performance of the *Update* function because this function makes references to 36 arrays out of 46 and has very little cache reuse. Nonetheless *Update* accounts less than 10 % of the execution time, overall array-specific region size provides 11 % performance improvement over the program global region size.

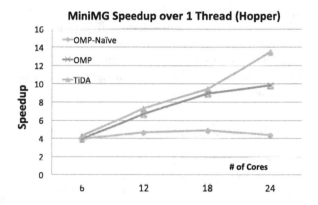

Fig. 7. Multigrid strong scaling results on a single Hopper node, finest grid size 256^3.

5.4 Performance Evaluation of Multigrid

MiniMG is a compact multigrid application that solves Poisson's equation with periodic boundary conditions. MiniMG iterates V-cycles, which uses Red-Black Gauss Seidel smooths at each grid level. Our original MiniMG implementation employs the data structures provided by Boxlib [30], a software framework for adaptive mesh refinement (AMR). A program written in Boxlib consists of distributed-memory arrays called *multiFabs*, each consisting multiple *Fabs* (Fortran Array Boxes). While *multiFab* can span across different processes, a *Fab* is contiguous in the local memory of a process.

We implemented the multigrid solver in TiDA and compared its performance against OMP. **(i) OMP-naive** parallelizes computations of each *Fab* using all the cores in a compute node without any locality optimizations such as first touch or thread binding. **(ii) OMP** employs a similar parallelization scheme as *OMP-naive* does. However, this variant initializes *Fabs* in parallel to take advantage of NUMA-aware initialization for locality. OpenMP threads execute tiles of a *Fab* in parallel. Similar to *OMP* and *OMP-naive*, there is no parallelism across *Fabs*. **(iii) TiDA** splits *Fabs* into regions (e.g. 4 regions on Hopper) to map each region to a NUMA node, then tiles each region using the *logical* tiling. This variant employs nested OpenMP parallelism. Both regions and tiles in each region are executed by OpenMP threads in parallel. Program global tile and region sizes are used.

Figure 7 shows the strong-scaling results of the MiniMG variants in a single compute node. For all cases, the solution grid is 256^3, divided to eight 128^3 *Fabs*. The poor performance of *OMP-naive* demonstrates the significance of data placement when multiple NUMA domains are present. *TiDA* outperforms other variants on 24 cores and reduces the execution time of *OMP*, a NUMA-aware OpenMP implementation, by up to 37 %. The reason is that *TiDA* does not suffer from the latency overhead caused by spanning the working set across the NUMA nodes. Specifically, *TiDA* overcomes the latency problem by assigning each region to a NUMA node, reducing the number of remote memory accesses. Moreover, given the speculation that an exascale machine will have hundreds of coherence domains, regional tiling will be even more advantageous. The performance of *TiDA* slightly drops on 18 cores due to load imbalance (i.e. assigning 8 *Fabs* to 3 NUMA nodes). In the future, TiDA will mitigate the impact of such load imbalance by supporting tile migration.

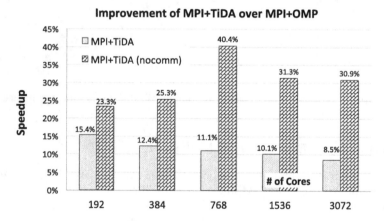

Fig. 8. Hybrid programming results for multigrid on Hopper, finest grid size is 1024^3.

We create hybrid variants that use *MPI+TiDA* and *MPI+OMP* to parallelize the multigrid solver across compute nodes. On-node communication is conducted via sharing memory, whereas off-node communication relies on message passing. Our original multigrid solver implements a truncated V-cycle. Thus, a fixed *Fab* size must be used so that all code variants run the same numerical algorithm. In this study we do not use a pure MPI variant, which employs one MPI process per core because that variant would require very small *Fabs*, reducing the convergence rate of the solution.

Figure 8 shows the strong-scaling study on 128 compute nodes (3072 cores) on Hopper, fixing the finest grid at 1024^3 and *Fab* size at 128^3. We can see that *MPI+TiDA* outperforms *MPI+OMP* on up to 3072 cores. However, the performance improvement of *MPI+TiDA* over *MPI+OMP* steadily reduces from

15.4 % on 192 cores to 8.5 % on 3072 cores. This is because the cost of off-node communication grows as the number of cores increases in strong scaling. Indeed on 3072 cores, the communication overhead accounts for 45 % of the execution time, thus the performance benefit of using TiDA becomes less significant. As shown in the same figure, without including the off-node communication time, the performance improvement by *MPI+TiDA* increases from 23.3 % to 30.9 % (going from 192 to 3072 cores). Currently Boxlib is responsible for handling inter-process communication. In the future, we plan to add a runtime support to hide communication overheads by overlapping with computation.

5.5   Programming Effort

The primary goal of TiDA is to enable data locality optimizations through abstractions without requiring extensive code changes in the legacy codes. The number of lines of code (#loc) added to existing implementations of the applications is insignificant compared to the size of the programs. For example, for the Heat, we added fewer than 10 lines to build metadata and tilearrays, and added six lines to extract the metadata per nested loop. Moreover, tiling can be performed over a function, which can contain multiple nested loops and no communication phase. Then the #loc can be even smaller because the retrieving tile bounds and pointer to its data can be performed at the function level, significantly reducing the #loc. For example, in the SMC code even though there are 28 nested loops, only four function calls containing those loops needed to be tiled, thus only about 50 lines of TiDA code are added to original 3780 lines of SMC code. When the presented applications ran on another platform, the programmer does not need to modify the source but tune the tile size and region size. Programming effort of using TiDA could be further reduced by elevating the tiling primitives to the level of a language construct (such as an attribute in a Fortran array descriptor) or an embedded directive (extension to OpenMP), but all of TiDA's performance and coding efficiency benefits are available via its library interface.

6   Related Work

OpenMP is the most common approach for shared-memory parallelism. OpenMP does not provide a simple abstraction for data decomposition or tiling. The *collapse* clause in OpenMP increases parallelism through flattening the multidimensional iteration space into a single dimension but it doesn't implement cache-blocking on the iteration space. The programmer has to introduce nested parallelism to be able to implement tiling however nested parallelism complicates the locality management because it is left to the OS to schedule the newly created threads within a nested region.

Recently, several interfaces and language extensions have emerged to provide data structure and layout abstractions for data locality. Kokkos [12] and Dash [14] support multi-dimensional arrays in C++ and address the intra-chip data layout changes using C++ meta-programming. GridTool [5] targets multi-stage regular grids that are common in complex weather and climate models and implements the methods with C++ template meta-programming. In both cases, the paradigm is packaged using intense C++ metaprogramming, which is not amenable to other languages such as C, Fortran, Python, etc. Given the installed base of existing code that is written in languages other than C++, TiDA offers language neutral access to these tiling abstractions.

Chen et al. [9] developed tiled MapReduce for large scale data processing with fault tolerance support. Application focus in TiDA is different; it targets structured grid problems, particularly Adaptive Mesh Refinement codes, which are challenging to optimize in large-scale systems. Hierarchically Tiled Arrays (HTA) [6] describes hierarchy and topology of data where computation and communication are represented by overloaded array operations. The array notations hide the cost of temporary arrays and layout transformations, often leading to severe performance penalties, which prevents HTA to be integrated into other parallel libraries. TiDA avoids operator overloading and array notations, and uses abstractions that balance productivity and performance.

Past work has also clearly demonstrated the performance and energy advantages of locality-aware task placement for on-chip data movement. Placements that exploit communication locality and Network on Chip (NoC) topology have been shown to increase effective communication bandwidth by reducing contention on NoCs by 53 % [21], decrease packet latency by 23 % [31], decrease energy by 60 % [18], and provide tighter quality-of-service guarantees compared to locality-agnostic placements [18]. However, past work lacks interaction with the application layer and thus typically resorts to heuristic algorithms or reactive techniques such as process migration [4] using predicted or observed communication graphs and requirements. TiDA improves on past work by generating data-centric and topology-aware mappings based on each application's data structure layout abstracted from the programmer.

7   Conclusion

We introduce TiDA as a durable tiling abstraction for data-centric computing. TiDA provides a simple API to describe tile size and data layout and isolates tuning parameters to a single point in the code where the data is instantiated, providing performance portability. The results for five stencil applications show its enhanced scalability potential on HPC systems. Moreover, TiDA's abstractions are forward looking. It supports layouts for alternative cache-coherence mechanisms as massively-parallel chip architectures move towards regional coherence models. Even though we implemented TiDA using Fortran and C++ as the base languages, the abstractions are not tied to these languages and can be implemented in any other languages. If the API is elevated to a language, the metadata retrieval and tuning for tile size and memory layout can be lifted from the programmer to the compiler and runtime, which would further reduce programmer burden.

We are currently developing a runtime system to hide communication overheads between TiDA regions and allow asynchronous execution of tiles. In addition, we plan to extend the current API to target GPU architectures.

Acknowledgments. Dr. Unat is supported by the Marie Sklodowska Curie Reintegration Grant 655965 by the European Commission. Authors from KU are supported by the Turkish Science and Technology Research Centre Grant No: 215E285. Authors from LBNL were supported by the SciDAC Program and the Exascale Co-Design Program under the U.S. DOE contract DE-AC02-05CH11231. This research used resources of the National Energy Research Scientific Computing Center, which is supported by the Office of Science of the U.S. DOE under Contract No. DE-AC02-05CH11231. We would like to acknowledge and thank John Bell and Hakan Memisoglu for their input.

References

1. PLuTo, A polyhedral automatic parallelizer and locality optimizer for multicores. Software. http://pluto-compiler.sourceforge.net
2. Real World Technologies: Knights Landing Details. http://www.realworldtech. com/knights-landing-details/
3. Balfour, J., Dally, W.J.: Design tradeoffs for tiled CMP on-chip networks. In: Proceedings of the 20th Annual International Conference on Supercomputing, ICS 2006 (2006)
4. Bertozzi, S., Acquaviva, A., Bertozzi, D., Poggiali, A.: Supporting task migration in multi-processor systems-on-chip: a feasibility study. In: Proceedings of Design, Automation and Test in Europe, 2006, DATE 2006, vol. 1, pp. 1–6, March 2006
5. Bianco, M., Cumming, B.: A generic strategy for multi-stage stencils. In: Silva, F., Dutra, I., Santos Costa, V. (eds.) Euro-Par 2014 Parallel Processing. LNCS, vol. 8632, pp. 584–595. Springer, Heidelberg (2014)
6. Bikshandi, G., Guo, J., Hoeflinger, D., Almasi, G., Fraguela, B.B., Garzarán, M.J., Padua, D., von Praun, C.: Programming for parallelism and locality with hierarchically tiled arrays. In: Proceedings of the Eleventh ACM SIGPLAN Symposium on Principles and Practice of Parallel Programming, PPopp, 2006, pp. 48–57. ACM, New York (2006)
7. Bondhugula, U., Hartono, A., Ramanujam, J., Sadayappan, P.: A practical automatic polyhedral parallelizer and locality optimizer. SIGPLAN Not. 3(6), 101–113 (2008)
8. Chen, J.H., Choudhary, A., de Supinski, B., DeVries, M., Hawkes, E.R., Klasky, S., Liao, W.K., Ma, K.L., Mellor-Crummey, J., Podhorszki, N., Sankaran, R., Shende, S., Yoo, C.S.: Terascale direct numerical simulations of turbulent combustion using S3D. Comput. Sci. Discovery 2(1), 015001 (2009)
9. Chen, R., Chen, H.: Tiled-mapreduce: efficient and flexible mapreduce processing on multicore with tiling. ACM Trans. Archit. Code Optim. 10(1), 3:1–3:30 (2013)
10. Das, R., Mutlu, O., Moscibroda, T., Das, C.R.: Application-aware prioritization mechanisms for on-chip networks. In: Proceedings of the 42nd Annual IEEE/ACM International Symposium on Microarchitecture, MICRO, pp. 280–291 (2009)
11. Datta, K., Murphy, M., Volkov, V., Williams, S., Carter, J., Oliker, L., Patterson, D., Shalf, J., Yelick, K.: Stencil computation optimization and auto-tuning on state-of-the-art multicore architectures. In: Proceedings of the ACM/IEEE Conference on Supercomputing, SC 2008, pp. 4:1–4:12. IEEE Press, Piscataway (2008)

12. Edwards, H.C., Sunderland, D., Porter, V., Amsler, C., Mish, S.: Manycore performance-portability: Kokkos multidimensional array library. Sci. Program. **20**(2), 89–114 (2012)
13. Emmett, M., Zhang, W., Bell, J.B.: High-order algorithms for compressible reacting flow with complex chemistry. Combust. Theor. Model. **18**(3), 361–387 (2014)
14. Fuchs, T., Fürlinger, K.: Expressing and exploiting multidimensional locality in DASH. In: Proceedings of the SPPEXA Symposium 2016. Lecture Notes in Computational Science and Engineering, Garching, Germany, January 2016
15. Goglin, B.: Managing the topology of heterogeneous cluster nodes with hardware locality (hwloc). In: International Conference on High Performance Computing and Simulation, HPCS 2014, Bologna, Italy, 21–25 July 2014, pp. 74–81 (2014)
16. Hall, M., Chame, J., Chen, C., Shin, J., Rudy, G., Khan, M.M.: Loop transformation recipes for code generation and auto-tuning. In: Gao, G.R., Pollock, L.L., Cavazos, J., Li, X. (eds.) LCPC 2009. LNCS, vol. 5898, pp. 50–64. Springer, Heidelberg (2010)
17. Hartono, A., Baskaran, M.M., Bastoul, C., Cohen, A., Krishnamoorthy, S., Norris, B., Ramanujam, J., Sadayappan, P.: Parametric multi-level tiling of imperfectly nested loops. In: Proceedings of the 23rd International Conference on Supercomputing, ICS 2009, pp. 147–157. ACM, New York (2009)
18. Jingcao, H., Marculescu, R.: Energy-aware mapping for tile-based NoC architectures under performance constraints. In: Proceedings of the Asia and South Pacific Design Automation Conference, ASP-DAC 2003, pp. 233–239 (2003)
19. Kim, D., Rajopadhye, S.: Parameterized tiling for imperfectly nested loops. Technical report CS-09-101, Department of Computer Science, Colorado State University (2009)
20. Kim, D., Renganarayanan, L., Rostron, D., Rajopadhye, S., Strout, M.M.: Multi-level tiling: M for the price of one. In: Proceedings of the ACM/IEEE Conference on Supercomputing, SC 2007, pp. 51:1–51:12. ACM, New York (2007)
21. Murali, S., De Micheli, G.: Bandwidth-constrained mapping of cores onto NoC architectures. In: Proceedings of the Conference on Design, Automation and Test in Europe - vol. 2, DATE '04, (2004)
22. Renganarayanan, L., Kim, D.G., Rajopadhye, S., Strout, M.M.: Parameterized tiled loops for free. SIGPLAN Not. **42**(6), 405–414 (2007)
23. Rogers, B.M., Krishna, A., Bell, G.B., Ken, V., Jiang, X., Solihin, Y.: Scaling the bandwidth wall: challenges in and avenues for CMP scaling. In: Proceedings of the 36th Annual International Symposium on Computer Architecture, ISCA, pp. 371–382 (2009)
24. Shalf, J., Dosanjh, S., Morrison, J.: Exascale computing technology challenges. In: Palma, J.M.L.M., Daydé, M., Marques, O., Lopes, J.C. (eds.) VECPAR 2010. LNCS, vol. 6449, pp. 1–25. Springer, Heidelberg (2011)
25. Unat, D., Cai, X., Baden, S.B.: Mint: realizing CUDA performance in 3D stencil methods with annotated C. In: Proceedings of the International Conference on Supercomputing, ICS 2011, pp. 214–224. ACM, New York (2011)
26. Unat, D., Chan, C., Zhang, W., Bell, J., Shalf, J.: Tiling as a durable abstraction for parallelism and data locality. In: Workshop on Domain-Specific Languages and High-Level Frameworks for High Performance Computing, 18 November 2013
27. Unat, D., Chan, C., Zhang, W., Williams, S., Bachan, J., Bell, J., Shalf, J.: Exasat: an exascale co-design tool for performance modeling. Int. J. High Perform. Comput. Appl. **29**(2), 209–232 (2015)
28. Unat, D., Shalf, J., Hoefler, T., Schulthess, T., Dubey, A., (eds.) et al.: Programming abstractions for data locality. Technical report (2014)

29. Vega, A., Cabarcas, F., Ramirez, A., Valero, M.: Breaking the bandwidth wall in chip multiprocessors. In: International Conference on Embedded Computer Systems, SAMOS, pp. 255–262 (2011)
30. Zhang, W., Almgren, A., Day, M., Nguyen, T., Shalf, J., Unat, D.: BoxLib with tiling: an AMR software framework. SIAM J. Sci. Comput. (2016)
31. Zhou, W., Zhang, Y., Mao, Z.: An application specific NoC mapping for optimized delay. In: Design and Test of Integrated Systems in Nanoscale Technology, DTIS 2006, 184–188, September 2006

Scalable Applications

OpenAtom: Scalable Ab-Initio Molecular Dynamics with Diverse Capabilities

Nikhil Jain[1]([✉]), Eric Bohm[1], Eric Mikida[1], Subhasish Mandal[2],
Minjung Kim[2], Prateek Jindal[1], Qi Li[3], Sohrab Ismail-Beigi[2],
Glenn J. Martyna[3], and Laxmikant V. Kale[1]

[1] Department of Computer Science, University of Illinois at Urbana-Champaign,
Champaign, USA
nikhil.jain@acm.org
[2] Department of Applied Physics, Yale University, New Haven, USA
[3] IBM TJ Watson Laboratory, Yorktown Heights, USA

Abstract. The complex interplay of tightly coupled, but disparate, computation and communication operations poses several challenges for simulating atomic scale dynamics on multi-petaflops architectures. OPE-NATOM addresses these challenges by exploiting overdecomposition and asynchrony in CHARM++, and scales to thousands of cores for realistic scientific systems with only a few hundred atoms. At the same time, it supports several interesting ab-initio molecular dynamics simulation methods including the Car-Parrinello method, Born-Oppenheimer method, k-points, parallel tempering, and path integrals. This paper showcases the diverse functionalities as well as scalability of OPENATOM via performance case studies, with focus on the recent additions and improvements to OPENATOM. In particular, we study a metal organic framework (MOF) that consists of 424 atoms and is being explored as a candidate for a hydrogen storage material. Simulations of this system are scaled to large core counts on Cray XE6 and IBM Blue Gene/Q systems, and time per step as low as $1.7\,s$ is demonstrated for simulating path integrals with 32-beads of MOF on 262,144 cores of Blue Gene/Q.

1 Introduction

Modern supercomputers have become larger and more complex with each successive generation. Although new platforms present novel opportunities, best use of these platforms can be made only by overcoming the challenges that each new architecture poses to the users. Scientific methods and their requirements also change as the domain of interest and goals of research evolve over time. Hence, applications used for simulating scientific phenomena on HPC systems need to grow continually in terms of their scientific capability and parallel scalability.

OPENATOM is a scalable implementation of the Car-Parrinello Ab-initio Molecular Dynamics (CPAIMD) method [7] implemented using the CHARM++ runtime system [23]. It is suitable for studying materials at the atomistic level wherein the electronic structure must be explicitly modeled in order to accurately simulate the behavior of the system being investigated. For example, Fig. 1

© Springer International Publishing Switzerland 2016
J.M. Kunkel et al. (Eds.): ISC High Performance 2016, LNCS 9697, pp. 139–158, 2016.
DOI: 10.1007/978-3-319-41321-1_8

shows the schematic of a metal-organic framework (MOF) that is the subject of materials research as a candidate for hydrogen storage [22], and is currently being simulated using OPENATOM in this regard. Typical studies at this level of detail are generally restricted to a few hundred atoms as they require numerous communication-intensive Fast Fourier Transformations (FFTs). This makes scalable parallelization of such methods challenging. In our previous work, we have shown that OPENATOM is able to make use of Charm++'s asynchrony and object-based overdecomposition approach to overcome these challenges for performing CPAIMD on IBM's Blue Gene/L and Blue Gene/P systems [5,6].

While the computational capacity of HPC systems has been increasing steadily, the size of scientific systems of interest (such as MOF) has not grown proportionately because the time scales of interest for the study of important phenomena have not been reached (minimal 100–1000 ps). This motivates a drive to achieve fastest time per step as the time step of the discrete time solver is order 0.1 femtosecond. Hence, it is critical that modeling software provide good *strong* scaling for the fixed sized problems being studied.

Fig. 1. Schematic representation of MOF with 43 H_2

On the other hand, scientific methods that enable faster convergence (e.g., parallel tempering [10]), or are capable of simulating more complex physical phenomena at atomic scale (e.g. quantum effects using path integrals [20]) require concurrent execution of weakly coupled atomic systems of the same size. Implementation and execution of such scenarios present productivity and performance challenges that also need to be addressed by software such as OPENATOM.

Our recent efforts in OPENATOM have been focused on finding solutions to the challenges described above so that scalable simulations can be performed on production HPC systems. This paper presents these recent additions and improvements to OPENATOM and highlights the following contributions:

– **Generalized topology-aware mapping schemes** for OPENATOM are proposed and their positive impact is demonstrated.
– **Charm-FFT**, a new scalable FFT library which uses 2D-decomposition and minimizes communication, is presented and its benefits are shown.
– **Multi-instance "Uber" method** is a novel scheme added to OPENATOM, which provides a powerful tool to seamlessly implement and execute new scientific methods/variations individually and concurrently. As a result, users can now run methods such as k-points, path integrals, and parallel tempering together in a single run of OPENATOM, if desired.
– **BOMD** [21] is presented as a new addition to OPENATOM's capability.
– **Performance results** that demonstrate the scalability of all scientific methods provided in OPENATOM are presented. A time per step of only 1.7 s is shown for simulating 32-beads of MOF on 262,144 cores of Blue Gene/Q.

2   Background and Related Work

OPENATOM is an implementation of the CPAIMD method [7] in CHARM++ [1], and has been described in [6,18,23]. The CPAIMD method is an effective technique to simulate atomistic dynamics on a ground state potential surface derived from a Kohn-Sham (KS) density functional theory formulation within a local or gradient corrected approximation. It has a wide range of applications in chemistry, biology, materials science, and geophysics, etc. [8,11]. CPAIMD computations involve many phases with complex dependencies, and as such have proven to be difficult to scale. OPENATOM utilizes CHARM++'s ability to naturally compose multiple dissimilar modules and thus allows various phases of CPAIMD to overlap in both time and space.

CHARM++ [1] is an adaptive runtime system built upon the idea of overdecomposed migratable parallel objects that communicate asynchronously via remote method invocations. A key principle in CHARM++ applications is that the programmer should not have to think in terms of nodes, cores, or some other hardware specific entity. A program is developed as a collection of parallel objects, called chares, that coordinate via messaging and are composed of both the data and the computation of the particular application. It is then the job of the runtime system to map these objects to the hardware, manage communication between these objects, and schedule them for execution as work becomes available for them. This allows the programmer to decompose the problem in a way that is natural to the algorithm itself, rather than decomposing based on the specific hardware that is being used in a given run.

2.1   Parallelization of OpenAtom in Charm++

Parallelization of the CPAIMD method follows directly from the expression of the density functional and overlap integrals between the KS electronic states [18,23]. There are over ten different kinds of chares, each representing different phases of the computation as shown in Fig. 2. Note that although the phase numbers are linearly increasing, different phases may overlap with each other based on their computation tasks as discussed next.

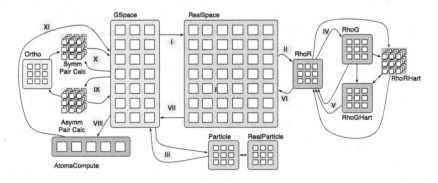

Fig. 2. Parallel structure of OPENATOM

KS Electronic States: Each state, I, has both a discrete real-space $(RS_I(x,y,z))$ and g-space $(GS_I(g_x, g_y, g_z))$ representation, where the latter is the Fourier expansion coefficients of the state in the plane wave basis. The representations are interconverted via concurrent 3D-FFTs (phases I and VII in Fig. 2). The real-space representation for each state is decomposed in 1D along planes of the 3D grid. However, application of a spherical cut-off to the g-space representation results in an imbalanced decomposition if 1D decomposition along planes is used. This imbalance is corrected by aggregating small "planes" into larger chunks of data as described in [18].

Electronic Density: The electronic density, ρ, is expressed using both a discrete real-space ($RhoR$) and g-space ($RhoG$) representation, where $RhoR(x,y,z) = \sum_I |RS_I(x,y,z)|^2$. As for the states, $RhoR$ is decomposed along planes, while imbalances in $RhoG$ due to spherical cut-off are corrected by aggregation of smaller planes into larger chunks. The application of the Euler-Exponential Spline method [19] to the computation of local electron-nuclear interaction creates another grid with real-space and g-space components ($RhoRHart$ and $RhoGHart$). In addition to being decomposed like $RhoR$ and $RhoG$, these grids are also decomposed along the number of atom types, $N_{atm-type}$. All these computations are overlapped with each other and contribute to the "Kohn-Sham potential" (phase V), which is communicated to RS (phase VI in Fig. 2).

Nonlocal Pseudopotential: The non-local pseudopotential energy accounts for the fact that the CPAIMD method mathematically eliminates "core" electrons and considers only the "valence" electrons. The interaction and the kinetic energy of non-interacting electrons is computed independently of the density-related terms by particle planes, and thus leads to adaptive overlap of phase III with phases II, IV, V, and VI.

Pair Calculators: Corrections are necessary to handle first order variations that cause deviations from orthogonality in $GS_I(g_x, g_y, g_z)$. To do so, the Λ matrix is computed and the forces, $F_{GS_I}(g_x, g_y, g_z)$, are modified:

$$\Lambda(I,K) = \sum_g F_{GS_I}(g_x, g_y, g_z)\, GS_K(g_x, g_y, g_z)$$
$$F_{GS_I}(g_x, g_y, g_z) -= \sum_K \Lambda(I,K)\, GS_K(g_x, g_y, g_z)$$

This task is performed by the PC_{asymm} chares, which concurrently compute matrix multiples for pairs of states (phase IX in Fig. 2). Further corrections in second order variations to orthogonality must be applied to the newly evolved states. The PC_{symm} chares perform this task by computing the overlap matrix and are assisted by the *Ortho* chares for computing the inverse square root of the overlap matrix. (phase X in Fig. 2).

Atoms: As the atom position data is needed by multiple phases, it is replicated throughout the platform as a *group*, i.e., a chare array with one chare on every processor. Given the small number of atoms, this does not add a significant memory overhead. Integration of the forces to adjust the position of the particles is parallelized up to N_{atms} and is trivial compared to the other operations. This computation is kicked off in phase VIII and is completed in phase XI.

2.2 Related Work

CPMD is an MPI-based implementation of ab-initio molecular dynamics developed through collaboration between IBM and the Max-Planck Institute, Stuttgart [9]. It has a large feature list which includes path integrals and support for excited states. However, in [3], it shows weak scaling up to 256 nodes only. QBox is another MPI-based implementation of first-principle molecular dynamics developed at UC Davis that demonstrated scaling up to 64 K nodes of Blue Gene/L for very large atomic systems [13]. Its feature list for performing CPAIMD and BOMD is similar to that of OPENATOM. However, to the best of our knowledge, it does not have native support for multi-instance methods that enables execution of ensemble methods such as k-points, path integrals, parallel tempering, etc. without code input from the users.

In HPC, several application and runtime system developers have studied techniques for mapping [2,5,12,14] to three-dimensional torus topologies with the emergence of supercomputers like the IBM Blue Gene and Cray XT/XE series. Bhatele [4] explore use of information about application's communication patterns and network's topology to create automated tools for generating better mappings. Hoefler and Snir [15] discuss generic mapping algorithms to minimize contention and demonstrate their applicability to torus, PERCS, and fat-tree networks. In addition to being custom designed for OPENATOM, mapping techniques presented in this paper differ from related approaches in two ways. First, mapping of a large number of objects of distinct types to processes is performed. Second, instead of being platform dependent, higher level mapping rules are defined to optimize performance on multiple platforms.

3 New Capabilities

The CPAIMD method has been commonly used to simulate nuclear motion on a ground state potential surface. Recently, researchers have extended the basic CPAIMD method in many ways to expand the scope of problems which can be effectively handled. Several of these extensions share a commonality in that they each consist of a set of slightly different, but mostly independent, instances of the standard CPAIMD computation. These include k-points sampling, quantum path integrals molecular dynamics, spin density functionals, and parallel tempering simulations. Depending on the extension, the instances interact in different ways among themselves, but those differences lead to relatively small changes in the overall flow of control. We refer to all these extensions as multi-instance methods.

3.1 Uber Scheme

To support different multi-instance methods, we have implemented an overarching Uber indexing infrastructure. This scheme allows multiple instances to reuse all the objects that implement CPAIMD in OPENATOM by creating distinct copies of the objects that are required by the instances. Objects that belong to a given instance are maintained as a distinct set of chare arrays and thus form an *Uber* comprising one simulation instance. Objects that are shared among different instances are referenced using shallow copies. Furthermore, Ubers are *composable* across different methods, i.e., multiple types of multi-instance methods can be used in any given simulation.

When multi-instance methods are executed, the first step taken by the Uber scheme is the division of compute resources among the instances. Given that the work performed by most of the Ubers is of similar load, a balanced division of compute resources is performed. Section 4.3 presents the schemes that can be used to select specific cores that are assigned to each of the Ubers. Next, objects required for performing simulation within each Uber are created. On any given process and from any of these objects, the variable *thisInstance* can be accessed to find more information about the Uber a given object belongs to. Currently, an Uber is identified by four indices, each of which refers to a type of multi-instance method supported in OpenAtom (discussed next). After the initial set up, all Ubers simulate the configurations assigned to them. Information exchange and synchronization among Ubers is efficiently performed using basic Charm++ constructs such as remote method invocation and collective operations.

In OpenAtom, an Uber is identified by four indices, which are the instance's offsets in four different types of multi-instance methods:

- *Path Integrals*: used to study nuclear quantum effects.
- *Parallel Tempering*: used for sampling to treat rough energy landscapes.
- *k-points*: enables sampling of the Brillion Zone (BZ) to study metals and/or small systems.
- *Spin Density Functional*: treats magnetic systems.

We now briefly describe each of these methods that have been added recently to OpenAtom, except Spin which is currently being implemented.

Path Integrals: In order to explore nuclear quantum effects, Feynman's Imaginary Time Path Integral method (CPAIMD_PI) [20] has been implemented. In this method, each classical nucleus is replaced by a ring polymer of P beads connected by harmonic links to their nearest neighbors. The method's computational complexity increases linearly with P as the inter-bead interactions are imaginary time ordered and each bead group forms a classical subsystem.

CPAIMD_PI has been integrated into OpenAtom such that each Uber has an independent electronic computation ($RS, GS, RhoRS$, etc.) associated with that bead's set of nuclei. Therefore, the entirety of the standard CPAIMD method shown in Fig. 2 is local to each Uber. The additional work required to evaluate and integrate the intrapolymer forces to evolve the ensemble is order P. It is implemented by force and position exchanges between each representation of the N nuclear particles from all the beads. This communication extends the standard CPAIMD nuclear force integration phase (phase XI in Fig. 2) such that the simulation cannot proceed until the bead forces are computed. Thus, it forces a synchronization across all beads in every time step.

Parallel Tempering: One widely used method to sample rough energy landscapes in statistical physics is Parallel Tempering (PT) [10]. In this method, a set of complete CPAIMD parallel simulations are initiated with different temperatures. The lower temperatures in the set explore low lying minima while the higher temperatures traverse the energy landscape. After every time step, the Ubers that are nearest neighbors in temperature space exchange temperatures via a rigorous Monte-Carlo acceptance rule. The computational complexity of this method also increases linearly with the number of temperatures being explored. However, a global synchronization is not needed at the end of each time step since the temperature exchange only happens among nearest neighbors.

k-points Sampling of the Brillion Zone: In a previous work, we studied large, insulating systems where computation at only the Γ-point of the Brillion zone (BZ) [7] was sufficient [23]. In small, metallic or semiconducting systems, more points are required, and that is the functionality k-points sampling provides. Away from the Γ-point, at finite $\mathbf{k}$, the states are complex and a set of n_k k-points with weights w_k are used to sample the BZ. Different k-points interact in the formation of the density - there is only 1 density summed over all k-points taking into account the weights. Hence different Ubers get their own copy of state chares, but all of them point to the same density chares ($RhoRS, RhoGHart$, etc.) and atoms. The parallel scalability of this method is typically bounded by the time spent in the density phase.

3.2 Born-Oppenheimer Method

Other than CPAIMD, the Born-Oppenheimer method [21] (BOMD) is the other common method used to generate the dynamics of nuclei on the ground state energy surface provided by Kohn-Sham density functional theory. Unlike the CPAIMD method which introduces a fictitious dynamics for the expansion coefficients of the KS-states, under BOMD, the density functional (and hence the expansion coefficients of the KS-states) is minimized and then the atoms are evolved using a straightforward symplectic integrator. This leads to a secular growth in the energy. We have added the capability of using BOMD as an alternative for performing simulations in OpenAtom. Use of BOMD impacts the flow diagram in Fig. 2 in the following way: instead of performing phase VIII in every time step, the system is first minimized and then phase VIII is performed.

Method comparison: Both CPAIMD and BOMD methods have been known to be stable and can be used to simulate important scientific phenomena. At any time, an improvement in one method can leap-frog the other as the preferred way to go. The advantage of the BOMD is its simplicity. The disadvantage is that the minimization procedure is truncated at a finite tolerance in practice, which can lead to higher aggregated error.

4 Parallel Optimizations

Parallel implementation of phases described in Sect. 2.1 leads to several communication intensive operations in OpenAtom. In any given phase, several FFTs, section-reductions, and multicasts are performed concurrently. Multi-instance methods exacerbate the situation by increasing the number of occurrences of these operations and by adding communication of their own. As a result, it is important that communication is well orchestrated and task-mapping is performed to maximize the network utilization and reduce the overheads.

4.1   Distance-Aware Mapping

Significant work had been done on mapping OPENATOM to compact the 3D-grid network topology used in systems such as IBM Blue Gene/P [16]. Since the 3D-nature of simulated space (e.g. 3D state grid) matched the 3D-grid of Blue Gene/P's torus, high performing precise mapping schemes were developed to obtain improved performance on those systems. However, the mappings from the past no longer lead to optimal performance because of (1) changes in dimensionality of the networks, e.g. Blue Gene/Q has a 5D-torus, and (2) irregular allocations, e.g. on Cray XE6/XK7 systems, typical allocations are not restricted to an isolated high bisection bandwidth cuboid. Hence, we have developed new schemes that improve upon the old schemes in two ways: portability to a larger set of current supercomputers and less time to compute the mapping.

Separation of Concerns: The main principle underlying the mapping improvements is the separation of logic that decides mapping from assumptions regarding the interconnect topology. For example, the new mapping schemes take decisions based on relative closeness of pairs of processes, but how the closeness is defined and computed is left to the topology manager. This separation enables us to define generic rules of thumb on relative placements of objects of various types with respect to other objects.

Boilerplate Mapping Algorithm: A typical mapping routine for a given chare type consists of three steps: find the available list, reorder/process the list based on the object type, and make assignments. The first step simply queries the topology manager to provide a distance-aware list of available cores/processors. Thereafter, to find suitable candidates among the available cores for the given objects, the available list is either divided among smaller sets or sorted in a particular order using the topology manager. Finally, suitable cores are assigned objects while accounting for load balance and exclusion among various cores. Throughout the process, a highly efficient exclusion list is maintained to down-select cores for mapping remaining objects of the same type or other types.

Distance-Aware Order of Processes: To obtain a list of available cores for an object type, we start with a list of all cores available to the current job. Thereafter, any exclusions defined by the previous mappings of other types of objects are applied. The exclusions are typically useful in assigning to different cores objects of different types that are expected to be active concurrently. In addition, they are used for excluding cores with special tasks, e.g. rank 0 is responsible for control flow management tasks, and is thus given fewer objects. We provide the option to override exclusions either by the user as a configuration parameter or due to lack of sufficient number of cores in the current job.

In the past, for mapping on Blue Gene/P, the ordering of the list was closely tied to the number of chares that host a state in the simulated system. By forcing the number of such chares to be a factor of the number of cores, the mapping was able to divide the available set of cores evenly. Given the isolated cuboidal allocations of Blue Gene/P, the mapping was also able to divide the available set of cores among smaller cuboids and assign them to the states [5], leading to high efficiency communication patterns.

In the new mapping scheme, all the above restrictions have been removed, while preserving the performance. The topology manager orders a given set of cores by making a pass through the set of processors in a topology-aware manner. For making the pass, the available cores are divided among small topologically-close units and ordered accordingly. For example, on Cray's XE6, the traversal is performed along the longest axis using small cubes of size $4 \times 4 \times 4$. The main advantage of such a traversal is the guaranteed topological proximity of the cores that are close in the list. At the same time, communication among a pair of cores, P1, that is reasonably distant from another pair of cores, P2, is less likely to interfere with the communication of the pair P2.

Mapping the States: The two types of state objects, RS and GS, play a central role in the control flow of OPENATOM. Forward and backward FFTs are performed between RS and GS in every iteration. After the forward FFT to RS, a plane-wise reduction on RS is performed to the density objects, which return the result via a multicast to RS. Following the backward FFT to GS, multicast and reductions are performed between GS and pair calculators. Given the plane-based nature of both these operations and the bisection bandwidth requirement of $O(\#states)$ FFTs between RS and GS, it is better to spread RS and GS on the given cores such that communication to/from the planes does not interfere, while the planes use as much bisection bandwidth as possible.

Hence, the mapping code divides the distance-aware ordered list of cores it obtains from the topology manager evenly among the planes of RS/GS using a block-mapping scheme. This mapping does not add any of the cores to the global exclusion list since every core in the system has at least one RS/GS object.

Mapping the Density: Contributions from all the RS objects are combined to create the density for $RhoR$ by a reduction operation. Given the plane-based division of RS, the aggregation is also performed along the planes. Hence, to improve the performance of the reduction, the density planes of $RhoR$ are placed near the cores that host the corresponding RS planes. These cores are added to the exclusion list for mapping the remaining density objects. Other density objects, $RhoG$, $RhoRHart$, and $RhoGHart$, are then evenly spread on cores sorted by their distance from the centroid of the cores that host $RhoR$.

Particle Planes and Pair Calculators: Both types of particle planes, RPP and GPP, are closely tied to the states. The GPP objects are co-located with GS objects since they work on a large amount of common data. The RPP objects are spread across the set of cores that host GS/GPP objects for corresponding plane. This helps improve the performance of FFTs between RPP and GPP.

Finally, to map the pair calculators, a new distance-aware list of cores is obtained from the topology manager and the pair calculators are mapped in that order while maintaining load balance. This scheme works well because it places the pair calculators for a given plane close to where its *GS* objects are mapped.

4.2 Overdecomposed FFTs with Cutoffs

The existing code for performing parallel FFTs in OPENATOM is based on 1D-decomposition of data. Hence, the amount of parallelism available for state and density FFTs are $O(\#states * \#planes)$ and $O(\#planes)$, respectively. In a typical OPENATOM simulation, the number of states is at the most 1000. Each of the states is represented using grids that contain at most $300 \times 300 \times 300$ points. This implies that the maximum parallelism available in state FFTs is $O(300,000)$, but is only $O(300)$ for density FFTs. Thus 1D-decomposition based density FFTs severely limits the scalability of OPENATOM, especially on large machines with many more compute nodes.

Charm-FFT Overview: To eliminate the scaling bottleneck due to density FFTs, we have developed a fully asynchronous Charm++ based FFT library, Charm-FFT. This library allows users to create multiple instances of the library and perform concurrent FFTs using them. Each of the FFT runs in the background as other parts of user code execute, and a callback is invoked when the FFT is complete. The key features of this library are:

1. *2D-decomposition:* Users can define fine-grained 2D-decomposition that increases the amount of available parallelism and improves network utilization.
2. *Cutoff-based smaller grid:* The data grid typically has a cutoff in g-space, e.g. density has a g-space spherical cutoff. Charm-FFT improves performance by avoiding communication and computation of the data beyond the cutoff.
3. *User-defined mapping of library objects:* The placement of objects that constitute the library instance can be defined by the user based on the application's other concurrent communication and placement of other objects.
4. *Overlap with other computational work:* Given the callback-based interface and Charm++'s asynchrony, the FFTs are performed in the background while other application work can be done in parallel.

Charm-FFT Details: The creation of an instance of the library is performed by calling `Charm_createFFT` from any process. The user is required to specify the size of the FFT grid and the desired decomposition. A cutoff and mapping of the FFT objects can also be specified. Optionally, a callback can be specified which is invoked when the distributed creation of the library instance is completed. Internally, three types of Charm++ objects are created: `D1`, `D2`, and `D3`. Each of these objects owns a thin bar (a pencil) of the FFT-grid in one of the dimensions, e.g. in Fig. 3(a), `D1` objects own pencils along Z axis. The decomposition of the FFT-grid among these objects is decided based on the user input.

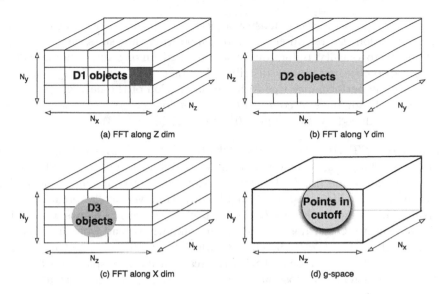

Fig. 3. Charm-FFT: concurrent cutoff-based FFTs with 2D-decomposition.

Typically, D1 objects are associated with the grid in the real-space, while D3 objects are used for the grid in the g-space. The D2 objects are not visible to the user as they are used for the intermediate transpose only. Before executing FFTs, the user is required to inform D1 and D3 objects about the memory where the grid resides by making local API calls in a distributed manner.

When the setup is complete, an FFT can be started on an instance by calling Charm_doForwardFFT or Charm_doBackwardFFT. These calls return immediately without actually performing the FFT, but after registering it with the library. If Charm_doForwardFFT is invoked, the FFTs are performed locally along Z dimension by D1 objects. Following this FFT, any data along Z axis that is beyond the cutoff is ignored, and *only the data within the cutoff is communicated* to D2 (Fig. 3(b)). On D2 objects, FFT along Y dimension is performed which further reduces the FFT-grid to a cylinder of thin bars as shown in Fig. 3(c). This data is communicated to D3 objects, where FFT along X dimension reduces the cylinder to a sphere (Fig. 3(d)). At this point, the user specified callback is invoked informing the application of FFT's completion. The distribution of pencils, which have grid points within the sphere, to D3 objects is performed such that the total number of grid points that are in the sphere are load balanced across D3 objects. For Charm_doBackwardFFT call, these steps are performed in reverse order. Note that if *FFTs are started on multiple instances one after the other, all of them are performed concurrently.*

Adapting OpenAtom to Use Charm-FFT: In order to use Charm-FFT with OPENATOM, a significant fraction of the density object implementation has been rewritten. This is because the decomposition of density objects is tied to the decomposition of the FFT-grid. The integration has provided three benefits:

(1) The decomposition of the density objects is no longer restricted to be a 1D-decomposition. Users can choose a decomposition that suits their system.
(2) The *RS* to density reduction is now divided among finer chunks and is targeted to objects that are distributed among more cores. This is likely to improve the performance due to better utilization of the network.
(3) The significant lines of code (SLOC) count for the control flow of density has been reduced by more than 50 % from $4,198$ to $1,831$.

Mapping of FFT Objects: To make the best use of the 2D-decomposition of density, a new mapping scheme has been developed for the density and Charm-FFT objects. Since the *RhoR* objects are no longer tied to only one plane of *RS*, they are evenly spread among the available cores. However, while spreading them uniformly, we attempt to keep *RhoR* objects close to the *RS* planes with which they communicate. Other density objects are similarly spread while maintaining their proximity to the *RhoR* objects with which they interact. The Charm-FFT objects, D1 and D3, are colocated with the real-space and g-space objects. The D2 objects are assigned in close proximity of the D1 objects they interact with.

4.3   Scaling Multiple Instances

When multiple instances, i.e., Ubers described in Sect. 3.1, are executed concurrently, two additional concerns arise: (1) How should the objects that belong to different Ubers be mapped? (2) What impact does presence of multiple instances have on the performance of OPENATOM? In this section, we explore these issues and discuss how they are addressed in OPENATOM.

   In Sect. 3.1, we have described the implementation of different multi-instance methods. From that description, it is easy to see that inter-Uber communication is infrequent and low volume. Hence, it is preferable to map objects of different Ubers on different cores, so that they do not interfere with each other. We have experimented with two types of mappings based on this idea:

(1) Disjoint Partitions (DPS): In this scheme, the ordered distance-aware list of cores created by the topology manager is divided evenly among the instances using a block-mapping scheme. Given the topologically sorted property of the list, this reduces interference among the intra-Uber communication of different Ubers. This also reduces the number of hops for communication within a Uber.

(2) Interleaved Partitions (IPS): This scheme divides the topologically sorted list of cores among various instances in a round-robin manner. Here, while the intra-Uber communication of different Ubers may interfere, the increased bisection bandwidth may improve the performance of the 3D-FFTs. This scheme may also benefit from overlap of computation time of one Uber with communication of other Ubers since cores connected to a router are assigned to different Ubers.

Performance Comparison: To compare the two schemes, DPS and IPS, we execute the MOF system (Sect. 5) with 2, 4, and 8 Ubers, where each Uber is allocated 2,048 cores of Blue Waters. When only two Ubers are executed, both schemes provide similar performance. However, as the number of Ubers is increased to four and eight, DPS reduces the time per step by up to 31 % and 40 %, respectively in comparison to IPS. From these results, we conclude that avoiding interference among intra-Uber communication of different Ubers is better, and thus DPS is used for all the remaining results in this paper.

Effect of Ubers on Performance: Figure 4b presents the time line view of Projections [17] obtained when OPENATOM is executed with four Ubers on a Blue Gene/Q system for one time step. Each horizontal bar in this figure shows the computation executed on a core (or process) colored using the legend shown in Fig. 4a. It can be observed that a significant fraction of the timeline is colored white, which implies high idle time.

High idle time is observed because the execution of different Ubers is not as synchronized as it should be given their similar workload. As seen in Fig. 4b, this is because the start of the time step in some Ubers is delayed (highlighted in the figure), which in turn is caused by these Ubers waiting on information computed by the multi-instance methods. Longer waits are observed for some Ubers since transmission of such information is blocked by forward progress made by other Ubers that have already received the information. To avoid these delays, we force all Ubers to wait at the end of each time step till all instances have received the data needed to perform the next time step.

Figure 4c shows another type of delay caused by inter-Uber interference. This delay is because, in Charm++, global operations such as broadcasts and reductions are implemented using optimized tree-based construction that spans all cores (as is done in most parallel languages). However, when multiple instances are executed, the global broadcasts and reductions are meant for only a subset of objects on some cores. Such operations may get delayed if intermediate cores, which are not part of the source Uber, are busy performing other work. This inefficiency is removed by replacing global broadcasts and reductions by Charm++'s sections-based operations. Use of these constructs ensures that only participating cores are used for forwarding data during global operations, and thus minimizes aforementioned delays.

After eliminating idle time due to inter-Uber interference, we observe that the small amount of additional work done for the multi-instance methods unexpectedly takes a very long time as highlighted in Fig. 4d. We find two reasons for this: (1) Excessive fine-grained division of work required by multi-instance methods leads to a large number of small-sized broadcasts and reductions, (2) Core 0 is overloaded since it is assigned work both as a member of an Uber and as the multi-instance method coordinator. These issues are solved first by increasing the granularity of the chare array that performs the multi-instance method; this reduces the number of broadcasts and reductions. Second, core 0 is excluded from being assigned work for any Uber.

Figure 4e presents the last performance issue we observe: as core 0 is offloaded, one of the cores in one of the Ubers (which gets one less core than others) gets overloaded with the pair calculator work resulting in some performance

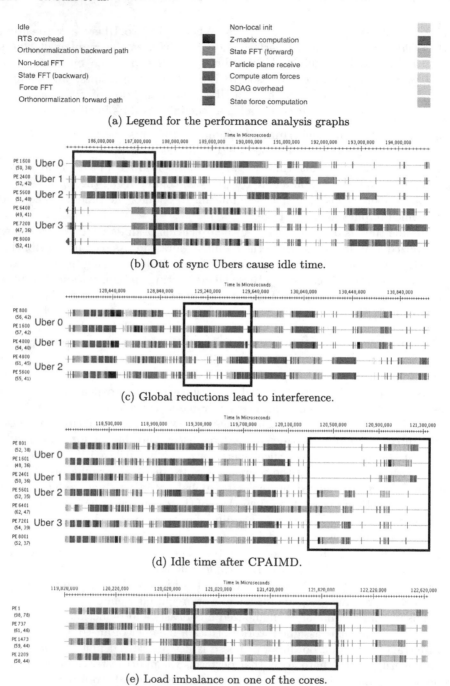

(a) Legend for the performance analysis graphs

(b) Out of sync Ubers cause idle time.

(c) Global reductions lead to interference.

(d) Idle time after CPAIMD.

(e) Load imbalance on one of the cores.

Fig. 4. Multi-instance performance optimization. (a) Legend for the performance analysis. graphs. (b) Out of sync Ubers cause idle time. (c) Global reductions lead to interference. (d) Idle time after CPAIMD. (e) Load imbalance on one of the cores. (Color figure online)

loss. To remove this inefficiency, we allow the affected Uber to place only pair calculators on core 0. This works fine because no other computation overlaps with the computation done by pair calculators.

5   Scaling Results

In this section, we present scaling results obtained by integrating capabilities and optimizations described in Sects. 3 and 4 into OPENATOM. All the experiments have been performed on Blue Waters, a Cray XE6/XK7 system, and Vulcan and Mira, IBM Blue Gene/Q systems. Most experiments were repeated five times to account for runtime variabilities, but only up to 1 % deviation was observed on both types of systems.

We use two systems of scientific interest in these studies: Liquid water and Metal-organic Framework (MOF). Water is a simple system which contains a box of water with 32 molecules. MOF is a more complex larger system used to study suitability of metal-organic frameworks (Fig. 1) for H_2 storage [22]. The MOF system used in this paper is MOF-5 which comprises $Zn_4O(BDC)_3$ (BDC 1,4 benzenedicarboxylate). It contains 424 atoms, 1552 electrons, and 776 KS states. We have found it to be stable at the cutoff of 50 Rydberg, which is used in our simulations. Each state is represented by a $220 \times 220 \times 220$ size grid.

5.1   Performance of Charm-FFT

The first set of results shows the performance of Charm-FFT as a FFT library. To understand the impact of decomposition on the time taken to compute a 3D-FFT, we perform a FFT of a $300 \times 300 \times 300$ size grid on 512 nodes of Blue Gene/Q using different decompositions. For these experiments, the baseline execution time is 76 ms, which is obtained when 1D-decomposition of the grid is performed, i.e., 300 objects are used. In Fig. 5, it can be seen that as we perform finer decomposition of the grid along two dimensions, the time to compute 3D-FFT reduces significantly. The best per-

#Objects	Decomposition	Time (ms)
100	10 × 10	80
300	300 × 1	76
300	75 × 4	69
300	20 × 15	45
400	20 × 20	35
900	30 × 30	24
1600	40 × 40	24
2500	50 × 50	22
3600	60 × 60	23

Fig. 5. FFT on a $300 \times 300 \times 300$ grid.

formance is obtained when the grid is divided among 2,500 objects that are arranged as a 2D grid of size 50×50. In this case, the time to perform FFT is reduced by 70 % in comparison to the baseline. Further decreasing the decomposition granularity leads to excess communication overhead.

Figure 6 (left) demonstrates that the choice of cutoff can have a significant impact on the time to perform FFT. For a grid of size $300 \times 300 \times 300$, up to 3x reduction in execution time can be seen on 512 nodes of Blue Gene/Q. While

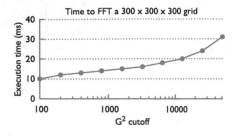
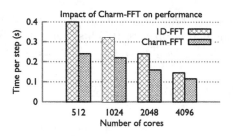

Fig. 6. (left) As the G^2 cutoff decreases, time to FFT reduces. (right) Charm-FFT improves the time per step of OPENATOM by up to 40 %.

cutoffs as low as 100 are unrealistic from a scientific perspective, G^2 values that eliminate as many as half the grid points are common. In Fig. 6 (left), the x-axis value of 6,400 represents this common scenario, where 41 % reduction in execution time is observed.

Finally, in Fig. 6 (right), we present the impact of using Charm-FFT in OPE-NATOM for the 32-molecule Water system scaled to core counts that are at the parallelization limits of the Water system. For most of the core counts, Charm-FFT is able to increase the available parallelism and reduces the time per step by 30–40 %. For core counts less than 400, we find that the performance of the default version of OPENATOM matches closely with the version that uses Charm-FFT. This is expected since for small core counts, the default 1D-decomposition is able to utilize most of the network bandwidth.

5.2   Single Instance Execution

In this section, we present performance results for simulating a single instance of MOF with OPENATOM. Figure 7 shows strong scaling results when the core count is increased from 512 to 32,768 on Blue Waters. It can be seen that the time per step decreases significantly from 11.7 s to less than a second as more cores are used. Our topology-aware mapping scheme consistently provides a performance boost of 16–32 % on all system sizes. Similar improvements are obtained on Mira where three hardware threads are utilized on every core. Best execution time of 0.67s per time step is obtained on 32,768 cores of Blue Waters for the MOF system which has only 776 electronic states. Note that topology aware mappings are computed once at the beginning of long running simulations. Hence, overhead due to such computations is minimal. For example, for a typical science run of several hours on 1,024 nodes, computing the mapping takes less than 3.2 s.

In Fig. 8, good scalability is shown for BOMD computation as we scale from 4,096 cores to 16,384 cores on Blue Gene/Q. Use of topology-aware mapping outperforms the default mapping by up to 32 % in these cases. In fact, with topology-aware mapping, 74 % reduction in time per step is obtained when the number of cores is increased by four times, i.e., perfect scaling is observed. These results strongly indicate that OPENATOM is able to provide scalable support to different simulation methods by exploiting their common characteristics.

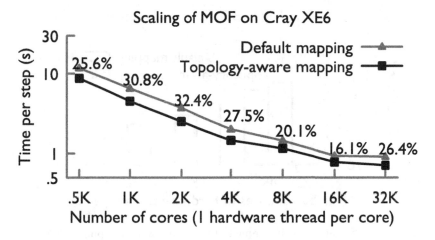

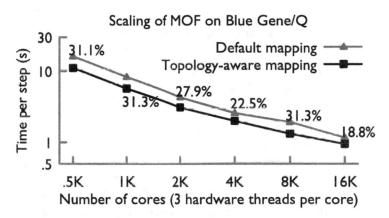

Fig. 7. OpenAtom shows good scaling on both Cray XE6 and Blue Gene/Q. Benefit of topology aware mapping is significant as shown by the % values. (Color figure online)

5.3 Scalability of Ubers

Now, we present performance results for simulating multiple instances of MOF on Blue Gene/Q. As a representative of multi-instance methods, we use the Path Integral method (CPAIMD_PI) in these experiments. Three configurations with 8, 16, and 32 Ubers are strong scaled from 8,192 cores to 262,144 cores, where three hardware threads are used on each core. For each of these configurations, Fig. 9 shows that an efficiency of 52 % is obtained when the core count is increased by 8× from the smallest configuration executed. For example, the 32 beads simulations observe a 4.2× speed up when core count is increased from 32,768 to 262,144. Time per step as low as 1.7s is obtained for executing 32 beads on 262K cores of Blue Gene/Q. For other configurations, time per step close to one second is obtained by making use of multiple hardware threads available on the system.

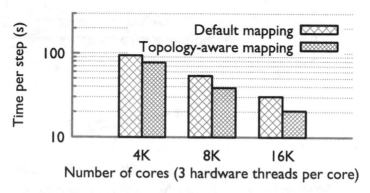

Fig. 8. Perfect scaling and positive impact of topology-aware mapping is demonstrated for BOMD computation.

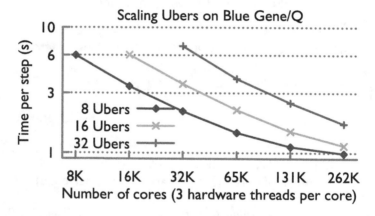

Fig. 9. By exploiting Uber infrastructure and topology-aware mapping, OPENATOM enables strong scaling of Path Integrals up to a quarter million cores on Blue Gene/Q. These are representative results that should extend to other multi-instance methods such as the k-points, Parallel Tempering, and Spin. (Color figure online)

In fact, due to the communication intensive nature of these simulations, one out of every three threads is dedicated to advancing communication asynchronously, while the other two threads perform computation.

6   Conclusion

In this paper, we have presented the capabilities and scalability of OPENATOM. New science capabilities, viz. multi-instance methods and BOMD, have been added to OPENATOM recently and are described in this paper. Positive impact of optimization techniques, namely distance-aware mapping, Uber indexing, and overdecomposed 3D-FFTs with spherical cutoff, has also been shown on two production HPC platforms, IBM Blue Gene/Q and Cray XE6. By leveraging these techniques, we have demonstrated that OPENATOM provides efficient strong scaling up to 32,768 cores for MOF, an important science system with only a few hundred atoms. Finally, a time per step of $1.7s$ and strong scaling up to 262,144 cores have been shown for multi-instance scientific simulations. These results strongly suggest that OPENATOM is a highly scalable simulation code with diverse capabilities.

Acknowledgments. This research is partly funded by the NSF SI2-SSI grant titled Collaborative Research: Scalable, Extensible, and Open Framework for Ground and Excited State Properties of Complex Systems with ID ACI 13-39715. This research is also part of the Blue Waters sustained-petascale computing project, which is supported by the National Science Foundation (award number OCI 07-25070) and the state of Illinois. Blue Waters is a joint effort of the University of Illinois at Urbana-Champaign and its National Center for Supercomputing Applications.

This research used resources of the Argonne Leadership Computing Facility at Argonne National Laboratory, which is supported by the Office of Science of the U.S. Department of Energy under contract DE-AC02-06CH11357. This research also used computer time on Livermore Computing's high performance computing resources, provided under the M&IC Program.

References

1. Acun, B., Gupta, A., Jain, N., Langer, A., Menon, H., Mikida, E., Ni, X., Robson, M., Sun, Y., Totoni, E., Wesolowski, L., Kale, L.: Parallel programming with migratable objects: Charm++ in practice. In: SC (2014)
2. Agarwal, T., Sharma, A., Kalé, L.V.: Topology-aware task mapping for reducing communication contention on large parallel machines. In: Proceedings of IEEE International Parallel and Distributed Processing Symposium 2006, April 2006
3. Alam, S., Bekas, C., Boettiger, H., Curioni, A., Fourestey, G., Homberg, W., Knobloch, M., Laino, T., Maurer, T., Mohr, B., Pleiter, D., Schiller, A., Schulthess, T., Weber, V.: Early experiences with scientific applications on the IBM Blue Gene/Q supercomputer. IBM J. Res. Dev. **57**(1/2), 14:1–14:9 (2013). doi:10.1147/JRD.2012.2234331
4. Bhatele, A.: Automating topology aware mapping for supercomputers. Ph.D. thesis, Department of Computer Science, University of Illinois, August 2010. http://hdl.handle.net/2142/16578
5. Bhatele, A., Bohm, E., Kale, L.V.: Optimizing communication for Charm++ applications by reducing network contention. Concurr. Computat.: Pract. Exp. **23**(2), 211–222 (2011)
6. Bohm, E., Bhatele, A., Kale, L.V., Tuckerman, M.E., Kumar, S., Gunnels, J.A., Martyna, G.J.: Fine grained parallelization of the Car-Parrinello ab initio MD method on Blue Gene/L. IBM J. Res. Dev.: Appl. Massively Parallel Syst. **52**(1/2), 159–174 (2008)
7. Car, R., Parrinello, M.: Unified approach for molecular dynamics and density functional theory. Phys. Rev. Lett. **55**(22), 2471 (1985)

8. Carloni, P., Bloechl, P., Parrinello, M.: Electronic structure of the Cu, Zn super-oxide dimutase active site and its interactions with the substrate. J. Phys. Chem. **99**, 1338–1348 (1995)
9. cpmd.org. http://www.cpmd.org/
10. Earl, D.J., Deem, M.: Parallel tempering: theory, applications, and new perspectives. Phys. Chem. Chem. Phys. **7**, 3910–3916 (2005)
11. Brugé, F., Bernasconi, M., Michele, P.: Ab initio simulation of rotational dynamics of solvated ammonium ion in water. J. Am. Chem. Soc. **121**, 10883–10888 (1999)
12. Fitch, B.G., Rayshubskiy, A., Eleftheriou, M., Ward, T.J.C., Giampapa, M., Pitman, M.C.: Blue matter: approaching the limits of concurrency for classical molecular dynamics. In: SC 2006: Proceedings of the 2006 ACM/IEEE Conference on Supercomputing. ACM, New York (2006)
13. Gygi, F., Draeger, E.W., Schulz, M., de Supinski, B.R., Gunnels, J.A., Austel, V., Sexton, J.C., Franchetti, F., Kral, S., Ueberhuber, C.W., Lorenz, J.: Large-scale electronic structure calculations of high-Z metals on the BlueGene/L platform. In: Proceedings of the 2006 ACM/IEEE Conference on Supercomputing, SC 2006. ACM, New York (2006). http://doi.acm.org/10.1145/1188455.1188502
14. Gygi, F., Draeger, E.W., Schulz, M., Supinski, B.R.D., Gunnels, J.A., Austel, V., Sexton, J.C., Franchetti, F., Kral, S., Ueberhuber, C., Lorenz, J.: Large-scale electronic structure calculations of high-Z metals on the Blue Gene/L platform. In: Proceedings of the International Conference in Supercomputing. ACM Press (2006)
15. Hoefler, T., Snir, M.: Generic topology mapping strategies for large-scale parallel architectures. In: Proceedings of the International Conference on Supercomputing, ICS 2011, pp. 75–84. ACM, New York (2011)
16. IBM Blue Gene Team: Overview of the IBM Blue Gene/P project. IBM J. Res. Dev. **52**(1/2) (2008)
17. Kale, L.V., Zheng, G., Lee, C.W., Kumar, S.: Scaling applications to massively parallel machines using projections performance analysis tool. Future Gener. Comput. Syst. Spec. Issue: Large-Scale Syst. Perform. Model. Anal. **22**, 347–358 (2006)
18. Kumar, S., Shi, Y., Bohm, E., Kale, L.V.: Scalable, fine grain, parallelization of the Car-Parrinello ab initio molecular dynamics method. Technical report, UIUC, Department of Computer Science (2005)
19. Lee, H.S., Tuckerman, M., Martyna, G.: Efficient evaluation of nonlocal pseudopotentials via Euler exponential spline interpolation. Chem. Phys. Chem. **6**, 1827–1835 (2005)
20. Marx, D., Parrinello, M.: Ab initio path integral molecular dynamics. Z. Phys. **B 95**, 143–144 (1994)
21. Payne, M.C., Teter, M.P., Allan, D.C., Arias, T.A., Joannopoulos, J.D.: Iterative minimization techniques for ab initio total-energy calculations: molecular dynamics and conjugate gradients. Rev. Mod. Phys. **64**, 1045 (1992)
22. Rosi, N.L., Eckert, J., Eddaoudi, M., Vodak, D.T., Kim, J., O'Keeffe, M., Yaghi, O.M.: Hydrogen storage in microporous metal-organic frameworks. Science **300**(5622), 1127–1129 (2003). http://www.sciencemag.org/content/300/5622/1127.abstract
23. Vadali, R.V., Shi, Y., Kumar, S., Kale, L.V., Tuckerman, M.E., Martyna, G.J.: Scalable fine-grained parallelization of plane-wave-based ab initio molecular dynamics for large supercomputers. J. Compt. Chem. **25**(16), 2006–2022 (2004)

SPRITE: A Fast Parallel SNP Detection Pipeline

Vasudevan Rengasamy$^{(\boxtimes)}$ and Kamesh Madduri

The Pennsylvania State University, University Park, PA, USA
{vxr162,madduri}@psu.edu

Abstract. We present SPRITE, a new high-performance data analysis pipeline for detecting single nucleotide polymorphisms (SNPs) in the human genome. A SNP detection pipeline for next-generation sequencing data uses several software tools, including tools for read alignment, processing alignment output, and SNP identification. We target end-to-end scalability and I/O efficiency in SPRITE by merging tools in this pipeline and eliminating redundancies. For a benchmark human whole-genome sequencing data set, SPRITE takes less than 50 min on 16 nodes of the TACC Stampede supercomputer. A key component of our optimized pipeline is PARSNIP, a new parallel method and software tool for SNP detection. We find that the quality of results obtained by PARSNIP (sensitivity and precision using high-confidence variant calls as ground truth) is comparable to state-of-the-art SNP-calling software. A prototype implementation of SPRITE is available at sprite-psu.sourceforge.net.

1 Introduction

In this work, we consider the pervasive *genetic variation detection* workflow in biomedical informatics. The goal of this workflow is to automatically determine genetic variations present in the genome of an individual (called the *donor*), by comparing it to a *reference* genome. SNPs are nucleotide differences at a single position and account for nearly 90 % of the total variations. Detecting SNPs with high accuracy plays a very important role in identifying disease risk, studying drug efficacy [31], etc. SNP detection using current state-of-the-art tools can take more than a day of sequential compute time, and the pipeline is typically I/O bound. In this paper, we focus on improving end-to-end efficiency and parallel scaling of this pipeline, and design new hybrid parallel algorithms and software (SPRITE, comprised of PRUNE, SAMPA, PARSNIP). The end-to-end running time of SPRITE on the Stampede supercomputer is 11.7 hours on a single compute node, and 48 min on 16 nodes, for a realistic input data set. In comparison, the end-to-end time using current state-of-the-art tools on a single compute node is 23 hours, and so we achieve a speedup of 1.97× and 28.7× using single node and 16 nodes respectively. We also show that the resulting SNP detection quality is comparable to two state-of-the-art variant detection pipelines. Further, we create SPRITE$^+$, an in-memory version that does not generate intermediate files. SPRITE$^+$ can be executed on just a few compute nodes (requiring about 105 GB aggregate main memory for the human genome).

© Springer International Publishing Switzerland 2016
J.M. Kunkel et al. (Eds.): ISC High Performance 2016, LNCS 9697, pp. 159–177, 2016.
DOI: 10.1007/978-3-319-41321-1_9

2   Background: Variant Detection Pipelines

The genome sequences of any two (human) individuals are highly similar. However, the small percentage of genetic variation (variants) is believed to have important biological and medical implications. Identifying an individual's single nucleotide genetic variants has become a standard first step in many biological and biomedical applications. In this section, we describe the three key steps in the workflow to detect genetic variants,

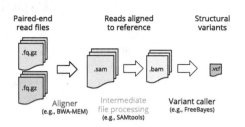

Fig. 1. A simplified view of computational stages in a SNP detection pipeline.

shown in Fig. 1, and mention prior approaches to exploit parallelism.

Alignment. The output of a DNA sequencer is a set of *reads*. A read is a short segment of the genome whose sequence is known, but whose location in the genome is not known. The first step of this pipeline, *Alignment*, refers to identifying the location of the donor genome's reads, by using an index built from the known reference genome. Alignment is the most computationally intensive task in the workflow. This step takes FASTQ (FQ) files containing the reads as input and produces output in the Sequence Alignment/Map (SAM) format [17].

There are several approaches to aligning reads against a reference genome. Usually, an alignment algorithm uses an index of the reference genome. The FM-index [7] is the index of choice for the most popular aligners of sequencing data [13,15,16,19]. It can be used to find if a query substring occurs in the reference in time independent of the length of the reference. The FM-index is a full-text index which is based on the Burrows-Wheeler transform [1,2] developed for text compression. An alternate to the FM-index is a hash-based index. In this approach, a hash table is created mapping all small strings (called seeds) to their locations in the reference (or, sometimes, in the reads). While initially popular [18,29], hash-based approaches have largely been replaced by the FM-index approach due to its superior performance.

Most alignment software tools exploit parallelism on a single node through multithreading [11,15], but do not directly support multi-node parallelism. For multi-node scaling, the coarse-grained strategy that is typically followed is to split the input gzipped FASTQ files into multiple equally-sized files, and concurrently execute the binary on each read partition file. The tool pMap [26], for instance, enables multi-node execution of different aligners such as BWA [16], SOAP [19], Bowtie [13], in this manner. Peters et al. [24] introduce the pBWA framework, which uses a master-slave approach to support multi-node execution of BWA.

Intermediate File Processing. In this step, SAM files are converted to a binary file format called Binary Alignment/Map (BAM). BAM files store the same information as SAM files, but using compressed binary-encoded records. BAM files are also sorted according to the alignment position, merged and indexed. SAMtools [17] and Picard [25] are two widely-used tools for SAM/BAM file processing. Both these tools support multithreaded execution for some of their SAM/BAM file processing stages.

Variant Calling. A variant caller takes a single BAM file as input and generates a list of variants (SNPs; Insertions and Deletions or *indels*). Roughly, this is done by a left-to-right scan of the BAM file. Locations where all alignments do not agree with the reference nucleotide are statistically analyzed to determine if the alternate nucleotide is due to a variant in the donor, or due to a sequencing error. The output of this step is a text file in the Variant Calling Format (VCF), containing a single line for every variant. While there are further downstream filtering and analysis steps that are often performed after variant calling, they are computationally less intensive, and so we do not discuss them here.

The variant callers in SAMtools [14] and FreeBayes [8] use a Bayesian statistical framework in their variant calling procedure. GATK [5] is another popular variant caller using a multistage variant calling strategy. It first performs *local realignment* around Indels and a routine called *base quality score recalibration* to output analysis-ready BAM output. In the next phase, GATK emits raw variants by discovering all sites with statistical evidence for the presence of an alternate allele. Finally, the raw variant calls are integrated with external data, such as known variants, to separate true variants from false positives.

Nielsen et al. [23] review various SNP-calling methods and classify them as either methods based on counting nucleotides or as probabilistic methods. Counting-based methods perform well when the sequencing *depth of coverage* is high ($> 20\times$). Our SNP detection algorithm PARSNIP is a counting-based method, and we show that its accuracy is comparable to probabilistic methods, for a benchmark data set with $50\times$ coverage. Liu et al. [21] evaluate the accuracy of four variant callers (SAMtools, GATK, glftools2 [10], and Atlas2 [3]) and observe that GATK often outperforms other methods for various objective metrics.

End-to-End Pipelines and Benchmarking. There are several recently developed variant detection pipelines using different tool combinations for the pipeline stages. SpeedSeq [4] uses BWA-MEM to perform alignment, SAM-BLASTER [6] to mark duplicates and extract discordant reads and split reads, Sambamba [30] for sorting the records, and FreeBayes to call variants. It supports single-node parallelism through multithreading and its speedup is mainly due to in-memory duplicate removal and sorting. BALSA [22] is an extension of the GPU-based alignment software SOAP3-dp [20], and performs read quality control, alignment, base score recalibration, de-duplication and realignment in memory. Therefore, it achieves high single-node performance. Churchill [12] is a variant detection pipeline using BWA-MEM for alignment, Picard for alignment output processing, and GATK to call variants. Churchill divides the reference genome into equally-sized regions, so that reads aligning to individual regions can be assigned to different nodes in order to improve scalability. The Isaac [27] pipeline requires high-memory compute nodes and supports multithreaded parallelism. In this paper, we perform direct comparisons of SPRITE to SpeedSeq and a reference pipeline constructed using state-of-the-art tools. We were unable to run all steps in Churchill and BALSA to completion for the data sets we evaluated. The reference pipeline and SpeedSeq outperform Isaac on the data sets we looked at.

There has been recent work to identify high-confidence variant calls that can be used to evaluate the accuracy of various pipelines. Zook et al. [33] develop a benchmark data set of SNP and Indel calls for the NA12878 human genome. They integrate variant calls using 14 data sets from five sequencing technologies, seven aligners, and 3 variant callers. SMASH [32] is another benchmarking effort consisting of synthetic and real genome data sets, and a set of variants for each data set.

3   SPRITE: Algorithms and Implementation Details

We now discuss our new SNP-calling pipeline SPRITE and explain the rationale behind creating new modules. SPRITE is made up of three tools, PRUNE, SAMPA, and PARSNIP, corresponding to the three key steps of alignment, intermediate file processing, and variant calling, discussed in the previous section. Figure 2 shows the pipeline stages. Note that the intermediate file formats have changed in this case, but we still work with the

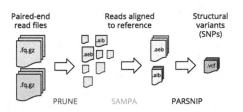

Fig. 2. The SPRITE pipeline with the new PRUNE, SAMPA, and PARSNIP tools. Note the new aeb/aib file formats used by SAMPA.

restriction of using FASTQ files as input and generating VCF-formatted output files. Our pipeline is designed to exploit both shared- and distributed-memory parallelism as much as possible. We use MPI for inter-node parallelism and POSIX threads within each node for exploiting shared-memory parallelism.

3.1   PRUNE: Alignment Parallelization

PRUNE is based on the BWA-MEM [15] aligner. We describe key changes to support multi-node parallelism and reduce I/O in subsequent stages of SPRITE.

Virtual Read Partitioning. In SPRITE, we do not explicitly partition reads and create smaller FQ files. This is the strategy used in pMap [26] and Churchill [12]. Instead, we create an index file in which we store offsets to *read* *blocks* within the original FQ file. We do not need to read the entire file in order to determine the offsets: if l is the read length (in bytes) and B is the desired block size, then finding the offset for read block i requires accessing the file roughly at the location $4Bli$, reading until the start of the next read, and writing the offset to the index file. This divides the FQ file into approximately equally-sized chunks. For a full human data set, this read partitioning completes in a few seconds on uncompressed FQ files, and we choose a block size B ensuring good load balance.

Hybrid Parallelism. We exploit hybrid MPI and pthreads parallelism in PRUNE to scale BWA-MEM across multiple nodes. Each read block is further partitioned across multiple threads within a process. The reference sequence is comprised of multiple *contigs* (or contiguous sequence without gaps), and there are about 100 contigs of different lengths in the reference human genome. Each MPI process creates a separate output file for each contig. This reduces the need for frequent inter-node communication and simplifies the other steps of SPRITE.

Exact and Inexact Alignment Records. We develop a new intermediate alignment output format that is based on inspecting the CIGAR string field in a SAM record. Our format classifies alignment records as being *exact* or *inexact*. A concatenation of these records results in the AEB (Alignment Exact Binary) and AIB (Alignment Inexact Binary) files indicated in Fig. 2. Creating separate files for exact and inexact alignments has the following benefits:

- AEB records require much less memory when compared to AIB records, since they do not require a CIGAR string. Since more than 90 % of the reads fall in the AEB category for high read depth data sets, separating the two types of records results in a significant output file size reduction. For instance, for the NA12878 data set used in all our experiments, the size of the SAM file created by BWA-MEM aligner is 448 GB, and the combined sizes of all exact and inexact alignment files created by PRUNE sums to 54 GB, which is a 88 % reduction in output size.
- Exact alignment records do not have any insertions, deletions, or soft/hard clipping, and as a result, are easier to process downstream.

We list the fields present in AEB and AIB records in Table 1. The fields #CigarOps and CigarStr are not needed for AEB records, since #CigarOps is 1, and CigarStr is lM for all AEB records (l is the read length). We restrict the maximum number of CIGAR operations to 10 per read in order to reduce the size of AIB output files. This does not impact SNP detection accuracy, since only a tiny fraction of reads have CIGAR strings with more than 10 CIGAR operations.

An upper bound on the number of AEB and AIB files to be generated is known beforehand. We do not store unaligned reads and zero quality alignments, and this reduces the file sizes for subsequent stages.

Table 1. Fields present in *Exact* and *Inexact* alignment records.

Field	Exact Alignment	Inexact Alignment	Size (Bytes)
Position	✓	✓	4
Flag	✓	✓	2
MapQuality	✓	✓	1
Sequence	✓	✓	30
ReadLength	✓	✗	1
#CigarOps	✗	✓	1
CigarStr	✗	✓	20

3.2 SAMPA: Intermediate File Processing

Once alignment completes, the AEB and AIB records are sorted according to the alignment position. The primary goal of sorting is to order reads for SNP calling. As the records aligning to different reference contigs are written to different output files in PRUNE, we can now sort records of each contig concurrently. This is not the case if a SAM file is created, and this is one of the reasons why the sort and index steps in the SAMtools software are time-consuming.

We use MPI-based parallelization for this step, with each process sorting alignment output files corresponding to a set of contigs. Our algorithm called SAMPA partitions alignment files among MPI tasks such that each MPI task gets approximately an equal number of alignment records, and all alignment files corresponding to a contig are processed by a single MPI task.

The time taken per MPI task by the sort step is linear in the number of AEB/AIB records assigned to the MPI process. In the first stage, SAMPA reads the alignment output files and counts the number of reads aligned to each position of a reference contig. Then, a prefix sum computation gives the position (in the sorted output file) of the first record corresponding to each alignment position. In the second stage, the position in the output file for each record is computed by using the calculated offset, and the records are written to an output buffer at that position. The output buffer is finally written to disk after processing all records.

In comparison to the SAMtools sort, our approach is done entirely in-memory. Hence, it is significantly faster. If alignment output files corresponding to a single contig are distributed across different MPI tasks, the sorted output of all such tasks have to be merged in a subsequent step. We avoid this by assigning each contig to a single task. However, doing so limits scalability, as the maximum number of MPI tasks is limited by the number of contigs in a reference genome. Due to in-memory sorting, memory becomes a bottleneck as the number of MPI tasks per node increases. Each MPI task sorts one contig at a time. The maximum memory required depends on the longest contig and the number of reads aligning to that contig. For the NA12878 data set, we require 5.5 GB to process the longest contig.

3.3   PARSNIP: Parallel SNP Detection

We now discuss our PARSNIP counting-based SNP detection algorithm and related optimizations. The inputs to this algorithm are the sorted binary alignment records (AEB and AIB records created using SAMPA) and the reference set of contigs. The output of the PARSNIP algorithm is a file containing SNP records in the VCF format. The output specifies the SNP position in a contig, the reference nucleotide and the alternate allele, a quality score assigned to the SNP call, and values for parameters used as quality filters. Our work currently considers just SNPs, and we do not yet support indel or other complex structural variation detection. Hence, we are able to modify the intermediate steps so that the input to PARSNIP is in an easy-to-parse format.

The key data structure used in our algorithm is a frequency table (denoted as $\mathcal{F}$). This array-based tabular representation is shown in Fig. 3. Each entry in this table corresponds to a single position in the reference contig and stores the number of occurrences of each type of base, the read depth at that position, and the number of alternate bases occurring in forward strand and reverse strand.

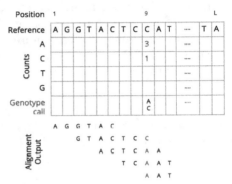

Fig. 3. Organization of the frequency table $\mathcal{F}$ used in PARSNIP.

While processing each AEB record, l consecutive entries in $\mathcal{F}$ starting from the alignment position of the read sequence are updated such that, in each of the table entries, the base count and the read depth are incremented by 1. Note that the CIGAR operation M (Match) indicates matches as well as single base flips, and so all read bases in the matched positions need not actually match with the corresponding bases in the reference sequence.

AIB records are processed by iterating through the CIGAR operations. If the operation is *Match*, the base count and depth fields of $\mathcal{F}$ are incremented for the matched positions, similar to the AEB case described previously. If the operation is *Deletion*, then the depth field alone is incremented for these positions, since it indicates a gap character in these positions.

Hybrid Parallelization. We use MPI and pthreads to parallelize PARSNIP. PARSNIP proceeds by assigning a set of contigs to each MPI process such that each process gets approximately an equal number of alignment records to process. After this initial step, each MPI process performs the following three tasks for each contig assigned to it: (1) Update $\mathcal{F}$ using AEB records, (2) Update $\mathcal{F}$ using AIB records, and (3) Call SNPs using $\mathcal{F}$. Tasks 1 and 3 are much more expensive than task 2, due to the low fraction of AIB records. We parallelize these two tasks using pthreads. For task 1, each thread is assigned a contiguous portion of the sorted AEB file to process. Let s_i be the alignment position of the first record assigned to thread i. Each thread processes the records assigned to it until it encounters the first record R satisfying the condition,

$$\text{AlignPosition}(R) + \text{ReadLength}(R) \geq s_{i+1},$$

where AlignPosition(R) is the position at which R is aligned to the reference, and ReadLength(R) gives the read length of R. This prevents different threads from modifying same locations in $\mathcal{F}$, thus avoiding race conditions. The records skipped in this manner are processed sequentially. For task 3, each thread calls SNPs present in a distinct region of contigs and hence, there is no race condition.

$\mathcal{F}$ is the major memory-consuming data structure. With PARSNIP, each MPI task requires only the current contig's frequency table $\mathcal{F}$ to be in memory. For the *hg19* human reference genome, the longest contig length is around 250 million base pairs, corresponding to the contig *chr1*. A row in $\mathcal{F}$, corresponding to one position of the reference contig, requires 28 bytes. So the largest contig requires approximately 7 GB memory, which would be the maximum memory required by any MPI process.

Filters. SNP calling requires applying filters to each entry of the table $\mathcal{F}$. Table 2 shows the filters used by PARSNIP and their default settings. A SNP is reported only when it passes all filters.

Table 2. PARSNIP SNP filters.

Filter	Description	Default setting
DP	Read depth	> 1
AAC	Alternate allele count	> 1
MQ	Average mapping quality of alternate allele	20
AAF	Fraction of alternate allele count to total read depth	20 %
SB	Strand bias	> 0

The filter *SB* filters out those SNPs which occur predominantly in either the forward or reverse strand, but not both. Values of SB ranges from 0 to 1, with 0 indicating that an alternate allele occurs in only one type of strand, and 1 indicating equal occurrence in both strand types. The rest of the filters are commonly-used in other tools as well.

4   SPRITE⁺: An In-Memory Version of SPRITE

To avoid I/O overheads between stages of the SPRITE pipeline, we have developed an in-memory version of SPRITE called SPRITE⁺. Our aim is to generate VCF file containing SNPs from input FASTQ files in a single step without creating intermediate files, as shown in Fig. 4.

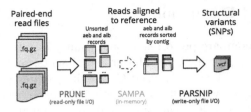

Fig. 4. SPRITE pipeline with in-memory processing.

Changes to PRUNE. Instead of writing AEB and AIB output records to disk, we modified PRUNE to store the alignment records in memory. Each thread within a MPI process has two buffers (*AEBBuffer, AIBBuffer*) for each contig, and all the buffers are expanded dynamically as required. Each thread uses separate buffers in order to avoid contention. Separate buffer for each contig enables independent processing of alignment records for each contig during the subsequent steps.

Intermediate Communication. PARSNIP requires all alignment records corresponding to a contig to be processed by the same MPI process. So, alignment records generated by all processes for a particular contig have to be transferred to a single node. Communication involves three stages:

1. Each process obtains the total number of AEB and AIB records present in all processes for each contig. Let *AlSize* denote the array containing the total number of alignment records for each contig.
2. Each process determines the set of contigs it should process by sorting the *AlSize* array and dividing it into P parts using recursive bisection.
3. Each process receives the alignment records for the contigs assigned to it from all other processes using the MPI_Alltoallv collective call.

Sort and SNP Calling. Once all processes receive the alignment records for the contigs assigned to them, the records are sorted according to the alignment positions using an in-place sort. Once sorted, each process invokes hybrid-parallel PARSNIP and outputs VCF files containing SNP calls.

For the NA12878 data set, SPRITE$^+$ requires 104 GB for single node execution, 137 GB per node for 2 nodes, 68.4 GB per node for 4 nodes, 34.3 GB per node for 8 nodes, and so on. The memory increase from 1 to 2 node run is due to the additional send/receive buffers needed for node count greater than 1. Hence, for systems with limited memory per node, SPRITE$^+$ can be run using larger node counts, since the memory required per node decreases with increasing node counts. The memory bottleneck can be substantially reduced by splitting the communication stage into multiple steps, each step involving transferring a single contig's alignment records to the appropriate MPI task.

5   Results and Discussion

In this section, we compare performance and quality results of our new SPRITE pipeline to two other pipelines. For all our experiments, we used the Stampede supercomputer at the Texas Advanced Computing Center (TACC). Stampede is a Dell Linux cluster with 6400+ Dell PowerEdge server nodes. Each node has two 8-core Intel Xeon E5 (Sandy Bridge) processors and an Intel Xeon Phi coprocessor (MIC architecture). We use the Lustre-based Scratch file system for file I/O. We do not use the Xeon Phi coprocessor. Each compute node has 32 GB DDR3 memory.

Table 3. Software tools used in experimental study.

Tool	Version	Purpose
BWA	0.7.12	BWT-based Aligner
SAMtools	1.1	SAM file to BAM file, sorting and merging BAM files
GATK	v3.2.2	Call variants using HaplotypeCaller tool
SpeedSeq	0.0.3b	Variant detection pipeline
vcftools	0.1.14	Filter out SNPs present in high confidence regions
vcflib		Convert complex variants to SNPs and INDELs
RTG Tools	3.5.2	Compare VCF files

Table 3 mentions the list of software tools used in our work along with their versions. We report performance results with the Illumina platinum genome sequence data set NA12878 in this paper. We have also experimented with other data sets, and please refer to the longer technical report version [28] for more details. The NA12878 data set was sequenced to 50× depth on an Illumina HiSeq 2000 system. We use the human genome version 19 (hg19) as the reference.

5.1   PRUNE Parallel Scaling

Figure 5 shows PRUNE's scalability for aligning reads in the NA12878 dataset when going from 1 compute node up to 32 nodes. For our multi-node experiments, we use 1 MPI process per node and 16 threads per process. We see that the throughput of PRUNE (measured in Mbp/s, million of bases aligned per second) increases almost linearly with MPI task counts. The fraction of I/O to compute time remains nearly constant (about 17%) across runs using 1 to 32 nodes, due to the high I/O bandwidth to the shared scratch filesystem of the Stampede system. The near-linear scaling indicates that our virtual read partitioning strategy results in good load balance. We chose the block size B to be around 5 million reads. We have run strong-scaling experiments up to 128 nodes (2048 cores) and observed good parallel efficiencies for PRUNE.

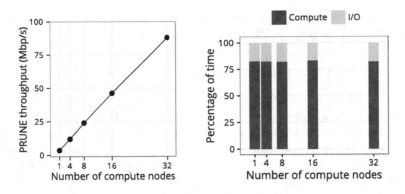

Fig. 5. PRUNE scales almost linearly with the number of compute nodes on Stampede. Both Compute and I/O time reduce with increasing parallelism.

5.2 SAMPA and PARSNIP Parallel Scaling

Figure 6 shows SAMPA's scalability across multiple nodes, and PARSNIP's scalability within a node and across nodes. The experiments are run using 1 process per node up to 16 nodes for multi-node experiments. With PARSNIP, we experiment with up to 16-way thread concurrency. Since all the reads mapping to a contig are assigned to a single MPI process, and since the majority of the reads map to only 23 contigs (out of 93), it becomes more difficult to perform fine-grained load balancing among MPI processes as the number of MPI processes increases. This load imbalance results in a decrease in speedup for SAMPA and PARSNIP when using more than 4 compute nodes.

SAMPA's parallel speedup is about 11× for 16 MPI processes. SAMPA's execution time is 615 s and 57 s for single-task and 16-way parallel runs, respectively.

The third plot in Fig. 6 shows the intra-node scaling characteristics of PARSNIP for the largest contig in hg19, *chr1*. It can be seen that just the compute time scales well up to 12 cores. For higher number of cores (> 8), I/O time dominates the overall time, and hence the overall speedup does increase beyond 8 cores. For *chr1*, PARSNIP's execution time is 52 s, of which I/O time corresponds

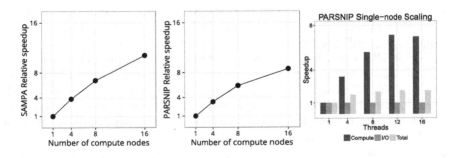

Fig. 6. SAMPA and PARSNIP scaling on Stampede: NA12878 data set.

to 20 s. Using 16 cores, the total time drops to 24.6 s, with I/O still taking 20 s. Parallel I/O for this stage is left to future work.

5.3   End-to-End Pipeline Execution

In this section, we compare the single-node execution time of SPRITE to two other pipelines supporting shared-memory parallelism. The tools used by individual pipelines for different stages are given in Table 4. RefPipeline is a pipeline we have put together using popular state-of-the-art tools for each stage. This conforms to "GATK best practices" [9] and the tools used are very popular in the bioinformatics community. In RefPipeline, all stages except SAM-to-BAM conversion are done using 16 threads. SAM-to-BAM conversion lacks multithreading support and is performed using a single thread.

Table 4. Tools used in each pipeline.

Stage	RefPipeline	SpeedSeq	SPRITE
Alignment	BWA-MEM 0.7.12	BWA-MEM v0.7.12	PRUNE
Alignment Output processing	SAMtools-1.1	SAMBLASTER v0.1.21, Sambamba v0.4.7	SAMPA
SNP Calling	GATK v3.2.2	FreeBayes v0.9.16-1	PARSNIP

Table 5 gives the single-node execution times for each stage of the three pipelines. Alignment is the dominant step in all three pipelines. The RefPipeline alignment time using BWA-MEM is 580 min. SpeedSeq's alignment time also includes alignment output processing time and it is 1.65× faster than the combined time for these two stages using the RefPipeline. PRUNE currently uses the BWA-MEM implementation in version 0.7.10 of BWA, which does not have compute-I/O overlap. Version 0.7.12 of BWA supports compute-I/O overlap, but we are yet to transition to this version. Also, the SAM records created by BWA are parsed in-order to create AEB and AIB records. Due to these reasons, PRUNE takes 692 min (Compute: 571 min, I/O: 71.5 min, SAM parsing: 49.5 min), as compared to RefPipeline's lower running time.

In our parallelized run of SpeedSeq SNP calling, each contig is assigned to a separate instance of a FreeBayes process. We follow the same approach to parallelize GATK-HC (HaplotypeCaller), by assigning one contig per process. Speed-Seq's multiprocess FreeBayes is 1.63× faster than RefPipeline's multiprocess GATK-HC. PARSNIP is significantly faster than both the parallelized versions of GATK-HC and SpeedSeq on a single node.

Due to in-memory duplicate marking and sorting, SpeedSeq achieves a speedup of 1.65× over RefPipeline. All stages of SpeedSeq are run using 16

Table 5. End-to-end pipeline execution times (in minutes) and speedup on a single compute node (16 cores) of Stampede for the NA12878 data set.

Pipeline	RefPipeline	SpeedSeq		SPRITE	
Stage	Time	Time	Speedup	Time	Speedup
Alignment	580	670	1.65×	692	0.84×
Alignment output processing	526			4	131.5×
SNP Calling	270	166	1.63×	3.5	77×
Overall	1376	836	1.65×	699.5	1.97×

cores. SPRITE is 1.97× faster and the majority of the overall speedup is due to SAMPA and PARSNIP speedup.

For single node execution of SAMPA and PARSNIP, alignment records are distributed among 4 single-threaded MPI processes. We restrict the number of MPI processes to 4 due to the memory limitation imposed by the output buffer for SAMPA and the $\mathcal{F}$ table for PARSNIP. SAMPA is 131.5× faster than SAMtools sort because SAMPA is an in-memory approach, whereas SAMtools sort writes temporary files to disk while sorting. PARSNIP's 77× speedup over GATK-HC comes from the simple counting-based in-memory algorithm, fixed-length alignment records, and fast processing of AEB records.

Table 6 shows speedup of 16-node execution of SPRITE and the in-memory version of SPRITE (SPRITE⁺) over single-node SPRITE execution time. Avoiding alignment file creation results in improving PRUNE's speedup from 12.67× to 14.78×. SAMPA and PARSNIP have less speedup with 16 nodes as compared to PRUNE, because of less work per process and some load imbalance issues. Since we do not implement hybrid parallelism for SAMPA, its speedup is lower than PARSNIP. SPRITE⁺ takes 48 min for FQ file ingestion to VCF creation for NA12878 dataset, and the majority of the time is spent in the alignment phase.

Table 6. End-to-end pipeline execution times (in minutes) and speedup on 16 compute nodes (256 cores) of Stampede for the NA12878 data set. Speedups are with respect to single-node performance of SPRITE (Table 5). SPRITE⁺ denotes version of SPRITE avoiding intermediate I/O.

Pipeline	SPRITE 16 nodes		SPRITE⁺ 16 nodes	
Stage	Time	Speedup	Time	Speedup
PRUNE	54.60	12.67×	46.80	14.78×
SAMPA	1.13	3.54×	0.80	5×
PARSNIP	0.68	5.14×	0.37	9.46×
Overall	56.40	12.4×	48.00	14.6×

5.4   SNP Calling Accuracy

In this section, we compare the accuracy of SNPs called by PRUNE with GATK's HaplotypeCaller (GATK-HC) and FreeBayes. For accuracy comparisons, we use two high-confidence SNP call sets as ground truth.

1. NIST GIAB v2.19: This data set consists of high-confidence SNP and Indel calls for NA12878. These calls are integrated from multiple executions of GATK-UG and GATK-HC on samples of NA12878 sequenced using several different technologies.
2. Illumina high quality calls v7.0: This data set is derived using high confidence variants called by several different analysis pipelines on all 17 Illumnina Platinum genome samples in the CEPH pedigree trio 1463.

Theses data sets also come with auxiliary files specifying high-confidence regions of the genome where the SNP and Indel calls are believed to be accurate. We extracted the variants in these regions using vcflib. We then converted complex variants into simple SNP and Indel valls using the vcfallelicprimitives tool in vcflib. All comparisons are done using the vcfeval tool available in the RTG Tools package.

Table 7. SNP calling quality comparison on NA12878. SNP_{hc}: SNPs in high confidence regions, SNP_{all}: Total SNPs reported.

Pipeline	SNP_{all}	NIST-GIAB v2.19			Illumina high quality calls v7.0		
		Sensitivity	Precision	SNP_{hc}	Sensitivity	Precision	SNP_{hc}
RefPipeline	4.04M	99.55	**99.48**	2.79M	97.5	**99.7**	3.53M
SpeedSeq	4M	99.51	99.32	2.79M	97.5	99.41	3.54M
SPRITE-1	3.97M	99.46	98.71	2.80M	97.3	98.88	3.55M
SPRITE-2	3.75M	98.93	99.35	2.77M	95.9	99.18	3.49M
SPRITE-3	4.85M	**99.63**	92.12	3.01M	**98.3**	97.53	3.63M

Comparing Accuracy. Table 7 compares PARSNIP's accuracy to GATK-HC (in Ref-Pipeline) and FreeBayes (in SpeedSeq). The table reports SPRITE's accuracy for three different configurations of filters used by PARSNIP.

- SPRITE-1 reports SNPs satisfying $MQ > 20$, $SB > 0.1$ and $AAF > 20\%$.
- SPRITE-2 reports SNPs satisfying $MQ > 30$, $SB > 0.2$ and $AAF > 25\%$
- SPRITE-3 reports SNPs satisfying $MQ > 0$, $SB >= 0$ and $AAF > 20\%$

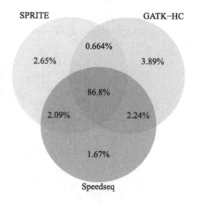

Fig. 7. SNP calling quality comparison on NA12878.

SPRITE-2 uses stringent filters and as a result, it gives the highest precision results among the three SPRITE configurations. SPRITE-3 on the other hand uses only the AAF filter, and as a result, it detects the maximum number of correct SNPs (high sensitivity) by sacrificing precision. The SPRITE-1 configuration strikes a balance between the other two configurations and has good precision and sensitivity values, which are comparable to the other two pipelines. Also, we can see that with more filtering criteria, the total number of SNPs reported (SNP$_{all}$) and the number of SNPs in high-confidence regions (SNP$_{hc}$) are much lower than the SNP counts obtained with fewer filters. In all our experiments, we used the $DP > 1$ and $AAC > 1$ filters.

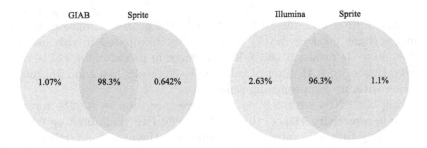

Fig. 8. PARSNIP's overlap with GIAB v2.19 and Illumina v7.0 base calls.

We compare all the SNPs reported by SPRITE-1 with those reported by Ref-Pipeline and SpeedSeq pipelines in Fig. 7. Figure 8 shows the percentage of overlap between the SNPs reported by SPRITE (using SPRITE-1 filter configuration) and the SNPs present in the high-confidence regions of the GIAB and Illumina data sets. With this configuration, we see that 98.3 % of the SNPs overlap with GIAB data and about 96.3 % overlap with Illumina calls. We observe that PARSNIP's overall accuracy is comparable to other tools.

5.5   PARSNIP Filter Tuning

In this section, we analyze the importance of each filter used in reducing the false positive count. Ideally, the filter should remove all false positives without removing true positives. We obtain raw SNPs by setting the initial filter conditions to values given in the SPRITE-3 configuration, which maximizes sensitivity. This configuration is shown as the leftmost point in each of the three plots in Fig. 9.

We can observe the drop in sensitivity as more SNPs are filtered out with the aim of improving the precision. In each of these plots, one of the three filters (AAF, SB, MQ) is varied, while setting other the two filter values to that of SPRITE-3 configuration. The precision and sensitivity values shown are obtained by evaluating SPRITE's accuracy with NIST-GIAB v2.19 call set.

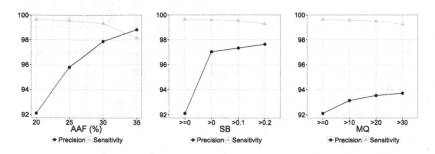

Fig. 9. Effect of various filters on PARSNIP's accuracy.

As the AAF filter is increased from 20 to 30, the precision improves by 5.77 % with only a slight decrease (.3 %) in sensitivity. Compared to this, increasing AAF from 30 to 35 results in .93 % improvement in precision for 1.17 % drop in sensitivity. Hence, an AAF filter of value up to 30 results in a good improvement in precision without compromising sensitivity.

Filtering out SNPs with $SB = 0$ improves precision by 4.92 % for a mere 0.04 % loss in sensitivity. Hence, this is highly effective in eliminating false positives. Increasing this filter value to 0.1 % improves the precision further by 0.3 % and decreases sensitivity by 0.05 %, and beyond this, the gain is insignificant.

Finally, filtering out SNPs with $MQ < 20$ improves precision by 1.42 % and decreases sensitivity by 0.13 %. Filtering out SNPs with $MQ < 30$ improves precision by 0.18 %, but the sensitivity drops by 0.25 % and hence not recommended.

5.6   Memory Requirement for SPRITE⁺

SPRITE⁺ implementation requires additional memory per node in order to buffer all alignment records created on a node, and also for temporary communication buffers required to send/receive alignment records to/from other processes. In this section, we give an account of maximum memory required per node to execute the SPRITE⁺ pipeline on the NA12878 data set.

During alignment, the maximum buffer size required per node for the output alignment records is 5.7 GB. The next stage involves communicating alignment records to other processes. In the worst case, each process sends all of its records to other processes and receives new set of data from others. Hence, the send and receive buffer sizes are upper-bounded by 5.7 GB. So, the maximum memory required per node during the communication phase is 17 GB (3 × 5.7). After the communication step, the send buffer is no longer required and can be freed, resulting in 11.4 GB of in-memory requirement after the communication stage.

The SAMPA stage does not require additional memory since we sort using an in-place quicksort. Finally, the PARSNIP step requires additional memory of 7.5 GB for the $\mathcal{F}$ table, and thus the maximum memory required per node for PARSNIP step is nearly 19 GB (11.4 GB + 7.5 GB), which is also the maximum memory required per node at any point of execution in the SPRITE$^+$ pipeline. For a single node run, since there is no communication stage, the maximum memory required for SPRITE$^+$ execution is 104 GB (5.2 GB for reference index $+16 \times 5.7$ GB for alignment output + 7.5 GB for $\mathcal{F}$ table).

6   Conclusions

In this paper, we presented the SPRITE pipeline for detecting single nucleotide variations present in a high-depth donor genome. We discussed three new tools in SPRITE: PRUNE (a scalable parallel implementation of BWA-MEM) to perform alignment, SAMPA (a counting sort-based in-memory method) for sorting the alignment records, and detecting SNPs using PARSNIP (a hybrid parallel counting-based SNP-calling algorithm). To reduce overheads due to intermediate file I/O operations, we have developed an in-memory version of SPRITE called SPRITE$^+$. We obtained a single-node speedup of 1.97× and 16-node speedup of 28.7× over a single-node reference pipeline implemented using state-of-the-art tools. Also, the SNP-calling accuracy of SPRITE is comparable to that of the reference pipeline and the SpeedSeq pipeline. Our results indicate that for high-coverage genomic data, counting-based SNP detection methods could be used instead of the more compute-intensive probabilistic methods, without sacrificing result accuracy.

Acknowledgments. This research is supported by the National Science Foundation award # 1439057. We thank members of our project research team for helpful discussions.

References

1. Adjeroh, D., Bell, T.C., Mukherjee, A.: The Burrows-Wheeler Transform: Data Compression, Suffix Arrays, and Pattern Matching. Springer, Heidelberg (2008)
2. Burrows, M., Wheeler, D.J.: A block sorting lossless data compression algorithm. Technical report 124, Digital Equipment Corporation, Palo Alto, CA (1994)
3. Challis, D., Yu, J., Evani, U.S., Jackson, A.R., Paithankar, S., Coarfa, C., Milosavljevic, A., Gibbs, R.A., Yu, F.: An integrative variant analysis suite for whole exome next-generation sequencing data. BMC Bioinformatics **13**(1), 8 (2012)
4. Chiang, C., Layer, R.M., Faust, G.G., Lindberg, M.R., Rose, D.B., Garrison, E.P., Marth, G.T., Quinlan, A.R., Hall, I.M.: SpeedSeq: ultra-fast personal genome analysis and interpretation. Nat. Methods **12**, 966–968 (2015)
5. Depristo, M., Banks, E., Poplin, R., Garimella, K., Maguire, J., Hartl, C.: A framework for variation discovery and genotyping using next-generation DNA sequencing data. Nat Genet **43**, 491–8 (2011)
6. Faust, G., Hall, I.: SAMBLASTER: fast duplicate marking and structural variant read extraction. Bioinformatics **30**, 2503–5 (2014)
7. Ferragina, P., Manzini, G.: Opportunistic data structures with applications. In: Proceedings Symposium on Foundations of Computer Science, pp. 390–398 (2000)

8. Garrison, E., Marth, G.: Haplotype-based variant detection from short-read sequencing (2012). http://arxiv.org/abs/1207.3907
9. GATK best practices. https://www.broadinstitute.org/gatk/guide/best-practices.php. Accessed May 2016
10. Abecasis Lab GLF tools. http://www.sph.umich.edu/csg/abecasis/glfTools. Accessed May 2016
11. Kathiresan, N., Temanni, M.R., Al-Ali, R.: Performance improvement of BWA MEM algorithm using data-parallel with concurrent parallelization. In: Proceedings of the International Conference on Parallel, Distributed and Grid Computing (PDGC) (2014)
12. Kelly, B., Fitch, J., Hu, Y., Corsmeier, D., Zhong, H., Wetzel, A., Nordquist, R., Newsom, D., White, P.: Churchill: an ultra-fast, deterministic, highly scalable and balanced parallelization strategy for the discovery of human genetic variation in clinical and population-scale genomics. Genome Biol. **16**(1), 6 (2015)
13. Langmead, B., Salzberg, S.L.: Fast gapped-read alignment with Bowtie 2. Nat. Methods **9**(4), 357–359 (2012)
14. Li, H.: A statistical framework for SNP calling, mutation discovery, association mapping and population genetical parameter estimation from sequencing data. Bioinformatics **27**(21), 2987–2993 (2011)
15. Li, H.: Aligning sequence reads, clone sequences and assembly contigs with BWA-MEM (2013). http://arxiv.org/abs/1303.3997v2
16. Li, H., Durbin, R.: Fast and accurate short read alignment with Burrows-Wheeler transform. Bioinformatics **25**(14), 1754–1760 (2009)
17. Li, H., Handsaker, B., Wysoker, A., Fennell, T., Ruan, J., Homer, N., Marth, G., Abecasis, G., Durbin, R.: 1000 Genome Project Data Processing Subgroup: The aequence alignment/map format and SAMtools. Bioinformatics **25**(16), 2078–2079 (2009)
18. Li, H., Ruan, J., Durbin, R.: Mapping short DNA sequencing reads and calling variants using mapping quality scores. Genome Res. **18**(11), 1851–1858 (2008)
19. Li, R., Yu, C., Li, Y., Lam, T.-W., Yiu, S.-M., Kristiansen, K., Wang, J.: SOAP2: an improved ultrafast tool for short read alignment. Bioinformatics **25**(15), 1966–1967 (2009)
20. Liu, C., Wong, T., Wu, E., Luo, R., Yiu, S., Li, Y., Wang, B., Yu, C., Chu, X., Zhao, K., Li, R., Lam, T.: SOAP3: ultra-fast GPU-based parallel alignment tool for short reads. Bioinformatics **28**(6), 878–879 (2012)
21. Liu, X., Han, S., Wang, Z., Gelernter, J., Yang, B.-Z.: Variant callers for next-generation sequencing data: a comparison study. PLoS ONE **8**(9), e75619 (2013)
22. Luo, R., Wong, Y.-L., Law, W.-C., Lee, L.-K., Cheung, J., Liu, C.-M., Lam, T.-W.: BALSA: integrated secondary analysis for whole-genome and whole-exome sequencing, accelerated by GPU. PeerJ **2**, e421 (2014)
23. Nielsen, R., Paul, J., Albrechtsen, A., Song, Y.: Genotype and SNP calling from next-generation sequencing data. Nat. Rev. Genet. **12**, 443–451 (2011)
24. Peters, D., Luo, X., Qiu, K., Liang, P.: Speeding up large-scale next generation sequencing data analysis with pBWA. J. Appl. Bioinform. Comput. Biol. **1**(1), 1–6 (2012)
25. Picard tools. http://broadinstitute.github.io/picard. Accessed Dec 2015
26. pMap: Parallel sequence mapping tool. http://bmi.osu.edu/hpc/software/pmap/pmap.html. Accessed May 2016

27. Raczy, C., Petrovski, R., Saunders, C.T., Chorny, I., Kruglyak, S., Margulies, E.H., Chuang, H.-Y., Kllberg, M., Kumar, S.A., Liao, A., Little, K.M., Strömberg, M.P., Tanner, S.W.: Isaac: ultra-fast whole-genome secondary analysis on Illumina sequencing platforms. Bioinformatics **29**(16), 2041–2043 (2013)
28. Rengasamy, V., Madduri, K.: Engineering a high-performance SNP detection pipeline. Technical report, The Pennsylvania State University (2015)
29. Rumble, S.M., Lacroute, P., Dalca, A.V., Fiume, M., Sidow, A., Brudno, M.: Shrimp: accurate mapping of short color-space reads. PLoS Comput. Biol. **5**(5), e1000386 (2009)
30. Sambamba: process your BAM data faster! http://lomereiter.github.io/sambamba/. Accessed May 2016
31. Single Nucleotide Polymorphism - SNPedia. http://www.snpedia.com/index.php/Single_Nucleotide_Polymorphism. Accessed May 2016
32. Talwalkar, A., Liptrap, J., Newcomb, J., Hartl, C., Terhorst, J., Curtis, K., Bresler, M., Song, Y.S., Jordan, M.I., Patterson, D.: SMaSH: a benchmarking toolkit for human genome variant calling. Bioinformatics **30**(19), 2787–2795 (2014)
33. Zook, J., Chapman, B., Wang, J., Mittelman, D., Hofmann, O., Hide, W.: Integrating human sequence data sets provides a resource of benchmark SNP and indel genotype calls. Nat. Biotechnol. **32**, 246–251 (2014)

Machine Learning

Predictive Modeling for Job Power Consumption in HPC Systems

Andrea Borghesi[1]([✉]), Andrea Bartolini[2,3], Michele Lombardi[1],
Michela Milano[1], and Luca Benini[2,3]

[1] DISI, University of Bologna, Bologna, Italy
{andrea.borghesi3,michele.lombardi2,michela.milano}@unibo.it
[2] DEI, University of Bologna, Bologna, Italy
luca.benini@unibo.it
[3] Integrated Systems Laboratory, ETH, Zurich, Switzerland
barandre@iis.ee.ethz.ch

Abstract. Power consumption is a critical aspect for next generation
High Performance Computing systems: Supercomputers are expected to
reach Exascale in 2023 but this will require a significant improvement
in terms of energy efficiency. In this domain, power-capping can signif
icant increase the final energy-efficiency by cutting cooling effort and
worst-case design margins. A key aspect for an optimal implementation
of power capping is the ability to estimate the power consumption of
HPC applications before they run on the real system. In this paper we
propose a Machine-Learning approach, based on the user and application resource request, to accurately predict the power consumption of
typical supercomputer workloads. We demonstrate our method on real
production workloads executed on the Eurora supercomputer hosted at
CINECA computing center in Bologna and we provide useful insights to
apply our technique in other installations.

1 Introduction

Supercomputers peak performance[1] is expected to reach the ExaFlops (10^{18})
scale in 2023 [20], as revealed by the exponential increase of the worldwide
supercomputer installation [16]. A key factor limiting their further growth is the
power consumption.

Indeed today's most powerful supercomputer is Tianhe-2 which reaches 33.8
PetaFlops with 17.8 MW of power dissipation [15]. Exascale supercomputers
built with today's technology would led to an unsustainable power demand
(hundreds of MWatts of power) while accordingly to [6] an acceptable range
for an Exascale supercomputer is 20 MW. For this reason, current supercomputer systems must significantly increase their energy efficiency, with a goal of
50 GFlops/W. Today "greenest" supercomputers achieve around 9 GFlops/W,
thus a wide gap still needs to be closed in order to satisfy Exascale requirements.

---

[1] Measured as FLOPS (floating point operation per second).

© Springer International Publishing Switzerland 2016
J.M. Kunkel et al. (Eds.): ISC High Performance 2016, LNCS 9697, pp. 181–199, 2016.
DOI: 10.1007/978-3-319-41321-1_10

The power consumed by a HPC systems is converted into heat therefore, beside the IT power strictly needed for the computation, the additional power consumption of the cooling infrastructure must be taken into account. The extra infrastructure needed for cooling down the HPC systems has been proved to be a decisively limiting factor for the energy performance; a common approach taken to address this problem is the shift from air cooling to the more efficient liquid cooling. To further reduce the cooling cost HPC systems uses hot water recycling and free-cooling solutions [19]. Indeed when ambient conditions allow it, it is possible to remove heat with direct exchange of heat with the ambient. The amount of heat removed with this approach is proportional to the temperature gradient between the supercomputer outlet temperature (water or air) and the inlet ambient temperature. During cold days the gradient increases, enabling a larger heat portion to be removed without switching on the chillers. At the same time an internal hot-temperature (i.e. hot-water cooling) increases the heat exchanged with the ambient.

A widely used metric for power efficiency is the *PUE index* (Power Usage Effectiveness), i.e. the ratio between the power consumption of the whole data center and the power consumption of the IT equipment alone. Common approaches for the design of the facility as well as for the PUE computation assume average or worst-case ambient parameters (temperature and humidity) as well as peak power consumption. However peak power consumption is rare event, which may not happen for the entire lifetime of the supercomputer. Moreover this static design approach becomes suboptimal when dealing with free-cooling. Indeed as early described in this circumstance the amount of IT power which can be removed without activating the chillers depends on the external temperature and humidity level, and thus varies across daily and night hours and seasons.

Current supercomputers cooling infrastructures are designed to withstand power consumption at the peak performance point. However, the typical super-computer workload is far below the 100 % resource utilization and also the jobs submitted by different users are subject to different computational require-ments [31]. Hence, cooling infrastructures are often over-designed. To reduce overheads induced by cooling over-provisioning several works suggest to optimize job dispatching (resource allocation plus scheduling) exploiting non-uniformity in thermal and power evolutions [5].

Hardware heterogeneity as well as dynamic power management have started to be investigated to reduce the energy consumption [17]. The idea is to limit the power consumed by a supercomputer exploiting the power variation which can be found across the computing resources of homogeneous [29] or heterogeneous [18] large-scale systems, in order to create energy and power aware schedulers.

A common approach to limit the amount of power consumed by HPC systems is *power capping* [21], which means forcing a supercomputer not to consume more than a certain amount of power at any given time. Power capping approaches are gaining popularity due the relatively simple implementation and the effective-ness in reducing the total power consumed by a supercomputer. We are especially interested in power capping techniques which do not require any change to the system components, nor to their performance, but only to jobs execution order alone. For these approaches a critical aspect is the possibility to know during the dispatching phase, *before* the actual execution, the amount of power consumed by a job. The key idea of this paper is therefore to provide a predictive model able to estimate with high accuracy the power consumptions of different applications running on a supercomputer. We evaluated our approach on a real supercomputer, with its own peculiar characteristics, but the methodology we employed is general and can be applied to different HPC systems.

The rest of the paper is organized as follows. Section 2 describes in more detail the power capping method and introduces the HPC machine considered in this work. In Sect. 3 we consider the nature of the applications running on supercomputers and the complications which may arise in a large system where multiple jobs may share the same resources. In Sect. 4 we present the prediction model and in Sect. 5 we evaluate the quality of the prediction w.r.t. real historical data. Finally Sect. 6 draws some conclusions and illustrates future research avenues.

2   Power Capping

Today's most common power budgeting techniques rely on the hardware components capacity to operate at different frequencies and therefore with different power consumptions. The main idea is to limit the computing nodes performance (i.e. through Dynamic Voltage Frequency Scaling, DVFS, the capacity of varying processor clock frequencies) when the total power consumption get closer to the critical threshold [13]. For example, in [26] an Integer Linear Programming (ILP) model is presented to enforce power capping in a HPC cluster. The goal is to combine power aware characteristics with CPU power capping to maximise job throughput of data centres where power is a constraint. Another possibility is the so called "overprovising". Supercomputer components such as CPU, GPU and memory have a vendor-specified Thermal Design Power (TDP) that corresponds to the maximal power required by the subsystem. Currently, maximum power consumption of an HPC system is determined by the sum of the TDP of its subsystems to take into account worst-case scenario where all components work at their TDP level. The ability to constrain the maximum power consumption of the subsystems below the vendor-specified TDP value allows to add more machines while ensuring that the total power consumption of the supercomputer does not exceed its power budget [23]. Today's processing elements can be configured to automatically limit they power consumption to a given budget. However this approach can severely degrade the performance of all the applications which will use the power capped resource, as they will run on a de-facto reduced performance HW.

Another strategy to impose a power constraint is to act on the job execution order alone, without requiring any HW modification nor any change in the operational frequencies of the computing nodes. Actually, this form of power capping may not exclude the HW one, because the HW one can still be required in case of optimistic misprediction. In general HW control can prevent power limit violations at a significant performance cost. Previous works have shown that extending current HPC system job dispatchers with power capping could lead to substantial energy savings without degrading the performance of the supercomputer and the QoS for the users [7,8]. The approaches studied in these work produce *proactive* schedules: they consider all the jobs which need to be run - and submitted in a job queue by the supercomputer users - and decide the starting time of each one of them in advance, according to a specified objective (i.e. QoS, maximal power savings, etc.). Compared to reactive power capping approaches which cannot prevent dangerous violations of the desired power budget as they are based on a posteriori measurement of the power consumption, proactive approaches can predict which one will be the power consumption of a future schedule and thus can ensure that the power budget is never exceeded.

Typically, job dispatchers need to know the power consumption (or at least an estimate) of each application before deciding a schedule - i.e. the order in which the job are executed. The goal is to guarantee *a priori* that the power constraint will not be violated in any moment (with a certain level of confidence). For this reason the capability of predicting the power consumptions of the jobs which need to be run is extremely important for the optimal implementation of a power capping method, as underlined by several works [22,30]. Furthermore, a greater prediction accuracy is related to a better performance of a power capped dispatcher (in terms of higher machine utilization and greater energy savings) [12]. Intuitively if we could exactly know the power consumed by each application we could generate optimal schedules and be sure that these schedules will never exceed the power budget; conversely, we may obtain sub-optimal solutions when we deal with imperfect estimates - we may want to be robust and never violate the power constraint (for example, employing a tighter power budget), or we can accept to exceed the power limit from time to time.

A common way to estimate an application energy or power consumption exploits hardware performance counters which monitors the system's components usage during the workload execution [11,14]. Despite the good accuracy obtained with these models the need to know the performance counters, which should be measured at runtime, clashes with the idea of having power consumption predictions available during the dispatching phase. A model to predict energy and power consumptions is presented in [28]. The authors propose an approach which does not require any application code instrumentation and allows for ahead of time power and energy consumption prediction. The main limit of the described method is that it considers only jobs which occupied entire computational nodes (this is due to the characteristics of the considered supercomputer). This on one hand simplifies the power consumption prediction but on the other hand cannot be directly generalized to different systems where multiple applications can possibly concurrently run on the same node.

Interest in power predictions is not limited to power capping. For example, the authors of [3] use DVFS in order to develop an energy aware scheduler able to reduce energy consumption of supercomputers. For this purpose they introduce a prediction model to forecast power and performance application in case of different execution frequencies. This model relies heavily on precise information about the application executables and requires the user to provide a tag identifying similar jobs. While we think this is an interesting direction, currently users provided information cannot be taken for granted.

In the rest of this section we describe the supercomputer which served as our case study.

2.1 The Eurora Supercomputer

The Eurora supercomputer prototype, developed by Eurotech and Cineca [1] has ranked first in the Green500 list in July 2013, achieving 3.2 GFlops/W on the Linpack Benchmark with a peak power consumption of 30.7 KW. Eurora has been supported by PRACE 2IP project [2] and it serves as testbed for next generation Tier-0 system. Its outstanding energy efficiency is achieved by adopting a direct liquid cooling solution and a heterogeneous architecture with best-in-class general purpose HW components (Intel Xeon E5, Intel Xeon Phi and NVIDIA Kepler K20). For its characteristics Eurora is a perfect vehicle for testing and characterizing next-generation "greener" supercomputers. As described in [4] Eurora has a heterogeneous architecture based on nodes (blades). The system has 64 nodes, each with 2 octa-core CPUs and 2 expansion cards configured to host an accelerator module: currently, 32 nodes host 2 powerful NVidia GPUs, while the remaining ones are equipped with 2 Intel Xeon Phi accelerators. Every node has 16 GB of installed RAM memory. A few nodes (external to the rack) allow the interaction between Eurora and the outside world, in particular a login node connects Eurora to the users and runs the job dispatcher (PBS). A key element of the energy efficiency of the supercomputer is a hot liquid cooling system, i.e. the water inside the system can reach up to 50° C.

Jobs are submitted by the users into one of multiple queues, each one characterized by different access requirements and by a different estimated waiting time. Users submit their jobs by specifying (1) the number of required nodes; (2) the number of required cores per node; (3) the number of required GPUs and Xeon Phi per node (never both of them at the same time); (4) the amount of required memory per node; (5) the maximum execution time.

Monitoring Infrastructure. Eurora features an integrated and low-overhead monitoring system composed by a set of software daemons and parsing scripts. The SW daemons run periodically (every 5 s) on each node to collect traces of the processing elements (CPUs, GPUs, Xeon Phi) activity by mean of HW performance counters. For each core they gather values from the Performance Monitoring Unit as well as the core temperature sensors, and the time-step counter. In addition, for each CPU it gathers the energy monitoring counters (power unit, core energy, dram energy, package energy) present in the Intel Running Average Power Limit (RAPL) interface. The parsing scripts process off-line the raw log of the performance counters to generate performance metrics (CPI, Load, Temperature, Power, etc.) and relate them with the job running on the node.

In addition to the physical information monitoring framework we also gather the information regarding the jobs which executed on the supercomputer; we consider parameters describing the job, such as the user who submitted it, the requirements (number of core requested, etc.), when it started and when it ended, etc. All the collected data are stored on a database hosted at CINECA.

A critical problem arises from the fact that multiple jobs can run concurrently on the same node: while we can directly measure only the power consumed by the CPUs the jobs can be allocate to single cores. Moreover, we know on which node a job run but we cannot distinguish the exact CPU it used (two CPUs per node). Therefore we cannot directly measure the power consumptions of applications which do not occupy entire nodes. The number of jobs which use only node portions is not negligible at all, since that is actually the majority of jobs which run on Eurora supercomputer[2]. This problem may emerge in many different HPC systems due to the various power measurements methodologies found in current supercomputers [27]. In the following sections we explain how we deal with such a problem.

3   Job Power Profiling

In this section we discuss and empirically validate two extremely important key concepts: (1) the power of a job can be approximated with its average value keeping a good accuracy; (2) a method to compute the power consumed by jobs which required only portion of nodes.

In this work we decided to consider only the power consumption of the CPUs, thus disregarding HW accelerators. We focused on the CPU consumptions because these are the most difficult to deal with, due to the fact multiple jobs can run on the same CPUs. Currently, HW accelerators cannot be shared by multiple jobs. Therefore from now on with "power" we are referring to the CPU power consumption. As already mentioned we must make a distinction between two kinds of problem: jobs which require entire nodes (one or more) and jobs which require only a portion of a node. In the first case we can simply use the power measures we collected; in the latter case we need a method to compute the power consumptions with the data at our disposal. This method is described in Sect. 3.1.

A HPC application power consumption may vary during its lifetime due to the nature of the applications itself and of the different phases which compose it, but the impact of such variability has not been extensively studied. Conversely, if the power consumption was constant - i.e. if we can associate to each job a precise, single value - the task of a job dispatcher would be greatly simplified[3].

---

[2] It is probably due to the fact that Eurora was originally a prototype and only later entered production phase.

[3] The proactive job dispatchers aforementioned require to know in advance the job power consumption as a single value; they could theoretically manage the power as a more complex object (i.e. a curve instead of a single value) but we risk to incur in significant performance losses.

Our idea is to use the *mean* power to represent the power consumption of a job, in the hope that the power variability is relatively low and the power consumption relatively constant or that when we add all the job power traces the variability of the power of each job is compensated by the others. This mean value is calculated as the average of all power measurements collected during the job lifetime.

In Fig. 1 we can see the power consumption profiles of three different jobs, A (Fig. 1a), B (Fig. 1b) and C (Fig. 1c). The first two jobs present a similar profile: their power consumption is quite constant and with a relatively small variability. In particular the power consumption of job B shows very little variability while job A powers have a higher variance - but still quite small compared to the mean value. As job C reveals, this is not always the case: there are also jobs whose power consumption changes more drastically during their lifetime (see the sharp increase in the power consumed by job C). Nevertheless, we can still estimate a job power consumption through its mean (average) value because the jobs with significant power variability are only the minority of all the jobs. The overwhelming majority of jobs show a low standard deviation in their power consumptions.

In Fig. 1d finally we see the histogram of the "normalized" standard deviations distribution. For each job we first compute the mean and the standard deviation of all the power measurements then we divide the standard deviation by the mean value to obtain a normalized standard deviation (to let us compare standard deviations of different jobs). We can easily see that for the vast majority of the jobs the standard deviation of the power consumptions is less than 10 % of the mean value - and in many cases even less than 5 %. This means that the standard deviation is, on average, very small and consequently the power variability is not too big. This is probably a characteristic of HPC jobs, which are generally carefully tuned to avoid big workload changes during the key computation.

This observation allows us to estimate the power consumption with the mean value without losing too much accuracy. It is clear that when associating a single power to a job we are going to lose some information about the real power consumption and therefore commit a certain (small) error. A job dispatcher with power capping is interested in the total power consumption of the system: when we sum all the jobs the errors tend to compensate each other thus the average error we commit is low.

3.1   Power Consumption of Jobs Not Using Entire Nodes

We describe now the technique to estimate the power of jobs running on portions of nodes. As discussed before we do not have a direct measurement of the power consumed by job using only a portion of a node. In this section we present a method to compute a power for these jobs. The main idea behind our approach is that each job consumes an amount of power proportional to its requirements (more specifically the number of requested cores).

An important requirement of our approach is the knowledge of the number of running jobs and "active" cores in each node at every time. Number of active

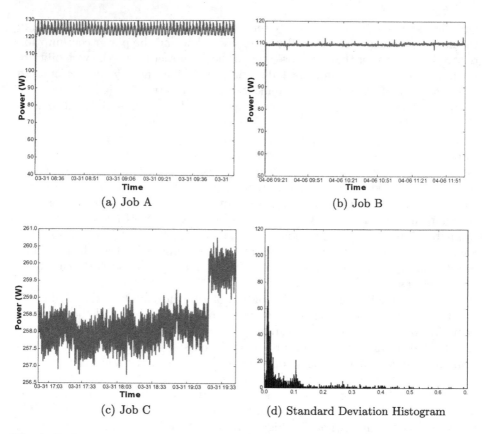

Fig. 1. Real power consumptions of 3 jobs (A, B and C) and standard deviation distribution histogram

cores means the number of cores that should be used in a node given the number of cores requested by all jobs running on such node. We therefore created these node profiles using the historical job traces. The information regarding the number of cores active on a node at any given time is fundamental for our approach since it allows us to understand the amount of power associated with a job: if a job j runs alone on node i the number of active cores is equal to the number of cores requested by job j and all the power consumption can be attributed to that job. Conversely if more jobs are running concurrently, each job will contribute to only a portion of the whole power (i.e. with 2 jobs sharing a node, using all the node cores, each job can be associated with half the measured power). This reasoning motivates the power we associate to each job as expressed in Eq. 1

$$P_j = \overline{P_{ij}} \frac{cr_j}{nca_{ij}} \qquad (1)$$

where P_j is the power associated to job j, cr_j is the number of cores required by job j, $\overline{P_{ij}}$ is the average power of the node i on which the job j has run during the job lifespan and nca_{ij} is the weighted average number of cores which were active on node i during the duration of job j. In practice this equations says that the power associated to a job depends on the amount of workload related to the job - i.e. how many of the active cores on the nodes were used by the job.

While $\overline{P_{ij}}$ and cr_j are information stored in our database and ready to be used, nca_{ij} needs to be computed. This value tells the average number of cores (related to the number of concurrent jobs) which were active during the lifetime of the job; this number can be computed using the node profiles described previously, which can tell us the number of active cores in any moment of the job duration. More precisely we divide the job lifespan in sub-intervals where the number of active cores is constant and then we compute the average number of cores, weighted by the sub-interval duration. To formalize, given a node i we suppose to have job j, with duration Dur_j, which starts at ST_j and terminates at ET_j. We then have a set of intervals $s \in j$, each one with duration Dur_s; in a sub-interval the number of active cores is nc_s. The weighted number of active cores can be computed as follows:

$$nca_{ij} = \sum_{s \in j} nc_s \frac{Dur_s}{Dur_j} \qquad (2)$$

We designed an experiment to test the accuracy of the approximation method for jobs using node portions. For a given time interval we compare the total real power of the system, computed as the sum of all the node power measurements at each given time (we use time sub-intervals of 5 min). Then, for every time considered we also compute the total estimated power, i.e. the sum of the powers of the jobs running at that time; the power of each job is calculated with the method discussed above. A clear limitation in this approach is the fact that we are comparing two aggregate metrics (total real power and total estimated power) and we do not calculate the single job error.

In Fig. 2 some results are shown - the trace corresponds to a one-day period. As we can see the results are remarkably good, for example in the period considered we can see that our power estimate has an accuracy around 99 %. The results can nevertheless be worse in general, but the accuracy for our whole data set is always between 95 % and 96 %. Part of the error we observe is not due to the method itself, but actually is caused by the imperfect data in our possession. For example, our algorithm strongly depends on the traces of the jobs which run on Eurora and particularly on the resource requirements declared by the jobs. This can be a source of error because users declare the peak requirement of their application but the average usage may be lower (i.e. asking for 4 cores but actually using just one on average).

The main weak point of our method is its reliance on the resource requirements, which are declared by the users. Hypothetically, users should make truthful declarations, but it turns out - as we discovered through previous analysis - that this is not always the case. This could also be due to the fact that we consider resource requirements as constant during a job lifespan whereas a job may not always employ all the requested resources. Nevertheless, there is a

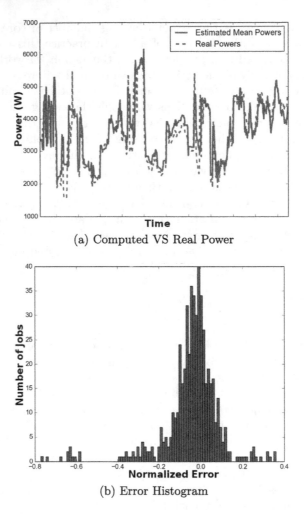

(a) Computed VS Real Power

(b) Error Histogram

Fig. 2. Comparison between the real aggregated power and the computed aggregated power. Mean error: 0.011

discrepancy between the resource requirements declared by the users and the resource actually used and such discrepancy is going to be a problem for the prediction model. We discuss this issue in Sect. 4.3.

4   Powers Prediction Model

In the previous sections we have seen that it is possible to describe a job power consumption with a single value - the mean value - and we are able to do that for every job running on the system, whether it occupies an entire node or not. With this information we can now create a prediction model to estimate jobs power consumptions. For this purpose we employed a machine learning approach (ML) which counts on the large amount of historical data in our possession: using the knowledge we have on the applications that run in the past we can learn a model able to predict the consumption of future jobs. We implemented our machine learning models with a Python module called *scikit-learn* [24].

The basic idea of a machine learning predictor is to learn a model which correlates a set of *input features*, or independent variables, with a *target*, or dependent variable. In our particular context we want to correlate the job characteristics (duration, requirements, etc.), i.e. the features, with the job power consumptions. This correlation can be learned by the model thanks to the large number of example which constitutes the training set, i.e. the data regarding past jobs, with their characteristics and power consumptions. After the learning phase the model can estimate the powers for new jobs (not seen during the training). A critical element for the success of ML techniques is the availability of large data sets for the training phase; in the Eurora's case we have a data set comprising tens of thousands of jobs (more or less 100k), which is more than enough to obtain good quality predictions.

We developed two different approaches, one to be used with jobs which require entire nodes (Sect. 4.1) and one to be used with jobs occupying only portion of nodes (Sect. 4.2). In this second case, we created multiple prediction models: one for each user with already enough collected data plus a generic one for new users.

4.1 Jobs on Entire Nodes

In the case of jobs on entire nodes we created a single model which takes into account the following features: user, queue, requested duration, number of requested nodes, number of requested cores, number of requested GPUs, number of requested Xeon Phi[4], amount of requested memory. The ML method we used for this model is called Random Forest Regression [10], which is an evolution of the classical and widely used Decision Tree [25]. Other than Random Forest we tried other supervised regression techniques, using the default implementations provided by sci-kit. We used Generalized Linear Model, Support Vector Machines, Decision Trees and ensemble methods (which combine the predictions of several base estimators) such as Bagging, AdaBoost and Gradient Tree Boosting. We then chose the approach with the better accuracy. The time required to train the model is very low, less than 3 s, and the time required to make a prediction is negligible, much less than a second. The training should be performed once with the available historical data and then the model could be updated regularly with the new jobs information collected during the normal execution.

A common way to compute the goodness of a prediction model is to split the data set into two subsets: the training set and the test set. With the training

---

[4] The number of requested HW accelerators is important because GPUs adn Xeon Phi are mounted on computing nodes with different power consumptions, i.e. a job requiring a GPU will necessary run on a CPU consuming more power than those with a Xeon Phi.

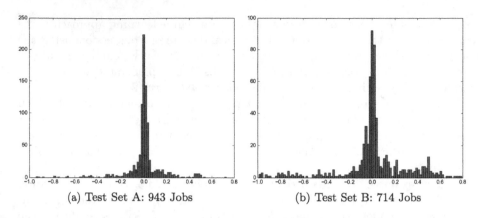

(a) Test Set A: 943 Jobs   (b) Test Set B: 714 Jobs

Fig. 3. Prediction errors histogram for two test sets

set we can learn the prediction model, which is then used to estimate the power consumptions of the jobs in the test set. These estimates are then compared with the real power consumptions of the jobs in the test set, computing the "prediction error" for each job in the test set[5]. The average of these prediction errors then measures the quality of the prediction, with lower values indicating higher quality. The average prediction error computed in this way is around 4 %–5 %, which guarantees a very accurate prediction. Figure 3a, b show the histograms of the prediction errors for two different test sets of jobs on entire nodes. These results were obtained with a training set of around 10k jobs and the test sets are, respectively, of 943 and 714 jobs (test and training sets randomly extracted from the whole data set).

4.2   Jobs on Portions of Nodes

In the case of jobs using only node portions the prediction turned out to be more difficult than the entire node case and that forced us to try with a different approach. In particular, we chose to create a prediction model for each user, since it is probable that a certain user will submit jobs with a similar pattern. Also in this case the best ML technique has been selected after a preliminary study and the best performance was obtained with Decision Tree Regression [9] - also a Decision Trees based method. The problem with having one predictor per user is that we split our training (and test) set and therefore the dimension of these sets decreases. If the test set dimension decreases too much the learning looses its effectiveness and consequently we cannot make good predictions. This problem happens particularly if there are users who submitted few jobs and thus we cannot actually learn a prediction model for them[6]. To solve this

---

[5] We actually used a normalized prediction error: $(real\_power - predicted\_power)/real\_power$.

[6] This is also a problem for new users to whom we cannot build any prediction model until a sufficient number of jobs are submitted.

issue together with the single user predictors we also have a "general" predictor, devised without splitting the test set and including all users. This generalized predictor is slightly less accurate than the specific ones, but it is an essential component in our prediction mechanism.

The input features of the generalized predictor are the same used for the entire nodes models plus the following: the job name, the number of jobs running on the system at the job start time, the number of cores used on the system at the job start time and the ratio between active cores and total number of cores on the system at job start time. These additional information mainly serve to characterize the supercomputer state and we also added the job name (the application executable) since jobs with similar names - by the same users - usually represent different runs of the same application (and probably are similar in terms of power consumption). The specific (per user) predictors have all the input features of the generalized predictor minus the user name: obviously, since it would be the same for all the jobs in the test set. The training time is very fast also in this case, usually less than 2 s for each user predictor.

The accuracy of the prediction has been computed as before, i.e. using the average prediction error. Now we have different accuracies for the different user predictors and to obtain an aggregate measure we calculate the mean of all the average prediction errors (one average prediction error user, plus the generalized one). The quality of the prediction is lower than in the case of jobs on entire nodes, with an average error around 15 % - for some user the error could be smaller than 3 % while for other users it could be up to 35 %. In Fig. 4 we can see the histograms of the prediction errors for two different users, User A and User B. In the case of User A (Fig. 4a) we see how the accuracy is very good since the errors are very small and centred on zero. Conversely Fig. 4b reveals that for User B the prediction is definitely less precise; it's easy to see that while the majority of jobs are well predicted (small error around zero), a few of them are extremely bad predicted (queue of errors much smaller than -1, on the left of the graph). In the following section we are going to describe the reason of this behaviour.

The predictor models devised for the jobs running on node portions could be also used without modifications also to predict the power of jobs running on entire nodes (jobs on entire nodes are a subset of jobs on node portions). Clearly, the accuracy of the prediction decreases w.r.t. to the dedicated predictor.

4.3 Outliers Management

After collecting the prediction results described previously we investigated them to understand why some predictions were so wrong. The first thing we noticed is that these bad estimated jobs have a small power (compared to the rest of the jobs). As we see in the next section, these "bad" jobs do not have a great impact on the aggregate prediction precision (that is, when we compare the total real system power consumption and the total predicted power) and could actually be disregarded. Furthermore we claim that these jobs are *outlier*, i.e. jobs not representing a typical Eurora workload. This is due to two factors. First, these jobs

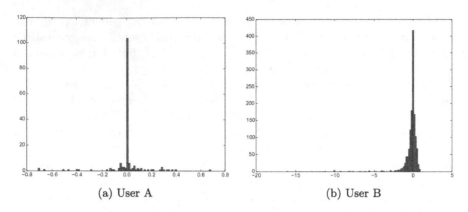

(a) User A   (b) User B

Fig. 4. Prediction error histogram for two different users

show "strange" behaviours: they usually have a very short duration (under 5 min and very often even less)[7]. This frequently means that these jobs did not have a correct execution and terminated abruptly, possibly without actually using the requested resources. The second issue is related to the discrepancy between the declared resource requirements and the resources actually used - due to both incorrect estimates by users and varying levels of resource utilization during the job execution. The jobs whose estimates are extremely wrong present a significantly higher level of discrepancy between the declared resource requirements and the resources actually used.

If we discard these outliers from the average prediction error computation, the accuracy increases sharply: the mean error becomes smaller than 4 %. This consideration leads us to formulate two simple guidelines to obtain better predictions: (1) it is extremely important that the users declare realistic requirements and should be incentivized to do that; (2) the job monitoring framework has to keep track of those jobs which did not terminate their execution correctly and must be able to distinguish them from the "successful" ones.

5   Results

In this section we present the conclusive results of the methods we introduced in the rest of the paper: estimate of a job power consumption with the mean value of multiple powers measures and prediction of such mean powers with a ML model. We want to know the final error we obtain after having applied all the stages of our method, each of them introducing some inaccuracy. For this purpose we tested our predictions against the real system power consumptions (again, we consider only CPU powers). The experiment set up is the same employed to compare mean power consumptions and real ones, that is we compare the

---

[7] We cannot just delete all jobs with short durations from the train set since in this way we could discard legitimate jobs.

total real power in the system at time t with the sum of all power predictions of job running at time t. The power predictions are obtained with the previously mentioned model and for the sake of simplicity we did not employ the dedicated predictor for the jobs running on entire nodes.

In our accuracy calculations we decided to disregard the outliers, as described in Sect. 4.3. In Fig. 5 we can see some results; the figure corresponds to a two-days period. On the left the predicted trend is compared to the real power trend and on the right we can see the histograms of the prediction errors. As we can see the results are very good, with a mean error smaller than 6 %. This is true also if we consider more extended period of times; the average error for the whole test period (a month) is around 8 % and 9 %.

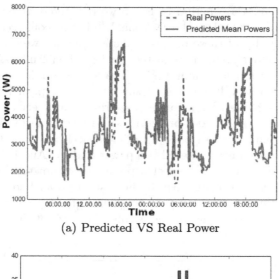

(a) Predicted VS Real Power

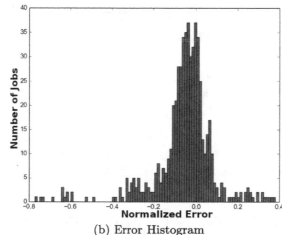

(b) Error Histogram

Fig. 5. Comparison between the real total power and the predicted total power. Period 2. Mean error: 0.056

While the average error is good with must consider the nature of our mispredictions in relation to the power capping. More specifically we can observe *under-prediction* and *over-prediction*. The first one could lead to emergencies (the real power actually exceeds the cap planned in the dispatcher) and the second one leads to machine under-utilization and it is undesirable as well. The concerns about underestimates is that they may lead to power and thermal overshoots. More in detail, when the predicted power is below actual power for a time significantly longer than the thermal time constants of the HPC machine, and the prediction error is above 10 %, then hardware power throttling would kick in at run time to prevent temperature overshoots, leading to undesirable performance losses and possible violations of service level agreements. We call these events "critical underestimates". Our error analysis reveals that critical underestimates would happen for less than 2 % of the operating time of the machine. For example, in the 2-days period of Fig. 5 we registered 37 periods when the predicted power was lower than the real one. While this could seem a high number, the great majority of these under-prediction periods were very short: 90 % of the times the under-predictions lasted for less than 2 min and 80 % of the under-predictions lasted less than 1 min. The longest under-prediction period lasted for 8 min. These values are very short w.r.t. a typical HPC application duration (i.e. a few hours). Even tough these results are very good we can nevertheless take into account under-predictions and there a few ways to cope with them. From one hand, we can back up our dispatcher with a HW power cap mechanism to ensure to never exceed the power budget. Another solution could be to require the dispatcher to respect a power constraint tighter than the real one, thus guaranteeing never to surpass the desired power budget.

An extremely important factor for the quality of the prediction is the availability of information regarding previous jobs. The size of the data set used to

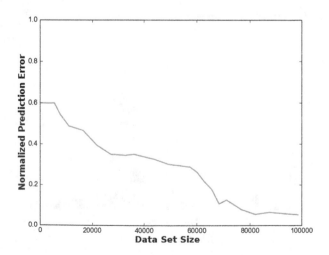

Fig. 6. Data set size and prediction error

train our learning machine models greatly influences the results accuracy. To give an idea of the relevance of this point we can look at Fig. 6. We have on the x-axis the increasing data set sizes (obtained through random sampling of our original data set) and on the y-axis the corresponding mean normalized error of the prediction. The mean error reported is the aggregated, final one. We can easily see that the prediction accuracy decreases (the error increases) when the data set size shrinks. A good dimension for the data set is around 80k entries (previously observed jobs)[8].

6   Conclusion

In this paper we presented a set of techniques which aim to improve the performance of power capping in HPC systems. Since job dispatchers need to know the power consumptions of the applications in order to create an optimal schedule here we proposed a method to predict such power consumptions. We have done that using techniques borrowed from the Machine Learning field and relying on the big quantity of data we collected on our case-study system - the Eurora supercomputer. The main results we obtained are the following.

First, we can approximate the power consumption of a job with a single value, the average of all the power measurements taken during its lifetime, with only a small loss of precision. Dealing with a single values instead of multiple ones is a great help for the job dispatcher. Then we tackled the problem of co-executing jobs, i.e. applications which run on the same node and using only a portion of the node resources. The problem arised from the mismatch between the minimal allocation unit in the system and the granularity of the power measures collected. We proposed an algorithm to estimated the mean power consumptions of such jobs and proved its efficacy. Finally we devised a method to predict the mean power consumption for every application obtaining a great prediction accuracy and we also provided guidelines to ensure the quality of the predictions.

As future work we plan to integrate the proposed solution in our previous job dispatchers with power capping. In order to do that we are also going to extend our model to consider the HW accelerators in our estimates.

Acknowledgement. This work was partially supported by the FP7 ERC Advance project MULTITHERMAN (g.a. 291125). We also want to thank CINECA and Eurotech for granting us the access to their systems.

References

1. Eurora page on the cineca web site. http://www.cineca.it/en/content/eurora. Accessed 14 Apr 2014
2. PRACE, the Partnership for advanced computing in europe

---

[8] In Eurora's case this corresponds to less than 3 months of observation.

3. Auweter, A., Bode, A., Brehm, M., Brochard, L., Hammer, N., Huber, H., Panda, R., Thomas, F., Wilde, T.: A case study of energy aware scheduling on SuperMUC. In: Kunkel, J.M., Ludwig, T., Meuer, H.W. (eds.) ISC 2014. LNCS, vol. 8488, pp. 394–409. Springer, Heidelberg (2014)

4. Bartolini, A., Cacciari, M., Cavazzoni, C., et al.: Unveiling eurora - thermal and power characterization of the most energy-efficient supercomputer in the world. In: Design, Automation Test in Europe Conference Exhibition (DATE), March 2014

5. Bartolini, A., Cacciari, M., Tilli, A., Benini, L.: Thermal and energy management of high-performance multicores: distributed and self-calibrating model-predictive controller. IEEE Trans. Parallel Distrib. Syst. $24(1)$, 170–183 (2013)

6. Bergman, K., Borkar, S., Campbell, D., et al.: Exascale computing study: technology challenges in achieving exascale systems, September 2008

7. Borghesi, A., Collina, F., Lombardi, M., Milano, M., Benini, L.: Power capping in high performance computing systems. In: Pesant, G. (ed.) CP 2015. LNCS, vol. 9255, pp. 524–540. Springer, Heidelberg (2015)

8. Borghesi, A., Conficoni, C., Lombardi, M., Bartolini, A.: MS3: a mediterranean-stile job scheduler for supercomputers - do less when it's too hot! In: International Conference on High Performance Computing & Simulation, HPCS, Amsterdam, Netherlands, 20–24 July 2015, pp. 88–95 (2015)

9. Breiman, L., Friedman, J., Stone, C.J., Olshen, R.A.: Classification and Regression Trees. The Wadsworth and Brooks-Cole Statistics-Probability Series. Taylor & Francis, Abingdon (1984)

10. Breiman, L.: Random forests. Mach. Learn. $45(1)$, 5–32 (2001)

11. Chetsa, G.L.T., Lefevre, L., Pierson, J., et al.: Exploiting performance counters to predict and improve energy performance of HPC systems. Future Gener. Comput. Syst. 36, 287–298 (2014)

12. Choi, J., Govindan, S., Urgaonkar, B., et al.: Profiling, prediction, and capping of power consumption in consolidated environments. In: IEEE International Symposium on Modeling, Analysis and Simulation of Computers and Telecommunication Systems, MASCOTS, pp. 1–10. IEEE (2008)

13. Cochran, R., Hankendi, C., Coskun, A.K., Reda, S.: Pack & cap: adaptive DVFS and thread packing under power caps. In: Proceedings of the 44th Annual IEEE/ACM International Symposium on Microarchitecture, pp. 175–185. ACM (2011)

14. Contreras, G., Martonosi, M.: Power prediction for intel xscaleprocessors using performance monitoring unit events. In: Proceedings of the International Symposium on Low Power Electronics and Design, ISLPED 2005, pp. 221–226. ACM, New York (2005)

15. Dongarra, J.J.: Visit to the national university for defense technology changsha, China. Technical report, University of Tennessee, June 2013

16. Dongarra, J.J., Meuer, H.W., Strohmaier, E.: 29th top500 Supercomputer Sites. Technical report, Top500.org, November 1994

17. Feng, W., Cameron, K.: The Green500 list: encouraging sustainable supercomputing. IEEE Comput. $40(12)$, 50–55 (2007)

18. Fraternali, F., Bartolini, A., Cavazzoni, C., et al.: Quantifying the impact of variability on the energy efficiency for a next-generation ultra-green supercomputer. In: Proceedings of the International Symposium on Low Power Electronics and Design, ISLPED 2014, pp. 295–298. ACM, New York (2014)

19. Jungsoo, K., Ruggiero, M., Atienza, D.: Free cooling-aware dynamic power management for green datacenters. In: 2012 International Conference on High Performance Computing and Simulation (HPCS), pp. 140–146, July 2012

20. Kogge, P., Resnick, D.R.: Yearly update: exascale projections for 2013, October 2013
21. Lefurgy, C., Wang, X., Ware, M.: Power capping: a prelude to power shifting. Cluster Comput. **11**(2), 183–195 (2008)
22. Pakin, S., Storlie, C., Lang, M., et al.: Power usage of production supercomputers and production workloads. Concurrency Comput.: Pract. Experience (2013)
23. Patki, T., Lowenthal, D.K., et al.: Exploring hardware overprovisioning in power-constrained, high performance computing. In: Proceedings of the 27th International ACM Conference on International Conference on Supercomputing, ICS 2013, pp. 173–182. ACM, New York (2013)
24. Pedregosa, F., Varoquaux, G., Gramfort, A., et al.: Scikit-learn: machine learning in Python. J. Mach. Learn. Res. **12**, 2825–2830 (2011)
25. Quinlan, J.R.: Induction of decision trees. Mach. Learn. **1**(1), 81–106 (1986)
26. Sarood, O., Langer, A., Gupta, A., et al.: Maximizing throughput of overprovisioned HPC data centers under a strict power budget
27. Scogland, T.R.W., Steffen, C.P., Wilde, T., et al.: A power-measurement methodology for large-scale, high-performance computing. In: Proceedings of the 5th ACM/SPEC International Conference on Performance Engineering, ICPE 2014, pp. 149–159. ACM, New York (2014)
28. Shoukourian, H., Wilde, T., Auweter, A., Bode, A.: Predicting the energy and power consumption of strong and weak scaling HPC applications. Supercomputing Front. Innovations **1**(2), 20–41 (2014)
29. Shoukourian, H., Wilde, T., Auweter, A., Bode, A.: Power variation aware configuration adviser for scalable HPC schedulers. In: 2015 International Conference on High Performance Computing Simulation (HPCS), pp. 71–79, July 2015
30. Storlie, C., Sexton, J., Pakin, S., et al.: Modeling and predicting power consumption of high performance computing jobs. arXiv preprint arXiv:1412.5247 (2014)
31. You, H., Zhang, H.: Comprehensive workload analysis and modeling of a petascale supercomputer. In: Cirne, W., Desai, N., Frachtenberg, E., Schwiegelshohn, U. (eds.) JSSPP 2012. LNCS, vol. 7698, pp. 253–271. Springer, Heidelberg (2013)

Towards Machine Learning on the Automata Processor

Tommy Tracy II[1]([⊠]), Yao Fu[2], Indranil Roy[3], Eric Jonas[4],
and Paul Glendenning[2]

[1] University of Virginia, Charlottesville, VA, USA
tjt7a@virginia.edu
[2] Micron Technology, Inc., Milpitas, CA, USA
{alfu,pglendenning}@micron.com
[3] Micron Technology, Inc., Boise, ID, USA
iroy@micron.com
[4] University of California, Berkeley, CA, USA
jonas@ericjonas.com

Abstract. A variety of applications employ *ensemble learning models*, using a collection of decision trees, to quickly and accurately classify an input based on its vector of features. In this paper, we discuss the implementation of such a method, namely Random Forests, as the first machine learning algorithm to be executed on the Automata Processor (AP). The AP is an upcoming reconfigurable co-processor accelerator which supports the execution of numerous automata in parallel against a single input data-flow. Owing to this execution model, our approach is fundamentally different, translating Random Forest models from existing memory-bound tree-traversal algorithms to pipelined designs that use multiple automata to check all of the required thresholds independently and in parallel. We also describe techniques to handle floating-point feature values which are not supported in the native hardware, pipelining of the execution stages, and compression of automata for the fastest execution times. The net result is a solution which when evaluated using two applications, namely handwritten digit recognition and sentiment analysis, produce up to 63 and 93 times speed-up respectively over single-core state-of-the-art CPU-based solutions. We foresee these algorithmic techniques to be useful not only in the acceleration of other applications employing Random Forests, but also in the implementation of other machine learning methods on this novel architecture.

Keywords: Automata processor · Machine learning · Random forest

1   Introduction

Recent research has shown that tree-based ensemble models, in particular Random Forests [3], are fast and accurate models of classification for a wide range

---

T. Tracy II and Y. Fu—Both authors contributed equally to this work.

© Springer International Publishing Switzerland 2016
J.M. Kunkel et al. (Eds.): ISC High Performance 2016, LNCS 9697, pp. 200–218, 2016.
DOI: 10.1007/978-3-319-41321-1_11

of applications including bioinformatics [11], computer vision [4], and sentiment analysis [19]. As data rates climb, accelerating the classification rate of these models is critical, but also presents a variety of challenges. While the non-uniform memory access patterns of tree traversal algorithms result in memory-bound CPU-based implementations, execution divergence while traversing different paths in the tree(s) prevents multiple threads on Single Instruction Multiple Data (SIMD) accelerators such as GPGPUs from executing in parallel.

Although parallelization on contemporary Multiple Instruction Multiple Data (MIMD) machines like CPU clusters is possible due to the independent computability of the individual trees, achieving good load balancing remains a challenge owing to different tree depths, deepest of which determines the overall runtime. Additionally, broadcasting a *feature vector* for every input to all the processors often makes the execution communication bound.

In spite of the above mentioned challenges, the classification rate is an important design metric for Random Forest-based applications. As the training and optimization is typically completed offline, the rate of classification determines the actual runtime performance of the algorithm. For example, the web search engine described by Asadi et al. [2] uses Random Forests in its innermost loop. Therefore, accelerating this loop for a search engine that processes billions of queries per day has a significant effect on the perceived latency experienced by the user. Similarly, a more efficient implementation leads to reduced power, infrastructure and cooling costs for the service providers.

The Automata Processor (AP) is a new non-Von Neumann processor based on the Multiple Instruction, Single Data (MISD) architectural taxonomy. It can compute thousands of user-defined Nondeterministic Finite Automata (NFAs) against a single data stream, in hardware and in parallel. We assert that this is an ideal architecture for accelerating Random Forests, because the values from a single feature vector (representing an input sample), need to be evaluated against the threshold conditions captured by the root-to-leaf paths in the decision trees. By creating a separate automaton for all possible root-to-leaf paths, and by executing thousands of such automata in parallel on the AP, significant acceleration may be achieved.

Nonetheless, executing Random Forest models on the AP required overcoming some fundamental challenges hitherto not addressed by previous AP work [12,13,17,20]. First, Random Forest feature values are often expressed as floating point numbers. Unfortunately, neither floating point numbers nor operations are supported on the AP. To address this limitation, we developed a labeling technique to represent floating point numbers using the symbol-space of the AP, and to operate on the same using the supported instruction set. Second, since all automata on the AP consume bytes from the input in the same order, each automaton was designed to process the feature values in a predefined ordered sequence. This deviates from the current Random Forest implementations, wherein the order of access to the feature values is determined by the tree traversal leading to non-uniform memory accesses.

Finally, in order to fit all of the automata required for large Random Forest models onto a single AP board, we adopted a compression technique called Automata Folding, which combines the address spaces of multiple features into as few State Transition Elements (STEs) as possible, reducing the automaton's size.

Having overcome the above mentioned challenges, we have expanded the use of this new processor to accelerate applications employing decision tree-based ensemble classifiers. As exemplars, we used these techniques to accelerate two applications: (1) the classification of handwritten digits and (2) characterization of a poster's sentiment behind a *Tweet*, a 140-character long message on the popular online social networking service *Twitter*. We hope that the techniques described in this paper catalyze further research on the acceleration of other applications using Random Forests, as well as other machine learning techniques on the Automata Processor.

The rest of the paper is arranged as follows. In Sect. 2, we briefly review decision trees and Random Forests, as well as the Automata Processor. Then in Sect. 3, we introduce our techniques to represent Random Forests as a set of automata that can be executed on the AP. In Sect. 4, we present our evaluation results, and finally we conclude with a discussion on avenues of future research in Sect. 5.

2   Background

2.1   Random Forest

The Random Forest [3] is a supervised classification algorithm. It is an ensemble technique, composed of multiple binary decision trees. Each tree is trained independently by using a random subset, with replacement, of the available training samples. A tree is built by iteratively choosing a *split feature* from a random subset of the feature space, and determining the best threshold value to maximize the entropy reduction per split. This threshold comparison for the split feature is captured as a *split node* in the tree, whose left child corresponds to the next state if the threshold qualification is met, and the right to the contrary. This learning process continues until a maximum depth or minimum error threshold has been met. Each leaf node in a tree represents a classification result. For example, the decision tree shown in Fig. 1a can be used to classify an input sample into one of the four classes: $Class$ 0 - $Class$ 3 based on the values of features $f1$–$f4$.

At runtime, a classification of the input sample, represented by a feature vector, is calculated for each tree. Starting at the root node, a root-to-leaf path is traversed based on the values of the features of the input sample. Since each of the split outcomes is mutually exclusive, there is only one root-to-leaf path per tree which can be traversed for any input feature vector. For example, the root-to-leaf path traversed in the decision tree in Fig. 1a for the input feature vector shown in Fig. 1b is highlighted in bold. The sample is therefore classified as belonging to $Class$ 2 by this tree. The net classification of the Random Forest is the *mode* of the results from all trees.

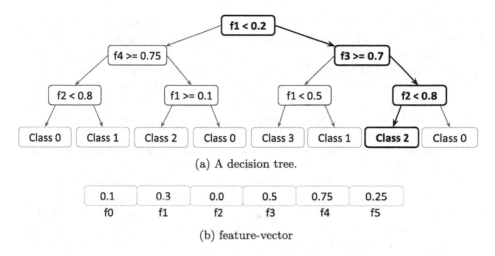

(a) A decision tree.

(b) feature-vector

Fig. 1. A decision tree.

Like most machine learning algorithms, Random Forests are trained offline
and then optimized for fast runtime classification. Current state of the art implementations run in super-linear time with decision tree depth. This non-linearity
arises from the limited locality of the memory access pattern. Computation at
each node requires non-uniform access to both the feature vector and the Random Forest model. This is because the split node features are unpredictable, and
so are the traversals of the root-to-leaf path for the trees. This unpredictability
makes current Random Forest implementations memory-bound, hampering the
scalability of the models.

Previous Work. The decision trees in Random Forest models are often non-
uniform in shape and significant in depth. This makes it impossible to fit an
entire decision tree as well as feature vector in the cache memory of modern
processors. Therefore, optimizing the traversal algorithm to maximize the spatial
and temporal locality has been widely studied.

Essen et al. [16] compare multi-core CPU, GPGPU and FPGA Random
Forest implementations for the highest classification rate, performance-to-power
and performance-to-cost ratios. They augmented the Compact Random Forest
(CRF) design [10] to improve the pipelinability of Random Forests on CPUs,
GPUS and FPGAs, and reported improvements in the classification rate by
clumping similar trees. Their results show that CRFs computed on FPGAs offer
the highest level of performance per watt, GP-GPUs to offer the best performance per dollar, and CPUs to offer the simplest, but lowest performing solution.

Researchers have also used ideas from modern compiler and database design
to maximize the efficiency of Random Forest models. For example, Asadi
et al. [2] use *predication* and *vectorization* to improve the net locality of decision tree traversal to maximize runtime performance. Predication is a technique

originating from compiler design to convert control dependencies into data dependencies. Vectorization is a technique originating from database research and batches decision tree computation to mask the cache misses that a sequential algorithm would incur. Although these techniques have shown considerable improvement over existing tree-based solutions, they are only incremental improvements on an algorithm that fundamentally lacks the data-locality necessary for high performance throughput on a von-Neumann architecture.

In [7], Lucchese et al. use an entirely different approach to accelerating additive ensembles of regression trees or a learn-to-rank model by representing tree traversals using bit vectors. Their algorithm, QuickScorer, uses the commutative property of the boolean *AND* operation to compute out-of-order tree traversals. We use a similar approach, ordering all feature thresholds to be used for simultaneous comparisons, but we pipeline the thresholding, effectively reducing the size of the resulting model, and simplifying the memory footprint. The authors report the fastest run-times to date by reducing the rates of control hazards and branch mispredictions over the previous state-of-the-art VPRED implementation [2].

2.2 Automata Processor

Micron's Automata Processor (AP) [5] is a re-configurable fabric of automata elements. The AP contains *State Transition Elements* (STEs) and *boolean elements* that can be configured to compute a set of Nondeterministic Finite Automata (NFA) in hardware. The AP also contains *counter elements* that give it more power than that available from pure NFAs. The programmer designs their application as automata, which are then compiled and loaded onto the processor.

Automata Representation. NFAs are represented as homogeneous automata on the AP with STEs and activation edges. STEs represent *states* and their corresponding state transition conditions; activation edges describe activation (transition-enabling) relationships between STEs. STEs with incoming edges from the *start state* are marked as *Start STEs*, and STEs with *final states* are marked as *Reporting STEs*. Start STEs can be configured as *start-of-data* STEs which process only the first symbol of the input data stream, or *all-input-start* STEs which process every symbol in the input data stream.

At runtime, all of the automata are loaded onto the processor, and the input data is streamed in as a *data flow*. This data flow broadcasts one symbol per cycle to all of the AP-chips in an AP *Rank*. On the first clock cycle, only the Start STEs are active which then match the input symbol against the character class of those STEs. If a match occurs, the matched STE activates all STEs connected to its outgoing connections. This process continues on the next cycle. The counter elements and boolean elements may be used to provide additional logic to these activation signals. If in a cycle one or more reporting STEs are matched, then an output is reported identifying the reporting STE(s) and the offset in the data flow where the match(es) occurred.

Programming Resources and Throughput. A single AP chip contains 49,152 STEs, 2304 boolean elements and 768 counter elements. An AP board contains 32 such chips, arranged in 4 ranks of 8 chips each. This cumulatively amounts to over 1.57 million STEs, 73,728 boolean elements and 24,576 counter elements. All of the chips in one rank can receive a broadcast from a single data flow or can be organized into two *logical cores* of 4 chips each. Each logical core processes the data flow at up to 1 Gbps, allowing a maximum data processing rate of 8 Gbps per board. Currently, ongoing work is continuing to increase this throughput to 16 Gbps by allowing logical cores of 2 chips each.

Current Status. The AP hardware is accompanied by a Software Development Kit (SDK) [1] which includes design tools to define, visualize, simulate, compile, load, and run user-defined NFAs on the AP. Using these tools, previous work including biological motif search [13], modeling Markov Chains [15], association rule mining [17], and Brill tagging [20] were developed. Although, these works inspired our research, we report results on actual hardware for the first time. In fact, the application for sentiment analysis has been showcased on hardware at the International Supercomputing Conference 2015 (ISC-15) and the Supercomputing Conference 2015 (SC-15), albeit with restrictions on prototype hardware which is currently in the validation phase.

3   Methodology

3.1   Overview

Figure 2 shows an overview of the execution pipeline. The classification process consists of three pipelined stages: labeling, model execution, and voting. In the first *labeling* stage, the floating point *feature vector* is converted into 8-bit labels. The labels corresponding to the feature values are concatenated to form a *label vector* delimited by the # symbol. The label vectors of the inputs serve as the input data flow.

In the second *model execution* stage, the automata loaded on the AP process this data flow in parallel to identify classifications for each tree in the model. Finally, in the *voting* stage, the classifications from all of the trees are combined to generate the final classification using a simple majority-consensus model for each input sample.

Currently, the labeling and voting stages are computed on the CPU and contribute to the overall runtimes. In the future, these will be computed on the FPGA present on the AP board. After porting labeling and voting to the FPGA, the *tree-classification* stage is estimated to become the rate-determining stage of the pipeline, hiding the runtimes of the other stages.

3.2   Automata Design

Given the AP's execution model, the most expeditious implementation of the Random Forest algorithm is obtained by representing each decision tree with one

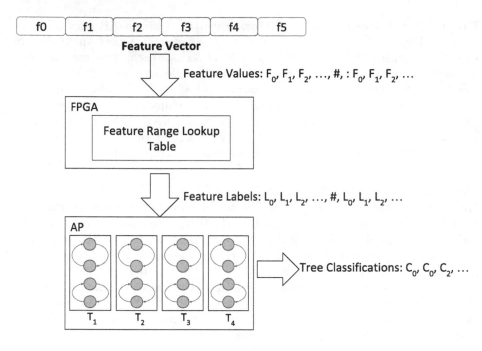

Fig. 2. Three stage execution pipeline

or more automata processing the same data flow in parallel. In order to achieve this we represent each root-to-leaf path in every decision tree in the Random Forest as a chain automaton, and execute all of the chain automata concurrently. In this section, we describe our techniques to generate such automata by overcoming three fundamental challenges. First, the feature vector values across all of the automata must be accessed on the same clock cycle(s). Secondly, a method to handle floating point numbers for feature values and split thresholds must be devised as no native support is present in the hardware. And thirdly, a compression technique must be adopted to arrest the expanded representation of all root-to-leaf paths in the trees. Throughout the rest of the section, We have used the decision tree shown in Fig. 1a as our running example to illustrate our techniques.

3.3   Enabling Parallel Execution of Decision Trees

We represent each root-to-leaf path in a decision tree as a chain of feature *evaluation nodes*. Each evaluation node represents one side of the decision tree's split node, and all possible paths are translated into chains. Because the evaluations are complete and exclusive, any feature vector will result in a single chain being traversed from top to bottom, and that one chain will return its associated classification. In this way, we've translated a tree-traversal to a set of exact-match automata.

Note that the order of the nodes in a chain does not affect the outcome of the computation, as the boolean AND operation is commutative; for this reason, we are free to re-order them. All automata on the AP must process feature values in the same order. Therefore, as the second step, the nodes in all of the chains are re-arranged in ascending order by feature id as shown in Fig. 3.

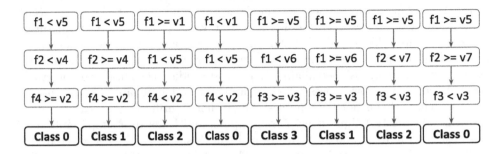

Fig. 3. Reordered chains representation of decision tree shown in Fig. 1a.

Next, the nodes representing identical features are combined, and new *satisfy-on-any-value* nodes are introduced for features that are not considered in a chain. The resultant chains are shown in Fig. 4. The satisfy-on-any-value nodes are depicted with a $*$ symbol. Notice that, in the resultant chains, all of the features are checked serially and in the same order, and hence these chains can be converted into automata executed in parallel on the AP. However, evaluating the thresholds for floating point numbers still remains a challenge; we discuss our solution next.

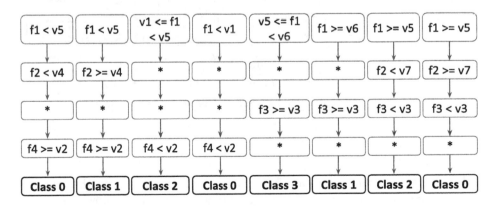

Fig. 4. Completed chains representation of decision tree shown in Fig. 1a.

3.4 Handling Floating Point Features and Threshold Values

Floating point feature values cannot be directly expressed on the AP, as there is
no native support. Scaling down these feature values to the 1-byte symbol space
of an STE (or a few STEs) is easy to achieve, but may lead to an unacceptable
loss of precision. We formulated an alternate approach by observing that the
feature values are only used by the Random Forest to determine which side of
a split threshold that value lies. Therefore, it is only necessary to know between
which two of the Forest's thresholds a feature value resides. For each feature,
we express the address space of floating point numbers as a set of intervals
demarcated by split thresholds used for the feature in *all the trees* in the forest.
Each interval is then assigned a label. In our case studies, the number of intervals
for each feature was always less than 255, and hence a 1-byte label could be used.
In cases where this is not true, multi-byte labeling is utilized.

This labeling technique is easy to compute, and leads to a simple automaton design without any loss of precision. Figure 5 shows the labels selected for
features $f1$–$f4$ of our running example. The address space of feature $f1$ is split
using the values $v1, v5$ and $v6$. Therefore, the intervals $(-\infty, v1)$, $[v1, v5)$, $[v5, v6)$
and $[v6, \infty)$ are labeled using 1-byte labels 0x0, 0x1, 0x2 and 0x3, respectively.
Similarly, the address-space for feature $f2$ can be labeled as 0x4, 0x5, 0x6; $f3$
as 0x7, 0x8; and $f4$ as 0x9, 0xa. A later section on Automata Folding will clarify the need for disjoint feature address spaces. Care is taken to avoid labeling
an interval with the delimiter symbol 0xff. Notice that, given a feature value,
its corresponding label can be computed in logarithmic time of the number of
intervals associated with that feature. This binary-search look up operation is
to be implemented on the on-board FPGA in the future.

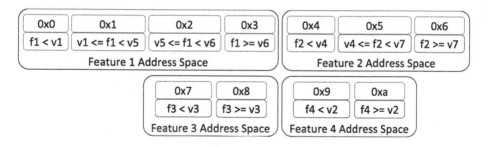

Fig. 5. Feature address space

Finally, these chains are ready to be converted into automata that can be
executed concurrently on the AP. The resultant automata are shown in Fig. 6.
The STEs in the automata are depicted using circles with labels placed inside.
A Start STE is demarcated using a solid triangle on the top-left corner. The ∞
sign inside the triangle marks the STE as an all-input-start STE. The reporting
STEs are outlined using double lines. STEs representing *satisfy-on-any-value*

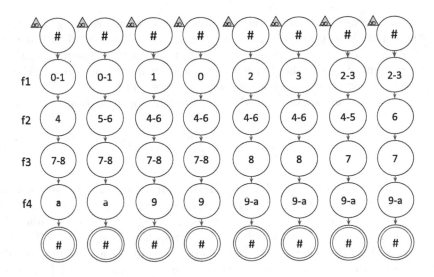

Fig. 6. Chains represented as automata executable on the Automata Processor

nodes are labeled to match any label for that feature. For example, for feature $f2$, the STEs are labeled as 0x4-0x6, $f3$ as 0x7-0x8 and $f4$ as 0x7-0x8.

For any input sample, the processing of all automata begins at the top Start STE. Because this STE is an all-input-start STE which is active on every clock cycle, it processes the end-delimiter 0xff, shown as #, at the end of the label vector of the previous input sample and activates the second STE to check the value of feature $f1$ in the next cycle. If the check is successful, the next STE is activated to check the value of feature $f2$, and so on. If the checks for all feature values are successful, then a report is generated by the reporting STE on encountering the delimiter at the end of the label vector.

The report contains the id of the reporting STE, which has an associated classification value. The report also contains the offset in the data flow where the report was generated which is used to determine the input sample associated with the classification. A simple majority of the classifications from all of the trees for an input sample is then declared as its final classification. These simple post-processing steps are scheduled to be migrated to the on-board FPGA.

3.5 Optimizing Automata for Higher Parallelism

The use of one STE per feature per automaton leads to significant resource requirements, even for moderately sized Random Forests. By realizing that the symbol space of an STE is typically much larger than the number of intervals associated with a feature, we used a compression technique called *AutomataFolding* to effectively combine features in a single STE. We did this by *folding* a chain into a loop.

Figure 7 shows the folded automata for our running example. The features in a typical Random Forest model have differing numbers of intervals associated with them. In general, the more relevant a feature is to determining the boundary between classifications, the more split nodes for that feature will exist in the forest, and the more intervals assigned to that feature. Assuming that the maximum number of thresholds used by a single feature is less than 255, it is possible to represent multiple features with a single STE!

Automata Folding works by solving the following optimization problem:

$$\min n : \forall i \in [1, n], \sum_{j=0}^{\lfloor m/n \rfloor} f_{nj+i} \leq C \qquad (1)$$

Where n is the number of STEs used in the automaton, i is the index of the current STE, f_{nj+i} is the number of intervals assigned to feature $nj+i$, m is the total number of features, and C is the capacity of the STE, 255. This optimization function returns the minimum number of STEs required to represent m features, where the STEs are chained to form a loop. In a simple case where two STEs are required, STE_1 checks feature 1. STE_2 then checks feature 2. STE_1 checks feature 3, STE_2 checks feature 4, and so forth.

Since the total number of labels for all of the features is less than 255[1], we need a single STE to check the labels of all of the features. This STE checks the first symbol of the label vector against the possible labels for feature $f1$. If a match occurs, it activates itself to check the second symbol in the label vector against the possible labels for $f2$ and so on. This is possible because the labels for different features are processed on separate clock cycles and the labels assigned to each feature are disjoint.

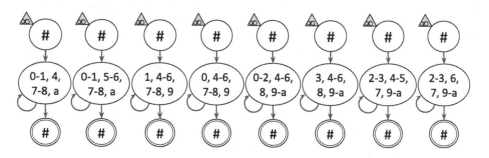

Fig. 7. Combining features into STEs.

4   Experimental Analysis

We implemented our automata-based Random Forest design on the AP as a proof of concept. We then compared our AP implementation against a state of the art Random Forest CPU implementation using two different models trained

---

[1] The symbol space of an STE minus one symbol reserved for the delimiter.

with differing data sets. The first data set, the MNIST handwritten digits database [6], contains labeled images of handwritten digits, where the classification for each image reflects the representative digit's value from 0 to 9. Each sample is represented by a 28×28 pixel 2-d array representing the image after being centered and scaled. Although we were able to successfully run our design on the AP hardware, because this is a prototype version, we were not able achieve the max performance expected from the hardware.

The second data set, the Sanders Twitter Sentiment Corpus [14], contains one large data set of Twitter messages with their associated sentiments. Three sentiments were considered in the set. The positive, neutral and negative classifications indicate the author's sentiment, while the irrelevant classification is reserved for Tweets in a different language, or those that have no meaning.

These two application data sets were used to train diverse Random Forest models using version 0.16.1 of the Scikit-Learn [9] machine learning framework, with differing tree counts, tree depths, and feature counts. We then took the generated models and converted them into our pipelined automata design to run on the AP. We chose to naively represent the handwritten digits with a 784-wide feature vector, one value per pixel. For the Tweet data, we used TF-IDF (Term Frequency, Inverse Document Frequency) vectorization with an experimentally-determined 1600 feature size.

The Random Forest models from both application were converted into space-efficient chain models that we loaded onto the AP. Knowing the number of STEs per chain, the feature vector size, and the number of trees in the ensemble, we could calculate the throughput of our models on future releases of the AP development board. There are 16 rows of STEs per block, 192 blocks per AP chip, 8 chips per rank, and 4 ranks per AP development board. The input symbol rate is 133 MegaSymbols per second. If the Random Forest model fits on a single rank, we can use inter-rank multiplexing to increase our throughput to 4x that. If the model is small enough to fit into two of chips in a rank, we can use rank logic core multiplexing and achieve an addition 4x speedup, with an effective throughput of 2.128 GigaSymbols per second!

The CPU throughput values were experimentally determined by using Scikit-Learn's Random Forest implementation (Scikit-Learn version 0.16.1) using the same Random Forest models we discussed above.

While benchmarking CPU performance using multi-cores, we found that the performance varies depending on the hardware configuration and the algorithm's parallel efficiency. In our analysis, Scikit-Learns performance did not scale well with core count. For example, with 16 cores, a speedup of no more than 3x was observed. Therefore, in order to provide a more reliable and stable comparison, we chose to use a single thread of the Intel Xeon CPU E5-2630 v3 @ 2.40 GHz processor for benchmarking CPU performance.

4.1   Results and Discussion

Random Forests Model Parameters and Accuracy.   Before comparing the AP and CPU implementations for the Twitter data set, we did a parameter exploration on the number of trees and number of leaves per tree and their impact on the sentiment model's accuracy. The goal was to find the elbow in the graph that maximized accuracy, while reducing the number of trees in the ensemble, and the number of leaves, which relates to the number of split nodes per feature. The experimental results on Twitter data show that the classification accuracy increases as the leaves per tree increases. We found that the maximum accuracy for our model saturated at 72 % with 800 leaves per tree. We also found the classification accuracy to increase from 5 to 40 trees, but no more significant increase of accuracy with more than 40 trees.

We performed the same parameter space exploration for the MNIST data set models. Our results show that increasing the number of leaves per tree in the ensemble has a similar effect as with the Twitter data, and we found our elbow with around 1000 leaf nodes per tree. Unlike the other data set, Twitter data models had a significant increase in accuracy when increasing the number of trees in the ensemble from 5 to 160 trees. Our highest experimental accuracy was calculated to be 97.1 % and was determined with 160 trees and 4500 leaves per tree (Fig. 8).

Throughput vs. Accuracy.   Generally, there is a trade-off between through-put and model accuracy for classification models. Random Forest models with fewer and shallower trees can achieve higher throughput, but at lower accuracy. Adding additional trees and training them to be deeper increases the accuracy to the model's saturation; adding any additional resources beyond this point just reduces the efficiency of the model and can yield over-fitting. The goal of model optimization is to find the trade-off between these parameters that maximizes throughput, while still achieving the required level of accuracy. This is often accomplished with design space exploration.

AP vs. CPU.   Figures 9 and 10 show that throughput is significantly affected by the number of trees in the Random Forest ensemble. As we discussed above, we saturate our accuracy with 40 decision trees, and therefore adding any more is unnecessary. With the same number of trees per model, the AP consistently performs with higher throughput than a single-threaded CPU on Twitter data. Figure 10 shows that, on MNIST data, the AP outperforms the CPU in most of the cases. With the number of trees greater than 20, and a large leaf number per tree (over 4000 leaves per tree), the throughput matches.

The AP architecture allows up to 16x multiplexing if the Random Forest model fits into two chips. As the model size increases, this multiplexing factor is reduced by factors of two (Tables 1 and 2). The steps in the graph indicate the model dimensions where the hardware cannot sustain the multiplexing factor. Future generations of the hardware will be able to fit larger models, therefore flattening the throughput curve.

For the Twitter models, the Random Forest implementations on the AP achieve from 2 times to 93 times the prediction throughput of a single CPU. For MNIST, the AP can achieve up to 63 times speed up over the CPU. The speed

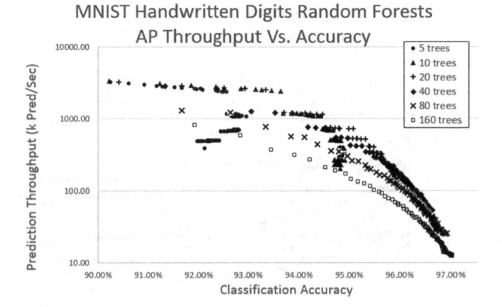

Fig. 8. MNIST handwritten digits random forests throughput on AP vs. accuracy

ups achievable using the AP are more significant with models that have fewer leaves per trees and fewer trees per forest.

The AP is a massively parallel device. With smaller Random Forests models, especially for models with lower numbers of leaves per tree, the AP's advantage of massive parallelism can be greatly taken as it can process hundreds of trees simultaneously. For the smaller models, we were able to achieve results with up to 93 times speedup against a single CPU thread. The AP's advantage decreases as

Table 1. Key data points of twitter results

Trees	Leaves	Accuracy	AP throughput (k pred/sec)	CPU throughput (k pred/sec)	AP speed up
5	40	66.9 %	14400	154	93
10	40	67.5 %	8130	129	63
20	40	67.7 %	5360	93.4	57
40	40	68.0 %	3750	58.5	64
5	600	70.4 %	2010	118	17
10	600	71.4 %	1530	86.4	18
20	700	71.7 %	385	51.5	7
40	700	71.9 %	194	32.4	6

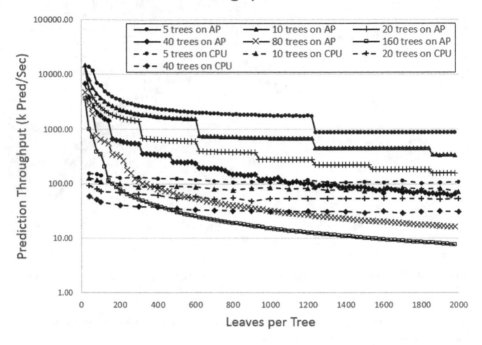

Fig. 9. Twitter sentiment random forests throughput on AP

Table 2. Key data points of MNIST results

Trees	Leaves	Accuracy	AP throughput (k pred/sec)	CPU throughput (k pred/sec)	AP speed up
5	50	82.2 %	13200	337	39
10	50	86.1 %	5980	242	25
20	50	87.8 %	4170	150	28
40	50	88.7 %	3350	86.5	39
80	50	89.2 %	2940	46.4	63
160	50	89.6 %	1350	25.0	54
10	500	93.3 %	2480	205	12
20	500	94.3 %	1160	125	9
40	750	95.2 %	420	68.0	6
80	1250	96.0 %	111	34.3	3
20	4000	96.1 %	129	98.9	1.3
40	4750	96.7 %	55.0	51.5	1.1
80	5000	96.9 %	25.0	26.6	0.9
160	5000	97.1 %	12.2	13.5	0.9

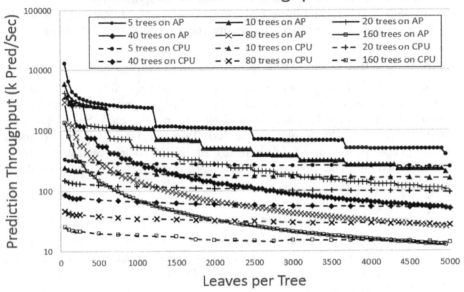

Fig. 10. MNIST handwritten digits random forests throughput on AP

the number of leaves per tree increase. With significantly decreased parallelism, a higher frequency CPU can reach similar performance as the AP.

With these properties in mind, it's important to focus on compacting ensemble models on the AP to maximize performance. Future applications of Random Forest-like models on the AP should focus on models that require smaller trees, but with large number of trees. As the AP scales with process nodes, we expect the hardware to achieve better scaling.

5   Future Work

5.1   Further Optimizations

Our first generation design addresses many important aspects of computing machine learning applications as automata on specialized hardware. Further optimizations include improving the performance by means of modifying the ensemble models and the automata algorithm. For example, reducing the size of the ensemble algorithms by using Compact Random Forest (CRF) [10] techniques would result in smaller trees utilizing fewer feature values, but achieving similar accuracies. Whereas Essen et al. constrain their CRFs to 6 levels to fit FPGAs, the AP allows us additional flexibility to choose larger tree depths and tree counts that may provide higher accuracy.

There are also potential algorithmic improvements that can be made. A denser binning technique could reduce the number of STEs used per tree, significantly increasing the size of forests that could be supported by one AP board. By potentially further combining feature address spaces, fewer symbols would need to be streamed per feature, improving the throughput of the system.

5.2 Accelerating Other Models

The techniques that we presented in this paper are not limited to Random Forests. Any decision-tree based ensemble technique can be ported to our automata design with little effort by a similar transformation. Some examples of models that could be accelerated include Boosted Trees [18] and Random Ferns [8]. These models are fundamentally similar in their tree traversal technique, but with emphasis on reducing the depth of trees or applying specialized learning techniques.

5.3 Automata on Other Hardware

Our automata design effectively reduces the run time complexity of the Random Forest algorithm by splitting the algorithm into floating point labeling and model computation. Splitting the critical path allows for the algorithm to be pipelined, accelerating the model.

This design could also work well on other hardware platforms including CPUs, GPGPUs and FPGAs. By considerably reducing the size of the Random Forest model, we could increase the cache utilization on a CPU or GPU. The thresholding operation could be computed in parallel on a subset of the available cores, while the model is executed on the remaining cores. Additional future work would include measuring the power-efficiency of this algorithm, and potentially using automata computation on low-power embedded applications. This work is left open for future research.

6 Conclusions

In this paper we present a technique for converting the Random Forest algorithm from a tree-traversal algorithm to a series of pattern matching automata in a pipelined system. This novel algorithm has effectively introduced a new design space for machine learning researchers. Whereby past research has focused on creating shallower decision trees to reduce the latency for tree traversal, our algorithm runs in linear time with the number of features, regardless of the depth of the decision trees! This potentially opens the door for future research into deeper trees on fewer features. We implemented our algorithm on Micron's AP and evaluated the runtime performance of our Random Forest implementation on AP. The results not only showed a promising avenue of applying tree-based ensemble classification methods on AP, but also provide information on the relationship between model settings and the runtime performance on the AP, which can be used to guide future research and development of more efficient classification models.

References

1. The micron automata processor developer portal, November 2014. http://www.micronautomata.com/
2. Asadi, N., Lin, J., de Vries, A.P.: Runtime optimizations for tree-based machine learning models. IEEE Trans. Knowl. Data Eng. **26**(9), 1 (2014)
3. Breiman, L.: Random forests. Mach. Learn. **45**(1), 5–32 (2001). http://dx.doi.org/10.1023/A3A1010933404324
4. Criminisi, A., Shotton, J., Konukoglu, E.: Decision forests: a unified framework for classification, regression, density estimation, manifold learning and semi-supervised learning. Found. Trends Comput. Graph. Vis. **7**(2–3), 81–227 (2012). http://dx.doi.org/10.1561/0600000035
5. Dlugosch, P., Brown, D., Glendenning, P., Leventhal, M., Noyes, H.: An efficient and scalable semiconductor architecture for parallel automata processing. IEEE Trans. Parallel Distrib. Syst. **25**(12), 3088–3098 (2014)
6. LeCun, Y., Cortes, C.: Mnist handwritten digit database. AT&T Labs (2010). http://yann.lecun.com/exdb/mnist
7. Lucchese, C., Nardini, F.M., Orlando, S., Perego, R., Tonellotto, N., Venturini, R.: Quickscorer: a fast algorithm to rank documents with additive ensembles of regression trees. In: Proceedings of the 38th International ACM SIGIR Conference on Research and Development in Information Retrieval, SIGIR 2015, pp. 73–82. ACM, New York (2015). http://doi.acm.org/10.1145/2766462.2767733
8. Ozuysal, M., Fua, P., Lepetit, V.: Fast keypoint recognition in ten lines of code. In: IEEE Conference on Computer Vision and Pattern Recognition, CVPR 2007, pp. 1–8, June 2007
9. Pedregosa, F., Varoquaux, G., Gramfort, A., Michel, V., Thirion, B., Grisel, O., Blondel, M., Prettenhofer, P., Weiss, R., Dubourg, V., et al.: Scikit-learn: machine learning in python. J. Mach. Learn. Res. **12**, 2825–2830 (2011)
10. Prenger, R., Chen, B., Marlatt, T., Merl, D.: Fast map search for compact additive tree ensembles (cate). Technical report, Lawrence Livermore National Laboratory (LLNL), Livermore, CA (2013)
11. Qi, Y.: Random forest for bioinformatics. In: Zhang, C., Ma, Y. (eds.) Ensemble Machine Learning, pp. 307–323. Springer US, New York (2012). http://dx.doi.org/10.1007/978-1-4419-9326-7_11
12. Roy, I.: Algorithmic techniques for the micron automata processor. Dissertation, Georgia Institute of Technology (2015)
13. Roy, I., Aluru, S.: Finding motifs in biological sequences using the micron automata processor. In: Proceedings of the 2014 IEEE 28th International Parallel and Distributed Processing Symposium, IPDPS 2014, pp. 415–424. IEEE Computer Society, Washington, DC (2014). http://dx.doi.org/10.1109/IPDPS.2014.51
14. Sanders, N.: Twitter sentiment corpus (2011). http://www.sananalytics.com/lab/twitter-sentiment/
15. Stan, J., Skadron, K.: Uses for random and stochastic input on microns automata processor. Technical report CS-2015-06, University of Virginia Department of Computer Science, Charlottesville, VA, September 2015
16. Van Essen, B., Macaraeg, C., Gokhale, M., Prenger, R.: Accelerating a random forest classifier: multi-core, GP-GPU, or FPGA? In: 2012 IEEE 20th Annual International Symposium on Field-Programmable Custom Computing Machines (FCCM), pp. 232–239. IEEE (2012)

17. Wang, K., Qi, Y., Fox, J., Stan, M., Skadron, K.: Association rule mining with the micron automata processor. In: IPDPS 2015, May 2015

18. Windeatt, T., Ardeshir, G.: Boosted tree ensembles for solving multiclass problems. In: Roli, F., Kittler, J. (eds.) MCS 2002. LNCS, vol. 2364, pp. 42–51. Springer, Heidelberg (2002)

19. Zhang, K., Cheng, Y., Xie, Y., Honbo, D., Agrawal, A., Palsetia, D., Lee, K., Keng Liao, W., Choudhary, A.: Ses: sentiment elicitation system for social media data. In: 2011 IEEE 11th International Conference on Data Mining Workshops (ICDMW), pp. 129–136, December 2011

20. Zhou, K., Fox, J.J., Wang, K., Brown, D.E., Skadron, K.: Brill tagging on the micron automata processor. In: 2015 IEEE International Conference on Semantic Computing (ICSC), pp. 236–239. IEEE (2015)

AutoMOMML: Automatic Multi-objective Modeling with Machine Learning

Prasanna Balaprakash[1,2]([✉]), Ananta Tiwari[3], Stefan M. Wild[1],
Laura Carrington[3], and Paul D. Hovland[1]

[1] Mathematics and Computer Science Division, Argonne National Laboratory,
Argonne, IL, USA
{pbalapra,wild,hovland}@mcs.anl.gov
[2] Leadership Computing Facility, Argonne National Laboratory, Argonne, IL, USA
[3] Performance Modeling and Characterization (PMaC) Laboratory,
San Diego Supercomputer Center, La Jolla, CA, USA
{tiwari,lcarring}@sdsc.edu

Abstract. In recent years, automatic data-driven modeling with machine learning (ML) has received considerable attention as an alternative to analytical modeling for many modeling tasks. While ad hoc adoption of ML approaches has obtained success, the real potential for automation in data-driven modeling has yet to be achieved. We propose AutoMOMML, an end-to-end, ML-based framework to build predictive models for objectives such as performance, and power. The framework adopts statistical approaches to reduce the modeling complexity and automatically identifies and configures the most suitable learning algorithm to model the required objectives based on hardware and application signatures. The experimental results using hardware counters as application signatures show that the median prediction error of performance, processor power, and DRAM power models are 13 %, 2.3 %, and 8 %, respectively.

1 Introduction

Modeling objectives such as performance, failures of critical subcomponents, power, and energy as functions of application and platform characteristics play a central role in managing extreme-scale computing goals. These models can be used to quantify meaningful differences across the decision space and to provide error bounds associated with their predictions; to offer a convenient mechanism for exposing near-optimal spots in the decision space; and to prune the decision space in autotuning. In a nutshell, multi-objective models can help compilers, operating systems, and runtime systems to make decisions proactively and/or reactively in order to best map applications to target platforms.

Analytical performance models based on first-principle, closed-form mathematical expressions may not be sufficiently accurate for all objectives of interest.

I'm an employee of the US Government and transfer the rights to the extent transferable (Title 17 §105 U.S.C. applies)

© Springer International Publishing Switzerland 2016 (outside the US)
J.M. Kunkel et al. (Eds.): ISC High Performance 2016, LNCS 9697, pp. 219–239, 2016.
DOI: 10.1007/978-3-319-41321-1_12

In such settings, data-driven (or "empirical") modeling can bridge the gap. In this approach, application and platform characteristics and their corresponding objectives are collected directly on the target platform, and a predictive model is built for each objective using statistical/machine-learning (ML) approaches.

The empirical models presented in the high performance computing (HPC) literature have been guided primarily by the expertise of the human modeler. It has become increasingly evident in the ML literature that success with ML algorithms depends not merely on the adoption of the suitable learning approach for a given data set, but also on the mastery of a more complex feature and algorithm engineering process [6]. Challenges in predictive modeling can be attributed to two major factors: the modeling complexity and the degrees of freedom modelers encounter when developing predictive models. Crucial aspects in predictive model development comprise variable selection, model selection, parameter tuning, cross-validation techniques, and background knowledge in disciplines such as machine learning, statistics, and mathematical optimization. Furthermore, even when several ML components and their implementations exist as open source software, assembling them for (multi-objective) predictive modeling task often requires ML expertise and domain knowledge; i.e., automating ML pipeline for a given data set is still a challenging task. This lack of automation in assembling a ML pipeline for modeling multiple objectives has meant that the adoption of ML approaches in HPC literature has mostly been ad-hoc.

We propose as a solution to the aforementioned problem an automated, end-to-end modeling framework called AutoMOMML (for Automatic Multi-Objective Modeling with Machine Learning). AutoMOMML employs a pipeline of statistical approaches in a systematic way to automate the predictive modeling process. The framework identifies the important variables, and selects and tunes the learning algorithms to model the required objectives based on hardware and application characteristics. Applications are characterized by using a set of performance hardware counters, which are counts of microarchitectural events. To generate training data, AutoMOMML uses a series of prepackaged microkernels to "probe" a target system to develop a comprehensive understanding of the degree to which application characteristics and hardware configurations affect component-level power draw and performance. That understanding is then encapsulated in models by using ML algorithms. The end-to-end framework greatly reduces the barrier to entry in model development for software developers, run-time designers, and hardware engineers and has the potential to bring modeling into the mainstream workflow of software and hardware stakeholders.

The key contribution of the paper is the general-purpose multi-objective modeling framework that comprises a pipeline of effective ML algorithms. We demonstrate the use of the framework for offline-modeling of performance and power. The proposed framework provides a systematic approach to compose ML components in an automatic way so that extensive ML expertise will no longer be a prerequisite for HPC predictive modeling tasks. In addition to being automatic and end-to-end, the framework is designed to produce analysis results after each stage of the pipeline that help understand what architectural factors affect the objectives, and how application signatures and objectives relate to each other.

2   The Problem and Setup

Given a target platform, the task of multi-objective modeling is to find a function

$$F(x) = [F_1(x), \ldots, F_m(x)]: \qquad x \in \mathcal{D} \subset \mathbb{R}^n, \tag{1}$$

where x is a vector of size n that parameterizes a hardware and application signature and $\mathcal{D}$ is a domain of possible values for x. The unknown function F takes the signature vector x as input and returns a vector $[F_1(x), \ldots, F_m(x)]$ quantifying m objectives, where each component corresponds to an objective of interest.

Approaches available for modeling F can be grouped into analytical and empirical modeling. The former deals with developing analytical approximations for each component function F_j using expert knowledge. The latter adopts statistical or ML methods to derive a surrogate model $S_j \approx F_j$ using a set of training points $\mathcal{T} = \{(x_1, y_1), \ldots, (x_l, y_l)\} = \{X, Y\}$ obtained from microkernels. Each point in the training set comprises the signature vector $x_{(.)}$ and its corresponding multi-objective vector $y_{(.)} \in \mathbb{R}^m$.

Modeling with ML typically requires a pipeline of methods such as data preprocessing, variable importance analysis, variable selection, and model selection. The complexity of employing an effective ML pipeline is beyond most HPC users because of the algorithmic choices available for each method; therefore, users tend to resort to rules of thumb, which often result in nonrobust models. We develop a methodology that automatically selects an ML pipeline for the multi-objective modeling problem.

We focus on a signature vector consisting primarily of hardware counters exposed by the underlying hardware and collected using the Performance Application Programming Interface (PAPI) [26]. Hardware counters provide a convenient mechanism to measure the extent to which applications utilize/stress different architectural elements—e.g., counters that measure the number of branch instructions can be used to assess the level of stress that different applications put on the branch predictors. As such, a vector of hardware counters can be used to describe an application. In addition, a given application's power and performance behavior are affected by power- and performance-related hardware settings (e.g., CPU clock frequency, and power caps). Consequently, we add CPU clock frequency to the signature vector.

3   Proposed Approach

AutoMOMML consists of a pipeline of algorithmic modules (shown in Fig. 1) that can be grouped into two stages. The first stage is the dimension reduction stage, which reduces the number of inputs and outputs required for modeling via correlation analysis, input importance, and input selection modules. This stage reduces modeling complexity. The second stage is the model selection stage, where several supervised-learning methods are evaluated and fine-tuned on the training set; high-performing methods are then composed to obtain the multi-objective models.

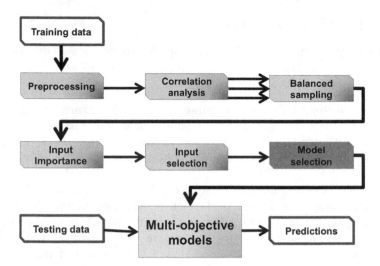

Fig. 1. AutoMOMML framework: multiple arrows after correlation analysis indicate that subsequent models are run for each objective.

3.1 Dimension Reduction

Data Preprocessing: Different entries in the signature vector x can take different ranges of values. For example, instruction-cache-related counts (e.g., L1 instruction cache misses) are usually orders of magnitude smaller than data-cache-related counts (e.g., L1 data cache misses). This difference in the range of values that entries in x can take affects several algorithmic modules in the pipeline. AutoMOMML adopts *range transformation* [11] to scale the values of each column in X to $[0, 1]$.

Correlation Analysis: This module computes the pairwise correlation to check for correlation among inputs. Given two input columns j and j' of X, the Pearson correlation coefficient $\rho \in [-1.0, 1.0]$ is given by the ratio of the covariance between j and j' to the product of the standard deviations of j and j'. When the value of $|\rho|$ is greater than a user-defined cutoff parameter `ccoff`, the input $x^{j'}$ that corresponds to column j' is removed from further analysis. The same analysis is applied on the output matrix Y to eliminate correlated outputs. Note that if two outputs are correlated, then it suffices to model only one of them. There are correlated outputs—power drawn by two sockets are correlated to each other and the same is true for the power drawn by two sets of DIMMs. Instead of modeling all these, it is enough to model only uncorrelated ones.

For each uncorrelated output u, AutoMOMML creates an output-specific training set $\mathcal{T}_u$. It comprises all uncorrelated inputs and the output u. After this analysis, the subsequent algorithmic modules are run for each $\mathcal{T}_u$; consequently, each $\mathcal{T}_u$ can be tackled independently.

Balanced Sampling: Heavily skewed distribution of response u in $\mathcal{T}_u$ can lead to unbalanced training points. This is due to the fact that we cannot explicitly control samples in performance counter (input) space and the corresponding outputs. When these points are used for predictive modeling, the model will have high prediction accuracy in high (probability) density regions but not in other areas. To address this issue, we adopt *over sampling* strategy, in which training points are sampled repeatedly from low-frequency ranges. Given an output-specific set T_u, we consider E equal-sized intervals for the output u. Let E_{max} be the number of points that belong to the high-frequency interval. For each of the remaining intervals, the number of points is increased to E_{max} by repeatedly sampling (with replacement) from that interval. Thus, for each output, the total number of points in the training set will be $E \times E_{max}$. We denote the resulting balanced training set by T'_u.

Input Importance: This module analyzes the impact of the uncorrelated inputs on the output and tries to remove some inputs from further consideration. The results can be used to understand (and rank) the application characteristics that affect the power and performance responses the most.

For this purpose, the random forest (**rf**) method [12], a state-of-the-art supervised-learning method for nonlinear regression, is adopted. The **rf** method uses a decision-tree-based approach that recursively partitions the multidimensional input space $\mathcal{D}$ into hyperrectangles such that inputs with similar output values fall within the same hyperrectangle. Partitions give rise to a decision tree of if-else rules as shown in Fig. 2. The tree shows that DRAM power is highly dependent on how the codes utilize on-chip and off-chip instruction and data caches, along with the behaviors of the TLB and branch predictor. High DRAM power is associated

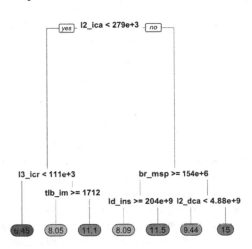

Fig. 2. Example decision-tree for DRAM power.

with a higher number of accesses to slower caches (L2 and beyond) and more TLB misses (more on this in Sect. 5). The depth of the tree is determined by a parameter **dpt**, which controls the learning ability of the tree.

Typically, a constant value is assigned to the leaf of the tree and is given by the mean of output values that fall within the same hyperrectangle. Prediction for a new input x^* is obtained by finding the hyperrectangle to which this point belongs using the decision tree and returning the constant value at the associated leaf. The strength of the **rf** method lies in using a set of decision trees because the ensemble corrects the instability of the individual trees. The predicted value for x^* is the average of leaf values obtained from each generated tree.

AutoMOMML deploys the permutation accuracy importance of **rf**. For a given training set T'_u, by randomly permuting the values of column j in X, the

---

Algorithm 1. Model-based input selection.

Input: Number of folds, K, for cross-validation, training points $\mathcal{T}_u''$, a set S of subset
    sizes, error tolerance percentage $\delta\%$, set $\mathcal{I}_u$ of inputs
    /* cross-validation phase */
1 create K folds $\{\mathcal{T}_{u1}'', \cdots, \mathcal{T}_{uK}''\}$ from $\mathcal{T}_u''$
2 **for** $k = 1 : K$ **do**
3      $\mathcal{T}_{out} \leftarrow \mathcal{T}_{uk}''; \mathcal{T}_{in} \leftarrow \mathcal{T}_u'' \backslash \mathcal{T}_{out}$
4      $u_{obsr} \leftarrow$ observed output in $\mathcal{T}_{out}$
5      $\mathcal{M}_{rf} \leftarrow$ fit($\mathcal{T}_{in}, \mathcal{I}_u''$)
6   compute *permut. acc. importance* of $\mathcal{I}_u''$
7   **for** each $s \in S$ **do**
8          $\mathcal{I}_s \leftarrow s$ most important inputs from $\mathcal{I}_u''$
9          $\mathcal{M}_{rf} \leftarrow$ fit($\mathcal{T}_{in}, \mathcal{I}_s$)
10        $u_{pred} \leftarrow$ predict($\mathcal{M}_{rf}, \mathcal{T}_{out}$)
11        $err_{ks} \leftarrow$ RMSE(u_{obsr}, u_{pred})
12   **end for**
13 **end for**
    /* subset selection phase */
14 $\overline{err}_s \leftarrow \frac{\sum_{k=1}^{K} err_{ks}}{K}$
15 $\overline{err}^* \leftarrow \min_{s \in S} \overline{err}_s$
Output: $s_{best} = \arg\min\{s \in S : \overline{err}_s \leq \overline{err}^* \times (1 + \delta\%)\}$

---

original relationship between input x^j and the response u will be broken. When X with permuted x^j is used to predict u, the prediction accuracy decreases substantially as compared with that of the original dataset with nonpermuted x^j. The impact of an input parameter x^j on the output o is computed as follows. For each tree, the random subsample $X' \subset X$ is split into in-bag and out-of-bag. The in-bag is used for building the tree, and the mean squared error (MSE) on the out-of-bag data is computed before and after permuting x^j in in-bag. The differences between the two are then averaged over all trees and normalized by the standard deviation of the differences. A significant increase in MSE after permuting values of x^j indicates that x^j has significant impact on u. When the increase in MSE is small (e.g., $<5\%$), x^j is removed from the set of inputs required for predicting u. Compared to other sensitivity analysis methods, this approach covers the impact of each input both individually and in combination with other inputs. Moreover, each tree is constructed only from a fraction of random inputs, thereby reducing the number of training points required. The resulting training set is denoted as $\mathcal{T}_u''$, which comprises only the significant inputs for output u.

Input Selection: Given the training set $\mathcal{T}_u''$ and a set S of input sizes, this module tries to find an input size $s \in S$ for predicting the output u. As shown in Algorithm 1, input selection is done in two phases.

    The first phase is K-fold cross-validation (lines 1–11). Training points are partitioned into K equal-sized folds by using random sampling without replacement. Out of the K folds, a single fold is retained as an out-of-bag set for validation;

the remaining $K - 1$ folds are used as in-bag points for training. Importance of each input in the in-bag points is obtained with the permutation accuracy importance of rf. For each candidate value $s \in S$, an rf model is retrained with the s most important inputs, and the root-mean-squared error (RMSE) for the prediction is obtained from the out-of-bag points. This process is repeated so that each of the K folds is used exactly once as out-of-bag.

The second phase of input selection consists of analyzing the results from the K folds to compute a single best subset size. The mean prediction error $\overline{err}_s$ for each $s \in S$ is obtained by averaging the prediction error over K folds. The algorithm chooses the smallest $s \in S$ whose prediction error $\overline{err}_s$ is not more than $\delta\%$ of the minimal mean prediction error $\overline{err}^*$. Smaller s values are preferred because they reduce the input space and can improve the predictive power of the model. Note that the s_{best} inputs for each fold can be different because the training points are different. This module handles such cases by computing the average rank of each input over all K folds and selects the top s_{best} inputs using the aggregated rank value.

Although Algorithm 1 relies on the rf method, it has been shown that for a number of modeling tasks input selection from the rf method is robust, and can improve the accuracy of other supervised-learning methods [20].

3.2 Model Selection

The model selection module consists of finding an appropriate method (and associated parameters) from a set of supervised-learning methods. A supervised-learning method that performs well on some predictive modeling tasks could be a bad choice for other tasks [6,11]. Moreover, choosing appropriate parameter settings for a given supervised-learning method is critical because it balances the bias-variance tradeoff [11] — high bias produces simpler models but leads to poor prediction accuracy, while high variance results in complex models with high prediction accuracy on the training set but can have poor prediction accuracy on the testing set.

Model selection is a difficult optimization problem. In ML research, this task has been traditionally tackled by using a trial-and-error process. New algorithmic methods have begun to emerge and have proven to be more effective than default settings and manual model selection [6]. The model selection module of Auto-MOMML considers a set of supervised-learning methods of varying complexities, tunes the parameters of each method, and combines the high-performing models to form a single model.

Algorithm 2 shows the model selection module. In addition to K and $\mathcal{T}$, it requires a set Z of supervised-learning methods and a subset $Q_z \in Q$ of parameter configurations for each method $z \in Z$. The module comprises three phases. First, for each method $z \in Z$ and for each parameter configuration $q \in Q_z$, the cross-validation phase consists of configuring z with q, training on the in-bag points and computing the prediction error on the out-of-bag points (lines 1–13). The second phase identifies the best configuration $\overline{q}_z$ for each method z by comparing the mean prediction error. In the third phase, the module selects the

---

Algorithm 2. Model selection.

Input: number K, training points $\mathcal{T}$, set Z of methods, set Q of parameter configurations for each method in Z

    /* cross-validation */

1 create K folds $\{\mathcal{T}_{u1}, \cdots, \mathcal{T}_{uK}\}$ from $\mathcal{T}_u$

2 **for** $k = 1 : K$ **do**

3      $\mathcal{T}_{out} \leftarrow \mathcal{T}_{uk}$; $\mathcal{T}_{in} \leftarrow \mathcal{T}_u \backslash \mathcal{T}_{out}$

4      $u_{obsr} \leftarrow$ observed output in $\mathcal{T}_{out}$

5   **for each** $z \in Z$ **do**

6          $Q_z \leftarrow$ subset of param configs in Q for z

7   **for each** $q \in Q_z$ **do**

8              $\mathcal{M}_z \leftarrow \texttt{fit}(\mathcal{T}_{in}, q)$

9              $u_{pred} \leftarrow \texttt{predict}(\mathcal{M}_z, \mathcal{T}_{out})$

10             $err_{kzq} \leftarrow \texttt{RMSE}(u_{obsr}, u_{pred})$

11   **end for**

12   **end for**

13 **end for**

    /* select best parameter setting for each method */

14 **for each** $z \in Z$ **do**

15   **for each** $q \in Q_z$ **do**

16          $\overline{err}_{zq} \leftarrow \frac{\sum_{k=1}^{K} err_{kzq}}{K}$

17   **end for**

18      $\overline{q}_z \leftarrow \arg\min_{q \in Q_z} \overline{err}_{zc}$

19 **end for**

    /* select best method(s) using statistical test */

20 $z^* \leftarrow \arg\min_{z \in Z} \overline{err}_{z\overline{q}_z}$

21 **for each** $z \in Z$ **do**

22   **if** $\texttt{t-test}(err_{(.)z\overline{q}_z}, err_{(.)z^*\overline{q}_{z^*}})$ cannot reject **then**

23          $\mathcal{M}_z \leftarrow \texttt{fit}(\mathcal{T}, \overline{q}_z)$

24   **end if**

25 **end for**

Output: $\mathcal{M} = \cup_z \mathcal{M}_z$

---

method z^* (configured with $\overline{q}_{z^*}$) with minimal mean prediction error as a baseline and adopts the statistical t-test to check the prediction errors of a method z ($err_{(.)z\overline{q}_z}$) is different from the baseline z^* ($err_{(.)z^*\overline{q}_{z^*}}$). The method z gets eliminated when the t-test rejects the null hypothesis that the difference is equal to zero. Note that the t-test is relatively robust to normality violations, one could easily replace the t-test with the Wilcoxon rank sum test to eliminate the low-performing learning methods automatically. The key idea behind the adoption of such a test is to remove the human from the pipeline. The methods that survive the elimination are configured with their corresponding best parameter setting and trained on all training points. The resulting models are returned as candidate models. For a given output, when there is more than one candidate model, the predictive value of a new testing point is given by the average of predicted values from each candidate model. This can be viewed as a systematic ensemble learning approach, a paradigm where multiple algorithms are used for learning from the same training set. The main difference from customary ensemble learning is that instead of using all the available models, the framework adopts only high performing ones.

In addition to `rf`, we consider five supervised-learning methods. A brief summary of each method is given below.

Linear regression (`lm`). takes the form $h(x) = c + \sum_{i=1}^{M} \alpha^i \times x^i$, where c is a constant and α^i is the coefficient of the input x^i. Training the model consists in finding the appropriate value of (c, α). This is obtained by minimizing the sum of differences between observed values in the training set and the corresponding values provided by the model.

$\mathcal{K}$-**nearest-neighbor** (`knn`) regression [11] computes the mean of the outputs of the $\mathcal{K}$ nearest (we use the Euclidean distance) points in the training set.

Support vector machines (`svm`) [22] for nonlinear regression project the input space of the training points into a higher-dimensional feature space and performing linear regression in that space. Training the `svm` consists of solving a quadratic programming problem. We adopt the widely used Gaussian radial basis function (RBF) as our kernel function. The cost v of constraint violation in the quadratic programming problem and the window parameter σ of the RBF provide tradeoffs between bias and variance.

Cubist (`cbt`) [1] is similar to `rf` but with the following differences. The **nt** trees are built sequentially such that the model of the bth tree is adjusted to correct the prediction error of the $(b-1)$th tree on the whole training set. This correction is done by adding the residuals of the $(b-1)$th tree to the response vector and fitting a new tree. Given a new testing point x^*, each tree can predict a value and nt predictions are averaged to give a final prediction. During prediction, it performs additional corrections based on **nn** nearest neighbors in the training set.

Stochastic gradient boosting (`sgb`) [17] is similar to `cbt`, in which nt trees are built sequentially but on a random subset of the training points. Each tree is generated with depth **dpt** and its leaves have at least min_o observations. At the bth iteration, a tree model is built to minimize the prediction error of the $(b-1)$th model. The key idea is that the residuals of the $(b-1)$th model are used as the negative gradient of the squared error loss function being minimized. Similar to gradient-descent algorithms, `sgb` generates a new model at the bth iteration by adding the bth tree that fits the negative gradient to the $(b-1)$th model. The bth model is multiplied by a parameter $0 < \lambda \leq 1.0$ to control the bias-variance tradeoff.

Except `lm`, all other supervised-learning methods require user-specified values for their respective parameters. Since promising values for each parameter are available for `knn`, `svm`, `rf`, `cbt`, and `sgb`, we define the set Q_z of parameter configurations for the method z using a grid. For example, if the method z has two parameters with 3 and 5 values, respectively, then we consider all possible combinations ($|Q_z| = 3 \times 5$). The set Q_z over all $z \in Z$ forms Q, which is given as input to Algorithm 2.

4   Experimental Setup

We now describe the hardware testbed, benchmarks and applications, data collection techniques, and other methodological decisions made for data collection.

Hardware Testbed Specifications: The testbed is a dual-processor node with two 8-core Intel Xeon E5-2650v2 (Ivy Bridge) processors. Each core has a 64 KB L1 cache (32 KB instruction cache and 32 KB data cache), a 256 KB combined L2 cache, and a 20 MB shared, last-level cache. The system has 64 GB of DDR3 DRAM. Hyperthreading and turbo boost are disabled for all the experiments. Each of the processors can be independently clocked at frequencies of 2.60 GHz to 1.20 GHz (at 100 MHz intervals). Processor clock frequency is changed by using the `cpufreq-utils` package available with many popular Linux distributions.

We use the RAPL (Running Average Power Limit) interface [16] to measure component-level power draw. For the processor, we collect "package power," which consists of power drawn by cores, the last-level cache and memory controller. We also collect power drawn by DRAM.

Model Training Benchmarks: AutoMOMML comes prepackaged with micro-kernels that exercise a target system's architectural components (e.g., CPU, and memory) in different ways[1]. Together, these computational kernels can be used to create power and performance profiles of the system and to learn what hardware events correlate with those profiles. These microkernels have different patterns of computation and memory access, and are highly prevalent in large-scale applications. Our hypothesis is that a sufficiently diverse set of computational kernels can be used as the basis for a general understanding of the impact that different computational properties have on performance and power draw.

Our suite draws compute kernels from a variety of scientific domains. Some of the kernels are modified versions of microkernels from the Polybench [31] and SPAPT suites [5], both of which are used to evaluate compiler-driven autotuning strategies [29]. Such kernels include matrix-matrix and matrix-vector operations, stencil kernels, and correlation and covariance calculation kernels. We also use the source code transformation framework CHiLL [14] to generate alternative implementations of a subset of Polybench kernels (dsyrk, dsyr2k, mm, mvt, and trmm). We apply cache tiling and loop unrolling code-transformation techniques to generate these variants.

The kernels are configured to run in an embarrassingly parallel mode using MPI and using all cores available on the testbed. Each MPI process initializes its own set of data structures and waits on a barrier for all the processes to finish initialization; all processes then do the exact same calculation. This configuration was motivated by two factors. First, RAPL power measurements can be made only at the per-socket level; per-core-level measurements are not available. Second, using node-level view enables our models to take contention on shared resources (e.g., last-level cache, TLB, and DRAM) into account.

---

[1] We will make the packages and the framework available on our website (http://www.sdsc.edu/~tiwari/AutoMOMML) at the time of publication.

Each kernel in our training suite is configured to run either in single or double precision. We also configure each of the kernels to work off of different levels in the memory hierarchy; that is, for each kernel, we have multiple working set sizes that fit in L1, L2, and last-level caches and main memory. This results in a total of eight configurations for each computational kernel.

Model Validation Applications: To validate the models, we use five application benchmarks (CG, FT, LU, MG, and SP) from the NAS parallel Benchmarks (NPBs) [3] and two co-design mini-applications from the Mantevo suite (miniGhost and CoMD) [23]. For all NPBs, we consider class C problems. We include all four stencil operations (5-, 7-, 9-, and 27-point) available in miniGhost in our evaluation. We consider both the Lennard-Jones (LJ) and embedded atom method (EAM) within CoMD. For all versions of miniGhost and CoMD, we consider a 128^3-sized grid for our evaluations. We compiled all our tests with *gcc-4.6.3* and the *-O2* flag.

For all the application benchmarks, we first profile the codes to determine hot-spot loops. We then manually instrument the source code to collect hardware counters around such loops. Intel's documentation states that RAPL counters are updated once every millisecond. However, others have noted that such updates do not occur at such intervals [21]. To ensure we have a sufficient number of power readings for each of the hot loops, we only consider loops that have per-visit lengths of more than 5 ms.

Tools: To measure the hardware counters, we wrote a simple library-based tool that allows us to "register" compute loops in kernels and applications for hardware counter data collection. Internally, the tool uses PAPI to collect the hardware counters. Each MPI process produces its own output file, and the outputs are merged to generate the node-level characterization for computations.

Data Collection: The models developed in this work are based on performance hardware counters. These counters are available on all modern processors and record low-level microarchitectural events (e.g., number of L1 cache accesses, number of mis-predicted branches) and are accessible via special-purpose model-specific registers. Hardware-level parameters (e.g., CPU clock speed and power caps on CPU and DRAM) also affect power draw and performance of computations. To also encapsulate the effects of those parameters, we measure power and performance of computations at different CPU frequencies.

Training kernels and application loops are instrumented to measure all PAPI-supported hardware counters. Hardware counter collection can be a noisy process, and care must be taken to reduce the noise in the measurements. We take two steps to limit this noise. First, we limit the number of hardware counters that we measure at a time to the number of counters that can be measured without multiplexing. This means measuring at most 11 compatible counters at a time on the Ivy Bridge testbed. Second, we measure each hardware counter five times; from among these five measurements, we take the average of the three values that are closest to each other and discard the remaining two.

Component-level power draw is measured by using PAPI. We reset the RAPL energy counters at the start of each computational loop. At the completion of the loop, the counters are read again to capture the per-component energy required to run the loop. To derive power, we divide the energy measurements with time. We express performance as cycles per instruction (`cpi`).

As a rule of thumb, ML methods require a number of training points that are roughly 10 times number of dimensions (or inputs). Our training set consists of approximately 1300 points; we generate multiple variants of the base 150 micro-kernels by using single and double precision modes and using different working set sizes (e.g., working set sizes that fit in L1 cache and L2 cache). The use of different precision modes and working set sizes produce variants that have markedly different computational signatures and performance/power profiles. We also run the kernels under multiple CPU clock frequencies. The assumption that we make when selecting the training set kernels is that these kernels cover the most common compute patterns in scientific applications (e.g., dense and sparse matrix computations, stencils, memory-intensive vs. compute-intensive kernels). For the scientific applications that we have focused on, the training set that we use provides good coverage. The implication of this underlying assumption is that when the framework encounters a computational signature that is not represented in the training set, the prediction will not be accurate enough. However, the automated nature of the framework will make it easy to incorporate this new computational signature into the existing training set.

Model Evaluation Metrics: To evaluate the predictive accuracy of the models, we rely on a set of metrics. The first of these is the arithmetic mean absolute prediction error (AMAPE), a simple and widely reported metric in the HPC literature. The main drawback of AMAPE is that it is sensitive to outliers and can even lead to misleading conclusions [36]. Given that the kernels and applications in our prediction set are diverse and have wide a range of run times and power draws, the distribution of prediction errors can be skewed. Therefore, we also rely on geometric mean absolute prediction error (GMAPE) and median absolute prediction error (MedAPE). We also report the usual ML metrics such as RMSE and R^2.

5   Experimental Results

We adopt a robust out-of-sample model validation strategy; first, from among all the microkernels, we select 75 % for training ($\approx$150 microkernels) and use them as the *kernel training set*—this is given as training data set $\mathcal{I}$ to the AutoMOMML. The remaining points in the kernel data set are tagged as the *kernel testing set*, which is then used to validate the models. This setup is based on an exploratory study in which we used 25 %, 50 %, 75 %, and 90 % for kernel training set and found that 75 % provides a reasonable coverage of input/output space. Note that sampling is done by using the names of the microkernels, which will ensure that all configurations of any given microkernel (single- and double-precision versions with working set sizes that fit in the L1, L2 and last-level

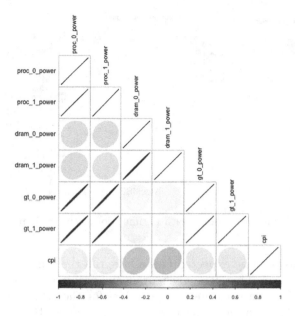

Fig. 3. Correlation analysis for output metrics.

caches and memory) belong to either the training or test set. Furthermore, we validate the models by using all points from the mini-applications, which are referred to as the *application testing set*.

AutoMOMML comprises few high-level component level parameters that can potentially affect the tradeoff between accuracy and the model building time. Based on component-level exploratory studies on the kernel training set, we set and recommend the following settings as default. The cutoff value in the correlation module is set to 0.90, and the number E of intervals in the balanced sampling module is set to 10. For the input selection, the number of folds K is set to 10, and the tolerance level, δ, is set to 1%. For each output, we generate 10 subset sizes by generating a sequence of 10 equally spaced values from 3 to $|\mathcal{I}_s|$. When the equally spaced value is not an integer, it is rounded off to the nearest integer.

5.1 Modeling Complexity Reduction

Data Preprocessing, Correlation Analysis, and Balanced Sampling: We observe that several inputs are highly correlated. Among the 40 PAPI counters, only 20 counters are uncorrelated. Highly correlated counters, for example, include data cache misses on L1 and L2 data cache accesses. These sets of counters effectively measure the same underlying phenomenon.

The results from the correlation analysis module for the outputs are shown in Fig. 3. Of 7 outputs, only 3 outputs are uncorrelated—dram_0_power and proc_0_power values are highly correlated to dram_1_power and proc_1_power,

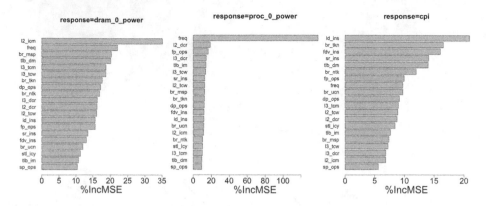

Fig. 4. Input importance with permutation accuracy importance.

respectively. This is to be expected because we run the same workload on both sockets of the testbed. Therefore, given dram and processor power for one socket, it will be straightforward to predict the values for the other socket. From this phase, AutoMOMML applies the rest of the modules in the pipeline for each of the three uncorrelated outputs (`dram_0_power`, `proc_0_power`, and `cpi`) independently.

Input Importance and Input Selection:
Fig. 4 shows the results from the input importance module. The plots show the impact of the input on the three outputs using permutation accuracy importance of the `rf` method. The x-axis shows percentage increase in MSE (%IncMSE) after permuting the input column x^i in the training set. For `dram_0_power`, we observe that on-chip (L1 and L2) and off-chip (L3) cache-related activities (reads/writes/accesses/misses for both data and instructions) emerge as the

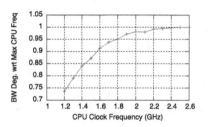

Fig. 5. Memory performance at different CPU clock frequencies.

most significant inputs. CPU clock frequency (freq) appears as the second most important input. To explain this counterintuitive observation, we took note of previous work [32] and used the lmbench benchmark [28] to measure memory read bandwidth across different CPU clock frequencies on our testbed. The results are plotted in Fig. 5. The curve shows that memory performance (measured in terms of the read bandwidth) degrades by roughly 26 % when CPU clock frequency is reduced to 1.2 GHz from 2.6 GHz. The power drawn by DRAM at 1.2 GHz is roughly 7 % lower than the power drawn at 2.6 GHz CPU clock frequency. A particularly interesting entry in the rankings is the branch mispredicted event. We attribute this to the potential of branch mispredictions to increase instruction cache misses by fetching the wrong instruction streams [1]. If the instruction footprint is larger than the exclusive L1 instruction cache, the trips to memory for instructions can significantly increase if instructions cached in inclusive L2 (and L3) caches are frequently evicted because of contention with data. TLB data misses also contribute to the DRAM power draw. Each TLB miss (on data or instruction) triggers a load from main memory in addition to a page walk. TLB misses will, therefore, also have implications for the cpi.

For the proc_0_power, the most significant parameter is freq, which is followed by memory, floating point, TLB, and cache-related events. For cpi, events related to memory (loads and stores) and branch units are the most significant. Memory and branch units contribute heavily to CPU stalls (or wasted cycles). Memory-related stalls are mainly due to poor data locality, which leads to poor cache usage. The performance of branch units is important because more than 10 % of the total instructions in the microkernels, on average, are branch instructions. Whether or not a given branch is accurately predicted therefore has a significant impact on performance. Even though branch predictor units in modern Intel processors are highly accurate, branch mispredictions incur a high penalty by requiring a complete flush of the deep instruction pipeline.

Using the results from this module, AutoMOMML removes inputs that do not have significant impact on the output. For each output, when %IncMSE for an input x^i is less than 5 %, it is removed from the predictor list for the corresponding output. Nevertheless, the results show that no input is insignificant for the three outputs. Note that the rf method is effective in identifying impactful parameters but it has limitations in detecting insignificant inputs [20].

Figure 6 shows the results from the input selection module. Algorithm 1 is run for each output with 10 subset sizes. The general trend is that increasing the number of inputs decreases RMSE, but the reduction becomes insignificant after a certain number of inputs. The results also show the number of inputs under various tolerance levels. For the adopted default tolerance of 1 %, AutoMOMML selects 8, 6, and 13 inputs for dram_0_power, proc_0_power, and cpi, respectively. The selected j inputs for an output correspond to the top j inputs for the same output in Fig. 4.

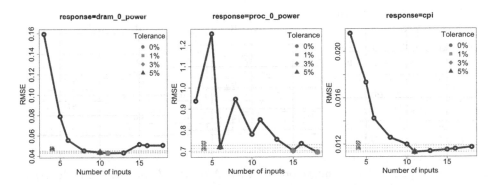

Fig. 6. Model-based input selection results.

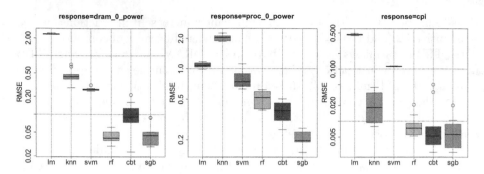

Fig. 7. Model selection results.

5.2   Model Selection

Each learning method is configured to run with 30 parameter configurations. The best parameter setting is obtained from the 10-fold cross-validation, as described in Algorithm 2. Figure 7 shows the box plots obtained from 10 RMSE values of each method with its best parameter setting. As evidenced by the box plot, the t-test establishes different model combinations based on the given output: for dram_0_power, rf and sgb are selected for bagging; for cpi rf, cbt, and sgb require being combined; for proc_0_power, sgb outperforms all other models.

To build the final predictive models, for each output, the selected methods are configured with their corresponding best parameter setting and retrained with the kernel training set (150 microkernels). Given an unseen point, the predicted value is given by the arithmetic mean of predicted values from the corresponding models — e.g., cpi prediction is given by the mean of predicted values from rf, cbt, and sgb models.

5.3   Model Validation

Table 1 summarizes the validation results on kernel and application testing sets. Recall that this is out-of-sample validation—i.e., the testing set points are not used in training the models. On the kernel testing set, we observe a high prediction accuracy

Table 1. Model validation results

Response	R^2	RMSE	AMAPE (%)	MedAPE (%)	GMAPE (%)
Kernel testing set					
proc_0_power	0.99	0.84	1.41	0.94	0.76
dram_0_power	0.89	1.00	4.60	1.23	1.50
cpi	0.93	0.19	17.4	13.3	8.57
Application testing set					
proc_0_power	0.95	1.98	3.11	2.30	1.87
dram_0_power	0.45	2.36	15.9	8.00	7.16
cpi	0.91	0.47	15.5	12.9	7.63

for dram_0_power and proc_0_power with AMAPE, GMAPE, and MedAPE values within 5 %. MAPE's sensitivity to a few outliers is evident in the case of cpi. While the MAPE for cpi is 17.4 %, GMAPE and MedAPE values are 8.57 % and 13.3 %, respectively. We also note that R^2 value for cpi is 0.93, which suggests that the model accurately captures the relationship between inputs and outputs well and that the model can be effective in comparing two competing code optimization strategies in an autotuning (e.g., selection of code variants) or run-time environment (e.g., selection of CPU clock frequency).

The results with the application testing set are promising and show a trend similar to that of kernel testing set. In particular, for `cpi` and `proc_0_power`, AMAPE, GMAPE, MedAPE, and R^2 values are similar to the values observed in the kernel testing set. Despite the fact that AMAPE for `dram_0_power` is 15.9 %, GMAPE and MedAPE are not more than 8 %. The RMSE value shows that, on average, the prediction is off only by 2.36 W. Closer examination of the results for `dram_0_power` prediction reveals that one instance of the NAS Parallel Benchmark, FT, shows a rather high prediction error ($\sim$30 %). Compared to other mini-applications and kernel testing set, FT's computational loops tend to have large number of function calls, which can affect instruction cache performance and execute significantly large number of branch instructions.

6   Related Work

The closest related work is the MuMMI [37] end-to-end automatic multi-objective modeling framework. MuMMI requires that training and testing points come from *the same* application. Thus, the data collection and modeling are needed for each application and obtained multi-objective models are application-specific. Consequently, modeling problem becomes relatively easy. MuMMI uses linear correlation for input selection, a linear model to capture the relationship between PAPI counters and performance, power, and energy. The major difference between AutoMOMML and MuMMI is that the models obtained from the former is not application-specific—i.e, within AutoMOMML, for a given system, model development is a one time process that consists of collecting training data using microkernels and using that data to train models.

From a methodological perspective, in [30] six supervised-learning methods are used to learn the relationship between hardware counters, source-code transformation parameters (tiling, parallelization, vectorization, and data locality improvement) and performance. It is a semi-automatic approach because input importance and selection and model selection are manually driven. In [34], kernel-specific surrogate models built by using artificial neural networks were used to model the relationship between compiler transformation parameters and objectives such as power draw, execution time, and energy usage of HPC kernels.

Research in model-guided autotuning has focused on developing online surrogate models for performance [18,27,33]. In [13,19], the authors developed online surrogate models for several scientific kernels on multicore architectures. In [7], the authors adopted boosted regression trees for obtaining online surrogate models for a GPU implementation of an image-filtering kernel.

Performance counters have been used to develop predictive power models in multiple research projects [9,10,24]. Bertran et al. [9] use the notion of "power components" (closely related architectural elements), develop microkernels that stress those components separately, identify a set of performance counters that can be used to quantify such stress, and use those performance counters to develop linear-regression-based power models. Isci and Martonosi [24] use a similar approach to identify a set of counters that can used to approximate the activities within key architectural components. The hardware counters are then used to develop component-level power models. Bircher and John [10] use performance hardware counters to develop power models that can predict system level power usage as a combination of component-level power usage. Lim et al. [25] developed a general approach for building system power estimation models based on hardware performance counters.

ML-based techniques have also been applied for multi-objective modeling in design space exploration—see [2, 15] and references therein. Their focus is in the adoption of supervised learning algorithms to maximize prediction accuracy and minimize the number of expensive simulations; they do not provide a pipeline of algorithmic components for end-to-end automated multi-objective modeling.

7   Conclusion

Automated modeling techniques have the potential to provide valuable hints for proactive and/or reactive steering of extreme scale systems towards better energy efficiency and reliability. To that end, this paper presented the AutoMOMML framework, a general-purpose machine-learning based framework for modeling multiple objectives. We applied the framework to model power and performance on a widely used Intel architecture and showed that the framework is capable of (1) producing highly accurate models that can predict power and performance of real-world application benchmarks, and (2) providing valuable information on how the modeled objectives relate to the properties of applications and power and performance related hardware parameters.

Our work in this area is only beginning. The fact that models trained using empirical data collected for microbenchmarks can predict power and performance of application benchmarks (i.e., out-of-sample prediction) across all CPU frequency settings is highly encouraging. Such predictions will form the cornerstones for developing, for example, intelligent runtime systems that can steer execution towards better energy efficiency by using model-guided selection of power-related hardware parameters. We are already pursuing multiple research avenues in this general genre: incorporating AutoMOMML within an autotuning framework [4], energy-aware computing framework [35], and the introspective and adaptive runtime systems envisioned for future extreme-scale systems [8].

Acknowledgments. This work was supported by the U.S. Department of Energy, Office of Science, Advanced Scientific Computing Research program under contract number DE-AC02-06CH11357.

References

1. Ailamaki, A., DeWitt, D.J., Hill, M.D., Wood, D.A.: DBMSs on a modern processor: where does time go? In: Proceedings of the International Conference on Very Large Data Bases, VLDB 1999, pp. 266–277, San Francisco (1999)
2. Azizi, O., Mahesri, A., Lee, B.C., Patel, S.J., Horowitz, M.: Energy-performance tradeoffs in processor architecture and circuit design: a marginal cost analysis. In: ACM SIGARCH Computer Architecture News, vol. 38, pp. 26–36. ACM (2010)
3. Bailey, D.H., Barszcz, E., Barton, J.T., Browning, D.S., Carter, R.L., Dagum, L., Fatoohi, R.A., Frederickson, P.O., Lasinski, T.A., Schreiber, R.S., Simon, H.D., Venkatakrishnan, V., Weeratunga, S.K.: The NAS parallel benchmarks-summary and preliminary results. In: Proceedings of ACM/IEEE Conference on Supercomputing, SC 1991, New York (1991)
4. Balaprakash, P., Tiwari, A., Wild, S.M.: Multi objective optimization of HPC kernels for performance, power, and energy. In: Jarvis, S.A., Wright, S.A., Hammond, S.D. (eds.) PMBS 2013. LNCS, vol. 8551, pp. 239–260. Springer, Heidelberg (2014)
5. Balaprakash, P., Wild, S., Norris, B.: SPAPT: search problems in automatic performance tuning. Proc. Comp. Sci. **9**, 1959–1968 (2012)
6. Bergstra, J., Bengio, Y.: Random search for hyper-parameter optimization. J. Mach. Learn. Res. **13**(1), 281–305 (2012)
7. Bergstra, J., Pinto, N., Cox, D.: Machine learning for predictive auto-tuning with boosted regression trees. In: Innovative Parallel Computing (InPar 2012), pp. 1–9. IEEE (2012)
8. Berry, M., Potok, T.E., Balaprakash, P., Hoffmann, H., Vatsavai, R., Prabhat: Machine learning and understanding for intelligent extreme scale scientific computing and discovery. Technical report (2015)
9. Dertian, R., González, M., Martorell, X., Navarro, N., Ayguadé, E.: A systematic methodology to generate decomposable and responsive power models for CMPs. IEEE Trans. Comp. **62**(7), 1289–1302 (2013)
10. Bircher, W.L., John, L.K.: Complete system power estimation: a trickle-down approach based on performance events. In: International Symposium on Performance Analysis of Systems and Software, ISPASS 2007, pp. 158–168. IEEE (2007)
11. Bishop, C.M.: Pattern Recognition and Machine Learning, vol. 1. Springer, New York (2006)
12. Breiman, L.: Random forests. Mach. Learn. **45**(1), 5–32 (2001)
13. Cavazos, J., Fursin, G., Agakov, F., Bonilla, E., O'Boyle, M.F., Temam, O.: Rapidly selecting good compiler optimizations using performance counters. In: IEEE International Symposium on Code Generation and Optimization (CGO 2007), pp. 185–197 (2007)
14. Chen, C., Chame, J., Hall, M.W.: CHiLL: a framework for composing high-level loop transformations. TR 08–897, Univ. of Southern California, June 2008
15. Chen, T., Guo, Q., Tang, K., Temam, O., Xu, Z., Zhou, Z.-H., Chen, Y.: Archranker: a ranking approach to design space exploration. In: ACM/IEEE 41st International Symposium on Computer Architecture (ISCA), pp. 85–96. IEEE (2014)
16. David, H., Gorbatov, E., Hanebutte, U.R., Khanna, R., Le, C.: Rapl: memory power estimation and capping. In: 2010 ACM/IEEE International Symposium on Low-Power Electronics and Design (ISLPED), pp. 189–194, August 2010
17. Friedman, J.H.: Stochastic gradient boosting. Comput. Stat. Data Anal. **38**(4), 367–378 (2002)

18. Fursin, G., Miranda, C., Temam, O., Namolaru, M., Yom-Tov, E., Zaks, A., Mendelson, B., Bonilla, E., Thomson, J., Leather, H., et al.: MILEPOST GCC: machine learning based research compiler. In: GCC Summit (2008)
19. Ganapathi, A., Kuno, H., Dayal, U., Wiener, J.L., Fox, A., Jordan, M., Patterson, D.: Predicting multiple metrics for queries: better decisions enabled by machine learning. In: IEEE International Conference on Data Engineering (ICDE 2009), pp. 592–603 (2009)
20. Genuer, R., Poggi, J.-M., Tuleau-Malot, C.: Variable selection using random forests. Pattern Recogn. Lett. **31**(14), 2225–2236 (2010)
21. Hähnel, M., Döbel, B., Völp, M., Härtig, H.: Measuring energy consumption for short code paths using RAPL. SIGMETRICS Perform. Eval. Rev. **40**(3), 13–17 (2012)
22. Hearst, M.A., Dumais, S.T., Osman, E., Platt, J., Scholkopf, B.: Support vector machines. IEEE Intel. Sys. App. **13**(4), 18–28 (1998)
23. Heroux, M.A., Doerfler, D.W., Crozier, P.S., Willenbring, J.M., Edwards, H.C., Williams, A., Rajan, M., Keiter, E.R., Thornquist, H.K., Numrich, R.W.: Improving performance via mini-applications. Sandia National Laboratories. Technical report SAND-5574 (2009)
24. Isci, C., Martonosi, M.: Runtime power monitoring in high-end processors: methodology and empirical data. In: International Symposium on Microarchitecture, MICRO 36, p. 93. IEEE Computer Society, Washington, DC (2003)
25. Lim, M.Y., Porterfield, A., Fowler, R.: Softpower: fine-grain power estimations using performance counters. In: Proceedings of the 19th ACM International Symposium on High Performance Distributed Computing, pp. 308–311. ACM (2010)
26. London, K., Moore, S., Mucci, P., Seymour, K., Luczak, R.: The PAPI cross-platform interface to hardware performance counters. In: Department of Defense Users' Group Conference Proceedings, pp. 18–21 (2001)
27. Magni, A., Dubach, C., O'Boyle, M.F.P.: A large-scale cross-architecture evaluation of thread-coarsening. In: Proceedings of the International Conference on High Performance Computing, Networking, Storage and Analysis, SC 2013 (2013)
28. McVoy, L., Staelin, C.: lmbench: portable tools for performance analysis. In: USENIX Annual Technical Conference, ATEC 1996, p. 23. USENIX Association, Berkeley (1996)
29. Norris, B., Hartono, A., Gropp, W.: Annotations for productivity and performance portability. In: Petascale Computing: Algorithms and Applications, pp. 443–462. Chapman & Hall (2007)
30. Park, E., Cavazos, J., Pouchet, L.-N., Bastoul, C., Cohen, A., Sadayappan, P.: Predictive modeling in a polyhedral optimization space. Int. J. Parallel Program. **41**(5), 704–750 (2013)
31. Pouchet, L.-N.: PolyBench: the polyhedral benchmark suite (2012). http://www.cse.ohio-state.edu/pouchet/software/polybench/
32. Schöne, R., Hackenberg, D., Molka, D.: Memory performance at reduced CPU clock speeds: an analysis of current x86 64 processors. In: Proceedings of USENIX Conference on Power-Aware Computing and Systems (2012)
33. Spillinger, O., Eliahu, D., Fox, A., Demmel, J.: Matrix multiplication algorithm selection with support vector machines (2015)
34. Tiwari, A., Laurenzano, M.A., Carrington, L., Snavely, A.: Modeling power and energy usage of HPC kernels. In: IEEE International Conference on Parallel and Distributed Processing Symposium Workshops (IPDPSW 2012), pp. 990–998 (2012)

35. Tiwari, A., Peraza, J., Laurenzano, M., Carrington, L., Snavely, A.: Green queue: customized large-scale clock frequency scaling. In: International Conference on Cloud and Green Computing, CGC 2012 (2012)
36. Tofallis, C.: A better measure of relative prediction accuracy for model selection and model estimation. J. Oper. Res. Soc. **66**, 1352–1362 (2014)
37. Wu, X., Lively, C., Taylor, V., Chang, H.-C., Su, C.-Y., Cameron, K., Moore, S., Terpstra, D., Weaver, V.: Mummi: multiple metrics modeling infrastructure. In: ACIS International Conference on Software Engineering, Artificial Intelligence, Networking and Parallel/Distributed Computing (SNPD), pp. 289–295 (2013)

Datacenters and Cloud

Supercomputing Centers and Electricity Service Providers: A Geographically Distributed Perspective on Demand Management in Europe and the United States

Tapasya Patki[1]([⊠]), Natalie Bates[2], Girish Ghatikar[3], Anders Clausen[4], Sonja Klingert[5], Ghaleb Abdulla[1], and Mehdi Sheikhalishahi[6]

[1] Lawrence Livermore National Laboratory, Livermore, USA
patki1@llnl.gov
[2] Energy Efficient High Performance Computing Working Group, Livermore, USA
[3] GreenLots and Lawrence Berkeley National Laboratory, Berkeley, USA
[4] University of Southern Denmark, Odense, Denmark
[5] The University of Mannheim, Mannheim, Germany
[6] Create-Net, Trento, Italy

Abstract. Supercomputing Centers (SCs) have high and variable power demands, which increase the challenges of the Electricity Service Providers (ESPs) with regards to efficient electricity distribution and reliable grid operation. High penetration of renewable energy generation further exacerbates this problem. In order to develop a symbiotic relationship between the SCs and their ESPs and to support effective power management at all levels, it is critical to understand and analyze how the existing relationships were formed and how these are expected to evolve.

In this paper, we first present results from a detailed, quantitative survey-based analysis and compare the perspectives of the European grid and SCs to the ones of the United States (US). We then show that contrary to the expectation, SCs in the US are more open toward cooperating and developing demand-management strategies with their ESPs. In order to validate this result and to enable a thorough comparative study, we also conduct a qualitative analysis by interviewing three large-scale, geographically-distributed sites: Oak Ridge National Laboratory (ORNL), Lawrence Livermore National Laboratory (LLNL), and the Leibniz Supercomputing Center (LRZ). We conclude that perspectives on demand management are dependent on the electricity market and pricing in the geographical region and on the degree of control that a particular SC has in terms of power-purchase negotiation.

1 Introduction

Current Supercomputing Centers (SCs) for High-Performance Computing (HPC) with peta-scale capabilities have high power demands, with peak requirements of over 30 MW and fluctuations of a few megawatts over short-time scales [4].

© Springer International Publishing Switzerland 2016
J.M. Kunkel et al. (Eds.): ISC High Performance 2016, LNCS 9697, pp. 243–260, 2016.
DOI: 10.1007/978-3-319-41321-1_13

This trend is expected to continue in the future as we push the limits of supercomputing further. As a result, Electricity Service Providers (ESPs) for such SCs need to support efficient electricity generation, transmission and distribution along with reliable grid operation. ESPs today already face reliability concerns for accommodating megawatt-level fluctuations from SCs and often require HPC client sites to forecast their electricity use. The acceptance and proliferation of renewable sources of energy further adds to the variability in electricity generation, making grid reliability even more challenging. A tighter integration and open communication between ESPs and their client SCs is thus critical as we proceed toward the next generation of supercomputing.

At present, most ESP-SC relationships are linear and unidirectional. Power is typically generated, distributed and delivered to customer sites without direct or active involvement, and most electricity pricing contracts are negotiated without any communication requirements. Going forward, however, it is expected that a multi-directional relationship will evolve between the ESPs and SCs. Communication and control will flow from end-customers to one or more of the electricity generation and distribution entities, and contract terms will enforce stringent usage requirements. The cloud and data center providers, such as Google, have already started to anticipate this multi-directional relationship and are taking advantage of this changing landscape. For example, Google's response suggests vertical integration, especially with Google's Energy Subsidiary which gives Google the right to sell energy within the United States [11]. Another example is the SmartGrid initiative [19] by the U.S. Department of Energy, which is making electricity delivery faster and more efficient by involving customers, adjusting to dynamic demands, and by providing automated solutions and quick responses to remote facilities. *Demand management* (DM) is a set of explicit actions taken by large-scale data centers, cloud providers, SCs and other entities in order to establish such multi-directional relationships with their ESPs. One key element is the *temporal* component that indicates the timescale requirements for the DM actions. The benefits of DM depend on the timescales of negotiation and implementation of this relationship with the ESPs. The Energy-Efficient High-Performance Computing Working Group (EE HPC WG) seeks to analyze the impact of DM implementations for SCs with HPC workloads and for their ESPs.

In our previous work, we focused on understanding how ESPs and SCs can work together to improve DM through grid-integrated services by surveying large-scale SCs in the United States [4]. We developed a questionnaire and surveyed 11 sites. We noted that none of the SCs are working directly with their ESPs to leverage the benefits of DM. Our main conclusion from this work was that SCs in the United States were interested in a tighter integration with their ESPs, but a business case for the same had not been well-demonstrated. In this work, we expand our analysis to include European SCs. We accomplish this by extending the aforementioned questionnaire and quantitatively surveying nine European SCs.

The main motivation for our geographical study lies in the way electricity is priced. In Europe, electricity is more expensive and is subject to more variability because of the larger mix of renewable sources. Additionally, the SCs in both geographical regions have different maximum power demands. For example, in the United States, four of the SCs we surveyed had HPC workloads of 10 MW or more. The remaining SCs in the United States as well as all the SCs in Europe had workloads of 5 MW of less. The size of demand and its variability have different and co-related impacts on the operation of the SCs and grid. Furthermore, the European grid is more integrated and differs in terms of its market interconnections than the United States, which impacts the benefits of DM for SCs [10].

The key objectives for this study thus included:

– Understanding the similarities and differences in the ESP-SC relationships based on geographical locations in Europe and the United States,
– Understanding how these relationships impact the motivation for DM and how the SCs under consideration can leverage the DM benefits, and,
– Determining any necessary regulatory and technology interventions for grid-integrated DM.

Our initial expectation was that the European SCs will be more tightly integrated with their ESPs because of the higher prices and more extensive use of renewables. Contrary to our expectations, however, we found that the United States shows more interest in responding to requests from their ESPs than Europe. The four SCs that needed 10 MW or more had active communication channels with their ESPs about responding to grid requests. None of the SCs in Europe had similar relationships with their ESPs. In this paper, we present these results and analyze the differences across the two geographies that may have led to this result. We first present results from our quantitative survey from 9 European SC sites and 11 United States SC sites, and then conduct a detailed qualitative analysis for three major SCs: Oak Ridge National Laboratory (ORNL), Lawrence Livermore National Laboratory (LLNL), and Leibniz Supercomputing Center (LRZ). The main goal for the qualitative analysis is to delve deeper into the electricity pricing structures as well as the available incentives for a tighter integration, and to understand what motivates the existing relationship between SCs and their ESPs to leverage the benefits from DM.

Section 2 motivates the need for an open multi-directional relationship between SCs and their ESPs and Sect. 3 presents an overview of DM actions. Section 4 presents the quantitative results from the questionnaire. In Sect. 5, we review our site-specific interviews and present a qualitative analysis of the DM options available to these sites. Section 6 presents related work, and Sect. 7 summarizes our results and discusses future research directions.

2   Motivation for Demand Management

We measured the power consumption of Sequoia, which is the world's third fastest supercomputer (17.1 petaflops) hosted at LLNL. Sequoia is a BlueGene/Q system with 98,304 16-core PowerPC A2 compute nodes and has a power rating of 7.9 MW. The data from Sequoia was collected at three-minute intervals over three days and the results can be seen from Fig. 1. Information about the workload being executed was not made available. The y-axis is the power consumed, and the x-axis represents the time samples. As can be noted from this figure, fluctuations of a few megawatts are fairly common. Some of these fluctuations may be related to maintenance cycles and could be scheduled or forecasted. However, there are other times where the fluctuations are not scheduled in advance and may occur as a result of the workload that is executing on the supercomputer.

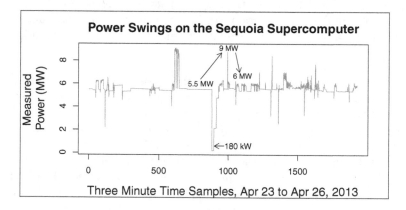

Fig. 1. Sequoia supercomputer power swings

We observe similar trends with data from Titan, which is the world's second-fastest supercomputer hosted at ORNL. Titan is a 17.6 petaflop system with a power rating of 8.2 MW. It comprises of 18,688 16-core AMD Opteron 6274 compute nodes, and each compute node has a NVIDIA Tesla K20X GPU. Figure 2 shows data gathered from identical WL-LSMS executions on the Titan supercomputer. WL-LSMS is a benchmark that performs thermodynamic calculations [15]. The graph in Fig. 2 has instantaneous power in MW on the y-axis and the benchmark execution time on the x-axis. The data is reported for a CPU-only run as well as a GPU-enabled run. The power samples for the CPU-only run were collected every 8 min, where as the samples for the GPU-enabled run were reported every second. The red line represents the GPU-enabled run and the blue line represents the CPU-only run. As can be noted from this data, substantial power swings are observed on Titan, both in the case of CPU-only as well as GPU-enabled runs.

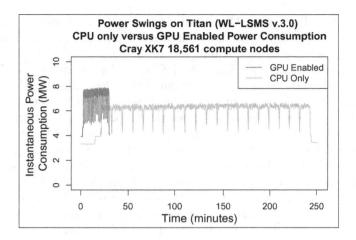

Fig. 2. Titan supercomputer power swings (Color figure online)

The energy efficiency improves by about seven times when the GPU is enabled as the application runs significantly faster. Note that the improvement in energy efficiency is application-dependent, and that the power swings observed here are a result of the ensemble runs of WL-LSMS. In this example, they occur when a new set of calculations is being initiated and there is a pause between the compute-intensive work phases. This trend is observed for both the GPU-enabled and the CPU-only runs. Peak power increased by about one megawatt with the GPU-enabled run. The net effect is that less energy is used to get the same amount of work done in the GPU-enabled case, but with slightly higher power draw and potentially higher power variability.

Both these datasets clearly indicate that power fluctuations occur in real production systems, and this can affect the reliability of the ESP grid. It is thus imperative to understand how such variable power demands can be managed better. In this context, demand management (DM) is one approach to mitigate the consequences of these power fluctuations that promotes a tighter relationship between ESPs and SCs.

3 Demand Management

Demand Management covers strategies, programs and methods that SCs and ESPs can employ to ensure grid reliability. We define *strategies* as power management techniques used by SCs to manage power and provide load flexibility. Strategies may or may not improve energy efficiency. For example, *Load Migration* is a strategy that SCs may use in response to an ESP's request, and while it helps manage power effectively, it does not impact the energy efficiency of the site. On the other hand, *fine-grained power management* techniques, such as using node-level power capping, or better job scheduling algorithms are likely to improve energy efficiency but may not be as useful in response to an ESP request. Almost all sites employ some power management strategies, especially the ones involving lighting, temperature, cooling, fine-grain power management and job scheduling.

Programs are incentives offered by ESPs to their customers and to SCs in order to motivate them to help balance the electrical grid and perform power managment. Common examples include peak shedding, peak shifting and dynamic pricing. Peak shedding describes the action where SCs (or consumers) reduce their electricity consumption in response to a request from the ESP. The reduction in electricity consumption does not lead to an increase in consumption at a later point in time. Peak shifting, on the other hand, moves load from one time slot to another, in response to a request from the ESP. Lastly, dynamic pricing is a mechanism used by the ESP to incentivize an increase or decrease in consumption by varying the price of electricity over time.

Methods are used by the ESPs to balance the electrical grid in the transmission and distribution phases. Examples of methods include regulation, frequency response, grid scale storage.

Another important aspect of DM is the wider acceptance of renewable sources of energy. In the current electricity mix, the benefits of *demand forecasting* (that is, predicting the amount of power required by an SC for a certain period of time) by the SCs and their communication with their ESPs for better capacity planning and electricity purchase negotiations have been shown. Such benefits can be exercised with active DM actions within a forecasted power band as described above. With increasing variable renewable generation in the electricity mix, more granular demand forecasting by the SCs can help ESPs to identify and plan for grid impacts during over- and under-generation conditions.

4   Quantitative Study

In this section, we discuss the results from our quantitative survey. We extended our questionnaire from our previous work [4] and contacted sixteen SCs in the European region. Appendix A provides an overview of the questionnaire. The detailed definitions for each of the demand management approaches and strategies can be found in our previous work [4]. Nine out of the sixteen European SCs that we contacted responded to the questionnaire. All except one of these sites were in Top 50 supercomputers in the world [1].

Figures 3 and 4 depict the total load in megawatts for each of the respondents in the United States and in Europe. Most supercomputing sites have a total load of under 5 MW (sixteen out of twenty). Four of the surveyed supercomputing sites had a total load of over 10 MW.

Both United States and Europe had power swings and fluctuations of a few megawatts. In our questionnaire, we asked respondents to report the maximum variability that they have experienced in their SCs. The results of these for United States as well as Europe are shown in Figs. 5 and 6 respectively. In the United States, three of the eleven sites surveyed had maximum variability of over 5 MW. For our United States respondents, the minimal option for reporting this

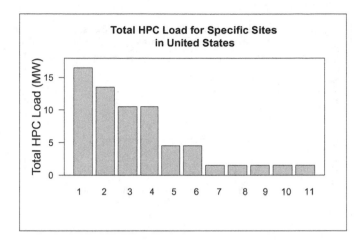

Fig. 3. Total load at SCs in United States

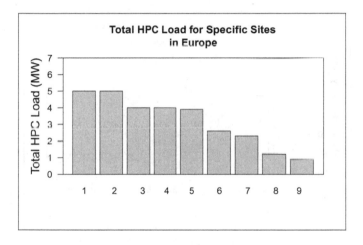

Fig. 4. Total load at SCs in Europe

was "Less than 3 MW", because of which we could not capture less intense power swings. In the European survey, we allowed the respondents to provide a more accurate value, and as shown in Fig. 6, we observed power swings in the range of half a megawatt to about 2 MW. Almost all of the respondents reported that this variability is due to maintenance cycles, and that it can be scheduled *day-ahead* if necessary.

In terms of demand management strategies, the survey indicated that there is moderate interest in grid integration strategies such as coarse- and fine- grained power management or temperature control in the United States, and low interest for the same in Europe. From the point of view of SCs, strategies such as cutting jobs or load migration have little or no interest.

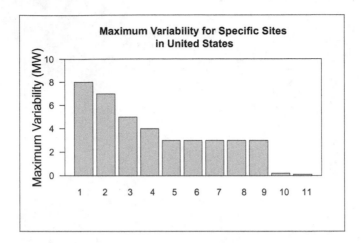

Fig. 5. Maximum variability at SCs in United States

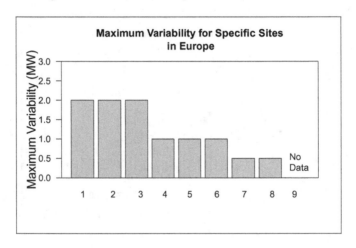

Fig. 6. Maximum variability at SCs in Europe

From our questionnaire, we also concluded that neither European nor the United States sites are engaged with peak shedding, peak shifting or dynamic pricing programs at present. More sites in the United States have communicated with their ESPs regarding these programs. While both European and United States SCs are interested in dynamic pricing, there is mixed interest in peak shedding and peak shifting. The European sites are more interested in peak shedding than peak shifting, but the United States sites are more interested in peak shifting. Both European and US sites are interested in discussing renewables with their ESPs, but there is little interest in communicating with regards to the other possible methods.

Table 1. Motivation for communicating with ESP (European respondents)

Ques: Please evaluate as high, medium or low the following motivations for your site's interest in pursuing a stronger relationship with your electricity service provider

	Low	Medium	High	Rating count
Economically justified	14.3 % (1)	28.6 % (2)	57.1 % (4)	7
Good citizen	14.3 % (1)	71.4 % (5)	14.3 % (1)	7
Adverse consequences	66.7 % (4)	16.7 % (1)	16.7 % (1)	6
Government regulation	71.4 % (5)	28.6 % (2)	0.0 % (0)	7

We also asked our European respondents to indicate what might motivate them to communicate with their ESPs. The results are shown in Table 1. As can be noted from this table, the main motivators are the financial incentives and the desire to be "good citizens". Thus, SC motivations are driven by market-based mechanisms that justify economics and social-responsibility, even under the absence of regulatory support.

Table 2. Communications with ESPs regarding available programs

Program	Europe	United States
Peak shedding	1	6
Peak shifting	0	4
Dynamic pricing	0	5

We noted that none of the European SCs communicated about grid integration potential, demand management and available flexibility with their associated ESPs. Additionally, there was little interest in a tighter integration with the ESPs. In general, the SCs in the United States seem to have a closer relationship with their ESPs than the ones in Europe. This can also be verified from Table 2, which shows that only 1 of the 9 respondents in Europe have had a discussion with their ESP.

4.1 Comments from Survey Respondents

From the comments section in our questionnaire, we noted that all SCs are already using *demand forecasting* to communicate their upcoming demands and maintenance cycle schedules with their ESPs. For example, one comment was "We project hourly average power at least a day in advance, within $+/-1MW$". Another interesting comment was "We've to ensure that our power load neither over- nor under-shoots the contracted power band. In any cases of foreseen power abnormalities we've to inform our grid provider at least two days ahead of schedule".

One of the SCs mentioned that they could not provide the forecast that was being asked by their ESP. More specifically, their comment indicated that their ESP asked for "multi-year forecast of energy requirements, additional detailed forecasting and ultimately real time data, and power projections, hour by hour, for at least a day in advance".

When it came to ESP programs, the United States SCs showed more interest. "Our site generates 30–35 MW of power yet still imports 5–10 MW. As a large generation source the utility providers see the campus as a highly attractive partner for offloading grid stress. automatic load shedding is being explored/deployed today", one of the SCs noted. Another comment was "[We are] working on load sharing of data with utility to provide better scheduling tools and address potential grid changes". One of the SCs mentioned that they demonstrated that peak shedding and shifting was possible, but not deployed due to its impact on HPC productivity.

The European SCs, on the other hand, did not have much knowledge about ESP programs. Some of the responses were "There are not so many related options and features offered by providers. We are open to further and pro-active efforts as long as providers have other kinds of programs to propose" and "With many of your questions I am wondering about the kind of contracts other centers might have and about the quality of some electricity providers".

The comments also indicated that the SCs in United States are investigating the impact of power fluctuations on the electrical grid. "[We are] working directly with provider to ensure that the effects of large load swings are understood. Have funded a simulation that accounts for all loads". and "Our provider has no problem with our load swings. They indicate no concern with our next system either, but we are still looking into possible options in case there actually is a problem". Were some of the interesting responses.

5   Qualitative Study: Site-Specific Interviews

The results presented in the previous section were based on data gathered through a questionnaire created for HPC centers based on experience from a United States context. The preliminary results of the comparison across the geographical regions gave the impression that European SCs had very limited communication with their ESPs with respect to grid integration. However, it was apparent that some SCs in Europe engage in collaboration with their ESPs in order to ensure minimal fluctuations as well as for forecasting of deviations from normal power consumption patterns. In order to shed light on the details of the relationships between SCs and ESPs that were not captured in the questionnaire, we designed a qualitative interview and surveyed ORNL, LLNL and LRZ. The thesis was that a qualitative analysis will yield more complete information and will enable us to present more thorough comparative study on the status of grid integration of SCs in Europe and the US. For each site, we asked the questions listed below. We present the information from each SC in the subsections that follow.

- What is your responsibility for negotiating the contract between your HPC facility and your ESP?
- Could you elaborate on the details of the pricing structure on your electricity? Note that for this question, we did not request specific information on the actual price the SC pays for electricity. We were interested in the type of pricing program they were enrolled in.
- Do you have any obligations towards your ESP, and if so, what is your incentive towards committing to these obligations? These obligations are characterized by being static and pre-smart grid, in the sense that no real-time communication is needed between ESP and SC. Examples include limits for allowed variability in power consumption and/or fixed power consumption limits. Examples for potential incentives include reduction in electricity price, enabling of direct payments and legislation benefits.
- Do you offer any kind of services for your ESP, and if so, what is your incentive for offering these services? These services are characterized by two way communication between the site and the ESP, where a consumer reacts to information sent by the ESP. Examples include load capping, powering up backup generations, etc.
- How do you envision your future relationship with your electricity provider? (Possible answers were: tighter, for example, by selling local generation capacity; or looser, for example, by being self-sufficient with regards to electricity needs.

5.1   Oak Ridge National Laboratory

For ORNL, DOE negotiates the contract with the ESP. ORNL gets its power from Tennessee Valley Authority (TVA), which generates, transmits and distributes the power. The DOE and TVA negotiate the power capacity that is being provisioned each year. Typically, a range for operation is chosen, for the current year, this range is 35 MW to 75 MW. In terms of electricity pricing, ORNL incurs two kinds of charges: a demand charge, which is fixed for a month, and an energy charge based on actual power consumption. The demand charge is determined by analyzing 30 min blocks and by determining the peak or maximum value for the month. The demand charge can be off-peak or on-peak based on the time of the day. It also has a time-of-use per day component. ORNL's provider, TVA, is not affected by power swings of a few megawatts (5 to 8 MW) and is very reliable. The goal for ORNL is to keep its HPC systems fully utilized in terms of power.

ORNL does not have any obligations and provide any services to its ESP. The only requirement is to operate in the range that was negotiated (35 MW to 75 MW). They have a model that explains their power usage that they provide to the TVA annually, but there is no two-way communication or forecasting. In general, the capital expenditure for the SC at ORNL dominates the operational costs. As the HPC system cost depreciates with time (for example, Titan's depreciation is about 20 K dollars per hour), there is little financial incentive to be flexible and to save on electricity costs. The goal is thus to keep their site fully utilized in terms of power.

5.2 Lawrence Livermore National Laboratory

In the case of LLNL, DOE negotiates the contract with the ESP with the help of a consulting company called Exeter. A bulk purchase of power is made for about 100 MW of power capacity from the California-Oregon Transmission Project (or COTP) and is shared between LLNL and two other DOE sites. Pacific Gas and Electric (PG&E) and Western Area Power Administration (WAPA) are used for transmission and distribution. In terms of electricity pricing, LLNL does not pay a demand charge, but only pays a flat energy charge of about 4.5 cents per kWh, which is on the lower side when compared to the industry. Forecasting is done on a regular basis in order to be a good citizen. For the scope of this questionnaire related to the HPC facility, there is not much financial incentive to save energy costs. Additionally, there are no obligations from the ESP and no services are provided. The goal is to keep the site fully utilized in terms of power and to minimize leftover power in order to be energy efficient.

5.3 Leibniz Supercomputing Center

The power contract between LRZ and *Stadtwerke München*, a Munich Power Company is the result of pan-European procurement. LRZ purchases a basic power band for one or multiple years at the European power stock exchange. Hence, the power price is determined by the European stock market. Additionally, there are charges for the power grid, renewable energy, concession levy as well as taxes which are significant. The charges for power generation and distribution constitute only 25 % of the power price in Germany. As a result, the energy costs are very expensive for LRZ.

LRZ operates in a 4 to 6 MW power band. They have a contracted power price of 0.16€ per kWh until 2018. A power grid usage fee is mainly determined by annual peak power consumption so large power swings result in much higher electricity cost. Power consumption measurements are averaged over 15 min time intervals. The annual power consumption maximum is also the average peak power consumed within a 15 min time interval. It is thus imperative to be able to forecast any power swings and to inform the ESP about the same. Better prediction models for power usage will definitely benefit LRZ in terms of electricity costs, as one of their goals is to save on energy costs. This is primarily because their energy costs dominate their operational costs. Typically, LRZ lets the ESP know about 2 days in advance for any scheduled downtimes. At present, there are no major obligations toward or services provided to the ESP, mostly because of the QOS guarantees that have to be adhered to for their users.

5.4 Analysis

The key goals for our qualitative analysis were to understand the power purchase relationships, energy use, and the level of demand management flexibility available to reduce electricity use and/or energy costs for the three SCs under consideration. Our interviews thus focused on the annual electricity purchase negotiations and pricing structure, and on characterizing SC's electricity use relative to larger campus. We also tried to identify the level of motivation for demand management for lowering peak power and energy use and for any services being offered. We observed that while some trends were common across all three sites, there were some differences. We summarize these similarities and differences below.

Similarities: An important common trend was that the power purchase negotiations were typically done by a third party (for example, DOE, Exeter or Stadtwerke München) and on an annual basis. Power capacity was negotiated by specifying an upper limit on the amount of power procured for all three sites. Additionally, in the case of ORNL and LRZ, a lower bound on the power capacity was also clearly specified. Negotiations for all three sites were done at the level of entire site or a set of collaborative sites, and not merely for the supercomputing facility that was located within the site.

Differences: We observed that the pricing structure was different in all three cases. In case of LLNL, there was a flat rate, which makes LLNL less sensitive to electricity cost variation. For ORNL, there was a variable rate, which makes it somewhat sensitive to electricity costs. LRZ, however, is very sensitive to the pricing structure because of the expensive energy costs as well as the impact of power swings on electricity costs. In terms of power fluctuations, LLNL used demand forecasting to be a good citizen. For both LLNL and ORNL, reliability was not a major concern and power variations were acceptable by the ESP. For LRZ, the electricity cost increases if there were more power swings, making them highly responsive to such variability and enabling the need for better forecasting. The electricity generation mix in the United States was mostly thermal, where as in Europe it was largely renewable sources of energy.

Overall, we believe that several factors drive the motivation for demand management. The key ones are the control that a site has when it comes to power purchase negotiations, their price sensitivity to power fluctuations, and financial as well as good-citizen-based intentions for communicating their demand with their ESP. One of the factors that was unclear in this analysis was the contribution of the electricity cost as a part of the site's annual budget or operation costs, which we plan to explore as part of our future work.

6   Related Work

The focus of our study is the relationship between ESPs and SCs. SCs are fundamentally different than data centers as they have stricter QoS and performance guarantee requirements and need to maintain high levels of utilization. At present, little research exists in the domain for demand management for SCs. Data centers are known to be capable of providing flexibility in their power consumption, and thus are great candidates to participate into energy market demand response (DR) programs. Wierman et al. [27] survey the opportunities and challenges for data center DR participation. Aikema et al.

[2] overview multiple types of ancillary service markets, and study the capacity and potential benefit by introducing a simple data center participation model. Siano [20] present a survey of DR for smart grids. Ghatikar et al. [13] exploit various load management techniques, such as load shedding and shifting for data center DR. Goiri et al. [14] propose GreenSlot, a workload scheduler to maximize the green energy consumption (that is, solar energy) while meeting the job deadline. Geographic load migration is another broadly studied data center management technique to help balance the grid, and reduce the energy cost exploiting the electricity price differences [9,16,17,24,25].

The participation of data centers in traditional DR programs, such as real-time dynamic energy pricing [12,18,26] and peak shaving [3,22,23], has been widely studied. Recently, there are a growing number of interests on the data center participation in emerging DR programs that are more profitable. Chen et al. [6] develop real-time dynamic control policies by leveraging both server level power management techniques and server state switches for data centers to provide regulation service reserves (RSRs). They also implement a prototype of the control policies on real-life server clusters with virtualized CPU resource limits [8]. Brocanelli et al. [5] propose the joint management of data center and employee Plug-in Hybrid Electric Vehicles (PHEVs) to increase the regulation profit. A systematic comparison shows that RSR is a more profitable program for data centers to participate than traditional programs such as peak shaving [7]. Clausen et al. [10] found that smaller data centers aggregated through a Virtual Power Plant are a potential resource in demand management, but no electricity markets that aimed to facilitate this type of resource existed in Denmark. However, Energinet.dk and other Nordic transmission system operators do recognize demand response and demand-side market participation as a resource in grid management, and have set forth initiatives to reducing market barriers towards this type of capacity.

DC4Cities [21] is a visionary project funded by the European Union to develop new scenarios within a smart city context, considering renewable energy availability, and a data center's energy needs. Through the development of energy management authorities (EMA) within smart cities, EMA admins can define energy goals for data centers. Workload managers at the level of each data center will then plan scheduling for applications according to energy goals and renewable energy availability, making data centers more energy adaptive.

7   Summary and Next Steps

In this paper, we conducted a quantitative and qualitative analysis on demand management perspectives in Europe and the United States from the point of view of supercomputing centers with HPC facilities. We surveyed 9 SCs in Europe and 11 SCs in the United States, most of which were part of the Top500 list. Our key findings were that contrary to our expectation, the SCs in Europe were not communicating actively with their ESPs with regards to demand management approaches. Our qualitative interviews with ORNL, LLNL and LRZ helped us understand the motivation and reasons behind this result. We observe that perspectives on demand management are dependent on the electricity market and pricing in the geographical region and on the degree of control that a particular SC has in terms of power-purchase negotiation.

In summary, we believe that the European ESP programs for DM need to be studied in greater detail and the awareness of the benefits for these programs needs to be raised among the SCs. As part of our future work, we want to explore the European ESP programs further, the lack of such closer relationships, and also conduct a similar study in Japan, which has different institutional and electricity supply challenges. We also want to conduct more qualitative analysis through in-person site interviews to understand the electricity markets and the available incentive better.

8   Additional Authors

Torsten Wilde, Leibniz Supercomputing Center
James H. Rogers, Oak Ridge National Laboratory
Ayse Coskun, Boston University
Hao Chen, Boston University
Peter M. Schwartz, Lawrence Berkeley National Laboratory
Gert Svensson, KTH Royal Institute of Technology
Bo Norregaard Jorgensen, University of Southern Denmark

Acknowledgments. The authors would like to thank Herbert Huber from the Leibniz Supercomputing Center (LRZ) and Anna Maria Bailey from Lawrence Livermore National Laboratory for the insights provided. This research used resources of the Oak Ridge Leadership Computing Facility at the Oak Ridge National Laboratory, which is supported by the Office of Science of the U.S. Department of Energy under Contract No. DE-AC05-00OR22725. This work was partially performed under the auspices of the U.S. Department of Energy by Lawrence Livermore National Laboratory under Contract DE-AC52-07NA27344 (LLNL-CONF-680495).

A   Appendix

The details of our questionnaire are presented below.

1. What is your total facility energy? This should be the same as the total facility energy number that is used for calculating PUE.
2. What is your total HPC load?
3. What is your facility PUE?
4. What is your facility's theoretical peak energy, as the infrastructure is currently fit up?
5. What is the maximum intra-hour variation in total facility energy that is likely to re-occur?
6. Do you employ coarse-grained power management strategies?
7. Do you employ fine-grained power management strategies?

8. Do you employ load migration as a strategy?
9. Do you employ job scheduling as a strategy?
10. Do you employ back-up scheduling as a strategy?
11. Do you employ shutdown as a strategy?
12. Do you employ lighting control as a strategy?
13. Do you employ increasing air temperature as a strategy?
14. Do you employ liquid temperature adjustment as a strategy?
15. Do you cut jobs as a strategy?
16. Are there any other strategies that you employ to manage and control your total facility energy in response to a request from your energy utility/provider?
17. Please evaluate each of the above strategies from questions 7 to 16 as high, medium or low, based on the MW impact of each of these strategies as a response to a grid request.
18. Have you had conversations with your electricity service provider about peak shedding?
19. Have you had conversations with your electricity service provider about peak shifting?
20. Have you had conversations with your electricity service provider about dynamic pricing?
21. Have you had conversations with your electricity service provider about grid scale storage?
22. Have you had conversations with your electricity service provider about power variability related to renewables and methods used for responding to such variability?
23. Have you had conversations with your electricity service provider about frequency response?
24. Have you had conversations with your electricity service provider about regulation?
25. Have you had conversations with your electricity service provider about congestion?
26. Is there information you would like from your provider that you are not getting? If yes, please describe what you would like to know.
27. Is your provider asking for information from you that you are not able to provide? If yes, please describe what they are asking for.
28. Do you experience any power quality issues at your HPC facility? If yes, please describe.
29. Do you know of any consequences between your site and your provider from either scheduled or un scheduled intra-hour power variations?
30. Please evaluate as high, medium or low the following motivations for your site's interest in pursuing a stronger relationship with your electricity service provider.
31. Please help us understand the economic aspects of power saving strategies. This is an open ended question and we encourage any feedback. For instance, what might it take to induce your site to participate in programs offered by your electricity service provider? What are the tradeoffs between savings and loss of scientific productivity and equipment depreciation.

References

1. Top500 Supercomputer Sites, November 2014. http://www.top500.org/lists/2014/11
2. Aikema, D., Simmonds, R., Zareipour, H.: Data centres in the ancillary services market. In: IGCC, pp. 1–10 (2012)
3. Aksanli, B., Pettis, E., Rosing, T.: Architecting efficient peak power shaving using batteries in data centers. In: IEEE 21st International Symposium on Modeling, Analysis and Simulation of Computer and Telecommunication Systems (MASCOTS), pp. 242–253 (2013)
4. Bates, N., Ghatikar, G., Abdulla, G., Koenig, G., Bhalachandra, S., Sheikhalishahi, M., Patki, T., Rountree, B., Poole, S.: Electrical grid and supercomputing centers: an investigative analysis of emerging opportunities and challenges. Inform. Spektrum **38**(2), 111–127 (2015)
5. Brocanelli, M., Li, S., Wang, X., Zhang, W.: Joint management of data centers and electric vehicles for maximized regulation profits. In: IGCC, pp. 1–10 (2013)
6. Chen, H., Caramanis, M.C., Coskun, A.K.: The data center as a grid load stabilizer. In: IEEE 19th Asia and South Pacific on Design Automation Conference (ASP-DAC), pp. 105–112 (2014)
7. Chen, H., Caramanis, M.C., Coskun, A.K.: Reducing the data center electricity costs through participation in smart grid programs. In: IEEE International Green Computing Conference (IGCC), pp. 1–10 (2014)
8. Chen, H., Hankendi, C., Caramanis, M.C., Coskun, A.K.: Dynamic server power capping for enabling data center participation in power markets. In: International Conference on Computer-Aided Design (ICCAD) (2013)
9. Chiu, D., Stewart, C., McManus, B.: Electric grid balancing through low cost workload migration. SIGMETRICS Perform. Eval. Rev. **40**(3), 48–52 (2012)
10. Clausen, A., Ghatikar, G., Jorgensen, B.N.: Load management of data centers as regulation capacity in denmark. In: International Green Computing Conference (IGCC), pp. 1–10. IEEE (2014)
11. Google Energy. Ferc order granting market-based rate authorization. Federal Energy Regulatory Commission (2010)
12. Ghamkhari, M., Mohsenian-Rad, H.: Data centers to offer ancillary services. In: 3rd International Conference on Smart Grid Communications, pp. 436–441. IEEE (2012)
13. Ghatikar, G., Ganti, V., Matson, N., Piette, M.A.: Demand response opportunities, enabling technologies for data centers: findings from field studies. LBNL-5763E. pdf (2012)
14. Goiri, Í., Haque, M.E., Le, K., Beauchea, R., Nguyen, T.D., Guitart, J., Torres, J., Bianchini, R.: Matching renewable energy supply and demand in green datacenters. Ad Hoc Netw. **25**, 520–534 (2015)
15. Oak Ridge National Laboratory. WL-LSMS Benchmark (2013). https://www.olcf.ornl.gov/wp-content/training/electronic-structure-2012/Eisenbach_OakRidge_February.pdf
16. Lin, M., Liu, Z., Wierman, A., Andrew, L.L.: Online algorithms for geographical load balancing. In: IGCC, pp. 1–10. IEEE (2012)
17. Liu, Z., Lin, M., Wierman, A., Low, S.H., Andrew, L.L.: Greening geographical load balancing. In: Proceedings of the ACM SIGMETRICS, pp. 233–244. ACM (2011)

18. Liu, Z., Liu, I., Low, S., Wierman, A.: Pricing data center demand response. In: ACM International Conference on Measurement and Modeling of Computer Systems, pp. 111–123 (2014)
19. US Department of Energy. Smart Grid (2015). https://www.smartgrid.gov/the_smart_grid/smart_grid
20. Siano, P.: Demand response and smart grids? A survey. Renew. Sustain. Energ. Rev. **30**, 461–478 (2014)
21. European Union. DC4Cities (2015). http://www.dc4cities.eu/en/
22. Urgaonkar, R., Urgaonkar, B., Neely, M.J., Sivasubramaniam, A.: Optimal power cost management using stored energy in data centers. In: Proceedings of the ACM SIGMETRICS Joint International Conference on Measurement and Modeling of Computer Systems, pp. 221–232 (2011)
23. Wang, D., Ren, C., Sivasubramaniam, A., Urgaonkar, B., Fathy, H.: Energy storage in datacenters: what, where, and how much? ACM SIGMETRICS Perform. Eval. Rev. **40**(1), 187–198 (2012)
24. Wang, H., Huang, J., Lin, X., Mohsenian-Rad, H.: Exploring smart grid and data center interactions for electric power load balancing. ACM SIGMETRICS Perform. Eval. Rev. **41**(3), 89–94 (2014)
25. Wang, R., Kandasamy, N., Nwankpa, C., Kaeli, D.R.: Data centers as controllable load resources in the electricity market. In: International Conference on Distributed Computing Systems (2013)
26. Wang, Y., Lin, X., Pedram, M.: A sequential game perspective and optimization of the smart grid with distributed data centers. In: Innovative Smart Grid Technologies (ISGT), pp. 1–6. IEEE (2013)
27. Wierman, A., Liu, Z., Liu, I., Mohsenian-Rad, H.: Opportunities and challenges for data center demand response. In: IGCC, pp. 1–10 (2014)

Resource Management for Running HPC Applications in Container Clouds

Stephen Herbein[1], Ayush Dusia[1], Aaron Landwehr[1], Sean McDaniel[1],
Jose Monsalve[1], Yang Yang[1], Seetharami R. Seelam[2], and Michela Taufer[1(✉)]

[1] University of Delaware, Newark, USA
taufer@udel.edu
[2] IBM T. J. Watson Research Center, Yorktown Heights, USA
sseelam@us.ibm.com

Abstract. Innovations in operating-system-level virtualization technologies such as resource control groups, isolated namespaces, and layered file systems have driven a new breed of virtualization solutions called containers. Applications running in containers depend on the host operating system (OS) for resource allocation, throttling, and prioritization. However, the OS is designed to provide only best-effort/fair-share resource allocation. Lack of resource management, as in virtual machine managers, constrains the use of containers and container-based clusters to a subset of workloads other than traditional high-performance computing (HPC) workflows. In this paper, we describe problems with the fair-share resource management of CPUs, network bandwidth, and I/O bandwidth on HPC workloads and present mechanisms to allocate, throttle, and prioritize each of these three critical resources in containerized HPC environments. These mechanisms enable container-based HPC clusters to host applications with different resource requirements and enforce effective resource use so that a large collection of HPC applications can benefit from the flexibility, portability, and agile characteristics of containers.

1 Introduction

While operating-system-based virtualization and containers are not new concepts, the emerging use of containers as a mechanism for operations across clusters in datacenters has the potential to change the computing landscape in HPC [26]. It also opens new research challenges in this field. Specifically, containers still need proper mechanisms for enforcing controlled resource allocation and management in containerized environments. This experimental paper describes mechanisms for the management of three key resources in containerized HPC applications: CPU, I/O, and network. The paper extends preliminary work presented in three posters at IEEE Cluster 2015 [9,11,19] by describing the mechanisms in a cohesive fashion and presenting their implementation in detail. Our implementation is based on Docker technology but can be adapted to other container technologies.

© Springer International Publishing Switzerland 2016
J.M. Kunkel et al. (Eds.): ISC High Performance 2016, LNCS 9697, pp. 261–278, 2016.
DOI: 10.1007/978-3-319-41321-1_14

Containers depend on the host OS for resource allocation and throttling. The fact that each container does not have its own kernel removes the kernel overhead from the container image and makes containers lighter weight in their memory and file system footprint as well as more easily portable than virtual machine (VM) images for HPC applications. On the other hand, the dependency on the host OS limits the containers' capability to control the allocation and management of HPC resources. Because traditional operating systems are designed to provide best-effort and fair-share resource allocation, they do not always support the workload requirements of containerized HPC applications. Thus, a containerized HPC application may, for example, experience substantial slowdowns because of the frequent context switching associated with the default fair-share scheduler, or they may suffer from high contention because of the fair-share bandwidth allocated by the OS kernel.

The contributions of this paper to the solution of resource managements problems in containerized HPC environments are threefold. First, we address the CPU allocation challenge for CPU-intensive applications running inside Docker containers that share the same compute node. By default, the host OS scheduling policy shares the node's CPUs between the containers using its fair-share quanta-based scheduling policy. In this policy each container is allowed to use a node's CPU for a predefined amount of time (typically 10 ms) before the next container is assigned to the CPU in a round-robin fashion. For applications such as LINPACK, this kind of fair sharing significantly slows the application performance because more time is spent on context switching than on real computation. To achieve better performance, we introduce a timeslicing mechanism [13] currently missing at the container level. When our mechanism is used, only a single container is scheduled at any time on shared resources for a prolonged period of time. This technique is akin to gang scheduling in HPC. With such a simple mechanism, we can improve an application's performance in a containerized environment by up to 4x.

Second, we address the challenge associated with disk I/O contention and disk I/O load imbalance in containerized applications across datacenter clusters. By default, containers are placed on nodes based only on available CPU and memory, ignoring the nodes' I/O load and capacity. This placement may result in poor I/O load balancing across the datacenter machines and ultimately in I/O hotspots for those nodes hosting containers with intensive I/O operations (e.g., frequent checkpointing). To prevent the formation of hotspots, we propose a two-tiered mechanism (i.e., at both the node and cluster levels) that extends Docker and Docker Swarm, making both capable of monitoring the containers' I/O activities and allocating containers based on I/O load balance across the datacenter nodes. We demonstrate how our two-tiered mechanism has the potential for higher bandwidth utilization without the contention effect.

Third, we address the challenge associated with network bandwidth throttling and prioritization. In order to ensure high-quality performance for critical, communication-intensive applications executed in containers, a required bandwidth level should be ensured without expanding or overprovisioning the network. By default in containers such as Docker, networks are configured to provide the "best effort" to all the traffic. Under these conditions, parameters such as bandwidth, reliability, and packets per second for a specific HPC application cannot be guaranteed. Consequently, a communication-intensive containerized application may experience unacceptable performance when hosted on nodes with other containerized applications. We address this problem by proposing a mechanism that enables bandwidth limits and preferential delivery service for critical applications in containers. Our solution can control latency and delay while providing a way to reduce data losses.

The rest of this paper is organized as follows. Section 2 presents our mechanism for dynamic CPU resource allocation among containers. Section 3 presents methods to enforce I/O constraints among containers. Section 4 describes our mechanism to manage the network among containers. Section 5 provides background on containers and Docker as well as relevant related work. Section 6 briefly summarizes our conclusions.

2   CPU Allocations in Containers

Docker builds on the Linux kernel to allocate CPU resources to containers. Specifically, Docker uses Linux control groups (*CGroups* [2]) to provide portions of CPU resource pools to containers. Users specify the number of *shares* to give to a container or group of containers a priori (or statically), and the Linux OS gives each container a CPU allocation proportional to the number of shares that the container was allocated. When the specified shares saturate the CPU resource pools, the kernel allocates a fair share across all containers. Traditionally, containers are given time slices of 10 ms before context switching. The frequent context switching imposes an overhead on the system and causes cache thrashing, ultimately leading to performance degradation. Figure 1 shows an example of execution times for different numbers of containers ranging from 1 to 5, when running the LINPACK benchmark with a default 10 ms time slice. The optimal execution time has a linear behavior (ideal); the observed executing time is superlinear (10 ms time slice). The fine-grained time-slice granularity defines the interval each container is allowed to run on the CPU resources before being preempted. Every time a container's context switch is performed, the new context thrashes the content of the cache memory and overwrites the previously running container's context, requiring storing all its applications' values and execution state. The shorter the cycle in which the containers' context switching occurs, the less locality that can be exploited by the containers' applications and the more context switches that are performed.

To mitigate losses in performance associated with static resource allocation and frequent context switching, we design and implement a mechanism that allows Docker to define and deploy a dynamic, coarse-grained time slice for each container. The mechanism serializes the containers' consumption of CPU resources and is particularly suitable for high-caching, compute-intensive HPC applications in containers.

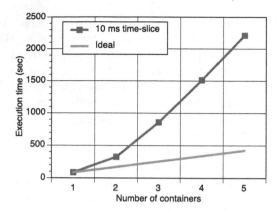

Fig. 1. Example of execution times for different numbers of containers running the LINPACK benchmark on an unmodified Linux OS with default 10 ms time slice.

2.1   CPU Allocation Mechanism

Current Docker containers support only static resource allocations. Shares are defined a priori and remain unchanged during the containers' executions. Our mechanism enables dynamic resource allocations at runtime by serializing the containers' execution for longer time-slice intervals. The serialization is obtained by increasing the shares of one container to 100 % and decreasing the shares of all other containers to 0 %. From an implementation point of view, we extend Docker with a simple but effective round-robin time-slice policy integrated into an Observe-Decide-Act (ODA) control loop [24] that schedules individual containers to be run one at a time for a defined time-slice interval. The round-robin policy first selects the container with the highest number of shares and allows it to run for the duration of the slice. The control loop then repeats, selecting containers in a round-robin fashion, each time reserving the entire pool of CPU resources for a single container.

With the ODA loop, we can collect container-specific information (e.g., priority information, application-specific information, and metadata on container requirements) that can serve as additional input for the decision-making process of the ODA loop. This is not possible if a third-party solution that runs outside Docker (e.g., in the Linux OS) is used. Moreover, the docker API and the command user interface are not changed, making the deployment of new capabilities for the user easier. Furthermore, we can leverage the Docker's client-server structure. The background Docker daemon provides the API to create, delete, or modify any container in the host OS; the Docker client provides the users with the command line interface, launches the daemon if necessary, and sends the commands to the daemon through the use of HTTP-like connections. In our implementation of the mechanism, a single Docker client can handle several Docker daemons, and a single ODA loop can handle multiple CPU resources in the distributed environment. Specifically, in our implementation, the CPU utilization is monitored at each step of the ODA loop; when overutilization is detected, the allocation mechanism decides whether to adjust the CPU shares to control which container is using the CPU resources of the corresponding machine.

To implement the allocation mechanism, we modify the Docker 1.6.1 source files at three levels. First, we modify the Docker daemon's driver by adding a new function that modifies CGroups' parameters for a given container. Specifically, at the driver level, we create a new update driver interface that updates the containers' CGroups configuration dynamically by pulling the current configuration (i.e., `libcontainer::Container::Config`) and pushing a new configuration with updated CPU shares allocation (i.e., `libcontainer::Container::Set`). We use the new function in the driver to make all of the necessary CGroup parameter modifications. Second, we add a new interface to the API of the server front-end that receives the `update` command for a specific container. Specifically, at the server front-end, we create a new POST handler that handles CPU share update commands sent from the client and initiates a new "update" job on the daemon. Third, we modify the Docker client by adding an additional command to the Docker command line interface. The new command handles the ODA loop, retrieves utilization information from the RESTful API, and pushes new CPU allocation information to the RESTful API. The source code of our implementation is available on GitHub at [22].

2.2 Empirical Results

To evaluate Docker when using our mechanism, we create containers for a high-caching, compute-intensive benchmark such as LINPACK [10] with a matrix of size 1000×1000 and a block size of 100×100. This is a large-enough problem size to represent a long term execution (i.e., longer than 60 s) on our 8-core nodes, one for each hardware thread. Each container utilizes 100 % of the CPU resources available on the host machine.

The first question we address in our assessment is the identification of an optimal time-slice size. To this end, we measure the execution time of the benchmark with different time-slice intervals ranging from 0.5 to 20 s and different numbers of containers ranging from 2 to 5. Figure 2a zooms in on the execution times for two containers; Fig. 2b zooms out for four configurations of 2, 3, 4, and 5 containers. For smaller time-slice intervals, we see no improvement in performance because of a delay in the reaction time for CGroups when used through Docker. Reaction time here is the amount of time elapsed between when a CGroup is changed and when the change results in altering the application performance. CGroup value changes do not instantaneously impact application performance because the OS scheduler does not pick them up as soon as they are changed. We observed an average delay time of approximately 700 ms. As the time-slice interval grows, we observe a performance sweet spot around 10 s for any number of containers considered in our tests.

The second question we address in our assessment is the impact of our mechanism on performance. To this end, we consider the optimal time-slice interval of 10 s (within the observed sweet spot window observed in Fig. 2b). Figure 3 shows the context switching of 5 containers when using our mechanism for the

LINPACK benchmark. In the test depicted in the figures, we start the adaptive scheduler after 10 s. The figure outlines the overlapping in the containers' executions before our mechanism is applied and the subsequent time-slice intervals. Within every ODA cycle, each container assumes complete control over the CPU resources for its time-slice interval. This process repeats until all the containers terminate their computation.

In Fig. 4 we compare the execution times of containers under differing levels of overallocation when using our mechanism (10 s time slice) versus using the traditional Linux implementation (10-ms time slice). For the sake of completeness we also add the ideal performance trend. As already outlined in Fig. 1, without our mechanism, as we increase the oversubscription of resources, the execution times

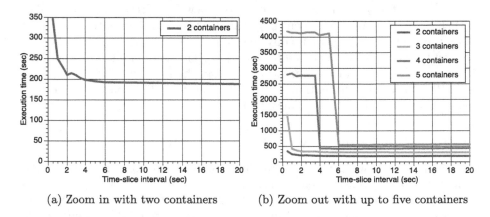

(a) Zoom in with two containers   (b) Zoom out with up to five containers

Fig. 2. Impact of time-slice intervals on execution times for different number of containers. (Color figure online)

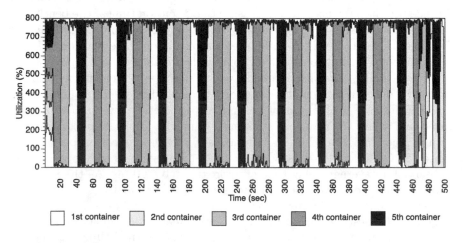

Fig. 3. Time slice of five containers and 10 s time slice.

significantly increases in a superlinear pattern because of caching and synchronization conflicts. With our mechanism, on the other hand, the performance is almost linear with the number of concurrent containers and improves by approximately a factor of 4 because of the mitigation of the aforementioned issues. With our mechanism, five containers take ∼5x the time of a single container whereas in the default model, five containers take over ∼20x times the time of a single container.

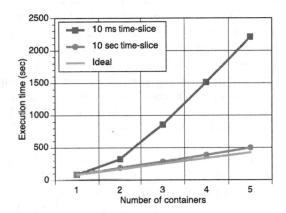

Fig. 4. Execution time for different numbers of containers with and without our mechanism with a time-slice interval of 10 s. (Color figure online)

We observe that our mechanism based on serializing applications in containers is efficient when there is an oversubscription of CPU resources and applications are highly optimized for maximal resource usage such as in LINPACK. The longer time-slice interval ultimately reduces cache thrashing and the overhead of context switching. Unlike the Linux scheduler, our time-slice intervals are on the order of seconds; performance sweet spots are observed for intervals ranging between 10 and 15 s. Under this time slice, a number of containers ranging between two and five are able to freely operate alone for long periods of time while taking full advantage of the locality during their execution. Our results demonstrate that an adaptive control scheme can positively affect the overall application performance. We are not suggesting that this mechanism is suitable for all applications; different application domains need different time slices. LINPACK is an example of compute-intensive applications where OS-based allocations is clearly not sufficient and a better CPU allocation results in a significant performance improvements when the application is executed in containerized workloads.

3   I/O Management of Container Clusters

HPC applications perform disk I/O operations (i.e., read and write) for various reasons such as reading the input parameters of a program, writing output results of a simulations, and periodically checkpointing the simulation state. The management of containerized applications is ignorant of the applications' load and nodes' I/O capacity. In other words, containers are placed on machines based only on available CPU and memory knowledge. When dealing with I/O-intensive applications, this naive placement of containers ultimately results in poor I/O load balancing across datacenter machines. Figure 5a shows an example of naive allocation of containers and its impact on the I/O bandwidth. The results in the figure refer to 90 containers executed in 14 virtual machines, each container hosting one I/O-intensive application. Each application continuously streams data to disk with different I/O rates: of 2 MB/s, 4 MB/s, or 8 MB/s. The I/O rate is randomly assigned at the container's launch time. The number of containers per VM depends on what containers are selected to be scheduled on the specific VM. In the figure we observe that after all the applications have been launched, the I/O bandwidth imbalance between nodes is significant, on the order of 50 MB/s. While the example in the figure depicts a load-imbalanced scenario across VMs, a similar behavior is expected across nodes in datacenter clusters.

To balance the load across nodes, we define a two-tier solution that combines a node-level mechanism and a cluster-level mechanism. At the node level, we change the Docker daemon to allow monitoring each container's I/O load, and we set absolute upper bounds on the container's I/O bandwidth. At the cluster level, we enable the scheduling system to perform load balancing by placing new containers across nodes based on the node's system I/O capability and utilized I/O bandwidth. Together these two mechanisms allow I/O-intensive applications to effectively execute with available I/O resources in HPC containerized environments.

3.1 Allocation Mechanisms

While kernels provide statistics on the I/O activity of each node and the Blkio CGroup has various parameters that allow us to control allocations such as I/O operations per second and bandwidth per second, container managers such as Docker do not provide API functions to leverage these capabilities [1]. At the node level, we extend the Docker API to capture the I/O device status for each container; the status includes disk utilization in terms of how much time the storage device has outstanding work (i.e., is busy), write bandwidth in terms of the number of bytes written to the device per second, read bandwidth in terms of the number of bytes read from the device per second, and wait time in terms of the average time (milliseconds) for I/O requests issued to the device to be served. To capture the I/O activities and to modify bandwidth limits for reads and writes in containers, we augment the client-side API of the Docker daemon in three ways. In our first modification, we add the ability for the Docker daemon to determine the maximum I/O bandwidth of the node it is running on. When a Docker daemon starts, it continuously performs unbuffered writes of 4 MB for 30 s and then calculates the effective bandwidth over that time period. In our second modification, we add the ability for the Docker daemon to determine the current I/O bandwidth utilization on each of the nodes. The Docker daemon parses the node's kernel information present at `/proc/diskstats`. Among the many statistics stored in `/proc/diskstats` is the number of sectors read and written to disk since boot. Every two seconds, the modified Docker daemon parses the number of sectors read and written, comparing the values between samples, and computes a running average of bytes accessed per second over 15 samples. We add this information, along with the maximum bandwidth, to the response for the `/info` Docker API call. For the third modification, we enable the Docker daemon to set the `blkio.throttle_write_bps_device` flag and the `blkio.throttle_read_bps_device` flag in the `Blkio` controller. Setting these flags under the `CGroup` directory named after the container ID allows us to limit the I/O bandwidth of a container.

At the cluster level, we ensure that the I/O load is being balanced across entire clusters. This task involves ensuring that the I/O load is distributed across the nodes of a cluster and that no node in the cluster is overburdened with I/O operations. To this end we monitor the average load of each node (i.e., CPU, memory, and I/O loads); the I/O load is monitored, and the I/O device status is stored with the modifications described above. When a new container is scheduled, it is allocated to the node with the lowest total load, where the weight of each load type is user configurable. We implement our solution on top of Docker Swarm. Note, however, that our method is generic to any other scheduling solution and can be easily extended to other schedulers such as Mesos and SLURM. While Docker Swarm includes the capability to monitor CPU and memory as well as to schedule containers across a cluster, it lacks knowledge of the I/O capacity and utilization of the containers. The node level mechanism described above extends the Docker daemon to make the I/O activity of each node and the I/O throttling of containers available through the `/info` Docker API call. The information is made available to Docker Swarm by augmenting the internal data structures of Swarm to store the I/O information for each node in the cluster and by increasing the frequency at which Swarm makes the `/info` API call to each Docker daemon so that Swarm always has an up-to-date view of the cluster's I/O state. We include the collected I/O information in Swarm's scheduling strategies and adapt the node weighting function that Swarm uses to determine the current load on a node to integrate the I/O weight together with the existing CPU and memory weights. These modifications to Docker Swarm allow us to determine when the I/O of a node is saturated and consequently stop scheduling containers on that specific node. The modifications also allow Swarm to better load balance container allocations across the cluster when using the *spread* scheduling strategy since it can include I/O when calculating the load on a node. The source code of the implementation of our node-level [20] and cluster-level [15] mechanisms is available on GitHub.

3.2   Empirical Results

To demonstrate the benefits of I/O knowledge once integrated in Docker Swarm, we repeat the test in Fig. 5a but with our modified Swarm. As described above,

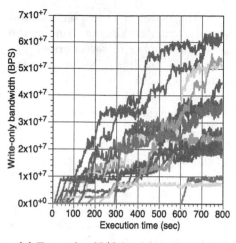
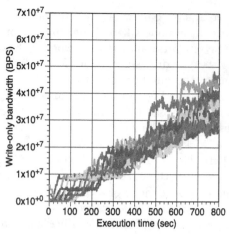

(a) Example of I/O load imbalance obtained with the original Docker and Docker Swarm.

(b) Example of balanced I/O load obtained with augmented Docker and Docker Swarm.

Fig. 5. Examples of imbalanced and balanced I/O load obtained with and without our augmented Docker and Docker Swarm. Each line represents the I/O used by one of 14 VMs running multiple I/O-intensive containerized applications. (Color figure online)

our test is performed on 14 VMs running 90 containers on the modified Docker daemons. Each VM had a dedicated core and dedicated hard drive to minimize contention. Figure 5b shows the results for the augmented Docker and Docker Swarm with full knowledge of the system's I/O. Contrary to the results in Fig. 5a, the I/O load across the 14 VMs is well balanced, and each VM is roughly using the same I/O bandwidth. More important, no single VM has maxed out its disk bandwidth. Under this balancing scheme, I/O-intensive containerized applications get their desired bandwidth easily and without contention. More generally, Fig. 5b provides a proof of concept to support the claim that the additional I/O knowledge allows Swarm to make better decisions at schedule time, which ultimately result in better load balancing and higher resource utilization. When applied to containers on HPC clusters, the same mechanism allows containerized applications to satisfy the I/O requirements and balance the load across the nodes of a datacenter.

4   Network Allocations in Containers

The Docker networking interface offers limited options to configure the network usage of containers. Docker networks are currently configured to provide the "best effort" to the network traffic. When Docker boots up, a single virtual Ethernet bridge, called docker0, is generated. By default, all the containers are configured to be in the same subnet and use docker0 to enable the communication with one another. Thus, no throttling or traffic prioritization is available. Without throttling, communication-intensive applications can starve other applications. Moreover, the lack in network traffic prioritization can cause poor performance in time-sensitive containerized applications. For example, a container hosting a real-time HPC application (e.g., a streaming application with fast Fourier transformations requiring iterative manipulations) may require more bandwidth than does a container hosting a batch or analytics applications. Figure 7a shows an example of a scenario with four containers with different traffic priorities: the first container has high network traffic priority, the second medium priority, and the last two low priority. Each container hosts an application that downloads a 450 MB file over FTP from an FTP server. Although we assign different priorities to the four containers a priori and the four download jobs start simultaneously (with one job in each container), the network bandwidths do not reflect the desired traffic prioritization with the default Docker networking.

To support different bandwidths and priorities for a pool of Docker containers with different network requirements, we implement two mechanisms that allow Docker to provide prioritization and throttling based on a network priority or rate limit assigned to containers by the user a priori. The two mechanisms can be used separately or in concert, since they complement each other.

4.1 Throttling and Priority-Based Allocation

Our priority-based mechanism extends Docker to include a priority scheme for network traffic. The priority scheme is enforced by using a packet classifier and scheduler. When using the packet classifier, packets are classified and added to one of three available priority queues (i.e., high, medium, or low). The medium level is the default level that is assigned to any container when no priority is defined by the user. The scheduler dequeues the packets and sends each packet to a container according to the queue's priority. Figure 6 provides a high-level overview of the mechanism.

We use the Linux traffic control (TC) utility to classify and then schedule the network traffic in and out of the docker0 interface [6]. Using the TC utility, we configure a network scheduling algorithm, also called a queuing discipline (qdisc), for both the ingress and egress directions [5]. Specifically, we use the PRIO qdisc, a scheduling algorithm that contains an arbitrary number of classes with priorities. We configured the PRIO qdisc to utilize three classes, where Class 1 has the highest priority, Class 2 (the default class) has a medium priority, and Class 3 has the lowest priority. In order for the PRIO qdisc to schedule packets based on priority, the packets must first be classified. We use TC filters to classify incoming and outgoing packets based on their IP address. A priority is assigned to containers when they are created. Since each container has an unique IP address, packets coming from or going to a container's IP address take on the priority of that container. For example, all the packets that have destination IP address of a container with high priority are enqueued to Class 1.

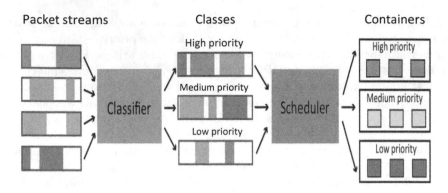

Fig. 6. Overview of the packet classifier and scheduler workflow.

Similarly, the packets with destination IP address of a container with default and low priority are added to Classes 2 and 3, respectively. Once the packets are properly classified and populate the appropriate class queues, the PRIO `qdisc` can begin scheduling the packets. The PRIO `qdisc` scheduler first checks for packets in the queue of Class 1; if no packets are available to dequeue, then the queue of Class 2 is checked; and if no packets are available to dequeue in the queue of Class 2, the queue of Class 3 is checked. The dequeuing of packets from the queue of different classes enforces the scheduling policy and priorities of containers. The problem with using just a PRIO `qdisc` is that individual connections, or "flows," within the same class can contend with one another and degrade performance. To avoid this scenario, we add a stochastic fairness queuing (SFQ) `qdisc` to each class. SFQ ensures fairness within each class by scheduling flows of the same class in a round-robin fashion, thus preventing any single flow from drowning out the rest of the flows.

Our throttle-based mechanism gives Docker the capability to throttle the rate at which the packets are sent or received by a given container. To throttle each container to its specified limit, we use TC to apply an independently configurable token bucket filter (TBF) `qdisc` to each container's packet queue. Each TBF has two required parameters. The first parameter is the traffic rate limit, specified by the users and assigned during the containers' initialization. The second parameter is the burst size, which determines the size of the buffer used by the TBF to queue packets when traffic is being throttled. If the buffer size is too small, packets may be dropped because more packets arrive than can be accommodated in the buffer. These dropped packets will cause an overhead to our throttling mechanism. We reduce this overhead by configuring the `qdisc` parameters for optimal performance—specifically, by setting the burst size to 10 % of the user-defined throttle rate. The source code of the implementation of both our network prioritization and throttling mechanisms is available on GitHub [12].

4.2 Empirical Results

We assessed our priority-based mechanism by repeating the test in Fig. 7a with the same four containers uploading a 200 MB file to the same FTP server but this time with the property-based mechanism in place. Figure 7b shows the network throughput observed for the four containers. In Fig. 7a we use the default Docker network, and the network throughput remains the same for all three containers despite the user-defined priorities. On the other hand, in Fig. 7b we observe different network throughput for the four containers because of our mechanism. Initially, the high-priority container (#1) has the highest share of the total throughput. When the file download completes for the high-priority container, the medium-priority container (#2) gets the highest share of the total throughput. Similarly, when the file download completes for the medium-priority container, the low-priority containers (#3 and #4) get all the bandwidth. The results also show that the low-priority containers get an equal share of the total throughput. These results prove that our mechanism implements priorities in containers and that the containers with equal priority get an equal share of the available bandwidth.

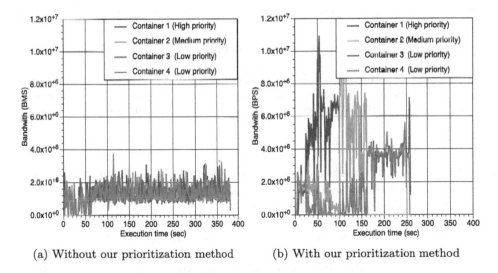

(a) Without our prioritization method   (b) With our prioritization method

Fig. 7. Network throughput of 4 containers downloading 450 MB over FTP with and without our network prioritization mechanism. Container 1 is assigned high priority, Container 2 medium priority, and Containers 3 and 4 low priority. (Color figure online)

To assess our throttle-based mechanism, we assign different bandwidth limits to three containers running on the same node and then monitor the network throughput experienced by each container. The containers' limits are 4.5, 3, and 1.5 MBps. The containers are configured to execute only a single job of uploading a file of size 200 MB to an FTP server. We use an FTP server to receive files from all the containers. The network throughput of all three containers is monitored for the duration of the uploads, first without throttle-based mechanism and then with the mechanism in place. Figure 8a shows the network throughput obtained by the three containers without our mechanism; Fig. 8b shows the throughput for the same test with our mechanism.

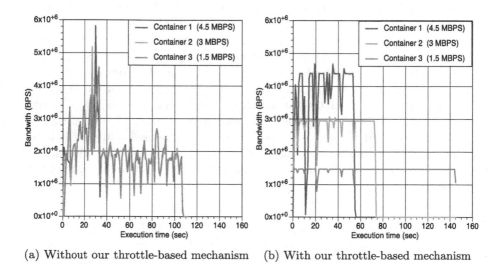

(a) Without our throttle-based mechanism   (b) With our throttle-based mechanism

Fig. 8. Network throughput of three containers without and with throttle-based mechanism. When the throttle-based mechanism is in place, the three bandwidth limits of 4.5, 3, and 1.5 MBps are observed for the three containers' uploads. (Color figure online)

Without the throttle-based mechanism, the network throughput is almost the same for all the containers. On the other hand, with limits, the network throughput is throttled to 4.5 MBps for Container 1, 3 MBps for Container 2, and 1.5 MBps for Container 3. The dips in the network throughput are due to the congestion control mechanism of TCP. In particular, if a packet loss occurs, multiple duplicate ACK signals are received, and the congestion window (cwnd) is reduced by the sender. The congestion window size estimates the congestion between sender and receiver and avoids overloading the link between sender and receiver with too much traffic.

The results of our empirical tests show that our Docker implementation with the throttle-based and priority-based mechanisms efficiently provides resource allocations to containers based on priorities and requirements. Specifically, our extension to Docker networking guarantees that containers' network bandwidth matches assigned priorities. Providing priority-based network allocation to containers has three advantages. First, container hosting bandwidth-intensive applications can be assigned a limit to prevent them from contending with other containers sharing the network. Second, operating costs can be reduced by using existing network resources more efficiently and thus delaying or reducing the need for expansion or upgrades. Third, time-sensitive and critical applications hosted in high-priority containers can now be assigned higher priority to get a higher share of network bandwidth, without starving other containers. Moreover, when containers host applications using UDP, which is not sensitive to network congestion, our mechanisms allow the associated containers to be throttled appropriately to achieve the desired level of bandwidth sharing.

5 Background and Related Work

This section provides background on container technologies, including container clouds. Also discussed in related work on Docker.

5.1 Containers, Docker, and Container Clouds

OS-based virtualization has supported containerization since the early 1980s, enabling users to isolate and customize their processes' environments (e.g., each container can have its own set of libraries while sharing resources of the system). FreeBSD Jails [18], Solaris Zones, AIX WPARs (Workload PARtitions), and HP UX containers are all examples of container technology used in various application domains.

Linux OS introduced resource control groups (i.e., *CGroups*) in 2007. *CGroups* are a set of features to measure, control, and isolate CPU, memory, disk I/O, network, namespace, and devices to a set of processes. Namespaces in particular allow the creation of containers with their own identify in terms of hostname, process identifiers, and network devices. *CGroups* are used to build isolated execution contexts called containers. Docker [21], Warden [3], Kubernetes [4], LMCTFY, LXC, LXD, and rkt are only a few examples of container technologies built on top of Linux *CGroups*. As of this writing, Docker is by far the most popular container technology. Figure 9 shows a typical system with Docker technology. The host operating system consists of the Docker Container Manager (i.e., Docker Engine). This engine can create, modify, and delete containers. Containers are created from file system packages called Docker images. A Docker image is a file system that contains all of the software necessary to run an application. The software includes the application code, dependent libraries, tools, and system libraries. There can be one or more docker containers per application on a given host, as shown in the figure. Other container technologies such as Warden and rkt are built on these same concepts. Although each container can have its own set of application codes and libraries, all the containers running on a host share the host kernel. Thus, the Container Manager depends on the host kernel for resource isolation, management, and enforcement. Linux kernels provide only fair sharing of resources across processes; advanced sharing policies are not normally implemented as part of the base kernel.

Container clouds are technologies that enable a cluster of Docker Engines to run on multiple hosts and offer the cluster resources as a service to multiple users

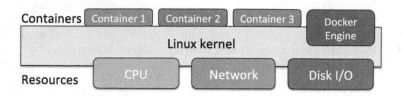

Fig. 9. Illustration of a typical container system. Docker Engine creates and manages the containers. The host OS provides the resource management functions.

with supporting tools for application composition, deployment, and operations. Docker Swarm is a clustering solution to group a set of Docker Engines. When an application composed of multiple containers is deployed to a Swarm cluster, different containers of the application may run on different nodes. In this context, efficient resource management has to be enforced across the multiple containers. Such efficient resource management is still missing for container-based clusters hosting HPC applications.

5.2   Related Work

The National Energy Research Scientific Computing Center (NERSC) developed Shifter [17], a system that allows for HPC centers and users to utilize Docker images in their normal workflows. It makes code deployment easier for users and software stack management easier for center administrators because application dependencies are integrated into the Docker images. Their system integrates with many existing HPC resources such as high-speed interconnects, parallel filesystems, batch job schedulers, resource managers, and HPC-specific operating systems (Cray Linux environment). Their work shows that Docker can be a valuable addition to the HPC workflow, but it lacks extensive testing of the overhead associated with containers.

Extensive analyses have been made of the overheads associated with containers compared with other virtualization methods and "bare metal" execution [8,14,23,27]. These analyses are usually limited to a single machine, however, and rarely study the effects of multiple containers running simultaneously. Soltesz et al. do study the contention caused by multiple containers on an overallocated system, but their work targets Linux-VServer, a virtualization technology that predates Linux containers and is limited to the CPU and I/O resources of a single machine [25].

Others have developed two-tiered systems for resource management of containers. Hong et al. developed a node-level system that monitors the CPU and memory usage of the containers running on each node in the cluster and a cluster-level scheduler that places new containers on nodes with the lightest load [16]. This is similar to how Docker Swarm schedules containers. Our two-tiered method is similar, with the crucial difference being that our method includes disk I/O in the load calculation. Blagodurov et al. developed a node-level system that pins memory-intensive applications to separate NUMA nodes in order to minimize contention and a cluster-level manager that migrates heavily contended applications to less contended nodes [7]. Their method does not directly integrate with the container scheduler, however, and thus they make decisions only at runtime, after the contention has occurred. Our method seeks to prevent contention before it happens, by integrating with the container scheduler and improving the scheduling decisions.

6 Conclusion

The resource management provided by the operating system is not sufficient for containerized workloads in HPC. We discuss resource management challenges in CPU, network, and I/O and describe solutions that achieve better application performance and system utilization. Our CPU management mechanism allows users to mitigate the performance slowdown due to frequent context switching and fair share. Our I/O management mechanism deals with I/O contention by allowing Docker to set up I/O bandwidth limits and to perform cluster-wide I/O load balancing. Our network management mechanism enables application-specific bandwidth priorities and bandwidth limits. Our results demonstrate that advanced resource management technologies are necessary to leverage containers for a broad set of HPC applications.

Acknowledgment. This work is supported by NSF grant #312259 and #312236. We also thank IBM for providing access to their Softlayer (http://www.softlayer.com) and Supervessel (https://ptopenlab.com) cloud platforms and for providing guidance on container technologies. Our code can be found on GitHub at [12, 15, 20, 22].

References

1. Block I/O Controller. https://www.kernel.org/doc/Documentation/cgroups/blkio-controller.txt
2. CGroups. https://www.kernel.org/doc/Documentation/cgroups/
3. Cloud Foundry Warden. https://github.com/cloudfoundry/warden
4. Kubernets by Google. http://kubernetes.io
5. Linux Advanced Traffic Control. http://lartc.org/howto/
6. Network Classifier CGroup. https://www.kernel.org/doc/Documentation/cgroups/net_cls.txt
7. Blagodurov, S., Fedorova, A.: Towards the contention-aware scheduling in HPC cluster environment. J. Phys. Conf. Ser. **385**(1), 012010 (2012)
8. Dandapanthula, N., Stanfield, J.: High Performance Computing - Containers, Docker, Virtual Machines and HPC. http://en.community.dell.com/techcenter/high-performance-computing/b/general_hpc/archive/2014/11/04/containers-docker-virtual-machines-and-hpc
9. Diaz, J.M.M., Landwehr, A., Taufer, M.: Poster: resource management layers for dynamic CPU resource allocation in containerized cloud environments. In: Proceedings of the IEEE Cluster 2015 Conference, pp. 1–2, September 2015
10. Dongarra, J.J.: Performance of various computers using standard linear equations software. SIGARCH Comput. Archit. News **20**(3), 22–44 (1992)

11. Dusia, A., Yang, Y., Taufer, M.: Poster: network quality of service in Docker containers. In: Proceedings of the IEEE Cluster 2015 Conference, pp. 1–2, September 2015
12. Dusia, A., Yang, Y.: Nework QoS Mechanism - Docker, May 2015. https://github.com/adusia/docker
13. Feitelson, D.G., Rudolph, L.: Parallel job scheduling: issues and approaches. In: Feitelson, D.G., Rudolph, L. (eds.) IPPS-WS 1995 and JSSPP 1995. LNCS, vol. 949, pp. 1–18. Springer, Heidelberg (1995)
14. Felter, W., Ferreira, A., Rajamony, R., Rubio, J.: An updated performance comparison of virtual machines and Linux containers. In: 2015 IEEE International Symposium on Performance Analysis of Systems and Software (ISPASS) (2015)
15. Herbein, S.: I/O QoS Mechanism - Docker Swarm, May 2015. https://github.com/SteVwonder/swarm
16. Hong, J., Balaji, P., Wen, G., Tu, B., Yan, J., Xu, C., Feng, S.: Container-based job management for fair resource sharing. In: Kunkel, J.M., Ludwig, T., Meuer, H.W. (eds.) ISC 2013. LNCS, vol. 7905, pp. 290–301. Springer, Heidelberg (2013)
17. Jacobsen, D., Canon, R.: Contain this, unleashing Docker for HPC. In: Cray User Group (CUG 2015), Chicago, IL, April 2015
18. Kamp, P.H., Watson, R.N.M.: Jails: confining the omnipotent root. In: Proceedings of the 2nd International SANE Conference (2000)
19. McDaniel, S., Herbein, S., Taufer, M.: Poster: a two-tiered approach to I/O quality of service in Linux. In: Proceedings of the IEEE Cluster 2015 Conference, pp. 1–2, September 2015
20. McDaniel, S.: I/O QoS Mechanism - Docker, May 2015. https://github.com/seanmcdaniel/docker/
21. Merkel, D.: Docker: lightweight Linux containers for consistent development and deployment. Linux J. **2014**(239), 2 (2014)
22. Monsalve, J., Landwehr, A.: CPU QoS Mechanism - Docker, May 2015. https://github.com/josemonsalve2/docker
23. Ruiz, C., Jeanvoine, E., Nussbaum, L.: Performance evaluation of containers for HPC. In: Hunold, S., et al. (eds.) Euro-Par 2015 Workshops. LNCS, vol. 9523, pp. 813–824. Springer, Heidelberg (2015). doi:10.1007/978-3-319-27308-2_65
24. Sironi, F., Bartolini, D., Campanoni, S., Cancare, F., Hoffmann, H., Sciuto, D., Santambrogio, M.: Metronome: operating system level performance management via self-adaptive computing. In: Design Automation Conference (DAC), 2012 49th ACM/EDAC/IEEE, pp. 856–865, June 2012
25. Soltesz, S., Pötzl, H., Fiuczynski, M.E., Bavier, A., Peterson, L.: Container-based operating system virtualization: a scalable, high-performance alternative to hypervisors. In: Proceedings of the 2nd ACM SIGOPS/EuroSys European Conference on Computer Systems 2007, pp. 275–287 (2007)
26. Vaughan-Nichols, S.: New approach to virtualization is a lightweight. Computer **39**(11), 12–14 (2006)
27. Xavier, M., Neves, M., Rossi, F., Ferreto, T., Lange, T., De Rose, C.: Performance evaluation of container-based virtualization for high performance computing environments. In: 2013 21st Euromicro International Conference on Parallel, Distributed and Network-Based Processing (PDP), pp. 233–240, February 2013

Communication Runtime

Mitigating MPI Message Matching Misery

Mario Flajslik[✉], James Dinan[✉], and Keith D. Underwood

Intel Corporation, Hudson, MA, USA
{mario.flajslik,james.dinan,keith.d.underwood}@intel.com

Abstract. To satisfy MPI ordering semantics in the presence of wild-cards, current implementations store posted receive operations and unexpected messages in linked lists. As applications scale up, communication patterns that scale with the number of processes or the number of threads per process can cause those linked lists to grow and become a performance problem. We propose new structures and matching algorithms to address these performance challenges. Our scheme utilizes a hash map that is extended with message ordering annotations to significantly reduce time spent searching for matches in the posted receive and the unexpected message structures. At the same time, we maintain the required MPI ordering semantics, even in the presence of wildcards. We evaluate our approach on several benchmarks and demonstrate a significant reduction in the number of unsuccessful match attempts in the MPI message processing engine, while at the same time incurring low space and time overheads.

1 Introduction

The Message Passing Interface (MPI) point-to-point ordering semantic ensures deterministic messaging between processes. This behavior eases the complexity of exchanging data in MPI applications and provides an efficient mechanism for sending ordered messages. While this semantic has contributed to the success of MPI, it may also pose performance challenges to applications that perform large volumes of communication without the need for point-to-point ordering.

To facilitate message matching, MPI implementations typically manage two queues: the posted receive queue and the unexpected message queue. These queues are implemented as linked lists to preserve the order in which receives are posted and unexpected messages are received. During the message matching process, these lists are searched for a match, starting with the oldest entry at the head of the list. However, the time to search through a linked list is known to linearly increase with the number of elements (i.e. searching a list has O(N) time complexity), which can pose a performance challenge for some applications.

Current hardware trends suggest that match queue depth is of growing concern. New processors are built with more cores, leading to more MPI processes per node and more threads per MPI process. But at the same time, those individual cores are not getting more powerful to deal with the increase in message rates resulting from higher network bandwidth available to the node.

© Springer International Publishing Switzerland 2016
J.M. Kunkel et al. (Eds.): ISC High Performance 2016, LNCS 9697, pp. 281–299, 2016.
DOI: 10.1007/978-3-319-41321-1_15

Faster implementations of current matching algorithms are difficult to derive, since searching through a linked list does not parallelize well. Instead, a new algorithm is needed, particularly for classes of applications that are susceptible to deep match queues.

Some applications post a small number of receive operations at a time, resulting in short queues. For those applications O(N) search complexity may not incur high overheads. However, we identify three classes of applications with communication properties that yield significant queue traversal overheads

1. Global communication patterns are characterized by most or all processes sending messages to most or all of their peers. In this work, we examine the LAMMPS molecular dynamics simulator [21] and the NAS Integer Sort benchmark [1]. Both of these applications perform all-to-all communication. LAMMPS directly makes point-to-point communication calls in its all-to-all exchange, while Integer Sort leverages MPI_Alltoall collective operation. Typical algorithms for MPI all-to-all collective limit the number of receive operations that are posted at any given time in order to balance overheads from unexpected message processing with the cost of posted receive queue traversal [24]. However, custom application-level, global communication patterns typically make no such effort, which makes them especially vulnerable to deep match queues.

2. Incast communication patterns (e.g. MPI_Gatherv) are characterized by processes that receive many messages at the same time from many other processes. Because these messages arrive from different processes in no particular order, they can lead to large unexpected message queues on the destination processes, or the messages are matched deep into the posted receive queue. In this work, we examine a Fire Dynamics Simulator (FDS) [14] that relies heavily on the MPI_Allgather operation. Because of this application's communication pattern, matching performance significantly impacts overall application performance and scalability.

3. Multithreaded communication is growing in importance as hybrid programming with MPI and threading systems gains popularity. The number of posted receive operations and unexpected messages can increase with the number of threads per process for fully multithreaded usage models, thus further exacerbating message matching overheads.

In this paper we present new matching algorithms and structures for traversing and storing posted receives and unexpected messages. Our solution replaces existing linked list approaches with a hash map. The hash map solution significantly reduces time spent searching for a message match; however, a simple hash map is not sufficient for ensuring the MPI ordering requirements in the presence of wildcard receive operations. Our algorithm efficiently stores additional metadata to maintain ordering, and is able to provide faster MPI message matching times, while at the same time maintaining correctness and performance in the presence of wildcards. Using this approach, we have reduced the number of match attempts per message by more than 50x for LAMMPS, 10x for Integer Sort, and 250x for FDS. In the case of FDS, this improvement in MPI matching performance resulted in an overall speedup of 3.5x.

To the best of our knowledge, this is the first solution that hashes on the full complement of MPI message matching parameters (communicator ID, source rank, and user-supplied tag) for both posted receives and unexpected message queues. For many applications, hashing on all matching parameters is critical to achieving a good distribution across bins and realizing the performance benefits of the hash map. Further, our approach is designed to enable efficient hardware offload implementations, as well as being suitable for fast software implementations. In such scenarios, limited space is available for storing ordering metadata; we present the first solution that is able to tolerate wrap-around and space exhaustion in the ordering metadata. In addition, the hash map approach breaks down message queues into multiple bins, resulting in an implementation that better lends itself to fine-grain locking of the matching structures and thereby relaxing a challenging serialization obstacle in multithreaded MPI implementations.

The rest of the paper is organized as follows: in Sect. 2 we present relevant MPI background and previous work on MPI message matching; Sect. 3 describes our binned algorithms that are evaluated in Sect. 4. We end the paper with a discussion in Sect. 5 and a conclusion in Sect. 6.

2 Background

The Message Passing Interface (MPI) [16] defines point-to-point message ordering between two processes based on the matching criteria of MPI messages: user-supplied tag, sending (a.k.a. source) process rank, and communicator identifier (typically an integer context ID). For a given sequence of send operations from process A to process B, receive operations performed by B — including those that use the any-tag and any-source wildcards — must attempt to match A's messages in the order in which they were sent. Additionally, when process B attempts to match a message sent by process A, B must select the oldest posted receive operation that matches A's message (i.e. same tag or any-tag, same source or any-source, and same communicator). If a matching posted receive is not found, B typically stores A's message in an unexpected message list for later processing. The corollary of these ordering rules is that MPI message matching is deterministic; nondeterminism only arises when the any-source wildcard is used and messages arrive from multiple senders.

This FIFO-like semantic and the presence of wildcards are the reason most MPI implementations store posted receive operations in a single message queue, implemented as a linked list that is ordered from oldest to newest. Upon message arrival, the queue is searched from oldest to newest, resulting in linear O(N) overhead. This is the approach used by the open source MPICH [18] MPI library, which provides the base for many commercial MPI implementations.

2.1 Related Work

MPI message ordering has historically presented a significant hurdle to the development of alternative MPI message matching structures. At the same time, the overhead of message matching has grown so important that the MPI Forum is considering a proposal to allow users to disable wildcards [17] as a means to enable optimizations that reduce matching overhead. As a result, the research community has closely tracked MPI match queue depth in the context of several applications [4,5,7,13], and investigated the latency impact of message queue length in relation to the message processing in offload engines [25] and processor speed [3].

One approach used in prior work is to fragment the unexpected message and posted receive queues based on communicator context ID [23]. Hashing or utilizing separate matching structures based on the context ID requires no special techniques, as communicators provide isolation and messages from one communicator cannot interact with operations on a different communicator. While this approach is well-understood, it has limited benefit in practice, as few applications spread traffic across communicators in a way that would yield a benefit, e.g. by using per-thread communicators.

MPI queues have also been fragmented based on the sender's rank [23]. Separate queues for local and remote processes are commonly used in practice to optimize shared memory communication [8,10,12]. These queues can be further fragmented into a set of queues, where each peer process has a separate queue or a hashing function is used to select a queue based on the sender's rank [9]. This method of splitting based on the sender's rank still presents challenges when any-source receive operations are performed, since an incoming message must match the oldest receive operation posted for that source or the any-source wildcard. For the posted receive queue, any-source wildcard receive operations can be appended to all lists and then removed from all lists on a successful match [23]; however, this approach results in an overhead that is proportional to the number of lists. Alternatively, wildcard receives can be stored in a separate list and when a wildcard operation is performed, subsequent non-wildcard operations can be queued in a single list to preserve ordering [9]. A third approach, used when matching messages sent over the OpenMPI [10] Byte Transport Layer (BTL), involves storing wildcard receive operations in a separate list and adding sequence numbers to all wildcard and non-wildcard operations to capture ordering information. During matching, both the per-process list and the wild list are searched and the matching entry with the oldest timestamp is selected [27]. For the unexpected message queue, fragmentation based on the sender's rank is straightforward; when the unexpected list is searched for a match to an any-source receive operation, deterministic behavior is not required and unexpected messages sent by all processes are searched in any order.

While per-peer queues can reduce matching times, they incur space overheads that are proportional to the number or processes. Recent work by Zounmevo and Afsahi [27] developed a new approach to hashing on the sender's rank that improves space scaling. Rather than utilizing a hash table, where collisions can result in searching through entries that cannot match a given query, their approach utilizes per-peer queues, resulting in a sparse vector of queue pointers. The process ID is decomposed into coordinates in a sparse vector representation, and a logarithmic set of levels of indexing lists are searched to locate the queue for receive operations posted to a given peer. This approach shortens posted receive lists dramatically; however, locating a given posted receive queue requires linear searches through multiple levels of indirection to reduce the space required to store the sparse set of per-peer posted receive queues. These additional levels of indirection complicate offload implementations and incur an overhead on all receive operations, which increases with the logarithm of the number of peers and can severely impact latency sensitive applications.

In contrast to the most advanced work on this topic [27], our approach utilizes hash tables, which incur a constant overhead in queue selection and have a fixed layout, thus adding modest overheads to latency sensitive communication patterns. Our approach is the first to hash based on the full set of matching criteria; previous approaches including [23,26,27] hash only on sender's rank and communicator ID. Finally, we use timestamps and overflow markers, rather than sequence numbers, providing the first solution for wrap-around and significantly reducing the space required to store ordering information. This more compact representation is especially important for MPI implementations where space considerations are important, such as implementations that pack data into a cache line or that utilize hardware offload. By eliminating overheads previously imposed by required handling of wildcard receive operations, our solution improves message matching overheads for most applications, while in the worst case maintaining the same level of performance as current solutions.

3   Binned Matching Algorithm

MPI message processing engines typically split message processing into two separate structures: one for handling posted receive operations and a second that is used to handle unexpected messages. The former structure captures information about which messages the receiver is ready to accept, whereas the latter stores information about messages that arrived but have not yet been received by the application.

3.1   Posted Receive Operations

We present a posted receive structure that provides fast search times by using multiple bins with a linked list within each bin. In other words, posted receives are stored in a hash map, but with a guarantee that the order within each bin is preserved. While this approach improves search time, it presents a challenge to provide MPI ordering in the presence of wildcard receives. First, we describe a general solution to the wildcards problem using marker list entries. We then optimize this approach to replace markers with embedded timestamps, and utilize markers to handle timestamps wrap-around. The resulting approach is more compact and amenable to efficient implementation.

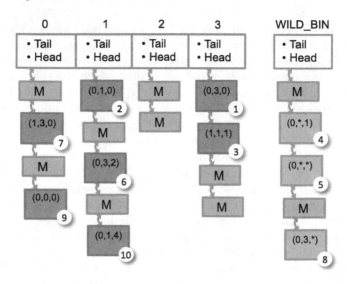

Fig. 1. Posted receive structure with 4 bins, containing receive entries with (c, s, t) parameters.

Capturing Ordering with Markers. In Fig. 1 we show the posted receive structure used in our binned algorithm. This structure is used to capture information about pending MPI receive operations. The programmer can explicitly post multiple pending operations through the use of nonblocking communication, e.g. by calling the MPI_Irecv function, or by having multiple threads perform receive operations at the same time. Nonblocking communication is an important optimization mechanism for MPI applications, which can be used to overlap communication with computation and pre-post receive operations to avoid overheads associated with unexpected messages. In addition to explicit receive operations, the MPI library may also implicitly post multiple pending receive operations while executing other MPI calls, such as blocking and nonblocking collectives or I/O operations.

Each of the bins in the structure contains a linked list. List entries are either markers (identified by letter M), or they are receive entries. Each receive entry is described with (c, s, t) tuple, which corresponds to communicator, source rank, and tag, where "*" describes wildcarded source or tag. In the corner of each receive entry in Fig. 1 is the insertion order number which establishes the order in which the entries were inserted into the structure. These numbers are for illustrative purposes only, and are not kept as state within each structure.

For the sequence of receive operations described by the insertion order numbers, current MPI implementations would create a linked list, where entry "1" is at the head of the list, followed by entry "2", and so on. In our approach, we create the set of lists shown in Fig. 1 by appending a posted receive descriptor for each receive operation to the list determined by a hash function. In this example, we use 4 bins and the hash function given by Eq. 1.

$$hash(c, s, t) = (c + s + t) \% NUM\_BINS \tag{1}$$

However, the hash function and the number of bins are configurable parameters. Descriptors containing wildcard receive entries are appended to a separate wild bin. Further splitting of the wild bin may be possible; however, most wildcard communication usage cases exhibit matching near the head of the list, limiting the potential benefit of this extension.

Figure 1 also demonstrates the use of markers to provide ordering between non-wild and wildcard entries. When a wildcard receive is appended to the wild bin, if the last item appended was not also a wildcard, markers are appended to all bins, including the wild bin, prior to appending the wildcard receive descriptor.

The sender cannot specify a wildcard in a message, thus searches through the posted receive structure are always performed using a (c, s, t) tuple that contains no wildcards. On a given search, both the selected bin corresponding to $hash(c, s, t)$ and the wild bin are searched for a match.

While searching through the selected bin and the wild bin for a match, the algorithm may encounter marker entries. Markers are used to recreate the ordering between entries in the bin list and the wild list. During the search, two timestamp counters are initialized to zero and maintained, one for the selected bin's list, and one for the wild list. As marker entries are encountered, the timestamp counter for the corresponding list is incremented, effectively counting how many marker entries have been encountered in the list up to that point. When matching receive descriptors are found in multiple lists (i.e. selected bin list and wildcard list), the descriptor in the list with the oldest (smallest) timestamp is selected. In cases where the timestamps are equal, the wild descriptor is selected. As receive descriptors are dequeued, markers move to the head of each bin. Markers can be periodically removed whenever a marker is present at the head of every bin. As an optimization, if all bins have N markers at their head, all N can be removed.

The algorithm for searching the binned posted receive structure is shown in Listing 1.1. In this formulation, we further shorten search times by searching both lists simultaneously to avoid continuing a search once a match has been found. If a match is not found in the posted receive structure, the message is appended to the unexpected message structure. The posted receive search and the unexpected message append must be accomplished atomically with respect to any other search or append.

Capturing Ordering with Timestamps. While markers are a sufficient means to establish ordering, they are not compact and can incur significant time and space overheads, as each marker is a separate list entry. We further refine our algorithm by embedding the timestamp value, dubbed *wild time* or WT, that would have been calculated via markers, into the receive descriptor. In this

```
elem *e   = get_head(hash(c,s,t));
elem *we  = get_head(WILD_BIN);
elem *match = NULL;
long e_ts = 0, we_ts = 0;

while (NULL != e || NULL != we) {
   if (is_marker(e)) {
      e_ts++;  e = e->next;
   }
   else if (is_marker(we)) {
      we_ts++;  we = we->next;
   }
   else if (NULL != e && (NULL==we || e_ts<we_ts)) {
      if (check_match(e, msg)) { match=e; break; }
      e = e->next;
   }
   else if(NULL != we) {
      if (check_match(we, msg)) { match=we; break; }
      we = we->next;
   }
}
```

Listing 1.1. Algorithm to search posted receive structure assuming message msg with matching parameters (c, s, t).

scheme, the current timestamp current_wt is maintained in a variable, and it is incremented whenever we would have appended markers. The current_wt value is stored as wild time in each receive descriptor, as they are appended to the structure.

For implementations where it is possible to use a large timestamp representation, e.g. a 64-bit integer, overflow may be virtually impossible. However, for implementations where the size of the receive descriptor must be compact, e.g. so that match list entries fit within a cache line or within limited memory in a hardware matching offload engine, timestamp overflows are possible and can be corrected using a combination of timestamps and markers. In this case, a marker is appended to every bin and current_wt is reset to 0 whenever current_wt has reached its maximum value. The matching algorithm is also extended to calculate the timestamp for a given descriptor using Eq. 2.

$$ts = wt + m\_cnt * WT\_MAX \tag{2}$$

where wt is the wild time embedded in a given descriptor, m_cnt is the number of markers encountered during the traversal of the descriptor's list, and WT_MAX is the maximum value that can be stored in a timestamp.

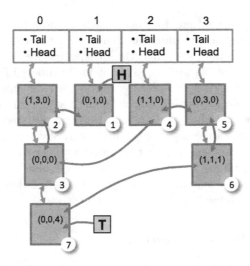

Fig. 2. Unexpected message structure with 4 bins, containing message entries with (c, s, t) parameters.

3.2   Unexpected Messages

Messages that arrive at the receiver before the corresponding receive operation has been performed are referred to as unexpected messages. It is possible for the MPI layer to reject unexpected messages and require the sender to retransmit them; however, this can result in significant overheads. Instead, most MPI implementations buffer unexpected messages in whole, or in part, allowing data to be either copied locally or requested from the sender when the corresponding receive operation is performed. When unexpected messages are buffered, the list of unexpected messages must be scanned before a receive operation is appended to the posted receive structure to determine if the message has already arrived. The unexpected message search and the posted receive append must be accomplished atomically with respect to any other search or append to preserve ordering.

Analogous to the posted receive queue, our unexpected message processing algorithm uses multiple bins to facilitate faster searching through the unexpected message structure. The receiver chooses the bin for each unexpected message based on a hash of the (c, s, t) tuple, which is comprised of the communicator ID, sender rank, and tag. Figure 2 shows a 4-bin example structure for handling unexpected messages. Each message is represented as a list entry that belongs to one of the bins. The number in the corner indicates the global order in which all messages were appended to the unexpected structure. This ordering number is for illustrative purposes only, and is not stored in the structure. In order to support wildcard receives, a globally ordered list is maintained (marked red in Fig. 2), in addition to per-bin lists (marked purple) and reusing the same list entries. Global list head and tail pointers are marked with H and T in Fig. 2. The round-robin hashing algorithm in Eq. 1 was used in this example.

Upon arrival, a message that does not match in the posted receive structure is appended to the unexpected message structure. First, the target bin is computed using a hash function, and then the unexpected message is added to the corresponding per-bin list, as well as to the globally ordered list.

When the application posts a receive operation, the unexpected message structure is searched for a possible match. If the receive contains wildcards for any field, by specifying either MPI_ANY_SOURCE or MPI_ANY_TAG, the global list is used to search for a message matching that receive operation. In the non-wildcard path, the bin is calculated first by hashing on the communicator, source, and tag values given in the receive operation. Then, the list corresponding to that bin is searched for a matching message. If a match is found through either type of search, the message is unlinked from both lists.

3.3   Analysis of Binned Algorithm

For an implementation with B bins, the average time spent searching the posted receive structure to match in incoming a message is $O(N/B)$. The worst case remains $O(N)$ when all posted receives are contained within the same bin or the wild bin. However, it is likely that such a list would contain entries with the same matching criteria and that the entry at the head of the list would match the incoming message, eliminating the $O(N)$ search. The cost of searching the unexpected list when posting a non-wildcard receive is similar. For a search of the unexpected list when posting a wildcard receive, the worst case is $O(N)$; however, wildcard receives are likely to match at the head of the unexpected list, eliminating this search cost.

To ensure that MPI ordering is preserved by the binned approach, we must maintain two safety properties for any pair of operations performed between processes A and B.

1. A message from process A that may match multiple receive operations at process B must attempt to match B's receive operations in the order in which they were posted.
2. A receive operation at process B that may match two messages sent by process A must attempt to match A's messages in the order in which they were sent.

Our algorithm, just like the linked list algorithm, guarantees that the posted receive and the unexpected message structures never contain receives and messages that match each other. This is true because the unexpected list is searched before appending a posted receive to the posted receive structure and vice versa. Further, these search and append operations are performed atomically. Additionally, the MPI library processes messages in the order they are sent, eliminating a reordering possibility outside of the matching algorithm. Therefore, it is enough to satisfy the two ordering requirements in each of the posted and unexpected structures independently.

For the posted receive structure, we observe that a receive operation matching a message with parameters (c, s, t) can be located only in the $H(c, s, t)$ bin or the wild bin. Posted receive operations within each bin are stored in a linked list that is ordered oldest to newest and ordering across bins is preserved through the use of a virtual timestamp. When a search is performed, all bins that could contain a matching operation are searched — in this case, the $H(c, s, t)$ and wild bins. If a match is found in both lists, the timestamp is used to select the oldest match, satisfying the first safety property.

Similarly, for the unexpected message structure, a message with parameters (c, s, t) can be located only in the $H(c, s, t)$ bin as a consequence of the deterministic hashing function H. The same message is also located in the global list. Both lists are ordered from oldest to newest. When a non-wildcard search is performed, the $H(c, s, t)$ bin is searched in order; this bin contains all unexpected messages that could potentially match the given non-wildcard receive operation. A wildcard search can potentially match an entry in any bin; thus, in this case, the global list is searched. In both cases, the ordered list property ensures that the second safety property is also maintained.

4   Evaluation

We evaluate our message matching scheme using the Fire Dynamics Simulator (FDS) application [14], the LAMMPS molecular dynamics simulator [21], and the NAS Integer Sort benchmark [1]. The evaluation was conducted on a 64 node cluster equipped with Intel® Xeon® E5-2697 v3 processors. Nodes are connected through Mellanox® ConnectX®-3* FDR InfiniBand host channel adapters. The operating system is Red Hat® Enterprise Linux® Server release 6.5, with gcc 4.4.7 compiler that is used throughout. Version 3.1.3 of the MPICH [18] MPI library was modified to include our binned matching algorithm in the common matching code across all network modules. As of the time of writing, MPICH does not directly include support for InfiniBand; thus, IPoIB was used in conjunction with the sockets network module.

We instrumented the MPI library to capture posted receive and unexpected message details. An average number of match attempts per message (i.e. the average match location in the structure) is kept at every rank. Additionally, for up to first 2048 matches, each rank keeps a log that records match location and queue depth for each message. We also used high-resolution timers to record the total amount of time spent traversing posted and unexpected structures. To gather more consistent numbers, we run no more than one process per hardware thread and disabled shared memory optimizations by setting the MPICH_NO_LOCAL environment variable.

We introduce a metric of match attempts per message, which provides a machine-independent measurement of an application's exposure to matching overheads. Match attempts per message includes attempts in both posted and unexpected message structures. Processing of each message always requires searching both structures: if a message is matched in the posted structure, the receiver had to search through the unexpected structure before posting that receive; alternatively, if the message is matched in the unexpected structure, the processing engine had to attempt to match that message with posted receives before appending it to the unexpected structure.

4.1 Fire Dynamics Simulator

Fire Dynamics Simulator (FDS) [14] is a computational fluid dynamics application that relies heavily on the MPI_Allgather() operation for communication. FDS is representative of a significant class of workloads, and as a result is included in the SPEC MPI® benchmark suite [19]. We run weak scaling experiments using the "circular burner" workload with up to 1792 ranks. The scaling results are presented in Fig. 3a,b shows the relative speedup of binned matching algorithm over the baseline case for varying numbers of bins.

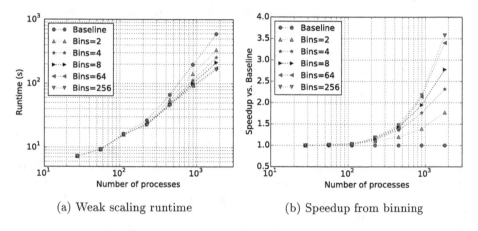

(a) Weak scaling runtime   (b) Speedup from binning

Fig. 3. Fire Dynamics Simulator results for the "circular burner" workload.

Figure 3a reveals that FDS encounters scalability challenges with the increase in number of ranks. Poor performance of the baseline matching algorithm is one of the reasons for the poor scaling, and our binned matching algorithm improves the large scale performance by more than a factor of 3.5x for 1792 ranks with 256 bins.

Figure 4 shows our match queue analysis of the FDS application. In Fig. 4a we show the number of match attempts per message versus the number of ranks for the baseline case. The baseline case is the unmodified MPICH matching algorithm that utilizes a single linked list. Along with displaying the average attempts per message computed across all ranks, we also show the values for worst and best case ranks. Match attempts in the worst case rank (rank 0) increase rapidly with number of ranks, reaching thousands of attempts per message.

The improvement from binned matching is shown in Fig. 4b. The improvements are greater with larger number of available bins, and the baseline case

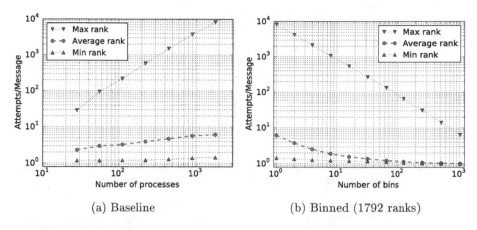

(a) Baseline   (b) Binned (1792 ranks)

Fig. 4. FDS match queue analysis, showing match attempts per message. (Color figure online)

is represented in this graph as the one bin case. The process that incurs the worst matching overheads (rank 0) especially benefits with the increased number of bins, as the number of match attempts per message drops linearly with the number of bins. With 256 bins, we are able to reduce search times from over 200 μs to less than 1 μs, resulting in more than 200x reduction in matching overheads.

4.2   LAMMPS

LAMMPS is a molecular dynamics simulator application [21]. In our evaluations we run the *rhodopsin* protein benchmark, which uses particle-mesh method to calculate long range forces [22]. As part of that method, it calculates a distributed 3-D FFT several times. This FFT calculation includes a matrix transpose, which in turn requires an all-to-all communication exchange along a dimension of the matrix. This global communication pattern is prone to deep match queues. This is in contrast to analysis in [4], which used *chains* workload that exhibits different match queue behavior.

In Fig. 5a we present a scatter plot showing how the number of match attempts per message depends on the number of MPI ranks for the baseline case. This is a strong scaling example with the size of the problem fixed at $15 \times 15 \times 15$ of basic rhodopsin blocks (benchmark replication factor is 15 along each dimension). Up to a certain number of ranks, the domain decomposition is such that during the FFT section, each process holds an entire 2-D slice of the matrix, and the decomposition is done only in one dimension. In this mode, the number of attempts per message grows linearly with number of processes (points connected with lines in Fig. 5a). For larger number of ranks (points without lines in Fig. 5a), the frequency domain matrix is decomposed in two dimensions, and each rank holds "pencil"-like chunks of the matrix. In that mode, the number

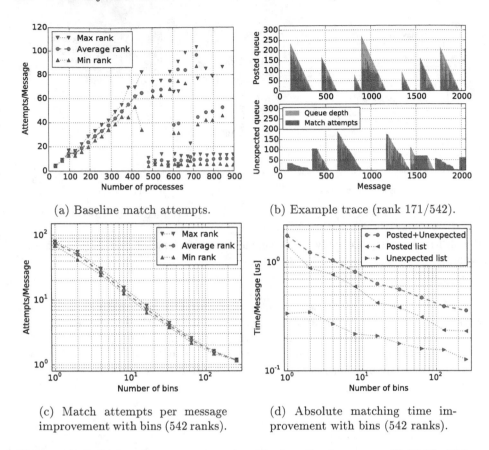

(a) Baseline match attempts.

(b) Example trace (rank 171/542).

(c) Match attempts per message improvement with bins (542 ranks).

(d) Absolute matching time improvement with bins (542 ranks).

Fig. 5. LAMMPS match queue analysis (workload replication: x,y,z = 15,15,15). (Color figure online)

of match attempts per message heavily depends on the domain decomposition; in particular on how well the number of ranks factorizes. The overall trend is for attempts per message to increase with the square root of number of ranks.

Our binned matching algorithm is capable of significantly improving the number of match attempts per message, depending on number of available bins, as shown in Fig. 5c. At the same time, it also improves the absolute time spent searching through posted and unexpected structures, as shown in Fig. 5d.

To further our understanding of the match queues, an example posted and unexpected queue trace for baseline matching is given in Fig. 5b. This example is for a representative rank (e.g. rank 171) out of 542 total ranks. The trace is recorded every time the queue is searched, but not on queue appends. This explains why queue depth values spike up and then ramp down. For example, in posted queue case, when the rank posts many receives back to back, that shows up as many trace entries in the unexpected queue (because unexpected queue is searched before receive is appended to posted queue). However, these receives do not show up in the posted queue until the next time a message is received and the posted queue is searched. At that time the trace records match attempts (blue) and queue depth (red) values. Large queue depth values are not necessarily a performance problem; the issue arises when there are large numbers of failed match attempts, which often correlates with large queue depths. In Fig. 5b, one can distinctly see several triangles which correspond to transpose sections of the application. For some transposes, the queue depth reaches over 200 elements.

4.3   Integer Sort

Integer Sort is taken from the NAS Parallel Benchmarks suite [1]. In our evaluations, we run the class "C" problem size. Integer sort makes use of MPI_Alltoall collective, with large message sizes. The all-to-all algorithm for large messages is to post multiple MPI_Irecv, one for each expected message, but up to a threshold value. Using this algorithm, no more than the threshold value of

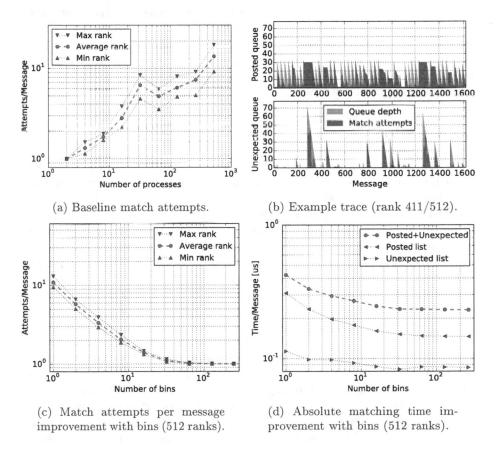

(a) Baseline match attempts.   (b) Example trace (rank 411/512).

(c) Match attempts per message improvement with bins (512 ranks).

(d) Absolute matching time improvement with bins (512 ranks).

Fig. 6. Integer Sort match queue analysis (alltoall threshold = 32). (Color figure online)

receives are pending at any time. The default threshold value in MPICH is 32. Additionally, care is taken to post receives in the order they are expected to be received at each node. The intent of this approach is to reduce the number of unsuccessful match attempts.

Figure 6a shows that the number of match attempts increases with the number of ranks in the baseline case. One can see a local peak at 32 ranks, which corresponds to the threshold value. However, as the number of ranks is increased further, the number of match attempts still increases. This is due to the unexpected queue not being bounded by the threshold value. As can be seen in Fig. 6b, the posted queue caps off at 32 entries, but the unexpected queue can grow beyond that limit, thus increasing the overall number of unsuccessful matches. Integer Sort was also evaluated in [7], where authors observe a continuous increase in posted and unexpected queue depths without posted queue depth capping off at the threshold value. This discrepancy is most likely due to a different implementation of the MPI_Alltoall collective algorithm that does not include the threshold optimization.

Using our binned approach, one can reduce the number of match attempts per message, as shown in Fig. 6c. Additionally, the improvement in absolute time spent on walking the posted and unexpected structures is shown in Fig. 6d. Another benefit of our binned algorithm is that it enables the user to increase the threshold value which may unlock more communication overlap without the match queue depth penalty.

5   Discussion

Selection of Parameters: The matching performance improvement is dependent on the number of bins and the distribution of message or receive descriptors across bins. More bins yield lower search times, but require additional space to store the state. The application behavior and hash function determine the distribution of messages across bins. Any hash function can be used, and it can use any or all of the matching criteria as inputs. For example, a cryptographic hash function, such as MD5, might provide best distribution of messages across all the bins. However, we observed that a simple, round-robin hash function, which is fast to compute, can work just as well across a broad set of usage models. The optimal hash function for assigning MPI messages to bins is a topic that is ripe for future investigation.

Implications to Multithreaded Message Processing: When a linked list is used, most MPI implementations utilize a single lock to synchronize accesses to the posted receive and unexpected message queues. By fragmenting these queues into multiple lists, the binned approach enables finer-grain locks to be used to synchronize each bin separately. If, for example, threads post receive operations that use different, non-wildcard tags, each thread accesses different bins in the unexpected message and posted receive structures, allowing them to perform these operations concurrently. It was previously believed that concurrent message processing by multiple threads is only possible when separate messaging structures are used for each communicator and threads use different communicators.

Implications to Offload Message Processing: Offloading MPI matching to specialized hardware has been investigated by the research community [6,26] and put into practice in several network interfaces, including the Myrinet*, Quadrics*, and Bull BXI* interfaces. As system-level and node-level scales increase, and implementors attempt to drive down MPI messaging latency, there is renewed interest in offloading MPI message matching. To enable the use of specialized hardware and software techniques, several current low-level networking APIs provide interfaces that include support for message matching [2,11,15,20]. Our work combines simple, well-understood data structures and algorithms in order to accelerate MPI message processing. While more sophisticated approaches are possible, we speculate that this practical approach is amenable to both hardware and software MPI matching engines.

6 Conclusion

We identify MPI message matching as a performance as a growing concern for applications, expecially those where MPI communication increases with the number of MPI processes or threads per MPI process. We presented new algorithms and data structures for storing MPI's internal posted receive and unexpected message queues. Our binned algorithm is based on a hash map, and it signif icantly accelerates searching through the structures for the case without wild cards. At the same time, even in the presence of wildcards, the binned algorithm maintains MPI message ordering semantics, while offering performance that is equivalent to, or better than the current implementations.

Our algorithm, with 256 bins, reduced the number of match attempts per message by more than 50x for LAMMPS, 10x for Integer Sort, and 200x for Fire Dynamics Simulator (FDS). In the case of FDS, this improvement in MPI matching performance resulted in an overall speedup of 3.5x.

References

1. Bailey, D.H., Barszcz, E., Barton, J.T., Browning, D.S., Carter, R.L., Dagum, L., Fatoohi, R.A., Frederickson, P.O., Lasinski, T.A., Schreiber, R.S., et al.: The NAS parallel benchmarks. Intl. J. High Perform. Comput. Appl. 5(3), 63–73 (1991)

2. Barrett, B.W., Brightwell, R., Hemmert, S., Pedretti, K., Wheeler, K., Underwood, K., Riesen, R., Maccabe, A.B., Hudson, T.: The portals 4.0.2 network programming interface. Technical report SAND2013-3181, Sandia National Laboratories, April 2013
3. Barrett, B.W., Hammond, S.D., Brightwell, R., Hemmert, K.S.: The impact of hybrid-core processors on mpi message rate. In: Proceedings of 20th European MPI Users' Group Meeting, EuroMPI 2013, pp. 67–71 (2013)
4. Brightwell, R., Goudy, S., Underwood, K.: A preliminary analysis of the MPI queue characterisitics of several applications. In: International Conference on Parallel Processing, ICPP 2005, pp. 175–183, June 2005
5. Brightwell, R., Pedretti, K., Ferreira, K.: Instrumentation and analysis of MPI queue times on the SeaStar high-performance network. In: Proceedings of 17th International Conference on Computer Communications and Networks, ICCCN 2008, pp. 1–7, August 2008
6. Brightwell, R., Riesen, R., Maccabe, A.B.: Design, implementation, and performance of MPI on Portals 3.0. Int. J. High Perform. Comput. Appl. **17**(1), 7–19 (2003)
7. Brightwell, R., Underwood, K.D.: An analysis of NIC resource usage for offloading MPI. In: Proceedings of Workshop on Communication Architecture for Clusters (2004)
8. Buntinas, D., Mercier, G., Gropp, W.: Design and evaluation of nemesis, a scalable, low-latency, message-passing communication subsystem. In: Proceedings of 6th International Symposium on Cluster Computing and the Grid, CCGrid, vol. 1, pp. 521–530, May 2006
9. Dózsa, G., Kumar, S., Balaji, P., Buntinas, D., Goodell, D., Gropp, W., Ratterman, J., Thakur, R.: Enabling concurrent multithreaded MPI communication on multicore petascale systems. In: Keller, R., Gabriel, E., Resch, M., Dongarra, J. (eds.) EuroMPI 2010. LNCS, vol. 6305, pp. 11–20. Springer, Heidelberg (2010)
10. Gabriel, E., Fagg, G.E., Bosilca, G., Angskun, T., Dongarra, J.J., Squyres, J.M., Sahay, V., Kambadur, P., Barrett, B., Lumsdaine, A., Castain, R.H., Daniel, D.J., Graham, R.L., Woodall, T.S.: Open MPI: goals, concept, and design of a next generation MPI implementation. In: Proceedings of 11th European PVM/MPI Users' Group Meeting, pp. 97–104. Budapest, Hungary, September 2004
11. Intel Corporation: Intel® True Scale Fabric Architecture: Enhanced HPC Architecture and Performance (2013)
12. Jin, H.W., Sur, S., Chai, L., Panda, D.: LiMIC: support for high-performance MPI intra-node communication on Linux cluster. In: Proceedings of International Conference on Parallel Processing, pp. 184–191, June 2005
13. Keller, R., Graham, R.L.: Characteristics of the unexpected message queue of MPI applications. In: Keller, R., Gabriel, E., Resch, M., Dongarra, J. (eds.) EuroMPI 2010. LNCS, vol. 6305, pp. 179–188. Springer, Heidelberg (2010)
14. McGrattan, K., Hostikka, S., Floyd, J.E.: Fire Dynamics Simulator, User's Guide. NIST Special Publication 1019 (2013)
15. Mellanox Technologies: Mellanox HPC-X™ Software Toolkit User Manual (2014)
16. MPI Forum: MPI: a message-passing interface standard version 3.0. Technical report, University of Tennessee, Knoxville, October 2012
17. MPI Forum Point-to-Point Working Group: No wildcards proposal to the MPI Forum, April 2015. https://svn.mpi-forum.org/trac/mpi-forum-web/ticket/461
18. MPICH: A high performance and widely portable implementation of the MPI standard, April 2015. http://www.mpich.org

19. Müller, M.S., van Waveren, M., Lieberman, R., Whitney, B., Saito, H., Kumaran, K., Baron, J., Brantley, W.C., Parrott, C., Elken, T., Feng, H., Ponder, C.: SPEC MPI2007-an application benchmark suite for parallel systems using MPI. Concurr. Comput.: Pract. Exp. **22**(2), 191–205 (2010)
20. Open Fabrics Alliance: Open fabric interfaces (OFI), April 2015. http://ofiwg.github.io/libfabric/
21. Plimpton, S.: Fast parallel algorithms for short-range molecular dynamics. J. Comput. Phys. **117**(1), 1–19 (1995)
22. Plimpton, S., Pollock, R., Stevens, M.: Particle-Mesh Ewald and rRESPA for parallel molecular dynamics simulations. In: Proceedings of 8th SIAM Conference on Parallel Processing for Scientific Computing, PPSC (1997)
23. Squyres, J.: The message passing interface (MPI). In: Gavrilovska, A. (ed.) Attaining High Performance Communications: A Vertical Approach, pp. 251–280. CRC Press, Boca Raton (2009)
24. Thakur, R., Rabenseifner, R., Gropp, W.: Optimization of collective communication operations in MPICH. Int. J. High Perform. Comput. Appl. **19**(1), 49–66 (2005)
25. Underwood, K., Brightwell, R.: The impact of MPI queue usage on message latency. In: International Conference on Parallel Processing, ICPP 2004, vol. 1, pp. 152–160, August 2004
26. Underwood, K.D., Hemmert, K.S., Rodrigues, A., Murphy, R., Brightwell, R.: A hardware acceleration unit for MPI queue processing. In: Proceedings of 19th International Parallel and Distributed Processing Symposium 2005, p. 96b (2005)
27. Zounmevo, J.A., Afsahi, A.: An efficient MPI message queue mechanism for large-scale jobs. In: Proceedings of 18th International Conference on Parallel and Distributed Systems, ICPADS 2012, pp. 464–471 (2012)

INAM²: InfiniBand Network Analysis and Monitoring with MPI

Hari Subramoni$^{(\boxtimes)}$, Albert Mathews Augustine, Mark Arnold,
Jonathan Perkins, Xiaoyi Lu, Khaled Hamidouche, and Dhabaleswar K. Panda

Department of Computer Science and Engineering, The Ohio State University,
Columbus, OH, USA
{subramoni.1,augustine.80,arnold.668,perkins.173,lu.932,
hamidouche.2,panda.2}@osu.edu

Abstract. Modern high-end computing is being driven by the tight integration of several hardware and software components. On the hardware front, there are the multi-/many-core architectures (including accelerators and co-processors) and high-end interconnects like InfiniBand that are continually pushing the envelope of raw performance. On the software side, there are several high performance implementations of popular parallel programming models that are designed to take advantage of the high-end features offered by the hardware components and deliver multipetaflop level performance to end applications. Together, these components allow scientists and engineers to tackle grand challenge problems in their respective domains.

Understanding and gaining insights into the performance of end applications on these modern systems is a challenging task. Several researchers and hardware manufacturers have attempted to tackle this by designing tools to inspect the network level or MPI level activities. However, all existing tools perform the inspection in a disjoint fashion and are unable to correlate the data generated by profiling the network and MPI. This results in a loss of valuable information that can provide the insights required for understanding the performance of High-End Computing applications. In this paper, we take up this challenge and design InfiniBand Network Analysis and Monitoring with MPI - $INAM^2$. INAM² allows users to analyze and visualize the communication happening in the network in conjunction with data obtained from the MPI library. Our experimental analysis shows that the INAM² is able to profile and visualize the communication with very low performance overhead at scale.

1 Introduction and Motivation

Across scientific domains, application scientists are constantly looking to push the envelope by running large-scale, parallel jobs on supercomputing systems.

This research is supported in part by National Science Foundation grants #CCF-1213084, #CNS-1419123, #CNS-1513120, #ACI-1450440 and #IIS-1447804.

© Springer International Publishing Switzerland 2016
J.M. Kunkel et al. (Eds.): ISC High Performance 2016, LNCS 9697, pp. 300–320, 2016.
DOI: 10.1007/978-3-319-41321-1_16

Supercomputing systems are currently comprised of thousands of compute nodes based on modern multi-core architectures. Interconnection networks have rapidly evolved to offer low latencies and high bandwidths to meet the communication requirements of parallel applications. InfiniBand (IB) has emerged as a popular high performance network interconnect and is increasingly being used to deploy some of the top supercomputing installations around the world. The Message Passing Interface (MPI) [27] is a very popular parallel programming model for developing parallel scientific applications that run on such high end supercomputing systems.

As IB clusters and the MPI-based applications that use these clusters have become increasingly complex, understanding how an HPC application interacts with the underlying IB network and the impact it can have on the performance of the application becomes ever more challenging. It is critical for the users and administrators of HPC installations as well as developers of high performance MPI middleware that run on these HPC installations to clearly understand this interaction. Such understanding will enable all involved parties (application developers/users, system administrators and MPI runtime developers) to maximize the efficiency and performance of the various individual components that comprise a modern HPC system and solve the various "grand challenge" problems. System administrators, application developers and developers of high performance parallel programming runtimes rely on a plethora of tools to accelerate and simplify the task of analyzing and understanding the various components of an HPC system.

One of the common questions system administrators tend to get from the users of the clusters they manage is: *Why is my application running slower than usual now?* Interaction with a concurrent job in the network or network based parallel file system is the most common cause for this behavior. Several tools exist in literature and as products which allow system administrators to analyze and inspect the IB fabric (e.g.: Nagios [4], Ganglia [1], Mellanox Fabric IT [34], INAM [8], BoxFish [10]). However, due to the lack of interaction with, and knowledge about the MPI library, no existing IB fabric monitoring tool can correlate network level and MPI level behavior to classify traffic as belonging or being generated by particular MPI primitives (e.g.: Point-to-point, Collective, RMA). Furthermore, they cannot classify network traffic as belonging to a particular job due to the lack of interaction with the job scheduler. Such classification would allow the system administrators to pin point the source of the conflict at a much finer granularity than what is possible with the existing set of tools.

Current generation high performance MPI runtimes are complicated pieces of software with hundreds of performance oriented features and knobs (e.g.: support for different high performance transport protocols, support for different collective communication algorithms and mechanisms, network topology aware communication, hardware offloaded communication, network hot spot avoidance). Some of these features have interdependencies and interactions with others. While the default setting of these features will deliver about 80 % of the maximum achievable performance in most cases, careful application specific tuning is required to extract that last 20 % of performance. This requires in-depth understanding of the workings of the MPI library and how it interacts with the underlying communication fabric. Existing MPI level profiling tools (like TAU [5], HPCToolkit [18], Intel VTune [13], IPM [2], mpiP [3]) give reasonable insights into the MPI communication behavior of applications. However, they have no knowledge about the underlying IB fabric and thus are not able to correlate network level and MPI level behavior to identify issues such as increased traffic levels on one link causing performance degradation for an MPI job whose communication is going over said link. Furthermore, most existing MPI profiling tools are unable to provide deep insights into the operations of the MPI library due to the lack of an interface that allows them to interact with the MPI library and identify the behavior of various internal components. To address this concern, the MPI forum recently proposed the MPI_T [26] interface which allows MPI profiling tools to track the performance of various internal components of the MPI library. Researchers have already begun to take advantage of this interface to provide optimization and tuning hints to the users [14]. However, these tools have no knowledge about the underlying IB fabric and thus suffer from the same drawbacks as other existing MPI tools.

As we can see, there is a gap in the support provided by existing network as well as MPI level profiling tools which must be filled. Any tool that is able to bridge this gap will enable end users to correlate the behavior of the IB fabric and the MPI runtime to gain true insights into the performance being delivered by high performance scientific applications. These issues lead us to the following broad challenge - *How can we design a tool that enables in-depth understanding of the communication traffic on the InfiniBand network through tight integration with the MPI runtime?*

2 Contributions

In this paper, we take up this challenge and design $INAM^2$ - a low-overhead profiling and visualization tool that is capable of presenting the profiling information obtained from the network and the MPI library in conjunction to allow users to gain more insights than afforded by existing tools that profile/visualize the network and MPI disjointly. We demonstrate how, through the profiling information provided by $INAM^2$, designers as well as users of high performance middleware can gain more insights into the communication characteristics of their runtimes allowing them to further fine tune the performance on a per application or per run basis. We show how, through the link analysis capabilities of $INAM^2$, system administrators can pin point the cause of network performance issues to a granularity of a process. Our experimental evaluation shows that the $INAM^2$ is able to profile and visualize the communication with very little performance overhead at scale. To summarize, $INAM^2$ provides the following major features:

- Analyze and profile network-level activities with many metrics (data and errors) at user specified granularity
- Capability to analyze and profile node-level, job-level and process-level activities for MPI communication (Point-to-Point, Collectives and RMA)
- Capability to profile and report several metrics of MPI processes at node-level, job-level and process-level at user specified granularity in conjunction with the MPI runtime
- Capability to analyze and classify the traffic flowing in a physical link into those belonging to different jobs in conjunction with the MPI runtime
- Capability to visualize the communication map at process level and node level granularities in conjunction with the MPI runtime
- "Job Page" to display jobs in ascending/descending order of various performance metrics in conjunction with the MPI runtime

Note that many of the features and capabilities described in this paper are already publically available as part of OSU INAM package for free download at http://mvapich.cse.ohio-state.edu/tools/osu-inam/. While we chose MVAPICH2 for implementing our designs, any MPI runtime can be enhanced to perform similar data collection and transmission.

The rest of the paper is organized as follows. Section 3 gives a brief overview of InfiniBand MPI over IB. In Sect. 4 we present the framework and design of $INAM^2$. We evaluate and analyze the correctness and performance of $INAM^2$ in various scenarios in Sect. 5. We present the possible use cases for $INAM^2$ in Sect. 6. The currently available related tools are described in Sect. 7. Finally we summarize the conclusions and possible future work in Sect. 8.

3 Background

In this section, we provide the necessary background information for this paper.

3.1 InfiniBand

InfiniBand is a very popular switched interconnect standard being used by almost 47 % of the Top500 Supercomputing systems [33] according to the Nov'15 listing. InfiniBand Architecture (IBA) [16] defines a switched network fabric for interconnecting processing nodes and I/O nodes, using a queue-based model. It supports two communication semantics: Channel Semantics (Send-Receive communication) over Reliable Connected (RC), Extended Reliable Connected (XRC), Dynamic Connected (DC), and Unreliable Datagram (UD); and Memory Semantics (Remote Direct Memory Access communication) over RC, DC and XRC. Both semantics can perform zero-copy transfers from source-to-destination buffers without additional host-level memory copies. RC is connection-oriented and requires dedicated QP for destination processes while the connection-less UD transport uses a single QP for all [22,24]. XRC optimizes QP allocation by requiring each process to create only one QP per node [23]. DC on the other hand combines the scalability of UD by providing the capability to use just on DC end point to communicate with an peer while providing the high-end RDMA/atomic features available with RC and XRC.

3.2 MPI

Message Passing Interface (MPI) [27], is one of the most popular programming models for writing parallel applications in cluster computing area. MPI libraries provide basic communication support for a parallel computing job. In particular, several convenient point-to-point and collective communication operations are provided. High performance MPI implementations are closely tied to the underlying network dynamics and try to leverage the best communication performance on the given interconnect. In this paper, we use modified MVAPICH2-X [25] based on the 2.2a release for our evaluations. However, our observations in this context are quite general and they should be applicable to other high performance MPI libraries as well.´

3.3 MPI_T

The MPI Tools Information Interface (MPI_T) provides a standard mechanism for MPI tool developers to both inspect and tweak the various internal settings and performance characteristics of MPI libraries. The MPI_T interfaces define two types of objects. The first type of object is the performance variable. Accessing the values of performance variables allows the software to peak under the hood of the MPI library to determine the state and how it is being affected by the MPI application. The second type of object is the control variable. This type of object is tied to a modifiable parameter of the MPI library. Accessing and modifying these will allow the software to change the behavior of the MPI library. Section 14.3 of the MPI 3 standard describes the MPI_T interface in full detail.

4   Design of INAM²

The overall architecture of InfiniBand Network Analysis and Monitoring with MPI (INAM²) is presented in Fig. 1. It consists of four major design components: (1) OSU INAM daemon (osuinamd), (2) OSU INAM Database, (3) Java-based Webserver, and (4) Web-based front end for visualization. We will go into the details of each in the following sections.

4.1   Design of OSU INAM Daemon

The OSU INAM daemon is the hub for all data collection related activities in $INAM^2$. As we saw in Sect. 2, one of the major capabilities of $INAM^2$ is its ability to interact with and extract information from the MPI processes and present data at network level, job level and process level granularities to the

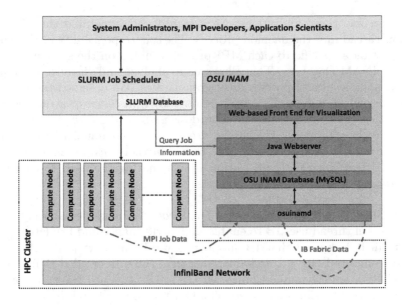

Fig. 1. Overall framework

end users. Apart from this, the daemon is also responsible for discovering the IB fabric and extracting data from various selected components in the IB fabric. Finally, it is also responsible for pushing all collected data elements into the OSU INAM database (described in Sect. 4.2). In order to allow these tasks to proceed in parallel and not bottleneck each other, we dedicate a thread for each activity.

MPI Data Collection Thread. While existing IB fabric monitoring tools like Nagios, Ganglia, and Mellanox Fabric IT are capable of displaying the overall state of the fabric, they're unable to break down the traffic and classify it at finer granularities (for instance at process level or as point-to-point or collective traffic) which can enable deep understanding. While one can theoretically use per virtual lane level counters and force MPI processes to use different virtual lanes to have process level granularity using existing tools, this method suffers from a fundamental issue — The IB standard only supports 16 virtual lanes. Given the current and emerging dense many-core nodes where the number of processes per node can be as high as 71, it becomes hard to perform a one-to-one mapping between processes and virtual lanes even at the node level. This fundamental bottleneck is further exacerbated by two mundane issues: (1) very few system administrators enable the use of multiple virtual lanes in practice on production supercomputing installations and (2) very few (if any) currently available IB products support per virtual lane level counters. Another advantage of using such an approach is that it frees us from the need to query the HCA on the node as the MPI process itself will send us the necessary details when the node is computing and while the node is not in use, we do not care about it as it is not expected to be contributing network traffic in a significant fashion.

To overcome these limitations, we designed and integrated the MPI data collection thread into the daemon process. The sole responsibility of this thread is to collect data specific to each MPI process running on the system and push it to OSU INAM Database. This allows us to analyze and visualize the data at job level, node level and process level granularities. We designed the thread to be a listener which accepts data from remote MPI processes to avoid the single point bottlenecks that can arise from a design where the thread actively polls each MPI process for data. The thread uses IB based communication to achieve high performance and low latency. The thread further uses the interrupt driven mode in IB to reduce CPU utilization by eliminating the need to continually poll to identify the arrival of new packets.

Design Choices for IB Transport Protocol: As mentioned above, the MPI data collection thread uses IB to enable high performance and low latency communication. It is known that IB supports several transport protocols such as Reliable Connected (RC), Unreliable Datagram (UD), Extended Reliable Connected (XRC), and Dynamic Connected (DC) [23,24]. Each transport protocol has different cost/performance tradeoffs. Our previous research has shown that using the UD and DC transport protocols over others can have significant benefits in terms of scalability and memory footprint [23,32]. Thus we eliminate RC and XRC from the pool of possible protocols. The choice of whether to use DC or UD depends on the communication requirements. From the point of view of the $INAM^2$, the communication requirements are similar to what one would expect from a high performance stock market application - typically small messages, high performance, high scalability, low latency and no requirement for absolute reliability. Our previous research has shown that [32], between DC and UD, UD is able to deliver high performance, high scalability, low latency better than DC when reliability is not an issue. Thus, we choose the UD protocol as the IB transport protocol for the MPI data collection thread.

Co-designing the MPI Runtime to Work with $INAM^2$. As we saw in Sect. 1, the MPI_T interface provides a convenient method to keep track of various internal states and metrics of an MPI library. We piggyback on this infrastructure and enhance it to enable monitoring for several more process level metrics. We introduce support in MVAPICH2-X [28] to keep track of: (1) CPU utilization of each process including idle time, user time, system time and the rest; (2) memory utilization of each process including current and maximum size of virtual memory consumed; (3) inter-node and intra-node communication buffer utilization including the maximum number of buffers that were required (high water mark); (4) intra-node bytes sent/received; (5) inter-node bytes sent/received; (6) total bytes sent/received for collective operations; and (7) total bytes sent for RMA operations. The MPI runtime collects this information and sends updates to the MPI data collection thread via UD Queue Pairs (QP) at user specified intervals (default value: 30 s). In addition to this, each packet sent has some meta data information about the process itself like rank, LID/GUID from which it's sending the data, time stamp when data was sent, job ID, etc., which will be used later to retrieve the data from the database. The MPI data collection thread dumps the UD QP and Local Identifier (LID) that it is listening on to a file. This location of this file is passed through environment variables set up by the system administrator to the MPI runtime. The runtime then uses this information while sending data out to the MPI data collection thread. While we chose MVAPICH2 for implementing our designs, any MPI runtime (e.g.: OpenMPI [12]) can be modified to perform similar data collection and transmission.

Fabric Discovery Thread. The *Fabric Discovery* (FD) thread is responsible for discovering the IB fabric and extracting data from various selected components in the IB fabric. The fabric discovery has multiple phases. In the first phase, the thread uses methods similar to what is used by the "ibnetdiscover" utility to identify the various IB devices present in the network and their current status. The data is stored in an easy to retrieve format in the database. Once all the devices have been identified, it computes the network path between each pair of hosts and pushes this information into the database as well. Once this is done, the fabric thread will monitor the network for any changes at a user specified interval. Then, the *FD* thread switches over to retrieving the performance counter information from the network.

Different design choices were explored to retrieve the performance counter information from the IB fabric. Using an OpenSM plugin in for the *performance manager* module to extract the performance counter information. However, this method will cause data to be extracted from all network devices (including the end nodes themselves). As the MPI data collection thread is already capturing information at a much finer granularity than what can be delivered by the network level counters, it would be prudent to avoid the useless query to retrieve this information. To avoid this, the *FD* thread issues queries to selected components in the network at user specified intervals. In our case, the selected components would be various switches in the network. By doing this, we also reduce the amount of high-priority management traffic that is generated on the network. Although the default value for the query interval is 30 s, we recommend that users set it to a lower value as the "Xmit Data" and "Rcv Data" counters are only 32-bit and can easily overflow depending on the volume of data being transferred. On receiving a response, the *FD* thread queues up the message in a FIFO queue to the database thread for eventual insertion into the database.

Database Thread. The *Database* (DB) thread is responsible for receiving information from the MPI data collection thread as well as the *FD* thread. When being run for the first time the *DB* thread will create all the tables in the schema that the given version of the tool expects. If an earlier version of the tool which used a different table scheme exists in the same system, it will automatically update them to avoid conflicts and make life easier for the user.

4.2   Design of OSU INAM Database

The Database design for $INAM^2$ is critical since all necessary data needs to be stored in and queried from it. A useful and scalable database schema plays a key role for the system to achieve the flexibility and high-performance needed to scale with large clusters. Figure 2 shows the design of the $INAM^2$ database. From this figure, we can see that through nine tables, $INAM^2$ is able to cover all the capabilities as mentioned in Sect. 2 and we believe all these tables and fields are necessary to maintain all the important statistical data for both the InfiniBand network and the MPI processes and their correlations.

For instance, the fields in the tables of "route", "links", "nodes", "port_data_counters", and "port_errors" can hold all the important data for InfiniBand network infrastructure, like links, nodes, ports and routes. On the other hand, in order to keep track of MPI process communication characteristics, we utilize the tables of "process_info", "process_comm_main", and "process_comm_grid" to store MPI library counters and the communication paths over the links. Through these, $INAM^2$ is able to analyze and profile node-level, job-level and process-level activities for MPI Point-to-point, collectives, and RMA communication. Further, this information can help to profile and report several important parameters/counters of MPI processes at the node-level, job-level and process-level as well as visualize the communication map at process-level and node-level granularities. Another example is analyzing and classifying InfiniBand network traffic flows in a physical link, through tables of "route", "link_route", and "links", we are able to distinguish the traffic into those belonging to different jobs in conjunction with the MPI runtime. More analysis examples and scenarios will be discussed in Sect. 6.

4.3   Design of Java Webserver and Web-Based Front-End Visualization

One of the most user-friendly features our $INAM^2$ tool provides is the Web-based visualization. Through $INAM^2$'s Web front-end, system administrators, MPI developers and end users can easily understand the statistics data of the activities over underlying InfiniBand network and MPI jobs, which are gathered from the OSU INAM daemon and acquired from the Slurm job scheduler as shown in Fig. 1. This information is organized and shown through Web pages in a way that can help users to correlate network level and MPI level behavior and identify the root causes of performance issues.

$INAM^2$ was not only designed for providing functionality, the high-performance design of the Web server and front-end will provide low latency as well as high throughput for users' queries, so that users can profile the network and MPI job performance during the job execution. As shown in Fig. 3, we designed the $INAM^2$ Web server based on the Spring [15] MVC (Model, View and Controller) architecture which can be integrated easily with a Java Tomcat server. On the client side, we choose to use the light-weight JQuery [21] library to send HTTP requests through AJAX [20]. With the help from JQuery and

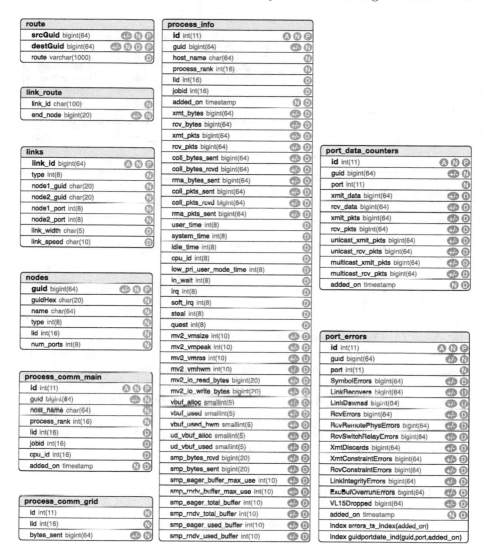

Fig. 2. Overview of OSU INAM database design

AJAX, $INAM^2$ pages can send data to and retrieve responses from the server asynchronously without interfering with the display and behavior of the existing page. Such a solution will dramatically improve the user experience because it hides a lot of the data processing and page rendering in the background.

The overall processing flow is as follows: (1) Whenever a user's action generates an HTTP request, it will be sent to the server side by Web browser or JQuery library with AJAX; (2) Once the Tomcat server receives the request, it is passed to the the Spring framework who will dispatch the coming request to the corresponding controller based on the mapping information of URL

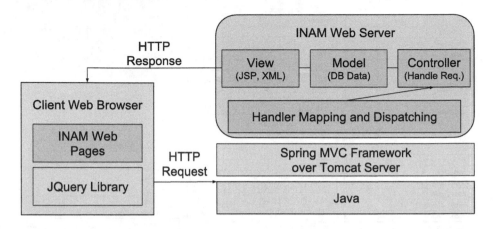

Fig. 3. Overall of INAM web server and front-end

(in the request) and Controller. The dispatcher has information about which controller needs to be invoked; (3) The selected controller will be invoked and it can query the model for some information, in most cases, about some data in database; (4) Once processing has been done, the Spring framework will get the response to build the view through JSP, XML, etc.; (5) Finally the HTTP response will be sent back to the browser at the client side. Then the Web page will be get updated. Note that the whole process is completed very fast since all the data has been stored in database through the OSU INAM daemon in advance and all the processing steps are configured and indexed in the database. As indicated earlier, many users' actions are handled through AJAX which alleviates the need to reload the page for fresh data.

5   Experimental Results

We describe the results of the various experiments carried out for this paper in this section.

5.1   Experimental Setup

Each node of our 184 node testbed has eight Intel Xeon cores running at 2.53 GHz with 12 MB L3 cache. The cores are organized as two sockets with four cores per socket. Each node also has 12 GB of memory and Gen2 PCI-Express bus. They are equipped with MT26428 QDR ConnectX-2 HCAs with PCI-Express interfaces. We used a Mellanox MTS3610 QDR switch, with 11 leafs, each having 16 ports. Each node is connected to the switch using one QDR link. The HCA, as well as the switches, use the latest firmware. The operating system used is Red Hat Enterprise Linux Server release 6.5 (Santiago), with the 2.6.32-431.el6.x86_64 kernel version. Mellanox OFED version 2.2-1.0.1 is used on all machines.

5.2 Impact of Profiling on Performance of Basic Microbenchmarks and NAS Parallel Benchmarks

In this section we study the impact the co-design of the MPI runtime with the MPI data collection thread of $INAM^2$ has on basic communication performance of different point-to-point as well as collective microbenchmarks and popular application kernels like the NAS parallel benchmarks [9]. Figure 4a compares the basic point-to-point inter-node latency obtained with and without the data collection happening in the MPI runtime. As we can see, the data collection adds less than 1 % degradation when compared to the native performance. In Fig. 4b, we depict the inter-node message rate obtained with the osu_mbw_mr microbenchmarks using a pair of processes. We see that the data collection and transmission adds about 6 % to 8 % overhead for messages less than 4,096 bytes. However, for larger messages, we see no significant impact at all (less than 1 %).

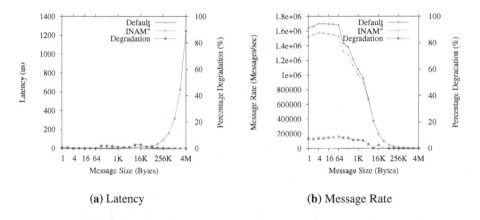

(a) Latency   (b) Message Rate

Fig. 4. Microbenchmark-level point-to-point performance

Figure 5a and b depict the performance impact the data collection and transmission has on some common collective communication patterns such as Broadcast and Alltoall, respectively. The evaluations were done at a scale of 512 processes. As we can see, the tool adds less than 5 % overhead for Broadcast. For Alltoall, we observe less than a 5 % degradation for messages up to 1,024 bytes. For larger messages the degradation is mostly around 7 % with only 4,096 byte message showing up to 12 % degradation.

Figure 6 compares the performance of the version of the MPI runtime with support for MPI level data collection with one which does not have the support. As we can see, at the application level, there is little to no impact on the performance due to the addition of the data collection and reporting. These are encouraging trends which positively advocate the use of such tools for end applications on modern supercomputing systems.

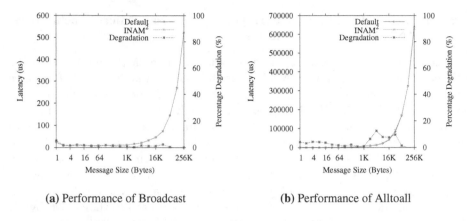

(a) Performance of Broadcast   (b) Performance of Alltoall

Fig. 5. Microbenchmark-level collective performance at 512 processes

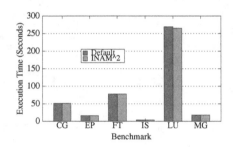

Fig. 6. Performance of class D NAS parallel benchmarks at 512 processes (Color figure online)

6   Discussion on Features of INAM^2 and Its Impact

In this section, we highlight some of the many features of INAM^2 and describe some of the potential impact it can have on the understanding and performance of applications.

6.1   Analyzing and Understanding Inter-node Communication Buffer Allocation and Use

Several high performance implementations of the the MPI programming model allocate a set of internal communication buffers that have been pre-registered with the IB HCA to enable fast small message communication. MVAPICH2, for instance, has been extensively tuned to ensure that the number and size of communication buffers is large enough to maintain good communication performance without significantly increasing the amount of memory consumed for these buffers. The memory footprint is even more important for these as they are always "pinned" to the physical memory and cannot be swapped out in case the application requires more memory to do its computation. However, at the level of end applications, one cannot assure that all the internal communication buffers that have been pre-allocated and pinned are being used by the application for communication. We use the INAM^2 tool to profile and understand the communication behavior of the NAS benchmarks and visualize how they use the internal communication buffers that MVAPICH2 allocates. Once the job has completed execution, we monitor the high water marker for the internal communication buffer usage over the lifetime of the job using the "historical job view" that INAM^2 offers. Table 1 shows the results of our analysis. It highlights the number of internal inter-node communication buffers taken for a 512 process run of class D NAS parallel benchmarks. The column "Default-Alloc" highlights the number of communication buffers pre-allocated with the default communication buffer tuning done for MVAPICH2. The "Default-HWM" column highlights the maximum number of communication buffers actually used by the application kernel in the default scenario. As we can see, there is a significant waste of communication buffers for several application kernels. With this insight, we perform application specific tuning and reduce the number of inter-node communication buffers pre-allocated at initialization time. "Tuned-Alloc" indicates the number of buffers allocated after we tuned the number of communication buffers with the insights gained from INAM^2. As we can see by comparing the memory taken for the default and tuned, we are able to save significant amounts of memory without any impact on the communication performance. Another observation is that the "Tuned-HWM" value is higher than "Default-HWM" in several cases even when the "Tuned-Alloc" is much less than "Default-Alloc" indicating better utilization of available communication buffer resources.

Table 1. Comparison of communication buffer utilization for default and tuned scenarios for 512-process class D NAS parallel benchmarks

Benchmark	Default-HWM (max value)	Default-alloc (max value)	Default-communication Buffer Memory (sum) (MB)	Tuned-HWM (max value)	Tuned-alloc (max value)	Tuned-communication Buffer-memory (sum) (MB)
CG	1	240	1570.20	2	48	409.33
EP	1	240	1570.20	3	48	348.22
FT	356	544	1735.49	295	320	647.24
LU	161	352	1584.74	152	192	503.76
MG	30	240	1570.20	32	80	561.33

6.2 Identifying and Analyzing Sources of Link Congestion

Existing IB fabric monitoring tools are capable of identifying congested links in the fabric. However, identifying the network "hot spots" alone is not good enough for system administrators. What they are looking for is the source of the congestion. Unfortunately, no tool offers the kind of automatic "reverse-lookup" feature that allows one to identify the various sources (end compute nodes) that could possibly have routes through the link in question. On a typical network with dynamic routing, doing this would prove to be a near insurmountable challenge. However, as IB networks are typically statically routed, it becomes a challenge that can be solved. We tackle and solve this challenge in INAM^2 using the various tables described in Fig. 2. Figure 7 depicts how one can identify the various routes going through the link. As we can see, the different paths that go through a given link gets highlighted in yellow. We actually go one step further and provide the capability to analyze and classify the traffic flowing in a physical link into those belonging to different jobs in conjunction with the MPI runtime allowing system administrators to identify exactly which job was contributing to the traffic going over a particular link. Users can view the link utilization by the jobs sending/receiving data through it in both directions in an absolute (in terms of number of bytes)or relative sense (as a percentage of total link capacity). Figure 8 depcits how, by selecting a job id, INAM^2 can process level link utilization for the selected job. Sections 4.2 and 4.3 describe how data is fetched from various tables to construct and display this novel feature.

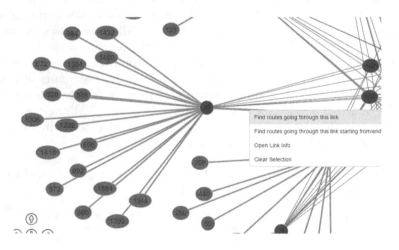

Fig. 7. Identifying communication routes going through a given link

6.3   Monitoring Jobs Based on Various Metrics

While typical job schedulers list what nodes are being used by which jobs, they do not list what each individual job is currently doing and how that impacts the different components of the HPC system. For instance, if a job is dumping a lot of data to the file system due to a checkpoint operation or because it has encountered a segmentation fault and is currently in the process of dumping cores, it is going to negatively affect all other processes in the system. Similarly, if a job is performing a network intensive communication operation, like an Alltoall, all jobs may get affected. Thus, it is in the best interest of all concerned that such"high-value" jobs be closely monitored by the system administrator. To address this concern, we introduce a "Live Job" page in INAM^2 which lists all

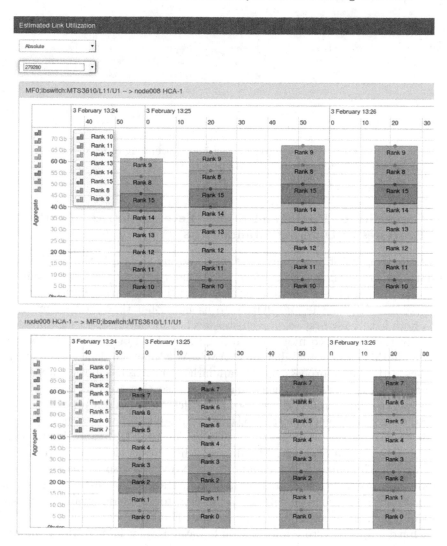

Fig. 8. Process level link utilization for a user specified job (Color figure online)

MPI jobs that are sending data to it through the MPI data collection framework. The page allows sorting the various jobs in ascending/descending order of the various metrics listed in the "process_info" table depicted in Fig. 2. Figure 9 shows an example of how this page would look like on a real cluster scenario with various jobs running. As we can see, each job ID is a hyperlink which takes the user to the "job page" for the corresponding job so that the user can get more details of what exactly is going on in the job.

Job ID	CPU User Usage	Virtual Memory Size	Total Communication	Total Inter Node	Total Intra Node	Total Collective	RMA Sent
270747	99	8.19 Mb	92.35 Gb	36.69 Gb	55.66 Gb	64.46 Gb	0.00 bytes
270748	99	15.12 Mb	149.98 Gb	58.23 Gb	91.76 Gb	102.78 Gb	0.00 bytes
270749	99	30.39 Mb	151.23 Gb	58.35 Gb	92.88 Gb	100.34 Gb	0.00 bytes
270759	99	17.99 Mb	58.71 Gb	37.29 Gb	21.43 Gb	303.73 Kb	0.00 bytes
270765	99	9.42 Mb	32.52 Gb	23.19 Gb	9.33 Gb	0.00 bytes	0.00 bytes

Showing 1 to 5 of 5 rows

Fig. 9. Live job page to display jobs in ascending/descending order of various performance metrics in conjunction with the MPI runtime

6.4 Capability to Profile and Report Several Metrics of MPI Processes at Different Granularities

One of the dangers of providing users with too much data is the possibility of inundating them with so much information that the high value data items get lost in the deluge of less relevant details. Thus, it is always helpful if one can aggregate and display the information to users so that they are first presented with a high level view first (e.g.: a cluster level or job level) and then allowed to slowly dig their way into more details (e.g.: node level or process level views). We provide this exact capability in INAM^2. Although the data from the MPI processes arrive at a process level granularity, once it has been entered into the database, things can be easily manipulated so that we can aggregate and display the details at much coarser granularities (e.g.: node level or job level). Figures 10 and 11 depict examples of the live job-level view of a given job and node level view of different processes that belong to a job respectively as rendered by INAM^2. Further, INAM^2 allows such analysis to be done in a "live" or a "historical" manner. This capability of INAM^2 to display historical information can prove very useful to system administrators. For instance, it is quite possible that the system or network administrator is made aware of an issue "post-mortem". In such scenarios, the current IB fabric monitoring tools, which do not have support to store information in databases for later retrieval, more or less leave the administrators helpless. However, if an administrator has access to a tool like INAM^2 which has the ability to "play back" events that occurred at a specified time in the past, it provides administrators the flexibility to inspect events "post-mortem" and identify the culprit(s) that caused the issue.

7 Related Tools

We believe that $INAM^2$ fills a void in the tools space as many do not monitor and correlate the impact of particular MPI jobs on the system. In principle, the pre-existing tool most closely related in design is *Lightweight Distributed Metric Service (LDMS)* [6] by Sandia. It strives to be a low overhead system monitoring tool which also correlates jobs to the impact on the system. LDMS

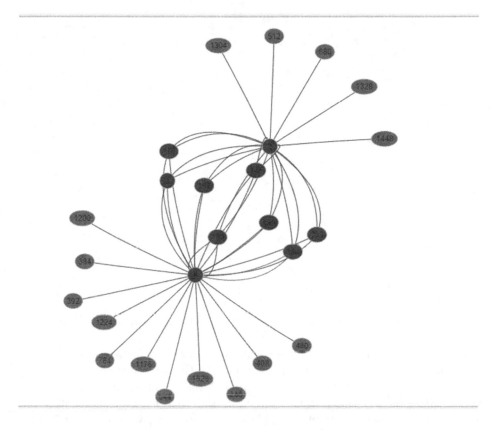

Fig. 10. Live job level view of a particular job

does not monitor the InfiniBand network directly as $INAM^2$ but does a good job monitoring other resources such as memory or filesystem I/O.

Another tool suite available is *HOlistic Performance System Analysis (HOPSA)* [7]. This suite is more focused on application on MPI but is designed in a way where each application or job may have different metrics monitored which may not allow for a full system view of how the set of jobs are interacting on the system.

The group at the Texas Advanced Computing Center have also developed a tool *TACC STATS* [31] to help them to explore job and system level reports. These reports help to identify jobs or system components that may need attention based on policies that they've set forth ahead of time. The main difference between this tool and $INAM^2$ is that *TACC STATS* does their analysis post-mortem whereas we try to make this information available in real time.

As mentioned earlier, several tools exist which allow system administrators to analyze and inspect the IB fabric such as Nagios, Ganglia, Mellanox Fabric IT, INAM, and BoxFish. However, due to lack of in-depth knowledge about the MPI library, no existing IB fabric monitoring tool can correlate the network level and MPI level behavior to classify traffic as being generated by particular MPI

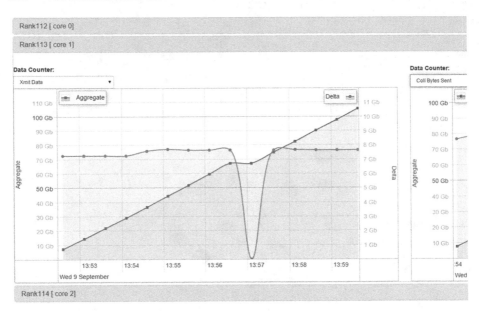

Fig. 11. Live node level view of different processes that are part of a particular job

primitives. Furthermore, they cannot classify network traffic as belonging to a particular job due to the lack of interaction with the job scheduler.

Also mentioned earlier, existing MPI level profiling tools like TAU, HPCToolkit, Intel VTune, IPM, and mpiP give reasonable insights into the MPI communication behavior of applications. However, they have no knowledge about the underlying IB fabric and thus are not able to correlate network level and MPI level behavior. With $INAM^2$ we strive to bridge the gap between the system level and MPI level profilers and monitors.

8   Conclusions and Future Work

In this paper, we presented the design of $INAM^2$ - a low-overhead profiling and visualization tool that is capable of presenting the profiling information obtained from the network and the MPI library in conjunction. We demonstrated how, through the profiling information provided by $INAM^2$, designers as well as users of high performance middleware can gain more insights into the communication characteristics of their runtimes allowing them to further fine tune the performance on a per application or per run basis. We showed how, through the link analysis capabilities of $INAM^2$, system administrators can pin point the cause of network performance issues to a granularity of a process. Several features of $INAM^2$ presented in this paper are already publically available in the released versions of the *OSU INAM* package which can be downloaded for free from http://mvapich.cse.ohio-state.edu/tools/osu-inam/. We plan to release the remaining features in upcoming releases of the *OSU INAM*. While the MPI data collection was designed and implemented using MVAPICH2-X, note that the same techniques are equally applicable to other MPI stacks.

As part of future work, we plan to incorporate support for additional MPI_T counters in conjunction with the MPI library. We would also like to extend INAM^2 to be capable of profiling and analyzing communication taking place to and from GPGPUs. Further, we would like to add the capability to profile various PGAS programing languages such as OpenSHMEM [29], UPC [35] and CAF [11] as well as different BigData frameworks like Apache Hadoop [17], MapReduce [19] and Spark [30].

Acknowledgements. We would like to thank Michael Knox from Cray and John Hanks from KAUST for their feedback on the OSU INAM package and thus enabling us to fix several bugs and performance issues.

References

1. Ganglia Cluster Management System. http://ganglia.sourceforge.net/
2. Integrated Performance Monitoring (IPM). http://ipm-hpc.sourceforge.net/
3. mpiP: Lightweight, Scalable MPI Profiling. http://www.llnl.gov/CASC/mpip/
4. Nagios. http://www.nagios.org/
5. Malony, A.D., Shende, S.: Performance technology for complex parallel and distributed systems. In: Kotsis, G., Kacsuk, P. (eds.) Proceedings of DAPSYS, pp. 37–46 (2000) ·
6. Agelastos, A., Allan, B., Brandt, J., Cassella, P., Enos, J., Fullop, J., Gentile, A., Monk, S., Naksinehaboon, N., Ogden, J., Rajan, M., Showerman, M., Stevenson, J., Taerat, N., Tucker, T.: The lightweight distributed metric service: a scalable infrastructure for continuous monitoring of large scale computing systems and applications. In: Proceedings of International Conference for High Performance Computing, Networking, Storage and Analysis, SC 2014, pp. 154–165. IEEE Press, Piscataway, NJ, USA (2014)
7. HOPSA Holistic Performance System Analysis. http://www.vi-hps.org/projects/hopsa/overview
8. OSU InfiniBand Network Analysis and Monitoring. http://mvapich.cse.ohio-state.edu/tools/osu-inam/
9. Bailey, D.H., Barszcz, E., Dagum, L., Simon, H.D.: NAS parallel benchmark results. Technical report 94-006, RNR (1994)
10. PAVE Software Boxfish. https://computation.llnl.gov/project/performance-analysis-through-visualization/software.php
11. Coarray Fortran (CAF). http://caf.rice.edu/
12. Open MPI: Open Source High Performance Computing. http://www.open-mpi.org
13. Intel Corporation. Intel VTune Amplifier. https://software.intel.com/en-us/intel-vtune-amplifier-xe
14. Gallardo, E., Vienne, J., Fialho, L., Teller, P., Browne, J.: MPI advisor: a minimal overhead MPI performance tuning tool. In: EuroMPI 2015 (2015)
15. Spring Framework. http://projects.spring.io/spring-framework/
16. Pfister, G.: Aspects of the InfiniBand architecture. In: IEEE International Conference on Cluster Computing (CLUSTER), pp. 369. IEEE Computer Society (2001)

17. Apache Hadoop. https://hadoop.apache.org/
18. HPCToolkit. http://hpctoolkit.org/
19. Dean, J., Ghemawat, S.: MapReduce: simplified data processing on large clusters. In: Proceedings of 6th Conference on Symposium on Opearting Systems Design and Implementation, OSDI 2004, vol. 6, p. 10. USENIX Association, Berkeley, CA, USA (2004)
20. Asynchronous JavaScript and XML. http://www.w3schools.com/Ajax/ajax_intro.asp
21. Jquery. https://jquery.com/
22. Koop, M., Jones, T., Panda, D.K.: MVAPICH-Aptus: scalable high-performance multi-transport MPI over InfiniBand. In: IPDPS 2008, pp. 1–12 (2008)
23. Koop, M., Sridhar, J., Panda, D.K.: Scalable MPI design over InfiniBand using extended reliable connection. In: IEEE International Conference on Cluster Computing (Cluster 2008), September 2008
24. Koop, M., Sur, S., Gao, Q., Panda, D.K.: High performance, MPI design using unreliable datagram for ultra-scale infiniband clusters. In: ICS 2007: Proceedings of the 21st Annual International Conference on Supercomputing, pp. 180–189. ACM, New York, NY, USA (2007)
25. Liu, J., Jiang, W., Wyckoff, P., Panda, D.K., Ashton, D., Buntinas, D., Gropp, W., Toonen, B.: Design and implementation of MPICH2 over InfiniBand with RDMA support. In: Proceedings of International Parallel and Distributed Processing Symposium (IPDPS 2004), April 2004
26. Schulz, M., MPIT: a new interface for performance tools in MPI 3. http://cscads.rice.edu/workshops/summer-2010/slides/performance-tools/2010-08-cscads-mpit.pdf
27. Message Passing Interface Forum: MPI: A Message-Passing Interface Standard, March 1994
28. MVAPICH2-X: Unified MPI+PGAS Communication Runtime over OpenFabrics/Gen2 for Exascale Systems. http://mvapich.cse.ohio-state.edu/
29. OpenSHMEM. http://openshmem.org/site/
30. Apache Spark. http://spark.apache.org/
31. TACC STATS. https://www.tacc.utexas.edu/research-development/tacc-projects/tacc-stats
32. Subramoni, H., Hamidouche, K., Venkatesh, A., Chakraborty, S., Panda, D.K.: Designing MPI library with dynamic connected transport (DCT) of InfiniBand: early experiences. In: Kunkel, J.M., Ludwig, T., Meuer, H.W. (eds.) ISC 2014. LNCS, vol. 8488, pp. 278–295. Springer, Heidelberg (2014)
33. Top 500 Supercomputers. http://www.top500.org/statistics/list/
34. Mellanox Technologies. Mellanox Integrated Switch Management Solution. http://www.mellanox.com/page/ib_fabricit_efm_management
35. Unified Parallel C (UPC). http://upc.lbl.gov/

Comparing Runtime Systems with Exascale Ambitions Using the Parallel Research Kernels

Rob F. Van der Wijngaart[1]([⊠]), Abdullah Kayi[1], Jeff R. Hammond[1],
Gabriele Jost[1], Tom St. John[1], Srinivas Sridharan[1], Timothy G. Mattson[1],
John Abercrombie[2], and Jacob Nelson[2]

[1] Intel Corporation, Hillsboro, OR, USA
rob.f.van.der.wijngaart@intel.com
[2] University of Washington, Seattle, WA, USA

Abstract. We use three Parallel Research Kernels to compare performance of a set of programming models(We employ the term *programming model* as it is commonly used in the application community. A more accurate term is *programming environment*, which is the collective of abstract programming model, embodiment of the model in an Application Programmer Interface (API), and the runtime that implements it.): MPI1 (MPI two-sided communication), MPIOPENMP (MPI+OpenMP), MPISHM (MPI1 with MPI-3 interprocess shared memory), MPIRMA (MPI one-sided communication), SHMEM, UPC, Charm++ and Grappa. The kernels in our study – Stencil, Synch_p2p and Transpose – underlie a wide range of computational science applications. They enable direct probing of properties of programming models, especially communication and synchronization. In contrast to mini- or proxy applications, the PRK allow for rapid implementation, measurement and verification. Our experimental results show MPISHM the overall winner, with MPI1, MPIOPENMP and SHMEM performing well. MPISHM and MPIOPENMP outperform the other models in the strong-scaling limit due to their effective use of shared memory and good granularity control. The non-evolutionary models Grappa and Charm++ are not competitive with traditional models (MPI and PGAS) for two of the kernels; these models favor irregular algorithms, while the PRK considered here are regular.

Keywords: Programming models · MPI · PGAS · Charm++

1 Introduction

With the stagnation of frequency scaling in modern processors and the emergence of power as a critical constraint in the design and deployment of supercomputers, hardware parallelism has been increasing dramatically. Managing expanded concurrency while maintaining voluminous validated legacy codes is a challenge, compounded by the expected increase in faults, and performance nondeterminism. These challenges have inspired the development of *dynamic runtime systems* (DRTS). While DRTS offer much promise for exascale, it is vitally

© Springer International Publishing Switzerland 2016
J.M. Kunkel et al. (Eds.): ISC High Performance 2016, LNCS 9697, pp. 321–339, 2016.
DOI: 10.1007/978-3-319-41321-1_17

important that they meet the needs of HPC applications at all relevant scales of parallelism. And even if DRTS prove more suitable for asynchronous and/or task-oriented algorithms, they must be able to support the regular/structured algorithms and more synchronous/procedural styles common in HPC.

Our goal is to study many relevant HPC programming models, evaluating them on their ability to support ubiquitous application patterns. The m by n complexity of this problem–m programming models and n application patterns– constrains the scope greatly. We have learned from the community that even mini-applications are difficult to port to new models and that many algorithms in different domains map to the same parallel programming patterns, meaning that porting many mini-applications may not produce a proportional understanding. On the other hand, studying a small number of programming models, or even treating MPI as a single programming model, does not sufficiently answer the question of how to implement HPC applications for peta- and exascale.

In this paper we evaluate a range of different programming models using the Parallel Research Kernels (PRK). The PRK comprise about a dozen different application *patterns*; we focus on the three that are most relevant to scientific computing applications running on modern HPC systems: Synch_p2p, Stencil and Transpose (details in Sect. 2). The models evaluated include:

- MPI1[1] and MPI+X models in the form of MPI1+OpenMP (MPIOPENMP) and MPISHM[2];
- established PGAS models SHMEM and UPC (Unified Parallel C), and the relatively new but semantically similar MPIRMA (MPI with direct Remote Memory Access); and
- the non-evolutionary programming models Charm++ and Grappa, both of which are oriented at irregular and unstructured computations, but which are still capable of implementing regular, structured computations.

In the rest of this paper we provide a detailed description of the PRK and motivate our choice of kernels. Next, we describe the programming models studied and how the PRK were implemented in each. We report experiments on one to 512 nodes of a state-of-the-art supercomputer, analyzing them in terms of the PRK implementation and observable runtime effects. We also reference the substantial body of related work and present our conclusions and future plans.

The novel contributions of this paper are: (1) an evaluation of four different usage models for MPI, including two using new features introduced in MPI-3; (2) the direct comparison of eight different programming models for three different parallel computing patterns on a platform (Cray* XC30) that is appropriate for all of them; (3) the demonstration that the PRK expose interesting behavior in programming models and are a viable alternative to the more complicated

---

[1] MPI refers to any model based upon the Message Passing Interface standard, while MPI1 refers to the usage of MPI two-sided communication.

[2] MPISHM refers to an MPI1-like program that uses shared memory within the node instead of explicit communication. It is similar to MPIOPENMP, but with significant differences related to locality and runtime overheads, among others. We use MPI-3 as our implementation of shared memory.

mini-applications currently used to evaluate programming models. In particular, the Cray* XC30 is the only mainstream HPC platform where the vendor provides MPI-3, UPC and SHMEM*, and where Charm++ and GASNet (used in Berkeley UPC) have been extensively tested and tuned, meaning that our data is less susceptible to runtime implementation quality effects. In our previous work, we found that comparing these models on InfiniBand* was problematic due to variation in implementation quality of all of the runtime systems except MPI.

2   Background and Motivation

In this section we provide context for our workloads, core programming models, and specific combinations of programming models used in our study.

2.1   Parallel Research Kernels

The PRK [36] are a suite of elementary operations (*kernels*) that can be used to study the suitability of parallel systems for parallel application programming. The full suite includes about a dozen kernels designed to expose various performance bottlenecks of a parallel system. In many cases, programmers can relate the observed performance of the PRK to the expected bottlenecks in their applications, allowing the PRK to serve as proxies for full applications.

The PRK are defined as paper-and-pencil operations independent of any particular implementation, although they do prescribe certain rules regarding data distribution on distributed memory systems. In addition to a canonical serial version, we provide reference implementations[3] using various parallelization techniques. The PRK implementations are self-contained, are arbitrarily scalable (problem size, compute resources), synthesize any data they need, and validate the results. They have been used to study new hardware architectures using simulators, as well as to evaluate new features in programming models [14].

For our study of programming systems for exascale computers, we use three kernels, in order of nominally increasing granularity: Synch_p2p, Stencil and Transpose. In our description of the reference implementations of the kernels we will refer to the units of execution generally as *ranks*. This should be replaced with *threads*, *chares*, or *PEs* as needed, depending on the particular programming model. For grid-based kernels we always opt for 2D over 3D. The reason is twofold. First, 2D problems typically have fewer options to exploit concurrency and more overhead than 3D (worse surface-to-volume ratios in domain decomposition problems, especially in the strong scaling case), which creates the extra stress for the runtime that we want to study. Second, 2D codes are more compact than 3D codes–a PRK design goal to maximize portability–but without sacrificing the realism that 1D codes do.

Synch_p2p involves a simple stencil-based problem. A two-dimensional array A of size $n \times m$, representing scalar values at grid points, is distributed

---

[3] PRK open source repository: https://github.com/ParRes/Kernels.

among the ranks in vertical strips. We apply the following difference stencil: $A_{i,j} = A_{i-1,j} + A_{i,j-1} - A_{i-1,j-1}$, with the condition that only updated array values or (fixed) boundary values may be used. The 2D data dependencies are resolved using a 1D software pipeline. Synch_p2p models the algorithmic structure of well-known benchmarks such as the LU-SGS NAS Parallel Benchmark (NPB) [3], and SNAP [37], but is even more stressful w.r.t. communication, as the kernel has only two spatial dimensions. It is not data-parallel, and must synchronize strictly on a point-to-point basis. Such synchronizations can be implemented using shared flags plus the `flush` directive in OpenMP, point-to-point messages in MPI1 and Charm++, put-wait in SHMEM and shared pointer access in UPC. In Grappa we use FullEmpty Bits (FEB) to implement producer/consumer synchronization. These techniques incur a forced write-to and read-from shared memory in OpenMP, and an inter-process communication latency for MPI1, SHMEM, UPC, Charm++, and Grappa. Performance is constrained by the overhead of frequent synchronization between ranks. Note: it is possible to increase the algorithm's granularity by grouping grid lines together explicitly, and our PRK implementation does indeed offer that option. But we do not consider that conforming, as we are interested in fine-grain application behavior.

The second kernel is **Stencil**, which applies a scalar, data-parallel stencil operation to the interior of a two-dimensional discretization grid of size $n \times n$. The stencil, which represents a discrete divergence operator, has radius r. In operator notation: $A = S(r)B$, where A and B are two-dimensional arrays and $S(r)$ is the stencil operator of radius r. The distributed-memory versions used in this paper employ two-dimensional domain decompositions to minimize the surface to volume ratio, and hence the communication volume. Communication is required to obtain ghost point values from logically nearest neighbors.

The third kernel is **Transpose**, in which a square matrix B of order n is divided into strips (columns) among the ranks, which store its transpose B^T in matrix A. The matrices are distributed identically, necessitating a *global* rearrangement of the data (all-to-all communication), as well as a *local* rearrangement (per-rank transpose of matrix tiles). Canonical execution of Transpose may lead to high numbers of cache and TLB misses, due to the strided nature of the data access of either A or B. To reduce this effect we employ blocking to implement the local transpose operation. For all programming models we use the same block size (32×32).

Each of the kernels' main operations is executed a number of times, and performance is computed by timing the entire sequence of operations, but skipping the first to reduce the effects of implicit initialization (e.g. network connections).

2.2   Programming Models

MPI1. The first version of the MPI standard [26] focused on message-passing functionality, defining point-to-point and collective operations as well as the critical infrastructure that makes MPI portable, extensible and composable. The set of functions in MPI-1 is quite complete with respect to practical parallel programming within Hoare's Communicating Sequential Processes (CSP) model. Contrary to popular belief, MPI-1 did not implement Valiant's Bulk Synchronous Parallel (BSP) model (this pattern was introduced in MPI-2 via MPI_Win_fence). Much of the success of MPI has been built upon the extensibility of the CSP model.

MPIOPENMP. MPI-2 [27] introduced an awareness of threads to MPI. Support for threads is not holistic; communication routines merely became thread-safe according to the user's request during initialization, but no changes to the communication routines were made that might make multithreaded MPI programs more efficient. For example, while the MPI standard does not explicitly require locks, most implementations use coarse-grain mutual exclusion for MPI_THREAD_MULTIPLE, which can have significant (negative) performance effects.

Because of the performance issues associated with concurrent access to MPI, many users only perform MPI calls outside of threaded regions. The fork-join model limits scalability, but the practical consequences of this are often relatively small if an MPI process is associated with each NUMA domain and threads are used only within that. For small numbers of threads, it is often the case that the overhead of mutual exclusion, which persists throughout the application, regardless of whether or not it is actually needed[4] is worse than the effect of joining (or merely serializing) all the threads to make MPI calls.

MPISHM: MPI Plus Interprocess Shared-Memory. While MPI+Threads is the most commonly applied solution to the multicore problem, an alternative model employs interprocess shared-memory. Heroux and coworkers proposed to use interprocess shared memory instead of threads in the context of MPI applications [20]. Members of the MPI Forum have elaborated upon this model [21] and it became part of MPI-3 [28]. This model is also referred to as MPI+MPI, as a way of connecting to MPI+X, where X equals MPI-3 shared memory.

SHMEM. Pioneered by Cray Inc. in the 1990s [17], SHMEM is a library specification that supports programming for a logically shared but physically distributed address space. All processes see variables in the global address space (symmetric variables), but also have their own local view in the partitioned global address space (PGAS). The SHMEM API provides a set of communication operations, similar to the MPI one-sided communication routines. SHMEM emphasizes one-sided communication features that can be mapped directly to hardware, which offers the potential for a more efficient implementation compared to MPI two-sided communication. Historically, SHMEM implementations have varied between vendor implementations, making it difficult to write portable SHMEM programs. Recently, OpenSHMEM [1] has emerged as a vendor-independent community standard and associated reference implementation, which has increased interest in SHMEM.

---

[4] MPI calls outside of threaded regions do not require mutual exclusion, but MPI has no way to know this.

MPIRMA: MPI One-Sided Communication. MPI-2 [27] introduced remote memory access (RMA), or one-sided communication, to MPI. This was not a successful effort, due to semantic constraints and implementation issues. With MPI-3 [28], the semantic issues were largely addressed, and MPIRMA is able to support the semantics of important PGAS models like SHMEM, Global Arrays (ARMCI), and Fortran coarrays, as demonstrated by OSHMPI[5], ARMCI-MPI[6], and OpenCoarrays[7], respectively, in addition to BSP and message-passing synchronization. We employ both passive- and active-target synchronization in the PRK. In all kernels we could use multiple styles of MPI-3 RMA, but we chose only one each for Synch_p2p and Stencil, and two for Transpose. The reason is that, to the extent that MPI-3 RMA can be *semantically* equivalent to SHMEM, the SHMEM implementation tells us what is possible with the passive-target motif, up to implementation differences (which may be substantial today).

UPC. UPC [34] is a PGAS extension to the the ISO C99 language. It handles shared and distributed memory with a uniform programming interface. Like SHMEM, UPC presents the abstraction of a global, shared address space. That space is partitioned among threads in a well-defined, user-prescribed way, allowing the programmer to exploit thread-to-data affinity and hence improve locality. Explicit put and get operations can also be used to increase granularity.

Charm++. The Charm++ programming framework [23] provides asynchronous remote method invocation (RMI) on persistent but migratable objects (*chares*) organized in multi-dimensional arrays. Communications between chares take place by specifying the parameters of the remote method (marshalling) or by sending the remote chare a message. While similar to MPI messaging, there are important differences. Chares are virtualized and may migrate between compute units transparently to the programmer. The flow of a program is not statically defined in terms of two-sided message passing; RMIs (with their data) are placed in task queues at the recipient, and are scheduled by the runtime, subject to an execution policy. Hence, messages may arrive in different order and well before they are needed, potentially providing substantial asynchrony. In addition, multiple chares may be assigned to the same compute unit (overdecomposition), which may provide more asynchrony and latency hiding. RMIs are nominally non-blocking, but may wait for certain events to occur if they contain *Structured Dagger* (SDAG) code. Messages and SDAG constructs generally offer the best performance and control. We use these for the Charm++ versions of the PRK.

Grappa. The Grappa runtime [30] is loosely based on innovations explored in the Tera* MTA [2] and Cray XMT [18] architectures, which allow very fast,

---

[5] https://github.com/jeffhammond/oshmpi.
[6] http://git.mpich.org/armci-mpi.git/.
[7] https://github.com/sourceryinstitute/opencoarrays.

hardware supported context switching between multiple instruction streams per core. This provides substantial latency hiding, but requires special hardware support. Grappa emulates these features in software using fast, user-level context switching, in addition to fine-grained communication and synchronization using FEBs across a partitioned global address space. The runtime watches for multiple asynchronous messages with a common destination from independent instruction streams, or from asynchronous communications in the same instruction stream, and batches them into a single transfer, transparently to the user. This can greatly improve the performance of fine-grain workloads.

3   Implementation and Performance Results

We performed three scaling experiments wherein problem size remains constant as more compute and memory resources are added for each kernel. For Stencil we select a star-shaped stencil of radius four (i.e. a 17-point star), and a grid of 49152×49152 points. We use the same dimensions for the grid of Synch_p2p and the matrix in Transpose. Problem sizes, numbers of ranks, and overdecomposition factors are chosen to allow for an even load across all processing elements when using all the cores on a node. An exception is made for Charm++, which performs better if one core per node is reserved for communication. This core is counted in the resource consumption, but does no computational work. To balance the load among the remaining cores on a node, we change the problem size for Charm++ to 47104 for all kernels. While strong-scaling from 1 to 512 nodes is not common in real applications, it exaggerates runtime overheads and allows us to draw conclusions about performance at much higher scale with a larger overall problem size but a per-node problem size within the range considered.

Our experiments were conducted on NERSC Edison, a Cray XC30 supercomputer with two 12-core Intel® Xeon® E5-2695 processors per node with the Aries interconnect in a Dragonfly topology. We used Intel 15.0.1.133 C/C++ compiler for all codes, except that Cray Compiler Environment (CCE) 8.4.0.219 was used for Cray UPC, and GCC 4.9.2 was used for Grappa. Berkeley UPC compiler 2.20.2 was used with the same Intel C/C++ compiler. System library versions were Cray MPT (MPI and SHMEM) 7.2.1, uGNI 6.0, and DMAPP 7.0.1. All MPIRMA transpose experiments enabled asynchronous progress; passive target RMA employed the DMAPP implementation[8]. While asynchronous progress in MPI may introduce overheads, it is the natural way to use one-sided communication and compares fairly to SHMEM and UPC, which make asynchronous progress on this platform.

All implementations of the PRK are derived from the same original MPI1 source code, and are functionally as similar as feasible, except for scheduling by the runtime, orchestration of communication, and data sharing. Although the implementations were written in a portable way, we consider them of high quality, since they were co-written and/or reviewed by the developers of the

---

[8] The environment variables are MPICH_RMA_OVER_DMAPP, MPICH_MAX_THREAD_SAFETY, and MPICH_NEMESIS_ASYNC_PROGRESS.

runtimes (Grappa, Charm++), or by the authors of this paper, who are experts in the other runtimes. All kernels are compiled with the same optimization flag (-O3). The use of Cray UPC and GCC C++ compilers (for Grappa) introduces a discrepancy that cannot be reconciled. However, sample trials using Gnu and Intel compilers for the same kernels show negligible performance differences, so we posit that this discrepancy does not substantively alter our results or conclusions with respect to Grappa.

Our methodology for presenting performance results is as follows. When a kernel is expected to show good scalability, we show normalized performance, in which absolute performance using P nodes is divided by P, as well as by the performance of the MPI1 code using a single node. This is the method we used for Stencil. When a kernel is expected to experience moderate to severe scalability problems, we show absolute performance on a log (cores)-linear (performance) scale, since this best depicts performance differences between the different models. This is the method we used for Synch_p2p and Transpose. For all kernels we report the *maximum* performance observed over a large number of experiments. This is because at the time of our experiments NERSC Edison experienced intermittent network issues, leading to a number of outliers that would unfairly penalize models that happened to run at an unfavorable time. Selecting the maximum over a large number of attempts produced the most consistent, fairest data.

3.1 Stencil Implementation Details and Performance

For the Stencil kernel we employ a 2D domain decomposition, where each MPI rank running on a processor core is assigned a tile within the overall grid that it updates in each iteration, based on the values computed in the previous iterations, as well as on values generated by logically nearest neighbor ranks. We employ the same method in Charm++, except that we allow an overdecomposition, which means that we divide the grid into more tiles–each assigned to a chare–than the number of processor cores employed. This technique is often used to provide overlap of computation and communication, since a core can work on updating the tile associated with one of its chares while the comunication needed for another of its chares is in progress. Overdecomposition could be applied in MPI as well, in principle, but would require explicit management of multiple tiles per rank, constituting a significant programming complication.

In all cases the tiles are chosen as close to square as possible to minimize their surface to volume ratio, which in turn minimizes the communication volume. An overdecomposition factor greater than 1 increases the number of tiles beyond the required minimum value, and hence increases the communication volume.

MPI1. Within each iteration an MPI rank determines whether it has a topological neighbor in each of four coordinate directions (+x, −x, +y, −y) and posts asynchronous receive calls (`MPI_Irecv`) for data from each of these neighbors. Subsequently, it copies data from its grid boundaries into communication buffers and posts asynchronous send calls (MPI_Isend) to each of its neighbors. Finally, it waits for all asynchronous communications belonging to the current iteration to finish (MPI_Wait) before copying the received data into ghost point locations and updating its tile values. It should be noted that the primary purpose of using asynchronous calls is to avoid deadlock. Since the load is fully balanced, all ranks engage in communication at effectively the same time, and negligible overlap of computation and communication occurs.

MPIOPENMP. We spawn one MPI rank per socket, and use OpenMP to parallellize the performance-critical loop nest in the code among the 12 cores (our experiments show that one MPI rank per node performs more poorly, due to NUMA effects). MPI communications only take place outside the threaded code regions. In a separate OpenMP-only experiment we determined that, for the granularities involved in this problem, OpenMP's fork-join overhead is negligible, justifying the use of omp parallel for.

MPISHM. The MPISHM implementation uses a hybrid communication method and a hierarchical domain decomposition. Ranks are grouped into a shared memory domain (spanning one socket in the case of MPISHM12 and two sockets for MPISHM24). As in the case of flat MPI, we use a two-dimensional domain decomposition that minimizes the surface to volume ratio and that produces one tile per rank. The tiles in this decomposition are grouped into logical rectangles (*super-tiles*), each of which is assigned to a group of ranks within the same subcommunicator. See Fig. 1a.

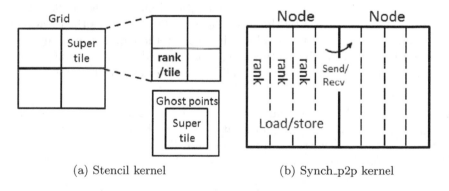

(a) Stencil kernel   (b) Synch_p2p kernel

Fig. 1. Hierarchical domain decompositions for MPISHM

One rank per subcommunicator allocates shared memory to store the data belonging to a super-tile. This memory includes ghost point values at the perimeter of the super-tile for communication with other super-tiles only. There is no explicit communication within a super-tile, only loads and stores, with proper synchronization. We synchronize via empty messages exchanged between logically nearest neighbors within the super-tile. If neighboring tiles are not in the same shared memory group, standard MPI1 communication is used to exchange ghost point values. This happens on a peer-to-peer basis, in which individual ranks at the boundary of their super-tile exchange messages with their topological neighbors in other super-tiles, unlike in the MPIOPENMP case, where individual threads do not communicate.

MPIRMA. For MPIRMA, we replaced non-blocking Send-Recv pairs with `MPI_Put` and added `MPI_Win_fence` synchronization where required (same location as calls to `MPI_Wait`). We could have instead used PSCW as in Synch_p2p, or passive target RMA with atomic counter synchronization as the SHMEM implementation does. In the future, we will implement and compare these different versions.

Charm++. The Charm++ implementation follows effectively the same strategy as MPI1. Virtually the entire program executed by a chare is cast as a single method invocation on the chare, comprising all iterations, including all communications with logically neighboring chares. Data is sent to neighbors asynchronously using messages, a special kind of RMI, and is received in an SDAG when construct. Such constructs are allowed to block until remote data has arrived. In that case the runtime can switch to work on another chare, if available, and execute its methods.

Grappa. The Grappa implementation also follows the MPI1 strategy, except that a core responsible for providing ghost point values to its neighbors writes those directly into those neighbors' communication buffers, to be scattered into actual ghost point locations by the receiving core. This bypasses the creation of communication buffers on the sending side, but at the expense of many small remote write operations (the runtime is capable of bundling these transparently, in principle). A single FEB word per buffer is used for synchronization.

SHMEM. The SHMEM implementation also closely follows the MPI1 version. We employ `shmem_putmem` for communication. For synchronization we use shmem atomic increments and `shmem_wait_until` until the required number of ghost point updates has been received.

UPC. The UPC implementation also closely follows the MPI1 version. We create shared ghost zones for each UPC thread. These are filled with neighbor data via `upc_memget`. Initial shared arrays are privatized for optimization. For synchronization we use `upc_barrier`. We refer to the Berkeley and Cray implementations of UPC as BUPC and CRAYUPC, respectively, in the text and figures.

Performance of Stencil. In Fig. 2 we show the performance of all runtimes for the stencil problem, divided by the peformance of single-node MPI1 and the number of nodes used. The numerals on Charm++ (1, 4, 16) indicate the overdecomposition factor. Those on MPISHM (12, 24) indicate the number of cores in a shared memory group. The graph mostly separates performance of implementations that rely on global barriers for synchronization and hence do not scale well (MPIRMA, BUPC, CRAYUPC), and those that use only point to point synchronization between nodes. Except for the highest core counts, performance of the latter is dominated by bandwidth to memory, forcing most of the performance curves together. Grappa has a lower absolute level because of its numerous small direct remote memory accesses. Charm++ uses a somewhat different problem size and hence a different data layout, which affects its absolute level of performance. Its scalability is good, except for an overdecomposition factor of 16, in which case runtime management and communication overhead of the wide ghost zones (4 points on all sides of a grid tile) limit performance.

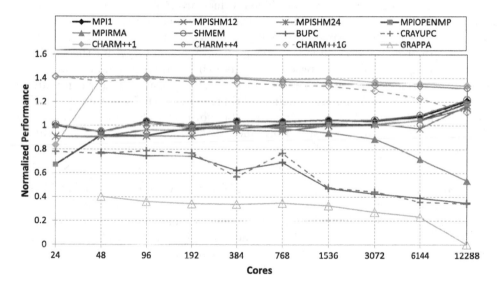

Fig. 2. Absolute performance of Stencil problem, divided by performance of single-node MPI1 and number of nodes used. (Color figure online)

3.2   Synch_p2p Implementation Details and Performance

The implementation of Synch_p2p follows the same principles as that of Stencil. Here the data dependencies dictate a 1D domain decomposition, where each rank is responsible for a vertical slice of the grid, see Fig. 1b. As mentioned in Sect. 2.1, the data dependency is resolved by updating values on only a single grid line segment before communicating one word with the logically neighboring rank. Implementation in MPI1 and Charm++ is obvious and will not be detailed.

MPIOPENMP. This kernel has no data parallelism, and hence we cannot use the simple fork-join mechanism of `omp parallel for` to parallelize the code among the threads within a rank. Instead, we use the method employed, for example, in the OpenMP version of the LU NPB, and documented in [9], for point-to-point synchronization between threads. Because there is no fork-join parallelism, the entire sweep over the grid is within a parallel OpenMP section (`omp parallel`), and threads within different ranks are required to communicate directly. A further complication is that the method for creating a dependence between successive sweeps over the grid involves a communication between the last thread on the last node, and the first thread on the first node. This necessitates use of `MPI_THREAD_MULTIPLE`, which typically hurts performance.

Grappa. In Synch_p2p all memory is private, except for a vector of ghost point values containing for each core all the rightmost grid point values that were produced by its predecessor in the pipelined solution process. These are FEB words for efficient synchronization. Their values are stored remotely using the `async write` method, which allows multiple individual writes to be combined automatically by the runtime into a single message, thus reducing latency costs. The programmer is responsible for setting an aggregation target for the runtime when building the code. Our best results were obtained for a bundling factor of 64 words, displayed in Fig. 3. Larger values of the aggregation factor can reduce latency more, but also increase pipeline fill time, so a non-trivial optimum usually obtains, which is not the same for all numbers of cores. Our optimum value of 64 was chosen to give the best performance at the highest core count for which we ran the Grappa version of the code.

MPISHM. The implementation of MPISHM is very similar to that of MPI1 and Grappa combined; communications between topologically neighboring ranks on different nodes uses blocking Send-Recv. Data exchange between neighboring ranks on the same node takes place via reads from the neighbor's shared memory window, supplemented with point-to-point synchronization via empty messages.

MPIRMA. The MPIRMA implementation of Synch_p2p is identical in form to MPI1, wherein Send-Recv pairs are replaced with the Post-Start-Complete-Wait (PSCW) pattern (see Ref. [28] for details). Data is transferred with `MPI_Put`. As there is essentially no semantic difference between MPI1 and MPIRMA for this kernel, we attribute any performance differences to implementation issues.

SHMEM. The SHMEM Synch_p2p implementation features two synchronization protocols, termed *handshake* and *no handshake*. The latter allows for relaxed synchronization, established via one fine-grain semaphore per grid line segment [35]. We only show results for this protocol, since it performs best.

UPC. The Synch_p2p implementation has two variations. One is portable, using a shared flag for communication between neighboring ranks. The other is more optimized but non-portable, using extensions in the Berkeley UPC compiler [8]. That version, denoted by *BUPCsem*, utilizes semaphores for synchronization within an iteration. However, both versions synchronize via a global barrier after each iteration.

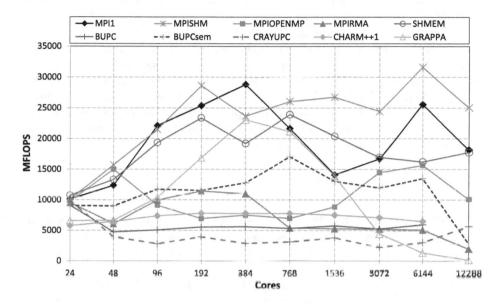

Fig. 3. Absolute performance of Synch_p2p problem (Color figure online)

Performance of Synch_p2p. Figure 3 shows performance of Synch_p2p. The results are dominated by two performance artifacts: efficiency with which runtimes can handle very frequent point-to-point synchronization, and the cost of doing global synchronization after each iteration. MPIRMA and both versions of UPC have barriers after each iteration, and clearly suffer the performance consequences at higher core counts. MPI1, SHMEM, Grappa, and MPISHM all function effectively the same, and their relative performances are close together (Grappa's scalability suffers beyond 64 nodes due to the current policy in the aggregator: it uses atomic operations to poll for messages to aggregate between cores in a node, which wastes significant inter-socket bandwidth at scale for problems with communications locality; new policies need to be added to serve sparse problems like Synch_p2p). The Charm++ runtime is designed for workloads that require flexibility, resilience, and dynamic load balancing. The overhead of such functionality results in higher latencies than for the other runtimes, and that effect is exaggerated by Synch_p2p. Finally, MPIOPENMP suffers from communication serialization within a rank due to the need for different threads within a rank to be able to communicate safely.

3.3 Transpose Implementation Details and Performance

Transpose requires all-to-all communication, wherein each processing element scatters pieces of its matrix columns to all other processing elements.

MPI1. This global exchange could be accomplished using `MPI_Alltoall`, but since the tiles of B are not contiguous in memory, and also need to be transposed locally, this would require a tripling of the memory footprint for matrix B to fit message buffers. Instead, we perform the transpose on N ranks in $N - 1$ communication phases. In each phase each ranks sends a different tile to a different recipient rank, using a conflict-free schedule that accomplishes a pairwise exchange. Message buffers are reused in each phase, which keeps the memory pressure small and improves locality. Local transposition of B tiles takes place as matrix elements are read from B and placed in the contiguous send buffer. Upon receipt of a tile, its data is scattered into the columns of A owned by the receiving rank, but no more transposition is required.

Charm++. This implementation exactly follows MPI1's.

MPIOPENMP and MPISHM. In the MPIOPENMP implementation we parallelize the loops that transpose, pack, and unpack the tile values using `#pragma omp parallel for`, but the MPI communications are carried out only by the master thread.

The MPISHM implementation closely follows MPIOPENMP. All ranks inside a node collaborate to transpose, pack, and unpack the tile values, and only a single rank within each node carries out the communication. We could have chosen to let all ranks participate in the communication, but then MPISHM would be conceptually identical to MPI1. Instead, ranks within a node synchronize before send and after receive so that a single rank can perform internode communication.

Grappa. Grappa communicates at the granularity of block rows directly into the destination matrix, so does not need a receive buffer, but issues many small asynchronous communication requests for the transport of column segments within each matrix tile. Synchronization at the end of iterations is via barriers.

UPC. The UPC implementation follows the MPI1 approach. However, tiles are communicated directly into the private space of each thread using `upc_memget`. For synchronization we use `upc_barrier`.

Performance of Transpose. Fig. 4 shows performance of the Transpose kernel. At smaller core counts it constitutes a coarse-grain workload. The message sizes decrease quadratically with the number of cores used; on 1536 cores,

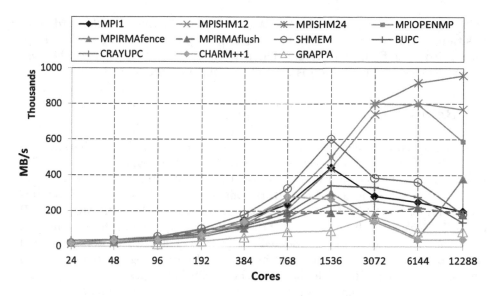

Fig. 4. Absolute performance of Transpose problem (Color figure online)

these are 4.5 MiB for 1 communicating rank per node (CRPN), 1.25 MiB bytes for 2 CRPN, and 8 KiB for the "flat" models (i.e. those with 24 CRPN), which is in the bandwidth-limited regime of the network. At 12288 cores, the message sizes associated with these models decrease to 72 KiB, 16 KiB, and 128 bytes, respectively. While 1 and 2 CRPN still use large messages, the other cases have become fine-grain. While Cray XC30 was designed to support fine-grain communication, it is still difficult to provide the same level of efficiency, and overheads are noticeable. This fact alone explains the most obvious trend in the data: only MPI+X models scale past 1536 cores. The figure shows data for MPISHM12 (2 CRPN, one on each socket), MPISHM24 (1 CRPN) and MPIOPENMP (2 CRPN for all cases except 12288, which used 1 CRPN). All the flat models taper off. Of the flat models, SHMEM is clearly the best at scale, in addition to being the best overall at 1536 cores and below. We attribute this to the low overhead of the SHMEM interface and the excellent support for SHMEM one-sided semantics in the Cray XC30 network. MPI1 is slightly worse than SHMEM, but follows a similar trend. Cray and Berkeley UPC also share a trend and flatten around 1536, reaching performance similar to the other flat models at high core counts. MPIRMA with flush synchronization, which is a similar semantic to the PGAS models, performs roughly on par with Cray UPC. MPIRMA with fence synchronization (collective) shows an anomaly at 12288 cores, which is hard to explain without detailed information about Cray MPI (we do not have it). It is possible that message aggregation permitted by the semantics of this synchronization motif becomes active at 128 bytes. Charm++ is competitive up to 768 cores, at which point it falls off and performs worst at scale, due to runtime overhead at fine granularities (cf. Synch_p2p). We evaluated Charm++ *with* overdecomposition, but it was no better than *without*, as expected, so we excluded the former from the figure for brevity. The performance of Grappa is poor, because its Transpose implementation is even finer grain than the other flat models.

4   Related Work

Cantonnet and coworkers evaluated UPC using NPB [3] and other benchmarks in [10,16]. Berlin and coworkers considered Pthreads, OpenMP, MPI and UPC using numerical (CG) and non-numerical (hash table update and integer sort) workloads in [7]. Coarfa and coworkers compared MPI, UPC and Coarray Fortran using the NPB in [11,12]. These papers considered the NPB MG, CG, SP and BT. Because of the generation of the hardware employed in the experiments, multicore effects were not considered. In [31], MPI and UPC were evaluated from both a productivity and performance standpoint using the power method on sparse matrices. Ref. [33] compares the HPCS languages (X10, Chapel and Fortress) using a simple version of the Hartree-Fock method found in quantum chemistry. In [13], the authors evaluate a wide range of programming models on their maturity (including tool support) and suitability to their applications. Performance experiments were not the focus of that paper. In [29], the authors present comparative experiments with Cilk, Go, TBB, and Chapel. Of these, only Chapel can run on clusters; however, in that study even on a single shared-memory node, Chapel did not show good performance or scalability. MPI, UPC and Coarray Fortran were compared in the context of the Cray Gemini interconnect in [32] using NPB FT and microbenchmarks. Dun et al. evaluated Chapel using a range of tests, from microbenchmarks to a molecular dynamics mini-application [15]. In [25], the authors compare Serial, OpenMP, MPI and CUDA against Chapel, Charm++, Liszt, and Loci when implementing LULESH. This interesting work focuses solely on the parallel pattern of the explicit stencil computation, which, while important, leaves out numerous patterns and applications. Moreover, at the cluster level, only weak-scaling results are presented, which do not fully stress scalability. In [4] the authors compare MPI against MPIOPENMP for an explicit stencil operation and use that as the motivation to create an MPI+X programming model, where X consists of asynchronously spawned tasks, based on overdecomposition of the computational domain. This approach shows promise and has the advantage that it is only a small departure from "classical" MPI1 style programming.

Our contribution differs from the above works in that each PRK focuses on a single, parameterized application pattern, allowing us to separate performance artifacts in different parts of an application. In addition, our work is unique in terms of the combinaton of number of *scalable* runtimes considered, and the extensiveness of the multiple-kernel tests. Previous studies using Synch_p2p include [6,14], which proposed new features for OpenSHMEM and MPI, respectively.

5   Conclusion and Future Work

We compared performance and scalability of eight programming models using three important patterns from the PRK. While there was no clear winner, a number of trends emerged. The incumbent models, MPI1 and SHMEM, performed well in general, although with Transpose both suffered at scale compared to MPISHM, which sends fewer and larger messages. SHMEM was better than MPI1 for Transpose, but otherwise they were roughly the same. The critical role of explicit aggregation of messages is clear from the Transpose results, with both variants of MPI+X winning by a large margin at scale, which is attributed to the message sizes. While MPIOPENMP is the easiest way for programmers to achieve aggregation and to take advantage of low-latency synchronizations in shared memory, we see evidence that MPISHM is the superior way to realize it, both from the empirical results of Synch_p2p and Transpose, and because of the challenges of mixing different runtimes (MPI and OpenMP). The success of SHMEM and MPI+X merits future investigation of SHMEM+X.

Both implementations of UPC delivered lower performance than the more explicit MPI1 and SHMEM, and the standard-compliant UPC implementation of Synch_p2p suffered due to lack of support for this synchronization motif (partly solved by a language extension). It may be possible to improve preformance by eliminating barriers, but that is non-trivial, due to the lack of explicit support for point-to-point synchronization in UPC (or other PGAS languages).

Charm++ performs best for Stencil at granularities for which it was designed, but fared poorly in Synch_p2p and Transpose. We do not observe much benefit from overdecomposition; The simple and naturally load balanced PRK are not well-suited to evaluate this feature. Grappa performed decently for the fine-grain Sync_p2p and medium-grain Stencil workloads, but scalability needs to be improved by better and more flexible message aggregation. In our kernels we found FEB most effective for synchronization through control variables, not directly through primary solution values.

The scope of this paper was limited in the kernels and models considered. All the kernels we used can be load balanced statically, which makes them amenable to easy implementation in MPI and derivatives. Asynchronous, adaptive models such as Charm++, Grappa, HPX (High Performance ParalleX) [22], and Legion [5] cannot demonstrate their strength with such simple workloads. We are developing a new PRK [19] that defies static load balancing, to explore this design space that is clearly less favorable for MPI and static PGAS models; the latter provide only low-level primitives for building dynamic load-balancing capability. None of the kernels we used tests fault tolerance, a feature that is today only provided by the Charm++ runtime, but that is gaining rapid importance. We are working on an objective framework, using existing PRK, to measure effectiveness and overhead of runtime error recovery mechanisms. We are also expanding our PRK implementations to Legion and HPX, and will include performance and scalability measurements of Fine-Grain MPI [24] in our next evaluation.

*Other names and brands may be claimed as property of others.
Intel and Xeon are trademarks of Intel Corporation in the U.S. and/or other countries. Software and workloads used in performance tests may have been optimized for performance only on Intel microprocessors. Performance tests, such as SYSmark and MobileMark, are measured using specific computer systems, components, software, operations and functions. Any change to any of those factors may cause the results to vary. You should consult other information and performance tests to assist you in fully evaluating your contemplated purchases, including the performance of that product when combined with other products. For more information go to http://www.intel.com/performance.
We used NERSC, a DOE Office of Science User Facility, DE-AC02-05CH11231.

References

1. OpenSHMEM Specification. http://www.openshmem.org
2. Alverson, R., et al.: The Tera computer system. In: International Conference on Supercomputing, pp. 1–6. ACM, New York, NY, USA (1990)
3. Bailey, D.H., et al.: The NAS parallel benchmarks. Int. J. High Perf. Comp. Appl. **5**(3), 63–73 (1991)
4. Barrett, R.F., et al.: Toward an evolutionary task parallel integrated MPI+X programming model. In: Proceedings of Sixth International Workshop on Programming Models and Applications for Multicores and Manycores, pp. 30–39. ACM (2015)
5. Bauer, M., Treichler, S., Slaughter, E., Aiken, A.: Legion: expressing locality and independence with logical regions. In: Supercomputing, p. 66. IEEE Computer Society Press (2012)
6. Belli, R., Hoefler, T.: Notified access: extending remote memory access programming models for producer-consumer synchronization. In: IPDPS, Hyderabad, India, May 2015
7. Berlin, K., et al.: Evaluating the impact of programming language features on the performance of parallel applications on cluster architectures. In: Rauchwerger, L. (ed.) LCPC 2003. LNCS, vol. 2958, pp. 194–208. Springer, Heidelberg (2004)
8. Bonachea, D., et al.: Efficient point-to-point synchronization in UPC. In: PGAS. ACM (2006)
9. Bull, J.M., Ball, C.: Point-to-point synchronisation on shared memory architectures. In: 5th European Workshop on OpenMP (2003)
10. Cantonnet, F., Yao, Y., Zahran, M., El-Ghazawi, T.: Productivity analysis of the UPC language. In: IPDPS, p. 254. IEEE (2004)
11. Coarfa, C., Dotsenko, Y., Eckhardt, J., Mellor-Crummey, J.: Co-array Fortran performance and potential: an NPB experimental study. In: Rauchwerger, L. (ed.) LCPC 2003. LNCS, vol. 2958, pp. 177–193. Springer, Heidelberg (2004)
12. Coarfa, C., et al.: An evaluation of global address space languages: co-array fortran and unified parallel C. In: PPoPP, pp. 36–47. ACM (2005)
13. Cook, R., Dube, E., Lee, I., Nau, L., Shereda, C., Wang, F.: Survey of novel programming models for parallelizing applications at exascale. Technical report LLNL-TR-515971, Lawrence Livermore National Laboratory (2011)
14. Dinan, J., Cole, C., Jost, G., Smith, S., Underwood, K., Wisniewski, R.W.: Reducing synchronization overhead through bundled communication. In: Poole, S., Hernandez, O., Shamis, P. (eds.) OpenSHMEM 2014. LNCS, vol. 8356, pp. 163–177. Springer, Heidelberg (2014)
15. Dun, N., Taura, K.: An empirical performance study of Chapel programming language. In: IPDPSW, pp. 497–506. IEEE (2012)

16. El-Ghazawi, T., Cantonnet, F.: UPC performance, potential: a NPB experimental study. In: Supercomputing, p. 17. IEEE (2002)
17. Feind, K.: Shared memory access (SHMEM) routines. In: CUG (1995)
18. Feo, J., et al.: Eldorado. In: Computing Frontiers, pp. 28–34. ACM (2005)
19. Georganas, E., Van der Wijngaart, R.F., Mattson, T.G.: Design and implementation of a parallel research kernel for assessing dynamic load-balancing capabilities. In: Parallel and Distributed Processing, ser. IPDPS, vol. 16 (2016, to appear)
20. Heroux, M.A., Brightwell, R., Wolf, M.M.: Bi-modal MPI and MPI+threads computing on scalable multicore systems (2011)
21. Hoefler, T., et al.: MPI + MPI: a new hybrid approach to parallel programming with MPI plus shared memory. Computing **95**(12), 1121–1136 (2013)
22. Kaiser, H., et al.: HPX: a task based programming model in a global address space. In : PGAS, p. 6. ACM (2014)
23. Kale, L.V., Krishnan, S.: CHARM++: a portable concurrent object oriented system based on C++, vol. 28. ACM (1993)
24. Kamal, H., Wagner, A.: FG-MPI: fine-grain MPI for multicore and clusters. In: IEEE International Symposium on Parallel and Distributed Processing, Workshops and Phd Forum (IPDPSW), pp. 1–8. IEEE (2010)
25. Karlin, I., et al.: Exploring traditional and emerging parallel programming models using a proxy application. In: IPDPS, pp. 919–932. IEEE (2013)
26. MPI Forum: MPI: a message-passing interface standard (1994)
27. MPI Forum: MPI-2: Extensions to the message-passing interface (1996)
28. MPI Forum: MPI: a message-passing interface standard. Version 3.0, November 2012
29. Nanz, S., et al.: Benchmarking usability and performance of multicore languages. In: International Symposium on Empirical Software Engineering. Measurement, pp. 183–192. IEEE (2013)
30. Nelson, J., Holt, B., Myers, B., Briggs, P., Ceze, L., Kahan, S., Oskin, M.: Latency-tolerant software distributed shared memory. In: 2015 USENIX Annual Technical Conference (USENIX ATC 2015). USENIX Association, Santa Clara, CA, July 2015
31. Patel, I., Gilbert, J.R.: An empirical study of the performance and productivity of two parallel programming models. In: IPDPS, pp. 1–7. IEEE (2008)
32. Shan, H., et al.: A preliminary evaluation of the hardware acceleration of the Cray Gemini interconnect for PGAS languages and comparison with MPI. ACM SIGMETRICS Perf. Eval. Rev. **40**(2), 92–98 (2012)
33. Shet, A.G., et al.: Programmability of the HPCS languages: a case study with a quantum chemistry kernel. In: IPDPS, pp. 1–8. IEEE (2008)
34. UPC Consortium: UPC lang. spec. v. 1.3, November 2013
35. Van der Wijngaart, R.F., et al.: Using the parallel research kernels to study PGAS models. In: PGAS. IEEE (2015)
36. Van der Wijngaart, R.F., Mattson, T.G.: The parallel research kernels: a tool for architecture and programming system investigation. In: HPEC. IEEE (2014)
37. Zerr, R., Baker, R.: Snap: Sn (discrete ordinates) application proxy: description. Technical report, Los Alamos National Laboratories, LAUR-13-21070 (2013)

Intel Xeon Phi

High Order Seismic Simulations on the Intel Xeon Phi Processor (Knights Landing)

Alexander Heinecke[1]([✉]), Alexander Breuer[2],
Michael Bader[3], and Pradeep Dubey[1]

[1] Intel Corporation, 2200 Mission College Blvd., Santa Clara, CA 95054, USA
alexander.heinecke@intel.com
[2] University of California, San Diego, 9500 Gilman Dr., La Jolla, CA 92093, USA
[3] Technische Universität München, Boltzmannstr. 3, 85748 Garching, Germany

Abstract. We present a holistic optimization of the ADER-DG finite element software SeisSol targeting the Intel® Xeon Phi™ x200 processor, codenamed Knights Landing (KNL). SeisSol is a multi-physics software package performing earthquake simulations by coupling seismic wave propagation and the rupture process. The code was shown to scale beyond 1.5 million cores and achieved petascale performance when using local time stepping for the computationally heavy seismic wave propagation. Advancing further along these lines, we discuss the utilization of KNL's core features, the exploitation of its two-level memory subsystem (which allows for efficient out-of-core implementations), and optimizations targeting at KNL's 2D mesh on-die interconnect. Our performance comparisons demonstrate that KNL is able to outperform its previous generation, the Intel® Xeon Phi™ coprocessor x100 family, by more than 2.9× in time-to-solution. Additionally, our results show a 3.4× speedup compared to latest Intel® Xeon® E5v3 CPUs.

Keywords: High-order · Vectorization · ADER · Discontinuous Galerkin · Finite Element Method · Intel Xeon Phi · Knights landing · KNL

1 Introduction

The understanding of earthquake dynamics is greatly supported by highly resolved, coupled simulations of the rupture process and seismic wave prop-

© Springer International Publishing Switzerland 2016
J.M. Kunkel et al. (Eds.): ISC High Performance 2016, LNCS 9697, pp. 343–362, 2016.
DOI: 10.1007/978-3-319-41321-1_18

agation. Requirements in resolution are pushed by detailed discretizations of complex geometric features, accurate representations of material heterogeneities and the need for resolved, high frequencies. This grand challenge of seismic modeling requires a large amount of computational resources. Optimal utilization by software is imperative.

Therefore, in addition to challenges from a numerical perspective, software packages that tackle this grand challenge, have to exploit the capabilities of state-of-the-art supercomputing architectures. In the past, simulations of seismic wave propagation used some of the largest supercomputers worldwide (e.g. [2,3,7–9,16–18,21,28,29]). However, only very few of the performed landmark-simulations coupled dynamic rupture propagation directly to seismic wave propagation (e.g. [10,16]). Taking the total number of simulation environments in the *SCEC/USGS Spontaneous Rupture Code Verification Project* [15] into account, a gap between latest physics-driven developments and HPC capabilities is visible. Reason is the required, high degree of algorithmic development, optimization and testing required to exploit all levels of parallelism offered by state-of-the-art supercomputing architectures [3].

The SeisSol software package[1] is the topic of this paper and uses, among other software (e.g. [1,27]), the Discontinuous Galerkin (DG)-Finite Element Method (FEM) for spatial discretization. Together with the use of unstructured tetrahedral meshes and the Arbitrary high-order DERivatives (ADER) scheme in time, this allows for accurate discretization of fault systems, surface topography and material heterogeneities [13,14,22].

In this paper, we present various improvements of the software package SeisSol for the new Intel Knights Landing architecture (KNL). To maximize application performance, equaling shortest time-to-solution, our optimizations address KNL's major enhancements over the current architecture, code-named Knights Corner, by (a) efficiently using both 512-bit wide vector processing units (VPU) per core, by (b) leveraging the low-bandwidth DDR4 memory and the high-bandwidth in-package multi-channel DRAM (MCDRAM) by an out-of-core application memory management, and finally by (c) balancing the on-die interconnect mesh-traffic for optimal throughput. In addition to our hardware-aware implementation, we demonstrate that advanced numerics and solvers are required for reduced time-to-solution. Here, SeisSol's computationally heavy wave propagation component was recently enhanced by a high performance Local Time Stepping (LTS) scheme to capture time step variations, commonly present in unstructured tetrahedral meshes [6]. Although the irregularities introduced by LTS normally contradict with the demands of modern and increasingly regular hardware architectures, such as KNL, we will demonstrate that our implementation is capable of running LTS efficiently on many-core processors with wide vector units.

---

[1] https://github.com/SeisSol/SeisSol, git-tag 201511 was used in this paper.

2   The Knights Landing Architecture

The Intel Xeon Phi x200 processor family, based on the KNL architecture, is the successor of the Intel Xeon Phi coprocessor introduced in 2012. It is fully binary compatible with latest Intel Xeon processors code-named Haswell and Broadwell, e.g. Xeon E5v3 and E5v4,[2] and is the first chip that offers support for the AVX512F, AVX512CD, AVX512PF and the AVX512ERI instruction set extensions, which double the width of Intel Architecture's (IA) vector computing capabilities. AVX512F and AVX512CD instructions will be also available on future Intel Xeon processors and increase the number of programable 512-bit wide vector-registers to 32. In contrast to the first generation Xeon Phi coprocessor, KNL is intended to be operated in self-booted fashion and has therefore no need for a host processor. An overview of a KNL-based processor is depicted in Fig. 1. The following descriptions are based on [25,26], which disclosed many detailed architectural information of KNL.

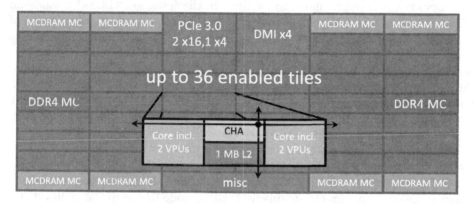

Fig. 1. Architectural overview of KNL: schematic die layout including the 2D-mesh of tiles and MCDRAM MC, DDR4 MC, IIO agents incl. a zoom into a tile.

KNL introduces many changes compared to KNC: up to 36 computing tiles (housing two cores with a shared L2 cache), 2 DDR4–2400 memory controllers (MC), 8 MCDRAM controllers (MCDRAM MC, accessing up to 16 GB in-package high-bandwidth memory) and a PCIe rootport with 36 PCIe3 lanes. All components are connected by a 2D mesh to ensure scalable communication within the die. Each DDR4 memory controller handles 3 channels with one DIMM each, allowing for up to 384 GB of system memory at 90 GB/s. The combined bandwidth of the eight high-bandwidth memory controllers exceeds 490 GB/s.

The computational heart of KNL is formed by an array of tiles. Each tile comprises two cores that share an 1 MB L2 cache and a Cache/Homing Agent (CHA). The latter one holds parts of a distributed tag directory which is used to maintain coherency across all L2 caches of all tiles. The cores are based on the Intel®

---

[2] TSX instructions, however, are not considered to be legacy x86 instructions.

Atom^{TM} architecture code-named Silvermont [19], but offer many enhancements for HPC workloads. The most important one is the tighly coupled floating point unit (FPU) implemented by two 512-bit wide vector processing units (VPU), which support the aforementioned AVX512 instruction set extensions. Additionally, the cores feature larger L1 caches (32 KB each for data and instructions), more aggressive out-of-order execution and optimized support for huge pages. The core itself is two-issue-wide at instruction level (decode, retire) and supports up to six concurrent micro operations (2 VPU-, 2 memory-, 2 integer-operations). Thus, a single thread per core can utilize the full VPU-performance. The higher execution width is needed to optimally load the machine, e.g. to handle bursts after cache misses.

KNL's mesh can be operated in three different cluster modes which are selectable at boottime. As pointed out above, each tile holds a fraction of the distributed tag directory. The goal of KNL's cluster modes is to provide different levels of affinity between the requesting tile, the tile which holds the corresponding tag entry, and the memory controllers. In the so-called ALL2ALL mode no affinities are enforced. This has the advantage that no explicit partitioning of memory controllers is required. However, this mode has also higher latencies as packages might travel through the entire chip. In QUADRANT mode the mesh is divided into four logical quadrants and an affinity between the tag directory and the memory controller is created by placing both in the same quadrant. Finally, Sub-NUMA-Clustering (or SNC4) is an extended version of the QUADRANT mode. Here, the four quadrants are exposed via NUMA domains to the OS such that applications can optimize memory access latencies even further.

KNL's memory subsystem is based on two different technologies. For capacity a 6-channel DDR4 is provided. For performance an up-to 16 GB large high-bandwidth in-package MCDRAM is provided. The MCDRAM can be used in different modes. The directly-mapped CACHE mode backs up the DDR4 memory. For applications that stay local or have a memory consumption of less than 16 GB, this is a simple solution to get nearly all benefits from the high-bandwidth memory. Hence CACHE mode introduces an additional hierarchy, MCDRAM cache-misses add latency to the corresponding accesses. The second mode is the so-called FLAT mode. Here, the MCDRAM is exposed as an additionally NUMA domain in the physical address space and the programmer can explicitly request memory in this region by using close-to-metal libnuma or Intel's memkind[3] library. Note that the default memory in this mode is DDR4, such that the MCDRAM cannot get polluted by OS housekeeping. Finally, the HYBRID mode is a mixture of the CACHE and FLAT mode.

3   Computational Core

SeisSol solves the elastic wave equations, a linear system of partial differential equations with variable coefficients, in stress-velocity formulation:

$$q_t + A^{x_1} q_{x_1} + A^{x_2} q_{x_2} + A^{x_3} q_{x_3} = 0. \tag{1}$$

---

[3] https://www.github.com/memkind/memkind.

$q(\boldsymbol{x}, t) = (\sigma^{11}, \sigma^{22}, \sigma^{33}, \sigma^{12}, \sigma^{13}, \sigma^{23}, u^1, u^2, u^3)^T$ is the space-time-dependent vector of quantities containing the six-dimensional stress tensor and the particle velocities. The quantities q are functions of space $\boldsymbol{x} = (x_1, x_2, x_3)^T \in \mathbb{R}^3$ and time $t \in \mathbb{R}$. Here, the three normal stress components are given by σ^{11}, σ^{22} and σ^{33}, the three shear stresses by σ^{12}, σ^{13} and σ^{23}, and the three particle velocities in x_1-, x_2-, and x_3-direction by u^1, u^2 and u^3. The subscripts in (1) denote partial derivatives with respect to t and x_1, x_2, x_3. $A^{x_c}(\boldsymbol{x})$ are the three space-dependent Jacobian matrices (size 9×9) carrying the influence of the heterogeneous material [14]. Extensions of (1) might include source terms, viscoelasticity, anisotropy, or dynamic rupture physics [12,14,20,22,23].

We obtain the fully discrete formulation by applying the DG-machinery to (1) for space discretization and the ADER scheme in time [14,20]. SeisSol uses static, unstructured tetrahedral meshes. Let Q_k (size $B_{\mathcal{O}} \times 9$) summarizes the per-element Degrees of Freedom (DOFs) for tetrahedral element k. The number of orthogonal basis functions $B_{\mathcal{O}}$ depends on the order of the overall scheme. In this work we present results for convergence rates $\mathcal{O} \in \{2, \ldots, 6\}$, leading to $B_2 = 4$, $B_3 = 10$, $B_4 = 20$, $B_5 = 35$ and $B_6 = 56$ basis functions. To advance an element k by its local time step, $t_k^{n_k+1} = t_k^{n_k} + \Delta t_k$, we compute the solution of SeisSol's time kernel, volume kernel and surface kernel.

Time: The time kernel predicts the evolution of the element-local DOFs within a time step. Following the Cauchy-Kowalewski procedure, we replace time derivatives by space derivatives and obtain:

$$\frac{\partial^{d+1}}{\partial t^{d+1}} Q_k(t_0) = -\sum_{c=1}^{3} \hat{K}^{\xi_c} \left(\frac{\partial^d}{\partial t^d} Q_k(t_0) \right) A_k^{\xi_c}. \tag{2}$$

$\hat{K}^{\xi_c}$ (size $B_{\mathcal{O}} \times B_{\mathcal{O}}$) are the three unique stiffness matrices, multiplied by the inverse, diagonal mass matrix in pre-processing. The stiffness matrices and the mass matrix are defined with respect to a reference element and in terms of the $\xi_1 \xi_2 \xi_3-$ reference coordinate system. The matrices $A_k^{\xi_c}$ (size 9×9) are linear combinations of the Jacobians. We use the DOFs at the current time step $t_k^{n_k}$ as initial condition for the recursive procedure in (2): $\partial^0/\partial t^0 Q_k(t_0) = Q_k^{n_k}$. The time derivatives $\mathcal{D}_k = \partial^d/\partial t^d Q_k$ allow us to integrate the DOFs in time as required by the volume and surface kernel:

$$\mathcal{T}_k(t_0, \hat{t}, \Delta t) = \sum_{d=0}^{\mathcal{O}-1} \frac{(\hat{t} + \Delta t - t_0)^{d+1} - (\hat{t} - t_0)^{d+1}}{(d+1)!} \cdot \frac{\partial^d}{\partial t^d} Q_k(t_0). \tag{3}$$

Integration of the DOFs via (3) is valid in arbitrary intervals $[\hat{t}, \hat{t} + \Delta t]$ within the stability limits imposed by the CFL-condition. This translates to the condition $t_k^{n_k} \leq \hat{t} < \hat{t} + \Delta t \leq t_k^{n_k} + \Delta t_k$, where our element-local time step Δt_k satisfies the CFL-requirements. Depending on an element's LTS configuration, it stores different, permanent time data for read-only access by face-neighboring elements. Here, an element might store the derivatives $\mathcal{D}_k$, or add the full time integrated DOFs of the time step, $\mathcal{T}_k^{\text{full}} = \mathcal{T}_k(t_k^{n_k}, t_k^{n_k}, \Delta t_k)$, to a permanent buffer $\mathcal{B}_k$, or store both.

Volume: The volume kernel uses $\mathcal{T}_k^{\text{full}}$ and computes the net-effects of the volume integration for an entire, element-local time step Δt_k:

$$\mathcal{V}_k(\mathcal{T}_k^{\text{full}}) = \sum_{c=1}^{3} \tilde{K}^{\xi_c}\left(\mathcal{T}_k^{\text{full}}\right) A_k^{\xi_c}. \tag{4}$$

$\tilde{K}^{\xi_c}$ (size $B_\mathcal{O} \times B_\mathcal{O}$) are the three non-transposed stiffness matrices, multiplied with the inverse mass matrix in pre-processing. Analogue to the time derivative computation (2), $A_k^{\xi_c}$ are linear combinations of the Jacobians.

Surface: Our last kernel is the surface kernel, computing the surface integration of the fully discrete ADER-DG formulation. The surface kernel uses the time integrated DOFs $\mathcal{T}_k^{\text{full}}$ of tetrahedron k and the time integrated DOFs $\mathcal{T}_{k_i}^{\text{part}}$ of the four face-neighboring tetrahedrons k_i. As discussed at the end of this section, $\mathcal{T}_{k_i}^{\text{part}}$ integrate face-neighboring derivatives $\mathcal{D}_{k_i}$ via (3), or directly use the buffer $\mathcal{B}_{k_i}$, containing one or multiple time integrated DOFs of the face-neighbor k_i. For a local face $i \in \{1, \ldots, 4\}$ of tetrahedron k, the kernel is given by:

$$\mathcal{F}_{k,i}\left(\mathcal{T}_k^{\text{full}}, \mathcal{T}_{k_i}^{\text{part}}\right) = \hat{F}^{-,i}\left(\mathcal{T}_k^{\text{full}}\right) \hat{A}_k^{-,i} + \hat{F}^{+,i,j_k(i),h_k(i)}\left(\mathcal{T}_{k_i}^{\text{part}}\right) \hat{A}_k^{+,i}. \tag{5}$$

$\hat{F}^{-,i}$ and $\hat{F}^{+,i,j,h}$ with $i,j \in \{1, \ldots, 4\}$ and $h \in \{1, 2, 3\}$ are the 52 unique flux matrices (size $B_\mathcal{O} \times B_\mathcal{O}$), multiplied by the inverse mass matrix in preprocessing. Here, the used indices j_k and h_k depend on the location of the elements' vertices in the reference element with respect to the shared face. As for the stiffness matrices and the mass matrix, the flux matrices are defined with respect to the unique reference element and thus shared among all elements. The matrices $\hat{A}_k^{-,i}$ (size 9×9) account for the element's own contribution to the numerical flux, while $\hat{A}_k^{+,i}$ (size 9×9) carry the contribution of the neighboring elements.

Update: By combining the individual kernels, we obtain the following two-step update scheme for an element-local time step $t_k^{n_k} \to t_k^{n_k+1}$:

$$Q_k^{*,n_k+1} = Q_k^{n_k} + \mathcal{V}_k - \sum_{i=1}^{4} \hat{F}^{-,i}\left(\mathcal{T}_k^{\text{full}}\right) \hat{A}_k^{-,i}, \tag{6}$$

$$Q_k^{n_k+1} = Q_k^{*,n_k+1} - \sum_{i=1}^{4} \hat{F}^{+,i,j_k(i),h_k(i)}\left(\mathcal{T}_{k_i}\right) \hat{A}_k^{+,i}. \tag{7}$$

Equation (6) summarizes all element-local contribution to the time step, while Eq. (7) accounts for the contribution of the face-neighboring elements.

Local Time Stepping: We use the Local Time Stepping (LTS) scheme introduced in [6] to account for heterogeneities in the CFL-imposed time step restrictions. This scheme trades some of the ADER scheme's flexibility, which in theory is able to advance each element with its optimal time step, for increased homogeneity. Here, we determine a fundamental time step equalling the global, minimal allowed time step of all elements. Afterwards, we assign every element to a cluster, such that it advances with an integer multiple of this fundamental time step. Considering the minimal, fundamental time step as Δt, the clustering reads as:

$$\mathcal{C}_1 = [\Delta t, r_1 \Delta t[, \ \mathcal{C}_2 = [r_1 \Delta t, r_1 r_2 \Delta t[, \ \ldots, \mathcal{C}_L = [r_1 \ldots r_{L-1} \Delta t, r_1 \ldots r_L \Delta t[. \quad (8)$$

With rates $r_l \in \mathbb{N}_{>1}$, we choose our L clusters to cover the entire interval of CFL-imposed time steps. In initialization all elements are assigned to their corresponding cluster. This work presents results for a clustering with fixed rates of $r_l = 2 \ \forall l$. Further, the LTS scheme of [6] limits cluster dependencies and complex, worst-case memory handling by a normalization step, which lowers the time step of corner-case elements. All elements of a cluster advance in time with the cluster's lower time step limit. Global Time Stepping (GTS) is a special case of our LTS scheme with a single cluster having rate $r_1 = \infty$. For GTS we store, in addition to the DOFs, the time integrated DOFs T_k^{full}, computed for the element-local contributions in (6). These are then used in the update step (7) by face-neighboring elements.

In contrast, elements being in LTS-relation with at least one of their face-neighbors require a more complex handling. Here, an element might have to sum and store consecutive time integrated DOFs, obtained via (3), over multiple element-local time steps in a buffer $\mathcal{B}_k$ to feed face-neighboring elements with larger time steps. Conversely, elements having face-neighbors with smaller time steps store the time derivatives $(\mathcal{D}_k)$, obtained using (2), which can then be evaluated by the face-neighbors in multiple evaluations of (7).

Summarizing, our LTS scheme is more challenging than GTS for the underlying hardware due to increased heterogeneity and memory requirements. In [6] we present full-machine results for a petascale, production character run on SuperMUC-2 (Haswell architecture). This run achieved 46 % of SuperMUC-2's HPL performance. Interpreting these results in terms of time-to-solution, rather than machine utilization, shows the real value of the LTS scheme. In the case of the rate-2, production character run, we reached a $4.1\times$ speedup over GTS.

4   Implementation

The discussion of the underlying ADER-DG discretization in SeisSol made clear that this algorithm is well suited for modern high-performance processors. The introduced update scheme requires dense compute capabilities (element-local operations in general) as well as high memory bandwidth for selected data structures ($\mathcal{B}_{k_i}$ and eventually $\mathcal{D}_{k_i}$ in the surface integral computation). In the upcoming subsections we will address how hardware features such as SIMD units and high-bandwidth memory can be leveraged to run high-order seismic simulations at high efficiencies. We discuss the following (co-)processors (Turbo mode being disabled):

HSX one Intel® Xeon® E5-2699v3 processor with 18 cores, 1.9 GHz at AVX-base frequency and up to 2.6 GHz Turbo frequency, 64 GB of DDR4-2133

KNC one Intel® Xeon Phi™ 7120A coprocessor in native mode with 61 cores, 1.24 GHz base and 1.33 GHz Turbo frequency, 16 GB of GDDR5, one core reserved for OS
KNL an Intel® Xeon Phi™ 7250 processor with 68 cores, 1.2 GHz AVX-base core-clock and 1.5 GHz all core Turbo frequency, 1.7 GHz mesh-clock, 16 GB MCDRAM@7.2 GT, 96 GB DDR4-2400, FLAT/(CACHE or QUADRANT), one core reserved for OS

4.1   Highly-Efficient Small Matrix Kernels

Small sparse and dense double precision matrix multiplication kernels form the computational back-bone of SeisSol. Single precision is possible but suffers from accuracy issues for higher orders [5], we therefore restrict ourselves to double precision in this work. As pointed out in previous work [5,7,16], the best strategy is to generate optimal code for these kernels. After an auto-tuning exercise, we found out that a fully dense backend is the best choice on KNL. Note that also on latest Intel Xeon processors (HSX) the sparse/dense tuning achieves only between 12 % (order 2) and 1.5 % (order 6) improvement with respect to time-to-solution. For the remainder of this section, we rely on regular BLAS notation: $C = \alpha A \cdot B + \beta C$, $C \in \mathbb{R}^{M \times N}$, $A \in \mathbb{R}^{M \times K}$ and $B \in \mathbb{R}^{K \times N}$. lda, ldb and ldc define the length of the leading memory dimension of each matrix, and therefore lda $\geq M$, ldb $\geq K$ and ldc $\geq M$. Since we only need the simple cases of $\alpha = 1$ and $\beta \in \{0,1\}$, we do not discuss the efficient integration of arbitrary α and β values into our kernels. A generalized version ($N \neq 9$) of the presented code generation approach is used in the back-end of the LIBXSMM open source project[4]. This library is already used in other scientific applications (e.g. CP2K [4] or Nek5000 [24]) which demand small matrix multiplications as well.

As we have discussed the implementation of SeisSol's kernels on older Intel architectures in detail in [5], we only focus on KNL in this article. Since KNL has 32 architectural registers available and we know that $N = 9$ holds always true, we decided to work in all cases on all columns of B and C simultaneously. A naive implementation might load 8 rows of column k of A into a register and then perform 9 FMA instructions, which broadcast the kth row of all 9 columns of B on the fly. After having processed all columns of A and rows of B, we would hold a 8×9 sub-matrix of C in 9 accumulator registers which are stored back to all 9 columns of C. However, such a kernel would suffer many instruction level dependencies which block efficient execution. An optimal AVX512 implementation needs to consider therefore two points: (a) eliminating dependencies by software pipelining to reduce pressure on micro-op level and (b) ensuring smallest possible instructions to reduce pressure on the frontend.

The problem of (a) is twofold. First, the innermost kernel consists of 9 FMA instructions which presumably run in throughput scenarios in 4.5 cycles as there are 2 VPUs per out-of-order core with a latency of 6 cycles. This puts high

---

[4] https://github.com/hfp/libxsmm.

pressure on the core as the same nine registers (e.g. zmm23-31) will be reused in the next iteration of the microkernel. As a solution we introduce a second temporary accumulator for C, zmm14-22, which is used in every other iteration. This ensures that the same register is only reused after at least 9 cycles. Before storing back to C we need to merge zmm23-31 and zmm14-23, however the overhead in case of a larger K is minor. Second, we pipeline the loads of rows per column k of A to get them as early as possible into the core's pipeline. This is easily doable as registers zmm0-13 are still unused: we implement a 6-register ring-buffer of A column-vectors.

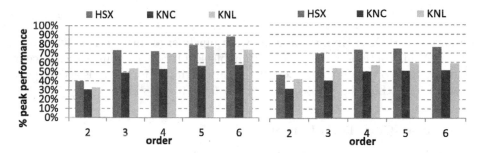

Fig. 2. Standalone matrix kernel performance running out of a hot L1 cache for HSX, KNC and KNL. Left: kernel performance for $B_\mathcal{O} \times 9 \times B_\mathcal{O}$ matrix multiplication shapes; right: kernel performance for $B_\mathcal{O} \times 9 \times 9$ matrix multiplication shapes. (Color figure online)

Issue (b), ensuring smallest possible instructions, is more problematic since we cannot afford to re-structure our data as it is normally done for large DGEMMs. We therefore have strided accesses (offset is ldb times 8), when reading B in the FMA-fused broadcast. If the offset exceeds 128 bytes, the length of the FMA instruction increases from 7 to 11 bytes which puts avoidable pressure on the fetch and decoder units. However, the instruction size can be fixed to 8 byte per FMA if the x86 SIB scale-index-base (SIB) addressing mode is utilized. Since we have spare general purpose registers, we can express the 9 column streams of B by SIB with different base registers (to the first, fourth and seventh column of B) and multiples ($\{1,2,4,8\}$) of ldb. Every 128th k we need to increase these pointers by 128 to remain in the one-byte offset range. In fact 128 elements in k-direction are possible as the AVX512 FMA instructions use a special encoding for the memory offest: they scale the offset value by the datatype size. For example, if the encoded offset is 55, then the offset used during the memory access is $55 \cdot 8 = 440$ (assuming double precision numbers).

Figure 2 compares the performance for the most often used kernel operations in SeisSol running single-threaded on HSX, KNC and KNL. HSX numbers are taken from [5]. For both operator shapes ($M \times N \times K$), $B_\mathcal{O} \times 9 \times B_\mathcal{O}$ and $B_\mathcal{O} \times 9 \times 9$, KNL clearly outperforms its previous generation (KNC). For $B_\mathcal{O} \times 9 \times B_\mathcal{O}$ nearly HSX performance is achieved. The governing reason for the lower performance

Table 1. Placements for all orders and the different data structures of SeisSol; DDR4/MCDRAM denotes if a particular data structure is placed in DDR4/MCDRAM.

Order	Q_k	$\mathcal{B}_k, \mathcal{D}_k$	$A_k^{\xi_c}, \hat{A}_k^{-,i}, \hat{A}_k^{+,i}$	$\hat{K}^{\xi_c}, \tilde{K}^{\xi_c}, \hat{F}^{-,i}, \hat{F}^{+,i,j,h}$
2	MCDRAM	MCDRAM	MCDRAM	MCDRAM
3	MCDRAM	MCDRAM	MCDRAM	MCDRAM
4	DDR4	MCDRAM	MCDRAM	MCDRAM
5	DDR4	MCDRAM	DDR4	MCDRAM
6	DDR4	MCDRAM	DDR4	MCDRAM

compared to HSX is KNL's two-issue-wide pipeline: all instructions which are not FMA instructions reduce the attainable FLOPS peak. Since these occur relatively more often for the $B_\mathcal{O} \times 9 \times 9$ operations, its performance is accordingly lower on KNL than the performance of the $B_\mathcal{O} \times 9 \times B_\mathcal{O}$ shapes.

4.2   Out-of-Core Time Kernel

SeisSol's wave propagation solver is implemented by two macro-kernels: the regular time kernel fused with the element-local volume kernel and element-local part of the surface kernel (6), and the contribution of the face-neighboring elements (7). In the case of high-order simulations the access frequency to Q_k, $\mathcal{B}_k$ or $\mathcal{D}_k$ and the element-local $A_k^{\xi_c}$, $\hat{A}_k^{-,i}$ in the computation of the local contributions is very low, as the data causing the majority of the compute ($\hat{K}^{\xi_c}$, $\tilde{K}^{\xi_c}$, $\hat{F}^{-,i}$ and temporary buffers) can be cached in each tile. However, gathering the neighboring contributions, $\mathcal{B}_{k_i}$ or $\mathcal{D}_{k_i}$, requires significantly more bandwidth than $\hat{A}_k^{+,i}$ for higher orders as they are bigger but have the same access frequency. These access patterns allow to overcome size limitations of the 16 GB MCDRAM by placing the 'slow-running' data structures in DDR4. Therefore, in FLAT mode and for higher order runs, we store $\mathcal{B}_k$ and/or $\mathcal{D}_k$ of every element into MCDRAM on the fly via the memkind library when computing them. As both memory types are seamlessly integrated into the architecture, we simply change the place of allocation, but not our macro-kernels. Thus pointers to $\mathcal{B}_k$ and/or $\mathcal{D}_k$ reference memory physically stored in MCDRAM whereas $A_k^{\xi_c}, \hat{A}_k^{-,i}, \hat{A}_k^{+,i}, Q_k$ reside in the DDR4 portion of the address space for orders $\mathcal{O} = 5$ and $\mathcal{O} = 6$. Additionally, we hold unique matrices, $\hat{K}^{\xi_c}, \tilde{K}^{\xi_c}, \hat{F}^{-,i}, \hat{F}^{+,i,j,h}$, including the 48 flux matrices required for neighboring elements' contribution to the surface kernel (7), in MCDRAM as well, as we expect local L2 cache evicts for higher orders. For lower orders, two to four, the bandwidth requirements of SeisSol for the element local matrices and Q_k increase. We therefore allocate more data structures in MCDRAM. In fact, for orders $\mathcal{O} = 2$ and $\mathcal{O} = 3$, all important data structures are placed in MCDRAM. Table 1 summarizes the used placements, when running on KNL in FLAT mode.

4.3   Optimizing the Mesh Traffic and Prefetching

KNL's last level cache (LLC) is not a shared cache level as it is implemented by a 2D mesh of up to 36 1 MB large slices of L2 caches, c.f. Sect. 2. These slices are kept coherent by a distributed tag directory in each tile's CHA. As we pointed out in the last section, for higher orders than four, the 48 flux matrices $F^{+,i,j,h}$ approach (500 KB for order five) or even exceed the size (1.5 MB for order $\mathcal{O} = 6$) of one tile's L2 cache. This can negatively effect the performance of (7) for two reasons: (a) especially for order $\mathcal{O} = 6$ this results into a high rate of CHA-to-CHA communication as the unstructured mesh causes unstructured accesses to the flux matrices (b) the hardware prefetcher cannot pick-up the unstructured accesses. Keeping the last section in mind, we know that we still have plenty of MCDRAM bandwidth available in higher orders. Therefore, we place several copies, one per two tiles, in MCDRAM. This ensures that the mesh traffic gets equally distributed and the access latency may not be limited by one CHA in the entire mesh holding the directory entries for one particular flux matrix. Additionally, we are using modified matrix kernel operations in (7), which allow for prefetching the flux matrix required for the next face-neighbor's contribution as well as the next $\mathcal{B}_{k_i}$ or $\mathcal{D}_{k_i}$. For best performance these prefetches are widely scattered throughout all eight matrix operations.

The effects of these tweaks are depicted in Fig. 3 when running a setup with LOH.1 characteristics, c.f. Sect. 5, using order $\mathcal{O} = 6$ in FLAT/QUADRANT mode on KNL. The plot shows scaling curves for the local part (6), the neighbor element's contribution (using no optimization and all optimization discussed above), and SeisSol's overall scaling using the optimized neighboring contribution (7). Its aforementioned performance tweaks roughly double the performance of (7) and result in nearly perfect scaling. For all operations the biggest scaling drop occurs when moving from one to two cores. The reason for this is the shared L2 cache per tile which allows for reading one line per cycle and writing a half line per cycle. This effects the performance of (7) more severe, since more data (flux matrices, time integrated DOFs/time derivatives, flux solvers) are read per element as in case of the element-local integrations. As for order $\mathcal{O} = 6$ the local part (6) takes up roughly 70 % of SeisSol's total runtime, the overall scaling follows the scaling of the (6). The full solver's performance is only slightly affected by the lower performance of (7).

5   Scenarios

In this section we evaluate the performance of three different scenarios. The first scenario, LOH.1, is a wave propagation benchmark, the second setting simulates seismic wave propagation in the volcano Mount Merapi, while the last configuration is a multi-physics dynamic rupture simulation of the 1992 Landers earthquake.

Our performance comparisons are carried out on a socket-to-socket basis for two reasons: (a) the power per KNL-socket is only ≈50 % higher than for a single-socket HSX and (b) Intel's reference platforms for KNL and HSX pack 4 sockets of each into 2U of rack-space. Furthermore, in case of KNL the socket

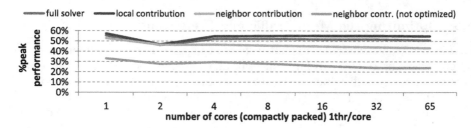

Fig. 3. Scaling of a setup with LOH.1 characteristics (c.f. Sect. 5) on KNL using global time stepping. Shown is the separated performance of the element local contribution (6) and the contribution of the face-neighboring elements (7) and the combined full solver for order $\mathcal{O} = 6$ (measured by a performance proxy application for single-node SeisSol executions with errors of less than 1 %). Additionally, we show the scaling of the neighboring elements' contribution to the surface kernel without our optimization for KNL's mesh and distributed LLC. (Color figure online)

power includes also MCDRAM power, therefore for a single-socket comparison roughly the same amount of energy is spent in the actual CPU. Additionally, SeisSol is known to run large-scale equivalents of the used Mount Merapi and Landers setups well to more than 100,000 cores [6,7,16].

5.1   LOH.1

The Layer Over Half-space benchmark [11] consists of two different material regions. The higher resolved layer is located at the flat surface and reaches 1 km deep into the computational domain. We use material parameters $\rho = 2600\,\text{kg/m}^3$, $\lambda = 20.8\,\text{GPa}$, and $\mu = 10.4\,\text{GPa}$ for the layer. The half-space covers the remaining part of the computational domain. Here, we use material parameters $\rho = 2700\,\text{kg/m}^3$, $\lambda = 32.4\,\text{GPa}$, and $\mu = 32.4\,\text{GPa}$. Figure 4 illustrates the 386,518-element mesh of the LOH.1 benchmark. The faces of the tetrahedral elements are aligned to the interface of the layer and the half-space, and are aligned to the boundary of the computational domain.

Boundary conditions are free-surface for the top of the computational domain ($z = 0$) and outflow everywhere else. We use a point dislocation at $(0,0,2\,\text{km})$ as seismic source.

The upper plot of Fig. 5 depicts the speed-up over global time stepping (GTS), executed on HSX, with respect to time-to-solution for the LOH.1 scenario. In terms of FLOPS, this translates into roughly 1.2 TFLOPS of raw performance on KNL which is $\approx$4× more than on HSX. However, we have to keep in mind, that we are using different sparse/dense switches for each operator on HSX, KNC and KNL (see Sect. 4.1, [7]). Therefore, the only fair comparison is time-to-solution. In this measure, KNL achieves a speed-up of 2.1–3.4× depending on the chosen order of convergence in global time stepping (GTS) runs and baseline architecture (upper plot of Fig. 5). We pad Q_k, $\mathcal{B}_k$ and $\mathcal{D}_k$ in their respective data structures on a per-element basis. On HSX we pad to the next 32-byte boundary and on KNL/KNC to the next 64-byte boundary and store $A_k^{\xi_c}$ dense on KNL, therefore the lower speed-up for lower orders (two to

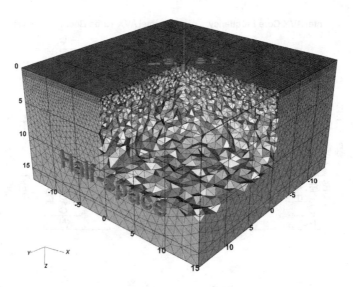

Fig. 4. Illustration of the Layer Over Half-space (LOH.1) setup. Shown is the domain $\Omega = [-15\,\mathrm{km}, 15\,\mathrm{km}]^2 \times [0, 17\,\mathrm{km}]$. The upper part of the domain is covered by the 1 Km thick layer (dark gray) and the remainder by the half-space (gray). The structure of the mesh is illustrated by removing the elements in $[0, 15\,\mathrm{km}]^2 \times [0, 10\,\mathrm{km}]$.

four) is expected. Here, the execution is memory bandwidth bound. In the case of $\mathcal{O} = 2$, KNL/KNC have to move roughly twice as much data as HSX. How heavily these low orders are bandwidth bound can also be seen from the $\approx 3\times$ faster computations resulting from execution out of MCDRAM. For higher orders the MCDRAM-benefit is measurable, but much smaller. It is worthwhile noting that the LOH.1 benchmark fits into MCDRAM for every order. At order 6 all data structures consume $\approx 6\,\mathrm{GB}$. Therefore it does not matter if the MCDRAM is used in the explicit FLAT or the implicit CACHE mode. When enabling rate-2 local time stepping (LTS) in SeisSol, a theoretical speed-up of 2.8× over GTS can be achieved. For higher orders HSX can achieve close to 95 % of this value and KNL can reproduce 95 % of HSX's LTS speed-up. The slightly lower speed-up is due to the cluster sizes and their distribution: the first and most often updated cluster contains less than 0.5 % of all elements whose calculations have to be parallelized across 67 cores on KNL instead of 18 on HSX. Nevertheless, when comparing to the HSX GTS baseline, KNL is able to execute the LOH.1 benchmark up to 7.7× faster.

5.2 Mount Merapi

Our second setting simulates seismic wave propagation in the volcano Mount Merapi. Except for the smaller mesh, now having 1,548,496 tetrahedral elements, this setting is identical to the one used in [6,7]. The origin $(0, 0, 0)$ of our setup is located at mean sea level below Mount Merapi's peak. For elements inside the

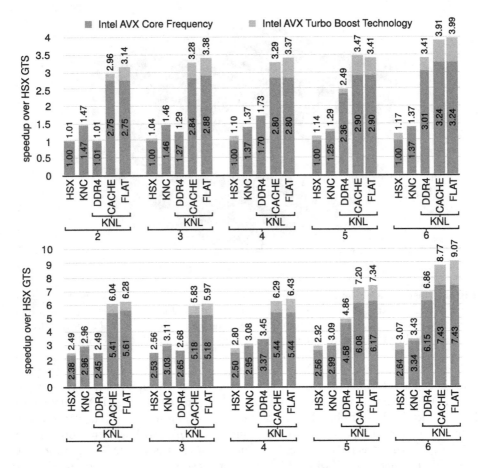

Fig. 5. Normalized time-to-solution speed-up in the LOH.1 scenario for HSX, KNC and KNL and orders 2–6. Upper plot: global time stepping, Lower plot: rate-2 local time stepping.

Fig. 6. Three LTS clusters of the Merapi configuration. Shown are, from left to right: $\mathcal{C}_2 = [2\Delta t, 4\Delta t[$, $\mathcal{C}_3 = [4\Delta t, 8\Delta t[$, $\mathcal{C}_4 = [8\Delta t, 16\Delta t[$.

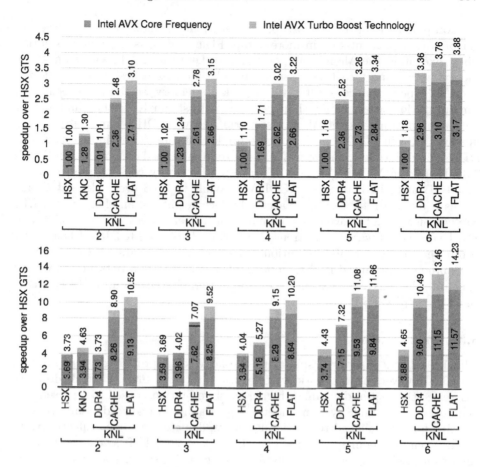

Fig. 7. Normalized time-to-solution speed-up in the Mount Merapi scenario for orders 2–6 and (co)processors HSX, KNC and KNL over HSX global time stepping. Upper plot: global time stepping, lower plot: rate-2 local time stepping.

volcano, being in the sphere with radius 5.1 km and center $(4\,\mathrm{km}, 0, 0)$, we use the material settings $\rho = 2400\,\mathrm{kg/m^3}$, $\lambda \approx 3.3\,\mathrm{GPa}$ and $\mu \approx 4.7\,\mathrm{GPa}$. All remaining elements have paramters $\rho = 2000\,\mathrm{kg/m^3}$, $\lambda \approx 2.3\,\mathrm{GPa}$ and $\mu \approx 2.4\,\mathrm{GPa}$. Two different characteristic lengths for element sizes are used inside and outside the volcano.

Figure 6 illustrates three different clusters for rate-2 clustering ($r_l = 2 \ \forall l$ in (8)). From the left to the right, we see the elements of clusters $C_2 = [2\Delta t, 4\Delta t[$, $C_3 = [4\Delta t, 8\Delta t[$ and $C_4 = [8\Delta t, 16\Delta t[$. The colors of the elements correspond to the element-local CFL-imposed time step. Boundary conditions are free-surface at the surface and outflow everywhere else. The faces of our tetrahedral elements are aligned to the surface topography, the material contrast and the spherical shape of the outflow boundary. We use a double-couple point source approximation at $(0, 0, 0)$ as seismic source in the Mount Merapi setup.

Compared to the LOH.1 setup, the larger mesh allows us to analyze our out-of-core implementation in more detail. Figure 7 depicts the time-to-solution when executing the Mount Merapi scenario, here rate-2 LTS can gain 4× in theory with respect to time-to-solution. The increased mesh size is reflected by KNC's performance results: due to lack of memory we can not execute the simulation for orders larger than two. In contrast, on KNL this limitation is no longer present. As the Merapi scenario achieves LOH.1-comparable speed-ups over HSX in FLAT, our out-of-core implementation is not limited by KNL's DDR4 bandwidth, e.g. for order $\mathcal{O} = 6$ the total consumed memory is 25 GB with 7.3 GB used in MCDRAM. For LTS the total memory consumption increases to 30 GB and 11 GB of used MCDRAM. While in GTS every element k only stores a buffer B_k for read-only access by face neighbors, an element k in LTS configurations might have to store buffers $\mathcal{B}_k$, or derivatives $\mathcal{D}_k$, or both $\mathcal{B}_k$ and $\mathcal{D}_k$. Even the software-transparent CACHE mode of the MCDRAM helps a lot compared to a pure DDR4 execution as its performance is always within 10 % of the manually optimized FLAT mode implementation. As a bottom line we can conclude that KNL can execute the Mount Merapi scenario up to 12.1× faster than the HSX GTS baseline.

5.3   1992 Landers

The 1992 Landers setup is similar to the large-scale, production configuration of [16]. However, in this work we only use a total of 466,574 tetrahedrons to discretize the spatial domain. A higher mesh resolution is used to represent the geometry of the fault system and the topography. We solve dynamic rupture physics for faces aligned to the fault system, depicted in Fig. 8. Effectively, we replace our Riemann solver, used in the surface kernel of Sect. 3, with a formulation explicitly enforcing a Godunov state, which satisfies a certain friction law [22]. Boundary conditions are free-surface at the surface and outflow everywhere else.

Material parameters in the domain are discretized using a one-dimensional, layered velocity profile. This velocity profile leads to gradually increasing wave speeds with increasing depth. The 1992 Landers setup uses global time stepping and orders 2–6 for the seismic wave propagation component. For the dynamic rupture computations a single quadrature point in time and multiple quadrature points in space are used [16]. Note that our computational core supports dynamic rupture physics only in GTS execution. While our considerations for the LTS wave propagation component in [6] directly translate to dynamic rupture elements, extensive benchmarking is required to validate local time stepping in dynamic rupture workloads. Here, one can either decide to follow the LTS approach of the scheme in [6] directly and perform a minimal impact normalization only. Other options could enforce neighboring dynamic rupture elements to have the same time step or enforce a shared, minimal time step for all elements with dynamic rupture faces. As in case of the LOH.1 scenario, all data structures would easily fit into MCDRAM any time as the total memory consumption at order 6 is 7.1 GB.

Fig. 8. Wave field of the 1992 Landers scenario after 12.5 s of simulated time. Shown is the fault system with a subsection of the unstructured tetrahedral mesh.

The GTS performance of the 1992 Landers setup is provided in Fig. 9. As this is a multi-physics scenario, we expect slightly lower performance than for the earlier pure wave propagation runs on a many-core processor. This is due to the fact that the dynamic rupture portion of the solver requires high scalar performance. Here, KNL's increased single-thread performance becomes visible. KNL reassembles more than 92 % of the pure wave propagation speed-up over HSX whereas the previous generation KNC chip is only able to attain 83 %. This results into a relative performance which is comparable to HSX. KNL's time-to-solution speed-up for executing the 1992 Landers earthquake simulations is 2.5–2.9× depending on the chosen order.

6   Conclusion

In this article, we presented a holistic optimization of SeisSol, a multi-physics simulation package for seismic simulations, which tightly couples seismic wave propagation, and dynamic rupture processes. First, we presented a deep-dive into KNL's architectural features and their challenges and opportunities for high-performance software. After a brief recapitulation of SeisSol's mathematical background, we discussed in detail how to exploit KNL's two VPUs per core efficiently and to leverage both memory subsystems for a novel out-of-core implementation in SeisSol's high-order wave propagation solver. The KNL-optimized implementation was evaluated for three different scenarios with distinct challenges and sizes. In case of global time stepping runs, KNL was able to outperform its predecessor, KNC, by 2.9× and the current most powerful Intel

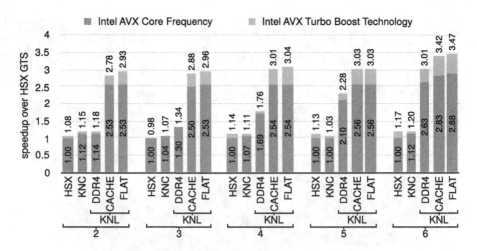

Fig. 9. Normalized time-to-solution speed-up over HSX for KNC and KNL and orders 2–6 when simulating the 1992 Landers scenario using global time stepping.

Xeon processor, E5v3, by more than 3.4×. Even more important, in contrast to KNC, KNL can maintain its speed-up over the E5v3 also when boosting time-to-solution via local time stepping, resulting into a more than 12.1× speed-up when comparing against global time stepping runtimes on Intel Xeon E5v3. Up to 3.1× faster execution on KNL is possible when taking local time stepping runtimes as a baseline. In summary, our results have demonstrate that for best time-to-solution we must not only rely on performance engineering (increasing achieved FLOPS) but also investments in algorithmic design achieving best asymptotic complexity (increasing the ratio of science/FLOP).

References

1. Benjemaa, M., et al.: 3-D dynamic rupture simulations by a finite volume method. Geophys. J. Int. **178**, 541–560 (2009)
2. Bielak, J., et al.: Parallel octree-based finite element method for large-scale earthquake ground motion simulation. Comput. Model. Eng. Sci. **10**(2), 99 (2005)
3. Bielak, J., et al.: The shakeout earthquake scenario: verification of three simulation sets. Geophys. J. Int. **180**(1), 375–404 (2010)
4. Borstnik, U., et al.: Sparse matrix multiplication: the distributed block-compressed sparse row library. Parallel Comput. **40**(5–6), 47–58 (2014)
5. Breuer, A., et al.: High-order ADER-DG minimizes energy- and time-to-solution of SeisSol. In: Kunkel, J.M., Ludwig, T. (eds.) ISC High Performance 2015. LNCS, vol. 9137, pp. 340–357. Springer, Heidelberg (2015)
6. Breuer, A., et al.: Petascale local time stepping for the ADER-DG finite element method. In: Proceedings of IPDPS 2016 (2016). To appear

7. Breuer, A., et al.: Sustained petascale performance of seismic simulations with SeisSol on SuperMUC. In: Kunkel, J.M., Ludwig, T., Meuer, H.W. (eds.) ISC 2014. LNCS, vol. 8488, pp. 1–18. Springer, Heidelberg (2014)
8. Carrington, L., et al.: High-frequency simulations of global seismic wave propagation using SPECFEM3D_GLOBE on 62K processors. In: Proceedings of SC 2008 (2008)
9. Cui, Y., et al.: Physics-based seismic hazard analysis on petascale heterogeneous supercomputers. In: Proceedings of SC 2013 (2013)
10. Cui, Y., et al.: Scalable earthquake simulation on petascale supercomputers. In: Proceedings of SC 2010 (2010)
11. Day, S.M., et al.: Tests of 3D elastodynamic codes: final report for lifelines project 1A02. Pacific Earthquake Engineering Research Center (2003)
12. de la Puente, J., et al.: An arbitrary high-order discontinuous galerkin method for elastic waves on unstructured meshes-IV. Anisotropy. Geophys. J. Int. **169**(3), 1210–1228 (2007)
13. de la Puente, L., et al.: Dynamic rupture modeling on unstructured meshes using a discontinuous Galerkin method. J. Geophys. Res. **114**, B10302 (2009)
14. Dumbser, M., et al.: An arbitrary high-order discontinuous Galerkin method for elastic waves on unstructured meshes-II. The three-dimensional isotropic case. Geophys. J. Int. **167**(1), 319–336 (2006)
15. Harris, R.A., et al.: The SCEC/USGS dynamic earthquake rupture code verification exercise. Seismol. Res. Lett. **80**(1), 119–126 (2009)
16. Heinecke, A., et al.: Petascale high order dynamic rupture earthquake simulations on heterogeneous supercomputers. In: Proceedings of SC 2014. Gordon Bell Finalist (2014)
17. Ichimura, T., et al.: Implicit nonlinear wave simulation with 1.08 T DOF and 0.270 T unstructured finite elements to enhance comprehensive earthquake simulation. In: Proceedings of SC 2015 (2015)
18. Ichimura, I., et al.: Physics-based urban earthquake simulation enhanced by 10.7 BLNDOF × 30 K time-step unstructured fe non-linear seismic wave simulation. In: Proceedings of SC 2014 (2014)
19. Intel Corporation: Intel(R) 64 and IA-32 Architectures Optimization Reference Manual, January 2016
20. Käser, M., et al.: An arbitrary high-order discontinuous Galerkin method for elastic waves on unstructured meshes-III. Viscoelastic attenuation. Geophys. J. Int. **168**(1), 224–242 (2007)
21. Komatitsch, D., et al.: High-order finite-element seismic wave propagation modeling with MPI on a large GPU cluster. J. Comput. Phys. **229**(20), 7692–7714 (2010)
22. Pelties, C., et al.: Three-dimensional dynamic rupture simulation with a high-order discontinuous Galerkin method on unstructured tetrahedral meshes. J. Geophys. Res. **117**, B02309 (2012)
23. Pelties, C., et al.: Verification of an ADER-DG method for complex dynamic rupture problems. Geosci. Model Dev. Discuss. **6**, 5981–6034 (2013)
24. Shin, J., et al.: Speeding up Nek5000 with autotuning and specialization. In: Proceedings of the 24th ACM International Conference on Supercomputing (ICS 2010), pp. 253–262. ACM, New York (2010)
25. Sodani, A.: Knights Landing (KNL): 2nd generation Intel(R) Xeon Phi(TM) processor. In: Hotchips-2015 (2015)
26. Sodani, A., et al.: Knights Landing (KNL): 2nd generation Intel(R) Xeon Phi(TM) processor. IEEE Micro, Hot Chips Special Issue, (2016, to appear)

27. Tago, J., et al.: A 3D hp-adaptive discontinuous Galerkin method for modeling earthquake dynamics. J. Geophys. Res. **117**, B09312 (2012)
28. Tu, T., et al.: From mesh generation to scientific visualization: an end-to-end approach to parallel supercomputing. In: Proceedings of SC 2006 (2006)
29. Wilcox, L.C., et al.: A high-order discontinuous Galerkin method for wave propagation through coupled elastic-acoustic media. J. Comput. Phys. **229**(24), 9373–9396 (2010)

Leveraging a Cluster-Booster Architecture for Brain-Scale Simulations

Pramod Kumbhar[1]($\boxtimes$), Michael Hines[2], Aleksandr Ovcharenko[1],
Damian A. Mallon[3], James King[1], Florentino Sainz[4], Felix Schürmann[1],
and Fabien Delalondre[1]

[1] Blue Brain Project, École Polytechnique Fédérale de Lausanne (EPFL),
Lausanne, Switzerland
pramod.kumbhar@epfl.ch
[2] Yale University, New Haven, USA
[3] Juelich Supercomputing Center, Jülich, Germany
[4] Barcelona Supercomputing Center, Barcelona, Spain

Abstract. The European Dynamical Exascale Entry Platform (*DEEP*)
is an example of a new type of heterogeneous supercomputing architecture that include both a standard multicore-based *"Cluster"* used to run
less scalable parts of an application, and an Intel MIC-based *"Booster"*
used to run highly scalable compute kernels. In this paper we describe
how the compute engine of the widely used NEURON scientific application has been ported on both the *DEEP* and the Intel MIC platform.
We discuss the design and implementation of the core simulator with an
emphasis on the development workflow and implementation details that
enable the efficient use of the new *"Cluster-Booster"* type of architectures. We describe optimizations of the data structures and algorithms
tailored to the Intel Xeon Phi coprocessor which contributed to improve
the overall performance of NEURON by a factor 5. Validation of our
implementation has first been done on STAMPEDE supercomputer in
order to emulate the DEEP architecture performance. Building on these
results, we then explored opportunities offered by the *DEEP* platform
to efficiently support complex scientific workflow.

Keywords: DEEP · NEURON · Intel MIC · Neuronal network
simulations · Performance analysis and optimization

1 Introduction

Current efforts toward Exascale systems show that the architecture trend has
changed considerably in comparison with Terascale to Petascale transition.
Designing *"bigger and faster"* processors by increasing clock speed is not possible
anymore due to the limitation of CMOS scaling [1]. To overcome this limitation,
we observe increasing efforts to build new architectures that combine both specialized low-power consumption accelerators and general purpose CPUs. As an
example, the CORAL collaboration [2] plans to build hybrid systems by combining CPUs with accelerators like NVIDIA GPUs and Intel MIC. An emerging

© Springer International Publishing Switzerland 2016
J.M. Kunkel et al. (Eds.): ISC High Performance 2016, LNCS 9697, pp. 363–380, 2016.
DOI: 10.1007/978-3-319-41321-1_19

consensus in the HPC community seems to indicate that a major refactoring of large-scale scientific applications will be needed to fully exploit the massive amount of parallelism offered by these new systems. As such a large refactoring may require considerable man-power resource, it seems critical to investigate alternative ways that can offer both performance and productivity for most of the scientific applications. Though typical HPC applications use cases are better described by Gustafson's law [3], there are several caveats that can possibly limit the scalability of parallel applications on future massively parallel systems. As such, a large part of the HPC applications running on to-date Petascale systems can be broadly categorized into two classes [4]:

- Limited number of applications with highly scalable code parts and regular communication patterns;
- Large number of applications with complex workflows and limited scalability.

Even though the second class of applications is traditionally harder to scale, it usually also offers optimization opportunities for a reduced set of kernels well represented by Amdahl's law. As such, these applications show more than one level of concurrency: highly scalable kernels with $O(N)$ concurrency and other kernels with only $O(K)$ concurrency ($1 \leq K \ll N$, where N is large number of cores). To overcome the performance and scaling challenges of these applications at Exascale and provide opportunities to also maintain scientific productivity, the European Dynamical Exascale Entry Platform (*DEEP*) project [5] is exploring a new type of supercomputing architecture consisting of an x86-based *"Cluster"* with Infiniband interconnect to run complex, less scalable code parts and an Intel MIC based *"Booster"* with EXTOLL network to run highly scalable compute kernels.

The Blue Brain Project *(BBP)* [6] at École Polytechnique Fédérale de Lausanne focuses on the systematic integration of the heterogeneous neuroscience data into a unifying model for simulation-based research. As part of this research effort, a comprehensive modeling software platform which support the building, simulation, analysis and visualisation of the models is being developed to facilitate neuroscience research. One of the main software component of this platform is the NEURON [7] simulator which is widely used by neuroscientists to model the electrical activity of large neuronal networks whose cable properties play an important role. As part of the co-design efforts carried out during the development of the *DEEP* platform, we have been porting and improving the performance of morphologically detailed, multi-compartment neuronal model simulation carried out by the BBP.

This paper is then organized as follows: In the second section, the DEEP platform as well as it programming models are first introduced. The third section presents our efforts in porting NEURON application on both Intel MIC and DEEP systems with an emphasise on non-traditional offload workflow. Performance optimisation of the application tailored to the DEEP/Intel MIC systems are then presented in Sect. 4 before its performance analysis using both timers and performance counters is described.

2 DEEP Platform

The DEEP platform consists of a hardware as well as a software stack including programming environment, libraries and performance analysis tools. The high level of the system architecture and parallel programming environment is described below.

2.1 Hardware

The simplified architecture of the DEEP system shown in Fig. 1 is based on the duality of the multi-core *Cluster* system complemented by the *Booster* of Intel MIC coprocessors. The cluster consists of 128 compute nodes, each with two eight-core Intel Xeon E5 CPUs, arranged in fat tree topology with the InfiniBand interconnect. The Booster part consists of 384 Xeon Phi coprocessors arranged in 3D torus topology with the *EXTOLL* network [8]. In addition to the MIC, the *Booster* carries *Booster Interface (BI)* cards with the *Intel Core i7* CPU which provides management functionality to *Booster* nodes as well as high bandwidth, low latency bridging functionality between *Cluster* and *Booster*. Unlike current clusters with Xeon Phi coprocessors, the *Booster* nodes are capable of running autonomously with the *BI*.

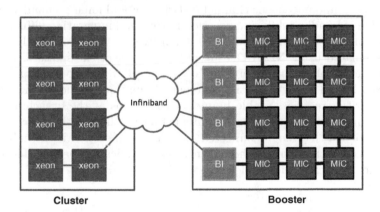

Fig. 1. The DEEP architecture shows the Intel Xeon *Cluster* with InfiniBand network on the left and the *Booster* of Xeon Phi coprocessors connected by the EXTOLL network on the right.

2.2 Software Stack and Programming Models

Parallel programming models are evolving slowly compared to hardware platforms and that presents a major challenge to developing applications with portable performance on heterogeneous HPC systems. In order to ease the application development, the DEEP software stack provides a runtime system and parallel programming models (based on MPI and OpenMP). When running on the *DEEP* system, applications need to offload and communicate between processes on the *Cluster* as well as the *Booster* nodes. The OmpSs [9] data-flow programming model developed by the Barcelona Supercomputing Center has been extended to support asynchronicity, heterogeneity and data movement between the *Cluster* and the *Booster*. Applications using *Message Passing Interface* (MPI) can use the dynamic process management interface, namely *MPI_Comm_spawn*, to offload kernels. To facilitate this, the MPI-3 compliant ParaStation MPI library has been extended and optimized on the architecture. This way, ParaStationMPI can work simultaneously over InfiniBand, EXTOLL, and bridges both fabrics with a custom developed protocol that guarantees low latency and high bandwidth. The DEEP hardware and software stacks have been discussed in more detail in [4]. Using this software stack six real-world HPC applications from different scientific areas are being ported as part of the co-design process, more information can be found in [8].

3   Porting NEURON's Core Engine

NEURON is a simulation environment developed over the last thirty years for modeling networks of neurons with complex branched anatomy including extra-cellular potential near membranes and biophysical properties such as multiple channel types, inhomogeneous channel distribution and ionic accumulation. It is also capable of handling diffusion-reaction models and integrating diffusion functions into models of synapses and cellular networks. Morphologically detailed models simulated using NEURON are able to represent the spatial diversity of electrical and biophysical properties of a neuron cell. Such models typically rely on the coupling of a set of partial differential equations modeling each branch of the dendritic tree via suitable boundary conditions at the branching points. Models of individual neurons are subdivided into individual compartments by the simulator via the tree of connected sections. Each section is the unbranched part of the cell with possibly inhomogeneous biophysical properties. The electrical behavior of each section is described by the cable Eq. 1.

$$c_m \frac{\partial v}{\partial t} = \frac{10^4}{4d(x)R_a} \frac{\partial}{\partial x}\left(d(x)^2 \frac{\partial v}{\partial x}\right) - I_{ion} + I_{syn}, \tag{1}$$

where the unknown $v[mV]$ represents the membrane potential, $c_m[\frac{\mu F}{cm^2}]$ is the membrane capacitance, $R_a[\Omega cm]$ is the section's axial resistivity (a constant), $d(x)[\mu m]$ is the diameter of the cross section as a function of the axial coordinate, I_{ion} $[\frac{mA}{cm^2}]$ is the current generated as a result of the flow of ions through the membrane via ion channels and ion pumps and I_{syn} $[\frac{mA}{cm^2}]$ is the current generated as a result of the flow of ions through the membrane as a consequence of a synaptic event. More detailed information about the simulator algorithm and its implementation can be found in [10].

The NEURON simulator is developed with a mixture of compiled (C, C++), interpreted (Python, HOC) and domain specific (NMODL) languages which helps building a flexible simulation framework. But porting the simulator to accelerators is a challenging task due to the following reasons:

- large codebase with complex application workflow;
- simulation environment allowing user to build and simulate models;
- complex data structures for offload programming models;
- hundreds of small compute kernels without a single hotspot.

In this section we describe efforts to refactor the core engine of the NEURON simulator and how we map it to the DEEP platform.

3.1 Extracting Core Engine of NEURON

The rat somatosensory cortex model currently investigated by computational neuroscientists of the BBP comprises approximately 217k neurons, with roughly 400 compartments and 3,500 synapses per neuron, and 3 to 5 channels per compartment. The BBP intends to use NEURON simulator to simulate very large models such as the rat and the human brain. A key issue to simulate network models with millions of cells is numerical efficiency and scalability, particularly with the use of the novel memory hierarchies and accelerators. Although the simulator has demonstrated scaling up to 64k core counts on the IBM Blue Gene/P system [11], solving morphologically detailed models of billions of neurons requires extensive changes in the simulator such as re-design of data structures to reduce memory footprint, enable vectorization and exposing more parallelism to take advantage of all available hardware threads.

In order to simulate the electrical activity of large scale neuronal networks, the in-memory network representation is built using morphologies of neuron cells. This part is very memory consuming and does not scale beyond the circuit of million cells. As part of the DEEP project we have contributed in factoring out the numerical engine of the NEURON simulator which enabled us to separate memory limiting model building part of the simulator from the core simulation engine. Figure 2 shows the workflow of the extracted NEURON simulator which is relevant for porting and optimization on supercomputing platforms. As part of a preprocessing step, neuroscientists can now use a model building workflow that relies on NEURON to build larger neuronal networks. Once the in-memory representation is built, NEURON dumps the circuit in binary and ASCII format to persistent storage. In this model building process, the input datasets are grouped into collection of cells so that every MPI rank or thread can load a pre-balanced dataset. The extracted simulator starts by reading binary circuit datasets and initializes necessary model data structures. The first I/O phase reads network connection topology information from the circuit and allocates memory for the required data structures. The second I/O phase reads all cell structures and parameters of the circuit into memory. In Fig. 2, the I/O phases are shown with the data size that they read, where *small* corresponds to a few megabytes per node and *large* means couple of gigabytes per node (depending upon the simulation network size).

The main timestep loop in the simulator represents a hybrid clock and event driven algorithm using optimal direct gaussian elimination to solve the large number of tree topology coupled algebric equations [12]. First, the matrix is built using contributions from *ion channels* and *synaptic current* computations. The membrane potential is obtained by solving the linear system and is used to update *channel state* variables. As *synaptic events* are not necessary to synchronize on every timestep, *spike exchange* is performed after *minimum network delay* which is typically four timesteps in our model. The percentage on the left for every phase in Fig. 2 shows the percent of simulation time spent in the individual phase for typical weak scaling simulation. The highlighted *reportingLib* component is used to write periodic compartment reports with *HDF5* file format which is currently under development and not ported yet.

3.2   Mapping the Simulator to Hardware

In current HPC platforms with accelerators applications typically start the execution on the host CPU and then offload compute expensive kernels to the accelerator. Offloading has some cost due to the initialization, kernel invocation, marshalling and transfer of data between host CPU and accelerator. Even if offloaded kernels execute

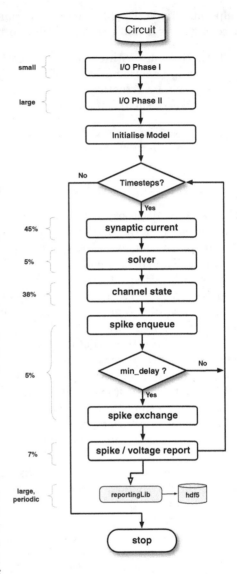

Fig. 2. Workflow of extracted core simulator of NEURON.

faster, offload may or may not provide speedup for overall application as it's profitability depends on a mixture of factors like offload runtime, application characteristics, accelerator performance etc. The initial plan for the NEURON simulator was to solve linear algebra and perform spike exchange on host CPUs and to offload computation of *synaptic and channel currents*, and *gating states* to the MIC. The NEURON simulator uses membrane model components developed by neuroscientists using NMODL [13] domain specific language (DSL). Our typical simulations have sixty to eighty compute kernels with each of them having less than 2 % of the total simulation time on the average. The detailed performance analysis using the Score-P performance analysis tool [14] showed that compute kernels take about a millisecond per timestep and also introduce strong synchronization between host CPU and accelerator due to the linear algebra solver. Implementing *traditional offload* (i.e. *Cluster* to *Booster* on the DEEP platform or CPUs to MIC on today's HPC cluster) would lead to a situation where simulator would offload lots of small kernels every timestep (with data copy for linear algebra on CPU). Interestingly, in addition to the *traditional offload* model, the DEEP programming model, with integration of job scheduling, provides the capability to implement the *Reverse Offload* where applications can start execution natively on the *Booster* nodes to execute compute expensive kernels and offload inefficient kernels to the *Cluster* nodes. This implementation allows the simulator to run large number of compute expensive kernels natively on the *Booster* and offload *"CPU friendly"* compartment report and initialization routines to the *Cluster*.

Multi-threading implementation and compiler vectorization of kernels (discussed in the next chapter) enables efficient use of Intel MIC coprocessor. The initialization phase and *reportingLib* library read/write gigabytes of data on every node. As I/O on the MIC is very slow, we adopted the *Reverse Offload* strategy to offload all I/O kernels to host CPUs or *Cluster*. We refactored the simulator code, and its offload implementation is shown in Fig. 3.

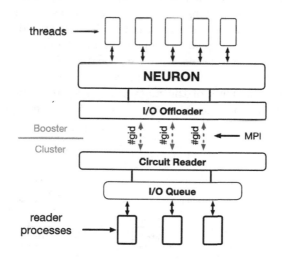

Fig. 3. I/O offload implementation in the simulator.

This newly developed *I/O Offloader* module transparently offloads I/O routines from the *Booster* to the *Cluster*. This is implemented using the *OmpSs offload* as well as *MPI_Comm_spawn* so that it can be run on the DEEP platform as well as today's HPC clusters. The *Circuit Reader* module is extracted and extended in order to handle I/O requests from threads of the simulator in *first come first serve* manner. The number of reader processes spawned depends on the number of nodes available and can be configured at runtime. Note that the efficient use of *DEEP* architecture with *normal* or *reverse* offload mode depends on the task granularity and suitability of the *Cluster* or the *Booster* nodes. One technique to evaluate the suitability of such a platform is to use the Paraver-Dimemas performance prediction toolset [15] which allows forecasting the effects of code optimization and can perform *what-if* analysis.

3.3   Offload Friendly Data Structures

One of the major challenges for application developers to adopt offload programming models like *Intel LEO*, *OmpSs* or *OpenACC* is complex, user defined data structures. Simple bitwise copyable C *struct* or C++ *class* without dynamically allocated members can be transparently copied to accelerators by current compilers. But data structures with multiple levels of pointer indirection are challenging as they require deep memory copy semantics [16] and are currently not supported by many compilers. The NEURON simulator has complex data structures to represent details of neuron cells such as branches of varying diameters and lengths, ionic channels, synapses, etc. This is a major challenge to implement the offload using OmpSs or other programming models. Figure 4 shows the schematic presentation of part of the data structure used in compute kernels. The *NeuronGroup* container loads group of cells from the circuit. Channel instances of different types are inserted into the cell and are represented by *MechList* with a linked list. Actual data for mechanisms is stored in the *MechData* vectors which are bitwise copyable. Depending on the type of the mechanism, additional data structures like *ion_data* are allocated. For linear algebra calculations additional vectors are allocated to store, for example, the right hand side *RHS* and *Diagonal* elements of the matrix. In order to transfer *NeuronGroup* for offload, one needs to either transfer individual bitwise copyable vectors or

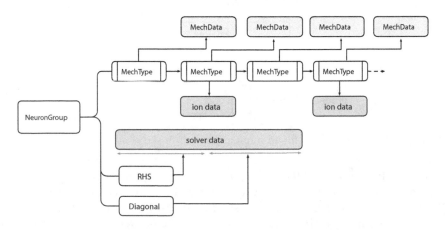

Fig. 4. Representation of data structure used in compute kernels.

needs to change the data structures. In the current implementation of the simulator changing data structures is a non-trivial task. Instead, we changed the *Circuit Reader* and the memory allocation strategy by packing data structures for compute kernels into contiguous vectors that allow us to easily transfer data structures using offload semantics.

4 Performance Optimization

After refactoring and porting the compute engine of the NEURON simulator on the DEEP platform, we optimized its performance on the MIC with the following changes.

4.1 Thread Parallelism

NEURON uses MPI to implement distributed memory parallelism and has demonstrated good scaling up to 64k cores on IBM BlueGene/P [11]. Although the simulator has threading implementation using pthreads, the pure MPI implementation is most commonly used due to a better scaling. Intel MIC card has 61 cores and each core has the ability to support 4 hardware threads. Applications can run in pure MPI mode without significant modification, but to reduce the memory footprint and the process scheduling overhead, it is recommended to use fewer MPI tasks per node. In the extracted core engine of the simulator we implemented OpenMP threading based on the existing shared memory threading APIs. Individual threads process a single cell or a group of cells in parallel which helps to expose on-node parallelism.

Figure 5 shows the comparison of the pure MPI implementation with the new OpenMP implementation. When 60 MPI ranks or threads per node are used, there is no significant performance difference. Once we use two or four MPI processes per core, OpenMP implementation shows approximately 12 % improvement.

4.2 Data Layout and Vectorization

Limited memory bandwidth is the first impediment to accelerating the performance of many real world applications. Figure 6 shows memory bandwidth utilization for few timesteps of the simulator on the Intel MIC. The simulator reach 140 GB/s which is close to the peak what many applications can achieve. This clearly shows that the compute kernels are memory bandwidth limited about 60 % of the simulation time. In order to better understand the nature of memory accesses and possible optimizations, we describe discretized structure of neuron cells and channels in Fig. 7. The complicated dendritic structures of neurons are divided into small compartments coupled to their adjacent compartments. The membrane channels or mechanisms (like K, Na, Ih) are inserted into different compartments of the cell. The number and types of channels vary from compartment to compartment.

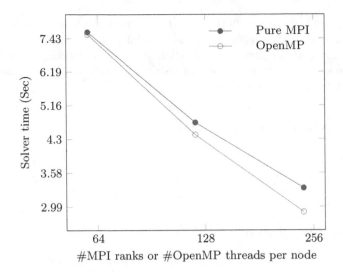

Fig. 5. Performance of pure MPI implementation compare to new OpenMP implementation on single MIC node for the simulation of 3200 cells. (Color figure online)

Fig. 6. Timeline view of a bandwidth utilization on MIC with original *AoS* memory layout when running core engine of the NEURON simulator. The first trace is a read bandwidth, whereas the second trace is the write bandwidth (in GB/s).

To efficiently compute the channels and exploit locality, the channels are grouped together by their type as shown in Fig. 7A. The original implementation of the simulator stores the properties of individual mechanisms (like *gna*, *tau*, *ik*etc.) in the *Array of Struct (AoS)* layout as show in Fig. 7B. Even though modern compilers can vectorize loops with *AoS* memory layout using gather-scatter instructions, this leads to the strided memory accesses which often have poor performance. In order to reduce the pressure on a memory bus and improve the performance of vectorization, channel properties are now re-arranged into the *Structure of Array (SoA)* layout as shown in Fig. 7C.

4.3   DSL Source to Source Compiler Changes

Due to the variety of models being developed by neuroscientists using *NMODL* domain specific language (which gets translated into *C* at compile time), it is not feasible to hand-tune kernels for different platforms. Instead, we have modified the *NMODL* source to source compiler to generate kernels with either *AoS* or *SoA* memory layout and provide hints to the compiler to auto-vectorize most of the compute kernels. New keywords like *CONDUCTANCE* have been

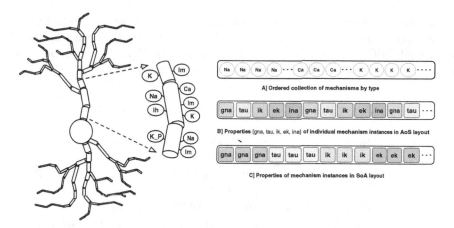

Fig. 7. Figure on the left shows schematic representation of dendritic structure of a neuron cell. The dendrites are divided into small interconnected compartments shown as cylinders. Different types of mechanisms are inserted into the compartment whose distribution changes for different cell types. On the right: [A] shows how the NEURON simulator groups the mechanism instances of the same type; [B] shows how properties of individual mechanism (e.g. *Na*) are stored in the *AoS* layout; [C] shows new *SoA* layout for storing mechanism properties in the extracted core engine of the simulator with the help of changes in the DSL compiler.

added which allow users to specify ohmic relation of current voltage to avoid the numerical derivative computation during the *NMODL* to *C* translation. In order to generate kernels with reduced pressure on memory ports, unnecessary intermediate variables in the *NMODL* files were removed.

5   Benchmarking and Performance Analysis

At the time of the performance analysis study the *Cluster* part of the DEEP hardware at Juelich Supercomputing Centre(JSC) was not fully in production to perform scaling studies. But since the core engine of NEURON is completely ported to run natively on MIC, we used the *Booster* for scaling studies. For the *Reverse* offload benchmarking we used the *Stampede* system at the Texas Advanced Computing Center [17]. On this system the simulator can start execution natively on MICs of allocated compute nodes and then use host CPUs to offload *Circuit Reader* routines. Note that OmpSs transparently manages offloading of kernels by spawning processes on available host CPUs but for the MPI offload implementation we used node allocation information from job scheduler to appropriately set *MPI_Info* keys with *MPI_Comm_spawn*. The Xeon Phi workstation at the JSC is used for hardware performance counter analysis. Table 1 shows details of benchmarking systems used for this study. Note that some nodes on the Stampede system have two MICs while others have a single MIC card. In order to compare the performance with the DEEP system, we considered a socket with MIC card as a node in order to mimic the DEEP architecture where we use only MIC and dynamically use CPUs for offload.

Table 1. Details of benchmarking systems

DEEP	Host	Sandy Bridge E5-2670 8 core CPU @ 2.6 GHz
	MIC	7120X Xeon Phi 61 core @1.23 GHz, 16 GB DRAM
	OmpSs toolchain	15.06 (with DEEP extensions)
	Intel toolchain	icc 15.2.164, Intel MPI 5.1 and Parastation MPI
	Network	InfiniBand + Extoll
Stampede	Host	Sandy Bridge E5-2680 8 core CPU @ 2.7 GHz
	MIC	Xeon Phi 61 core @1.1 GHz, 8 GB DRAM
	Intel toolchain	icc 14.0.1 and Intel MPI 4.1.0
	Network	InfiniBand
Xeon Phi workstation	Host	Sandy Bridge E5-2670 8 core CPU @ 2.6 GHz
	MIC	7120A Xeon Phi 61 core @1.23 GHz, 16 GB DRAM
	OmpSs toolchain	15.06 (with DEEP extensions)
	Intel toolchain	icc 15.0.1 and Intel MPI 4.1.2.040
	Network	InfiniBand

For the performance analysis of the simulator we used a circuit of 115k neuron cells produced by the neuroscientists at the BBP. In order to get the detailed on-node performance and hardware counter analysis we focus on results of ten representative kernels from five models written in NMODL. The majority of these computationally expensive models have two types of kernels that closely match with the code structure shown in Listings 1.1 and 1.2. First, the *nrn_state* kernel represents a channel state update and is dominated by exponential and division operations. Second, the *nrn_current* kernel represents a synaptic current calculation with very low arithmetic intensity and strided memory access due to the branched structure of a neuron cell.

Listing 1.1. Structure of compute intensive *nrn_state* kernel

```
1   _PRAGMA_FOR_VECTOR_LOOP_
2   for( i = 0; i < node_count; i++) {
3
4       int idx = node_index[i];
5       double v = vec[idx];
6       p3[i] = data[ion_index[i]];
7       double qt = 2.952882641412121;
8       double mAlpha = (0.182*(v+32.0)) / (1.0-(exp(-v-32.0)/6.0));
9       double mBeta = (0.124*(-v-32.0)) / (1.0-(exp(v+32.0)/6.0));
10      double mInf = mAlpha/(mAlpha+mBeta);
11      double mTau = (1.0/(mAlpha+mBeta))/qt;
12      p1[i] = p1[i] + (1.0-exp(dt*(-1.0/mTau))) *
            (-(mInf/mTau)/((-1.0/mTau)-p1[i]));
13      vec[idx] = v + _update_;
14  }
```

Listing 1.2. Structure of *nrn_current* kernel dominated by strided memory accesses with indirect index

```
1   _PRAGMA_FOR_VECTOR_LOOP_
2   for( i = 0; i < node_count; i++) {
3
4       int idx = node_index[i];
5       v = vec[idx];
6       p3[i] = data[ion_index[i]];
7       double gNaTs2 = p0[i]*p1[i]*p1[i]*p1[i]*p2[i];
8       double ina = gNaTs2*(v-p3[i]);
9       data[ion_index1[i]] += gNaTs2;
10      data[ion_index2[i]] += ina;
11      vec_rhs[idx] -= ina;
12      vec_d[idx] += gNaTs2;
13  }
```

For both kernel types the compiler assumes data hazards for storing array variables with indirect indexing (like *vec[idx]*, *vec_rhs[idx]*, *data[ion_index1[i]]* etc.). For channel models, there is generally only one instance of the same channel type in a given compartment. In order to enable compiler auto-vectorization, NMODL source to source compiler is modified to provide compiler dependent vectorization hints (like *ivdep* with icc, *ibm independent_loop* with xlc, *_CRI ivdep* with craycc etc.) using the macro *_PRAGMA_FOR_VECTOR_LOOP_*.

Figure 8 shows the speedup for the *nrn_state* and the *nrn_current* kernels in comparison with the original implementation (referred as *"Orig"*) of the extracted core engine of NEURON simulator. The *"SoA"* implementation represent the simulator version with the *SoA* memory layout and compiler vectorization, and the *"SoAOpt"* represent the version with additional optimisations discussed in Sect. 4.3. The vectorized *SoA* implementation shows 6x to 8x performance improvement which is expected with the use of a full 512-bit vector

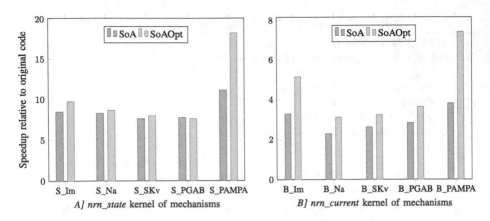

Fig. 8. The figure on the left shows the speedup for the *nrn_state* kernels. The figure on the right shows the speedup for the *nrn_current* kernel compared to the original implementation of NEURON simulator. (Color figure online)

instructions on the Intel MIC. The runtime of these kernels is dominated by exponential and division operations whose throughput is limited due to the limited pipelining in hardware functional units. That is why the *SoAOpt* implementation with memory access optimisations does not show significant improvement for *nrn_state* kernels. The Intel VTune Amplifier is used in order to measure performance counters to derive Cycles Per Instruction (CPI) and Vectorisation Intensity (VPU_ELEMENTS_ACTIVE per VPU_INSTRUCTIONS_EXECUTED) which are shown in Table 2. When a vector instruction with two full vector registers is performed, the *VPU_ELEMENTS_ACTIVE* event is incremented

Table 2. Cycles per instruction and vectorisation intensity

Kernel type	Compute kernel	Cycles per instruction			Vectorisation intensity	
		Orig	SoA	SoAOpt	SoA	SoAOpt
nrn_state	S_Ih	4.04	4.52	4.52	9.15	9.26
	S_Im	4.10	4.85	4.81	8.90	9.03
	S_Na	4.01	4.82	4.71	9.18	9.27
	S_SKv	3.84	4.86	4.96	9.00	9.10
	S_PGAB	19.30	9.61	7.31	8.32	8.44
	S_PAMPA	23.46	8.15	6.57	8.34	8.43
nrn_current	B_Ih	4.13	6.20	9.63	6.50	3.21
	B_Im	4.51	8.64	13.34	5.39	3.49
	B_Na	4.48	7.33	11.76	5.48	3.97
	B_SKv	4.26	7.77	12.78	5.29	3.55
	B_PGAB	5.48	4.20	4.27	6.39	4.68
	B_PAMPA	4.16	4.48	3.76	8.01	6.96

by 16 and 8 for the single and the double precision respectively. The *VPU_INSTRUCTIONS_EXECUTED* includes instructions for floating-point operations, memory load/store operations, instructions to manipulate vector mask registers, etc. The *CPI* for *nrn_state* kernels with *AoS*, *SoA* and *SoAOpt* implementations does not change significantly due to the high latency division and exponential operations which, even if implemented with intrinsics, have latencies that are one or two orders of magnitude higher comparing to addition or multiplication operations. The vectorization intensity around eight shows the full use of vector units (values greater than eight might be due to the use of math library functions).

The *nrn_cur* kernels have very low arithmetic intensity and strided memory accesses with indirect indexes as shown in Listing 1.2. Even if these kernels are vectorized, the compiler needs to use non-optimal vector gather-scatter instructions. Due to memory bandwidth saturation, these kernels show 3x to 4x speedup when compared to the original implementation. The *SoAOpt* implementation shows the improved performance for these kernels due to the reduced memory accesses described in Sect. 4.3. Note that the addition of the *CONDUCTANCE* keyword eliminates the computation of numerical derivative (strided memory accesses remains the same) and hence we can see the increase in CPI and the decrease in vectorisation intensity. The *S_PAMPA* and *B_PAMPA* kernels represent the synapse model. Synapses are responsible for receiving electrical or chemical signals from other neurons. These mechanisms are more computationally expensive since the number of synapses are three orders of magnitude higher than the number of other mechanisms. We optimized memory accesses and also precomputed some parameters during the initialization phase. These optimizations with the *SoA* memory layout and vectorization improved the performance by a factor of 20 for *nrn_state* and by a factor of 8 for *nrn_current* kernel of the synapse mechanism.

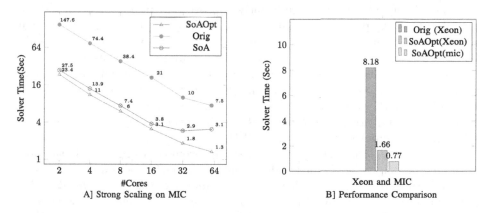

Fig. 9. On the left: Strong scaling of the simulator on a MIC node with two threads per core. On the right: Performance comparison of the 8-core Sandy Bridge CPU with the 61-core Xeon Phi coprocessor. (Color figure online)

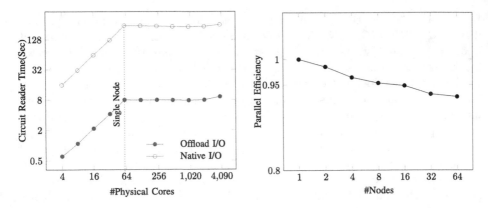

Fig. 10. On the left: the performance comparison of the *Circuit Reader* using native I/O vs offload I/O (61 cores per node, up to 64 nodes). On the right: the parallel efficiency of the simulator running natively on up to 64 nodes. (Color figure online)

Figure 9A shows strong scaling performance of *Orig*, *SoA* and *SoAOpt* implementations using two OpenMP threads per core on a single MIC node. Even though the original code exhibited good scaling, the on-node performance was very low due to the *AoS* memory layout and non-vectorized kernels. For small core counts the *SoA* implementation improves the performance by a factor of 6 due to vectorization and efficient memory bandwidth utilization. But as we increase the number of OpenMP threads, the memory bandwidth saturates after 32 cores and hence limits the scaling. Memory optimizations in the *SoAOpt* implementation reduces memory bandwidth pressure and helps improving the performance by a factor of 2. Overall we can see the 5.5x speedup when compared to the original code.

Although in this paper we focused on the Intel MIC architecture, the optimizations discussed have also significantly improved the performance on the x86 and Blue Gene/Q platforms. Figure 9B shows the performance of the original code on a CPU compared with the latest optimized version on the 8-core Sandy Bridge CPU and the 61-core Intel MIC. This simulation involves 3200 neuron cells with the biological time of one millisecond. The optimizations including memory layout changes and vectorization have improved the performance by a factor of 4.4 and 5 on the Blue Gene/Q and the x86 platforms respectively. As the memory bandwidth on the Intel MIC is significantly higher, the Intel MIC is 2.2x faster comparing to the 8-core CPU.

In order to measure the performance improvement using the offload programming model, we performed scaling studies up to 64 nodes on the Stampede system. Figure 10 (on the left) shows the performance of the *Circuit Reader* with I/O offload to CPUs and MIC native I/O on Stampede system. This simulation loads about 1850 neuron cells (about 3.5 GB) per node from the circuit. Note that loading circuit data involves a lot of small I/O operations due to a mixture of ASCII and binary data. As native I/O on the MIC is very slow in comparison with host CPUs, the *Circuit Reader* with offload is 30x faster than the native I/O on the MIC. In the weak scaling simulation the I/O size increases with the number of threads. However, since the I/O size per node remains constant beyond 61 cores, the time to load the circuit remains the same. Currently we use offload only for the *Circuit Reader* module during circuit loading but we believe this implementation will allow us to transparently ship periodic comparement reports generated with the *reportingLib* library. The parallel efficiency of the simulator (initialization excluded) up to 64 nodes is shown in Fig. 10 (on the right). The multi-threading implementation at the cell level exposes sufficient parallelism to allow using a single MPI rank per node with 120 OpenMP threads. The input circuit is balanced as part of the pre-processing step, which achieves excellent load balancing (98 %) across the threads as well as the MPI ranks. One can observe on the right side of the Fig. 10 that the simulator shows good scaling behaviour with parallel efficiency of 0.93 when using 64 nodes. The difference from ideal scaling is due to non-scaling behaviour of *MPI_Allgather* and spike event queueing mechanism.

6   Conclusion and Future Work

In this paper we presented our results of porting and optimizing the core engine of the widely used NEURON simulator on both the Intel MIC system and the DEEP platform. We discussed algorithmic workflow and low level optimizations that improved the overall performance of the application by a factor of 5. Building on the results, we provided a detailed performance of the application using hardware counters, demonstrating that the application is reaching peak bandwidth performance. Finally we showed how the different programming models offered by the DEEP software stack allowed the easy offload of the I/O intensive part of the application from booster to cluster nodes, as opposed to traditional cluster to booster offload offered by for example NVidia GPU systems. The latter allows exploring future scientific workflow development opportunities that could include run time data analysis and interactive in-situ visualization.

Acknowledgements. The research leading to these results has received funding from the European Community's Seventh Framework Programme (FP7/2007-2013) under Grant Agreement no. 287530. The EPFL Blue Brain Project as well as parts of this study are funded by the ETH board. The scaling studies were performed on the Stampede supercomputer hosted at the Texas Advanced Computing Center (TACC) and funded by the National Science Foundation (award OCI-1134872). We thank Jochen Kreutz for supporting benchmarking work on the *DEEP* system and Estela Suarez for reviewing the manuscript.

References

1. Taur, Y.: CMOS design near the limit of scaling. IBM J. Res. Dev. **46**(2.3) (2002). doi:10.3389/fncom.2011.00049
2. Department of Energy: DOE Awards $425 Million for Next Generation Supercomputing Technologies. 2014. http://energy.gov/articles/department-energy-awards-425-million-next-generation-supercomputing-technologies. Accessed 14 Nov 2014
3. Gustafson, J.L.: Reevaluating Amdahls law. Commun. ACM **31**(5), 532–533 (1998)
4. Eicker, N., et al.: The DEEP project: pursuing cluster-computing in the many-core era. In: HUCCA (2013)
5. DEEP project. http://www.deep-project.eu. Accessed 10 Oct 2015
6. Markram, H.: The blue brain project. Nat. Rev. Neuro-Sci. **7**(2), 153–160 (2006). doi:10.1038/nrn1848
7. Migliore, M., et al.: Parallel network simulations with NEURON. J. Comput. Neurosci. **21**(2), 119–129 (2006). doi:10.1007/s10827-006-7949-5
8. Mallon, D.A., et al.: Programming model and application porting to the dynamic exascale entry platform (DEEP). In: EASC (2013)
9. Duran, A., et al.: Ompss: a proposal for programming heterogeneous multi-core architectures. Parallel Proc. Lett. **21**(2), 173–193 (2011)
10. Hines, M.: NEURON — a program for simulation of nerve equations. In: Eeckman, F.H. (ed.) Neural Systems: Analysis and Modeling, pp. 127–136. Springer, New York (1993)
11. Hines, M., Kumar, S., Schurmann, F.: Comparison of neuronal spike exchange methods on a Blue Gene/P supercomputer. Front. Comput. Neurosci. **5**(49) (2011). doi:10.3389/fncom.2011.00049
12. Hines, M.: Effcient computation of branched nerve equations. Int. J. Bio-Med. Comput. **15**(1), 69–76 (1984)
13. Hines, M., Carnevale, T.: Expanding NEURON's repertoire of mechanisms with NMODL. Neural Comput. **12**(5), 995–1007 (2000)
14. Knüpfer, A., et al.: Score-P: a joint performance measurement run-time infrastructure for Periscope, Scalasca, TAU, and Vampir. In: Brunst, H., Müller, M.S., Nagel, W.E., Resch, M.M. (eds.) Tools for High Performance Computing, pp. 79–91. Springer, Heidelberg (2012). doi:10.1007/978-3-642-31476-6_7
15. Badia, R.M., et al.: DIMEMAS: predicting MPI applications behavior in grid environments. In: Workshop on Grid Applications and Programming Tools (GGF8) (2003)
16. Beyer, J., Oehmke, D., Sandoval, J.: Transferring user-defined types in OpenACC. In: CRAY User Group Proceedings (2014)
17. Texas Advanced Computing Center: Stampede Supercomputer. (2015). https://www.tacc.utexas.edu/stampede/. Accessed 22 Sept 2015

Manycore Architectures

Efficient and Predictable Group Communication for Manycore NoCs

Karthik Yagna, Onkar Patil, and Frank Mueller[✉]

North Carolina State University, Raleigh, USA
mueller@cs.ncsu.edu

Abstract. Massive manycore embedded processors with network-on-chip (NoC) architectures are becoming common. These architectures provide higher processing capability due to an abundance of cores. They provide native core-to-core communication that can be exploited via message passing to provide system scalability. Despite these advantages, manycores pose predictability challenges that can affect both performance and real-time capabilities.

In this work, we develop efficient and predictable group communication using message passing specifically designed for large core counts in 2D mesh NoC architectures. We have implemented the most commonly used collectives in such a way that they incur low latency and high timing predictability making them suitable for balanced parallelization of scalable high-performance and embedded/real-time systems alike. Experimental results on a single-die 64 core hardware platform show that our collectives can significantly reduce communication times by up to 95 % for single packet messages and up to 98 % for longer messages with superior performance for sometimes all message sizes and sometimes only small message sizes depending on the group primitive. In addition, our communication primitives have significantly lower variance than prior approaches, thereby providing more balanced parallel execution progress and better real-time predictability.

1 Introduction

The future of computing is rapidly changing as manycore processors are becoming ubiquitous. Massive manycore platforms with NoC architectures are starting to penetrate high-performance systems, three-tier servers, network processing and embedded/real-time systems. These architectures provide a significant advancement due to an abundance of cores, which requires mesh-based NoCs for scalability. This allows a large number of cooperating tasks to be scheduled together. Tasks can employ group communication via messages over the NoC to achieve scalability and reduced latency. Their on-chip mesh NoC speeds are at par with processor clock frequencies as a hop between neighboring tiles/cores takes 1–2 cycles, which is a game changer in terms of communication.

This work was supported in part by NSF grants 0905181 and 1239246.

© Springer International Publishing Switzerland 2016
J.M. Kunkel et al. (Eds.): ISC High Performance 2016, LNCS 9697, pp. 383–403, 2016.
DOI: 10.1007/978-3-319-41321-1_20

But such meshes are not without challenges as link contention and flow control become potential bottlenecks.

Poor group communication implementations can result in increased and highly variant latency due to NoC contention resulting in loss of predictability and imbalance in execution progress across cores. When multiple pairs of cores communicate, they may experience contention due to wormhole routing: After opening a source-destination path along a route, any other communication trying to use links on this path remains blocked until the former connection is closed. Such situations can be avoided using intelligent scheduling of each round of message exchanges.

For example, consider 9 cores taking part in all-to-all communication as in Fig. 1. The task on core 3 is trying to send to the task on core 8, and the task on core 4 is trying to send to the task on core 2. This results in 2 messages, one from $3 \rightarrow 8$ and another from $4 \rightarrow 2$. When sent at the same time, contention on link $4 \rightarrow 5$ due to wormhole routing results in a delay for one of these messages as they are arbitrated within the NoC hardware routers. Thus, sending tasks experience highly variable latencies. The effect shown in this example is amplified with increasing NoC mesh sizes. Such situations can be avoided using intelligent scheduling of each round of message exchanges.

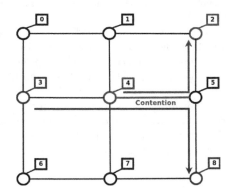

Fig. 1. NoC contention (Color figure online)

Furthermore, NoC architectures provide multiple message queues and networks [1–4]. On the TilePro64 [2], the User Dynamic Network (UDN) uses dynamic routing to forward messages from a source core to a destination core on Manhattan path following first the X- and then the Y-direction (X/Y-dimension ordered routing). The Static Network (SN) uses statically configured routes to forward packets received on each link. SN is faster than UDN in terms of packet forwarding speed (1 vs. 2 cycles), but is difficult to program and has route setup overhead.

This work contributes the design and implementation of group communication for large core counts utilizing 2D mesh NoC architectures. We employ efficient algorithms to reduce communication latency and exploit advanced NoC hardware features to provide better performance. We also ensure that communication uses contention-free paths and that no deadlock may occur. Deadlocks may occur due to head-of-line and path-based blocking, they are avoided by credit-based backpressure monitoring [5,6] or by ensuring absence of link contention (this work, for collectives, only). We have implemented five commonly used group communication primitives [7].

Our Barrier, Broadcast and Reduce use a communication tree in which the cores are arranged as nodes and share a parent-child relationship. The communication tree is used to send messages to/from the root. The Barrier and Reduce implementations utilize the UDN, whereas Broadcast uses the SN. Our implementation of Alltoall exploits simple pattern-based communication, common in MPI [7] runtime system implementations, to send messages concurrently, yet without contention, to reduce communication latency. This neither requires dynamic computation of a routing schedule nor incurs scheduling overhead or memoization of large routing tables. Our implementation uses message passing over the NoC of a TilePro64 and Intel SCC but is generic enough to be adopted to any 2D mesh NoC.

Experimental results on the TilePro hardware platform show that our implementation has lower latencies and less timing variability (lower variance) than prior work. We compared the performance of our implementation in micro-benchmarks against OperaMPI [8], a reference MPI implementation for the Tilera platform. Performance improvements of up to 95 % are observed in communication for single packet messages with significantly higher timing predictability (lower variance), which supports more balanced execution progress for high-performance computing (HPC) and helps meet deadlines in embedded/real-time scenarios. Our port to the Intel SCC achieves similar results compared to the vendor libraries [9].

2   Design and Implementation

Our work assumes a generic, generalized 2D mesh NoC switching architecture similar to existing fabrics with high core counts [1–3,9]. Each core is composed of a compute core, network switch, and local caches.

NoC Message Layer (NoCMsg): Our implementation provides an MPI-style message passing interface for NoCs. This facilitates basic point-to-point communication and supports our group communication. The NoC message layer implementation optionally provides flow control support. In our design, we turn off flow control when not required by program logic to further improve performance.

Group Communication Primitives: The key ideas behind our design of group communication primitives are to (1) reduce contention in the NoC; (2) exploit pattern-based communication to exchange messages concurrently; (3) reduce the number of messages by aggregation; and (4) leverage hardware features to improve performance. Due to these objectives, it is not feasible to simply resort to binomial trees for most collectives or other algorithms such as recursive doubling for allreduce since these algorithms are contention agnostic and will result in reduced performance over contention-sensitive NoCs.

We implemented the group communication on the Tilera TilePro64 and ported it to the Intel SCC [9] to demonstrate that our implementation is generic and can be extended to any 2D mesh NoC architectures.

2.1 Alltoall and Alltoallv

Alltoall/Alltoallv employ pattern-based communication, which allows several sets of tasks to exchange messages concurrently without contention as many exchanges split into multiple rounds.

The rounds are comprised of (1) direct (2) left and (3) right rounds. The direct round is further split into two subrounds. In subrounds, each task sends messages only along a straight path to its partner task. Tasks exchange messages along the X direction in direct subround 1 and along the Y direction in direct subround 2. In left rounds, each task sends messages along the X direction followed by the Y direction such that their path follows a counter-clockwise direction. In right rounds, each task sends messages along the X direction followed by the Y direction such that their paths follow a clockwise direction. These cases are depicted in Fig. 2. The XY dimension routing ensures that these directions are maintained consistently.

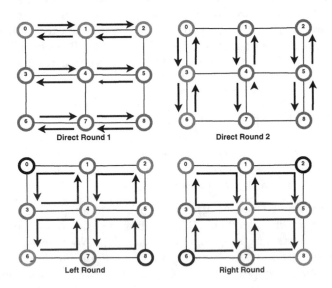

Fig. 2. Alltoall rounds (Color figure online)

The implementation details are sketched in Algorithm 1. In each round, the number of hops the message is forwarded is incremented until all tasks are covered. To begin, each task starts the direct subround one with one hop. The current column is selected by function Select-col. Tasks exchange messages with their neighbors one hop away along the X direction. This is done to ensure that the exchange is free of contention. The select functions operate as follows: Given a horizontal distance (e.g., two), determine the subset of cores via modulo arithmetic (example: every even core / rank modulo 2) that are active, followed by others round (example: every odd core / rank+1 modulo 2). Once the round has been completed, a barrier is forced between all tasks. The barrier ensures absence of contention across rounds. Subsequent rounds for other

---

Algorithm 1. Alltoall: x,y are task ranks; myrow,mycol are Cartesian coordinates of x.

```
 1: function NoCMsG-ALLTOALL
 2:     Xmax ← gridwidth; Ymax ← gridheight
 3:     for xhops ← 1, Xmax do // DIRECT SUBROUND 1 (DR1)
 4:         currcol = Select-col(DR1, xhops) // SELECT COLUMN FOR THIS ROUND
 5:         if mycol == currcol then                              ▷ my column's turn
 6:             UDN-xchg(x+xhops, y); UDN-xchg(x-xhops, y)
 7:         end if
 8:         Barrier()
 9:     end for
10:     for yhops ← 1, Ymax do // DIRECT SUBROUND 2 (DR2)
11:         currrow = Select-row(DR2, yhops) // SELECT ROW FOR THIS ROUND
12:         if myrow == currrow then                              ▷ my row's turn
13:             UDN-xchg(x, y+yhops); UDN-xchg(x, y-yhops)
14:         end if
15:         Barrier()
16:     end for
17:     for yhops ← 1, Ymax do // LEFT ROUND (LR)
18:         for xhops ← 1, Xmax do // SELECT ROW, COLUMN FOR THIS ROUND
19:             currrow = Select-row(LR, yhops); currcol = Select-col(LR, xhops)
20:             if myrow, mycol == currrow, currcol then
21:                 UDN-xchg(x-xhops, y+yhops); UDN-xchg(x+xhops, y-yhops)
22:             end if
23:             Barrier()
24:         end for
25:     end for
26:     for yhops ← 1, Ymax do // RIGHT ROUND (RR)
27:         for xhops ← 1, Xmax do // SELECT ROW, COLUMN FOR THIS ROUND
28:             currrow = Select-row(RR, yhops); currcol = Select-col(RR, xhops)
29:             if myrow, mycol == currrow, currcol then
30:                 UDN-xchg(x+xhops, y+yhops); UDN-xchg(x-xhops, y-yhops)
31:             end if
32:             Barrier()
33:         end for
34:     end for
35: end function
```

directions follow. The algorithm is unique in its absence of contention, which is key to the performance improvements we observed compared to naive exchange sequences with contention.

2.2   Barriers

We utilize modified 3-ary tree-based barriers that distribute the work evenly among nodes to minimize cycle differences upon barrier completion. In a 2D mesh, nodes have a most 4 neighbors so that in a barrier tree, any interior node receives a message from one neighbor and relays this message to 3 others. This provides maximal link coverage with minimal tree height (which is optimal). Hence, the tree is 3-ary on the interior, 4-ary for the root (to be precise) and of lower degree (2/1/0) for nodes close to the leaves and leaves themselves. The root of this tree is placed in the center of the NoCMsg grid to minimize latency (hops). The tree is constructed as part of the initialization process. Children notifying their parents when they have entered the barrier, up to the root. Once the root has received notifications from all children, it broadcasts a notification back down the tree by replying to its children and returns from the barrier call, as do the children. UDN is used to send/receive synchronization packets and their replies. Figure 3 shows an example of a barrier tree for a 4×4 grid.

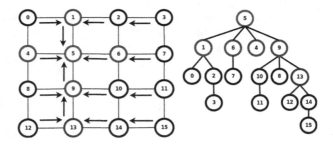

Fig. 3. Barrier tree: setup (Color figure online)

Flow control is not needed in barriers as a prerequisite of entering a barrier is that all outstanding sends/receives of local cores have completed. The synchronization packet is small enough so that the core can drop an entire synchronization packet into its output queue. It can then start a blocking send operation that halts the core's pipeline until synchronization packets become available. This technique significantly reduces synchronization costs when all cores are ready, yet conserves power when they are not.

2.3   Broadcast

Our Broadcast uses the SN of the TilePro64. The SN is more intricate to program and suffers from route setup overhead. However, message forwarding incurs zero

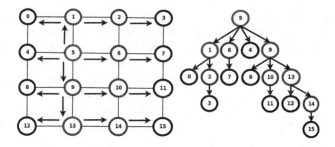

Fig. 4. Broadcast tree: static routes configuration (Color figure online)

overhead (due to a static route configuration). Since broadcast has a single sender and multiple receivers, the number of route configurations is low. This was the motivation behind using SN for the broadcast implementation.

We designed a tree-based algorithm rooted at the task performing the broadcast. Each task determines the root's row and column and configures the SN route. The route setup in the root is such that the message from the core is sent on its available links. All the tasks in the same column as the root have their route configured such that they receive from the root along the Y direction and send the message along other available links. Tasks in other columns receive along one X direction and send the message along the other X link.

For example, let the task with rank 5 initiate a broadcast. Then, its routes are set up to send the message from the core to all the links. The routes of tasks on cores in column one will be set up such that they send out the received message along the X and Y directions. The routes in all the other tasks will be set up in such a way that they will receive and forward along the X direction. This results in a broadcast tree as shown in Fig. 4. Different nodes have different route setup depending on their relative position to the root node. The root node is highlighted in red. The blue nodes receive along the Y direction and send along X direction (East and West). The green nodes receive along the X direction (from West) and send along the X direction (toward East). All the other nodes have receive along the X direction.

The static route of each task is configured inside the Broadcast call such that the message from the root flows to each leaf task. Our current implementation requires only a single route configuration per task and is contention-free.

2.4 Reduce and AllReduce

Our Reduce is similar to the barrier. The reduction operation is performed along the tree. Each child task sends its partial result upward toward the root. The root reduces the partial results to obtain the final result. The construction of the reduction tree is different from that of the Barrier. The reduction tree maps to a NoC grid such that the root task becomes the root of the tree. The tasks along its row become first-level children. The tasks in each column become second-level children to the first-level ones. Via recursive refinement, the algorithm extends to larger meshes, where more levels would be employed.

For example, let rank 5 be the root for the reduction operation. The tasks along its row become the first-level children (in this case, tasks with rank 4, 6 and 7). These first-level children become children of the root. Each column will therefore have a root or a first-level child. All the other tasks become children of the root or first-level children along their column. In the example, rank 5 becomes the root with ranks 1, 4, 6, 7, 9 and 13 as its first-level children. Rank 4 will have ranks 0, 8 and 12 as 2nd-level children etc. This reduction-tree setup is shown in Fig. 5. To avoid contention we impose rounds of communication per level and distance: distance 2 cores to level 1 send their values first (e.g., core 15), followed by distance 1 (e.g., core 11); followed by distance 2 cores to root (e.g., core 7) and distance 1 (e.g., core 6). Each of these four rounds has no link contention by tree construction.

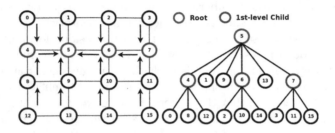

Fig. 5. Reduction tree: setup (Color figure online)

A reduction tree constructed in this fashion has two major advantages: (1) The implementation is simple and scalable and (2) the entire reduction takes place in two steps irrespective of the size of the NoC grid. The first step occurs in parallel for the root and its 1st-level children, where they receive and reduce values from their respective 2nd-level children. In the second step, the root will receive partial results from the 1st-level children and perform the reduction operation.

AllReduce is an extension of Reduce. It is implemented by performing a Reduce relative to rank 0, followed by a broadcast from rank 0 to all other tasks in the group.

3   Framework

Experiments were conducted on a 700 MHz 64-core Tilera TilePro processor (TilePro 64) and the Intel SCC. Our implementation is written in C and the programs were compiled with Tilera's MDE 3.03 tool chain/Intel's ICC at the O3 optimization level with respective C/C++/Fortran compilers. Some cores are used for specific purposes and are not available to run user programs restricting the maximum grid size to 7 × 7 on Tilera. In our experiments, grid sizes ranging from 2 × 2 to 7 × 7 were utilized allowing for a total of six configurations (omitting rectangular, non-square configurations, which are also valid).

OperaMPI implements the MPI 1.2 standard [10] for C. It is layered over Tilera's iLib, an inter-tile communication library that utilizes the UDN NoC network. The iLib library is vendor-supplied software and allows developers to easily take advantage of many features provided by the Tilera architecture. Message passing is one such feature. Point-to-point messages are directly supported by iLib closely resembling the equivalent MPI semantics. Internally, iLib utilizes interrupt-based virtual channels and complex packet encodings to synchronize senders and receivers to set up such point-to-point communication. However, iLib only supports a limited number of collective operations, namely broadcast and barrier. Hence, OperaMPI creates virtual overlays (e.g., binomial trees for reductions, recursive doubling for allreduce) to implement more complex MPI collectives, which result in NoC contention in contrast to our approach. OperaMPI has been evaluated against the IBM, Intel, MPICH and SPEC MPI test suites. Some of these results and implementation details (such as tree reduce/alltoall) are discussed in [8], which provides a fair foundation for comparison to OperaMPI. Furthermore, OperaMPI is the only working MPI implementation on Tilera and other ports (MPICH or Open MPI) are not only beyond the scope of this work but would be subject to the same NoC design/implementation choices we made.

Results of NoCMsg, our scalable and predictable NoC messaging framework, and the third-party OperaMPI and RCKMPI [11,12] were compared for Tilera and SCC, respectively. NoCMsg traffic is routed over the UDN/SN with 1–2 cycles and 1 cycle per hop, respectively, using polling instead of relying on iLib/OperaMPI interrupts with messages packaged in 128 byte flits.

4   Experimental Results

We experimented with of NoCMsg group communication repeating each run 21 times and reporting averages on the Tilera TilePro64 and also the Intel SCC [9] to demonstrate portability. We report the Tilera results first.

4.1   Single Packet Messages

The benchmark timing results for single packet messages are depicted in Figs. 6, 7, 8, 9 and 10 for 5 collectives. Time on the y-axis is plotted logarithmically in microseconds for averaged benchmark runs over different number of tasks (equal to cores) in the range from 4 to 49. Tables 1 and 2 depict execution time variances for each micro-benchmark for varying number of tasks for NoCMsg and OperaMPI, respectively.

We observe that as the number of tasks increases, the execution time of group communication increases. In case of Opera, the increase in runtime is significant for larger number of tasks. In comparison, our NoCMsg implementation is highly efficient, and increases in runtime are gradual. For Alltoall, our pattern-based approach effectively eliminates network contention resulting in a reduction of execution time by about 62 % (from 2027 down to 761) for a 7×7 grid size with a variance of 0.4 to 5.6 depending on the numbers of cores used. This variance is several orders of magnitude lower than that of the OperaMPI particularly for larger number of cores.

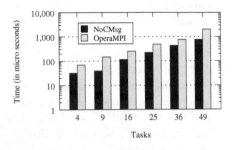

Fig. 6. Timing results for alltoall

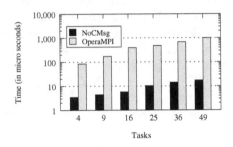

Fig. 7. Timing results for reduce

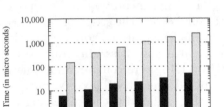

Fig. 8. Timing results for allreduce   **Fig. 9.** Timing results for barrier

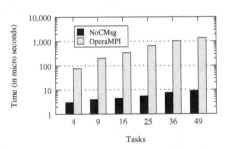

Fig. 10. Timing results for broadcast

Table 1. NoCMsg runtime var. $[\mu s^2]$

Num tasks	4	9	16	25	36	49
Alltoall	0.7	0.4	0.7	5.6	1.3	1.6
Barrier	0.5	0.8	0.4	1.6	1.1	5.6
Broadcast	0	0	0.2	0.24	0.53	0.12
Reduce	0.2	0.12	1.1	1.06	3.96	7.27
AllReduce	1.34	2.29	2.49	26.77	31.55	50.82

Table 2. OperaMPI runtime variance $[\mu s^2]$

Num tasks	4	9	16	25	36	49
Alltoall	3	984	18	2277	133330	622903
Barrier	750	303	29385	1838	2911	32117
Broadcast	7	57	259	4541	3004	3869
Reduce	545	686	21	2007	9980	3431
AllReduce	11	51	49	3839	5536	7517

Barrier and Broadcast are our most efficient collectives with up to 98 % reduction in execution time, i.e., Opera takes up to two orders of magnitude longer due to contention. Broadcast uses the SN with a single route setup (to configure the communication tree, setup time included) and minimal routing overhead. The SN is typically faster than the UDN, which makes Broadcast our most efficient and predictable collective in comparison. (Over UDN, broadcast would be close to the time of a barrier.) Execution time increases only by a factor of 3.5 as the grid size is gradually changed from 2×2 to 7×7 with a variance of less than 0.6 for all cases.

Our implementations of Reduce and Allreduce have 97 % and 98 % lower execution time, respectively, than OperaMPI for all tested grid sizes, i.e., OperaMPI is up to nearly two orders of magnitude slower. However, these collectives have a larger variance than others due to the two-step reduction employed by Reduce operations.

4.2 Varying Message Sizes

Figures 11, 12, 13, 14 and 15 depict the averaged performance for varying message sizes and number of tasks (cores) for both our NoCMsg implementation and OperaMPI, the reference implementation. Notice that execution times are plotted on a logarithmic scale on the y-axis. The solid lines represent execution times for NoCMsg while the dotted lines represent execution times for OperaMPI. The legend further indicates the number of tasks, i.e., key N4 represents NoCMsg with 4 tasks while O4 depicts OperaMPI with 4 tasks with the same color coding for identical grid sizes (in the same order as the line graphs). The range of grid sizes ranges from 4 to 49 total number of tasks (cores).

Figure 11 shows the execution time of the Alltoall collective for message sizes up to 4 KB, which is an inset to Fig. 12, the latter of which extends to 1 MB sizes. The execution and communication times increase with an increase in message size for both NoCMSg and OperaMPI. Our NoCMsg implementation of Alltoall performs very well for small messages with savings between 43 %–62 % up to a threshold (256 Bytes to 4 KB depending on message size and number of tasks, see Fig. 11). Yet, as message sizes increase, performance degrades, and for message sizes greater than this threshold, OperaMPI outperforms NoCMsg (see Fig. 12). This is because our Alltoall implementation is split into rounds of exchanges followed by barrier synchronization to ensure absence of contention. For large messages, this results in noticeable overhead. OperaMPI's Alltoall implementation is split into N-1 stages, where N is the total number of tasks. At each stage, one task takes a turn to send to a partner. While their setup is subject to contention to create a virtual channel, transmission proceeds without contention once a channel has been created, which provides higher bandwidth for large messages. Yet, prior work has shown that typical applications tend to utilize collectives with very small message payloads [13], which indicates that our NoCMsg covers the critical path for most applications and nicely complements OperaMPI's advantage for large messages.

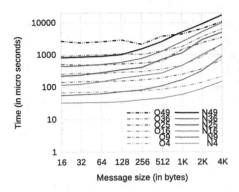

Fig. 11. Alltoall: inset msgs ≤ 4 KB (Color figure online)

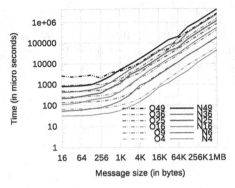

Fig. 12. Alltoall: varying msg sizes (Color figure online)

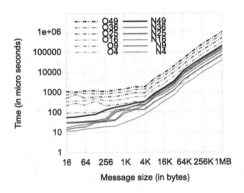

Fig. 13. Reduce: varying msg sizes (Color figure online)

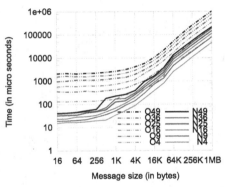

Fig. 14. AllReduce: varying msg sizes (Color figure online)

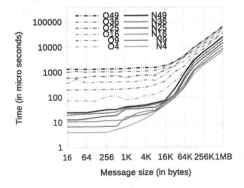

Fig. 15. Broadcast: varying msg sizes (Color figure online)

# tasks	reduce+bcast	recursive doubling
4	13.57	4
9	16.29	6
16	25.43	10
25	26.71	26
36	30.29	51
49	33.00	56

Fig. 16. Allreduce variants: avg. time [usec]

The timing results for Reduce and Allreduce are shown in Figs. 13 and 14, respectively. The execution time of our implementation is 48 %–98 % lower than that of OperaMPI for all message sizes up to 1 MB (and beyond), i.e., OperaMPI is up to two orders of magnitude more costly. However, the gap gradually decreases to about one order of magnitude difference. Asymptotically, the performance results of the two implementations approach each other for very large (but, in practice, unrealistic) message sizes. The implementation of Reduce in OperaMPI uses a communication tree but does not map it to the NoC in a contention-free manner. The resulting contention causes larger communication/execution times. The same observation also holds for AllReduce, a Reduce followed by a Broadcast. Since Reduce dominates the communication and execution time in AllReduce, its behavior is the same as Reduce.

We also compared our version to one that uses recursive doubling. Figure 16 indicates that the former outperforms the latter for larger core sizes while the latter to results in less setup overhead and thus better performance for smaller number of tasks. Collectives tend to involve all tasks in a code, so scalability is key. At 49 cores, the former is almost twice as fast as the latter and has lower asymptotic behavior indicating a higher potential for scalability. We identified the absence of contention in our design as the main contributor of the reduced time over doubling.

Figure 15 represents the execution time of Broadcast for different message sizes. OperaMPI implements Broadcast using a tree-like communication pattern, where the root task initiates the broadcast by sending the message to another task. The two tasks send the message to another two tasks. This transitive distribution of messages continues and eventually terminates after $log(N)$ steps, where N is number of tasks. This communication tree approach is efficient but does not map to the NoC in a contention-free manner. Similar to Reduce, there is always contention resulting in larger communication and execution time. Our Broadcast implementation uses SN unlike OperaMPI, which uses UDN. Routing overhead in SN is lower than that in UDN. This also contributes to better performance and lower execution time. From the NoCMsg curve, we can see that the execution time remains constant for message sizes up to 256 Bytes since only 1–2 flits are required (latency bound). Beyond 256 Bytes, the execution time of NoCMsg Broadcast increases at a higher rate than that of OperaMPI as it transitions from being latency to being bandwidth bound. This continues up to a message size of 128 KB, after which the rate of increase in execution time with increase in message size is nearly same for both NoCMsg and OperaMPI (bandwidth bound). Again, the execution times of the two implementations approach each other asymptotically for very large (but, in practice, unrealistic) message sizes.

Overall, these results show that our NoCMsg implementation is ideal for all/small message sizes depending on the collective primitive. As prior work has indicated, typical MPI applications utilize collectives with very small message payloads [13], and embedded/real-time applications follow a similar trend for numerical, actuator-based control systems. This underlines the contribution of our work for high-end and embedded/real-time applications alike as NoCMsg provides better performance and timing predictability than prior related work for the common case, and, moreover, for realistic 2D meshes without wrap-around network links at grid boundaries.

4.3 NAS Parallel Benchmark

We used NPB version 3.3 to evaluate our implementation. NPB by default uses strong scaling, where input sizes stay fixed for different numbers of cores. We used strong scaling due to input constraints for MG (input class A, to mostly remain on chip in L2 cache) and our own weak scaling inputs for all other benchmarks [14]. Weak scaling ensures that the computational work per core remains the same as the number of cores cooperating in a parallel application is increased. We choose inputs to remain resident in private L2 so that results measure the NoC properties rather than being dominated by off-chip memory traffic.

Figure 17 depicts the results for MG with strong scaling. MG is memory intensive and uses long- and short-distance inter-processor communication. The number of processes grows as a power of 2 resulting in 5 different grid sizes. We observe that NoCMsg is faster than OperaMPI for all grid sizes. Strong input scaling causes the total time to reduce as the number of tasks increases. For small task sizes, NoCMsg is much faster than OperaMPI. As the number of tasks increases, the time difference decreases. This is because MG is memory intensive with limited inter-process communication, and for large grid sizes the performance improvement due to efficient communication declines.

We used weak scaling for IS, FT, CG and LU. IS sorts integer numbers and perform frequent all-to-all collective communication for rebalancing. FT is a discrete 3D Fast Fourier Transform solver for partial differential equations using all-to-all communication. CG estimates Eigenvalues using the conjugate gradient method with irregular memory accesses and communication. LU is a computational fluid dynamics code with stencil-style point-to-point communication.

For IS and CG (Figs. 18 and 19), the execution time of NoCMsg is lower than that of OperaMPI. Performance benefits include both collectives and point-to-point improvements with improvements due to collectives (this paper) and point-to-point messages (for the latter, see [5,6]). The difference in execution time increases with as the number of tasks grows since inter-process communication dominates. For FT (Fig. 20), small differences in execution time between NoCMsg and OperaMPI are due to larger messages sizes.

For LU (Fig. 21), OperaMPI is faster than NoCMsg for small numbers of tasks when computation dominates total execution time. As the number of tasks increases, the inter-task communication starts to dominate the total execution time. The execution time of NoCMsg grows slower than that of OperaMPI, indicating that for larger numbers of tasks NoCMsg provides better performance.

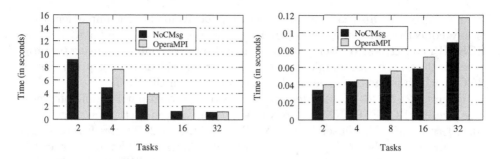

Fig. 17. NPB MG: strong scaling

Fig. 18. NPB IS: weak scaling

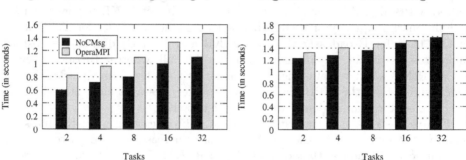

Fig. 19. NPB CG: weak scaling

Fig. 20. NPB FT: weak scaling

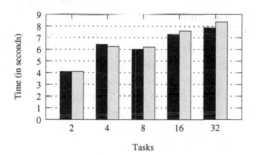

Fig. 21. NPB LU: weak scaling

4.4 Portability

The Intel SCC is a single chip with 48 cores connected by a 6×4 mesh with x/y dimension-ordered routing, where each of the 24 routers is attached to one tile with two local cores [9,15]. There is no cache coherence across the mesh; instead, message passing is supported via bare-bones message with RCCE and MPI-style communication with RCKMPI [11,12]. The mesh is subject to link contention (as was Tilera) but also core contention due to two cores sharing a single router. We ported NoCMsg to the Intel SCC using the same design philosophy in that link (and, for the SCC, also core) contention should be avoided in the implementation of any collective communication primitive, which is not the case for RCCE and RCKMPI collectives. We were able to ensure absence of contention using pattern-based collectives in communication rounds over one-sided put/get primitives of RCCE, which is the lowest level of communication on the SCC.

Figures 22, 23, 24 and 25 depict the effective throughput for different message sizes for RCCE, RCKMPI and NoCMsg (from bottom to top), averaged over 10,000 runs each. We observe that NoCMsg results in 2–5 times higher maximum throughput depending on the type of collective as NoCMsg approaches the theoretical bandwidth of the SCC. (Figure 22 is lacking RCCE results since the API does not support alltoall natively.) This throughput is constrained by the shared MPB SRAM buffer of 384 KB, which is split into 8 KB regions per tile, and the mesh frequency of 1066 MHz. Peaks are reached earlier for [All]Reduce (4 KB) than for Broadcast/Alltoall (128 KB and 196 KB) due to the cost of reductions vs. significant link contention for Alltoall, whereas Broadcast levels out at 15 MB/s but remains high. This is larger than the individual MPB size, which shows that the MPB streams multi-packet messages efficient as long as the data is L2 cache resident, i.e., not exceed 256 KB.

Figure 26 shows that the execution time of broadcasting a 236 KB message remains constant even as the number of cores increases due to pattern-based communication whereas that of RCCE and RCKMPI is one to four orders of magnitude higher for 48 cores. (Notice that 16 or more cores show nearly the same performance. The mesh only has 24 routers, and from 24 to 48 cores, a single copy between core pairs over their pair-wise local bus interconnect suffices.) Fig. 27 depicts the time of a 48-core barrier for each core involved in this collective. We observe that barriers are also 2–3 orders of magnitude faster under NoCMsg compared to RCCE/RCKMPI. We also see that barrier completion varies between even and odd cores, which is visible by the jagged curve for NoCMsg. This is due to two cores sharing a router, where the odd core is served first and then signal its sibling (even) core. The jagged lines for RCCE/RCKMPI are not visible since the y-axis is logarithmic.

Overall, NoCMsg is shown to be portable in its code base and results in significantly better throughput and performance for collectives than contention-oblivious communication methods.

5   Related Work

Communication patterns and communication trees as a means to implement collective operations have been well studied [16]. Barnett's broadcast [17] is loosely based on spanning binomial trees. Yang's tree-based multicast [18] constructs a quad-branch multicast (QBM) tree, a logic tree rooted at the source node of a multicast and has four subtrees. Our implementation of Broadcast uses a communication tree in a contention-free manner. But unlike QBM, our approach does not require special registers/buffers in the routers, support of double-X/Y routing and changes to message headers. QBM also cannot handle alltoallv. Topology-aware collectives [19] reduce but cannot eliminate congestion for HPC interconnect whereas our work eliminates any contention.

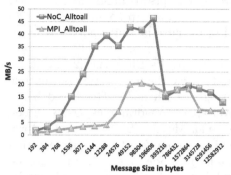

Fig. 22. Throughput for alltoall (Color figure online)

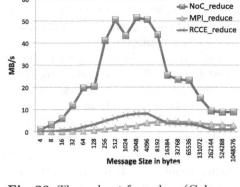

Fig. 23. Throughput for reduce (Color figure online)

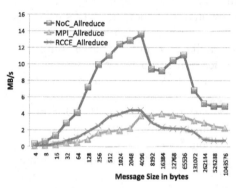

Fig. 24. Throughput for allreduce (Color figure online)

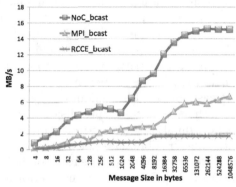

Fig. 25. Throughput for broadcast (Color figure online)

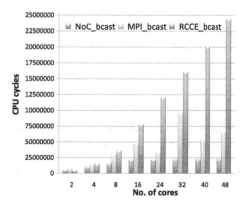

Fig. 26. Broadcast timing over cores (Color figure online)

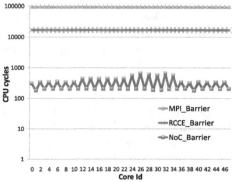

Fig. 27. Timing results per core for barrier (Color figure online)

Several approaches apply graph theoretic concepts to build efficient trees, e.g., a multi-level broadcast tree using extended dominator nodes (EDN) [20] but requires an expensive all-port instead of the current single-port NoC communication architectures.

Barriers were implemented in hardware for IBM's BlueGene [21]. Router-based barriers [22,23] require long headers to carry the information of multiple destinations and incur additional processing at each node. Tree-based barriers [24] partition the 2D mesh into four overlapping quadrants using the chosen root node as the origin whereas Barrier Tree for Meshes (BTM) utilizes a 4-ary synchronization tree constructed in a recursive manner [25]. Our implementation of barrier also uses a tree rooted at a chosen root node, but, unlike the others, neither requires a 2D division into submeshes nor relies on special registers for tree construction.

Our implementation of alltoall exploits pattern-based communication to concurrently exchange messages between partners. On the surface, this approach shares design strategies with Thakur's direct algorithm [26], which assigns mesh nodes ordinal numbers 0..N-1 in a row-major fashion. During step k, for $k = 1..N - 1$, the node with ordinal number i sends a message to the node whose ordinal number is an exclusive or (XOR) of i and k. This results in a communication pattern similar to ours under dimension order routing. Unlike our approach, their direct algorithm suffers from link contention, which is also the case for BG/L's random lists [27].

Others split tasks into disjoint communication groups [28–31]. Our implementation also uses a bottom-up approach, but neither requires a grid division into smaller submeshes nor results in contention.

More recent approaches focus on building static schedules for alltoall communication [32]. Some approaches perform path selection, core mapping and time-slot allocation intelligently to resolve conflicts on shared networks [33]. Others exploit time-division multiplexing on NoCs to solve the slot and path selection problem and this avoid contention [34]. Unlike these approaches, our implementation neither requires dynamic route calculations nor offline pre-calculations nor storage of large routing tables. Our tree-based implementations rely on the relative position of nodes to the root and take advantage of 2D mesh topology to map a tree in a contention-free manner, which is novel. This keeps our implementation simple, generic and scalable with minimum overhead.

6   Conclusion

We designed a set of efficient and predictable group communication primitives using message passing utilizing NoC architectures. The primitives employ highly efficient algorithms to provide contention-free communication and utilize advanced NoC hardware features. These primitives improve performance and reduce imbalance for HPC applications while providing higher timing predictability for embedded/real-time systems.

Our implementation of the most commonly used collectives reduces the communication time over a reference MPI implementation on TilePro64 by up to

95 % for single packet messages and up to 98 % for larger messages. NoCMsg has superior performance over OperaMPI irrespective of message size for all but one collective: For Alltoall, NoCMsg performs better for message sizes up to 256 Bytes while OperaMPI performs better for larger messages. The evaluation of NPB codes shows that NoCMsg outperforms OperaMPI for actual workloads. Our NoCMsg for the Intel SCC shows orders of magnitude increases in performance and 2–5 times higher throughput. NoCMsg thus nicely complements prior work that is efficient at larger (yet less common) message sizes for this case. Additionally, the variance of execution times for our implementation is several orders of magnitude lower than that of the reference MPI implementation, making our implementation ideal for balanced high-end as well as embedded/real-time applications. And instead of assuming ideal NoC symmetry with wrap-around links on the 2D boundaries, our work addresses realistic 2D meshes without wrap-around, such as present in contemporary NoC hardware designs.

References

1. Intel: Tera-scale research prototype: connecting 80 simple cores on a single test chip. ftp://download.intel.com/research/platform/terascale/tera-scaleresearchprototypebackgrounder.pdf
2. Tilera: Tilera processor family. www.tilera.com/products/processors.php
3. Wentzlaff, D., Griffin, P., Hoffmann, H., Bao, L., Edwards, B., Ramey, C., Mattina, M., Miao, C.C., Brown III, J.F., Agarwal, A.: On-chip interconnection architecture of the tile processor. IEEE Micro **27**, 15–31 (2007)
4. Adapteva: Adapteva processor family. www.adapteva.com/products/silicon-devices/e16g301/
5. Zimmer, C., Mueller, F.: NoCMsg: scalable NoC-based message passing. In: International Symposium on Cluster Computing and the Grid (CCGRID), pp. 186–195 (2014)
6. Zimmer, C., Mueller, F.: NoCMsg: a scalable message passing abstraction for network-on-chips. ACM Trans. Archit. Code Optim. **12**(1), 1 (2015)
7. Gabriel, E., et al.: Open MPI: goals, concept, and design of a next generation MPI implementation. In: Kranzlmüller, D., Kacsuk, P., Dongarra, J. (eds.) EuroPVM/MPI 2004. LNCS, vol. 3241, pp. 97–104. Springer, Heidelberg (2004)
8. Kang, M., Park, E., Cho, M., Suh, J., Kang, D.I., Crago, S.P.: MPI performance analysis and optimization on Tile64/Maestro. In: Workshop on Multi-core Processors for Space – Opportunities and Challenges, July 2009
9. Mattson, T., van der Wijngaart, R., Riepen, M., Lehnig, T., Brett, P., Haas, W., Kennedy, P., Howard, J., Vangal, S., Borkar, N., Ruhl, G., Dighe, S.: The 48-core SCC processor: the programmer's view. In: Supercomputing, November 2010
10. Gropp, W., Lusk, E., Doss, N., Skjellum, A.: A high-performance, portable implementation of the MPI message passing interface standard. Parallel Comput. **22**(6), 789–828 (1996)
11. Wijngaart, R.V.D., Mattson, T.: RCCE: a small library for many-core communication (2010)
12. Comprés Ureña, I.A., Riepen, M., Konow, M.: RCKMPI – lightweight MPI Implementation for intel's single-chip cloud computer (SCC). In: Cotronis, Y., Danalis, A., Nikolopoulos, D.S., Dongarra, J. (eds.) EuroMPI 2011. LNCS, vol. 6960, pp. 208–217. Springer, Heidelberg (2011)

13. Vetter, J., Mueller, F.: Communication characteristics of large-scale scientific applications for contemporary cluster architectures. In: International Parallel and Distributed Processing Symposium, April 2002
14. Gustafson, J.L.: Reevaluating Amdahl's law. Commun. ACM **31**(5), 532–533 (1988)
15. Howard, J: A 48-Core IA-32 message-passing processor with DVFS in 45nm CMOS. In: IEEE International Solid-State Circuits Conference, pp. 108–109, February 2010
16. McKinley, P.K., Tsai, J.I., Robinson, D.F.: A survey of collective communication in wormhole-routed massively parallel computers. IEEE Comput. **28**, 39–50 (1994)
17. Barnett, M., Payne, D.G., van de Geijn, R.A.: Optimal broadcasting in mesh-connected architectures. Technical report, Austin, TX, USA (1991)
18. Yang, J.S., King, C.T.: Efficient tree-based multicast in wormhole-routed 2D meshes. In: Proceedings of the 1997 International Symposium on Parallel Architectures, Algorithms and Networks, ISPAN 1997, Washington, DC, USA, pp. 494–500. IEEE Computer Society (1997)
19. Sack, P., Gropp, W.: Faster topology-aware collective algorithms through non-minimal communication. In: ACM SIGPLAN Symposium on Principles and Practice of Parallel Programming, pp. 45–54 (2012)
20. Tsai, Y.J., McKinley, P.K.: Broadcast in all-port wormhole-routed 3D mesh networks using extended dominating sets. In: Proceedings of the 1994 International Conference on Parallel and Distributed Systems, Washington, DC, USA, pp. 120–127. IEEE Computer Society (1994)
21. Ramakrishnan, V., Scherson, I.D.: Efficient techniques for nested and disjoint barrier synchronization. J. Parallel Distrib. Comput. **58**(2), 333–356 (1999)
22. Lin, X., McKinley, P.K., Ni, L.M.: Deadlock-free multicast wormhole routing in 2D mesh multicomputers. IEEE Trans. Parallel Distrib. Syst. **5**(8), 793–804 (1994)
23. Panda, D.K.: Fast barrier synchronization in wormhole k-ary n-cube networks with multi destination worms. In: Proceedings of the 1st IEEE Symposium on High-Performance Computer Architecture, HPCA 1995, Washington, DC, USA, pp. 200–209. IEEE Computer Society (1995)
24. Yang, J.S., King, C.T.: Designing tree-based barrier synchronization on 2D mesh networks. IEEE Trans. Parallel Distrib. Syst. **9**(6), 526–534 (1998)
25. Moh, S., Yu, C., Lee, B., Youn, H.Y., Han, D., Lee, D.: Four-ary tree-based barrier synchronization for 2D meshes without nonmember involvement. IEEE Trans. Comput. **50**(8), 811–823 (2001)
26. Thakur, R., Choudhary, A.: All-to-all communication on meshes with wormhole routing. In: Proceedings of the 8th International Parallel Processing Symposium, pp. 561–565 (1994)
27. Almási, G., Heidelberger, P., Archer, C.J., Martorell, X., Erway, C.C., Moreira, J.E., Steinmacher-Burow, B., Zheng, Y.: Optimization of MPI collective communication on BlueGene/L systems. In: International Conference on Supercomputing, pp. 253–262 (2005)
28. Bokhari, S., Berryman, H.: Complete exchange on a circuit switched mesh. In: Proceedings of the Scalable High Performance Computing Conference, SHPCC 1992, pp. 300–306 (1992)
29. Sundar, N.S., Jayasimha, D.N., Panda, D., Sadayappan, P.: Complete exchange in 2D meshes. In: Proceedings of the Scalable High-Performance Computing Conference, pp. 406–413 (1994)
30. Suh, Y.J., Shin, K.G.: All-to-all personalized communication in multidimensional torus and mesh networks. IEEE Trans. Parallel Distrib. Syst. **12**(1), 38–59 (2001)

31. Suh, Y.J., Yalamanchili, S.: All-to-all communication with minimum start-up costs in 2D/3D tori and meshes. IEEE Trans. Parallel Distrib. Syst. **9**(5), 442–458 (1998)
32. Brandner, F., Schoeberl, M.: Static routing in symmetric real-time network-on-chips. In: International Conference on Real-Time and Network Systems, pp. 61–70 (2012)
33. Hansson, A., Goossens, K., Rădulescu, A.: A unified approach to constrained mapping and routing on network-on-chip architectures. In: Proceedings of the 3rd IEEE/ACM/IFIP International Conference on Hardware/Software Codesign and System Synthesis, CODES+ISSS 2005, New York, NY, USA, pp. 75–80. ACM (2005)
34. Stefan, R., Goossens, K.: An improved algorithm for slot selection in the ethereal network-on-chip. In: International Workshop on Interconnection Network Architecture: On-Chip, Multi-Chip, pp. 7–10 (2011)

Distributed Job Allocation for Large-Scale Manycores

Subramanian Ramachandran and Frank Mueller[✉]

North Carolina State University, Raleigh, NC 27695-8206, USA
mueller@cs.ncsu.edu

Abstract. Contemporary operating systems heavily rely on single system images with shared memory constructs that may not scale well to large core counts. We consider the challenge of distributed job allocation, where each job is comprised of a set of tasks to be mapped to disjoint cores. A naive solution performing fragmented allocations may quickly escalate to deadlocks, where jobs hold and wait for cores in circular dependencies. To tackle these challenges, we propose a deadlock free distributed job allocation protocol. We have devised two policies for avoiding deadlocks, namely *active cancellation* and *sequencer-based atomic broadcast*. The protocol and the two policies have been implemented and evaluated on a Tilera TilePro64 processor with 64 cores on a single socket. Results show sparse job allocations to incur lower overhead for *active cancellation* while *sequencer-based atomic broadcast* has less overhead for denser allocations.

1 Introduction

While Moore's law has held for a considerable time in microprocessor design, it has reached its limits and may not keep pace with the ever increasing processing demand. Nonetheless, multicore/manycore processors have the potential to enjoy continued performance increases to meet future processing needs while reducing/constraining power consumption. Current trends in the industry indicate that the number of cores that fit on a single chip is rapidly increasing. With current single microprocessor chips packing 64+ cores on a die [1–3] and specialized computing devices, e.g., graphic processing units (GPUs), already support over 1000 core today.

Current multicores fall short of their scalability potential. One reason for this stems from reusing conventional Single System Image (SSI) OS designs for multicore architectures. With SSI, resources are aggregated to present a single view of the OS environment while data access and communication are realized via shared memory over traditional bidirectional buses. This approach delivers some performance increases in the natural evolution from single core up to 16 cores, but it deteriorates rapidly when the number of cores increases further [4]. Recent work [4–6] shows that coherent shared memory may not scale

This work was supported in part by NSF grants 0905181 and 1239246.

© Springer International Publishing Switzerland 2016
J.M. Kunkel et al. (Eds.): ISC High Performance 2016, LNCS 9697, pp. 404–425, 2016.
DOI: 10.1007/978-3-319-41321-1_21

well to large core counts. They instead promote the usage of scalable message passing for OS communication in large-scale manycores. Intel's Knights Landing (KNL) next-generation Xeon Phi provides L2 cache coherence via SSI, which may lead to contention at the mesh interconnect, similar to the overheads of shared memory shown to exceed those of simple message passing over the network-on-chip (NoC) for 16 cores or more in previous Tilera research [4,7]. Based on these observations, we conjecture that future large-scale NoCs may support shared memory partitions only for partitions of 8–16 cores complemented by message passing across partitions. This would depart from an SSI design and necessitate a distributed paradigm, which then requires a distributed job allocation approach for parallel codes to be executed, the focus of this work. An alternative solution would be hierarchical locks for non-uniform memory access (NUMA) systems [8], but this would still require a centralized job allocation strategy with limitations on scalability whereas a distributed approach is more general We believe that research on distributed designs for NoCs is essential for now as the implications of scalability limitations persist.

In this work, we propose a novel protocol to tackle the challenges of job allocation in a distributed system. Allocating jobs of tasks on a partitioned multi-resource system is known to be NP-hard, even for prioritized jobs [9]. The problem is further complicated in a distributed system due to the distributed nature of job generation. A naive approach allowing fragmented allocations could quickly lead to deadlocks in the job allocation algorithm. Our distributed job allocation protocol with two policies, *active cancellation* and *sequencer-based atomic broadcast*, takes a well disciplined approach in solving these issues. First, we avoid deadlocks by enforcing a globally unique order to resolve conflicting job allocations. Second, we split the job allocation problem into two subproblems: (1) query and reserve available resources; (2) find a good task-to-core mapping. Such a split enables effective heuristics [10,11] to tackle NP-hard task-to-core mapping while our distributed job allocation protocol reserves cores for the job.

While our distributed job allocation protocol is generic in scheduling any application, we use Message Passing Interface (MPI) [12] applications as our standard workload in this work for the following reasons: All ranks (tasks) of an MPI program need to start execution at the same time. Such a workload demands guaranteed availability of cores to start execution or waits until they are available. This allows us to model the job wait time as the overhead of the distributed job allocation protocol. And enables more flexible execution models where tasks are dynamically created in a distributed manner, e.g., using fine-grained task graphs to track dependencies.

In summary, this paper, makes the following contributions: (1) We propose the Pico-kernel Adaptive and Scalable Operating System (PICASO) to address the scalability challenges of future manycore processors. (2) We analyze the distributed job allocation problem and present a protocol with two policies, *active cancellation* and *sequencer-based atomic broadcast*. (3) We evaluate the solutions on the Tilera TilePro64 through a set of benchmarks to analyze the performance and scalability.

2   PICASO

PICASO features a distributed message passing system comprised of pico-kernels per core. Pico-kernels are worker cores that execute a job's user tasks. A set of pico-kernels are managed by a micro-kernel. Micro-kernels are dedicated cores for control purposes, e.g., to manage a set of pico-kernels and schedule jobs in coordination with other micro-kernels. Let a *micro-kernel domain* be the set of pico-kernels governed by this micro-kernel. Micro-kernels are typically topographically centered within its domain.

A pico-kernel reports only to its parent micro-kernel. A micro-kernel, on the other hand, apart from controlling its set of pico-kernels, also co-ordinates with other micro-kernels. An advantage of such a system is the decentralization of control, where each micro-kernel may engage in fast and autonomous decisions on managing its set of pico-kernels. Since pico-kernels are just worker cores, we use the terms pico-kernels and cores interchangeably in this work. Figure 1 shows how a PICASO system with micro- and pico-kernel abstraction can be organized in a large-scale manycore system. In contrast to other manycores, PICASO partitions the available cores into different domains represented by different colors. Each domain has a topologically centered core chosen to be the micro-kernel. The chosen micro-kernels (in red) manage their set of pico-kernels. All external interactions occur only between micro-kernels.

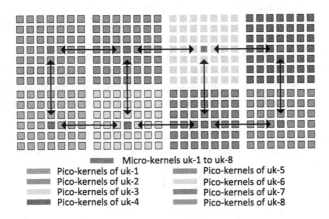

Fig. 1. Sample micro kernel (uk) plus pico kernel abstraction for manycores (Color figure online)

3   Distributed Job Allocation

We use the following terminology in our discussion: (1) A *task* is the basic unit of execution. (2) A *job* consists of a collection of tasks. (3) The *home micro-kernel* of a particular job is the micro-kernel where the job submission was initiated.

Assumptions: In this work, we consider jobs that require to be co-scheduled, i.e., these jobs consist of inter-dependent tasks that need to be concurrently executed on different nodes/cores. An example would be jobs of MPI programs, where all associated tasks need to start execution at the same time. Such a job allocation process can be divided into two steps: (1) Query available idle cores and reserve them for this job. (2) Devise the best possible task-to-core mapping from the available cores. Our focus in this paper is on the former part. Once enough cores are reserved for a job, methods and results from prior work [10, 11] can be applied to find the best task-to-core mapping for a given job. However, the problem becomes more complicated when extended to a distributed system due to the nature of job generation.

Conventional solutions involve a centralized resource manager that handles all job allocations. All cores continuously report their availability to this entity. Such an approach does not scale to a large number of cores due to (1) contention at the centralized entity (because of the incessant status updates) and (2) a single point of failure. More importantly, it allows for only a single job submission portal. These restrictions are undesirable for large core counts where jobs generate allocations queued up at different cores throughout the system.

Our proposed pico-/micro kernel distributed system abstraction partitions the available cores between different micro-kernels. This domain-specific delegation of scheduling capabilities to micro-kernels enables jobs that can be locally satisfied within a single micro-kernel domain to be handled by fast and autonomous decisions.

For jobs requiring more cores than can be locally satisfied, the *home micro-kernel*, where the particular job is submitted, co-ordinates with other micro-kernels to devise the allocation of cores to this job. Multiple job requests submitted at different micro-kernels could compete with each other for resources. Hence, we need a co-ordination protocol to resolve these conflicts and to choose the next job to execute loosely based on a globally unique order. This global unique order could be based on user-defined priority or a First Come First Serve (FCFS) policy. Such an ordering guarantees fairness and avoids starvation. Adhering to loose ordering rather than strict allows non-conflicting job allocations to proceed in parallel, thereby increasing the system utilization.

But a lack of such co-ordination protocols may lead to deadlocks. Deadlocks can happen when multiple jobs submitted at different micro-kernels hold different subsets of cores and wait for more cores to become available. Yet, none are able to proceed because all cores have been allocated to jobs without meeting the full allocation request of any single job in full. Figure 2 shows a deadlock condition with two micro-kernel domains. Each domain has initially 8 pico-kernels (worker cores) available. In step 1, two job submissions require 12 and 16 cores, respectively. In step 2, each job first holds on to available local cores and sends out a request for more cores. In step 3, each micro-kernel is blocked waiting indefinitely for responses to their requests. Since none of the job requests are fully satisfied, the system remains deadlocked.

Random back-off schemes could be used to recover in case of potential deadlocks. In such a method, different micro-kernels yield their cores and retry their job allocations after waiting for a randomly chosen back-off time. This probabilistically avoids a deadlock again, but fails to guarantee a bound on completion

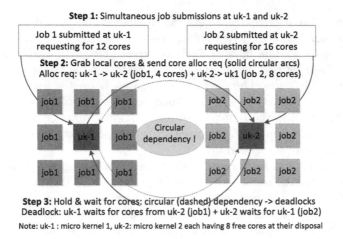

Fig. 2. Deadlock: 2 simultaneous jobs submissions (uk = micro-kernel)

time for the allocation algorithm. A more serious issue is potential starvation of jobs that require large allocations as they might never be satisfied. Therefore, a job allocation algorithm that avoids starvation with an upper bound on completion time is required.

4   Deadlock-Free Job Allocation

We have devised a distributed job allocation protocol for large-scale manycores. Two policies for deadlock avoidance are proposed, namely (1) active cancellation and (2) sequencer-based atomic broadcast. Both of these policies require that a globally unique order be established. For example, we could use timestamps of the job submission time along with the micro-kernel identifier to devise a globally unique job identifier, or we could use user-defined priorities in conjunction with a method to break ties for matching priorities. For the discussion in this work, we will refer to job priority based on a globally unique job ordering rather than a user-defined priority. In the following sections, we examine the two different approaches, compare their capabilities and finally conclude with a detailed performance evaluation.

4.1   The Main Scheduling Loop

Algorithm 1 shows the main scheduling loop. It performs two main functions: (1) Process any incoming message, and (2) in the absence of an incoming message, schedule pending job requests submitted at this micro-kernel.

The scheduling loop uses message passing as the only means of communication between micro-kernels, and between a micro-kernel and its set of pico-kernels. There can also be architecture-specific optimizations for micro- to pico-kernel communication, not shown here.

Algorithm 1. Scheduling loop at each micro-kernel

```
while TRUE do
    post nonblocking receive for fixed size header
    repeat
        if policy == active cancellation then
            schedule job via active cancellation // (2)
        else if policy == atomic broadcast then
            schedule jobs via atomic broadcast // (2)
        end if
    until fixed size header is received
    receive entire message body (blocking) // (1)
    call respective message handler routine
end while
```

The significant message types of the distributed job allocation protocol are as follows: *Core Allocation Request:* Sent by the *home micro-kernel* of the job. The request is propagated to all micro-kernels via an efficient request propagation scheme. *Core Allocation Response:* Sent by a micro-kernel when it commits certain cores to a particular job. *Job Spawn Request:* Sent by the *home micro-kernel* when it devises the best task allocation for the given job. This request follows the same propagation path earlier traversed by the *Core Allocation Request*. Micro-kernels that are not part of an allocation, release their reservations for this job when they receive this request. *Job Cancel Request:* When the *active cancellation* policy is used, this message is sent by the *home micro kernel* if it determines that there is an higher priority job to be satisfied first (see Subsect. 4.2). *Submit Job to Sequencer:* Under the *sequencer-based atomic broadcast* policy, all micro-kernels use this message to submit their job requests to the fixed sequencer (see Subsect. 4.3).

4.2   Active Cancellation

The periodic *active cancellation* procedure works as follows: Any micro-kernel that launches a job requiring more than the locally satisfiable cores sends a core allocation request to all its neighbors. This request is propagated to all other micro-kernels via an efficient request propagation scheme (see Sect. 4.4). A greedy policy is employed, i.e., the request to *each* micro-kernel always asks for the total number of cores required for the job, even if other micro-kernels have already simultaneously allocated a subset of cores for this job. This policy frequently allocates more cores than needed for a job, but guarantees a successful allocation (of cores committed to this job) and facilitates termination (unlike non-greedy approaches).

The algorithm handles the arrival of a higher priority core allocation request as follows: Each micro-kernel maintains a wait queue based on the globally unique order consisting of both the job requests it has sent out and the job requests it has received. All incoming job requests are inserted in the wait queue as per the globally unique ordering. If the new request is the head of the wait queue, it first checks if this request has a higher priority than any job request it has sent out earlier. If so, it engages in active cancellation of the lower priority job changing it to the BLOCKED state pending a renewed request. This frees up resources otherwise allocated to unsuccessful lower priority job requests. Finally, the micro-kernel commits as many cores as it can afford for this job request by responding with the committed cores to the *home micro-kernel* of this particular job request. The micro-kernel contributes new cores to this commitment whenever its resources become free. This scheme satisfies multiple job requests *loosely* based on the global ordering but also offers a relaxation to this hard criteria by allowing a lower priority request to proceed if its allocation is satisfied quickly enough before a higher priority job overrides it in the wait queue. This relaxation is allowed under the assumption that any job using a successful allocation will *eventually* complete, after which time the resources it was given becomes available for the next high priority job in the wait queue (bounded by the longest job).

4.3   Sequencer Based Atomic Broadcast

This method is inspired by the sequencer based atomic broadcast as explained in Défago et al. [13]. In this method, a micro-kernel is elected to be the single sequencer of the system. All job requests, even if submitted at different micro-kernels, are in turn forwarded to the sequencer to ensure globally unique ordering. The sequences sends the request to all the micro-kernels only once it has determined which job to execute next. Our approach differs here. Instead of broadcasting the request, we use a custom built request propagation scheme as explained in Sect. 4.4. This ensures that the job allocations happen in order without any collisions. Less conflicts directly translate to fewer messages compared to *active cancellation*. But since each micro-kernel has to send requests to the sequencer, it leads to contention at the sequencer and additional delays even for small allocation requests, which could have been solved with just a few neighboring micro-kernels. As we show in Sect. 7, this additional overhead translates into real performance benefits only in case of dense and large job allocations.

4.4   Pattern-Based Message Propagation

An efficient method for propagating request messages, such as core allocation and job spawn requests from any given source to all other micro-kernels in a 2D mesh topology, is required. Multi-casting messages from a given source to all micro-kernels is inefficient as this involves sending individual messages to each micro-kernel, unless hardware support for multi-casting exists [14]. Therefore, we have designed and implemented two alternatives: (1) a fixed pattern-based propagation scheme and (2) an adaptive pattern-based propagation scheme. We use the term *nodes* when introducing these schemes, as they not only apply to micro-kernels but any set of nodes in a 2D mesh topology. The adaptive pattern-based propagation scheme has the advantage that it does not expect nodes to be arranged in a 2D mesh topology.

Fixed Pattern-Based Propagation. When a message needs to be sent to all nodes in a 2D mesh processor NoC, the source sends the message only to its neighboring nodes. Each neighbor in turn propagates the request to its next set of unvisited neighbors following a predefined pattern over a minimum spanning tree. The pattern depends on the placement of the initial source of the message. Consider Fig. 3(a). The source initially sends the request to all its neighbors with an embedded information to propagate the request toward the East (and North if in column 1). Each node receiving this message propagates the request as per the embedded information. Similarly, if the source is located at bottom-right, the propagation will be toward West(+North) etc. Fig. 3(b) shows the pattern when the source is located at the center, in which case each arm takes the responsibility of propagating the request in all four directions. Following such a predefined pattern avoids duplicate requests, which waste link resources and increase processing time at the nodes.

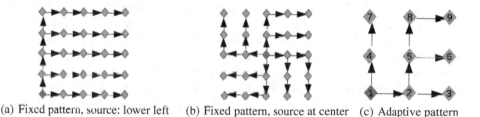

(a) Fixed pattern, source: lower left   (b) Fixed pattern, source at center   (c) Adaptive pattern

Fig. 3. Pattern-based request propagation schemes

Adaptive Pattern-Based Propagation. This scheme involves an initialization phase responsible for forming the adaptive pattern. In this phase, an empty message is forwarded from the given source to all its neighbors. Each neighbor in turn broadcasts the message to all of its next set of neighbors until all the nodes have been visited. At this point, each node has received the given message from multiple sources. It chooses one among these sources as a preferred source and informs it. The preferred source remembers this decision and forwards all messages it receives to this node. The criteria to choose the preferred source can be based on various policies, e.g., the first received request or shortest distance from the source to this node, to name a few. At the end of the first phase, every node has identified its preference from which source it wishes to receive a request in the future; or, alternatively, each node has remembered a list of neighbors to forward a message to that was received from a particular source. This forms an adaptive pattern (spanning tree) ensuring each node receives a message only once. An advantage of such adaptive patterns compared to fixed patterns is that the patterns could be adaptively rearranged in case of link failures. The initialization phase needs to be run only once during the system startup or when recovering from faults, hence reducing the overhead by amortizing the costs.

As an example, consider the pattern shown in Fig. 3(c) for a 3×3 tile with numbered nodes. This pattern is formed with 1 as the source node and forwarding paths from nodes 1 to 2 & 4, 2 to 3 & 5, 4 to 7, 5 to 8 & 6 and 8 to 9.

5   Implementation

The distributed job allocation protocols are applicable to any system of inter-networked cores, even heterogeneous cores [1,14]. But for the purpose of implementation and experimentation alone, the job allocator has been optimized for a 2D-mesh architecture, such as the Tilera TilePro64 [1,2]. The Tilera TilePro64 processor has 64 tiles interconnected with a 2D-Mesh NoC interconnect. Each tile has a processor engine running at 700 MHz, a switch engine for routing on the NoC over five different network interconnects and a cache engine. The User Dynamic Network (UDN) interconnect is the only one available for user-generated messages. We use the services of the NoCMsg [4] library. NoCMsg provides a deadlock free, scalable and efficient low-level message passing layer over UDN with an MPI like interface. This motivated our design choice and, hence, our scheduling loop. The protocols and the messages were designed entirely around these MPI like interfaces. This, in itself, makes our design generic enough to be ported to other message passing libraries as well.

For our experiments, we use an ordering based on a FCFS policy. Each tile on the TilePro64 has synchronized clocks. Hence, we use the time-stamp of the job submission along with the unique micro-kernel identifier of the job's home micro-kernel as a tie breaker for job submissions.

6   Evaluation Framework

We use the TilePro64 processor [1] for our evaluation. While the TilePro64 supports 64 tiles, at least two tiles are reserved exclusively by Tilera's hypervisor for administrative tasks and Input/Output operations. The maximum square tile size that can be reserved for user tasks is 7×7. We choose a square tile size so as to eliminate possibilities of discrepancies due to other asymmetric tile sizes. Overall, the Tilera platform limits our evaluation to 49 cores. Tilera supports a subset of Linux (but not a fully compatible Linux design) for system calls that go through the hypervisor. Job allocation, however, becomes the responsibility of the user to pin tasks to specific cores. We lift this burden via our distributed job allocation design, which is agnostic of Tilera's Linux layer and generalizes to any distributed OS design.

We support two different experimental frameworks for testing the performance of the job allocator, (1) a *real task* mode, and (2) a *partial simulation* mode. The *real task* mode supports execution of jobs that are MPI programs from the NAS Parallel benchmarks (NPB). Figure 4 shows the *real task* mode on the Tilera TilePro64 processor. This small PICASO system on a 6×6 tile has been divided into four regions. Each region has a topologically centered micro-kernel managing a set of 8 pico-kernels. Thus, a combination of NPB of power of two sizes (1,2,4,8,16 and 32) can be executed. This platform is primarily used to assess the schedulability of real user tasks.

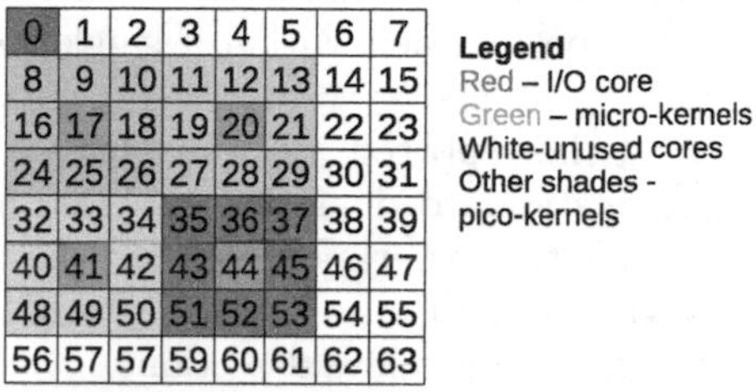

0	1	2	3	4	5	6	7
8	9	10	11	12	13	14	15
16	17	18	19	20	21	22	23
24	25	26	27	28	29	30	31
32	33	34	35	36	37	38	39
40	41	42	43	44	45	46	47
48	49	50	51	52	53	54	55
56	57	57	59	60	61	62	63

Legend
Red – I/O core
Green – micro-kernels
White-unused cores
Other shades -
pico-kernels

Fig. 4. PICASO system, 6×6 tile on TilePro64 (Color figure online)

The limited number of usable cores on the TilePro64 constraints our scalability tests on the *real task* mode. To overcome this, we have developed a *partial simulation* framework, where we consider all cores in the reserved tile as micro-kernels without pico-kernels. Task execution is simulated by timers triggering a job completion message after a certain user-defined execution time. This simulation platform is justified by the fact that the distributed job allocation protocol requires only micro-kernel interaction. Our results could be directly translated to the *real task* mode combining them with the pico-kernel management overheads obtained in the *real task* mode. *Partial simulation* assesses our protocol with up to 49 micro-kernels on a 7×7 tile.

The following sections detail the experiments/results under the *real task* mode and the *partial simulation* mode for different job allocation mixtures.

7   Experimental Results

The distributed job allocator and user programs are compiled as applications with O3 optimizations using Tilera's C/C++/Fortran compilers of the Multicore Development Environment (MDE) 3.03.

7.1   Performance Analysis

We first analyze the performance of both proposed schemes under *partial simulation*. We execute a set of job loads. For each job, we measure the job allocation overhead as the wait time of the job from the time of submission to the time it receives all the resources to execute. This wait time includes both the overhead of the distributed job allocation protocol and the time spent waiting for the earlier job allocations to terminate and to release its cores. Our focus is to measure the overhead of the distributed job allocation protocol in isolation. Hence, for performance tests, we use an initial state where no jobs are active. We then trigger simultaneous job submissions from different micro-kernels as they have the highest probability to result in fragmented allocations. This creates a workload for our protocol triggering its deadlock avoidance subsystem. Note that all our experiments cover cases where the job allocations require large numbers of cores that need more than one micro-kernel domain to be fully satisfied. Recall that job allocations, which could be satisfied within a single micro-kernel domain, have a constant overhead.

For all our experiments, the reported job wait times are averaged over 15 runs. The maximum relative standard deviation observed in these experiments was less than 20 %, except for the experiment in Fig. 5(b) with a relative standard deviations of up to 41 %. We discuss this exception and other significant experimental details in the following relevant sections.

In our experiments, we compare both our proposed polices, *active cancellation* and *sequencer-based atomic broadcast*, against one another. When reporting the relative performance improvement or degradation, we always follow the convention of comparing *active cancellation* against *sequencer-based atomic broadcast* as follows: Let the overhead of *active cancellation* be denoted as O_{ac} and the overhead of *sequencer-based atomic broadcast* be denoted as O_{ab}. Then the relative performance change of *active cancellation* is given by: $\frac{(O_{ab}-O_{ac})}{O_{ab}} \times 100\,\%$

7.2   Overhead for Sparse Job Allocations

This experiment uses the *partial simulation* mode. Job allocation requests are generated simultaneously from the four extreme corners of a 7×7 tile. These requests can be satisfied with just a few nearby micro-kernels even before the conflicting job requests arrive from the other corners. Hence, in most of these cases, cancellation of the lower priority job request may not even be required as all the simultaneously submitted jobs are satisfied without the need for global ordering. Conversely, with *sequencer-based atomic broadcast*, all requests have to still go to the single sequencer, which can only serve one request at a time so that serialization delays impact these small job allocations. This experiment proves that *active cancellation* provides best performance in scenarios where sparse job submissions can proceed in parallel.

In the following set of experiments, we consider two scenarios: Jobs that can be execute in parallel and jobs that need to be executed serially one after another.

Jobs Executing in Parallel. Figure 5(a) and 5(b) depict the scenario where each job can proceed in parallel. For the four jobs (x-axis), their corresponding job wait times are depicted (y-axis). The job wait time does not include execution times of prior jobs as all these jobs execute in parallel. Hence, the measured job wait time can be considered as the exclusive protocol overhead. We observe a relative decrease in the job wait times for *active cancellation* when compared to *sequencer-based atomic broadcast*.

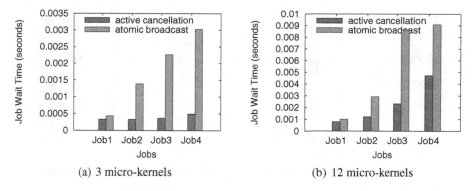

(a) 3 micro-kernels   (b) 12 micro-kernels

Fig. 5. Overhead for parallel allocations (a) 3 micro-kernels (b) 12 micro-kernels (Color figure online)

In the 1st experiment (Fig. 5(a)), each job requires a number of pico-kernels (cores) that is satisfied with available cores from 3 out of a total of 49 micro-kernel domains. We observed a relative performance improvement for *active cancellation* over *sequencer-based atomic broadcast* of 23 % for the 1st job, 76 % for the 2nd job and 83 % for the 3rd and 4th jobs. The serialization at the sequencer results in "backpressure" that aggregates latency (compared to resolving requests in parallel).

In the 2nd experiment (Fig. 5(b)), each job requires a number of pico-kernels (cores) that is satisfied with available cores from 12 out of the total 49 micro-kernel domains. The relative performance improvement of *active cancellation* over *sequencer-based atomic broadcast* for the four jobs were: 21 % for the first job, 58 % for the second job, 73 % for the third job and 48 % for the fourth job. For *active cancellation*, we observe a maximum relative standard deviation of 41 % in this experiment, which is explained as follows: The wait time of each job depends on how many cancellations are required after the first job has been successfully allocated. In some runs, we observe that a lower priority job request propagated fast enough to succeed in its allocation before a higher priority job triggers cancellation. In these cases, the job wait times for the lower priority jobs are reduced. They are otherwise above average if more cancellations occur.

Jobs Executing Serially. When jobs execute serially, job wait times depend largely on execution times of preceding jobs. When prior jobs take a long time, this becomes the main contributor to the job wait time. Conversely, when the execution time is lower than the minimum job allocation overhead, then the overhead of the distributed job allocation protocol is the main contributor to the job wait time. Hence, for the next two experiments, we consider both short and long running jobs. Short running jobs help assess the actual overhead of the two polices. Long running jobs demonstrate that for serially executing jobs, this performance improvement is not entirely carried over as a reduction in the job wait times.

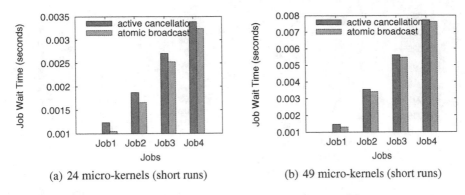

(a) 24 micro-kernels (short runs)   (b) 49 micro-kernels (short runs)

Fig. 6. Overhead for short jobs (a) 24 micro-kernels (short runs) (b) 49 micro-kernels (short runs) (Color figure online)

Short Running Jobs: We set the job execution times to 0.001 seconds, which is below the minimum overhead observed. Figure 6(a) depicts a case where each job requires a number of pico-kernels (cores) that is satisfied by exactly 24 out of the total 49 micro-kernel domains. Hence, two out of the four jobs can run in parallel. As not all jobs can run in parallel, allocations of the lower priority jobs require cancellation so that the allocation of higher priority jobs is satisfied. This results in an additional overhead for *active cancellation* compared to *sequencer-based atomic broadcast* of ≈ 17 % and ≈ 12 %, respectively, for the first two jobs, but considerably less for the next two jobs (7 % and 4 %, respectively). Figure 6(b) depicts the case where all jobs require a number of pico-kernels (cores) that is satisfied by exactly all available 49 micro-kernel domains and, hence, execute serially one after another. Here, *active cancellation* incurs additional overhead as lower priority job allocations need to be canceled to enforce the globally unique order. The overhead for *active cancellation* is ≈ 12 % for the 1st job and reduces considerably to 4 % for the 2nd job, and then to ≈ 1 % for the 3rd/4th jobs.

Long Running Jobs: For these experiments, we set the job execution times to 0.5 seconds, which is much higher than the overhead of the distributed job allocation protocol. Hence, in these cases, the execution time is the main contributor to the job wait time. During the initial execution delay for the spawned jobs, the job allocation protocol reorders the job wait queue. Therefore, subsequent jobs are spawned as soon as the earlier jobs complete with a minimal overhead. Figure 7(a) depicts a case where each job requires a number of pico-kernels (cores) that is satisfied by exactly 24 out of the total 49 micro-kernel domains. Hence, two out of the four jobs can run in parallel. Job wait times are depicted on the y-axis on a *logarithmic* scale. Here, *active cancellation* incurs an additional overhead of 17 % and 13 %, for the first two jobs, respectively. The additional overhead for the next two jobs is very minimal (0.03 % to 0.05 %). Figure 7(b) depicts the case where all jobs require a number of pico-kernels (cores) that is satisfied by exactly all available 49 micro-kernel domains and, hence, execute serially one after another.

Job wait times are depicted on the y-axis on a *logarithmic* scale again. Here, *active cancellation* incurs an additional overhead of $\approx 12\,\%$ for the first job but only $0.01 - 0.04\,\%$ for subsequent jobs. Hence, the above experiments show that for long running jobs, which execute serially one after another, the performance gain achieved by *sequencer-based atomic broadcast* is minimal.

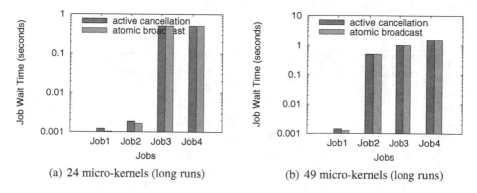

(a) 24 micro-kernels (long runs)   (b) 49 micro-kernels (long runs)

Fig. 7. Overhead for long jobs (a) 24 micro-kernels (long runs) (b) 49 micro-kernels (long runs) (Color figure online)

7.3 Job Allocation Overhead for Increasing Tile Sizes

In this experiment, we scale the tile size ($n \times n$) from 2×2 to the maximum supported size of 7×7. Per tile size, we generate n simultaneous job requests, each requiring pico-kernels (cores) satisfied by exactly n micro-kernel domains. E.g., in a tile size of 2×2, there will be 2 simultaneous job requests requiring pico-kernels (cores) satisfied by 2 micro-kernels each, and in a tile size of 7×7, there will be 7 simultaneous job requests requiring pico-kernels (cores) satisfied by 7 micro-kernels each. This experiment shows the additional overhead for jobs that can ideally execute in parallel.

The results depicted in Fig. 8 compare the job wait times of the first and last jobs for *active cancellation* and *atomic broadcast*. Here, the job wait times are depicted on the y-axis for different tile sizes on the x-axis. We observe that the wait time for the first among the n jobs is consistently lower for *active cancellation* as it does not incur the overhead of submitting all job requests at the sequencer. We observe a reduction in the job wait time of the first job from $6\,\%$ for a tile size of 2×2 to up to $60\,\%$ for a tile size of 7×7. For the sake of analysis, let us assume that the highest priority job overrides all other jobs in their home micro-kernels before any of the lower priority jobs gets a chance to execute. In this case, there will be one initial request sent for the highest priority job. For all other lower priority jobs, there will be $n - 1$ initial requests plus $n - 1$ cancel and finally $n - 1$ repeat requests sent in total. Thus, all subsequent jobs incur this additional overhead. Notice that significant performance gains in spawning the first job compensates for this additional overhead for subsequent jobs to a large extent. Compared to *sequencer-based atomic broadcast*, we observe a slight increase in the job wait times for *active cancellation* ($1 - 12\,\%$ for smaller tile sizes, i.e., 2×2 and 3×3). But for larger tile sizes, we observe a more significant reduction in the overhead for *active cancellation* (up to $15\,\%$). This experiment reinforces our earlier finding that as long as multiple simultaneous job submissions can execute in parallel, *active cancellation* has a lower overhead compared to *sequencer-based atomic broadcast*.

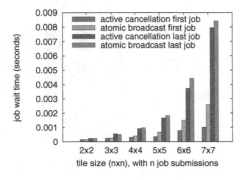

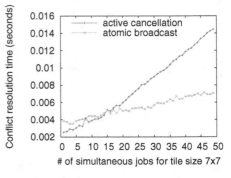

Fig. 8. Job allocations as tile size increases (Color figure online)

Fig. 9. Worst case for n simultaneous jobs

7.4   Worst-Case Conflict Resolution for N Simultaneous Jobs

In this experiment with n simultaneous job submissions, we measure the conflict resolution time for the first job to execute. We use a fixed tile size of 7×7 in the *partial simulation* mode. As all the cores are considered to be micro-kernels in this mode, a maximum of 49 micro-kernels are available. All job submissions require a large number of pico-kernels (cores) that can only be satisfied by the cores available in all the 49 micro-kernel domains. In this worst-case scenario, the *sequencer-based atomic broadcast* scheme provides the best performance. The *sequencer-based atomic broadcast* scheme just has to wait for the job allocation request with the highest priority to arrive. It can then send out core allocation requests one after another. The maximum overhead occurs when the highest priority job request is the one that reaches the sequencer last. Compare this to the considerable overhead in *active cancellation*. Here, in the worst-case, the $n - 1$ lower priority job requests together could have reserved all available cores in all micro-kernels. But none would have reserved enough to proceed executing. Hence, for the highest priority job request to execute, it has to override each of the lower priority job request in all other micro-kernels by sending job cancel requests. In the worst-case, $n - 1$ cancellation requests need to be sent before the first job can get enough cores for its allocation to be satisfied. We see this reflected in Fig. 9. The wait time for the first job is shown on the y-axis and x-axis depicts n, the number of simultaneous job submissions. We observe that the worst-case performance is better for the *sequencer-based atomic broadcast* scheme once the number of micro-kernels simultaneously requesting allocations exceeds $1/4^{th}$ of the total number of micro-kernels.

7.5   Experiments with NPB Codes in Real Task Mode

The *real task* mode on the TilePro64, introduced in Sect. 6, consists of 4 micro-kernels, each managing a set of 8 pico-kernels. We can execute jobs that require a maximum of 32 cores in this mode. To confirm the pattern observed under the *partial simulation* mode, we conduct similar, yet scaled down experiments in *real task* mode.

Job Allocations Executing in Parallel. Here, two jobs (NPB FT Class = S size = 16) run in parallel in two different micro-kernel domains with inputs chosen to be L2 resident (to ensure that experiments are not dominated by DRAM memory latencies). Each job requires 16 cores, which can be satisfied in parallel. We measure the average job wait time. This wait time is exclusively due to the protocol overhead as it does not include any resource wait time. This experiment is an approximation of the sparse job allocations explained in the context of the *partial simulation* mode. We observe results following the same pattern: Under *active cancellation*, less overhead is incurred compared to *sequencer-based atomic broadcast*. These results are shown in Fig. 10. The y-axis depicts job wait time for the two jobs executing in parallel (x-axis).

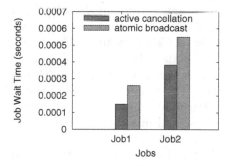 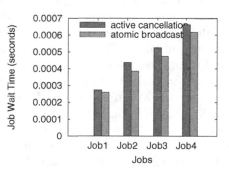

Fig. 10. Real task mode: parallel job alloc. (Color figure online)

Fig. 11. Real task mode: Serial Job Alloc. (Color figure online)

Job Allocations Executing Serially. In this experiment, four jobs (NPB FT Class = S size = 32) requiring all the 32 cores available from all of the four micro-kernels are submitted simultaneously. These job submissions compete for all resources and are eventually serialized to execute one after another. Thus, this experiment is similar to the *partial simulation* mode experiment in Sect. 7.4, which measured the worst-case conflict resolution time for n simultaneous job submissions. We obtain similar results, where *sequencer-based atomic broadcast* performs much better than *active cancellation*. Figure 11 shows these results with the exclusive job wait time on the y-axis for the four jobs on the x-axis. Exclusive job wait time is calculated here as the actual job wait time minus execution times of all prior jobs. This metric provides the job allocation overhead in isolation. A purely centralized approach should perform inferior. But our sequencer approach uses a centralized approach enhanced by contention-free communication over a spanning tree of micro-kernels (Fig. 3), which scales further.

7.6   Performance of Pattern-Based Propagation

To evaluate the impact of scalability of pattern-based message propagation, a simple experiment was devised. A request is broadcasted to all nodes (cores) in a 7×7 tile (max. 49 nodes). The time to broadcast this request and receive a reply from all endpoints in the reverse path of broadcast is measured. The results in Fig. 12 compare the time taken on the y-axis against the number of nodes to which the message is broadcast on the x-axis. Four different schemes are compared: (1) A naive broadcast scheme (The source sends m individual messages to m recipients.); (2) distributed flooding (The source sends the message to all its neighbors who multi-cast the message to their neighbors until all nodes have received the message.); (3) fixed pattern-based propagation (see Sect. 4.4); and (4) adaptive pattern-based propagation (see Sect. 4.4). We resort to analysis to determine scalability in number of cores on our single chip platform.

For our analysis, let us assume a tile size of $n \times n$. One sender needs to broadcast the message to the remaining $n^2 - 1$ recipients. Among the different schemes, the naive broadcast scheme tends to be the most time consuming. In this scheme, a single source node sends the message to all the recipients and waits for replies from each of them. This increases the load on the single source. The number of individual end-to-end messages on the NoC equals the number of recipients of the broadcast, i.e., $n^2 - 1$. But it is important to note that, on a 2D mesh topology with X-Y dimension ordered routing, the messages are sent over the same link multiple times resulting in unnecessary link utilization. We can easily observe that as the same X-Y path is traversed multiple times, there is heavy contention on a few links that become the bottleneck.

Distributed flooding performs slightly better. In this method, the load on the single source node is reduced as all nodes contribute to forwarding the message. Also, the message is sent exactly once over each link. But the number of individual messages on the NoC is comparatively larger than that of the naive broadcast scheme. For a tile size of $n \times n$, the total number of messages equals the total number of links on the NoC, i.e., $2n(n - 1)$. Hence, after a threshold point, the cost of distributed flooding tends to increase and is as costly as the naive broadcast scheme. This trend was observed in Fig. 12, when the number of nodes is greater than 43.

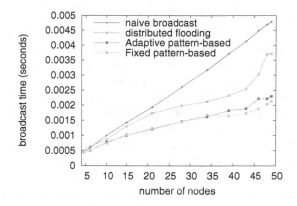

Fig. 12. Different request propagation schemes (Color figure online)

Fixed pattern-based propagation, where messages propagate in a predefined pattern, uses the least number of individual messages, namely $n^2 - 1$. The fixed pattern reduces the number of links used to $n^2 - 1$ and the message is sent exactly once on each link. Also, the load on the single source node is considerably reduced as each recipient forwards the message further. Hence, pattern-based propagation consumes the least amount of time (see Fig. 12).

In the adaptive pattern-based propagation scheme, the number of individual messages is $n^2 - 1$, which is the same as in the fixed pattern-based scheme. Also, the scheme ensures that the message is sent only once per link. Even the additional cost in setting up the adaptive pattern is amortized over multiple runs. Hence, the adaptive pattern-based scheme performs as good as the fixed pattern-based scheme (see Fig. 12). The adaptive pattern-based scheme is only slightly costlier than the fixed pattern-based scheme. This is explained as follows: Depending on the adaptive pattern formed, certain nodes may need to forward the message to more than one recipient (unlike the fixed pattern-based scheme). E.g., nodes 2 and 5 incur this additional processing time in Fig. 3(c).

8   Related Work

Manycores have sparked many OS redesigns [5,6,15–20]. Our micro-kernel and pico-kernel abstraction is design for larger number of cores and was inspired by FOS and Barrelfish [6,15], where application and OS services run on physically separate cores. In contrast to FOS, we benefit more from spatial locality as pico-kernels (cores) only need to communicate with their parent micro-kernel. We follow the core of the design principles postulated by Peter et al. [21] for designing multi-core schedulers. We even go one level further and take a purely distributed message passing approach as the primary means of communication via adoption of NoCMsg [4] for low-level messaging. Boyd-Wickizer et al. [20] analyze and fix scalability issues in the Linux kernel for several system applications and show that good scalability up to 48 cores could be achieved by modest changes. However, their workload consisted of embarrassingly parallel codes, such as independent Apache threads and parallelized "make" commands.

The compute chip of BlueGene/Q [22,23] has 16 cores for executing application tasks, one core dedicated to OS services and one (disabled) to increase manufacturing yield. This is similar to our approach of dedicated micro-kernels for OS services and applications. Our design differs as we propose multiple dedicated micro-kernels managing the cores in a manycore chip rather than across nodes. Kobbe et al. [24] provide agent-based allocation on a multicore for malleable applications, where cores of a job are governed by a single agent. ADAM [25] also uses an agent-based approach but requires a global (centralized) agent coordinating smaller agents per cluster of cores. Our approach is much finer grained with multiple micro-kernels coordinating the allocation of a job in a distributed manner. It is also lighter weight than agent-based allocation in Grid/Cloud computing, which use complex allocation schemes with high latency unsuitable for on-chip allocation [26,27].

Job schedulers for HPC clusters, such as the TORQUE resource manager [28], SLURM [29] and the Maui scheduler [30], use similar algorithms for resource allocation and employ backfilling algorithms to increase utilization. These cluster schedulers are centralized while Mesos [31] only allocates a subset of requested resources and Omega [32] allows parallel schedulers to access shared state in a lock free manner. All of them have scalability limitations due to shared/centralized state (covered by our sequences-based approach in experiments), while our advanced design follows a distributed/message passing design and scales. Omega employs an optimistic concurrency control and has parallel scheduling capabilities. But atomic updates to the shared state serialize scheduling decisions. Instead, we allow individual micro-kernels to be scheduled in parallel and resolve conflicts only when needed. Our techniques and algorithms also have been tailored and optimized to benefit from the on-chip communication of NoC processors. Job co-scheduling for High-end computing (HEC) systems often use a single job submission portal [33,34], which requires a centralized resource manager that does not scale. Tang et al. [35] propose a distributed job co-scheduler for HEC systems. They propose to resolve deadlocks by yielding the resources after a predefined wait time subject to deadlock (see Sect. 3). Our approach differs as we avoid deadlocks in job allocation and guarantee a definite completion time for the distributed job allocator. NoC architectures like the Kalray MPPA-256 [14] have specialized support for multi-casting, which can vastly improve the performance of our distributed job allocation protocol as job requests propagate fast resulting in fewer cancellations for *active cancellation*. Most NoC architectures ([1,3]) lack hardware support for multi-casting, while our efficient pattern-based request propagation schemes can be applied to them.

9   Conclusion

We introduce PICASO, a distributed message passing system, to meet the scalability challenges of future manycore processors and demonstrate the ease and usability of such a system in managing large numbers of cores on a single chip. We study the distributed job allocation problem and propose a protocol with two policies, *active cancellation* and *sequencer-based atomic broadcast*. Both policies avoid fragmented allocations (that would otherwise lead to deadlocks) and guarantee allocations loosely following a global order. Experimental TilePro64 results indicate that for sparse job allocations the *active cancellation* scheme provides lower overhead while for denser job allocations the *sequencer-based atomic broadcast* scheme provides lower overhead.

References

1. Tilera tile64 processor family. https://en.wikipedia.org/wiki/TILE64
2. Wentzlaff, D., Griffin, P., Hoffmann, H., Bao, L., Edwards, B., Ramey, C., Mattina, M., Miao, C.C., Brown III, J.F., Agarwal, A.: On-chip interconnection architecture of the tile processor. IEEE Micro. **27**, 15–31 (2007)
3. Howard, J., et al.: A 48-core IA-32 message-passing processor with DVFS in 45nm CMOS. In: Solid-State Circuits Conference Digest of Technical Papers (ISSCC), pp. 108–109 (2010)
4. Zimmer, C., Mueller, F.: Nocmsg: scalable noc-based message passing. In: International Symposium on Cluster Computing and the Grid (CCGRID) (2014)
5. Baumann, A., Barham, P., Dagand, P.E., Harris, T., Isaacs, R., Peter, S., Roscoe, T., Schüpbach, A., Singhania, A.: The multikernel: a new OS architecture for scalable multicore systems. In: Symposium on Operating Systems Principles, pp. 29–44 (2009)
6. Wentzlaff, D., Agarwal, A.: Factored operating systems (fos): the case for a scalable operating system for multicores. SIGOPS Oper. Syst. Rev. **43**, 76–85 (2009)
7. Zimmer, C., Mueller, F.: NoCMsg: a scalable message passing abstraction for network-on-chips. TACO **12**(1), 1–24 (2015). doi:10.1145/2701426
8. Chabbi, M., Fagan, M., Mellor-Crummey, J.: High performance locks for multi-level numa systems. In: ACM SIGPLAN Symposium on Principles and Practice of Parallel Programming, pp. 215–226 (2015)
9. Davis, R.I., Burns, A.: A survey of hard real-time scheduling for multiprocessor systems. ACM Comput. Surv. (CSUR) **43**(4), 35 (2011)
10. Zimmer, C., Mueller, F.: Low contention mapping of real-time tasks onto tilepro 64 core processors. In: IEEE Real-Time Embedded Technology and Applications Symposium, pp. 131–140 (2012)
11. Agarwal, T., Sharma, A., Kale, K.: Topology-aware task mapping for reducing communication contention on large parallel machines. In: International Parallel and Distributed Processing Symposium, April 2006
12. Snir, M., Otto, S., Huss-Lederman, S., Walker, D., Dongarra, J.: MPI: The Complete Reference, vol. 1, 2nd edn. MIT Press, Cambridge (1998)
13. Défago, X., Schiper, A., Urbán, P.: Total order broadcast and multicast algorithms: taxonomy and survey. ACM Comput. Surv. (CSUR) **36**(4), 372–421 (2004)
14. de Dinechin, B.D., de Massas, P.G., Lager, G., Léger, C., Orgogozo, B., Reybert, J., Strudel, T.: A distributed run-time environment for the Kalray MPPA-256 integrated manycore processor. Procedia Comput. Sci. **18**, 1654–1663 (2013)
15. Baumann, A., Peter, S., Schüpbach, A., Singhania, A., Roscoe, T., Barham, P., Isaacs, R.: Your computer is already a distributed system. why isn't your OS? In: HotOS (2009)

16. Gamsa, B., Krieger, O., Appavoo, J., Stumm, M.: Tornado: maximizing locality and concurrency in a shared memory multiprocessor operating system. In: OSDI, pp. 87–100 (1999)
17. Boyd-Wickizer, S., Chen, H., Chen, R., Mao, Y., Kaashoek, M.F., Morris, R., Pesterev, A., Stein, L., Wu, M., Dai, Y.H., et al.: Corey: an operating system for many cores. In: OSDI, pp. 43–57 (2008)
18. Nightingale, E.B., Hodson, O., McIlroy, R., Hawblitzel, C., Hunt, G.: Helios: heterogeneous multiprocessing with satellite kernels. In: Proceedings of the ACM SIGOPS 22nd Symposium on Operating Systems Principles, pp. 221–234. ACM (2009)
19. Liu, R., Klues, K., Bird, S., Hofmeyr, S., Asanovic, K., Kubiatowicz, J.: Tessellation: space-time partitioning in a manycore client OS. In: HotPar 2009, vol. 3, Berkeley, CA (2009)
20. Boyd-Wickizer, S., Clements, A.T., Mao, Y., Pesterev, A., Kaashoek, M.F., Morris, R., Zeldovich, N.: An analysis of Linux scalability to many cores (2010)
21. Peter, S., Schüpbach, A., Barham, P., Baumann, A., Isaacs, R., Harris, T., Roscoe, T.: Design principles for end-to-end multicore schedulers. In: 2nd Workshop on Hot Topics in Parallelism, Berkeley, CA, USA (2010)
22. Haring, R.A., Ohmacht, M., Fox, T.W., Gschwind, M.K., Satterfield, D.L., Sugavanam, K., Coteus, P.W., Heidelberger, P., Blumrich, M.A., Wisniewski, R.W., et al.: The IBM BlueGene/Q compute chip. IEEE Micro. **32**(2), 48–60 (2012)
23. Boyle, P.: The BlueGene/Q supercomputer. In: PoS LATTICE 2012, vol. 20 (2012)
24. Kobbe, S., Bauer, L., Lohmann, D., Schröder-Preikschat, W., Henkel, J.: Distrm: distributed resource management for on-chip many-core systems. In: Proceedings of the Seventh IEEE/ACM/IFIP International Conference on Hardware/Software Codesign and System Synthesis, pp. 119–128 (2011)
25. Al Faruque, M.A., Krist, R., Henkel, J.: Adam: run-time agent-based distributed application mapping for on-chip communication. In: Design Automation Conference, pp. 760–765
26. Cao, J., Jarvis, S.A., Saini, S., Kerbyson, D.J., Nudd, G.R.: Arms: an agent-based resource management system for grid computing. Sci. Program. **10**(2), 135–148 (2002)
27. Berman, F., Wolski, R., Casanova, H., Cirne, W., Dail, H., Faerman, M., Figueira, S., Hayes, J., Obertelli, G., Schopf, J., Shao, G., Smallen, S., Spring, N., Su, A., Zagorodnov, D.: Adaptive computing on the grid using apples. IEEE Trans. Parallel Distrib. Syst. **14**(4), 369–382 (2003)
28. Staples, G.: TORQUE resource manager. In: Supercomputing, p. 8 (2006)
29. Yoo, A.B., Jette, M.A., Grondona, M.: SLURM: simple linux utility for resource management. In: Feitelson, D.G., Rudolph, L., Schwiegelshohn, U. (eds.) JSSPP 2003. LNCS, vol. 2862, pp. 44–60. Springer, Heidelberg (2003)
30. Jackson, D.B., Snell, Q.O., Clement, M.J.: Core algorithms of the maui scheduler. In: Feitelson, D.G., Rudolph, L. (eds.) JSSPP 2001. LNCS, vol. 2221, p. 87. Springer, Heidelberg (2001)
31. Hindman, B., Konwinski, A., Zaharia, M., Ghodsi, A., Joseph, A.D., Katz, R., Shenker, S., Stoica, I.: Mesos: a platform for fine-grained resource sharing in the data center. In: USENIX Conference on Networked Systems Design and Implementation, pp. 295–308 (2011)
32. Schwarzkopf, M., Konwinski, A., Abd-El-Malek, M., Wilkes, J.: Omega: flexible, scalable schedulers for large compute clusters. In: European Conference on Computer Systems, pp. 351–364 (2013)

33. Huedo, E., Montero, R.S., Llorente, I.M.: A framework for adaptive execution in grids. Softw.: Pract. Exp. **34**(7), 631–651 (2004)
34. Kannan, S., Roberts, M., Mayes, P., Brelsford, D., Skovira, J.F.: Workload management with loadleveler. IBM Redbooks **2**, 2 (2001). http://www.redbooks.ibm.com/redbooks/pdfs/sg246038.pdf
35. Tang, W., Desai, N., Vishwanath, V., Buettner, D., Lan, Z.: Job coscheduling on coupled high-end computing systems. In: ICPP Workshops, pp. 317–326 (2011)

Extreme-Scale Computations

Many-Core Acceleration of a Discrete Ordinates Transport Mini-App at Extreme Scale

Tom Deakin[1]([✉]), Simon McIntosh-Smith[1], and Wayne Gaudin[2]

[1] Department of Computer Science, University of Bristol, Bristol, UK
`tom.deakin@bristol.ac.uk`, `simonm@cs.bris.ac.uk`
[2] High Performance Computing,
UK Atomic Weapons Establishment, Aldermaston, UK
`Wayne.Gaudin@awe.co.uk`

Abstract. Time-dependent deterministic discrete ordinates transport codes are an important class of application which provide significant challenges for large, many-core systems. One such challenge is the large memory capacity needed by the solve step, which requires us to have a scalable solution in order to have enough node-level memory to store all the data. In our previous work, we demonstrated the first implementation which showed a significant performance benefit for single node solves using GPUs. In this paper we extend our work to large problems and demonstrate the scalability of our solution on two Petascale GPU-based supercomputers: Titan at Oak Ridge and Piz Daint at CSCS. Our results show that our improved node-level parallelism scheme scales just as well across large systems as previous approaches when using the tried and tested KBA domain decomposition technique. We validate our results against an improved performance model which predicts the runtime of the main 'sweep' routine when running on different hardware, including CPUs or GPUs.

1 Introduction

Deterministic discrete ordinates neutral particle transport is a balance equation which describes the movement of neutral particles through materials of varying properties. As the particles move through the material, they can collide with material atoms causing a change in direction of movement and/or a change in energy level of the particle. Additionally, the particle may be absorbed and potentially a fission reaction can occur, resulting in the loss or gain of particles. The governing equation for this balance of particles, the *transport equation*, is solved via a numerical method resulting in an approximate solution due to the complexity of finding an analytic solution in all but the simplest cases. Therefore this is a computationally intensive problem which requires High Performance Computing in order to find solutions in a tractable time. Indeed, it is estimated that 50–80 % of simulation time is devoted to transport codes on United States Department of Energy systems [14] making this a very important problem.

The solution of the transport equation involves a matrix-free inversion of an operator which forms a sweep across the grid; it is this part of the algorithm

© Springer International Publishing Switzerland 2016
J.M. Kunkel et al. (Eds.): ISC High Performance 2016, LNCS 9697, pp. 429–448, 2016.
DOI: 10.1007/978-3-319-41321-1_22

which takes up the majority of the computation time in transport codes. In this paper we investigate applying our previous attempts to accelerate the intra-node updates to run a transport mini-app at large scale using many-core processors such as GPUs. A mini-app removes the complexity of a production application whilst also providing a proxy for performance. We use the KBA algorithm for spatial decomposition, the de facto algorithm to provide the benchmark for the performance of transport codes [15], see Sect. 2.1. We show weak scaling results for our accelerated scheme requiring storage of the angular flux in device memory, and discuss the challenges of strong scaling.

In particular we make the following contributions:

1. We present weak scaling results using an improved node level scheme running on GPUs. The results show that the KBA algorithm is still a solution at scale.
2. We improve on a performance model to predict the running time of our accelerated transport sweep at scale.
3. Results are presented for two leading GPU enabled supercomputers, the two largest in the world at the time of writing. We demonstrate up to a 4× speedup of a GPU accelerated time-dependent deterministic transport application at scale compared to an optimised CPU version.

The rest of the paper is structured as follows. In Sect. 2 we introduce the SNAP mini-app and the KBA algorithm used for spatial decomposition. Section 3 introduces the current state of the art. Our implementation is discussed in Sect. 4. Our performance model is introduced in Sect. 5 and we present weak and strong scaling results in Sect. 6 before concluding in Sect. 7.

2   SNAP: Sn Application Proxy

The Discrete Ordinates (S_N) Application Proxy (SNAP) [24] is a proxy application (mini-app) from Los Alamos National Laboratory based on their deterministic discrete ordinates neutral particle transport code, PARTISN. It maintains the performance characteristics of PARTISN, without the complexity of a production application; in particular the input data is deliberately arbitrary and non-physical. Deterministic transport models the movement and interaction of neutral particles, such as neutrons or photons, through a mesh with varying material properties. As the particles move in straight lines within the material, they may interact with the material and change energy and/or direction. It is the net balance of these neutral particles that is governed by the Boltzmann transport equation (1) solved in the proxy application; the authors would recommend that readers unfamiliar with the solution of the transport equation consult the Lewis and Miller textbook for an introduction [16]. Whilst the transport equation can in general include fission terms, the equation solved in SNAP does not include this.

$$\left[\frac{1}{v}\frac{\partial}{\partial t} + \hat{\Omega}\cdot\boldsymbol{\nabla} + \sigma(\boldsymbol{r},E)\right]\psi(\boldsymbol{r},\hat{\Omega},E,t) = \qquad (1a)$$

$$q_{\text{ex}}(\boldsymbol{r},\hat{\Omega},E,t) + \qquad (1b)$$

$$\int dE' \int d\Omega' \sigma_{\text{s}}(\boldsymbol{r},E'\to E,\hat{\Omega}'\cdot\hat{\Omega})\psi(\boldsymbol{r},\hat{\Omega}',E',t) \qquad (1c)$$

The transport equation operates over seven dimensions: time (t), three-dimensional space $(\boldsymbol{r})$, two angular $(\hat{\Omega})$ and energy (E). The net movement of the neutral particles in these dimensions is called the *angular flux* ψ. Integrating over the angular dimensions yields the *scalar flux* ϕ. q_{ex} defines an external source of particles. A large number of particles are assumed so that each dimension can be considered as a continuum. However in order to solve the equation using numerical methods they must be discretised; SNAP uses finite difference in space and time, multi-group in energy and discrete ordinates in angle.

The application seeks to solve numerically the equation for the unknown ψ. This is done by iteration on the scattering source: a simple iteration where the value of ψ for the previous iteration is used in (1c) in order to update the values for ψ in (1a). Jacobi is used in energy groups [6]. This results in two implicit solve iteration loops for each time-step, typically called *outer* and *inner* iterations. The update of the value on the right hand size of (1) is partially updated in the outer and inner iterations. The outer updates the group-to-group scattering whilst the inner updates only the within group scattering.

It is the inversion of the streaming-collision operator (1a) that results in a *sweep* across the mesh and consists of the vast majority of the runtime of the SNAP proxy application. The discrete ordinates and spatial discretisation results in a data dependence between cells, as pictured in Fig. 1. In order to calculate the angular flux at the centre of each cell, the incoming face values are required from upwind neighbours. Outgoing fluxes are then calculated to satisfy downwind neighbour dependencies.

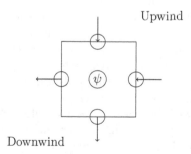

Fig. 1. Data dependency of the sweep algorithm

The original implementation of SNAP uses OpenMP threads to run in parallel over energy groups, and relies on automatic SIMD compiler vectorisation over angles. The spatial domain is decomposed across MPI ranks according to the KBA algorithm, discussed in more detail in Sect. 2.1. The sweep within each MPI rank is conducted in serial.

SNAP is designed to perform both time-dependent and time-independent deterministic transport solves. For the purposes of this paper we consider a time-dependent solution and therefore require storage of the full angular flux, rather than just the scalar flux and face angular fluxes. This imposes a significant memory capacity requirement and it is important that this is taken into account for discrete accelerators. The angular flux in a time-dependent solution requires storage for two time-steps each containing all points in the six-dimensional space/energy/angle domain.

2.1   The KBA Schedule

The data dependency between cells during the sweep requires some degree of sequential computation. Given that the angular flux is spatially decomposed across multiple compute nodes we require an algorithm or schedule to orchestrate the computation which adheres to the data dependency whilst maximising the concurrency in the wavefront.

Such a schedule was developed by Koch, Baker and Alcouffe (KBA) [5,7,15]. This method decomposes the spatial domain in one dimension less than the total dimension of the problem: a 1D decomposition for a 2D problem and a 2D decomposition for a 3D problem. Each node therefore contains the full domain of a single spatial dimension, and a portion of the remaining spatial dimensions. This is visualised in three-dimensions in Fig. 2. Each coloured $2 \times 2 \times 6$ block of the spatial domain is placed onto a separate compute node. Due to their long, thin, shape these sub-domains are often described as *pencils*.

A sweep begins from a corner of the grid, with a single angle. The schedule performs the sweep over all angles in this octant before sweeping all angles in the octant starting from the cell at the opposite end of the pencil. The next corner is then chosen until all angles are swept.

The communication occurs when a calculation reaches a sub-domain boundary; once a value of the angular flux is calculated on a boundary edge for a given angle, this value is communicated to the neighbouring node so that it may begin or continue with the sweep. This results in a natural over-decomposition or tiling of the spatial domain. Note that cells within a pencil on a given node are operated on in serial in the original algorithm.

The data dependency of the sweep gives a simple task dependency graph for the sweep of each angle. By combining the graphs of each angle, the workload can be *pipelined* so that the number of idle stages is reduced; as soon as one processor finishes their portion of work for one angle they begin the graph for the next angle.

This algorithm has been extended to consider more modern architectures with vector units on each processor [6]. Vector units allow for angles within an octant to be solved concurrently in a data parallel fashion.

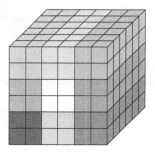

Fig. 2. KBA spatial decomposition in three dimensions

3   Related Work

Denovo is a three-dimensional steady state discrete ordinates code from Oak Ridge National Laboratory [12]. It is designed to solve the time independent version of the Boltzmann transport equation. Denovo uses the KBA algorithm for spatial decomposition (see Sect. 2.1) and a GMRES solve for within-group solves in contrast to the traditional iteration on a scattering source. The sweep routine occupies over 80 % of typical Denovo execution time. As the Denovo code solves only the steady state version of the transport equation, only the scalar flux need be stored.

The Denovo code has also been ported to GPUs using CUDA, in particular targeted at the Titan supercomputer [4]. Octants and energy groups are decoupled so that they may be solved on different portions of the machine. The spatial domain is decomposed according to the KBA algorithm using MPI. The KBA algorithm is also applied to thread blocks to exploit spatial parallelism within the sub-domains. Each moment in the scalar flux is assigned to a warp.

The reference [4] shows scaling results on the early upgrade of the Jaguar supercomputer in preparation for the full upgrade to Titan when the system was installed with NVIDIA Fermi X2090 GPUs. Weak scaling results on this system show that the GPU version of the sweep was up to 3.5× faster than the CPU sweep. The same Denovo code was later run on Titan, which contains NVIDIA Tesla K20X GPUs. The sweep routine on the GPU was 4–6× faster than the CPU sweep running on 8 (of 16) cores per node, however the total code obtained an overall 2× speedup for the benchmark problems [11].

Whilst these results show good speedup, Denovo does not require storage of the angular flux as it is not time-dependent, and so is not constrained by this challenging memory capacity requirement. Due to the limited memory capacity of the many-core devices compared to CPU DRAM capacity, a solution which requires storage of the angular flux requires a solution with better scalability in order to provide the total memory footprint by using many more nodes.

Additionally, because energy groups are decomposed into separate sets in Denovo they are solved on separate parts of the machine and so a fixed problem size artificially requires a large node count. Because of the speedup in the sweep routine from the GPU code, the majority of computation time shifts to other portions of the code which require all-to-all communication to distribute updated vectors.

A direct port of the SNAP mini-app using the CUDA framework by Wang et al. exists and uses a similar parallelisation scheme to the original code [23]. In our previous work we showed that on a single node this approach did not improve the performance over our benchmark CPU despite the use of GPUs [9].

4   A Many-Core Implementation

The KBA schedule discussed in Sect. 2.1 describes the spatial decomposition between compute nodes but stipulates little about the computation within a node. It was shown that a hybrid approach where each MPI rank should utilise a number of cores to improve the scalability of the transport application [6], and this approach is implemented in the original SNAP implementation.

The authors have previously demonstrated that the intra-node solve of SNAP can be accelerated using many-core devices, such as GPUs [9,10] providing single node speedups in line with the improved memory bandwidth of such devices. Our previous work was, to the best of our knowledge, the first time that such a significant speedup was achieved for a SNAP-like transport code using a many-core processor. The within-cell concurrency of angles within an octant and of energy groups via Jacobi was combined with the spatial concurrency of the wavefront within a node's spatial domain (as pictured in Fig. 3) in order to provide an effective scheme to exploit the increased resources of the many-core device over the multi-core CPU. However these improvements will not necessarily transfer to a multi-node domain.

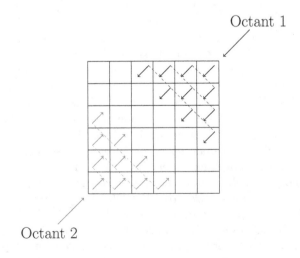

Fig. 3. Parallel sweep

KBA is used as a baseline for sweep scheduling algorithms, and so it is important to begin with combining this schedule with our accelerated intra-node scheme. However, this does not necessarily yield equivalent scaling results for many-core. Sweep algorithms rely on pipelining the work to maximise the number of busy processors while minimising the start up and tear down costs associated with the data dependency across the decomposed spatial domain; not all processors can begin at the start of the simulation and must wait until some internal boundary data reaches them before they can begin. The approaches to obtain good intra-node performance on accelerated devices require large aggregation factors in the angular and energy dimensions, and so if the length of the pipeline relies on these dimensions then the number of sweeps available to overlap is severely reduced and hence predicted scaling is poor; this is the case for the algorithms of Adams et al. [1, 2]. The KBA algorithm was originally designed to allow for aggregating all angles in one octant [15]; the original authors of KBA found that while this reduced the theoretical parallel efficiency it performed better in practice. The SNAP mini-app uses KBA and so a fair comparison with the same spatial decomposition is required to test how our accelerated intra-node scheme performs at scale.

Our implementation of KBA and accelerated intra-node transport sweep uses MPI and OpenCL. OpenCL [18] is a parallel programming framework for heterogeneous platforms. The basic model consists of a host and a device such as a GPU, CPU, FPGA, etc. The host CPU and device have separate memory regions and memory must be explicitly managed by the programmer.

Units of work are defined, called work-items. Similar to OpenMP, this unit of work is typically the body of a loop. The work-items are mapped onto vector-lanes of the device architecture. In general these lanes are called processing elements, and operate in groups called compute units.

A kernel defines the problem size (number of work-items) and if required the work-group size. A work-group is a collection of work-items. Synchronisation is only possible within a work-group on the device and between work-groups via the host at the end of kernels. On a CPU, each work-group would be assigned to a core, and the work-items to vector lanes within that core. The kernel is enqueued on (offloaded to) the device as a whole and the OpenCL runtime schedules the computation of work-groups. The host controls the compute offload and memory transfer through the use of a command queue.

OpenCL therefore allows a very fine grained parallel programming notation of concurrent work. This means that it is very portable and can run on a variety of supported architectures from different vendors. In other work we have compared the performance of OpenCL and CUDA versions of this code and they are within a few percent of each other.

The computation of the angular flux kernel is designed so that each work-item computes the angular flux for one angle and energy group in one cell. The number of work-items is the number of angles in the octant multiplied by the number of energy groups, multiplied by the number of cells in the wavefront.

The original SNAP mini-app is written in Fortran, however OpenCL provides a C API, and so the required parts of the mini-app were rewritten in C. This includes the MPI communication routines so that the energy groups can be included in the kernel solve. The original SNAP calls the MPI routines from within the OpenMP parallel region, something which is not possible when using an offload model such as that in OpenCL. Moving the MPI calls outside of the group iteration loop allows us to send a single (larger) message containing data from all energy groups, rather than one message per energy group reducing the number times the penalty of message latency is paid.

Within a pencil sub-domain of the array according to the KBA decomposition, the many-core implementation runs in parallel over all cells within the local wavefront. We are free to choose how many XY-planes, or *chunks*, we compute before communicating to neighbouring nodes. Figure 4 shows a 2D pencil shape where six planes numbered 1–6 are computed before communication of downwind fluxes occurs. The numbers show which wavefront the cells are in. Notice that the widest (and thus most parallel) wavefront in this example occurs at the third and fourth wavefront. There is a start-up time until this maximum wavefront size is reached, and also a tear down cost returning back to a single cell just before the communication.

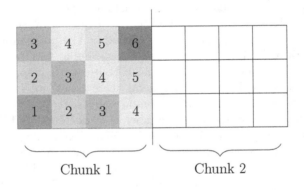

Fig. 4. Chunking of KBA communication

The original SNAP implementation operates in serial over cells in the chunks and so the start-up/tear-down costs do not appear there. For the many-core version the number of cells in the wavefront helps to generate enough independent work-items to keep the GPU saturated with enough work; we are running just a single cell's worth of work-items at the start and end of every chunk. Kernel invocations of wavefronts consisting of just a few cells will likely under-utilise the GPU, however generates a simpler communication pattern than an approach suggested by Pennycook et al. for non-perpendicular chunking which avoids this repeated start-up cost [20].

As we are performing a time-dependent solve of the transport equation we require storage of two instances the angular flux. Our implementation requires that this data is stored resident on the accelerator device. We will therefore be limited by the memory capacity of the device. It is the subject of a future study to stream the data from host memory to the device memory. However, note that future self-hosting many-core systems, such as Intel's upcoming Knights Landing, may require a fully resident scheme such as presented in this paper.

5   Performance Model

The performance model proposed by Bailey and Falgout [3] predicts the runtime of transport sweeps derived from the number of stages in the sweep multiplied by the time to complete a stage. The time per stage is defined as the sum of the computational time per stage C, the communication time per stage B and the latency time per stage L. Whilst the model is just for the sweep time rather than total application time, given that the sweeps form the majority of the runtime of the application it should provide a reasonable approximation to runtime.

The latency time per stage L can be given as αK, for K messages per stage and a machine dependent value α representing the time to send a message (network latency). Likewise the communication time per stage B can be given as $\beta m \Gamma$, where Γ is the total number of cells in the communication faces, m is the number of bytes to communicate per cell, and β is a machine dependent value representing the time to send a byte (inverse network bandwidth). Both α and β are running micro-benchmarks on the machine in question.

We define the number of cells in a given three dimensional problem by the values N_x, N_y, N_z, the number of energy groups by N_g and the number of angles per octant N_m. We employ a two dimensional decomposition across $P_x \times P_y$ processors. We also define the number of chunks (XY-planes per communication) as η.

The number of stages is derived from the KBA scheduling algorithm. A stage consists of calculating a chunk of the KBA pencil and communicating the values to the neighbouring processors. Octants are pipelined in pairs where the sweeps start from the same processor in the four corners of the processor grid. Each one of the pairs behaves symmetrically. The processor in the opposite corner of the processor grid must wait to receive its first message. This is $P_x + P_y - 2$ stages before the final processor can begin. Once the processor in the opposite corner to the starting processor starts we assume that it can complete its work uninterrupted as messages will arrive on time (this fact was demonstrated by Adams et al. [1]). The workload is the number of chunks in the pencil for each of the two octants.

Therefore the total time T for S stages of the sweep is given in the model (2):

$$T = S(C + B + L) \tag{2a}$$

$$B = \beta m \Gamma \tag{2b}$$

$$L = \alpha K \tag{2c}$$

$$S = 4 \left(P_x + P_y - 2 + \frac{2N_z}{\eta} \right) \tag{2d}$$

Finally we must define the computational time per stage C. For a code which uses the CPU for the sweeps we use the metric suggested by Bailey and Falgout (3). This is the product of a 'grind time', γ, per value of the angular flux to update in a stage. This γ gives us a tuning parameter to the model that is related to machine characteristics. This value allows us to use regression analysis to assist fitting the model to the data.

$$C_{\text{CPU}} = \gamma N_m N_g \eta \frac{N_x}{P_x} \frac{N_y}{P_y} \qquad (3)$$

We alter this model for our GPU accelerated version. We hope to capture the idea that running a kernel on a GPU with few work-items takes similar time to a kernel with enough work-items to saturate a GPU device. Therefore the work per stage is related to the number of kernel enqueues, rather than the amount of work per cell, as specified in (4). Notice that the number of kernel enqueues is the number of wavefronts in each chunk, and γ represents an average kernel execution time.

$$C_{\text{GPU}} = \gamma \left(\frac{N_x}{P_x} + \frac{N_y}{P_y} + \eta - 2 \right) \qquad (4)$$

The model requires three machine dependent parameters: network latency (α), inverse bandwidth (β) (time to send a byte) and an estimate of the compute cost (γ). In order to obtain the first two metrics the benchmark b_eff was run on 2048 nodes of Titan, with one MPI rank per node [21]. The benchmark reported a network latency of $\alpha = 3.327\,\mu s$ and an effective bandwidth of 575 MBytes/s per node, and so $\beta = 1/(575 \times 10^6)$.

We also ran the benchmark on 64 nodes of Piz Daint, with one MPI rank per node and achieved a network latency of $\alpha = 1.735\,\mu s$ and an effective bandwidth of 6354 MBytes/s per node, and so $\beta = 1/(6354 \times 10^6)$. These network benchmarks show that Piz Daint has a higher performing network than Titan.

6   Results

6.1   Supercomputers

The Swiss National Supercomputing Centre supercomputer, *Piz Daint*, is a Cray XC30 supercomputer consisting of 5,272 nodes, each containing one 8-core Intel Xeon E5-2670 CPU and one NVIDIA Tesla K20X GPU. The nodes are connected with the Aries interconnect according to a Dragonfly topology. The machine has an RMAX of 6.3 PFLOPS/s [22]. Piz Daint has CUDA 6.5 with OpenCL driver version 340.87.

The Oak Ridge National Laboratory supercomputer, *Titan*, is a Cray XK7 consisting of 18,688 nodes, each containing one 16-core AMD Opteron 6274 CPU and one NVIDIA Tesla K20X GPU. The nodes are connected with the Gemini interconnect according to a three-dimensional torus topology. The machine has an RMAX of 17.6 PFLOPS/s [22]. Titan has CUDA 7.0 with OpenCL driver version 346.99.

6.2   Weak Scaling

In order to assess the weak scaling of our implementation we drew inspiration from previous weak scaling transport studies [6]. The problem is chosen with sub-domains representing pins in a reactor, and so by weak-scaling the pencil-shaped blocks of work per node by increasing the number of pencils one can begin to build a model of a full reactor core. This means that both the total amount of work and the nature of that work per node remains constant as the problem is scaled up. We therefore use the following parameters:

- $4 \times 4 \times 400$ cells per MPI rank with mesh size of $1.0\,\mathrm{cm} \times 1.0\,\mathrm{cm} \times 100.0\,\mathrm{cm}$
- S_{32}: 136 angles per octant and 32 energy groups
- 1 time-step of $0.01\,\mathrm{s}$ with inner convergence criteria of $1.0\mathrm{E} - 5$
- 2 orders of scattering expansion
- Computation of 4 XY planes before communication

We found that this problem requires four outer iterations, with between four and two inner iterations per outer. Each MPI rank requires 3.6 GBytes for storage of the angular flux. Note that we always perform an inner for each energy group in our implementation. Each NVIDIA Tesla K20X GPU has 6 GBytes of memory, of which 5.6 GBytes is usable by OpenCL. Our current implementation requires the data be fully resident on the GPU and so we are limited by the memory capacity of the GPU; our experiments are chosen to remain within this limit.

The scaling studies begin at 4 MPI ranks, and we assign one GPU per MPI rank. This requires both vertical and horizontal communication across the interconnect in the 2D MPI rank layout according to KBA. We also run the original implementation of SNAP on the CPUs in an appropriate configuration given the memory capacity per compute node. We found that two MPI ranks per socket/NUMA region provided the fastest run time on the CPU. On Titan this is four MPI ranks per node, and on Piz Daint this is two MPI ranks per node. This will allow some threading over the energy groups whilst also providing more spatial parallelism than a layout with fewer MPI ranks.

Titan. The results from Titan can be seen in Fig. 5. It is clear that the GPU implementation provides a speedup of around 4× over the CPU implementation. The STREAM benchmark [17] achieves a memory bandwidth of 32 GBytes/s on the Opteron CPUs, whilst GPU-STREAM [8] achieves 182 GBytes/s on the K20X GPUs, a 5.7× improvement in memory bandwidth of the GPU over the CPU. These benchmarks have no communication costs associated with them as they are simply run on a single node. We previously showed that we obtained a 4× speedup of single node performance of our intra-node accelerated scheme on Titan [9], and we can see here that this speedup is maintained as we weak-scale up to thousands of GPUs.

Our performance model can be used as a comparison to the results. For the CPU version of the model, we set $\gamma_{\mathrm{CPU}} = 1.8 \times 10^{-8}$ in (3), and for the GPU version we set $\gamma_{\mathrm{GPU}} = 8.0 \times 10^{-6}$ in (4). Note again that γ is a tuning parameter

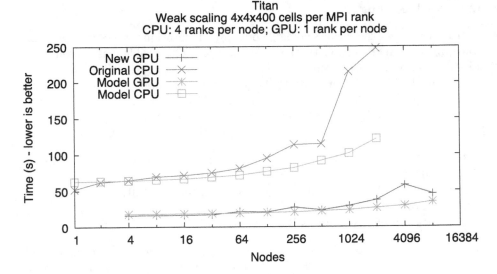

Fig. 5. Weak scaling SNAP on Titan

to the model that we cannot directly benchmark, and so we must choose a value with regression. We use the benchmarked values for network latency and bandwidth as given in Sect. 5.

The model predicts the runtime of eight octant sweeps, and so we multiply the prediction by the number of these as reported by the application; for the CPU this was 348 sweeps and for the GPU this was 11 sweeps. The number of sweeps is the same as the number of inners performed, noting that the CPU version sweeps (and counts) energy groups independently whereas the GPU code always sweeps all groups.

The model is plotted in Fig. 5 alongside the data collected from the implementation and it is clear that our scaling results are validated by the model. Given the choice of γ in the performance model, the scaling results are accurate on average to 17.6 % for the GPU, and 18.8 % for the CPU runs; these accuracies are across a very wide range of scales, from 1 to 8,192 nodes. Note that we would *not* expect 'perfect' weak scaling of a horizontal line parallel to the x-axis in the figure. The achieved times of the CPU runs at large scale do start to deviate from the model, however this is likely due to network considerations on Titan, rather than being attributed to inaccuracies the model.

It should be noted that even on four nodes the accelerated implementation spends 55 % of the sweep time in communication. At 8192 ranks with a total grid size of 512 × 256 × 400, 84 % of the sweep time is spent in inter-node communication. At this scale, we obtain 35 % weak-scaling efficiency comparing the time for four nodes to 8192. This efficiency is similar to that obtained by the original implementation running on the CPUs. Therefore the benefits of our improved node-level scheme utilising GPUs have successfully carried across to the MPI version at scale, whilst running four times as fast.

The running times on Titan can be very variable, often up to a 2× difference. Whilst the time taken to complete the sweeps increases this is only in the network time; the computation portion remains the same. There seems to be large variability in the network performance of the Titan supercomputer at scale, as has been shown previously for the Gemini network with the torus topology [13, 19]. In our results we have taken the minimum time across five runs. We see the variability even within consecutive runs within the same job allocation; node placement is not the major factor in the variability.

Piz Daint. The results of the same weak scaling experiment run on Piz Daint can be seen in Fig. 6. The GPU implementation provides a speedup of up to 2× over the original implementation running on the CPU. The STREAM benchmark [17] achieves a memory bandwidth of 41 GBytes/s on the single socket Xeon compared to 182 GBytes/s for GPU-STREAM on the K20X [8].

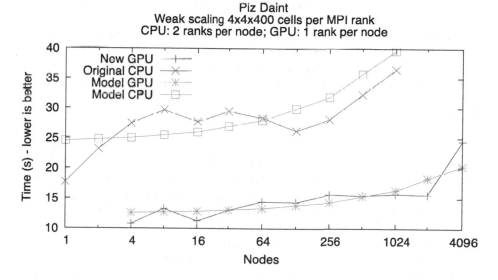

Fig. 6. Weak scaling SNAP on Piz Daint

Piz Daint performs much better than Titan when it comes to time spent communicating. At the initial point of four nodes, 42 % of the sweep time is spent in the communications compared to 55 % on Titan. At 2048 nodes this has risen to 60 % on Piz Daint compared to 80 % on Titan demonstrating that Piz Daint has better network performance at scale. The communication time then doubles when doubling the number of nodes to 4096, but the compute time stays constant. Piz Daint consists of 5272 nodes and so this experiment is over

75 % of the whole machine. The figure also shows that parallel efficiency was at around 70 % up to 2048 nodes. This is an improvement over Titan, and this is likely due to the better interconnect. Communication times are between 1.3 and 3.2 times *faster* on Piz Daint than Titan over the weak scaling experiment. The computation time of the sweep is also around 14 % faster on the GPUs in Piz Daint than those in Titan; this may be due to driver versions and the improved host CPUs in Piz Daint as the GPUs between the two machines are identical.

As before, our performance model can be used as a comparison to the results as is shown in Fig. 6. For the CPU version of the model, we set $\gamma_{CPU} = 9.0 \times 10^{-9}$ in (3) (half of what we chose for Titan), and for the GPU version we set $\gamma_{GPU} = 1.4 \times 10^{-4}$ in (4). The GPU scaling results match well to the predicted values, with an average of a 8.6 % difference. The CPU model lies within 11.9 % of the achieved values, but does not capture the wave-like trend of the obtained results; importantly the upward curve indicating an increase at node counts beyond 128 is captured by the model showing the scaling performance as a whole with enough accuracy to be of use.

After each inner and outer iteration the convergence of the solution is compared. The maximum change since the previous iteration of the scalar flux per energy group is computed and shared between all MPI nodes. This requires an `MPI_Allreduce` operation. For the outer iteration convergence check, only the maximum change overall is needed and so only a reduction operation over a single value is required. As we weak scale to more nodes, the time to perform these reduction operation increases from less than 1 % to approximately 8 % of the runtime. The sweep still dominates the solution time requiring around 90 % of the total time.

6.3   Choice of Chunk Size

The larger the chunk size, the fewer times we have to exhibit the start-up/teardown costs (see Fig. 4) and so the total time spent in the computation kernel reduces. Note the total amount of work remains constant for all chunk sizes. However by increasing the chunk size we increase the size of the messages that we need to send and hence copy from the GPU to the CPU, over the network and back onto the neighbouring GPU. Figure 7a shows the effect that chunk size has on performance. The time to copy the data is negligible at small chunk sizes, but the computation time is larger than the minimum achievable with a larger chunk size. We are also not using much network bandwidth as we are sending many comparatively small messages; approximately 140 kilobytes per message for a chunk size of one.

Conversely for large chunk sizes the data transfer time over PCIe becomes noticeable and the network is required to send fewer, larger messages; approximately 28 megabytes per message for a chunk size of 200. Note that in this case we are also holding the sweep up and the MPI rank starting the sweep will sit idle for much of the sweep execution time.

The minimum height bar in Fig. 7a will give the best trade-off between computation time per node, network bandwidth *and* latency, and keeping all nodes busy throughout the sweep by providing enough chunks along the pencil length for spatial over-decomposition. Due to the data dependency of the wavefront sweep MPI communications cannot be overlapped with computation as each rank must always have a blocking receive. As can be seen from Fig. 7a, for Titan the best chunk size we found was eight; on Piz Daint we found the best was 20.

Our performance model from Sect. 5 (using $\gamma_{GPU} = 8.0 \times 10^{-6}$ as before) also shows this increase in running time with larger chunk size, as pictured in Fig. 7b. The model predicts the lowest running time could be achieved with chunk size of 2, however most small chunk sizes are very similar in runtime. The predicted values are most sensitive to the bandwidth parameter β.

6.4 Strong Scaling

The strong scaling of deterministic transport has always presented a challenge in the real world. The limit imposed by memory capacity means a realistic starting point for a strong scaling study (at a few nodes) is difficult.

To begin an investigation into strong scaling, a relatively large grid was chosen with common angular and energy group fidelity. The physical spatial and time dimensions were chosen only so that the problem converged within a short amount of time. We therefore use the following parameters which has a memory footprint of approx. 690 GBytes:

- $256 \times 256 \times 256$ cells with mesh size of $2.56\,cm \times 2.56\,cm \times 2.56\,cm$
- S_8: 10 angles per octant and 32 energy groups
- 1 time-step of $0.01\,s$ with inner convergence criteria of $1.0E - 5$
- 2 orders of scattering expansion
- Computation of 4 XY planes before communication

When running this problem on Titan it was not possible to run the original CPU code with hybrid MPI + OpenMP as the original code would hang, and so the results were collected in this section with flat MPI with 16 ranks per node. The original code required 347 inners to converge.

Figure 8a shows the strong scaling results obtained on Titan with the original CPU implementation and in Fig. 8b our new version running on the GPUs. Predicted times for both implementations are added, using predicted grind times of $\gamma_{CPU} = 1.8 \times 10^{-8}$ and $\gamma_{GPU} = 3.0 \times 10^{-5}$.

A linear line is also plotted to demonstrate that the model (and obtained times) are not expected to scale linearly with node count; this shows that strong scaling is a real challenge for transport code. Note that the CPU version scaled nearly linearly to begin with; this implies that in order to improve the scalability of the many-core version we must reduce the node count by increasing the potential memory capacity of each GPU node. However, our solution strong scales at least as well as the state of the art for deterministic transport.

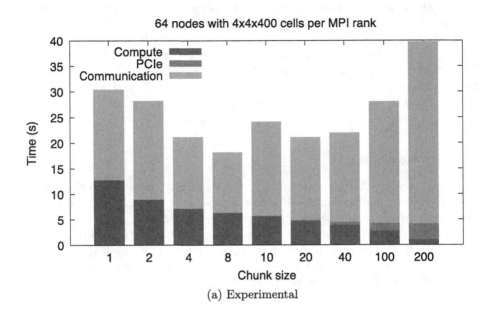

(a) Experimental

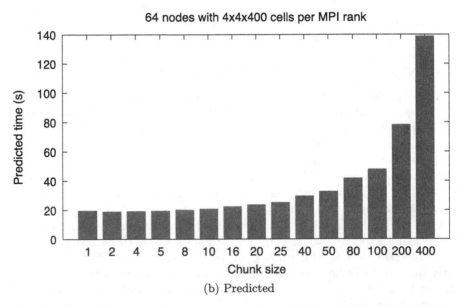

(b) Predicted

Fig. 7. Sweep timings for various chunk sizes on 64 nodes of Titan (Color figure online)

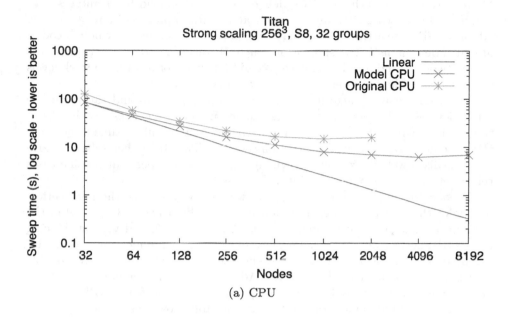

(a) CPU

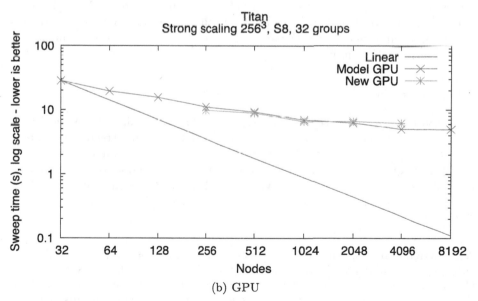

(b) GPU

Fig. 8. Sweep timings for strong scaling

7 Conclusion

Many-core devices such as GPUs deliver memory bandwidth advantages over traditional multi-core CPU architectures along with improved hiding of memory latency and so are attractive for increasing performance of memory bound codes, of which deterministic transport is one such. However, deterministic transport is also network bound and is sensitive to careful balance of intra-node work levels in order to obtain good performance on a large system.

We used the KBA algorithm for spatial decomposition and saturated the GPU devices with work by solving all angles and energy groups for all cells in the local wavefront. We have shown that good scaling is still possible when using GPUs to accelerate the computation on the node. The GPUs themselves are also being utilised well as we have shown they are obtaining performance increases relative to their memory bandwidth.

By accelerating the intra-node solve, we do however make the final performance of the transport code more dependent on the network. Over half of the running time is spent in communication with our accelerated version. Placing more GPU devices in a single node to avoid network communication and providing increased bandwidth and lower latency network interfaces are two possible solutions for this at a hardware level. Additionally if the memory capacity of GPU devices was increased it would be possible to run on fewer MPI ranks.

Our accelerated version of the SNAP mini-app shows that time-dependant solves of the transport equation scale well enough using the regular KBA algorithm. This approach is therefore valuable in the preparation of transport solvers for the upcoming many-core Department of Energy CORAL procurement systems, Sierra and Summit.

7.1 Future Work

We intend to investigate schemes to improve the strong scalability by increasing the size of the spatial sub-domain per MPI rank. We can stream the data to the device so we are not limited by the memory capacity of the device, instead using the larger memory capacity of the host and thus reducing the number of MPI ranks required. Additionally we will implement our scheme in OpenMP 4.5 to compare a single source implementation across GPUs and Knights Landing Xeon Phis.

Acknowledgements. This work has been financially supported by A.W.E. The authors would like to thank the University of Bristol High Performance Computing Group and Intel Parallel Computing Center; and Maria Grazia Giuffreda of CSCS at the Swiss National Supercomputing Centre for access to Piz Daint. This research used resources of the Oak Ridge Leadership Computing Facility at the Oak Ridge National Laboratory, which is supported by the Office of Science of the U.S. Department of Energy under Contract No. DE-AC05-00OR22725.

References

1. Adams, M.P., Adams, M.L., Hawkins, W.D., Smith, T., Rauchwerger, L., Amato, N.M., Bailey, T.S., Falgout, R.D.: Provably optimal parallel transport sweeps on regular grids. In: International Conference on Mathematics, Computational Methods and Reactor Physics, pp. 2535–2553 (2013)
2. Adams, M.P., Adams, M.L., Mcgraw, C.N., Till, A.T., Bailey, T.S.: Provably optimal parallel transport sweeps with non-contiguous partitions. In: Joint International Conference on Mathematics and Computation (M&C), Supercomputing in Nuclear Applications (SNA) and the Monte Carlo (MC) Method, pp. 1–19. No. ANS MC2015, American Nuclear Society, Nashville, Tennessee (2015)
3. Bailey, T.S., Falgout, R.D.: Analysis of massively parallel discrete-ordinates transport sweep algorithms with collisions. In: International Conference on Mathematics, Computational Methods, and Reactor Physics, pp. 1–15. American Nuclear Society, New York, USA (2009)
4. Baker, C., Davidson, G., Evans, T.M., Hamilton, S., Jarrell, J., Joubert, W.: High performance radiation transport simulations: preparing for TITAN. In: 2012 International Conference for High Performance Computing, Networking, Storage and Analysis, pp. 1–10 (2012)
5. Baker, R., Koch, K.: An Sn algorithm for the massively parallel CM-200 computer. Nucl. Sci. Eng. **128**, 312–320 (1998)
6. Baker, R.S.: An Sn algorithm for modern architectures. In: Joint International Conference on Mathematics and Computation (M&C), Supercomputing in Nuclear Applications (SNA) and the Monte Carlo (MC) Method. No. ANS MC2015, American Nuclear Society, Nashville, TN (2015)
7. Baker, R., McGhee, J., Koch, K., Morel, J.: Two Sn algorithms for the massively parallel CM-200 computer. Submitted to Nuclear Science and Engineering (1996)
8. Deakin, T., McIntosh-Smith, S.: GPU-STREAM: benchmarking the achievable memory bandwidth of Graphics Processing Units (poster). In: Supercomputing, Austin, Texas (2015)
9. Deakin, T., McIntosh-Smith, S., Gaudin, W.: Expressing parallelism on many-core for deterministic discrete ordinates transport. In: Workshop on Representative Applications at IEEE Cluster, Chicago (2015)
10. Deakin, T., McIntosh-Smith, S., Martineau, M., Gaudin, W.: An improved parallelism scheme for deterministic discrete ordinates transport. Int. J. High Perform. Comput. Appl. (Spec. Issue) (2015, in press)
11. Evans, T.M., Joubert, W., Hamilton, S.P., Johnson, S.R., Turner, J.A., Davidson, G.G., Pandya, T.M.: Three-Dimensional Discrete Ordinates Reactor Assembly Calculations on GPUs. In: Joint International Conference on Mathematics and Computation (M&C), Supercomputing in Nuclear Applications (SNA) and the Monte Carlo (MC) Method. No. ANS MC2015, American Nuclear Society, Nashville, Tennessee (2015)
12. Evans, T.M., Stafford, A.S., Slaybaugh, R.N., Clarno, K.T.: Denovo: a new three-dimensional parallel discrete ordinates code in SCALE. Nucl. Technol. **171**, 171–200 (2010)
13. Freed, J., Gupta, S., Tiwari, D.: An analysis of network congestion in the Titan supercomputers interconnect (poster). In: Supercomuting, pp. 1–2 (2015)
14. Hoisie, A., Lubeck, O., Wasserman, H.: Performance and scalability analysis of teraflop-scale parallel architectures using multidimensional wavefront applications (2000)

15. Koch, K., Baker, R., Alcouffe, R.: Solution of the first-order form of three-dimensional discrete ordinates equations on a massively parallel machine. Trans. Am. Nucl. Soc. **65**, 198–199 (1992)
16. Lewis, E., Miller, W.J.: Computational Methods of Neutron Transport. American Nuclear Society, La Grange Park (1993)
17. McCalpin, J.D.: Memory bandwidth and machine balance in current high performance computers. In: IEEE Computer Society Technical Committee on Computer Architecture (TCCA) Newsletter, pp. 19–25, December 1995
18. Munshi, A.: The OpenCL Specification, Version 1.1 (2011)
19. Pedretti, K., Vaughan, C., Barrett, R., Devine, K., Hemmert, K.S.: Using the Cray Gemini performance counters
20. Pennycook, S.J., Hammond, S.D., Mudalige, G.R., Wright, S.A., Jarvis, S.A.: On the acceleration of wavefront applications using distributed many-core architectures. Comput. J. **55**(2), 138–153 (2012)
21. Rabenseifner, R., Schulz, G.: B_eff v3.6. https://fs.hlrs.de/projects/par/mpi/b_eff/
22. Strohmaier, E., Simon, H., Dongarra, J., Meuer, M.: Top 500, November 2015. http://www.top500.org
23. Villa, O., Johnson, D.R., OConnor, M., Bolotin, E., Nellans, D., Luitjens, J., Sakharnykh, N., Wang, P., Micikevicius, P., Scudiero, A., Keckler, S.W., Dally, W.J.: Scaling the power wall: a path to exascale. In: Supercomputing (2014)
24. Zerr, R.J., Baker, R.S.: SNAP: SN (discrete ordinates) application proxy - proxy description. Technical report, LA-UR-13-21070, Los Alamos National Labratory (2013)

Efficiency of High Order Spectral Element Methods on Petascale Architectures

Maxwell Hutchinson[1]([✉]), Alexander Heinecke[2], Hans Pabst[3], Greg Henry[4], Matteo Parsani[5], and David Keyes[5]

[1] Department of Physics, University of Chicago, Chicago, IL, USA
maxhutch@uchicago.edu
[2] Intel Corporation, Santa Clara, CA, USA
[3] Intel Semiconductor AG, Zurich, Switzerland
[4] Intel Corporation, Hillsboro, OR, USA
[5] Extreme Computing Research Center, KAUST,
Thuwal 23955, Kingdom of Saudi Arabia

Abstract. High order methods for the solution of PDEs expose a trade-off between computational cost and accuracy on a per degree of freedom basis. In many cases, the cost increases due to higher arithmetic intensity while affecting data movement minimally. As architectures tend towards wider vector instructions and expect higher arithmetic intensities, the best order for a particular simulation may change.

This study highlights preferred orders by identifying the high order efficiency frontier of the spectral element method implemented in Nek5000 and NekBox: the set of orders and meshes that minimize computational cost at fixed accuracy. First, we extract Nek's order-dependent computational kernels and demonstrate exceptional hardware utilization by hardware-aware implementations. Then, we perform production-scale calculations of the nonlinear single mode Rayleigh-Taylor instability on BlueGene/Q and Cray XC40-based supercomputers to highlight the influence of the architecture. Accuracy is defined with respect to physical observables, and computational costs are measured by the core-hour charge of the entire application. The total number of grid points needed to achieve a given accuracy is reduced by increasing the polynomial order. On the XC40 and BlueGene/Q, polynomial orders as high as 31 and 15 come at no marginal cost per timestep, respectively. Taken together, these observations lead to a strong preference for high order

© Springer International Publishing Switzerland 2016
J.M. Kunkel et al. (Eds.): ISC High Performance 2016, LNCS 9697, pp. 449–466, 2016.
DOI: 10.1007/978-3-319-41321-1_23

discretizations that use fewer degrees of freedom. From a performance point of view, we demonstrate up to 60 % full application bandwidth utilization at scale and achieve ≈1 PFlop/s of compute performance in Nek's most flop-intense methods.

Keywords: High order · Vectorization · Spectral element method · Nek5000

1   Introduction

The solution of partial differential equations (PDEs) is a core problem in HPC, with particular application to computational materials science and fluid dynamics. PDEs are solved by discrete approximation: space and time are sampled and the PDEs is translated into a relation on those samples. From a mathematical point of view, these approximations are characterized by stability conditions and convergence rates. Schemes which do not satisfy stability conditions usually fail catastrophically with values that diverge to infinity. The convergence rate describes the relationship between the resolution and the error. For a characteristic inter-sample spacing h, a method is of order p if the error goes as h^p. High order methods are schemes with convergence rates higher than third order [21], many of which expose the order as a user input.

From a computational point of view, the approximations are characterized by sparsity, locality, and arithmetic intensity. As the order increases, the sparsity and locality typically decrease while the arithmetic intensity increases. The improved convergence rates are 'paid for' with more floating point operations (FLOP), on a per sample basis, while, for a given error tolerance, the number of samples can be decreased. The relationship between these computational characteristics and computational cost is complicated by features common to modern architectures: vector instructions, deep caches, and arithmetic-to-data movement imbalance.

Here, we explore the relationship between order, accuracy, cost, and architecture. We identify the user-facing properties of high order methods: the accuracy in observables, time to solution, resource usage, and required scale. We also identify the user-defined inputs: the physical problem, the order, the total number of samples, the number of processors, and the computer architectures. To make the study more practical, we focus on the specific task of optimizing a study of the single-mode Rayleigh-Taylor instability (smRTI) as a parameter sweep over Grashof and Prandtl numbers. This is a high throughput use-case, where the relevant cost is resource usage and scale is fixed with respect to the size of the problem and assumed to not be a limitation. This leaves us with the accuracy and resource usage versus the order, number of samples, and computer architectures.

We select the NekBox version of the Nek5000 code (together: Nek), which implements the spectral element method (SEM) [18] with tunable order, is known to scale to a million ranks [16], and has been used for Rayleigh-Taylor problems in the past [9]. NekBox takes advantage of static, uniform meshes to solve the coarse part of the preconditioner with FFTs or DCTs, improving efficiency and scalability. We extract representative order-dependent kernels from Nek and analyze their performance on BlueGene/Q and Cray XC40 supercomputers.

We also conduct a set of application benchmarks to measure the cost and accuracy. The cost is computed in core-hours, in the same way most users are charged. The accuracy is computed with respect to the smRTI's bubble height and mix volume, which are the most common observables studied in the smRTI community. The benchmarks vary the order and total number of samples, and are conducted on the Mira and Shaheen XC40 supercomputers at Argonne Leadership Computing Facility (ALCF) and KAUST Supercomputing Laboratory (KSL), respectively.

1.1 Outline

In Sect. 2, we review the SEM as implemented in Nek. In Sect. 3, we introduce LIBXSMM for hardware-aware implementation of Nek's performance critical kernels, and demonstrate their performance in isolation. In Sect. 4, we perform a convergence/performance study of SEM discretizations for the smRTI problem and present full-application performance at scale. Section 5 concludes with a discussion of preferred orders on the BlueGene/Q and Cray XC40 supercomputers.

2 Nek's Computational Core

2.1 Governing Equations and Time-Splitting

Nek5000 and NekBox solve the incompressible Navier–Stokes equations:

$$\frac{\partial u}{\partial t} + u \cdot \nabla u = -\frac{1}{\rho}\nabla p + \nu\nabla^2 u + f \qquad \nabla \cdot u = 0, \tag{1}$$

where u is the flow velocity, ρ is the fluid density, p is the pressure, ν is the kinematic viscosity, and f consists of user-defined forcing terms. Additionally, Nek can solve advection-diffusion equations for scalars, such as the temperature or mass fraction:

$$\frac{\partial \phi_i}{\partial t} + u \cdot \nabla\phi_i = \alpha_i\nabla^2\phi_i + q_i, \tag{2}$$

where ϕ_i is the scalar value, α_i is the diffusivity, and q_i is a user-defined source term, each for the ith scalar.

The time derivative is discretized with a backward difference formula (BDF), within which the nonlinear and forcing terms are extrapolated (EX):

$$\sum_{j=0}^{k} \frac{\beta_i}{\Delta t} M u_i^{n-j} = -\frac{1}{\rho}D_i p^n + \nu K u_i^n + \sum_{j=1}^{n} a_j \left[M f_i^{n-j} - (Cu_i)^{n-j} \right], \tag{3}$$

where M is the mass matrix, C is the convection matrix, K is the stiffness matrix, D is the gradient matrix, $i \in \{1, 2, 3\}$ are the spatial dimension indexes, n is the time level index, and k is the formal order of accuracy of the BDF/EX scheme. The pressure is decoupled from the new velocity, u^n, by taking the divergence:

$$Kp^n = D_i \sum_{j=1}^{n} a_j F_i^{n-j}, \qquad (4)$$

where $F_i^n = M f_i^n - (C u_i)^n$, which results in the Poisson pressure equation. Finally, the pressure is incorporated back into (3):

$$\left[\nu K + \frac{b_0}{\Delta t} M \right] u_i^n = -D_i \frac{p^n}{\rho} + \sum_{j=1}^{k} \left[a_j F_i^{n-j} + \frac{b_j}{\Delta t} M u^{n-j} \right], \qquad (5)$$

which results in three Helmholtz velocity equations.

These steps are the core of Nek5000 and NekBox: the explicit calculation of right-hand sides, a Poisson solver for the pressure, (4), and a Helmholtz solver for the three components of the velocity, (5).

2.2   Spectral Element Method

Nek5000 and NekBox implement SEM: a two-level discretization constructed from tensor products of Gauss-Lobatto-Legendre (GLL) quadrature points within elements and continuity across elements, forming a mesh. Fields are represented as

$$u(x, y, z) = \sum_{i=0}^{p} \sum_{j=0}^{p} \sum_{k=0}^{p} \tilde{u}_{i,j,k,e} h_i(x) h_j(y) h_k(z), \qquad (6)$$

where p is the polynomial order of the method, $e(x, y, z)$ is the index of the element in the mesh, and $h_i(x)$ is the ith Lagrange polynomial through the GLL points of element e. The choice of Lagrange polynomials leads to diagonal mass matrices and related geometric factors. The spectral basis within each element enjoys exponential convergence with respect to the polynomial order. GLL points do not sample space uniformly, so concatenating elements is more effective at reducing grid spacing than increasing spectral order. Many small elements are also better able to match complex geometries than fewer larger ones. The spectral element method is able to satisfy both the demand for geometric flexibility with quasi-uniform coverage and spectral convergence, but the particular choice of the spectral order versus the number of elements can be difficult to optimize.

In SEM, operators are written as the product of a local operator and *direct stiffness summation*, which enforces continuity at the shared element boundaries. The local operators are decomposed into tensor products of 1D operators. The general form of an operator A is:

$$A = (A_x \times I_y \times I_z) + (I_x \times A_y \times I_z) + (I_x \times I_y \times A_z), \qquad (7)$$

where A_x, A_y, A_z are 1D projections of the operator A and I is the identity matrix. In this way, linear operators from $R^{N \times N \times N} \to R^{N \times N \times N}$ can be evaluated in $O(N^4)$ operations instead of $O(N^6)$ [20]. This reduces the arithmetic intensity of operator evaluation in SEM to $O(p)$.

2.3   Computational Profile

The spectral element method, as implemented in Nek5000 and NekBox, spends its time in three computational motifs: sparse communication, vector-vector, and matrix-matrix. The sparse communication comes from the direct stiffness summations and the coarse part of the pressure preconditioner. The vector-vector workload comes from inner products in the solvers and frequent rescaling by geometric factors, which are shaped like the diagonal mass matrix. The matrix-matrix workload comes from local operator evaluation.

The direct-stiffness summation is handled by a stand-alone library [11,17]. In Nek, the pressure solve takes roughly 30 % of the run-time, distributed between operator application, inner products, and the preconditioner. The preconditioner is multigrid with a local additive Schwarz part and the global coarse part [13]. In NekBox, the coarse part of the pressure preconditioner is solved directly with FFTs or fast cosine transforms, and typically takes less than 5 % of the total runtime. Local communication makes up a small portion of NekBox's run time at moderate numbers of points per processor, and Nek5000 and NekBox weak scale effectively to millions of ranks [9].

The efficiency of the vector-vector computation is generally left to the compiler, aided by aggressive loop merging in the solvers. For architectures that support them, the compiler needs help issuing non-temporal stores, which are performance optimal only if the working set is larger than the last level cache. These stores are used in parts of the solver and local element evaluation, and are discussed further in Sect. 3.

Matrix-matrix is the most accessible and performance critical portion of the workload. In particular, it is the only part of Nek that depends on the order, holding the total degrees of freedom (DOFs) fixed.

2.4   Order-Dependent Kernels

There are two matrix-matrix routines that sit inside of the iterative solvers: the Helmholtz operator and a basis transformation.

The Helmholtz operator is found on the left-hand side of (4) and (5):

$$Hu = (h_1 K + h_2 M)u,$$

where the special case of $h_2 = 0$ is the Poisson operator.

1: **procedure** LOCAL HELMHOLTZ OPERATOR(Hu, u, h_1, h_2)
2:     $(Hu)_{i,j,k} \leftarrow (G_x)_{i,j,k} * \sum_l (K_x)_{i,l} u_{l,j,k}$ ▷ matrix-multiply size (p^2, p, p)
3:     **for** $k = 0 \rightarrow p$ **do**
4:         $(Hu)_{i,j,k} \mathrel{+}= (G_y)_{i,j,k} * \sum_l (K_y)_{j,l} u_{i,l,k}$ ▷ matrix-multiply size (p, p, p)
5:     **end for**
6:     $(Hu)_{i,j,k} \mathrel{+}= (G_z)_{i,j,k} * \sum_l (K_z)_{k,l} u_{i,j,l}$ ▷ matrix-multiply size (p, p^2, p)
7:     $(Hu)_{i,j,k} \mathrel{+}= h_1 (Hu)_{i,j,k} + h_2 M_{i,j,k} u_{i,j,k}$
8: **end procedure**

G is a constant diagonal matrix derived from geometric terms and subscripts within parenthesis refer to spatial directions. Matrix sizes are given in BLAS notation: rows in result, columns in result, inner dimension.

The basis transformation is used to diagonalize the local Poisson operator in the overlapping Schwarz preconditioner, to restrict and interpolate the solution and residual in the multigrid preconditioner, and to dealias the convection operator.

1: **procedure** TRANSFORM(v, u)
2:     $f_{i,j,k} \leftarrow \sum_l (A_x)_{i,l} u_{l,j,k}$ ▷ matrix-multiply size (p^2, p, p)
3:     **for** $k = 0 \rightarrow p$ **do**
4:         $g_{i,j,k} \leftarrow \sum_l (A_y)_{j,l} f_{i,l,k}$ ▷ matrix-multiply size (p, p, p)
5:     **end for**
6:     $v_{i,j,k} \leftarrow \sum_l (A_z)_{k,l} g_{i,j,l}$ ▷ matrix-multiply size (p, p^2, p)
7: **end procedure**

3   Kernel Analysis and Optimization

3.1   Small Matrix Multiplications

The implementation of fast matrix multiplications, i.e., the BLAS library's GEMM routines, and dense linear algebra more generally is one of computer science's best studied fields. However, large matrices [7] have been the primary focus and, as a result, vendor-tuned BLAS implementations do not provide optimal performance when used for the small GEMMs in Nek. Several BLAS libraries recently introduced so-called batched interfaces to speed-up series of independent and small multiplications by exploiting parallelism and amortizing calling overheads [10]. As Nek performs dependent GEMMs within each element, batched execution would necessarily be inter-element, inhibiting important caching optimization and consuming significantly more memory bandwidth. Therefore, most of Nek's computer science related work was devoted on speeding up small GEMMs [19]. Parts of Nek5000 and the related NekCEM codes have been independently ported to OpenACC [14,17] to speed-up small GEMMs.

Today, Nek5000 and NekBox ship with a FORTRAN-based matrix-matrix implementation called mxm_std. By default, mxm_std explicitly defines multiple interfaces corresponding to values of the inner dimension k, and provides unrolled FORTRAN primitives to the compiler. For IBM's BlueGene series, common sizes are manually implemented for best performance in FORTRAN assembly-intrinsics in mxm_bgq. Similarly, mxm_std features some special case optimizations targeting AMD's Opteron processor, which is used in the United States' largest system, Titan, at Oak Ridge National Laboratory.

In order to ensure the best possible performance on a range of modern Intel processors, featuring different versions of Advance Vector Extensions (AVX) instructions, we would need to conduct a long and complicated tuning effort of Nek's mxm_std akin to the narrow customizations already present. Instead, we integrated an early prototype of the LIBXSMM library [1,8] into

NekBox. LIBXSMM provides highly-optimized single-threaded small matrix-multiplication routines tuned for all recent Intel processors. It is already successfully used in the quantum chemistry application CP2K and high-order finite element seismic wave equation solver SeisSol [4].

In contrast to mxm_std, LIBXSMM creates a specific kernel implementation for each small matrix multiplication size and optimizes that kernel specifically for each set of vector extensions. Each kernel is composed from a-priori known and best-performing basic blocks. Remainder handling can be performed either explicitly by application-side padding or internally by slightly less efficient fill-in basic blocks. We rely on the latter in our integration of LIBXSMM into NekBox.

We leverage LIBXSMM's experimental just-in-time (JIT) compilation feature to adapt at runtime to Nek's spectral order. The JIT feature generates a small matrix multiplication when its size is requested for the first time and caches compiled code until the application process is terminated. Additionally, LIBXSMM can expose the function pointer to the application to bypass future dispatches when call patterns are simple.

As an example, we provide the integration of LIBXSMM into NekBox's local Helmholtz kernel from Sect. 2.4 in Listing 1.1. This fragment is called within a loop over elements that is typically long enough to amortize overheads. When entering the element-local operator for the very first time, we request the required kernels from the LIBXSMM library, which JIT compiles them internally, and store the corresponding functions pointers into persistent variables to avoid dispatching in subsequent calls. Compared to the pseudo-code fragment, cf. 2.4, we use temporary buffers to separate matrix-matrix from vector-vector operations, which are performed in one step at the end of each element. The other common matrix-matrix motifs, basis transformation in particular, are optimized analogously.

3.2   Enhancing Element Update Performance by Streaming Stores

Caches in Intel processors are designed as write-back caches with read-for-ownership (RFO). Therefore, writing to a vector in main memory costs two operations: a load into the cache and the write. Nek performs many such element updates, cf. Listing 1.1, and long vector updates in linear solvers. Compiling the Helmholtz element update leads to 5 streams being explicitly read (gx, gy, gz, b, u), one RFO of au and one write of au. As we stream through all elements the RFOs are harmful for two reasons: (a) they consume bandwidth and therefore can cause a $\approx 16\%$ performance drop; and (b) they unnecessarily occupy cache space and might evict useful data.

Since the SSE2 instruction set, the Intel architecture offers so-called non-temporal stores (NTS). These special instructions write data directly into main memory without generating RFOs and consuming cache. They operate best when being executed on vector-length aligned addresses, as cache-line splits are impossible. The compiler cannot fulfill the alignment requirement for all orders, because Nek stores field data compactly, which prohibits semi-automatic generation of NTS. Therefore, we implemented a FORTRAN interface module with a

Listing 1.1. Integration of LIBXSMM into NekBox's element-local Helmholtz operator. xmm1, xmm2, xmm3 are persistent functions pointers to amortize LIBXSMM's dispatching overhead. The libxsmm_dispatch call JITs the requested kernel and populates the persistent function pointers.

```
logical, save :: init = .false.
type(LIBXSMM_DMM_FUNCTION), save :: xmm1, xmm2, xmm3

! lazy initialization of function-private function pointers
! to eliminate dispatching overhead
if (.not. init) then
  call libxsmm_dispatch(xmm1, nx, ny*nz, nx, 1.0_dp, 0.0_dp)
  call libxsmm_dispatch(xmm2, nx, ny, ny, 1.0_dp, 0.0_dp)
  call libxsmm_dispatch(xmm3, nx*ny, nz, nz, 1.0_dp, 0.0_dp)
  init = .true.
endif

! element-local operation
call libxsmm_call(xmm1, C_LOC(wddx), C_LOC(u(1,1,1)), C_LOC(work1))
do iz=1,nz
    call libxsmm_call(xmm2, C_LOC(u(1,1,iz)), C_LOC(wddyt), C_LOC(work2(1,1,iz)))
enddo
call libxsmm_call(xmm3, C_LOC(u(1,1,1)), C_LOC(wddzt), C_LOC(work3))

! element update
au(:,:,:) = h1* ( work1*gx + work2*gy + work3*gz ) + h2*b*u
```

C-backend and x86 intrinsics that applies loop-peeling to leverage NTS for the majority of stores in long, potentially unaligned updates. This module covers the important kernels of Nek by offering NTS-enhanced primitives to: (a) set an 1d-array to a fixed value (b) copy an 1d-array (c) multiply component-wise an 1d array, and (d) perform the Helmholtz element update, including the special case of the Poisson operator, $h_2 = 0$. For case (b), Listing 1.2 depicts Intel AVX2 code.

3.3   Discussion of Performance Reproducers

In order to analyze the performance of LIBXSMM integration and the NTS module, we have implemented standalone reproducers of the identified small matrix multiplication motifs. They are included in the LIBXSMM library as examples and performance tests. In contrast to NekBox, they are parallelized via OpenMP instead of MPI, but the performance agrees within 10 % of a full NekBox execution at scale. We used a single node of the Cray XC40 and BlueGene/Q, cf. Sect. 4.1, for generating performance data in this section.

Figure 1 compares the performance of Intel MKL 11.2.1, Nek's own mxm_std, and LIBXSMM with and without non-temporal stores. For all element sizes, LIBXSMM offers the best performance, but the difference for orders ≤16 are very small as the execution is heavily memory bandwidth bound. A significant boost is possible by leveraging NTS: we are able to sustain 100 % of the STREAM triad bandwidth (101.6 GiB/s) up to an element size of 16. For larger problems, the small GEMM performance is more important. Here LIBXSMM is up to 2× faster than mxm_std und up to 40 % faster than Intel MKL.

Listing 1.2. Loop peeling approach including determining the middle section for which aligned NTS instructions can be used.

```
void stream_vector_copy( const double* i_a,
                         double*       io_c,
                         const int     i_length) {
  int l_n = 0;
  int l_trip_prolog = 0;
  int l_trip_stream = 0;

  /* init the trip counts to determine aligned middle section */
  stream_init( i_length, (size_t)io_c, &l_trip_prolog, &l_trip_stream );

  /* run the prologue */
  for ( ; l_n < l_trip_prolog;  l_n++ ) {
    io_c[l_n] = i_a[l_n];
  }
  /* run the bulk, using streaming stores */
  for ( ; l_n < l_trip_stream;  l_n+=8 ) {
    _mm256_stream_pd( &(io_c[l_n]),   _mm256_loadu_pd(&(i_a[l_n]))   );
    _mm256_stream_pd( &(io_c[l_n+4]), _mm256_loadu_pd(&(i_a[l_n+4])) );
  }
  /* run the epilogue */
  for ( ; l_n < i_length;  l_n++ ) {
    io_c[l_n] = i_a[l_n];
  }
}
```

In case of very low orders the benefit of NTS is greater than 16%, which we attribute to NTS avoiding cache pollution. For medium sized orders we exactly see the expected 16%, and large problems have additional bandwidth available such that RFOs are less harmful.

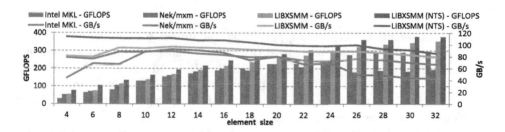

Fig. 1. Performance of the Helmholtz reproducer running on a single node of Shaheen for different implementation of small matrix multiplications. NTS denotes the usage of the non-temporal store optimized module. (Color figure online)

The performance numbers for the basis transformation on Shaheen are comparable to the Helmholtz operator and therefore not plotted. To summarize them, LIBXSMM-based GEMMs are the fastest and, due to higher computational demand, NTS are only important of for very small 1d sizes. LIBXSMM is able to achieve 50% of maximum floating-point performance for moderate orders. LIBXSMM ranges from 4× faster than mxm_std and Intel MKL at the smallest order to 40% faster at the largest.

The performance of the Helmholtz kernel is representative of the basis transformations kernel on Mira as well. To compare with Shaheen, Fig. 2 repeats the Helmholtz operator reproducer experiment on a single node of Mira. IBM ESSL version 5.1.1 is used as the vendor library in place of Intel MKL. In place of LIBXSMM, mxm_bgq, which features QPX SIMD instructions, is used for the sizes that it supports. When no QPX implementation is available, mxm_bgq falls back to mxm_std. Up to element size 16, Nek's mxm_std and mxm_bgq libraries are a better choice compared to IBM ESSL. For larger element sizes (except 22 and 24) the performance is comparable. However, the fraction of available bandwidth used is significantly worse than on Shaheen. Even at high element sizes, Shaheen is at 80 % bandwidth utilization with LIBXSMM and 50 % without, whereas Mira runs at 17 %. The relative efficacy of mxm_bgq on Mira, where available, highlights the strength of LIBXSMM: the ability to automatically issue the best available vector instructions at any size.

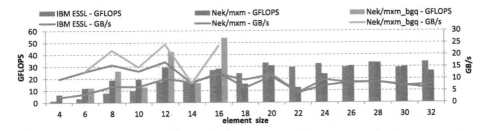

Fig. 2. Performance of the Helmholtz operator reproducer running on a single node of Mira for different implementation of small matrix multiplications. (Color figure online)

Figure 3 depicts corresponding performance numbers for the basis transformation reproducer in three use cases: (a) unitary transformation from element size to element size, (b) prolongation/dealiasing from 1d size to (3/2) the element size, and (c) restriction/aliasing from 1d size to (2/3) the element size. Note that the (3/2) factor implies some dimensions are significantly larger then the element size shown on the x-axis.

As with the Helmholtz reproducer, the LIBXSMM-based executions are the fastest and due to higher computational demand; NTS are only important of for very small 1d sizes. LIBXSMM is able to achieve 50 % of maximum floating-point performance for medium sized orders In direct comparison to mxm_std and Intel MKL, the speed-up of LIBXSMM varies between close to 4× at very small order to roughly 40 % at very large order.

4   Scenarios and Performance

4.1   Architectures

We run on two supercomputers: Mira at the ALCF and Shaheen XC40 at the KSL. Mira is a IBM BlueGene/Q with 49,152 nodes. Each node has 16 cores with

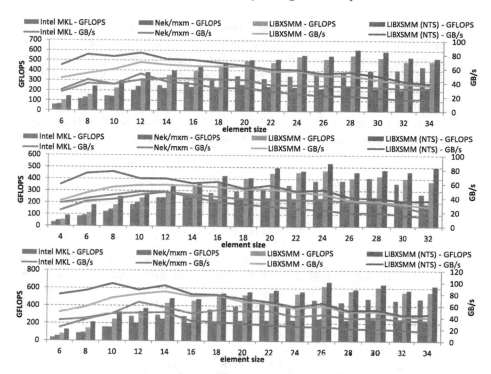

Fig. 3. Performance of the basis transformation reproducers using different implementation for the small matrix multiplications. NTS denotes the usage of the aforementioned non-temporal store optimized module. The top plot shows the diagonalization in the local Poisson operator, the middle one the prolongation and the bottom one the restriction case. (Color figure online)

4 hardware threads per core and can support 204.8 GFLOPS and 30 GiB/s main memory bandwidth, measured by [15]. Shaheen is a Cray XC40 with 6144 nodes. Each node has two Intel® Xeon® E5-2698v3 (code-named Haswell) processors with 16 cores each and can support around 1177.6 GFLOPS and 101.6 GiB/s main memory bandwidth, measured by [15]. Shaheen's cores therefore have 2.9× the floating point and 1.7× the memory bandwidth of Mira's BlueGene/Q cores.

4.2   Single Mode Rayleigh-Taylor Instability

The Rayleigh-Taylor instability (RTI) occurs when the pressure and density gradients point in opposite directions, as in the canonical case of a heavy fluid supported on top of a lighter fluid in a gravitational field. The Rayleigh-Taylor growth rate is an increasing function of the wave-number, up to a viscous cutoff, making the smallest scales grow fastest. Because energy is pumped into the system at small scales, the RTI is notoriously difficult to model numerically [5].

The RTI describes how the dense fluid is pushed through and mixes with lighter fluid. This dynamic mixing process is essential to the behavior of flows found in exploding stars [3], the oceans and atmosphere [12], and inertial confinement fusion. In the latter case, dense plastic ablator is pushed into and mixed with the lighter hydrogen fuel. The carbon-laden ablator radiates energy much more quickly than the fuel, reducing hot-spot temperature and preventing ignition. The study of the RTI and related mixing is a priority research direction for inertial confinement fusion performance [6].

Nek5000 and NekBox [2] are used to model the incompressible Boussinesq equations, which approximate the RTI at low density contrasts:

$$\frac{\partial u}{\partial t} + u \cdot \nabla u = -\nabla p + \nu \nabla^2 u + \tilde{g}T \tag{8}$$

$$\frac{\partial T}{\partial t} + u \cdot \nabla T = \alpha \nabla^2 T \tag{9}$$

$$\nabla \cdot u = 0, \tag{10}$$

where T is a scalar that can be interpreted as a temperature, in which case α is the thermal diffusivity and $\tilde{g}$ is the product of the gravitational acceleration and the thermal expansion coefficient.

The single-mode Rayleigh-Taylor instability (smRTI) restricts the initial perturbation of the interface to be sinusoidal, and is generally considered in periodic span-wise boundary conditions:

$$T(x, y, z, 0) = A \cdot \operatorname{erf}\left[\frac{z + a_0 \cos(2\pi x/\lambda) \cos(2\pi y/\lambda)}{\delta}\right], \tag{11}$$

where $A \in (0, 1]$ is the Atwood number, λ is the wavelength, a_0 is the initial interface amplitude, and δ is the initial interface width. This simplification allows the problem to be defined by only two dimensionless numbers in the limit of $a_0, \delta \to 0$, the Grashof number (Gr) and the Prandtl number (Pr):

$$\mathrm{Gr} = \frac{A\tilde{g}\lambda^3}{\nu^2}, \qquad \mathrm{Pr} = \frac{\nu}{\alpha}. \tag{12}$$

Even under these simplifications, the late-time behavior is not well understood. Experiments are prone to spurious low-wavelength modes that dominate the dynamics at late times, while the cost of direct numerical simulations is quadratic with the domain's aspect ratio.

It would be valuable to systematically sample the Grashof-Prandtl space with high fidelity simulations at late-time/high-aspect-ratio to better inform experimental design and model development. Such a study would be very expensive, so it is important to select a cost-minimizing strategy.

We take this problem, the selection of a cost-minimizing strategy for the late-time smRTI, as our motivation. In addition to the isolated reproducers discussed in Sect. 3, we present NekBox application benchmarks based on smRTI with typical Nek settings. The aim of these benchmarks is to identify minimum cost discretizations that attain a given accuracy.

The benchmarks are conducted for combinations of the element size taken from $\{4, 6, 8, 10, 12, 14, 16, 32\}$ and span-wise mesh size taken from

$\{2, 4, 8, 12, 16, 24, 32, 48, 64, 96, 128\}$. The total number of points ranges from around 1 million to 4 billion. The problem is weak-scaled: the number of elements per rank is chosen as to consume approximately half of the available main memory, or around 16k and 262k points per rank on Mira and Shaheen, respectively. The problems are constrained to fill an integer number of nodes, which puts a lower bound on the mesh size and excludes some cases that would partially fill nodes. The domain is a box with dimension $[0, .5]^2 \times [-1, 1]$, and the elements are cubic. The span-wise boundary conditions are symmetric and the vertical boundary conditions are no-slip in velocity and no-flux (insulating) in the scalar. The initial condition is stationary in velocity with a scalar given by (11), the Grashof number is 17,324, and the Prandtl number is 1. The timestep is calculated based on a Courant number of 0.4, which scales linearly with the number of elements and quadratically with the size of the element due to the spacing of the GLL nodes. The Courant condition is defined only in a linear limit, so during the initial exponential growth regime the Courant number is computed using the stagnation velocity, $\sqrt{A\tilde{g}/(\pi\lambda)}$.

Outputs are written at regular intervals in simulated time, constant across problem sizes. Therefore, smaller problems perform a greater share of I/O, as is the common case in CFD. Nek5000 and NekBox write separate files for separate ranks. The number of ranks that participate in I/O is a fixed proportion of the total number of ranks.

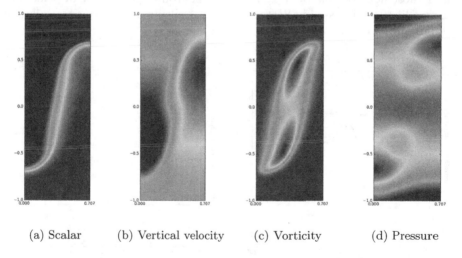

(a) Scalar   (b) Vertical velocity   (c) Vorticity   (d) Pressure

Fig. 4. Scalar, velocity, vorticity, and pressure fields at end of simulation. (Color figure online)

Slices of the end of the simulation are shown in Fig. 4. Two observables are calculated in post-processing: the *bubble height* and the *mix volume*:

$$H = \sup \left\{ z : \min_{x,y} T(x, y, z) < T_0 \right\}, \qquad \Theta = \int |T - T_0| \, dV, \qquad (13)$$

where T_0 is the volumetric average temperature. These two observables are common to smRTI models and lie at opposite ends of the locality spectrum: the bubble height is defined by the neighborhood of the bubble tip while the mix volume is an integral over the entire domain. The root mean square error in each observable is computed over all the outputs.

4.3 Time to Accuracy

For each simulation, we compute the FLOP rate and aggregate memory bandwidth. NekBox includes explicit FLOP and memory operation counters and timers in the most performance critical regions of the code. Memory operations are counted assuming single-element intermediate data stays in cache, and therefore does not contribute to main memory bandwidth. These counters are consistent with those used in the reproducers. The whole application is not covered, so the counters can be considered lower bounds on the whole-application performance.

The attained memory bandwidth per core on Shaheen and Mira are plotted in Fig. 5. On Shaheen, bandwidth is constant with respect to the number of elements and a weak function of the order, ranging from around 65 to 75 % of peak. On Mira, bandwidth is still constant with respect to the scale, but varies more strongly with polynomial order, especially at orders greater than 16 and those not divisible by 4. It ranges from around 15 to 50 % of peak. The mxm_bgq library, discussed in Sect. 3, is used, resulting in performance spikes at QPX-supported orders, e.g. 8.

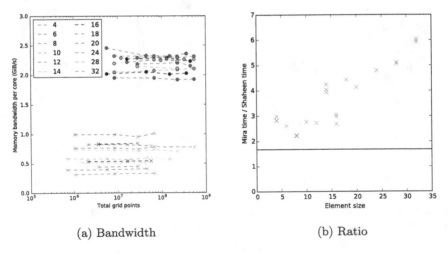

(a) Bandwidth   (b) Ratio

Fig. 5. Weak scaling of bandwidth on Shaheen and Mira. In (a), circles and crosses indicate memory bandwidth per core on Shaheen and Mira, respectively, vs the problem size labeled by element size. In (b), the ratio of the bandwidths are shown vs element size for common discretizations. The solid line indicates ratio of STREAM memory bandwidth. (Color figure online)

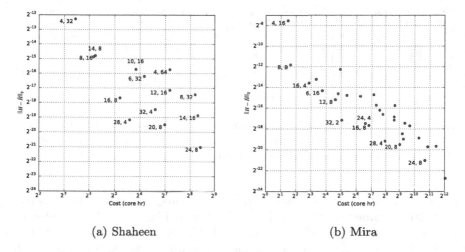

(a) Shaheen   (b) Mira

Fig. 6. Error with respect to bubble height, (13), vs. the computational cost, in processor hours, on Shaheen (a) and Mira (b). Points are labeled as $(p+1, e)$ pairs, where p is the order, $p+1$ is the element size, and e is the number of elements in one dimension. More runs are present on Mira due to the smaller BGQ nodes evenly dividing more problem sizes.

The accuracy is plotted versus the computational cost for a variety of discretizations in Fig. 6. The error in bubble height and mix volume are strongly correlated, so only the error in the height is plotted. As expected, doubling the the spectral order while keeping the number of elements fixed, e.g. $(4, 32) \rightarrow (8, 32)$ and $(8, 8) \rightarrow (16, 8)$, significantly improves the accuracy, but also increases the cost by 16–32×. The first 8× is due to an increase in the number of degrees of freedom, the next 2× is due to the shorter timestep, and, when compute-bound, the final 2× is due to an increase in the floating point load. Doubling the spectral order while keeping the number of points fixed, e.g. $(16, 8) \rightarrow (32, 4)$ and $(8, 8) \rightarrow (16, 4)$, increases the cost by 2–4×, as expected, but also improves the accuracy. Doubling the spectral order while halving the number of points in each direction, e.g. $(8, 32) \rightarrow (16, 8)$ and $(14, 16) \rightarrow (28, 4)$, reduces the cost by 4–8× while maintaining or slightly improving the accuracy.

We define the *efficiency frontier* as the set of discretizations that minimize computational cost for fixed accuracy or, equivalently, minimize error given fixed computational cost. The efficiency frontiers on Mira and Shaheen are comprised of discretizations with very high orders, given our constraints. The most efficient schemes are those with element size greater than 16, except for very low accuracy simulations.

4.4   Whole Application Performance

To date, our largest calculation on Shaheen occupied 131,072 cores as depicted in Fig. 7 for element size 32. NekBox achieved 197 TiB/s memory bandwidth

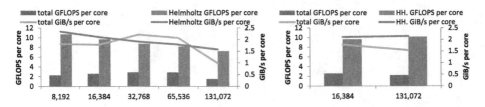

Fig. 7. Strong scaling (left) and weak scaling (right) on Shaheen on up to 131,072 cores (2/3) of the full 7 PFLOPS machine using an element size of 32. To avoid log plots we show per-core performance. (Color figure online)

and 290 TFLOPS in weak scaling. This corresponds to 47.8 % of peak memory bandwidth sustained over the entire application at high order. In case of strong scaling these numbers are slightly lower with 130 TiB/s and 195 TFLOPS. However, the Helmholtz operator, as the most compute intense sub-routine, is able to achieve up to 0.94 PFLOPS in strong and 1.33 PFLOPS in weak-scaling on 131,072 cores. We also consider 65,536 cores runs, occupying 1/3 of Shaheen. These runs achieved at least 135.6 TiB/s memory bandwidth and 184.9 TFLOPS. This corresponds to 67.5 % of peak memory bandwidth sustained over the entire application at high order. Finally, extrapolating to full machine, NekBox would reach at least 406.8 TiB/s and 554.6 TFLOPS. At the same scale, a weak scaling of the Helmholtz operator would result into 1.9 PFLOPS out of 7 PFLOPS performance.

5   Conclusion

NekBox enhanced by LIBXSMM generated kernels on Shaheen XC40 executes the performance critical, order-dependent components of Nek above 80 % of peak memory bandwidth. For comparison, compiled code on the BlueGene/Q architecture is only able to reach 50 % of peak and for many polynomial orders operates around 30 %. Therefore, despite only having 1.7× the memory bandwidth, Shaheen's cores outperform Mira's cores by 3–6× with the greatest improvement at high order and for sizes that are not divisible by the vector width, 4 in this case. NekBox is able to scale 67.5 % utilization rates to 65,536 cores on Shaheen.

For the smRTI, the efficiency frontier, i.e. the discretizations that minimize cost given accuracy or minimize error given cost, have polynomial orders between 15 and 31, higher than are typically used in spectral element schemes. The presence of high order schemes on the efficiency frontier can be understood by the combination of two effects. First, the increase in arithmetic intensity is hidden by the imbalance between floating point capabilities and memory bandwidth, providing high order at no marginal cost on a per time-step basis. Second, higher order schemes with fewer degrees are freedom are more accurate than lower order schemes with more degrees of freedom. It is generally possible to maintain accuracy by increasing the order while decreasing the total degrees of freedom, and, consequently the total cost.

Generally the order should be chosen to be at least large enough to saturate the floating point capabilities of the architecture in the order-dependent kernels, because increasing the order to that point significantly improves accuracy at no marginal computational cost. On BlueGene/Q, this mark is polynomial order 15, while on the Cray XC40 it is 31.

For many problems and observables, the calculation may additionally benefit from increasing the order until just before single-element operations spill out of cache. The improvement in accuracy is exponential with the polynomial order, so the degrees of freedom needed to achieve a level of accuracy can decrease. The increase in the cost with respect to order for compute-bound orders is linear, so if the decrease in the number of degrees of freedom needed is super-linear, the net result is a less expensive calculation. Usage in this way, which exceeds the largest element sizes that we ran on Shaheen, warrants further study.

More generally, high order methods with high locality, the structured elements in SEM being only one example, are able to take advantage of wider vectors and higher compute to memory ratios to reach higher order at little to no marginal cost on a per-step basis. However, increases in cost can come in through coupling to the choice of time-step and an increase in iteration counts in the solvers. These increases can often be mitigated by reducing the total number of degrees of freedom, relative to an equivalent lower-order calculation.

The next generation will include supercomputers featuring the Xeon Phi processor code-named Knights Landing, e.g., Cori at NERSC with more than 20 PFLOPS. As the architecture continues to evolve, we can see that updated node-level optimizations and order-sensitivity studies are key to helping scientists continue to perform large scale, high efficiency simulations.

Acknowledgment. This research used the resources of the Supercomputing Laboratory at the King Abdullah University of Science and Technology (KAUST) in Thuwal, Saudi Arabia. This research used resources of the Argonne Leadership Computing Facility, which is a DOE Office of Science User Facility supported under Contract DE-AC02-06CH11357. We acknowledge useful conversations with Paul Fischer, James Lottes, Aleksandr Obabko, Oana Marin, Michel Schanen, Scott Parker, Vitali Morozov, Matthew Otten, and Robert Rosner.

References

1. LIBXSMM v1.0.2 (2015)
2. NekBox v2.0.0 (2015)
3. Bell, J.B., et al.: Direct numerical simulations of type Ia supernovae flames. II. The Rayleigh-Taylor instability. Astrophys. J. **608**(2), 883–906 (2004)
4. Breuer, A., Heinecke, A., Rannabauer, L., Bader, M.: High-order ADER-DG minimizes energy- and time-to-solution of seissol. In: Kunkel, J.M., Ludwig, T. (eds.) ISC High Performance 2015. LNCS, vol. 9137, pp. 340–357. Springer, Heidelberg (2015)

5. Dimonte, G., Youngs, D.L., Dimits, A., Weber, S., Marinak, M., Wunsch, S., Garasi, C., Robinson, A., Andrews, M.J., Ramaprabhu, P., Calder, A.C., Fryxell, B., Biello, J., Dursi, L., MacNeice, P., Olson, K., Ricker, P., Rosner, R., Timmes, F., Tufo, H., Young, Y.-N., Zingale, M.: A comparative study of the turbulent RayleighTaylor instability using high-resolution three-dimensional numerical simulations: the Alpha-Group collaboration. Phys. Fluids **16**(5), 1668 (2004)
6. Gocharov, V., et al.: Panel 3 report: implosion hydrodynamics. LLNL report LLNLTR-562104, pp. 22–24 (2012)
7. Goto, K., et al.: Anatomy of high-performance matrix multiplication. ACM Trans. Math. Softw. **34**(3), 12:1–12:25 (2008)
8. Heinecke, A., et al.: LIBXSMM: a high performance library for small matrix multiplications. In: Poster and Extended Abstract Presented at SC 2015 (2015)
9. Hutchinson, M.: Direct numerical simulation of single mode three-dimensional Rayleigh-Taylor experiments (2015). arXiv:1511.07254
10. Intel Corporation: Intel MKL 11.3 Release Notes. Introduced (S/D)GEMM_BATCH and (C/Z)GEMM3M_BATCH functions to perform multiple independent matrix-matrix multiply operations (2015)
11. Ivanov, I., et al.: Evaluation of parallel communication models in Nekbone, a Nek5000 mini-application. In: 2015 IEEE International Conference on Cluster Computing (CLUSTER), pp. 760–767. IEEE (2015)
12. Linden, P.F.: On the structure of salt fingers. Deep Sea Res. Oceanogr. Abstr. **20**, 325–340 (1973)
13. Lottes, J.W., et al.: Hybrid multigrid/Schwarz algorithms for the spectral element method. J. Sci. Comput. **24**(1), 45–78 (2005)
14. Markidis, S., et al.: OpenACC acceleration of the Nek5000 spectral element code. Int. J. High Perform. Comput. Appl. **29**(3), 311–319 (2015)
15. McCalpin, J.D.: STREAM: sustainable memory bandwidth in high performance computers. Technical report, University of Virginia, Charlottesville, Virginia, 1991–2007. A continually updated technical report. http://www.cs.virginia.edu/stream/
16. Offermans, N., Marin, O., Schanen, M., Gong, J., Fischer, P., Schlatter, P., Obabko, A., Peplinski, A., Hutchinson, M., Merzari, E.: On the strong scaling of the spectral element solver Nek5000 on petascale systems. In: Solving Software Challenges for Exascale, pp. 57–68. Springer (2016)
17. Otten, M., et al.: An MPI/OpenACC implementation of a high-order electromagnetics solver with GPUDirect communication. Int. J. High Perform. Comput. Appl. (2016). http://hpc.sagepub.com/content/early/2016/02/01/1094342015626584.abstract. doi:10.1177/1094342015626584
18. Patera, A.T.: A spectral element method for fluid dynamics: laminar flow in a channel expansion. J. Comput. Phy. **54**(3), 468–488 (1984)
19. Shin, J., et al.: Speeding up Nek5000 with autotuning and specialization. In: Proceedings of the 24th ACM International Conference on Supercomputing, ICS 2010, pp. 253–262. ACM, New York (2010)
20. Tufo, H.M., et al.: Terascale spectral element algorithms and implementations. In: Proceedings of the 1999 ACM/IEEE Conference on Supercomputing, p. 68 (1999)
21. Wang, Z.J., et al.: High-order CFD methods: current status and perspective. Int. J. Numer. Meth. Fluids **72**(8), 811–845 (2013)

Resilience

Scalability of Partial Differential Equations Preconditioner Resilient to Soft and Hard Faults

Karla Morris[1]([✉]), Francesco Rizzi[1], Khachik Sargsyan[1], Kathryn Dahlgren[3],
Paul Mycek[2], Cosmin Safta[1], Olivier Le Maître[4],
Omar Knio[2], and Bert Debusschere[1]

[1] Sandia National Laboratories, Livermore, CA, USA
{knmorri,fnrizzi,ksargsy,csafta,bjdebus}@sandia.gov
[2] Duke University, Durham, NC, USA
{paul.mycek,omar.knio}@sandia.gov
[3] UC Santa Cruz, Santa Cruz, CA, USA
kmdahlgr@ucsc.edu
[4] LIMSI-CNRS, Orsay, France
olm@limsi.fr

Abstract. We present a resilient domain-decomposition preconditioner for partial differential equations (PDEs). The algorithm reformulates the PDE as a sampling problem, followed by a solution update through data manipulation that is resilient to both soft and hard faults. We discuss an implementation based on a server-client model where all state information is held by the servers, while clients are designed solely as computational units. Servers are assumed to be "sandboxed", while no assumption is made on the reliability of the clients. We explore the scalability of the algorithm up to ~12k cores, build an SST/macro skeleton to extrapolate to ~50k cores, and show the resilience under simulated hard and soft faults for a 2D linear Poisson equation.

1 Introduction

As computing platforms evolve towards exascale, several key challenges are arising related to resiliency, energy consumption, memory access, concurrency and heterogeneous hardware [1,6,7,10,11]. There is no consensus or clear idea yet on what a "typical" exascale architecture might look like [1]. One of the main concerns is understanding how the hardware will affect future computing systems in terms of reliability, communication and computational models, and which ones will emerge to become the main reference for exascale.

Exascale simulations are expected to rely on thousands of CPU cores running up to a billion threads [6,7]. This framework will lead to systems with a large number of components, and large communication cost for data exchange. The presence of many components and the increasing complexity of these systems,

---

© Springer International Publishing Switzerland 2016 (outside the US)
J.M. Kunkel et al. (Eds.): ISC High Performance 2016, LNCS 9697, pp. 469–485, 2016.
DOI: 10.1007/978-3-319-41321-1_24

e.g. more and smaller transistors, and lower voltages, can become a liability in terms of system faults. Exascale systems are expected to suffer from errors and faults more frequently than the current petascale systems [6,7]. Current parallel programming models and implementations will require a resilient infrastructure to be suitable for fault-free simulations across many cores in reasonable amounts of time.

In general, system faults can be grouped under two main categories, namely hard and soft faults [6,16]. Hard faults can cause partial or full computing nodes to fail, or the network to crash. These faults have an evident impact on the run and the system itself. Soft errors, on the other hand, are more subtle because some of them can be undetected, e.g. in the case of silent data corruption (SDC). The reason is that their effect is simply to alter information where it is stored, transmitted, or processed. The key feature of silent errors is that, when undetected, there is no opportunity for an application to directly recover from the fault when it occurs.

Currently, application checkpoint-restart is the most commonly used tool for fault-tolerance [6]. This approach is in fact straightforward and robust, but it is anticipated that in future extreme scale systems it will not be suitable because the time for checkpointing and restarting will exceed the mean time to failure [6,7,21]. Also, check-pointing can lead to substantial overhead depending on the simulation size [4]. Improving reliability and efficiency for future extreme scale systems is thus becoming increasingly important. This is crucial in the context of large-scale scientific problems, ranging from climate predictions, to nano-engineering, medicine and biology, where complexity can only be tackled with large computing power and time.

In this paper, we present a domain-decomposition preconditioner for the solution of 2D partial differential equations (PDEs) targeting resilience to both hard faults and silent data corruption in the form of bit-flips. This work is part of Resilient EXtreme Scale Scientific Simulation (REXSSS), a project focusing on developing novel approaches for resilient extreme scale computing. The algorithm presented consists of recasting the original PDE as a sampling problem, followed by a resilient data manipulation to achieve the final solution update. One of the main features is that the algorithm does not need to detect all types of system faults that can occur, but focuses solely on the information that a simulation provides.

For the implementation, we rely on a server-client model (SCM) grouping MPI processes into servers and clients. For the purpose of this work, the servers are assumed to be safe (or "sandboxed") units holding the data. The clients are designed solely to accept and perform work without any assumption on their reliability. A client is simply defined as a set of MPI processes, which can take up part or all of a computing node. A key advantage of this structure is its inherent resiliency to hard faults, provided that the MPI framework is fault-tolerant. Since the actual data is safely held by the servers, the SCM is inherently resilient to clients crashing (partial or complete node failures), as this translates to missing tasks.

We analyze the scalability of the algorithm and implementation up to $\sim 12k$ cores, and complement it with an SST/macro [32] skeleton of our application to extrapolate the performance up to $\sim 50k$ cores. To test resilience, two different types of faults are considered: hard faults modeling clients crashing, and soft faults in the form of bit-flips occurring on the clients during task execution. These faults are modeled using a Poisson process with a failure rate extracted from the literature. We demonstrate the resiliency of the algorithm for a 2D linear elliptic PDE, and explore the effect of the faults.

The main innovations of this work are: (a) the reformulation of the PDE solve so it is reduced to a number of independent tasks to increase concurrency and parallelism, and (b) the ability to inherently mitigate the effects of both hard and soft faults that may occur in the execution of those tasks. To frame this work in the proper context, our approach is intended for future exascale platforms, with fault rates so high that checkpoint-restart will not be a viable option, and current solvers will fail to adequately scale due to system size. As such, the current version of our application is not meant to be competitive with current state-of-the-art solvers on today's computational platforms. Rather, it is an early version of a novel domain-decomposition-based approach targeting scaling and resilience to soft and hard faults on exascale platforms. Our approach can be seen as a preconditioner that will enable today's solvers to be used effectively on future architectures by operating on subdomain levels.

The paper is organized as follows. In Sect. 2, we discuss related work; in Sect. 3, we describe the mathematical formulation; in Sect. 4, we illustrate the implementation details; in Sect. 5, we present the results, focusing on the scalability Sect. 5.1, and resilience Sect. 5.2. Finally, Sect. 6 presents the conclusions.

2   Related Work

On the path to extreme-scale computing, one of the main efforts being pursued is resiliency and fault-tolerance at various levels, namely solutions based on hardware, software and combinations of the two [30]. In the case of hardware solutions, developers consider mechanisms for preventing hardware errors as well as the detection and subsequent correction of errors, e.g. through the re-execution of failed instructions. The increased cost and overhead associated with node reliability is potentially mitigated through the construction of computing systems with a heterogeneous infrastructure [30].

Approaches to fault-tolerance also include algorithm-based fault tolerance (ABFT) [4,8,12], process-level redundancy [28], and algorithmic error correction code [23]. ABFT is labeled as a non masking approach because algorithms need to integrate ABFT by incorporating some level of redundancy [6]. If an error or a fault occurs, data redundancy allows reconstruction of the missing part of the result. It is increasingly recognized that new approaches need to be incorporated at the algorithm's level to account for potential faults, so that the algorithms themselves are made more robust and resilient, without relying exclusively on hardware.

Domain decomposition methods [19] are easy to parallelize. While the scalability and convergence of these methods have been extensively studied in both PDE, see e.g. [24,31], and linear solvers, see e.g. [2,15,18], we are not aware of any fault resilience study specific to domain decomposition algorithms. Chen et al. [8] proposed an algorithm-based recovery method for iterative system solvers to enable resilience to fail-stop failures based on data partitioning tailored to the characteristics of the iterative scheme, while Larson *et al.* [20] achieved fault tolerance by combining solutions on sparse grids. Both approaches can in principle be reformulated in a domain decomposition paradigm, but with a distinct flavor of fault-detection or redundancy present.

Most of the work related to the development of resilient algorithms relies on the detection of a fault and the process to overcome its effect [5,13,29]. The work we present here circumvents the need for fault and error detection and at the same time exploits the foreseen heterogeneity of the future extreme-scale platforms to enable the resiliency of the overall algorithm.

3   Mathematical Formulation

We present the formulation for a generic 2D elliptic PDE of the form

$$\mathcal{L}y(\mathbf{x}) = g(\mathbf{x}), \tag{1}$$

where $\mathcal{L}$ is an elliptic differential operator, $g(\mathbf{x})$ is a given source term, and $\mathbf{x} = \{x_1, x_2\} \in \Omega \subset \mathbb{R}^2$, with Ω being the target domain region. We focus on Dirichlet boundary condition $y(\mathbf{x})|_{\mathbf{x} \in \Gamma} = y_\Gamma$ along the boundary Γ of the domain Ω. A formulation of the algorithm focusing on 1D elliptic PDEs can be found in [26]. Elliptic equations are chosen as a test case because they represent fundamental problems encountered in physics, and also pose challenges within many scientific simulations, e.g. the pressure Poisson equation for the incompressible Navier-Stokes equations, or the solution of the electrostatic configuration in molecular dynamics. The algorithm below is conceptually not limited to elliptic PDEs, and we are currently working on its extension to parabolic and hyperbolic PDEs, which will be the subject of future publications. Moreover, it can be readily extended to 3D domains as well.

Figure 1 shows a high-level schematic of the algorithm's workflow. The starting point is the *discretization* of the computational domain. In general, the choice of the discretization method is arbitrary, potentially heterogeneous across the domain, e.g. uniform, or non-uniform rectangular grid, or a finite-element triangulation, etc.

The second step is the *partitioning* stage. The target 2D domain, Ω, is partitioned into a grid of $n_{x_1} \times n_{x_2}$ *overlapping* regions (or subdomains), with n_{x_k} being the number of subdomains along the x_k-th axis. The size of the overlap does not need to be equal and uniform among all partitions, and can vary across the domain. The partitioning stage yields a set of $n_{x_1} \times n_{x_2}$ subdomains Ω_{ij}, and their corresponding boundaries Γ_{ij}, for $i = 0, \dots, n_{x_1} - 1$, and $j = 0, \dots, n_{x_2} - 1$, where Γ_{ij} represents the boundary set of the ij-th subdomain Ω_{ij}.

One of the advantages of the above decomposition for the elliptic problem in Eq. (1) is that if we know the solution along the subdomain boundaries, then this information can be used as boundary condition within each subdomain,

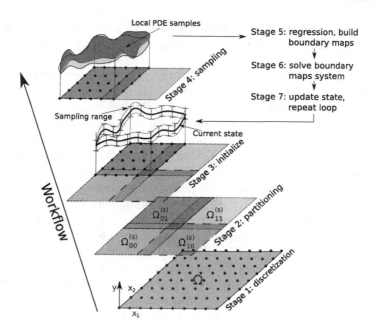

Fig. 1. Schematic of the workflow of the algorithm. For clarity, starting with stage 2 we only show the steps for Ω_{01} but the same "operations" are applied to all subdomains.

to perform a single local solve that yields the full solution over the full domain, Ω. Consequently, we define as our object of interest the set of solution fields along the boundaries, which we denote $y(\mathbf{x})|_{\mathbf{x}\in\Gamma_{ij}}$ for $i = 0, \ldots, n_{x_1} - 1$, and $j = 0, \ldots, n_{x_2} - 1$. Due to the overlapping, each subdomain Ω_{ij} includes *inner* boundaries, Γ_{ij}^{in}, i.e. the parts of the boundaries contained within Ω_{ij} that belong to the intersecting (neighboring) subdomains. The core of the algorithm relies on exploiting within each subdomain Ω_{ij} the *map* relating the solution at the subdomain boundaries, $y(\mathbf{x})|_{\mathbf{x}\in\Gamma_{ij}}$, to the solution along the inner boundaries, $y(\mathbf{x})|_{\mathbf{x}\in\Gamma_{ij}^{in}}$. These maps can be written compactly as

$$y(\mathbf{x})|_{\mathbf{x}\in\Gamma_{ij}^{in}} = f^{(ij)}\left(y(\mathbf{x})|_{\mathbf{x}\in\Gamma_{ij}}\right), \tag{2}$$

for $i = 0, \ldots, n_{x_1} - 1$, and $j = 0, \ldots, n_{x_2} - 1$. The system of equations assembled from these *boundary-to-boundary maps* collected from all subdomains, combined with the boundary conditions on the full domain $y(\mathbf{x})|_{\mathbf{x}\in\Gamma}$, yields a fixed-point problem of the form

$$\mathbf{y}(\mathbf{x}) = \mathcal{F}\mathbf{y}(\mathbf{x}), \tag{3}$$

where $\mathbf{y}$ represents the vector of the solution values at all subdomains boundaries. This problem is only satisfied by the solution of Eq. (1). We remark that these boundary maps $f^{(ij)}$ relate the y-values, since they are built from the restrictions of the subdomain solutions at the corresponding boundaries. As outlined in [26], even though general (non-)linear solvers can solve the fixed point problem, this approach is not the best because it involves an overhead due to global communication and would require on the fly subdomain solutions to evaluate the maps.

The method adopted in [26] for 1D problems, which we carry over in the current work, is to construct *approximations* (or surrogates) of the boundary-to-boundary maps, which we call $\tilde{f}^{(ij)}$. One of the key features of the algorithm is that the construction of these maps can be done for each subdomain *independently* from all the others. This allows us to satisfy data locality and avoid the overhead due to communication, which is crucial to achieve scalability on extreme scale machines. To build these surrogate maps, given a current "state" of the solution at the subdomains boundaries, we use a sampling strategy to solve the target PDE equation locally within each subdomain for sampled values of the boundary conditions on that subdomain, see stage 3 in Fig. 1. These samples are used within a regression approach to "infer" the approximate boundary-to-boundary maps. For non-linear problems, the maps are non-linear and using linear surrogate maps will carry an additional source of discrepancy, due to the linear approximation of a generally non-linear map. For linear PDEs, instead, as shown in [26], the boundary maps are linear as well.

The construction of the boundary-to-boundary maps plays a key role for addressing soft faults. As shown in [26], when inferring linear maps, using a suitable ℓ_1-error model one can seamlessly filter out the effects of few corrupted data. The ℓ_1 noise model allows us to find the solution with as few non-zero residuals as possible. Under the assumption that faults are rare and provided that the case targeted is linear, the inferred maps will fit the non-corrupted data exactly while effectively ignoring the corrupted data. In the present work, we employ an iteratively reweighted least squares (IRLS) method, which is effectively equivalent to a ℓ_1 minimization [9].

Following the construction of the surrogate boundary-to-boundary maps, we can then solve the *approximate* version of the fixed point system in Eq. (2), which provides us with the new solution state at all the subdomains boundaries and represents an approximation of the solution. In the case of linear PDEs, because the boundary-to-boundary maps are linear and assuming an ideal scenario where no faults occur, the approximate solution obtained after one iteration is exact. An important measure of the accuracy of the current solution $y(\mathbf{x})|_{\mathbf{x} \in \Gamma_{ij}}$ is the *residual* vector, defined as

$$\mathbf{z}^{(T)} = \mathcal{F} \mathbf{y}^{(T)} - \mathbf{y}^{(T)}, \tag{4}$$

which can be computed by extra subdomain solves using boundary conditions defined by the current solution $\mathbf{y}^{(T)}$, and subtracting the corresponding current solutions $\mathbf{y}^{(T)}$ from the resulting values at all boundaries. Given the fixed-point problem in Eq. (3), the residual in Eq. (4) vanishes if $\mathbf{y}^{(T)}$ is the exact solution. The above outline of the algorithm shows that the original PDE problem is practically recast as a sampling problem, followed by a resilient data manipulation to achieve the final solution update.

4   Implementation Details

We have developed a parallel, C++ implementation of the algorithm using a server-client model (SCM). In this section, we describe the SCM and its resilience properties; how we implement each stage of the algorithm to exploit the inherent SCM model's resilience; and an SST/macro [32] skeleton model of the algorithm that we use for performance and scalability analysis.

4.1   Server-Client Model

Figure 2 shows a schematic of our SCM structure. We adopt a cluster-based model, namely the MPI ranks are grouped into separate clusters, with each cluster containing a server and, for resource balancing purposes, the same number of clients. These clusters are designed such that all servers can communicate between each other, while the clients within a cluster are only visible to the server within that cluster. Moreover, within any given cluster, clients are independent, i.e. each client handles a different work unit and they cannot communicate with each other. This design allows us to have clients failing without affecting any other clients. Only the work being executed by that client is affected. From a practical standpoint, this structure is enabled by constructing an inter-server communicator, which links all the servers and is only visible to the servers; a cluster communicator, shared among a server and its clients; and an intra-client communicator defined for each client, which is only visible to the ranks defining that client. The data is distributed among the servers, and these are assumed to be highly resilient (safe or under a "sandbox" model implementation). The sandbox model assumed for the servers can be supported by either hardware or software. The former assumption is supported by hardware specifications on the variable levels of resilience that can be allowed within large computer systems. In the case of software support, a sandbox effect can be accomplished by a programming model relying on data redundancy and strategic synchronization [5,14,22].

This sandboxing model implies an overhead both in terms of needing extra nodes, and the cost to make those extra nodes safe to faults. This overhead and its cost should be examined with respect to the benefits this would yield for resilience purposes. In other words, one should explore whether investing in sandboxing a subset of the machine components offsets the cost one would have to face if adopting a different model. The sandboxing model also has potential benefits for energy purposes, since it would allow variable energy consumption across the machine. For example, while the servers could be run in a highly reliable hardware/software configuration, the client nodes could be run in less reliable configuration (lower voltage, less error correction levels, etc.), which would result in a lower energy cost that may offset the server overhead. Effective approaches for sandboxing servers to make them safe to faults are the subject of ongoing research in the community.

Since the servers hold the data, they are responsible for generating tasks, dispatching them to their pool of available clients, as well as receiving and

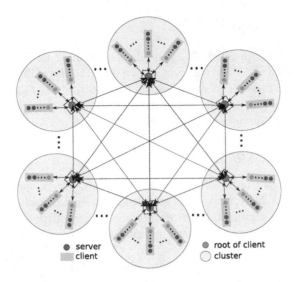

Fig. 2. Schematic of the server-client structure. (Color figure online)

processing tasks. Currently, the framework is designed such that data is distributed among the servers once during the setup stage. We are currently working on relaxing this constraint to allow dynamic load balancing, i.e. designing the servers such that they can exchange/steal work during runtime.

A client is defined as a set of MPI processes, and is designed solely to accept and perform work without any assumption on its reliability. To minimize communication, the root rank of a client is the only one receiving from the server a new task to perform. This paradigm can be exploited in certain hardware configurations because leveraging local communication within a client is more efficient than having the server communicate a task to all the MPI ranks in a client. One example is the case where all ranks of a client live in the same node, so that one can exploit in-node parallelism and faster memory access. After receiving the task, the root process then broadcasts it to all the other ranks in the client, so that the client as a whole works in parallel to solve the task. The implementation also supports the capability of having the root rank of a client receiving multiple tasks, and distributing them among all the children ranks of that client so that each child rank works on an individual task. This working mode is useful when tasks are lightweight such that it becomes more efficient to have all ranks in a client solving individual tasks, rather than having all ranks working together to solve in parallel the same task. All communications between a server and its clients are done with non-blocking operations, allowing us to overlap them on the server side with the computational operations involved in the creation and processing of the tasks. Given that our code is based on complex C++ objects, e.g. the tasks objects themselves, we leverage the Boost serialization/MPI library to enable object communication via MPI.

A key property of the SCM structure is the inherent resiliency to hard faults, provided that the MPI framework is fault-tolerant. This is because clients crashing (partial or complete node failures) only translates into missing tasks. Of course, this needs to be complemented by making the application resilient to hard faults, i.e. designing the algorithm so that it can deal with missing data.

4.2   Algorithm Implementation

The algorithm described in Sect. 3 involves four main stages: sampling, regression, fixed-point solve, and updating. As illustrated before, sampling and regression can be performed within each subdomain independently and concurrently. This feature reveals their task-based nature, and is therefore implemented in the form of tasks executed by the clients. On the other hand, the fixed-point solve of the boundary-to-boundary maps system and the updating of the subdomains are executed by the servers, since they fully own the state information. The system of equations built from the boundary maps is much smaller than the original discretized PDE system over the full domain grid, and so it fits on a small number of servers. Moreover, the servers are "sandboxed", allowing us to circumvent any potential data corruption during these operations.

4.3   Skeleton Model for Performance Analysis Without Faults

We have developed a skeleton of the algorithm by stripping away all operations except for communication and control statements. This skeleton is useful for identifying the basic control flow of the algorithm, and allows the estimation of the algorithm's performance through the SST/macro library [32]. SST/macro is a library for simulating applications running on architectures using network discrete events. More specifically, relying upon models of a target architecture, SST/macro estimates the performance of processing and network components without incurring the cost of doing actual message passing or computation operations. Accordingly, SST/macro skeletons only need to contain the control flow and message passing behavior of actual applications. The library can thus be used to estimate the performance of a given application on new or existing architectures without launching the application on the actual target machines.

5   Results

As a test case, we rely on the following 2D linear elliptic PDE

$$\frac{\partial}{\partial x_1}\left(k(\mathbf{x})\frac{\partial y(\mathbf{x})}{\partial x_1}\right) + \frac{\partial}{\partial x_2}\left(k(\mathbf{x})\frac{\partial y(\mathbf{x})}{\partial x_2}\right) = g(\mathbf{x}), \tag{5}$$

where $k(x_1, x_2)$ is the diffusivity, and $g(x_1, x_2)$ is the source term. This PDE is solved over a unit square $\Omega = (0,1)^2$, with homogeneous Dirichlet boundary conditions. The diffusivity and source fields are defined as

$$k(x_1, x_2) = 8.0 * \exp(-d(x_1, x_2)/0.025) + 2.0, \tag{6}$$
$$g(x_1, x_2) = 2.0 * \exp(-d(x_1, x_2)/0.050) - 1.0, \tag{7}$$

where $d(x_1, x_2) = (x_1 - 0.35)^2 + (x_2 - 0.35)^2$. To solve the above PDE within each subdomain, we employ a structured grid and second-order finite differences to discretize Eq. (5). The resulting linear system stemming from the finite-difference discretization of the local problem is solved using the parallel solver AztecOO in Trilinos [17].

5.1 Nominal Scalability

In this section, we concentrate on the scalability achieved in the absence of faults, and focus on the communication-intensive stages of the algorithm. The scalability tests were performed on Edison (NERSC), a Cray XC30, with.Peak performance of 2.57 Petaflops, Cray Aries high-speed interconnect with Dragonfly topology with ~8 GB/sec MPI bandwidth (http://www.nersc.gov). Table 1 lists the parameters used for the scalability runs strategically chosen to complete the tests we envisioned within the available allocation time.

Table 1. Scalability tests.

	Weak	Strong
Subdomains	12^2, 18^2, 24^2, 30^2, 48^2	32^2
Total cores	3088, 6948, 12352, 19300, 49408	3088, 12352, 49408
Subdomain grid size	$\sim115^2$	$\sim115^2$
Overlap (# cells)	12	12
Servers	16, 36, 64, 100, 256	16, 64, 256
Number of clients/server	48	48
Size of each client	4	4

Weak Scaling. Due to the properties of the SCM, the weak scaling can be setup in two possible ways. The first involves fixing the number of servers, and as the problem size increases, the number of clients is proportionally increased. One drawback of this approach is that it limits the size of the problem that one can tackle, because the number of servers is fixed. This configuration would work well for small problems, but in the limit of the problem size increasing, the memory of the servers would impose a constraint. The alternative is a configuration where the number of clients per server and the amount of data owned by each server is fixed, and the problem size is increased by adding increasingly more clusters. This setting imposes no constraint on the problem size. This is the case that we adopt in this work, as shown in Table 1.

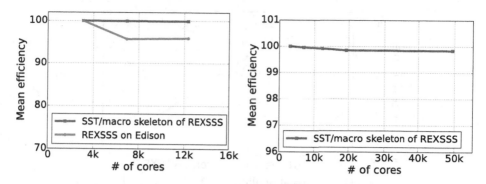

Fig. 3. Nominal weak scaling results (i.e. without faults): left panel shows the comparison between the results obtained with the SST/macro skeleton and REXSSS, while the right panel shows the results obtained with the SST/macro skeleton only. (Color figure online)

Figure 3 shows the results for the weak scaling. The full REXSSS code has been tested up to $\sim 12k$ cores, while the SST/macro skeleton was used to extrapolate the behavior up to $\sim 50k$. The efficiency stays within 95 % for the REXSSS code, and the behavior is qualitatively well reproduced by the SST/macro skeleton. The discrepancy is partially due to the fact that the skeleton only approximates the full code, and that while the skeleton relies on regular MPI, the full code uses the Boost serialization/MPI library, which introduces overhead. The excellent weak scalability is further confirmed by the extrapolation run with the SST/macro model, showing approximately the same efficiency up to $\sim 50k$.

Strong Scaling. For a given fixed problem size, the strong scaling can be setup in three different ways. One involves fixing the number of servers and the size of each client, and increasing the computational power by adding more clients per server. The second involves fixing the number of servers and number of clients per server, and increasing the size of each client to increase the overall computational power. The third involves defining a cluster as the reference computational unit, and increasing the numbers of clusters to add computational power. In this work, we focus on the third scenario because it is consistent with the setup used for the weak scaling, namely having a cluster as reference unit.

Figure 4 shows the strong scaling results obtained through the SST/macro skeleton up to $\sim 50k$. The plot shows that the scaling is excellent, only slightly deviating from the ideal trend. This result confirms that the application is not limited by communication. Tests with REXSSS are ongoing to confirm this strong scaling behavior.

5.2   Resiliency

The key property of our algorithm is its resilience. In this section, we now focus on showing the resiliency of the algorithm under simulated system faults, and

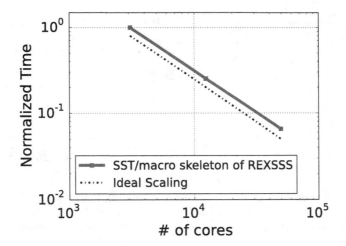

Fig. 4. Nominal strong scaling results (i.e. without faults). (Color figure online)

explore the effect of the faults on the algorithm performance. We focus on two different types of faults: hard faults, which can only affect the clients (servers are safe), and cause a client to crash; and SDC during computation while a client is performing work. We evaluate the resilience against SDC affecting the numerical data used in the algorithm and we exclude other types of faults, e.g. in data structures or control flow, since these issues represent a different problem. All the runs are performed with the full REXSSS code.

Failure Distribution. To simulate the occurrence of faults, we assume a Poisson process, defined by a constant average rate, r (failures/time), and a failure distribution, $F(t) = 1 - \exp(-rt)$. Using an exponential distribution implies that the process is assumed "memoryless", i.e. each event is independent of the other. If a different model was used, this would not affect the results of this study as our focus is on how our approach handles faults, regardless of how they occur in time.

To define suitable failure rates for modeling the occurrence of the faults, we rely on the data in [27]. We extract failure rates by scaling up the results found in [27] assuming future architectures to have a 10^4-way local concurrency within nodes (stemming from a combination of cores and threads), and comprising 10^5 nodes. From the analysis, we obtain for hard faults $r_1 = 5 \cdot 10^{-5}$ and $r_2 = 1.8 \cdot 10^{-4}$ ($n_{\text{faults}}/\text{sec}$), while for SDC we have $r_1 = 4 \cdot 10^{-5}$ and $r_2 = 1.7 \cdot 10^{-4}$ ($n_{\text{faults}}/\text{sec}$).

From an implementation standpoint, to simulate the occurrence of a fault for a target operation we proceed as follows. For a given failure rate, we draw a sample from a standard uniform random number, and extract from the corresponding failure density $F(t)$ the amount of time until the next fault occurs. We then measure the execution time for the target operation to complete, and if that time exceeds the next failure time, then a fault is triggered. Once the fault is triggered, if it is a SDC, then the result of the task is corrupted. If it is a hard fault, then all ranks of that client are set idle to mimic the case of a lost (crashing) client. This enforces no further communication between that client and its server since the client is no longer visible to the server. We are currently working on an implementation using *User Level Fault Mitigation* (ULFM) MPI [3], a fault tolerance capability proposed for the MPI standard. This will allow us to actually kill MPI ranks without causing the MPI framework to exit with failure. Some of the complications related to fault tolerant MPI implementations stem from the need to reconstruct broken MPI communicators, which is required by a regular SPMD application to proceed after the loss of an MPI rank. The advantage of the SCM we are proposing is that this can be circumvented by simply not rebuilding a lost client, and having the server distributed tasks among the remaining clients.

Test Problem and Discussion. To show resiliency, we consider a problem involving 48^2 subdomains, distributed among 48 servers. Each server-client cluster includes 48 clients each made of 1 rank. The local grid within each subdomain is $\sim 100^2$. We consider three runs, one with no faults that is used as a reference, and two runs with faults based on the rates defined before. The corresponding number of cores is in all cases 2352, and all runs are performed on Edison. We anticipate that to have a more statistically meaningful analysis an ensemble of runs would be needed, but this objective was prohibitive to obtain on Edison. However, a resilience analysis based on ensemble runs was performed for a smaller PDE test and can be found in [25].

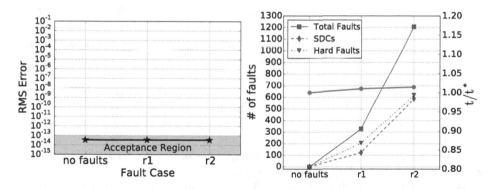

Fig. 5. (Left): root-mean-square (RMS) error of the residual in Eq. (4); (Right): blue is used to show the number of faults broken down by category, while red is used to visualize the time to converge t normalized by t^*, which is the corresponding time for the faultless case. (Color figure online)

Figure 5 shows key results obtained for the resilience runs. The left panel shows the root-mean-square (RMS) residual in Eq. (4) for each test run, computed from the value of the residual at each boundary location. Color-coded blue is the region of acceptance, i.e. the region of RMS values where the runs are considered successful. The reason this envelope is very tight around very small RMS is that, as anticipated before, when the algorithm is applied to a linear PDE, the boundary-to-boundary maps are linear and are inferred exactly. Consequently, when the fixed-point system is solved with sufficiently small tolerance, the final error is close to machine precision. The figure shows that in all cases, the solution converges, regardless of the number of faults occurring. The right panel shows in blue the number of faults affecting each run, broken down by category, while in red we plot the time to converge, t, normalized by t^*, which is the corresponding time for the no faults case. Despite the fact that in the r_2 case about 600 clients are lost out of an initial pool of 2304, and the simulation is affected by about 600 SDCs, the results show that the runtime stays approximately constant. At first glance, this result seems to imply that the run-time is bound by communication costs. In the present work, however, as seen from the scalability plots, the SST/macro model allowed us to determine that the messages are indeed small enough to not cause any bottleneck for the application. The negligible effect of the faults on the runtime is due to the overhead caused by the Boost serialization/MPI library, which tends to make the effective communication costs much higher than with pure MPI. These results show that using the Boost serialization library prevents us from quantifying the real overhead of the resiliency. We are currently working on addressing this question using regular MPI.

6   Conclusions

This study presented a domain-decomposition PDE preconditioner that is resilient to hard and soft faults, and showed its application to a 2D elliptic problem involving a steady diffusion equation with variable coefficients. The algorithm exploits a novel reformulation of the problem that allows us to cast it into a sampling problem over a set of subdomains such that "data" is generated, and then suitably manipulated to yield the final updating of the solution state.

We discussed a server-client-based implementation, and presented its scalability. The weak scaling showed a 95 % efficiency up to $12k$ cores. The analysis was complemented by building a SST/macro skeleton of our application which allows us to estimate both weak and strong scalability to $50k$ cores. The results showed excellent scalability over the range explored.

The paper finally showed the resilience of the algorithm under the SCM implementation with both simulated hard faults and SDCs. The results showed convergence in all cases. They also revealed that the overhead due to the presence of faults is negligible, being within 2 %, even though up to 35 % of the clients die and about 600 SDCs occur during the run performed for the largest failure rate. This effect, however, is due to the use of the Boost serialization/MPI library.

Acknowledgments. Sandia National Laboratories is a multi-program laboratory managed and operated by Sandia Corporation, a wholly owned subsidiary of Lockheed Martin Corporation, for the U.S. Department of Energy's National Nuclear Security Administration under contract DE-AC04-94AL85000. This material is based upon work supported by the U.S. Department of Energy, Office of Science, Office of Advanced Scientific Computing Research, under Award Numbers 13-016717. This research used resources of the National Energy Research Scientific Computing Center, a DOE Office of Science User Facility supported by the Office of Science of the U.S. Department of Energy under Contract No. DE-AC02-05CH11231.

References

1. Ang, J.A., Barrett, R.F., Benner, R.E., Burke, D., Chan, C., Cook, J., Donofrio, D., Hammond, S.D., Hemmert, K.S., Kelly, S.M., Le, H., Leung, V.J., Resnick, D.R., Rodrigues, A.F., Shalf, J., Stark, D., Unat, D., Wright, N.J.: Abstract machine models and proxy architectures for exascale computing. In: Proceedings of the 1st International Workshop on Hardware-Software Co-Design for High Performance Computing. Co-HPC 2014, pp. 25–32. IEEE Press, Piscataway, NJ, USA (2014). http://dx.doi.org/10.1109/Co-HPC.2014.4

2. Benzi, M., Frommer, A., Nabben, R., Szyld, D.B.: Algebraic theory of multiplicative schwarz methods. Numerische Mathematik **89**(4), 605–639 (2001)

3. Bland, W., Bouteiller, A., Herault, T., Bosilca, G., Dongarra, J.: Post-failure recovery of mpi communication capability: design and rationale. Int. J. High Perform. Comput. Appl. **27**(3), 244–254 (2013). http://dx.doi.org/10.1177/1094342013488238

4. Bosilca, G., Delmas, R., Dongarra, J., Langou, J.: Algorithm-based fault tolerance applied to high performance computing. J. Parallel Distrib. Comput. **69**(4), 410–416 (2009)

5. Bridges, P.G., Ferreira, K.B., Heroux, M.A., Hoemmen, M.: Fault-tolerant linear solvers via selective reliability. ArXiv e-prints, June 2012

6. Cappello, F., Geist, A., Gropp, B., Kale, L., Kramer, B., Snir, M.: Toward exascale resilience. Int. J. High Perform. Comput. Appl. **23**(4), 374–388 (2009)

7. Cappello, F., Geist, A., Gropp, W., Kale, S., Kramer, B., Snir, M.: Toward exascale resilience: 2014 update. Supercomput. Front. Innovations **1**(1) (2014). http://superfri.org/superfri/article/view/14

8. Chen, Z.: Algorithm-based recovery for iterative methods without checkpointing. In: Proceedings of the 20th International Symposium on High Performance Distributed Computing, HPDC 2011, pp. 73–84. ACM, New York, NY, USA (2011). http://doi.acm.org/10.1145/1996130.1996142

9. Daubechies, I., DeVore, R., Fornasier, M., Güntürk, C.S.: Iteratively reweighted least squares minimization for sparse recovery. Commun. Pure Appl. Math. **63**(1), 1–38 (2010). http://dx.doi.org/10.1002/cpa.20303

10. DOE-ASCR: Exascale programming challenges. Technical report, July 2011. http://science.energy.gov/~/media/ascr/pdf/program-documents/docs/ProgrammingChallengesWorkshopReport.pdf

11. DOE-ASCR: Top ten exascale research challenges. Technical report, February 2014

12. Du, P., Bouteiller, A., Bosilca, G., Herault, T., Dongarra, J.: Algorithm-based fault tolerance for dense matrix factorizations. In: Proceedings of the 17th ACM SIGPLAN Symposium on Principles and Practice of Parallel Programming, PPoPP

2012, pp. 225–234. ACM, New York, NY, USA (2012). http://doi.acm.org/10.1145/2145816.2145845

13. Du, P., Luszczek, P., Dongarra, J.: High performance dense linear system solver with soft error resilience. In: IEEE International Conference on Cluster Computing (CLUSTER), pp. 272–280, September 2011

14. Engelmann, C., Naughton, T.: Toward a performance/resilience tool for hardware/software co-design of high-performance computing systems. In: 2013 42nd International Conference on Parallel Processing (ICPP), pp. 960–969, October 2013

15. Griebel, M., Oswald, P.: Greedy and randomized versions of the multiplicative schwarz method. Linear Algebra Appl. **437**(7), 1596–1610 (2012)

16. Gupta, R., Iskra, K., Yoshii, K., Balaji, P., Beckman, P.: Introspective fault tolerance for exascale systems. Technical report, Argonne National Laboratory, 9700 South Cass Avenue, Argonne, IL 60439 (2012)

17. Heroux, M., Bartlett, R., Hoekstra, V.H.R., Hu, J., Kolda, T., Lehoucq, R., Long, K., Pawlowski, R., Phipps, E., Salinger, A., Thornquist, H., Tuminaro, R., Willenbring, J., Williams, A.: An overview of trilinos. Technical report, SAND2003-2927, Sandia National Laboratories (2003)

18. Holst, M.: Algebraic schwarz theory. Technical report CRPC-994-10, California Institute of Technology (1994)

19. Keyes, D.: How scalable is domain decomposition in practice? In: Proceedings of the 11th International Conference on Domain Decomposition Methods, pp. 286–297. Domain Decomposition Press (1999)

20. Larson, J.W., Hegland, M., Harding, B., Roberts, S., Stals, L., Rendell, A.P., Strazdins, P., Ali, M.M., Kowitz, C., Nobes, R., Southern, J., Wilson, N., Li, M., Oishi, Y.: Fault-tolerant grid-based solvers: combining concepts from sparse grids and mapreduce. Proc. Comput. Sci. **18**, 130–139 (2013)

21. Li, D., Vetter, J.S., Yu, W.: Classifying soft error vulnerabilities in extreme-scale scientific applications using a binary instrumentation tool. In: Proceedings of the International Conference on High Performance Computing, Networking, Storage and Analysis, SC 2012, pp. 57:1–57:11. IEEE Computer Society Press, Los Alamitos, CA, USA (2012). http://dl.acm.org/citation.cfm?id=2388996.2389074

22. Li, M.L., Ramachandran, P., Sahoo, S.K., Adve, S.V., Adve, V.S., Zhou, Y.: Understanding the propagation of hard errors to software and implications for resilient system design. SIGOPS Oper. Syst. Rev. **42**(2), 265–276 (2008). http://doi.acm.org/10.1145/1353535.1346315

23. Malkowski, K., Raghavan, P., Kandemir, M.: Analyzing the soft error resilience of linear solvers on multicore multiprocessors. In: 2010 IEEE International Symposium on Parallel Distributed Processing (IPDPS), pp. 1–12 (2010)

24. Quarteroni, A., Valli, A.: Domain Decomposition Methods for Partial Differential Equations. Numerical Mathematics and Scientific Computation. Clarendon Press, Oxford (1999)

25. Rizzi, F., Morris, K., Sargsyan, K., Mycek, P., Safta, C., LeMaitre, O., Knio, O., Debusschere, B.: Partial differential equations preconditioner resilient to soft and hard faults. In: IEEE International Conference on Cluster Computing (CLUSTER), pp. 552–562, September 2015

26. Sargsyan, K., Rizzi, F., Mycek, P., Safta, C., Morris, K., Najm, H., Maître, O.L., Knio, O., Debusschere, B.: Fault resilient domain decomposition preconditioner for PDES. SIAM J. Sci. Comput. **37**(5), A2317–A2345 (2015)

27. Schroeder, B., Gibson, G.: A large-scale study of failures in high-performance computing systems. IEEE Trans. Dependable Secure Comput. **7**(4), 337–350 (2010)

28. Shye, A., Moseley, T., Reddi, V., Blomstedt, J., Connors, D.: Using process-level redundancy to exploit multiple cores for transient fault tolerance. In: 37th Annual IEEE/IFIP International Conference on Dependable Systems and Networks, 2007, DSN 2007, pp. 297–306 (2007)
29. Sloan, J., Kumar, R., Bronevetsky, G.: Algorithmic approaches to low overhead fault detection for sparse linear algebra. In: 2012 42nd Annual IEEE/IFIP International Conference on Dependable Systems and Networks (DSN), pp. 1–12, June 2012
30. Snir, M., Wisniewski, R.W., Abraham, J.A., Adve, S.V., Bagchi, S., Balaji, P., Belak, J., Bose, P., Cappello, F., Carlson, B., Chien, A.A., Coteus, P., DeBardeleben, N., Diniz, P.C., Engelmann, C., Erez, M., Fazzari, S., Geist, A., Gupta, R., Johnson, F., Krishnamoorthy, S., Leyffer, S., Liberty, D., Mitra, S., Munson, T., Schreiber, R., Stearley, J., Hensbergen, E.V.: Addressing failures in exascale computing. IJHPCA, 129–173 (2014)
31. Toselli, A., Widlund, O.: Domain Decomposition Methods - Algorithms and Theory. Springer Series in Computational Mathematics. Springer, Heidelberg (2005). http://link.springer.com/book/10.1007/b137868
32. Wilke, J.J., Kenny, J.P.: Using discrete event simulation for programming model exploration at extreme-scale: macroscale components for the structural simulation toolkit (SST). Technical report, Sandia technical report SAND2015-1027 (2015)

Multi-versioning Performance Opportunities in BGAS System for Resilience

Nan Dun[1], Dirk Pleiter[2(✉)], Aiman Fang[1], Nicolas Vandenbergen[2], and Andrew A. Chien[1]

[1] Department of Computer Science, University of Chicago, Chicago, USA
{dun,aimanf,achien}@cs.uchicago.edu
[2] Jülich Research Centre, JSC, 52425 Jülich, Germany
{d.pleiter,n.vandenbergen}@fz-juelich.de
http://gvr.cs.uchicago.edu

Abstract. Resilience has become a major concern in high-performance computing (HPC) systems. Addressing the increasing risk of latent errors (or silent data corruption) is one of the biggest challenges. Multi-version checkpointing system, which keeps multi-version of the application states, has been proposed as a solution and has been implemented in Global View Resilience (GVR). The resulting more sophisticated management of data introduces overheads and the resulting impact on performance need to be investigated. In this paper we explore the performance of GVR for an HPC system with integrated non-volatile memories, namely Blue Gene Active Storage (BGAS). Our empirical study shows that the BGAS system provides a significantly more efficient basis for flexible error recovery by using GVR multi-versioning features compared to using a standard external storage system attached to the same Blue Gene/Q installation. Using BGAS especially achieves at least 10× performance boost for random traversal across multiple versions due to significantly better performance for small random I/O operations.

Keywords: Resilience · Multi-versioning · Global view resilience · BGAS · Parallel file-system

1 Introduction

Resilience has already become a major concern while top high performance systems continue to progress towards 10^{18} Flops/s performance. Current large-scale systems are comprised of millions of components, leading to significant growing error rates. It is anticipated that the mean time between failures (MTBF) could soon become less than an hour [39,48,51]. Future exascale systems are projected to have the mean time to interrupt (MTTI) as low as 10 to 30 min [8,9,20,41].

Checkpoint/restart has been the classical approach to tolerate failures. However, as the size of checkpoints scale up, the limited disk bandwidth becomes the critical bottleneck of performance, e.g., I/O bandwidth as high as 60 TBytes/s

© Springer International Publishing Switzerland 2016
J.M. Kunkel et al. (Eds.): ISC High Performance 2016, LNCS 9697, pp. 486–504, 2016.
DOI: 10.1007/978-3-319-41321-1_25

is required to meet checkpointing demand [37]. Various checkpoint/restart techniques have been efficiently applied to improve the performance of checkpointing [4,6,12,15,19,41,50]. Using high bandwidth non-volatile memories (NVM) can reduce both checkpoint cost and lost computation dramatically upon recovery from failures (due to reduced optimal checkpointing interval, or "micro-checkpointing"), which enables systems to tolerate high rates of "fail-stop" (immediately detected) errors [47].

To this end, we have proposed Global View Resilience (GVR), an approach using *versioned*, distributed arrays to enable computational scientists to build portable, resilient applications [14,27]. The goal of the GVR project is to address a larger class of errors, including not only fail-stop (immediately detected failures such as an ECC or checksum detected partial data loss) or node crash addressed by classical checkpoint/restart [28], but also growing concerns about *latent errors*, or often called silent data corruption (SDC). Latent errors are errors which are not detected immediately, but may eventually manifest as incorrect results, severe performance degradations, or even application crashes [21,49]. Multi-versioning is especially useful during recovery from latent errors [38]. Checkpoint/restart keeps only the latest checkpoint by assuming checkpointed data is correct. But checkpointed data can be already corrupted by latent errors. If the application detects a latent error after a checkpoint has been taken, it has to restart the whole computation from the beginning.

In this work, we exploit how multi-versioning can benefit from integrating NVM into high performance system architectures, particularly in the Blue Gene Active Storage (BGAS) system — an extension of the Blue Gene/Q architecture. Adding BGAS to a Blue Gene/Q installation with a standard external storage system results in a hierarchical storage system. The external storage system is based on hard disk drives and is accessed through the General Parallel File System (GPFS). In this paper we specifically focus on understanding

1. How BGAS helps the multi-version rollback recovery, where its efficiency is determined by the performance of reading/writing the whole versions of data.
2. How BGAS helps the multi-version *flexible recovery*, where its efficiency is determined by the performance of reading/writing partial data across multiple versions with different access patterns.

Experimental results show that using BGAS achieves $1.2\times$ speedup for whole version access and at least $10\times$ speedup for random partial version access comparing to the use of the external storage system. Therefore, GVR multi-versioning is able to harness the power of NVM to enable efficient flexible recovery for applications to tolerate growing error rates in future extreme-scale systems.

The rest of this paper is organized as follows. Section 2 describes the GVR programming model and especially its versioning feature that enables flexible error recovery. The BGAS system is illustrated in Sect. 3. In Sect. 4, we elaborate the evaluation of GVR versioning performance on both BGAS and GPFS and present the experimental results. Finally, Sect. 5 discusses the related work and Sect. 6 summarizes our conclusions.

2   Global View Resilience

2.1   Global View Resilience and APIs

The Global View Resilience (GVR) model enables portable application-controlled resilience. In GVR, applications control redundancy (per data structure), error checking, and recovery (exploit application semantics) in a portable fashion with *versioned* distributed arrays [38]. GVR's interface has two parts: (1) basic data access, update, and version creation, and (2) error signaling and handling, which achieves the following key features:

- Multi-version distributed arrays that enable complex and latent error recovery.
- Multi-stream versioning that gives the programmer control of when versions are created for an array.
- Unified error signaling and handling, customized per GVR distributed array, that enable algorithm-based fault-tolerance (ABFT) error-checking and recovery.

GVR distributed arrays each have a global name but are distributed across multiple nodes [5,42,43]. The *Global Array Interface* comprises array data access and versioning APIs. The global name supports flexible programming of irregular applications and, in the context of resilience, eases recovery programming when the number of physical resources has changed. In addition to distributed array creation, GVR supports block-based access operations (*put/get*) on multi-dimensional arrays, synchronization operations (*wait/fence*), and accumulate operations (*acc/get_acc*). Beyond these traditional operations, GVR adds novel operations to create and label versions as well as to navigate between different versions.

GVR includes the *Open Resilience* (OR) interface, designed to support flexible application and cross-layer handling. Open resilience supports a wide variety of error types, including process crash, node failure, memory error, network error, and application-detected error, and is extensible to more as they arise. The OR interface allows applications to define error-checking and recovery routines, exploiting both application and system semantics for efficiency and robust recovery. The interested reader can find a full description of GVR APIs and usage examples in the GVR documentation [27].

The versioning feature of GVR is implemented using different techniques such as flat array or log-structured array [24,25]. Log-structured arrays allow for a more efficient implementation of versioning as version updates are recorded as logs. This improves the use of BGAS in different aspects. First, log-structured array reduce space costs for bookkeeping changes between versions, thus requiring lower I/O bandwidth for versioning persistence. Second, less versioning space costs allows more versions to be stored in the persistent storage layer. Third, since the lifetime of non-volatile memories is also a critical concern, less version writes improves the overall lifespan of NVM storage.

We have applied GVR approach to several scientific applications, including ddcMD, Trilinos/PCG, Chombo, and OpenMC [14]. Figure 1 illustrates an example of flexible recovery in OpenMC [45], a Monte Carlo particle transport code, by using partial data of versioned arrays. In GVR enabled OpenMC, the tally data is accumulated to a versioned global array. At the end of each batch simulation tally data can be snapshotted as a version and thus a history of tally data is created. Since the tally scoring is Monte Carlo accumulation only, if a latent error is detected at the latest batch but this error occurred in some batch, then we are able to correct the contaminated tally data by removing the contribution caused by this latent error. This *forward error correction* allows the application to recover from latent errors without rolling back to a previous state and thus conserves the computational efforts. For example, if we use checkpoint/restart then we have to roll back to a correct batch and restart all computations. Within the proposed forward error recovery scheme, not the entire array but only a small portion of array requires correction. Furthermore, using GVR to implement the tally data achieves superior parallel performance and scalability, i.e., 85 % efficiency at 16,384 processes comparing to 1,000 processes with 2.39 TBytes mesh tally across 1,366 nodes on Cray XC30 supercomputer, comparing to other data decomposition implementations [17,45].

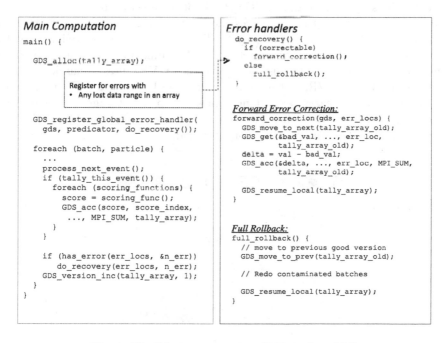

Fig. 1. Flexible recovery using GVR in OpenMC.

2.2   Scalable Checkpointing Restart

Scalable Checkpoint Restart (SCR) is a multi-level checkpointing system designed to reduce the overhead of checkpointing and meet the scalability requirements [2,41]. In future high performance computing systems, checkpointing to an external storage system becomes extremely expensive as the checkpoint size keeps increasing while the disk bandwidth is limited. On large systems it can already take hours to write one single checkpoint [11]. The idea of SCR is to write inexpensive but less resilient checkpoints in memory and higher layers of a hierarchical storage system. Only the most resilient checkpoints are kept in the lowest layer, which is typically accessed through a parallel file system (PFS). Here the creation of checkpoints is most expensive. Therefore SCR can exploit the use of different memory and storage technologies that feature different bandwidth and capacity characteristics. This allows, in particular, to increase checkpoint frequency and reduce checkpoint costs exploiting new NVM technologies.

2.3   Input/Output Organization

GVR uses SCR interfaces to store versions across the storage hierarchy. Essentially SCR serves as a file manager. The overview of the utilization of SCR in GVR is illustrated in Fig. 2. In GVR's implementation, an array is a set of chunks held by participating processes. By a versioning procedure, a version of the array is first created in memory by GVR. Second, to flush a version to SCR, GVR uses SCR to create a file name for each chunk. GVR defines the suffix of the file name and records this metadata, thus GVR maps a chunk to a file. Given the file name, GVR writes chunks to files on local disks. SCR then manages these files and creates redundant copies within the storage hierarchy. The frequency at which SCR flushes files to the lower-level storages, e.g., NVM or PFS, is determined by the runtime configuration.

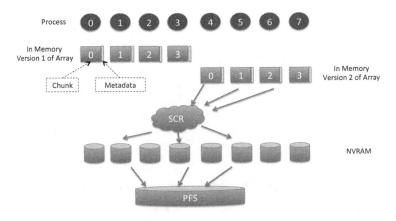

Fig. 2. Usage of SCR in GVR.

GVR manages metadata of versions and therefore can access them flexibly. For example, to read an element from an array, GVR first checks whether it is in memory or not:

– If it is in memory, GVR simply returns that element.
– If it is not in memory, GVR first calculates which chunk that element resides in. Given the metadata, GVR creates the suffix of the file name for the target chunk and uses SCR to obtain the full path of that file, which allows to locate the file. Finally, GVR opens the file and uses the offset metadata to read the element and returns its value.

3   Blue Gene Active Storage System

The Blue Gene Active Storage (BGAS) extends the IBM Blue Gene/Q (BG/Q) architecture [22,23,31] by integrating I/O nodes (ION) equipped storage-class-memory in between the compute nodes and the external storage, i.e., GPFS, as shown in Fig. 3. Each BGAS node is connected via I/O links to 2 compute nodes. The bandwidth of these links is roughly matched by the bandwidth to NVM device attached to each BGAS node and thus the aggregate I/O band-width scales with the number of BGAS nodes. BGAS thus has the potential of significantly improving the I/O capabilities of a BG/Q installation in terms of higher bandwidth and access rates. The first BGAS system worldwide was attached to the JUQUEEN supercomputer at Jülich Supercomputing Centre (JSC) in 2013 [34].

The JUQUEEN system consists of 28 racks with a total of 458,752 processor cores providing a peak performance of 5.9 PFlops/s. Each node (either compute node or I/O node) comprises one processor with 16 IBM A2 cores, which are based on the PowerPC ISA and run at 1.6 GHz. Each nodes features 16 GiBytes of SDRAM-DDR3 memory (thus 448 TBytes memory in total).

The BGAS system attached to JUQUEEN consists of 32 I/O nodes each equipped with a newly designed Hybrid Scalable Solid State Storage (HS4) PCIe card comprising 2 TBytes of SLC NAND flash memory. All these nodes are interconnected by a 3-dimensional torus network. Furthermore, each node is connected to 2 of the 28 JUQUEEN racks, i.e. 2048 compute nodes, and an external storage. Following the design of Blue Gene/Q the bandwidth between a BGAS node and the directly connected compute nodes matches the bandwidth to the I/O device, i.e. the bandwidth to the flash memory plus the Ethernet fabric. The nominal bandwidth to the flash memory is about 2 GB/s and therefore roughly equal to 2 10-Gigabit Ethernet links. It is worthwhile noting that this design point differs from those of burst buffers, where the bandwidth to compute nodes and NVM memory is chosen to be significantly larger compared to the bandwidth towards the external storage.

In the configuration of BGAS considered here, direct access to the storage attached to the BGAS nodes is only possible for processes running on the BGAS nodes. These can either use a POSIX interface to a local file system or use the new Direct Storage Access (DSA) interface [40], which provides RDMA APIs to the flash memory. Since for this installation we are not using a parallel file system there is no shared namespace. Furthermore, compute node processes have to interact with service processes on the BGAS nodes to access the flash memory. For this the capabilities of the BG/Q system software stack can be used to, e.g., delegate POSIX file I/O requests or to communicate with processes running on the BGAS nodes via named pipes. Alternatively, proprietary service daemons can be used, which are currently being implemented as Jülich BGAS Runtime (BGRT) and provide access to the DSA RDMA interfaces through split transactions [33]. In the following we will not consider this option.

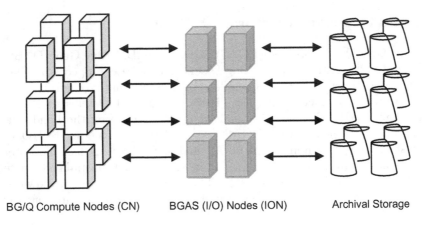

BG/Q Compute Nodes (CN)   BGAS (I/O) Nodes (ION)   Archival Storage

Fig. 3. Overview on the BGAS architecture.

4   Evaluation

To measure the GVR version create and traversal performance on BGAS, we first use the IOR benchmark to understand the base I/O performance of BGAS. Then we synthesize a micro-benchmark simulating various version access patterns to evaluate how GVR versioning performs on BGAS.

4.1   Experimental Settings

We run the experiments only on the IONs and use either the BGAS storage devices or the external storage, which are accessed through a local POSIX file system or GPFS, respectively. As external storage the scratch file system of the JUST4 storage system at JSC is used. This file system is provided through 28 IBM GSS-24 systems, each equipped with 6 dual-port 10 GE adapaters. For the current (experimental) BGAS installation the number of Ethernet ports towards the external storage thus exceeds those towards the BGAS nodes by a factor of about 20. For GPFS and the local file system a file system block size of 1 MiByte and 4 kiBytes are used, respectively. It should be noted that the HS4 card internally operates with blocks of size 8 kiBytes. We use GCC 4.4.7, MVAPICH2 2.1, IOR 2.10.3 [1], GVR 1.0.1, and SCR 1.1.7 [2]. The BGAS driver version is D14, and is still under active development and based on the hardware capabilities performance improvements are feasible.

4.2   Base I/O Performance

Cache Effects. To understand the cache effects on the I/O nodes, we perform benchmark runs using IOR for different file sizes to exhaust the on-node buffer cache and therefore to find the optimal file size for further investigation. We measure the aggregated I/O bandwidth on *one single* I/O node for a total of 16 processes using one file per process/core on various file size (by setting `blockSize` in IOR), where `transferSize` is set to 2 MiBytes. Figure 4 shows the results for GPFS and BGAS, respectively. For GPFS, when the aggregated file size reaches 2 GiBytes (16 · 128 MiBytes), the file read throughput saturates at around 2 GiBytes/s. For BGAS, the stable throughput is achieved at around 2.5 GiBytes/s when the aggregated file size reaches 8 GiBytes (16 · 512 MiBytes). To eliminate the cache effects for both GPFS and BGAS, we from now on consider 1 GiBytes file size per process, only.

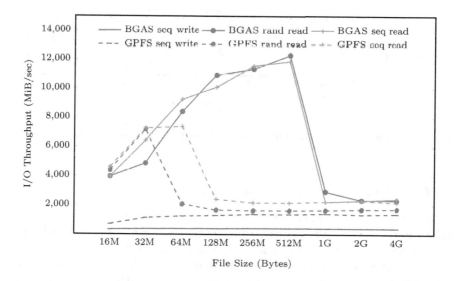

Fig. 4. POSIX I/O performance varying file size, one file per process, 16 processes, transfer size of 2 MiByte.

Basic I/O Performance. In the following we use a file size per process of 1 GiByte. The number of concurrent processes is varied with each process writing/reading to/from a separate file. Two different access patterns are used:

sequential and random access. We use 1, 2, and 4 BGAS IONs in the experiments and spawn 2 processes on each node.

As shown in Fig. 5, for sequential write, GPFS generally outperforms BGAS when transfer size is larger than 16 kiBytes. The lower performance of the HS4 storage devices for large transfer sizes reflect the high costs of the erase and program operations required for writing data to flash as well as some inefficiencies of the block device driver. Using the DSA interface bandwidth exceeding the GPFS performance can be achieved. As shown in and Figs. 6 and 7, BGAS has better overall read performance than GPFS, at least 2× for sequential read and 10× for random read.

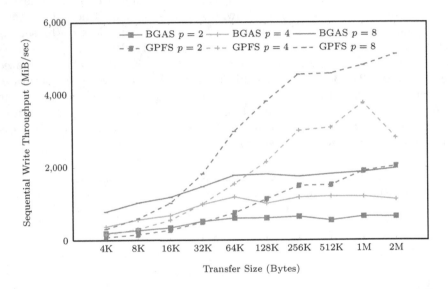

Fig. 5. Sequential write performance, 1 GiByte per process.

4.3   GVR Version Traversal Performance

To understand the version traversal performance under different access patterns during the recovery, we developed a micro-benchmark to read versions that are already persisted by SCR as files stored on BGAS or GPFS.

These synthesized microbenchmarks are motivated by real applications and are representative for major array access patterns during the error recovery [14]. For example, OpenMCs forward error recovery generally issues a few small random read operations to get a portion of global array data across different versions. If we directly measure OpenMCs recovery performance on BGAS and GPFS, the difference will be quantitatively invisible because the overall runtime is much larger than array access time. But with discrepancies in performance of different storage layers increasing, we expect these differences to become significant. In addition, other applications may use contiguous large reads for recovery,

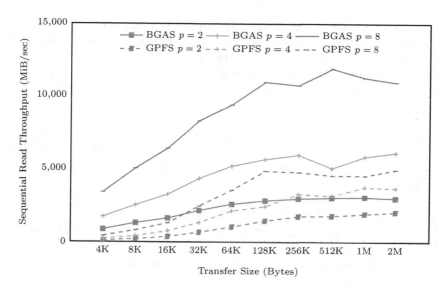

Fig. 6. Sequential read performance, 1 GiByte per process.

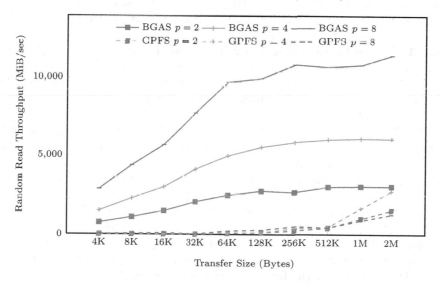

Fig. 7. Random read performance, 1 GiByte per process.

so we also synthesized this access pattern in our microbenchmarks. In general, the performance of application-specific flexible recovery can be determined by many factors. By separating the I/O contribution of storage layer from other factors, we are able to quantitatively justify the performance gain by using BGAS.

In the following experiments, we use 4 BGAS IONs and scale the number of processes from 1 to 8 on each node, i.e., 4 to 32 processes in total. The array size is proportional to the number of processes, i.e., weak scaling, by 256 MiB per process. Since GVR uses block distribution by default, each process is responsible for exposing 256 MiBytes of memory as subarray and managing its versions. SCR is configured to flush *every* version to the lower-level storage, i.e., disabling in-memory versions, so that only the current version of the array is held in memory. Then we apply a series version creation and traversal operations on the array as follows:

Increase versions. Create 10 versions of the array using GDS_version_inc(), e.g., version 0 to 9 in chroicle order. The element type is equivalent to CHAR. Each version is flushed to files on the lower-level storage by the configuration of SCR.

Read previous version. Read entire previous version, i.e., version 0, of the array using *one* GDS_get() call to copy the whole array to local buffers. Each process loads 256 MiB chunk of the version from the files stored on lower-level storage.

Read latest 5 versions. Read entire previous 5 versions, i.e., version 0 to 4, of the array using GDS_get(), for each version only one GDS_get() is called to copy the whole array to local buffers.

Read oldest 5 versions. Read entire oldest 5 versions, i.e., version 5 to 9, of the array using GDS_get(), for each version only one GDS_get() is called to copy the whole array to local buffers.

Read 1 MiByte From latest 5 versions. Read 1 MiByte segment at random offsets from each version of latest 5 versions of the array using GDS_get() on each process. This access pattern represents use cases where users try to flatten specific data structures and store them as contiguous segments in versioned array.

Read 1 MiByte From oldest 5 versions. Read 1 MiByte segment with random offsets from each version of oldest 5 versions of the array using GDS_get() on each process

Read random 64 words from latest 5 versions. Read 64 words at random offsets from each version of latest 5 versions of the array using GDS_get() on each process. This access pattern represents use cases where application stores an array of numerical values (e.g., integer or double type) globally addressable by all processes. For example, in OpenMC, each element in the tally data array is a score value of specific physical quantity at some point in 3D space. During the forward correction (see Sect. 2), elements with corrupted values can be fixed by using values stored in previous versions.

Read random 64 words from oldest 5 versions. Read 64 words at random offsets from each version of oldest 5 versions of the array using GDS_get() on each process.

Figure 8 shows results of measuring elapsed time of versioning. The performance of version increment is consistent with the observation of sequential write performance shown in Figs. 4 and 5: GPFS is slightly better than BGAS for sequential write.

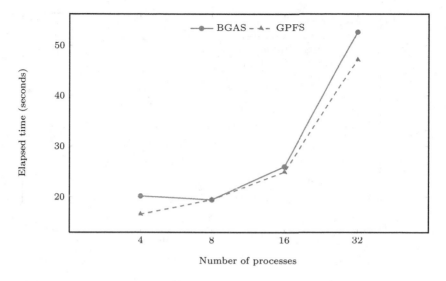

Fig. 8. Create 10 versions on 4 nodes, weak scaling, 256 MiBytes/process.

Figure 9 shows the comparison for reading previous, recent 5, and oldest 5 versions, respectively. Notice that accessing older versions generally has extra latency. This may be due to cache effects of underlying I/O stacks.

Figures 10 and 11 show the partial version traversal performance. In general, using the local BGAS storage devices result in at least 10× speedup, especially for random words read, compared to the external GPFS storage system.

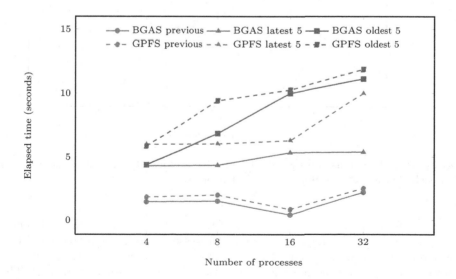

Fig. 9. Entire versions traversal on 4 nodes, weak scaling, 256 MiBytes/process.

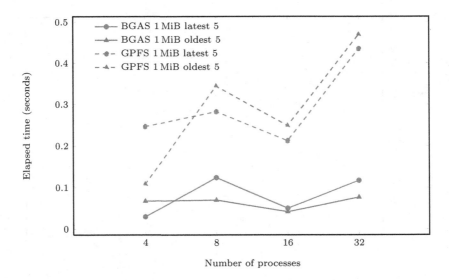

Fig. 10. Partial versions traversal on 4 nodes by reading 1 MiByte at random offsets from each version, weak scaling, 256 MiBytes/process.

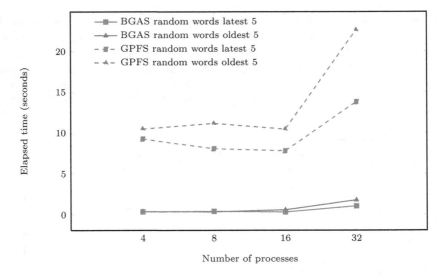

Fig. 11. Partial versions traversal on 4 nodes by reading 64 words at random offsets from each version, weak scaling, 256 MiBytes/process.

To shed some light in the reasons for this significant performance difference, we repeated the benchmark run using 32 processes using the scalable HPC I/O characterization tool Darshan [13]. In Table 1 we compare the time spent in reading and writing data, metadata operations as well as other operations. The time spent on other operations includes GVR creating the copy of the array and invoking SCR calls to store, search, and retrieve files from lower-level storage system. Note that the performance difference comes from two major parts: the read itself and metadata operations. In particular, using BGAS shows about $20\times$ and $60\times$ speedup for 1 MiByte and random words reads, respectively. For both types of operations the total amount of read and written data is (almost) identical, however, the I/O patterns of both cases differ significantly. In case of random reads the number of seek and file open operations is about $20\times$ and $60\times$ larger compared to the contiguous reads case. This is consistent with the observed difference in execution time.

The impact of non-sequential small I/O requests on GPFS performance has been discussed before [29,32]: GPFS prefers large request size, when request size is smaller than GPFS block size, a significant portion of data will be wasted. One solution is to use a higher-level I/O library to reorder and combine small requests before sending them to GPFS.

Table 1. Time spent on different types of operations during GVR partial version traversal on 4 IONs as reported by Darshan.

Elapsed time (sec)	Read contiguous 1 MiB		Read 64 random words	
	BGAS	GPFS	BGAS	GPFS
Read	0.19	0.32	0.19	4.77
Write	6.23	3.94	5.87	3.82
Metadata	0.01	0.20	0.13	6.59
Others	19.56	17.54	20.82	28.82

5   Related Work

There have been years of studies on checkpoint/restart [18] and NVM research effort has been focused on using hybrid memory systems to improve the performance of checkpointing. Li et al. discussed the opportunities for NVM in scientific applications [36]. Dong et al. used a hybrid Phase-Change Random Access Memory (PCRAM) based checkpointing to reduce the overhead to less than 4% on a projected exascale system [16]. Zhou et al. proposed an approach for multi-core system by using writeback-aware analysis to partition the bandwidth of PCM [52]. However, as pointed out by Gao et al. these hybrid systems can still have prohibitively high checkpoint overhead and system downtime, especially when checkpoints are taken frequently and therefore a partial checkpointing approach is proposed to further improve the checkpointing efficiency [26].

Checkpoint restart (C/R) system can also use SCR to manage and flush its checkpoints to low-level external storage system. However, C/R will not be able to provide the same flexibility as GVR to do application specific flexible recovery, e.g., partial data recovery where GVR can explore more benefits than C/R. How to recover communicators and execution after node failures is beyond the scope of this paper. But GVR can restore all consistent versions available in NVM after node loss. This is because (1) GVR has internal redundancy schemes which skew versions across nodes to create redundancy. This guarantees there are consistent versions available even after node loss. (2) the metadata is replicated in all nodes so that GVR can use it to recover any consistent versions and discard corrupted versions.

Recently, NVM-based burst buffers have been proposed as a high-bandwidth, storage tier between compute nodes and traditional disk storage. It serves as I/O offloading layer that absorbs bulk data produced by applications, while seamlessly draining the data to the PFS in the background. The advanced architecture features of burst buffer systems have been recognized. Several next generation of supercomputers are going to deploy burst buffers. Cori [4] is National Energy Research Scientific Computing (NERSC) Center's next supercomputer system (NERSC-8). The phase 1 system will provide approximately 750 TBytes of burst buffer storage. Summit [3] is Oak Ridge National Laboratory's next high performance supercomputer. It will consist of approximately 3,400 nodes, each with at least 512 GBytes memory and 800 GBytes NVM-based storage. With this layer of burst buffers, applications can dump data quickly and return to computation without waiting data to be moved to disk. Recent works including Bent et al. [7], Brown et al. [10], Liu et al. [37], and other works [35,44,46] have explored utilizing burst buffers to improve the resilience.

6   Summary and Future Work

We studied the performance opportunities of multi-versioning, a GVR approach to add flexible resilience to applications, using BGAS. The NVM-based BGAS system provides a more efficient basis and opportunities for GVR versioning comparing to an traditional external storage systems attached to the same system, especially for flexible error recovery using random version access.

We used Blue Gene/Q and BGAS as an available vehicle to get a better understanding of what will be possible on future architectures. We believe the results of the paper to be relevant beyond the considered system as it shows the capabilities of a system providing a fast storage layer that has properties, which support fast traversal between different copies of data objects. For the considered system this was mainly achieved by avoiding the parallel file system, exploiting locality properties and having a relatively high bandwidth. We further highlighted the opportunities of exploiting data processing capabilities within the storage. All this should be taken into account for future architecture designs and coincides nicely with the roadmaps of next generation pre-exascale systems.

Equipped with additional compute resource, e.g., idle cores on ION, in-situ analysis could be off-loaded to the ION. Such active storage concepts can potentially be exploited for enabling algorithm-based fault-tolerance (ABFT) error-checking (see, e.g., [30] for an approach that could benefit from such an architecture). Though using BGAS via the file system interface is the most portable way for applications, we look forward to exploiting more efficient alternatives of using the BGAS system such as Direct Storage Access (DSA) from compute nodes.

Acknowledgments. This work was supported by the Office of Advanced Scientific Computing Research, Office of Science, the U.S. Department of Energy, under Award DE-SC0008603 and Contract DE-AC02-06CH11357. This work was completed in part with resources provided by Jülich Supercomputing Centre and we would like to thank in particular Michael Stephan for his support. We gracefully acknowledge the collaboration with IBM Research on the BGAS architecture in the context of the Exascale Innovation Center (EIC). In particular, we want to thank Blake Fitch for his continuous support and for many helpful discussions. Part of the work has been done within the Joint Laboratory for Extreme Scale Computing (JLESC).

References

1. IOR benchmark. http://ior-sio.sourceforge.net
2. Scalable checkpoint/restart (SCR) library. https://github.com/hpc/scr
3. Summit compute system. https://www.olcf.ornl.gov/summit/
4. Antypas, K., Wright, N., Cardo, N.P., Andrews, A., Cordery, M.: Cori: a Cray XC pre-exascale system for NERSC. In: Cray User Group Proceedings. Cray (2014)
5. Bariuso, R., Knies, A.: SHMEM user's guide for C. Cray Research, Inc. (1994)
6. Bautista-Gomez, L., Tsuboi, S., Komatitsch, D., Cappello, F., Maruyama, N., Matsuoka, S.: FTI: high performance fault tolerance interface for hybrid systems. In: Proceedings of the 2011 ACM/IEEE International Conference for High Performance Computing, Networking, Storage and Analysis, SC 2011 (2011)
7. Bent, J., Grider, G., Kettering, B., Manzanares, A., McClelland, M., Torres, A., Torrez, A.: Storage challenges at Los Alamos National Lab. In: IEEE 28th Symposium on Mass Storage Systems and Technologies, pp. 1–5, April 2012
8. Bergman, K., Borkar, S., Campbell, D., Carlson, W., Dally, W., Denneau, M., Franzon, P., Harrod, W., Hiller, J., Karp, S., Keckler, S., Klein, D., Lucas, R., Richards, M., Scarpelli, A., Scott, S., Snavely, A., Sterling, T., Williams, R.S., Yelick, K.: Exascale computing study: technology challenges in achieving exascale systems. Technical report DARPA IPTO (2008)
9. Borkar, S., Chien, A.A.: The future of microprocessors. Commun. ACM **54**, 67–77 (2011)
10. Brown, D.L., Messina, P., Keyes, D., Morrison, J., Lucas, R., Shalf, J., Beckman, P., Brightwell, R., Geist, A., Vetter, J., et al.: Scientific grand challenges: crosscutting technologies for computing at the exascale. Office of Science, U.S. Department of Energy, pp. 2–4, February 2010
11. Cappello, F.: Fault tolerance in petascale/exascale systems: current knowledge, challenges and research opportunities. Int. J. High Perform. Comput. Appl. **23**(3), 212–226 (2009)
12. Cappello, F., Casanova, H., Robert, Y.: Preventive migration vs. preventive checkpointing for extreme scale supercomputers. Parallel Process. Lett. **21**(02), 111–132 (2011)
13. Carns, P., Latham, R., Ross, R., Iskra, K., Lang, S., Riley, K.: 24/7 characterization of petascale I/O workloads. In: IEEE International Conference on Cluster Computing and Workshops, pp. 1–10, August 2009

14. Chien, A.A., Balaji, P., Beckman, P., Dun, N., Fang, A., Fujita, H., Iskra, K., Rubenstein, Z., Zheng, Z., Schreiber, R., Hammond, J., Dinan, J., Laguna, I., Dubey, A., Hoemmen, M., Heroux, M., Teranishi, K., Siegel, A.: Versioned distributed arrays for resilience in scientific applications: global view resilience. In: Proceedings of International Conference on Computational Science (2015)

15. Daly, J.T.: A higher order estimate of the optimum checkpoint interval for restart dumps. Future Gener. Comput. Syst. **22**(3) (2006)

16. Dong, X., Muralimanohar, N., Jouppi, N., Kaufmann, R., Xie, Y.: Leveraging 3D PCRAM technologies to reduce checkpoint overhead for future exascale systems. In: Proceedings of the Conference on High Performance Computing Networking, Storage and Analysis, SC 2009, pp. 57:1–57:12 (2009)

17. Dun, N., Fujita, H., Tramm, J., Chien, A.A., Siegel, A.R.: Data decomposition in Monte Carlo particle transport simulations using global view arrays. Int. J. High Perform. Comput. Appl. March 2015

18. Egwutuoha, I.P., Levy, D., Selic, B., Chen, S.: A survey of fault tolerance mechanisms and checkpoint/restart implementations for high performance computing systems. J. Supercomput. **65**(3), 1302–1326 (2013)

19. Fang, A., Chien, A.A.: How much SSD is useful for resilience in supercomputers. In: Proceedings of the 5th Workshop on Fault Tolerance for HPC at eXtreme Scale (2015)

20. Ferreira, K., Stearley, J., Laros III, J.H., Oldfield, R., Pedretti, K., Brightwell, R., Riesen, R., Bridges, P.G., Arnold, D.: Evaluating the viability of process replication reliability for exascale systems. In: Proceedings of 2011 International Conference for High Performance Computing, Networking, Storage and Analysis (2011)

21. Fiala, D., Mueller, F., Engelmann, C., Riesen, R., Ferreira, K., Brightwell, R.: Detection and correction of silent data corruption for large-scale high-performance computing. In: Proceedings of 2012 International Conference on High Performance Computing, Networking, Storage and Analysis, pp. 78:1–78:12 (2012)

22. Fitch, B.G.: Exploring the capabilities of a massively scalable, compute-in-storage architecture (2013). http://www.hpdc.org/2013/site/files/HPDC13_Fitch_BlueGeneActiveStorage.pdf

23. Fitch, B.G., Rayshubskiy, A., Pitman, M.C., Ward, T.J.C., Germain, R.S.: Using the active storage fabrics model to address petascale storage challenges. In: Proceedings of the 4th Annual Workshop on Petascale Data Storage (2009)

24. Fujita, H., Dun, N., Rubenstein, Z.A., Chien, A.A.: Log-structured global array for efficient multi-version snapshots. In: Proceedings of 2015 15th IEEE/ACM International Symposium on Cluster, Cloud and Grid Computing, pp. 281–291 (2015)

25. Fujita, H., Iskra, K., Balaji, P., Chien, A.A.: Empirical comparison of three versioning architectures. In: Proceedings of IEEE Cluster 2015 (2015)

26. Gao, S., He, B., Xu, J.: Real-time in-memory checkpointing for future hybrid memory systems. In: Proceedings of the 29th ACM on International Conference on Supercomputing, pp. 263–272 (2015)

27. GVR Team.: Global View Resilience (GVR) API documentation, version 1.0.1. Technical report, University of Chicago, Department of Computer Science, October 2015

28. Hargrove, P.H., Duell, J.C.: Berkeley lab checkpoint/restart (BLCR) for Linux clusters. J. Phys. Conf. Ser. **46**, 494 (2006)

29. Heger, D., Shah, G.: IBM's general parallel file system (GPFS) 1.4 for AIX. Technical report, IBM Corporation, November 2001

30. Huang, K.H., Abraham, J.: Algorithm-based fault tolerance for matrix operations. IEEE Trans. Comput. **C–33**(6), 518–528 (1984)

31. IBM Blue Gene Team: The IBM Blue Gene project. IBM J. Res. Dev. **57** (2013)
32. Jones, T., Koniges, A., Yates, R.K.: Performance of the IBM general parallel file system. In: Proceedings of 2000 IEEE International Parallel and Distributed Processing Symposium (2000)
33. Jülich Supercomputing Centre: BGAS user documentation. https://trac.version. fz-juelich.de/EIC/wiki/bgas-user
34. Jülich Supercomputing Centre: Blue Gene Active Storage boosts I/O performance at JSC. http://www.fz-juelich.de/SharedDocs/Pressemitteilungen/UK/EN/2013/ 13-11-18bgas.html
35. Kulkarni, A., Manzanares, A., Ionkov, L., Lang, M., Lumsdaine, A.: The design and implementation of a multi-level content-addressable checkpoint file system. In: 2012 19th International Conference on High Performance Computing, pp. 1– 10, December 2012
36. Li, D., Vetter, J.S., Marin, G., McCurdy, C., Cira, C., Liu, Z., Yu, W.: Identifying opportunities for byte-addressable non-volatile memory in extreme-scale scientific applications. In: Proceedings of the 2012 IEEE 26th International Parallel and Distributed Processing Symposium, pp. 945–956 (2012)
37. Liu, N., Cope, J., Carns, P., Carothers, C., Ross, R., Grider, G., Crume, A., Maltzahn, C.: On the role of burst buffers in leadership-class storage systems. In: Proceedings of the 2012 IEEE Conference on Massive Data Storage (2012)
38. Lu, G., Zheng, Z., Chien, A.A.: When is multi-version checkpointing needed? In: Proceedings of the 3rd Workshop on Fault-Tolerance for HPC at Extreme Scale, pp. 49–56 (2013)
39. Martino, C.D., Kalbarczyk, Z., Iyer, R.K., Baccanico, F., Fullop, J., Kramer, W.: Lessons learned from the analysis of system failures at petascale: the case of Blue Waters. In: Proceedings of the 2014 44th Annual IEEE/IFIP International Conference on Dependable Systems and Networks, pp. 610–621 (2014)
40. Metzler, B., Trivedi, A.: Prototyping byte-addressable NVM access. In: Proceedings of 11th OpenFabrics Developers Workshop (2015)
41. Moody, A., Bronevetsky, G., Mohror, K., de Supinski, B.R.: Design, modeling, and evaluation of a scalable multi-level checkpointing system. In: Proceedings of the 2010 ACM/IEEE International Conference for High Performance Computing, Networking, Storage and Analysis, pp. 1–11 (2010)
42. Nieplocha, J., Palmer, B., Tipparaju, V., Krishnan, M., Trease, H., Aprà, E.: Advances, applications and performance of the global arrays shared memory programming toolkit. Int. J. High Perform. Comput. Appl. **20**(2), 203–231 (2006)
43. Numrich, R.W., Reid, J.: Co-Array Fortran for parallel programming. SIGPLAN Fortran Forum **17**(2) (1998)
44. Ouyang, X., et al.: Enhancing checkpoint performance with staging I/O and SSD. In: Proceedings of 2010 International Workshop on Storage Network Architecture and Parallel I/Os, May 2010
45. Romano, P.K., Forget, B.: The OpenMC Monte Carlo particle transport code. Ann. Nucl. Energy **51**, 274–281 (2013)
46. Sato, K., Mohror, K., Moody, A., Gamblin, T., de Supinski, B.R., Maruyama, N., Matsuoka, S.: A user-level InfiniBand-based file system and checkpoint strategy for burst buffers. In: Proceedings of 2014 14th IEEE/ACM International Symposium on Cluster, Cloud and Grid Computing (2014)
47. Schlichting, R.D., Schneider, F.B.: Fail-stop processors: an approach to designing fault-tolerant computing systems. ACM Trans. Comput. Syst. **1**(3), 222–238 (1983)

48. Schroeder, B., Gibson, G.A.: A large-scale study of failures in high-performance computing systems. In: Proceedings of 2006 IEEE/IFIP International Conference on Dependable Systems and Networks (2006)
49. Shantharam, M., Srinivasmurthy, S., Raghavan, P.: Characterizing the impact of soft errors on iterative methods in scientific computing. In: Proceedings of Supercomputing (2011)
50. Young, J.W.: A first order approximation to the optimum checkpoint interval. Commun. ACM **17**(9) (1974)
51. Zheng, Z., Yu, L., Tang, W., Lan, Z., Gupta, R., Desai, N., Coghlan, S., Buettner, D.: Co-analysis of RAS log and job log on Blue Gene/P. In: Proceedings of 2011 IEEE International Parallel and Distributed Processing Symposium (2011)
52. Zhou, M., Du, Y., Childers, B.R., Melhem, R., Mosse, D.: Writeback-aware bandwidth partitioning for multi-core systems with PCM. In: Proceedings of the 22nd International Conference on Parallel Architectures and Compilation Techniques, pp. 113–122 (2013)

Author Index